Lecture Notes in Computer Science 13056

More information about this subseries at http://www.springer.com/series/7409

Jannicke Baalsrud Hauge · Jorge C. S. Cardoso ·
Licínio Roque · Pedro A. Gonzalez-Calero (Eds.)

Entertainment Computing – ICEC 2021

20th IFIP TC 14 International Conference, ICEC 2021
Coimbra, Portugal, November 2–5, 2021
Proceedings

 Springer

Editors
Jannicke Baalsrud Hauge ⓘ
Bremer Institut für Produktion und Logistik
GmbH (BIBA)
Bremen, Germany

KTH
Stockholm, Sweden

Licínio Roque ⓘ
University of Coimbra
Coimbra, Portugal

Jorge C. S. Cardoso ⓘ
University of Coimbra
Coimbra, Portugal

Pedro A. Gonzalez-Calero ⓘ
Complutense University of Madrid
Madrid, Spain

ISSN 0302-9743   ISSN 1611-3349 (electronic)
Lecture Notes in Computer Science
ISBN 978-3-030-89393-4   ISBN 978-3-030-89394-1 (eBook)
https://doi.org/10.1007/978-3-030-89394-1

LNCS Sublibrary: SL3 – Information Systems and Applications, incl. Internet/Web, and HCI

This Springer imprint is published by the registered company Springer Nature Switzerland AG
The registered company address is: Gewerbestrasse 11, 6330 Cham, Switzerland

Preface

With pride we present the conference proceedings of ICEC 2021, the 20th edition of the IFIP International Conference on Entertainment Computing. It was hosted by the Department of Informatics Engineering of the University of Coimbra in Portugal. The mission of ICEC is to bring together researchers and practitioners from diverse backgrounds in the fields of entertainment computing and serious games to discuss and learn from each other's experiences in order to achieve more attractive and meaningful applications. Consequently, for ICEC 2021, all working groups in TC14 on entertainment computing contributed with article submissions, tutorials, interactive installations, and workshops, so that we are very happy to present contributions showing the variety of research that is required to develop good entertainment computing applications. In addition, there's a continuing desire to create a real global community, connecting researchers from all parts of the world to further the science of entertainment computing and serious games with industry, which was reflected in the invited keynotes. Furthermore, we were celebrating the 20th ICEC conference, and at the same time IFIP was celebrating it's 60 anniversary with a set of activities, so we are happy to host one of these events as part of the conference.

Entertainment computing and serious games operate on the multidisciplinary intersection of design, art, entertainment, interaction, computing, psychology, and numerous serious application domains, bringing together researchers in all these fields, and therefore the program mirrors this diversity. The conference received a total of 83 submissions, and after an extensive review process 26 full papers, 13 works in progress papers, 3 interactive entertainment/experiential works, 3 student competition papers, 4 workshop papers, and 1 tutorial were accepted. The ICEC 2021 Program Committee was composed of 84 experts from 23 different countries, comprising a unique representation of the global entertainment computing and games communities. We thank all the members of this committee and all the additional external reviewers for their work and commitment. The importance and credibility of these proceedings are sustained by the competence and dedication of these professionals.

The conference program was furthermore enriched by two keynote speakers. Ana Paiva (University of Lisbon) gave a talk on how to make robotics social, namely the problem of engineering agents that exhibit specific social capabilities, including aspects such as emotions, personality, culture, non-verbal behavior, empathy, collaboration, and others. Josué Monchan (Pendulo Studios) spoke on narrative writing and other creative challenges behind games, helping us to understand several aspects of managing the creative process. Moreover, we inaugurated a special track of invited talks to recognize some of the most influential papers published through the Entertainment Computing journal.

We wish to recognize the hosting institution, the University of Coimbra, the cooperation of Sociedade Portuguesa das Ciências dos Videojogos, and the support of Instituto Pedro Nunes in helping to facilitate several aspects of this year's conference organization.

November 2021

Jannicke Baalsrud Hauge
Jorge C. S. Cardoso
Licínio Roque
Pedro Gonzalez-Calero

Organization

General Chairs

Licínio Roque   University of Coimbra, Portugal
Pedro Gonzalez-Calero   Universidad Complutense Madrid, Spain

Program Committee Chairs

Jannicke Baalsrud Hauge   KTH Royal Institute of Technology,
                                     Sweden/BIBA, Germany
Jorge C.S. Cardoso   University of Coimbra, Portugal

Works in Progress Chairs

Paula Alexandra Silva   University of Coimbra, Portugal
Valentina Nisi   University of Lisbon/ITI, Portugal
Teresa Romão   Nova University of Lisbon, Portugal

Workshops Chairs

Mitsuru Minakuchi   Kyoto Sangyo University, Japan
Elif Surer   Middle East Technical University, Turkey
Pedro Martins   University of Coimbra, Portugal

Tutorials Chairs

Esteban Clua   Universidade Federal Fluminense, Brazil
Eddie Melcer   University of California, Santa Cruz, USA

Interactive Entertainment/Experiential Works Chairs

Drew Davidson   Entertainment Technology Center, Carnegie
                                     Mellon University, USA
Troy Kohwalter   Universidade Federal Fluminense, Brazil

Student Competition Chairs

Erik van der Spek   TU Eindhoven, The Netherlands
Nelson Zagalo   University of Aveiro, Portugal

Doctoral Consortium Chairs

Liliane Machado   Federal University of Paraíba, Brazil
Artur Lugmayr   Umea University, Sweden/University of Western
                          Australia, Australia/UXMachines Pty Ltd,
                          Australia

Communication Chairs

Nuno Correia   Nova University of Lisbon, Portugal
Zhigeng Pan   Hangzhou Normal University, China

Local Organization Committee

Ana Paula Afonso   CISUC, Universidade Aberta, Portugal
Luís Lucas Pereira   CISUC, University of Coimbra, Portugal
Mariana Seiça   CISUC, University of Coimbra, Portugal
Rui Craveirinha   CISUC, University of Coimbra, Portugal/Player
                          Research, UK

Steering Committee

Rainer Malaka   University of Bremen, Germany
Helmut Hlavacs   TU Wien, Austria
Erik van der Spek   TU Eindhoven, The Netherlands
Esteban Clua   Universidade Federal Fluminense, Brazil
Nuno Correia   Nova University of Lisbon, Portugal

Program Committee

Abdennour El Rhalibi   Liverpool John Moores University, UK
Aidong Lu   University of North Carolina at Charlotte, USA
André Miede   Hochschule für Technik und Wirtschaft des
                          Saarlandes, Germany
André Perrotta   University of Coimbra, Portugal
Andreas Scalas   CNR IMATI, Italy
Andrés Adolfo Navarro Newball   Pontificia Universidad Javeriana, Colombia
Antonio J. Fernández Leiva   Universidad de Málaga, Spain
Artur Lugmayr   Umea University, Sweden/University of Western,
                          Australia/UXMachines Pty Ltd, Australia
Barbara Göbl   University of Vienna, Austria
Carlos Caires   University of Saint Joseph, China
Cristina Sylla   University of Minho/ITI/LARSyS, Portugal

Michela Mortara	CNR IMATI, Italy
Mitsuru Minakuchi	Kyoto Sangyo University, Japan
Naoya Isoyama	Nara Institute of Science and Technology, Japan
Nelson Zagalo	University of Aveiro, Portugal
Nick Graham	Queen's University, Canada
Nikitas Sgouros	University of Piraeus, Greece
Nour El Mawas	Université de Lille, France
Nuno Correia	Universidade Nova de Lisboa, Portugal
Paula Alexandra Silva	University of Coimbra, Portugal
Pedro Gonzalez-Calero	Universidad Complutense Madrid, Spain
Pedro Martins	University of Coimbra, Portugal
Per Backlund	University of Skövde, Sweden
Philipp Jordan	University of Hawai'i at Mānoa, USA
Qingde Li	University of Hull, UK
Ralf Doerner	RheinMain University of Applied Sciences, Germany
Robert Wendrich	University of Twente, The Netherlands
Rui Craveirinha	University of Coimbra, Portugal/Player Research, UK
Rui Prada	Universidade de Lisboa, Portugal
Ryohei Nakatsu	Kyoto University, Japan
Sara Kunz	Portuguese Catholic University, Portugal
Sheng Li	Peking University, China
Sobah Abbas Petersen	Norwegian University of Science and Technology, Norway
Stefan Goebel	TU Darmstadt, Germany
Teresa Romão	Nova University of Lisbon, Portugal
Theodore Lim	Heriot-Watt University, UK
Theresa-Marie Rhyne	Consultant, USA
Troy Kohwalter	Universidade Federal Fluminense, Brazil
Valentina Nisi	University of Lisbon/ITI, Portugal
Vanessa Cesário	ITI/LARSyS, Portugal
Wolfgang Mueller	University of Education Weingarten, Germany
Xiaosong Yang	Bournemouth University, UK
Youquan Liu	Chang'an University, China
Xun Luo	Tianjin University of Technology, China

Additional Reviewers

Alvaro Gutierrez, Spain
Ehtzaz Chaudhry, UK
Feijoo Colomine, Venezuela
Jorge Quiñones
Mara Catalina Aguilera-Canon, UK

Neerav Nagda, UK
Sascha Müller, Germany
Susanne Haake, Germany
Yanhui Su, Sweden
Yu Xi, UK

Contents

Works in Progress

Interactive Entertainment/Experiential Works

Student Game and Interactive Entertainment Competition

ICEC Tutorial

Full Research Papers

Comparison of Viewing Contents Using Large LED Display and Projector by Psychological Evaluation

Ryohei Nakatsu[1](✉), Naoko Tosa[1], Hiroyuki Takada[2], and Takashi Kusumi[1]

[1] Kyoto University, Kyoto 606-8501, Japan
ryohei.nakatsu@design.kyoto-u.ac.jp, {tosa.naoko.5c,
kusumi.takashi.7u}@kyoto-u.ac.jp
[2] TELMIC Corp, Tokyo 110-0016, Japan
h.takada@telmic.co.jp

Abstract. Displaying content on a large screen using an LED display or projector has many possible applications including entertainment. Therefore, which one is appropriate depending on the various situation is an important theme. In this research, a psychological experiment was conducted to compare the cases where video contents were displayed on a 200-inch LED display and a 200-inch screen with a projector under three different brightness conditions. As the content, we used 6 kinds of lecture videos with a wide variety including science, technology, psychology, art, etc. by Kyoto University professors. We asked 34 subjects to watch each lecture video for 20 min and then fill out a questionnaire. As a result, the brighter the LED display, the better the evaluation result, while the brighter the projector, the lower the evaluation result. Also, a further detailed analysis was performed by analysis of variance (ANOVA).

Keywords: Projector · LED display · Large display · Lighting · Psychological experiment · Two-way ANOVA

1 Introduction

Displaying images and videos on a large screen is suitable as a means of appealing image information to many people. Such display method is suitable for events, conference presentations, street advertisements, entertainment, art exhibitions, etc. As a method of displaying a large screen image or video, there are a method of displaying on a large LED display and a method of projecting with a projector. Although large LED displays are expensive, they have excellent visibility even in bright conditions, so they are often used in places with high daytime traffic such as train stations and street corners. On the other hand, the method of displaying using a projector has the drawback that it is difficult to see in a bright situation but has the advantage that it can be displayed without changing an existing wall or building. In particular, projection mapping [1], which projects a three-dimensional image using the shape of a building as it is, is attracting attention as a new

© IFIP International Federation for Information Processing 2021
Published by Springer Nature Switzerland AG 2021
J. Baalsrud Hauge et al. (Eds.): ICEC 2021, LNCS 13056, pp. 3–14, 2021.
https://doi.org/10.1007/978-3-030-89394-1_1

display method and is often used in entertainment and other situations [2]. On the other hand, as the price of large LED displays has fallen and the brightness of projectors has improved, the scenes in which both are used are beginning to overlap.

In this study, we conducted a comparative experiment between LED displays and projectors showing contents on a large screen. For the experiment, several conditions were set for the brightness, and various video contents to be displayed were prepared. And the experiment was conducted using the framework of the psychological experiment in which the subjects filled out questionnaires. In this paper, we will describe the experimental contents, analysis results, and consideration based on them. This paper is useful in that it presents reference data on which condition is to be used when images/videos are displayed on a large screen using LED displays and projectors.

2   Related Work and Background

Psychological studies on the visibility of displayed images have been conducted for long time. Gilinsky showed that the distance to the image and the size of the image have a great effect on visibility [3]. Since then, as display methods, projectors, LED displays, and LCD televisions have become widespread, research on the visibility of displayed images/videos has been actively conducted.

For example, regarding display by a projector, research on the effect of screen size and distance to the screen on visibility [4] and research on screen size suitable for building a VR environment were conducted [5]. Regarding LED displays, visibility when used for signs was studied [6]. In addition, researches on the visibility of high-resolution image/video display using HDTV were conducted [7, 8].

However, it seems that no experiment has been reported so far that directly compares the display by the LED display and the projector under various conditions. As we think it is necessary to systematically carry out such a comparative experiment, in our previous research we carried out the psychological experiment in which we asked the subjects to watch contents on the LED display and the projector and to comparatively evaluate the two methods [9]. In the experiment, a comparative experiment was conducted using two types of contrasting content, art content [10, 11], and text-based content. In addition, as for the lighting conditions, there were two conditions; with lighting and without lighting. As a result, when the art content was viewed using the LED display under the condition without lighting, it was highly evaluated, followed by the condition of art content × LED display × lighting and art content × projector × no lighting. The results showed that the art content was highly evaluated compared to the case of text-based content.

On the other hand, however, the fact that the art content is used has a great influence on the evaluation result. Also, the presentation time of the content was as short as 1 min. Since most of the viewing using a large display/screen is a scene such as a lecture or a conference presentation, we received requests to carry out a comparative experiment under such realistic conditions. To meet such demands, we assumed more realistic scenes such as lectures and conference presentations and conducted a comparative experiment using an LED display and a projector when viewing such scenes for a certain period.

3   Method

3.1   Experimental Condition

Two types of display methods and three types of lighting conditions were arranged, and as a result, six types of experimental conditions combining these were arranged.

(1) Display Method

To simulate the content displayed on a large screen and to make an accurate comparison between the LED display and the projector, a method of displaying contents on a 200-inch LED display and a 200-inch screen using a 10,000-lm projector are used. The size of both the display and the projector is 4.43 m in width and 2.5 m in height (ratio 16:9). The LED display is made by arranging SMD elements at a pitch of 2.5 mm, and the total resolution is 1760 pixels × 960 pixels, which is almost full HD resolution. The brightness is 1200 cd/m^2. The 10,000-lm projector is also full HD resolution. All projected images were in HD.

Figure 1 shows the 200-inch LED display and Fig. 2 shows the screen and projector. The LED display, projector, and screen necessary to realize these environments were installed in a laboratory with an area of about 300 m^2.

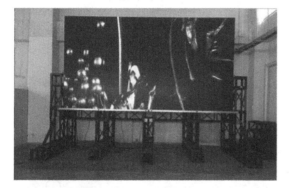

Fig. 1. 200-inch LED display used for the experiment.

Fig. 2. 200-inch screen and projector used for the experiment.

(2) Lighting Condition
To compare the difference between a bright environment and a dark environment, in a laboratory equipped with an LED display and a projector + screen, three types of bright environments were prepared: full lighting, half lighting, and no lighting. A comparative experiment was conducted under the above conditions. To realize complete darkness, the experiment was conducted at night after sunset, and the lighting of the entire laboratory was controlled in a way of fully turned on, half turned on, or turned off. As a result, complete darkness could be realized when the lights were turned off. Under this condition, the illuminance at the subject's position is about 400 lx when all the lights are turned on, 200 lx when half the lights are turned on, and 0 lx when all the lights are turned off.

The subject sat in a chair 5 m away from the display and screen in front of their center and watched the content displayed on them. This is within the range of 5 m to 6 m calculated from the screen size (inch) × 0.3 to 0.25, which is the optimum viewing distance generally referred to. When the subject looks at the projection plane, the elevation angle is 27° and the viewing angle is 42° (Fig. 3).

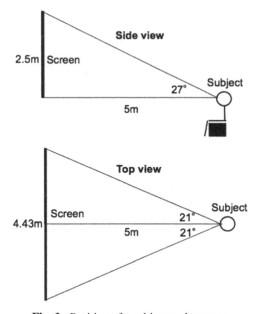

Fig. 3. Position of a subject and a screen

(3) Content
In the previous experiment, we compared art content and text-based content. On the other hand, since displays and screens of about 100 inches to 200 inches are often used in the case of lectures and presentations, in this research the content was selected assuming such a situation. Six lecture videos are used: science, engineering, medicine, philosophy, psychology, and art from Kyoto University OCW (https://ocw.kyoto-u.ac.jp), which are the lecture videos released by Kyoto University faculty members.

3.2 Experimental Procedure

(1) Subject
The subjects were 34 students from Kyoto University (23 males and 11 females). All of them are in their late teens and twenties (avg. = 20.6, sd = 1.68).

(2) Image/Video Presentation Procedure
There are 6 conditions that combined the experimental conditions described in 3.1 (1) and (2). For each of the subject all of these conditions were presented randomly as 6 trials. For each trial the above contents were assigned in well-balanced way using the design of experiment [12]. Each trial consists of; break (30 s) → content viewing (10 min) → intermediate evaluation (5 min) → content viewing (10 min) → final evaluation (5 min) (Fig. 4).

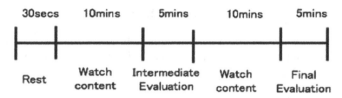

Fig. 4. Procedure of content viewing and evaluation

(3) Measurement Method
The semantic differential (SD) method was adopted as the subjective evaluation method. The SD method uses an evaluation scale in which adjectives with opposite meanings are placed at both ends and the space between them is divided into 7 or 5 stages. In this experiment, a 7-stage evaluation scale was used.

(4) Evaluation Items
While referring to subjective evaluation items of the previous studies [4, 5, 7, 8], we adopted the 6 subjective evaluation measurement items shown in Table 1 and asked each subject to fill out a questionnaire.

When displaying on a large screen, whether or not a sense of presence is realized is often used as an evaluation item [13]. However, assuming that the large screen display is becoming normal and that it will be used in lectures and classes, we did not include items related to the sense of presence. In addition, considering the wide range of subjects' fields of study, the content was selected equally from the science and humanities, rather than the content biased to some fields. In addition, since the degree of understanding of the lecture content will affect the evaluation results, the content was selected from a slightly higher level of lecture content for students in specialized fields rather than for the general public. Instead of having subjects evaluate their comprehension, we used general evaluation items such as "Is it easy to see" or "Is it possible to concentrate?"

As mentioned above, the content is presented as shown in Fig. 4 under 6 kinds of experimental conditions given in random order. During 20 min of viewing, an intermediate evaluation was done at the middle of 10 min and the final evaluation was done after watching. As there was no evaluation difference between these two evaluations, the final evaluation result was used for the analysis.

Table 1. Subjective evaluation item

Satisfied – unsatisfied
Easy to watch – difficult to watch
Awakened – sleepy
Concentrated – not concentrated
Motivated – not motivated
Want to watch longer – don't want to watch longer

4 Results and Discussion

4.1 Average Value of Subjective Evaluation Items

Six types of experimental conditions were compared for each subjective evaluation item. Figure 5 shows a comparison of two display methods and three lighting conditions for the six evaluation items.

4.2 Consideration of the Average Value of Subjective Evaluation Items

(1) Regarding Overall Satisfaction
The evaluation score of the LED display decreased as it got darker, while the projector increased. The LED display has a high score of 5.29 for full lighting condition, but it decreases to 5 for half lighting and 4.56 for no lighting. In a comparison experiment between art content and text-based content, the darker the LED display, the higher the evaluation [5], but in this experiment, the evaluation score decreases as the illuminance decreases. In the case of art content, lowering the illuminance had the effect of making details look clearer. But in the case of content such as lectures and presentations, when the illuminance is lowered, probably the contrast between the text and the background is strongly felt. On the other hand, in the case of a projector, the average score is 3.68 for full lighting, but for half lighting it is 4.18, which exceeds the center value, and when the lights are off, the evaluation score is 4.97, higher than LED display.

From these, it is necessary to pay attention to the following when displaying contents on a large screen in the case of presentations and lectures.

- LED display is excellent under the condition of the brightness of 200 lx or more.
- However, it is desirable to adjust the brightness of the LED display in dark conditions.
- It is desirable to use the projector under conditions where the lights are turned off as much as possible.
- Under the condition of the brightness of 200 lx or more, it is necessary to use the projector with high brightness.

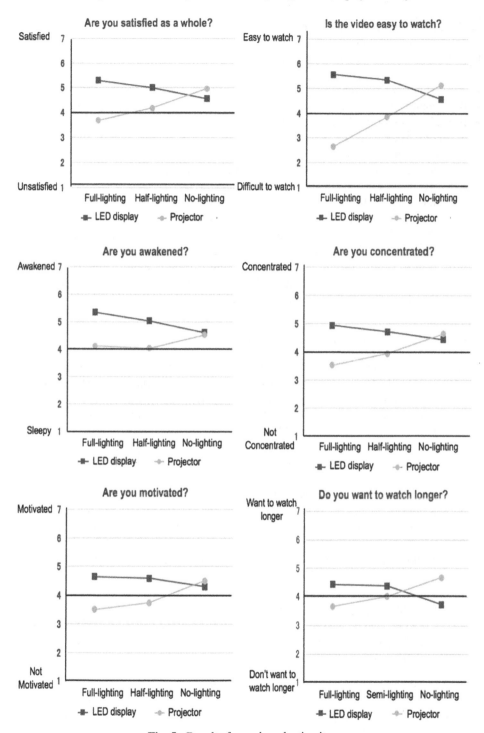

Fig. 5. Results for each evaluation item

(2) Regarding Other Evaluation Items

For the other evaluation items, similar results as the overall satisfaction were obtained for all the evaluation items. In particular,

- All evaluation items show that the evaluation score of the LED display decreases as the illuminance decreases, and conversely the evaluation score of the projector increases.
- In the case of full lighting and half lighting, the LED display always gets a higher evaluation score than the projector.
- When the light is off, the evaluation values of the LED display and the projector are close to each other, or for several evaluation items, the scores are reversed.

The tendency of the score of each evaluation item shows almost the same tendency as the result of overall satisfaction. However, concerning "whether the video is easy to watch", the result is that the value of the projector changes greatly. It is a low value of 2.65 for full lighting, but it is 3.84 for half lighting, and 5.12 for no lighting, which exceeds that of the LED projector. Probably this is because the evaluation item "whether the video is easy to watch" is not an emotional evaluation item but a quantitative evaluation item so that the effect of illuminance on the projector is directly exerted.

4.3 Two-Way Analysis of Variance (Two-Way ANOVA)

Factors affecting the results of this experiment include two conditions related to the display method (LED display/projector) and three conditions related to the lighting conditions (full-lighting/half-lighting/no-lighting). Therefore, to perform a more detailed analysis, two-way ANOVA (analysis of variance) was performed. Table 2 shows a summary of the results of two-way ANOVA.

Since it is considered that the results related to the total satisfaction are representative one from Fig. 5, the results of the two-way ANOVA regarding the total satisfaction will be mainly described.

The results showed that the main effect on lighting conditions ($F(2,66) = 1.27$, $p = .289$) was not significant, whereas the main effect on display method ($F(1,33) = 15.75$, $p < .001$), the interaction between the display method and the lighting conditions ($F(2,66) = 23.50$, $p < .001$) was found to be significant.

The result of the simple main effect is that the simple effect of the lighting condition when using the LED display ($F(2,132) = 5.09$, $p = .007$) and also the simple effect of the lighting condition when using the projector ($F(2,132) = 15.83$, $p < .001$) were significant. Regarding the lighting conditions, the simple effect for full-lighting ($F(1,99) = 44.55$, $p < .001$) and the simple effect for half-lighting ($F(1,99) = 11.55$, $p = .001$) are significant. However, the simple effect ($F(1,99) = 2.89$, $p = .092$) for no lighting was off was not significant.

Table 2. Results of two-way ANOVA

		Are you satisfied?	Is it easy to watch?	Are you awakened?	Are you concentrated?	Are you motivated?	Do you want to watch longer?
Main effect	Display method	**	**	**	**	**	ns
	Lighting condition	ns	**	ns	ns	ns	ns
Interaction	Display method×Lighting condition	**	**	*	**	**	**
Main effect of a factor for each level of another factor	Display method at full-lighting	**	**	**	**	**	*
	Display method at half-lighting	**	**	**	**	**	ns
	Display method at no-lighting	ns	*	ns	ns	ns	**
	Lighting condition display＝LED	**	**	*	ns	ns	*
	Lighting condition at display＝Proj	**	**	ns	**	**	**
Multiple comparison	Full-lighting: LED - Proj	**	**	**	**	**	*
	Half-lighitng: LED - Proj	**	**	*	*	**	ns
	No-lighting: LED - Proj	ns	*	ns	ns	ns	*
	LED: Full - Half-lighting	ns	ns	ns	ns	ns	ns
	LED: Full - No-lighting	*	**	*	ns	ns	*
	LED: Half - No-lighting	ns	**	ns	ns	ns	ns
	Proj: Full - Half-lighting	*	**	ns	ns	ns	ns
	Proj: Full - No-lighting	**	**	ns	**	**	**
	Proj: Half - No-lighting	*	**	ns	*	**	ns

**: p<.01, *: p<.05, ns:Not statistically significant

For the multiple comparisons using the Holm method, when using the LED display, the comparison between full-lighting and no-lighting (p = .012) is significant, but the comparison between full-lighting and half-lighting and between half-lighting and no-lighting are not significant. When using a projector, the comparison between full-lighting and no-lighting (p < .001) is significant, but the comparison between full-lighting and half-lighting (p = .044) and between half-lighting and no-lighting (p = .014) were significant. Figure 6 shows the result of total satisfaction including these results.

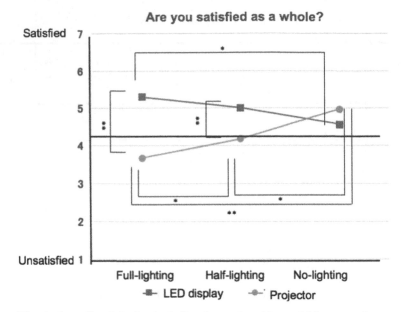

Fig. 6. Overall satisfaction including the results of the multiple comparisons.

5 Conclusion

Which is more advantageous, LED display or projector when displaying content on a large screen is an important issue, as showing contents using large display is becoming popular in many occasions including entertainment. But few experiments have been reported so far that directly compare the projector and the LED display under various conditions.

We are approaching this problem by using a 200-inch LED display and a 200-inch screen + projector. In the previous research [6], we conducted an evaluation experiment on what kind of environmental conditions are suitable while comparing art content with text content. As a result, based on the average score and the result of multiple comparisons, "art content × LED × no-lighting" gives a very high score.

However, LED displays and projectors are mainly used for presentations at academic conferences, lectures, etc. In such cases, there are many situations where images and videos are used together with text. Conventionally, projectors have often been used in such situations, but as large LED displays have become cheaper, there are increasing opportunities for LED displays to be used. As it is useful to compare the LED display and the projector in such a situation, we conducted a comparative experiment in such an environment.

In this research, the content was displayed under a total of 6 environmental conditions that combined the conditions of a 200-inch LED display/200-inch screen + projector, and full-lighting/half-lighting/no-lighting. The SD method was applied to 34 subjects. As the content, we assumed the scene of lectures and presentations and considered avoiding the influence of the content by using multiple contents. As a result, lecture videos covering a wide range of fields such as science, engineering, medicine, psychology, philosophy, and art were selected from the lecture videos by Kyoto University faculty members and used in the experiments.

As a result, we obtained an interesting result that the evaluation score decreases as the lighting conditions become darker when using an LED display, whereas it increases as the lighting condition becomes darker in the case of a projector. In addition, the LED display obtained a higher evaluation score than the projector under bright conditions, but the difference between the two became smaller as the lighting became darker, and the results were the same under the no-lighting condition, or the evaluation score of the projector was higher than LED display.

Furthermore, by performing two-way ANOVA, detailed results were obtained on how each factor interacts with other factors and influences the evaluation score under various conditions. We believe that we have obtained guidelines for using LED displays and projectors when giving lectures and presentations.

In this experiment, the subjects were students in their 20s, and it is thought that the sensibilities of the young generation are reflected in the results. As our future research, it is necessary to conduct experiments using subjects of other generations.

References

1. Blokdyk, G.: Projection mapping a complete guide. 5STARCooks (2018)
2. Schmitt, D., Thebat, M., Burczykowski, L. (eds.): Image Beyond the Screen: Projection Mapping. Wiley-ISTE (2020)
3. Gilinsky, A.G.: Perceived size and distance in visual space. Psychol. Rev. **58**, 460–482 (1951)
4. Narita, N., Masaru, K., Okano, F.: Optimum screen size of viewing distance for viewing ultra high-definition and wide-screen images. J. Inst. Image Inform. TV Eng. **55**(5), 773–780 (2001)
5. Ni, T., Bowan, D.A., Chen, J.: Increased display size and resolution improve task performance in information-rich virtual environments. Proc. Graph. Interface **2006**, 139–146 (2006)
6. Liou, J.-J., Huang, L.-L., Wu, C.-F., Yeh, C.-L., Chen, Y.-H.: A study of vision ergonomic of LED display signs on different environment illuminance. In: Proceedings of the 9th International Conference on Engineering Psychology and Cognitive Ergonomics, pp. 53–62 (2011)
7. Sakamoto, K., Sakashita, S., Yamashita, K., Okada, A.: Influence of high-resolution 4K displays on psychological state during content viewing. In: Proceedings of the 16th International Conference on Human Computer Interaction International, pp. 363–367 (2014)
8. Narita, N., Kanazawa, M.: Psychological factors of 2D/3D HDTV sequences and evaluation method of their overall impressions. J. Inst. Image Inform. TV Eng. **57**(4), 501–506 (2003)
9. Nakatsu, R., Tosa, N, Kusumi, T., Takada, H.: Psychological evaluation for images/videos displayed using large led display and projector. In: IFIP International Conference on Entertainment Computing 2020, pp. 382–390. LNCS 12523 (2020)
10. Pang, Y., Zhao, L., Nakatsu, R., Tosa, N.: A study on variable control of sound vibration form (SVF) for media art creation. In: 2015 Conference on Culture and Computing. IEEE Press (2015)
11. Tosa, N., Pang, Y., Yang, Q., Nakatsu, R.: Pursuit and expression of Japanese beauty using technology. Arts J. MDPI **8**(1), 38 (2019). https://doi.org/10.3390/arts8010038

12. Fisher, R.A.: The Design of Experiments, 9th edn. Macmillan (1971)
13. Duval, T., Nguyen, H., Fleury, C., Chauffaut, A., Dumont, G., Gouranton, V.: Embedding the features of the users' physical environments to improve the feeling of presence in collaborative virtual environments. In: IEEE 3rd International Conference on Cognitive Infocommunications (2012)

CS:Show – An Interactive Visual Analysis Tool for First-Person Shooter eSports Match Data

Robin Horst[✉], Stefan Manuel Zander, and Ralf Dörner

RheinMain University of Applied Sciences, Wiesbaden, Germany
{Robin.Horst,Ralf.Doerner}@hs-rm.de

Abstract. Electronic Sports (eSports) is a fast-growing domain within the entertainment sector and becomes economically relevant in terms of a paying audience, merchandise, and major tournaments with highly endowed prize money. First-person shooter (FPS) games represent a dominant discipline. Professional training methodologies such as post-match analyses and tactics discussions are becoming essential in training sessions besides pure mechanical-oriented exercises such as aiming and movement. Furthermore, professional sports coaches are involved in the training of players. In this paper, we are investigating this newly developing profession, specifically, how multimedia systems can be built to support coaches and players in analyzing data of previous matches for preparing for future ones. In the example of Counter-Strike: Global Offensive (CS:GO), we identified a set of six criteria that can be incorporated into tools to support the analysis of FPS matches. We describe user interface functionalities that allow to interactively analyze the highly multivariate data of FPS matches. We show our concepts' technical feasibility by implementing them within a tool – *CS:Show*. Within an expert user study, evaluate our concepts with professionals. We conclude that our proposed eSports analysis tool was preferred over analysis functionalities built in in CS:GO. Supported by statistically significant evidence, our participants rated our tool more efficient, more usable, and assigned the tool with higher analytical ability than an average tool for analyzing FPS eSports matches.

Keywords: eSports · Information visualization · Competitive games · Match analysis · Coaching tools · First-person shooter · Visual analytics · Counter-strike · Global offensive

The work is supported by the Federal Ministry of Education and Research of Germany in the project Innovative Hochschule (funding number: 03IHS071).

J. Baalsrud Hauge et al. (Eds.): ICEC 2021, LNCS 13056, pp. 15–27, 2021.
https://doi.org/10.1007/978-3-030-89394-1_2

1   Introduction

Electronic Sports (eSports) is a developing industry and is growing rapidly in recent years [6]. Competitive gaming is becoming professional and profitable for teams, managers, and other stakeholders such as event and streaming hosts [12]. Furthermore, traditional sports clubs are already investing in eSports teams [22]. There is also investment in the teams' professional training, for example, coaches who plan and lead the athletes' training sessions [4]. However, only little is scientifically investigated concerning the professional training of eSports athletes when it comes to using the plethora of multivariate data that can be obtained from past matches. It could be used to draw conclusions for future ones, for example, by analyzing upcoming opponents in a league, identifying weaknesses of the team, and developing new tactics.

In this paper, we investigate analyzing matches of first-person shooter (FPS) games and make the following contributions:

- We propose six criteria that allow professional coaches and players to analyze FPS matches systematically.
- In the example of Counter-Strike: Global Offensive (CS:GO), we show the feasibility of our criteria based on available eSports data and implement a match analysis tool – *CS:Show*. We employ the tool within a user study with CS:GO professionals. Based on our study's results, we evaluate our proposed tool and point out other functionalities that should be considered within the design of future eSports match analysis systems.

The paper is organized as follows. We briefly review related work in the next section. Then, we present six criteria we identified for analyzing FPS matches. After that, we describe how we designed and implemented our CS:Show tool. Before we conclude, we report and discuss our findings from our expert user study.

2   Related Work

The training of eSports athletes can easily occupy between 12 and 14 h per day [9,18]. However, Kari and Karhulahti [14] could point out that only less than half of this time on average is spent actively playing eSports games. That leaves a significant amount of training time for team meetings, review sessions, video analyses, strategic discussion, etc. [14].

Work by Snavely [21] states that coaches prepare such theory-oriented training sessions by considering past matches of both their own and opposing teams and analyze the players' abilities and habits, such as typical positioning, aim, angles that are observed, decision making, communication between players, among others. The results of their analyses are discussed in the following sessions with the players, where various aspects and situations are pointed out, reviewed, and visually supported by utilizing recorded demos and map-data.

Finally, coaches try to develop overall guidelines and strategies with the players based on their analyses.

Overall, map-visualizations and demos are used within the theory-sessions emphasize the analyses and work out novel strategies with the players. A common task that coaches perform during these sessions is drawing rough layouts of player movements and potential routes onto visual map-representations using standard painting programs [7]. These drawings are performed iteratively based on the personal feedback of the players [2].

With regard to software tools that are used for training and analysis, besides painting and drawing programs, there also exist eSports-specific tools that aim at supporting coaches and players in developing new strategies and analyzing matches. Concerning FPS games and CS:GO, we identified tools such as Noesis [3], Skybox.gg [20], Scope.gg [19], AkiVer CS:GO Demo Manager [1], and demoanalyzer-go [16] as current examples. All of these tools support analysts (i.e., coaches or players) similarly to parse the contents of demo files and present the results to the analysts.

In the CS:GO community, the use of demos is established due to their capability of reviewing matches from different perspectives, including any player's perspective, and they usually have a smaller file size compared to video recordings [5]. However, the demo files and their data can only be used and reviewed using proprietary tools or functionalities built within the competitive games themselves. For example, the built-in CS:GO and Overwatch replay viewer provides basic functionalities for loading and reviewing recorded demos. However, they lack advanced analysis features. Providing the analysts with more in-depth information about their games and their opponents would allow them to learn more about their matches and perform better in future matches [15].

Except for demoanalyzer-go, a command-line program, the mentioned tools provide analysts with a graphical user interface (GUI). In terms of functionality, demoanalyzer-go is the only program that provides an automated ranking prediction based on the demo file's statistical data [16]. Noesis, Skybox.gg, and Scope.gg each provide a timeline where analysts can jump to single points in time and get the positions of players and metadata visualized [3,19,20]. A selection of multiple timeframes for further exploration [26] of the multivariate and temporal data is not provided. AkiVer CS:GO Demo Manager and demoanalyzer-go do not offer timelines [1,16].

Noesis, Scope.gg, and CS:GO Demo Manager all feature heat maps for visualizing the data [1,3,19], although their implementations differ from tool to tool. They either visualize the players' kills or deaths. Scope.gg's implementation provides its heat maps based on zones, which are customarily defined areas for each map of CS:GO.

The AkiVer CS:GO Demo Manager, Noesis and Scope.gg and all feature a mini-map on which player positions are drawn [1,3,19]. On this map visualization, the players' view directions are visualized by lines indicating solely the direction or cones indicating the viewing angle of players. Compared to the 2D map representation of AkiVer CS:GO Demo Manager, Noesis, and Scope.gg, Skybox.gg does not provide a common top-down map view but a 3D view.

Finally, there exists substantial work that focuses on psychological aspects of eSports players (e.g., [11]) or economic and management perspectives (e.g., [8]). Results from related work concerning training and coaching practices and methodologies support the importance of theoretical preparation and the potential of using software tools to support coaches and players in it. However, we identified a research gap in this area since little scientific work was found. Within the investigation of existing tools for practitioners, we pointed out common functionalities that should be considered as a start for investigating tools for pre- and post-analyses of FPS matches.

3   FPS Match Analysis Criteria

In this section, we present six criteria we identified for analyzing FPS games. We do not claim to present a complete list of criteria, but an initial set that serves as a foundation for our FPS match analysis tool.

Criteria 1 – Location Awareness: A common objective in FPS games (e.g., CS:GO, Overwatch, Battlefield, etc.) is to target certain areas or objectives in the level [17]. One team must prevent the other team from accomplishing the objectives. A common tactic for the defending team is *camping*, where players would find hiding spots and wait there for the attacking (*rushing*) team to approach the objective [25]. Within match analysis procedures, it is crucial being able on the one hand to point out hiding spots of the defending team to anticipate their behavior and prepare for them when attacking, and on the other hand, to foresee which routes the attacking team will take to get to the objective to find the best hiding spots when defending.

Criteria 2 – Blind Spots: Due to the dominant shooting mechanics within FPS games, analyzing the vision can give advantageous insights into what areas are commonly watched by the opponents and avoid these areas [13]. This is particularly important in FPS games where single shots can be lethal (e.g., CS:GO) since the first shot may be the fatal one without the possibility to react to fire. Players in FPS games only have a certain view angle (in CS:GO fixed to 90°) so that blind spots exist (e.g., behind the player or far left/right of the viewing direction). Furthermore, even areas that lie within the current viewing direction of players might not be fully perceived. For example, players watch closer areas more thoroughly than farther areas. Information about these blind spots can be aggregated over certain time spans, for example, to provide analysts with information about which areas are more or less observed throughout a match.

Criteria 3 – Patience: Our third criteria, patience, is also related to the location of players. It describes the players' movement behavior in terms of a player's average resting time in one location before switching locations. Knowing the patience factor of specific players may enable coaches to develop tactics to counteract their actions. Patience is not only applicable to positions but also to the actions of players, for example, how frequently players perform weapon switching, jumping, or crouching, etc.

Criteria 4 – Aggressiveness: Aggressiveness is a criterion that measures how brisk a player acts. On the one hand, patience is a sub-aspect, for example, when a player has a low patience factor, a player may be attributed aggressive. But on the other hand, we incorporate another factor in aggressiveness that states how players react to friendly or opponent team members' actions. Such insight can give coaches information for deciding how enemy players can be disrupted and lured into actions. Furthermore, this criterion can be used to coach the own team and give advice on when to be more aggressive and when to stay calm, and carefully consider reactions to enemy activities such as shots fired or grenades thrown.

Criteria 5 – Weapons: The use of different weapons is another elementary mechanic in FPS games, with each weapon having various characteristics [24]. Different weapons can have different trade-offs, such as damage done vs. projectile range vs. accuracy vs. bullet spread, etc. The knowledge of what weapons are preferred by opponents can be used by coaches to make informed decisions on which weapons are suitable and advantageous to the enemies' tactics (e.g., sniper vs. close combat shotgun). However, such decisions are also dependent on the level design.

Criteria 6 – Utility: Our last criteria is the players' use of utilities. As utilities of FPS games, we summarize weapon mechanics and game objects that are not primary shooting or hitting weapons, such as grenades that inflict damage, grenades that impair the vision (e.g., flash grenade), grenades that impair the movement (e.g., stun grenades), or utilities that effect a whole area (e.g., flame (molotov) grenades or smoke grenades). The utility aspect includes when and where such utilities are used and give insight into their trajectories. The anticipation of such utilities can help coaches and players developing strategies to avoid the opponents' successful use of them, for example, avoiding particular routes where opponents regularly use such utilities or dodging them.

4   CS:Show Tool

In this section, we describe the GUI design of CS:Show – an FPS match analysis tool in the example of CS:GO.

Our tool's multi-view GUI consists of eight elements further described in the following. Figure 1 illustrates them. The (1) *top menu bar* at the top of the GUI (Fig. 1) provides system functionality such as loading a demo file into the tool, handling the multiple windows, or closing the application.

The (2) *player list* (Fig. 1 upper left) displays all players that were part of the match. It also illustrates their status with respect to the currently selected timeframe (in CS:GO called *tick*). For example, it reveals whether players are already dead at the current tick. Furthermore, the menu shows which team the players belong to and lets users select one or more players. Based on the player list selection, our tool provides additional information on demand about the current state within the (3) *statistics view* (Fig. 1 lower left).

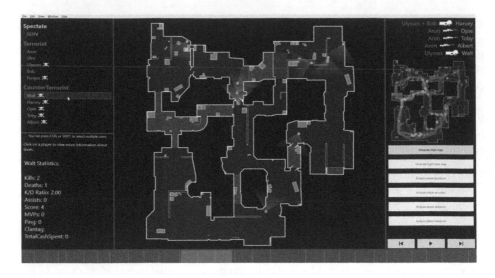

Fig. 1. A screenshot of the CS:Show GUI.

The (4) *timeline* (Fig. 1 bottom) provides users with the ability to jump to a specific tick of the match, so that information about the players within the statistics view can display tick-specific information. Furthermore, multiple ticks can be selected as a coherent range of ticks (Fig. 1 bottom, orange bar within the timeline). This functionality enables our users to create a heat map from a selected time range of the match rather than only from the data of an entire match. The timeline also can display important match events such as a round start, bomb plantings, etc., directly on the timeline. For example, the grey strokes in Fig. 1 show the start of rounds to help users get an overview of the data.

The (5) *mini-map view* (Fig. 1 middle) illustrates outlines and important zones of a certain CS:GO level such as bomb or hostage zones and player spawns. Furthermore, it visualizes the players' positions at the current tick of the match and shows players' view frustums to illustrate potential blind spots at a given time.

The (6) *kill feed* shows the sequence of a round's kills. Pictographs visualize which weapon was used for the kill. The order of the player names encodes who was killed by whom similarly to the in-game visualization of kills in CS:GO.

The (7) *heat map view* displays a small version of the mini-map with a heat map overlay. This gives users a glimpse in the match data over the selected range of ticks and the selected players concerning a specific aspect such as the positioning, death, vision, etc. This view can be detached, for example, to view it on a second monitor to see both the mini-map view and the heat map view simultaneously during the analysis process. Furthermore, it can also be switched with the mini-map view so that the heat map is displayed in the middle and the mini-map is displayed smaller and on the side.

Finally, the (8) *meta tools* allow users of our tool to alter the current mini-map or heat map view. For example, drawing tools are provided to draw lines, basic forms, or freehand lines to prepare a specific tick for discussing it within a review session with the team later. Besides drawing-related meta tools, we also provide meta tools that guide users by analyzing specific match aspects and criteria such as player accuracy, patience, or fine-grained heat map adjustments. The latter includes altering the brush stroke size of heat maps. Fine-grained brush strokes help to analyze the individual players' movements (Fig. 2 left), whereas a coarse brush stroke size is suitable for providing a general overview of the map and its hot spots (Fig. 2 right).

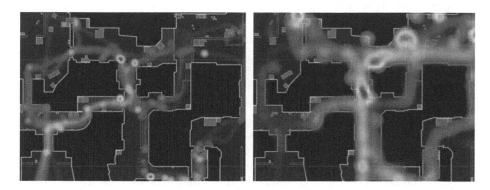

Fig. 2. Two situations with different heat map brush stroke sizes.

We used C# and the GUI framework Windows Presentation Foundation (WPF) to implement the CS:Show visual analysis tool. Each of the mentioned elements was implemented as separate WPF user control to preserve their reusability in future versions of the tool. For drawing functionality such as the heat map generation, we utilized a native heat map library exported as DLL and called via Platform Invocation (P/Invoke).

5   Evaluation

Within an expert user study, we evaluated our proposed CS:Show tool. The study involved ten unpaid and voluntary participants (aged between 16 and 32 years with Ø 22.90 and SD 4.65). They were recruited from professional service providers (e.g., Fiverr and social media platforms (e.g., Reddit). We selected them based on their subjective classification as professional CS:GO coaches and players and objective skill measures (e.g., competitive CS:GO ranking as Global Elite (highest possible rank), total CS:GO playtime, or currently being a professional CS:GO team's coach.). The user study was conducted as a moderated remote study using Discord.

The procedure of the study took place as follows. Firstly, participants were welcomed and then informed about the topic of the study. We introduced them to the UI of the tool and the process of the evaluation. Then the actual task phase of the study started. In this phase, our participants were asked to perform nine tasks with the tool, such as familiarizing with the tool for several minutes, loading and analyzing demos, and drawing conclusions on tactical aspects that could be derived with the tool. Finally, we asked our participants to fill out a questionnaire.

We evaluated four aspects with this questionnaire:

[A1] *Ease of use*: How usable is our tool?

[A2] *Analysis ability*: How well enables our tool analysts to conduct analyses based on the provided functionalities?

[A3] *Efficiency*: How well does the analysis approach with our tool justifies the time it takes?

[A4] *Product character*: The product character [10] is a measure incorporating both pragmatic and hedonic qualities.

Relating to the product character (A4), we utilized the abbreviated AttrakD-iff questionnaire [23] as an established tool for measuring it. Aspects 1–3 were captured with seven questions Q1–Q7 on a 7-point semantic differential scale. They were concerned with (Q1) the GUI quality, (Q2) the analysis ability of our tool compared to other analysis procedures, (Q3) the performance, (Q4) the task efficiency, (Q5) the heat map visualization, (Q6) the displayed statistics, and (Q7) the analysis of player behavior. The questions were clustered to the aspects 1–3, whereas Q1, Q3, and Q4 were clustered to A1, Q5, Q6, and Q7 to A2, and Q4 and Q2 to A3. Finally, space for written comments and demographic questions concluded the questionnaire. A single session of the study was performed within a roughly one hour timeframe.

5.1   Analysis of the Results

Figure 3a (left) represents the value distributions of the single items Q1–Q7. The box-whisker plots show that the mean values of all single questions lie above the hypothetical neutral value of 3. Wilcoxon signed-rank tests were conducted on the items to analyze how CS:Show was rated by the participants compared to a neutral rating. With a threshold for statistical significance of 5%, the tests for Q1, Q3, Q4, and Q6 did confirm statistically significant differences (Table 1). Furthermore, Fig. 3a (right) shows the value distributions of the three observed aspects 1–3. Again, all mean values lie above 3. Further Wilcoxon signed-rank tests were conducted to test the outcome for the aspects against a neutral rating. All tests confirm significant differences.

The written comments from the questionnaire, observations, and oral statements during the study were used to capture additional information and were assigned to A1–A3. Concerning A1, we noticed difficulties creating the heat map. For example, two out of ten participants failed to select the players from the player list before creating the heat map. Furthermore, one participant did not figure out that a time span selection on the timeline must be made prior as

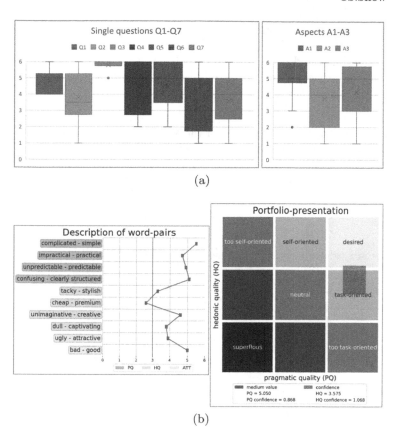

Fig. 3. (a) Box-whisker plots for the single questions 1–6 and the aggregated aspects 1–3. (b) Description of word-pairs and portfolio-presentation of the AttrakDiff values.

well. Finally, several minor negative comments were given about the prototypical look of the interface.

Concerning A2, our participants proposed to exclude the *freeze time* from the heat map generation (the time in which players spawn and are unable to move to give the teams sufficient time to communicate purchasing gear). Furthermore, they suggested also providing heat maps for player deaths, kills, and *entry frags* (first kill in a round). Our participants also noted that the money players carry and have spent would allow the analysis of an individual player's economy. Finally, one participant asked for insights in data about flashbang grenades, for example, at which times players threw such grenades, which areas were affected, and which players were blinded by them.

Concerning A3, six out of ten stated that they would prefer CS:Show over the built-in demo viewer they often use and found our tool more efficient. Still, they also stated that the workflow would benefit from using drag-and-drop actions, for example, for loading demo files. Furthermore, it was suggested to add fast-forward playback functionality to speed up finding specific demo sections. Some participants also noted that zooming into both the timeline and the map visualization would be beneficial. Finally, it was proposed to add functionality to enter a particular tick by its number to jump to it directly rather than navigating to it using the timeline.

Table 1. Mean values, SD, and output of the Wilcoxon signed-rank tests for Q1–Q7 and A1–A3. All values are rounded to four decimal places.

Questions/aspects	Ø-values	SD	P-values
Q1	4.8	0.7888	$p = 0.0020$
Q2	3.8	1.6865	$p = 0.1563$
Q3	5.8	0.4216	$p = 0.0020$
Q4	4.5	1.5811	$p = 0.0195$
Q5	4.5	1.5092	$p = 0.0195$
Q6	3.2	1.7512	$p = 0.7422$
Q7	3.6	1.6465	$p = 0.3828$
A1	5.0333	1.1592	$p \leq 0.0001$
A2	3.7667	1.6750	$p = 0.0230$
A3	4.1500	1.6311	$p = 0.0042$

The outcome of the AttrakDiff questionnaire was analyzed concerning the product character of CS:Show (A4). The portfolio-presentation (Fig. 3b right) shows that CS:Show was placed within the graph's 'task-oriented' region. The square is shifted towards the 'desired' area, and the confidence rectangle overlaps slightly with it. The word-pair visualization (Fig. 3b left) shows that all mean values lie above 3 and thereby on the positive side of the graph, except 'cheap–premium', which lies between 2 and 3.

5.2   Discussion of the Results

The evaluation results show that professional eSports coaches and players could successfully use CS:Show to analyze CS:GO matches. The ease of use (A1) of our tool was rated the most positive of the three aspects. The overall positive perception is supported by statistical significance and the AttrakDiff evaluation. However, both the medium deviation of Q1 and the AttrakDiff items 'ugly–attractive' and 'cheap–premium' suggest improving the visual GUI quality in future versions of our tool.

Concerning the analysis ability (A2), the results indicate that our participants could develop novel strategies with our tool and that the visualizations within our heat map we provided were positively accepted. This claim is also backed by statistical significance. However, our participants also suggested several aspects that would be beneficial, which we did not include in CS:Show.

Furthermore, we could also not find the mentioned functionality in most of the analyzed tools in Sect. 2. This indicates that improvements such as economic- and utility-related aspects should be investigated in future work.

The efficiency (A3) was also rated positively. While this could also be backed by statistical significance, our participants noted that our tool would be more efficient than existing tools when including the additional functions mentioned in A2. Q2's deviation range also supports this claim.

Finally, concerning our tool's product character (A4), the AttrakDiff results support the high usability of our tool with the pragmatic qualities items. Still, hedonic qualities could be improved. For example, re-implementing the tool with modern web GUI frameworks such as vue.js or react might help creating a more contemporary look and providing subtle visual improvements such as fade- and button animations and layout styles.

6   Conclusion and Future Work

In this paper, we investigated interactive eSports FPS match analysis procedures. In the example of CS:GO, we introduced six criteria that can be incorporated in tools to support the analysis of FPS matches. We described a suitable GUI and aspects concerning the implementation and provision of the criteria concepts for coaches and players within an interactive analysis tool – CS:Show. Based on our user study's results with professional eSports coaches and players and backed by statistical evidence, we conclude that CS:Show could be used successfully by our participants. Furthermore, we pointed out novel features that should be included in future match analysis tools.

Future work should investigate the novel identified features and how CS:Show can include them. Furthermore, based on our work, it should be explored how match data from other FPS eSports games can be included within our analysis tool. We have shown the feasibility in the example of CS:GO, but other competitive FPS games such as Overwatch, Rainbow Six Siege, Call of Duty, Battlefield, etc., might be analyzed using our criteria as well. Finally, the analysis of matches from different FPS games might also bring up novel criteria that can be used to support CS:GO coaches and players. This way, a comprehensive pool of FPS analysis criteria that experts can choose of establishes, and the growing eSports field will further professionalize and advance.

References

1. Akiver: Akiver analysis tool (2021). https://github.com/akiver/CSGO-Demos-Manager. Accessed 15 Sept 2021
2. Andreasen, M.S., Caspersen, T.B.: The human factor in eSport: Esport psychology. BoD-Books on Demand (2019)
3. Bang & Jensen ApS: Noesis analysis tool (2021). https://www.noesis.gg/. Accessed 15 Sept 2021

4. Bányai, F., Griffiths, M.D., Király, O., Demetrovics, Z.: The psychology of eSports: a systematic literature review. J. Gambl. Stud. **35**(2), 351–365 (2019). https://doi.org/10.1007/s10899-018-9763-1
5. Bednárek, D., Kruliš, M., Yaghob, J., Zavoral, F.: Data preprocessing of eSport game records. In: Proceedings of the 6th International Conference on Data Science, Technology and Applications, pp. 269–276. SCITEPRESS-Science and Technology Publications, Lda (2017)
6. Block, S., Haack, F.: eSports: a new industry. In: SHS Web of Conferences, vol. 92. EDP Sciences (2021)
7. Fanfarelli, J.R.: Expertise in professional overwatch play. Int. J. Gaming Comput. Mediat. Simul. (IJGCMS) **10**(1), 1–22 (2018)
8. Hallmann, K., Giel, T.: eSports-competitive sports or recreational activity? Sport Manage. Rev. **21**(1), 14–20 (2018)
9. Jacobs, H.: Here's the insane training schedule of a 20-something professional gamer (2015). https://www.businessinsider.com/pro-gamers-explain-the-insane-training-regimen-they-use-to-stay-on-top-2015-5. Accessed 15 Sept 2021
10. Hassenzahl, M.: The thing and I: understanding the relationship between user and product. In: Blythe, M., Monk, A. (eds.) Funology 2. HIS, pp. 301–313. Springer, Cham (2018). https://doi.org/10.1007/978-3-319-68213-6_19
11. Hung, J.C., Lin, Z.-Q., Huang, C.-H., Lin, K.-C.: The research of applying affective computing based on deep learning for eSports training. In: Hung, J.C., Yen, N.Y., Chang, J.-W. (eds.) FC 2019. LNEE, vol. 551, pp. 122–129. Springer, Singapore (2020). https://doi.org/10.1007/978-981-15-3250-4_15
12. Jenny, S.E., et al.: eSports venues: a new sport business opportunity. J. Appl. Sport Manage. **10**(1), 8 (2018)
13. Jordan, C.: Information Models in Multiplayer Gaming: Teaching New Players the Complex In-game Economy of Counter-Strike: Global Offensive. Ph.D. thesis, Auckland University of Technology (2020)
14. Kari, T., Karhulahti, V.M.: Do e-athletes move? A study on training and physical exercise in elite e-sports. Int. J. Gaming Comput. Mediat. Simul. (IJGCMS) **8**(4), 53–66 (2016)
15. Larsen, L.J.: The play of champions: Toward a theory of skill in eSport, pp. 1–23. Sport, Ethics and Philosophy (2020)
16. Quancore: demoanalyzer-go analysis tool (2021). https://github.com/quancore/demoanalyzer-go. Accessed 15 Sept 2021
17. Rayner, D.C.F.: Analysing openings in tactical simulations. Ph.D. thesis, University of Alberta (2008)
18. Stanton, R.: The secret to eSsports athletes' success? Lots - and lots - of practice (2015). https://www.espn.com/espn/story/_/id/13053116/esports-athletes-put-hours-training-reach-pinnacle (2015). Accessed 15 September 2021
19. Scope.gg. CS:GO Analytics.: Scope.gg analysis tool (2021). https://scope.gg/. Accessed 15 September 2021
20. Skybox Technologies ApS: Skybox analysis tool (2021). https://landing.skybox.gg/. Accessed 15 Sept 2021d
21. Snavely, T.L.: History and analysis of eSport systems. Ph.D. thesis, University of Texas at Austin (2014)
22. Ströh, J.H.A.: The eSports market and eSports sponsoring. Tectum Wissenschaftsverlag (2017)
23. User Interface Design GmbH: AttrakDiff questionnaire (2021). http://attrakdiff.de/index-en.html. Accessed 15 Sept 2021

24. Vorderer, P., Bryant, J.: Playing Video Games: Motives, Responses, and Consequences. Routledge, London (2012)
25. Weber, R., Behr, K.M., Tamborini, R., Ritterfeld, U., Mathiak, K.: What do we really know about first-person-shooter games? An event-related, high-resolution content analysis. J. Comput. Mediat. Commun. **14**(4), 1016–1037 (2009)
26. Yi, J.S., Ah Kang, Y., Stasko, J., Jacko, J.A.: Toward a deeper understanding of the role of interaction in information visualization. IEEE Trans. Vis. Comput. Graph. **13**(6), 1224–1231 (2007)

Fun to Enhance Learning, Motivation, Self-efficacy, and Intention to Play in DGBL

Gabriella Tisza(✉) ⓘD, Sijie Zhu, and Panos Markopoulos ⓘD

Faculty of Industrial Design, Eindhoven University of Technology, Groene Loper 3,
5612 AE Eindhoven, The Netherlands
g.tisza@tue.nl

Abstract. Digital Game-Based Learning (DGBL) has been attracting increasing attention from researchers and educators, especially as related studies suggest it can enhance learning and positively affect students' motivation, attitude, self-efficacy, and intention to play similar games. However, research into DGBL is not explicit about the role of fun in DGBL. In our study we hypothesized that the perceived fun while playing with an educational game has a positive impact on children's measured- and perceived learning, motivation, attitude, self-efficacy and intention to play similar games. We conducted an online survey study with secondary school students (N = 28, mean age = 13.54) before and after playing with an online educational game on the topic of biology. The results indicate that the fun they experience while playing the game has a significant and positive effect on the perceived learning, the change in students' motivation and self-efficacy, and the intention to play similar games. However, no significant effect was found on the measured learning and the change in attitude towards the subject. Our findings partially support the contention that making DGBL more fun improves learning. Future research should seek further empirical evidence in other topic areas and for different ages, and to explore how DGBL can help improve attitudes towards the topic as well.

Keywords: Digital game-based learning · Educational game · Fun · Motivation · Attitude · Self-efficacy · Intention · Biology

1 Introduction

Digital learning games have gained popularity [1] due to the increased availability of computer and multimedia technologies at schools. A recent systematic review by Hainey et al. [2] indicated that digital game-based learning (DGBL) has been widely applied to various topics in science, mathematics, languages, social issues, history, and music. There is a growing body of empirical evidence showing that DGBL enhances students' learning [3, 4] and their motivation to learn [5–8]. Additionally, DGBL is associated with increased self-efficacy [5, 9–12], increased attitude toward the subject [10, 13] and increased intention to play learning games in the future [14].

© IFIP International Federation for Information Processing 2021
Published by Springer Nature Switzerland AG 2021
J. Baalsrud Hauge et al. (Eds.): ICEC 2021, LNCS 13056, pp. 28–45, 2021.
https://doi.org/10.1007/978-3-030-89394-1_3

Teaching with digital games builds on the idea that learning with digital games resembles the leisure time that people spend playing video games: it is fun and intrinsically motivating [15]. Accordingly, in DGBL literature the assumption that educational games are fun is rarely doubted or verified through measurement. As follows, empirical research with measured entities is scarce on the possible effects on fun in DGBL, and often contradictory. For example, Sim, MacFarlane and Read [16] found that the fun seven and eight years-old children experienced while learning with a digital game was not correlated with learning. Iten and Petko [17] reported similar results with primary school children: their regression analysis revealed that the enjoyment of the game is not associated with the self-reported learning, nor to the measured learning. However, a meta-analysis on computer games as learning tools [18] and a literature review on game-based learning suggested a direct link between learning and enjoyment [4]. Additional to the aforementioned findings, previous research on serious games pointed out that children's interest to engage with similar subjects increased according to the perceived enjoyment, and that children's intention to use similar games was significantly influenced by their attitude (anticipated simplicity and usefulness) toward the game [17]. Given the wide interest in this topic, the empirical research on the role fun plays in DGBL is quite limited and the results are inconclusive.

In this study, we set out to investigate how the experienced fun while playing a digital game influences students' learning, motivation, attitude, self-efficacy, and intention to play similar games. We recruited secondary school students to play a biology educational game – Code Fred: Survival Mode. Before and after playing the game, we administered a knowledge assessment test, students' motivation, attitude, and self-efficacy, and after playing the game we additionally measured students' perceived learning, intention to play similar games and we asked them to report on the fun they have experienced while playing. In the following sections of the paper we introduce related research, followed by the study methods, results and the discussion of the herein introduced findings.

2 Related Research

2.1 Digital Game-Based Learning

Digital game-based learning (DGBL) is a recently emerged term that refers to acquiring knowledge and skills through playing engaging computer games [19]. It is frequently used interchangeably with other terms such as educational games, learning games, serious games, and edutainment. Throughout the paper we use the term DGBL, and we refer to games as educational games.

Nowadays, educational games are being used across a wide range of subjects. In a recent literature review Boyle et al. [3] found that science, technology, engineering, and mathematics (STEM) are the most popular subject disciplines where DGBL is applied. This confirms earlier studies [2, 4, 20] and is of particular relevance as STEM abilities are seen as crucial for future development of oneself as well as the society [21].

2.2 Fun in DGBL

In this paper we operationalize fun based on the work of Tisza and Markopoulos [47]. Accordingly, any learning activity, including game-based learning is fun when one is intrinsically motivated for participation, feels in control of the activity, immersed in the experience by losing sense of time and space, the level of skills meets the level of challenge, the activity evokes positive and not negative emotions, and it supports the abandonment of social inhibitions.

It is often assumed that DGBL is fun. However, Yee [22] argued that educational games require players to do many tasks, making students feel tired and tedious. In other cases educational games were found to take too long and were no longer fun to play after the novelty effect was gone [23].

The effect of fun on learning with digital games is more controversial. Some studies found a positive association [4] and others no relation at all [16, 17]. Long [24] reported on a game for learning to program from which 80% of the study participants learnt something, while Sim, MacFarlane and Read [16] examined three educational applications for young children and reported no significant correlation between the observed or the reported fun and students' learning. When an educational game reaches its purpose and it is indeed fun to play with then the perceived enjoyment of the game motivates students to continue learning about the subject taught in the game [17] and increases students' attitude about the subject [17]. Additionally, previous research found that a higher level of game enjoyment is correlated with a higher motivation to learn [17]. However, the same article [17] reported that the enjoyment of the game had no influence on students' intention to play again, despite other studies suggesting the opposite [16]. There appears to have been no prior studies examining the possible relationship between fun in DGBL and self-efficacy.

2.3 Learning in DGBL

As mobile technology advances, digital games are no more bound to desktop computers and video consoles and can be played at different locations and times of the day [3, 25, 26]. Learners are having ample opportunities to play digital games, which has spawned the interest in their potential benefits regarding knowledge and skill acquisition, but also their affective, motivational, perceptual, physiological and cognitive outcomes [3, 4]. Research in DGBL has mostly focused on learning outcomes [3, 4, 27]. Empirical findings to date are divided. Some studies indicate that digital games are suitable for learning purposes for varied subjects including math, science, biology and psychology [3, 4, 20, 24, 28–30], while other studies report an adverse effect of digital games on learning [31–33]. For the assessment of learning in DGBL, researchers use either knowledge tests [15, 34–37] or measure learning based on the learners' self-report [17, 38].

2.4 Motivation, Attitude, Self-efficacy, and Intention to Play in DGBL

DGBL can enhance motivation to acquire certain knowledge [39, 40], which is a key element of successful learning [41]. Tüzün et al. [42] found that primary school students had a significantly higher intrinsic motivation and lower extrinsic motivation in a geography DGBL environment as compared to their motivation in the traditional school context. Others reported that students' motivation for mathematics was significantly higher for students learning in a mathematical game-based learning environment in comparison to a control group [5]. Such a positive relationship between students' learning motivation and DGBL is further supported by other studies [6–8]. On the other hand, Huizenga, Admiraal, Akkerman, and Dam [35] reported no significant differences in motivation between children learning in a DGBL and those in control groups.

Earlier research demonstrated that learning in DGBL can improve participants' attitude toward the subject [10, 13, 17]. Iten and Petko [17] found that the more children enjoy playing a DGBL the more they get interested in the subject matter. Akinsola and Animasahun [13] also found that students' achievement and positive attitude toward mathematics can be improved by the use of simulation-games environments. Sung and Huwang [10] developed a mindtool-integrated collaborative educational game, which was found to promote students' learning related attitudes.

Self-efficacy refers to students' perceptions and beliefs about their academic capabilities [43], and was found to be an effective predictor of academic motivation and achievements [44]. Hun, Huang, and Hwang [5] reported that students gained more self-efficacy in a mathematical game-based e-book learning environment compared with traditional instruction methods. Afari, Aldridge, Fraser, and Khine [12] measured students' academic efficacy before and after playing a mathematics game, and reported a significant improvement. Meluso, Zheng, Spires, and Lester [9] also suggested that after playing an educational game students demonstrated an increase in self-efficacy toward science.

Another study investigating serious games [17] reported that the anticipated usefulness and the anticipated simplicity of the learning game – which they labeled as attitude – are significant and positive predictors of the intention to play similar games. This is in accordance with Çankaya and Karamete [45] who found that DGBL had a positive influence on participants' intention to play the game again and with Rambli, Matcha and Sulaiman [46] who reported on children's strong willingness to play again with an augmented reality learning game.

The contradictory results of previous research on the effect of fun in DGBL may be attributed to inconsistent conceptions and measurement of fun and enjoyment in earlier studies. For many of the studies reported above, the notion of enjoyment and fun are left implicit [16, 17, 24]. Additionally, some of them used measures that may lack a theoretical basis, and consist of a single item [16, 24] where the predictive validity is questionable. Others used informal observations [16], which are not sufficient in conceptualizing and quantifying the role of fun in DGBL. The only study that comes close is that of Iten and Petko [17], however, despite using multi-item measures, they did not provide a clear definition of fun, which they use interchangeably with enjoyment. Nevertheless, they questioned the role of fun in serious games and called for research to investigate possible aspects of engagement from different angles.

2.5 Hypotheses

To address the apparent gap in earlier research regarding the potential benefits of DGBL we conducted a study aiming to understand how fun can impact students' learning, motivation, attitude, self-efficacy, and intention to play similar games in DGBL.

Accordingly, we hypothesized that:

H1: The experienced fun during DGBL positively affects students' reported learning.

H2: The experienced fun during DGBL positively affects students' measured learning.

H3: The experienced fun during DGBL positively affects students' motivation.

H4: The experienced fun during DGBL positively affects students' attitude.

H5: The experienced fun during DGBL positively affects students' self-efficacy.

H6: The experienced fun during DGBL positively affects students' intention to play similar games.

3   Methods

3.1   Participants

We recruited students from a Dutch bilingual secondary school. Our selection criteria were to have a good level of English comprehension and to be between age 13 and 14. The study was approved by the Ethical Board of Eindhoven University of Technology, Department of Industrial Design and informed consent was obtained from the participants and their parents before the study took place. In total, 28 of the second-year students participated in the study (12 boys, 16 girls, mean age = 13.54, SD = 0.508).

3.2   Procedure

The study took place in the spring of 2020. Since all formal educational activities took place online due to the COVID19 pandemic, participants took part in this study (i.e. played the game and responded the questionnaires) in an online classroom setting instead of the traditional physical environment. All students had access to laptops and had experience with using laptops to follow online lessons. Before the study started, the students were informed about the procedures by the teacher and informed consent was obtained. At the beginning of the lesson, students received a step-by-step guide to follow. This instructional document introduced the steps to take during the lesson and provided links to the questionnaires and the game. Throughout the lesson all participants were present in an online group meeting, so whenever a question or a problem emerged, students could ask help directly from the researcher and the teacher.

The study consisted of three sections: the pre-game data collection followed by playing the game Code Fred: Survival Mode, and the post-game data collection. Responding to the questionnaires before and after the game took approximately 7 min each. Students had approximately 25 min to complete the game. Ten minutes before the end of the lesson we asked students to stop playing the game – if they were still busy at that time – and do the post-game questionnaire.

3.3   Measures

To assess the interaction between the experienced fun and students' learning, motivation, attitude, self-efficacy, and intention to play similar games, we adopted validated measures and collected data from the study participants before and after playing the game. The pre-game questionnaire investigated students' motivation, attitude, and self-efficacy, along with a knowledge assessment test for the measured learning. The post-game questionnaire additionally investigated students' self-reported (i.e. perceived) learning, the fun they have experienced during playing the game and their intention to play similar games. The used measures, their operational definition, the items we used, and their respective sources are presented in Table 3 in the Appendix.

For the assessment of fun we used FunQ [47]. FunQ is a recently developed theoretically founded and validated questionnaire that specifically assesses adolescents' perceived fun. In our study, we excluded three items referring to social interactions given that participants played the game alone. Accordingly, participants rated their agreement on a 5-point scale (1 – Strongly disagree; 5 – Strongly agree) along fifteen items.

According to Bloom's taxonomy [50], six levels of learning can be distinguished. In this study we addressed two levels by collecting data on knowledge acquisition (*Knowledge*) and perceived learning (*Evaluation*). For the assessment of knowledge acquisition, we designed a test consisting of six multiple choice, single selection questions. The six test questions refer to six chapters of the game by asking about the knowledge and the related task to save Fred. For example, in chapter one the message appears on the screen "Danger is detected. Send adrenaline to these organs to escape: eye, hearth, liver". In the knowledge test we ask students the following: When your body detects danger, it reacts by sending adrenalin to the following body parts to escape EXCEPT: eyes/lungs/liver/brain. To gain a point, students must select the correct response (lungs). For each question participants could gain one point, resulting in a maximum of six points. We used the difference between the pre-game and the post-game scores as an indication of learning (i.e. measured learning).

The perceived learning was measured by a single item measure adopted from previous research [51, 52]. Participants were asked 'Have you learned something new today about biology?' and they could indicate their agreement on a 5-point scale (1 – Not at all; 5 – A whole lot).

To evaluate students' attitude toward biology, we adapted three items from the Motivated Strategies for Learning Questionnaire [53]. During adaptation we slightly changed the original items to fit better the study purpose (e.g. instead of 'It is important for me to learn the course material in this class.' we used 'It is important for me to learn what's taught in the biology class.' as we were interested in students' general attitude toward biology classes, not the specific gamified class we conducted for the study). Students indicated their agreement with the items on a 5-point Likert scale (1 – Strongly disagree; 5 – Strongly agree).

For the assessment of students' motivation toward biology we adapted three items from the Attitudes toward Mathematics Inventory [54]. During the adaptation we exchanged the word 'mathematics' into 'biology' to fit the study purpose (e.g., original item: 'I am willing to take more than the required amount of mathematics'; adapted item: 'I am willing to take more than the required amount of biology'). Students rated their agreement with the items on a 5-point scale (1 – Strongly disagree; 5 – Strongly agree).

For the measurement of students' self-efficacy, we adapted three items from the Motivated Strategies for Learning Questionnaire [53] to have the focus on biology classes in general and not the gamified learning setup applied for the study (e.g., original item:

'I expect to do well in this class.'; adapted item: 'I expect to do well in biology class').
Students were asked to indicate on a 5-point scale their agreement with the items (1 –
Strongly disagree; 5 – Strongly agree).

To address students' intention to play similar games we adapted three items from
the Motivated Strategies for Learning Questionnaire [53], which were evaluated on a
5-point scale (1 – Strongly disagree; 5 – Strongly agree). For this dimension, we used
original items that indicate task value and extended it to become a reasoning for playing
similar games again (e.g., original item: 'I think the course material in this class is useful
for me to learn.'; adapted item: 'I want to do similar activities in my biology classes
because I think these kinds of activities are useful').

Cronbach's alpha values indicate a good internal consistency for all used scales (see
Appendix).

3.4   The Game

To test these hypotheses, we asked children to play Code Fred: Survival Mode (see
Fig. 1). In choosing the game we had several requirements:

- The subject covered is equally suited for boys and girls. Research has shown that
  among STEM subjects, biology is most equally appealing for both genders [48, 49].
- The length of a game session is suitable for classroom use, taking no longer than
  30 min.
- The game covers a certain topic sufficiently, so that knowledge acquisition can be
  measured meaningfully.
- The game is fun and educative and aligns well with participants' knowledge and
  curriculum.

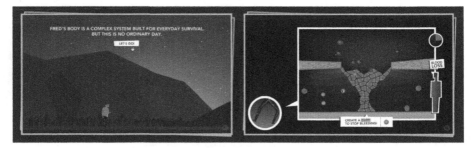

Fig. 1. Screenshots of code Fred: Survival mode. Left: opening scene. Right: episode 5 – gather
elements from across the body to quickly heal the wound.

The game is developed by the Museum of Science + Industry Chicago and it teaches
the player about the human body. The player leads the injured Fred through twelve
episodes, e.g., to get oxygen to the muscles, to stop bleeding, to heal a wound, to inspect
and disable bacteria, and to maintain a stable blood sugar level. The game is completed
when the player completes all twelve episodes and brings Fred safely back to his camp.

The game takes about 25 min, it has a well-defined topic and connects well to the curriculum, and it is fun to play for both boys and girls.

4 Results

To assess the fun experienced during the herein introduced study we calculated the FunQ scores by summing the values after correcting for the values of the reversed items. This resulted in an average score of 51.43, (SD = 12.04) from the possible range of 15–75, from which we conclude that students had fun while playing the game. Correlation analysis between the FunQ and the item "During the activity, I had fun" indicates a significant correlation ($r = 0.910$, $p < 0.001$), supporting the validity of the aforementioned claim.

Regarding the measured learning, we first calculated the scores for the pre-game and the post-game knowledge assessment tests ($mean_{pre-game} = 2.39$, $SD = 0.96$; $mean_{post-game} = 3.57$, $SD = 1.40$). Independent sample t-test found no gender difference in the knowledge test scores ($p_{pre-game} = 0.781$; $p_{post-game} = 0.266$). Then, we subtracted the pre-game test scores from the post-game scores. This resulted in an average score of 1.18 ($SD = 1.16$) for the measured learning. Paired sample t-test indicates that this difference is significant ($p < 0.001$), thus we conclude that based on the measured learning scored students have learned by playing the game.

To address participants' perception about their learning and test we asked them after playing the game whether they thought they had learned something new about biology. Students self-rated their learning on average 2.93 ($SD = 1.09$) on a 5-point scale, which translates to having learnt 'something'.

To compare students' reported learning with the measured learning scores we applied correlation analysis. We did not find a significant correlation between the measured and the perceived learning ($r = 0.246$; $p = 0.206$).

The reported average score for students' motivation at the beginning of the study was 2.64 ($SD = 0.81$), and it was 2.82 ($SD = 1.04$) on a 5-point scale after playing the game. We did not find any gender difference (independent sample t-test, $p_{pre-game} = 0.110$; $p_{post-game} = 0.865$). The average change in the motivation score is 0.18 ($SD = 0.67$). Paired sample t-test indicates that the change is not significant ($p = 0.170$).

As for students' attitude toward biology, the average score at the beginning of the study was 3.60 ($SD = 0.80$), and it was 3.63 ($SD = 1.00$) on a 5-point scale after playing with the game. Independent sample t-test indicates no gender difference in the scores ($p_{pre-game} = 0.708$; $p_{post-game} = 0.930$). The average change in the attitude toward biology score is 0.04 ($SD = 0.53$). Paired sample t-test indicates that the change is not significant ($p = 0.725$).

Regarding the self-efficacy, the reported average score at the beginning of the study was 3.58 ($SD = 0.49$), and it was 3.64 ($SD = 0.70$) on a 5-point scale after playing with the game. No gender difference was found (independent sample t-test, $p_{pre-game} = 0.203$; $p_{post-game} = 0.741$). The average change in the self-efficacy score is 0.06 ($SD = 0.58$). Paired sample t-test indicates that the change is not significant ($p = 0.592$).

Regarding students' intention to play similar games, the reported average score at the end of the game was 3.43 ($SD = 1.19$) on a 5-point scale.

For a summary of the pre- and post-game scores and the related statistics see Table 1.

Table 1. Pre- and post-game mean scores of measured learning, motivation, attitude, self-efficacy, and intention to play. All items were evaluated on a 5-point scale (1 – strongly disagree; 5 – strongly agree).

	Pre-game	Post-game	p	Cohen's D	Gender difference
Measured learning	Mean = 2.39 SD = 0.96	Mean = 3.57 SD = 1.40	<0.001	0.984	p_{pre} = 0.781 p_{post} = 0.266
Motivation	Mean = 2.64 SD = 0.81	Mean = 2.82 SD = 1.04	0.170	0.192	p_{pre} = 0.110 p_{post} = 0.865
Attitude	Mean = 3.60 SD = 0.80	Mean = 3.63 SD = 1.00	0.725	0.039	p_{pre} = 0.708 p_{post} = 0.930
Self-efficacy	Mean = 3.58 SD = 0.49	Mean = 3.64 SD = 0.70	0.592	0.099	p_{pre} = 0.203 p_{post} = 0.741

4.1 Fun and Learning

To quantify the effect of fun on the measured learning and test hypothesis 2, we conducted a regression analysis. The analysis reveals that the experienced fun explains 7.1% of the variance in the measured learning scores ($R^2 = 0.071$; $\beta_{std} = 0.266$, p = 0.172). In other words, the effect of the experienced fun on the measured learning is small and non-significant.

To understand how the experienced fun affects the perceived learning and test hypothesis 1, regression analysis was applied. The analysis reveals that the experienced fun explains the 42.4% of the variance in the perceived learning scores ($R^2 = 0.424$; $\beta_{std} = 0.651$, p < 0.001). In other words, children who experienced more fun with the game report to have learnt more compared to those who experienced less fun.

4.2 Fun and Motivation

To test hypothesis 3 regarding the effect of fun on students' motivation, a regression analysis was applied. Results indicate that the experienced fun while learning with a digital game explains 21.2% of variance in the motivation change ($R^2 = 0.212$; $\beta_{std} = 0.460$, p = 0.014). Thus, having fun while learning significantly contributes to students' increased motivation toward the subject.

4.3 Fun and Attitude

To quantify the effect of fun on students' attitude and to test hypothesis 4, we conducted regression analysis. Results show that 13.4% of the variance in the attitude change is explained by the experienced fun ($R^2 = 0.134$; $\beta_{std} = 0.366$, p = 0.055), but this effect is not significant. In other words, having fun while playing a digital learning game does not contribute significantly to students' attitude change.

4.4 Fun and Self-efficacy

To assess the relationship between fun and self-efficacy and to test hypothesis 5, a regression analysis was applied. The analysis indicates that fun accounts for 14.9% of the variance in the self-efficacy change scores ($R^2 = 0.149$; $\beta_{std} = 0.386$, p = 0.042). Thus, having fun while playing with an educational game significantly contributes to students' increased self-efficacy.

4.5 Fun and Intention to Play

To test the final hypothesis (H6) regarding the effect of fun on students' intention to play similar games we applied regression analysis. Results show that 70.3% of the variance in the intention to play similar games scores is explained by the experienced fun ($R^2 = 0.703$, $\beta_{std} = 0.838$, p < 0.001). In other words, having fun while learning with a digital game has a considerable impact on students' willingness to play similar games.

For a summary of all regression analysis results see Table 2.

Table 2. Summary of the regression analysis results. The effect of fun on students learning, motivation, attitude, self-efficacy, and intention to play.

	R^2	β_{std}	p
Measured learning	0.071	0.266	0.172
Perceived learning	0.424	0.651	<0.001
Motivation	0.212	0.460	0.014
Attitude	0.134	0.366	0.055
Self-efficacy	0.149	0.386	0.042
Intention to play	0.703	0.838	<0.001

5 Discussion

Our study investigated the role that fun plays in DGBL, for which earlier research is scarce and results are contradictory. Some researchers found no relationship between fun and learning while playing with an educational game [16, 17], while others [4, 18, 24] report on a significant association between the two. While we did not find a significant relationship between the experienced fun and the measured learning (H2), we did find that the experienced fun while playing a digital learning game has a significant and positive effect on students' perceived learning (H1). Hence, hypothesis 1 is supported and hypothesis 2 is refuted. A possible explanation by Koriat and Bjork [55] is that perceived learning often does not reflect the actual learning achievement since the judgment of learning is influenced by various factors. Furthermore, we suggest that students' perception of their learning might not only refer to factual knowledge but includes other skills that are not part of the knowledge assessment test. Additionally, the two measures address different levels of learning according to Bloom's taxonomy [50], which also explains the discrepancy between the two scores.

As for the effect of fun on students' motivation, our results provide an explanation to previous findings [5–8, 39, 40, 42], as we found that having fun while learning with a digital game has a significant and positive influence on students' motivation (H3). Thus our results support hypothesis 3. While previous studies on DGBL found that DGBL enhances students' motivation, they did not investigate from where exactly this relationship derives from. Our findings suggest that experiencing fun while learning with a digital game affects significantly students' motivation, resulting in the previously often found positive effect of DGBL on students' motivation.

Nonetheless, the effect of fun on attitude toward biology was not significant in our study (H4), contrary to an earlier report of a significant effect of fun on students' subject-related attitude [17]. Since research is scarce on this matter, we call on further research to for a thorough understanding.

Our results indicate that having fun while learning with an education game has a significant influence on students' self-efficacy (H5). Thus hypothesis 5 is justified. We propose that this finding refines and explains earlier reports [5, 9], that DGBL enhances students' self-efficacy.

Regarding the effect of the experienced fun while learning with a digital game on students' intention to play similar games in the future (H6), our findings support previous research [16] and concur with the one of Iten and Petko [17] as we found that fun is a strong influencer on students' willingness for engaging with similar games in the future. Accordingly, hypothesis 6 is supported by the results.

In sum, our study supports designers, researchers and educators in making digital game-based learning fun as our research demonstrated a positive effect of fun on students' motivation, self-efficacy and intention to engage with similar games, which are considered as key factors to successful learning. On the other hand, our results also shed light on the underlying effect of fun on the often-found positive association between DGBL and motivation and self-efficacy. Moreover, we provided a possible explanation for the disputed effect of fun on learning. To end with, we encourage both designers and researchers to not take fun granted in DGBL and we call for future research for a better understanding of fun in digital game-based learning.

6 Limitations and Future Work

This study has been conducted as an online class, which is different from the traditional formal learning environment. Nevertheless, since the game was online and students had access to the researcher and their class teacher during the study, we argue that student's experience was not hindered by the setup. The use of the single-item measure for the perceived learning, we believe, did not hinder the predictive validity given that the item was successfully used in previous research and it measures a concrete and simple construct. Nevertheless, future research is required focusing on the differences between the measured and perceived learning. Furthermore, while there was a clear increasing tendency in students' motivation, attitude and self-efficacy scores, the difference between the pre-game and post-game scores were not significant. We attribute this finding to the properties of the game and speculate that a different topic or a more fun game would have resulted in a stronger increase in the aforementioned scores. Accordingly, we call for future research with different games and on different subjects to investigate the herein revealed effects.

Acknowledgements. We are grateful to the anonymous participants for their contribution and to their class teacher for the help and support he provided. This project has received funding from the European Union's Horizon 2020 research and innovation programme under grant agreement NO 787476. This paper reflects only the authors' views. The Research Executive Agency (REA) and the European Commission are not responsible for any use that may be made of the information it contains.

Appendix

Table 3. The measured factors, their sources, operational definitions, and respective questions. All items were evaluated on a 5-point scale (1 – strongly disagree; 5 – strongly agree)

Factor and source	Operational definition	Item/question
Fun [47] ($\alpha = 0.940$)	The degree to which students experienced fun during the activity	I did this activity because I had to. (reversed item) I did this activity because I wanted to I want to do something like this again During the activity… I knew what to do I felt I was good at this activity I did something new I was curious I had fun I was happy I felt that time flew I forgot about school I felt good I felt bad. (reversed item) I felt angry. (reversed item) I felt sad. (reversed item)

(continued)

Table 3. (*continued*)

Factor and source	Operational definition	Item/question
Perceived learning [51]	The degree to which students indicate their learning during the activity	Have you learnt something new today about biology?
Motivation [54] ($\alpha_{pre} = 0.789$; $\alpha_{post} = 0.912$)	The degree to which students indicate their motivation toward the subject	I am willing to take more than the required amount of biology I plan to take as much biology as I can during my education The challenge of biology appeals to me
Attitude [53] ($\alpha_{pre} = 0.822$; $\alpha_{post} = 0.850$)	The degree to which students indicate their attitude toward the subject	I think what we are learning in biology class is interesting It is important for me to learn what's taught in the biology class I think what I'm learning in the biology class is useful for me to know
Self-efficacy [53] ($\alpha_{pre} = 0.608$; $\alpha_{post} = 0.757$)	The degree to which students indicate their self-efficacy toward the subject	I'm certain I can understand the ideas taught in the biology class I expect to do very well in biology class I know that I will be able to learn the material for the biology class
Intention [53] ($\alpha = 0.945$)	The degree to which students indicate their willingness to play similar games	I want to do similar activities in my biology classes because I find these kinds of activities are interesting I want to do similar activities in my biology classes because I think these kinds of activities are useful I want to do similar activities in my biology classes because I feel these kinds of activities are important

(*continued*)

Table 3. (*continued*)

Factor and source	Operational definition	Item/question
Measured learning [n.a.]	The difference between the post- and pre- score on the knowledge test	1. When your body detect danger, it reacts by sending adrenalin to the following body parts to escape EXCEPT: *eyes / lungs* / liver / brain* 2. Your body delivers oxygen from the lungs to leg muscles by the help of: *neuroglobin / cytoglobin / hemoglobin* / myoglobin* 3. When your body is losing blood, it needs to quickly heal the wound by gathering the following elements EXCEPT: *platelet / clotting factor / fibroblast / epithelium** 4. When your body is invaded by bacteria, it will inspect the bacteria in your: *blood / infected cells / lymph node* / spinal cord* 5. When your body sends an 'infection alert', the following happens: *your body warns you to take a paracetamol / your body releases antibodies to disable bacteria before they multiply and infect cells* / your body makes you thirsty, so you'll drink a lot and flush the bacteria away / your body releases antihistamine to kill bacteria before they attack your organs* 6. When your body has high blood sugar, it needs to release: *glucose from pancreas / glucose from liver / insulin from pancreas* / insulin from liver*

*Indicates the correct answer for the knowledge test.

References

1. Erhel, S., Jamet, E.: Digital game-based learning: impact of instructions and feedback on motivation and learning effectiveness. Comput. Educ. **67**, 156–167 (2013). https://doi.org/10.1016/j.compedu.2013.02.019
2. Hainey, T., Connolly, T.M., Boyle, E.A., Wilson, A., Razak, A.: A systematic literature review of games-based learning empirical evidence in primary education. Comput. Educ. **102**, 202–223 (2016). https://doi.org/10.1016/j.compedu.2016.09.001
3. Boyle, E.A., et al.: An update to the systematic literature review of empirical evidence of the impacts and outcomes of computer games and serious games. Comput. Educ. **94**, 178–192 (2016). https://doi.org/10.1016/j.compedu.2015.11.003
4. Connolly, T.M., Boyle, E.A., MacArthur, E., Hainey, T., Boyle, J.M.: A systematic literature review of empirical evidence on computer games and serious games. Comput. Educ. **59**(2), 661–686 (2012). https://doi.org/10.1016/j.compedu.2012.03.004
5. Hung, C.-M., Huang, I., Hwang, G.-J.: Effects of digital game-based learning on students' self-efficacy, motivation, anxiety, and achievements in learning mathematics. J. Comput. Educ. **1**(2–3), 151–166 (2014). https://doi.org/10.1007/s40692-014-0008-8
6. Burguillo, J.C.: Using game theory and competition-based learning to stimulate student motivation and performance. Comput. Educ. **55**(2), 566–575 (2010). https://doi.org/10.1016/j.compedu.2010.02.018
7. Dickey, M.D.: Murder on Grimm Isle: the impact of game narrative design in an educational game-based learning environment. Br. J. Educ. Technol. **42**(3), 456–469 (2011). https://doi.org/10.1111/j.1467-8535.2009.01032.x
8. Harris, K., Reid, D.: The influence of virtual reality play on children's motivation. Can. J. Occup. Ther. **72**(1), 21–29 (2005). https://doi.org/10.1177/000841740507200107
9. Meluso, A., Zheng, M., Spires, H.A., Lester, J.: Enhancing 5th graders' science content knowledge and self-efficacy through game-based learning. Comput. Educ. **59**(2), 497–504 (2012). https://doi.org/10.1016/j.compedu.2011.12.019
10. Sung, H.Y., Hwang, G.J.: A collaborative game-based learning approach to improving students' learning performance in science courses. Comput. Educ. **63**, 43–51 (2013). https://doi.org/10.1016/j.compedu.2012.11.019
11. Wang, M., Zheng, X.: Using game-based learning to support learning science: a study with middle school students. Asia Pacific Educ. Res. **30**(2), 167–176 (2020). https://doi.org/10.1007/s40299-020-00523-z
12. Afari, E., Aldridge, J.M., Fraser, B.J., Khine, M.S.: Students' perceptions of the learning environment and attitudes in game-based mathematics classrooms. Learn. Environ. Res. **16**(1), 131–150 (2013). https://doi.org/10.1007/s10984-012-9122-6
13. Akinsola, M.K., Animasahun, I.A.: The effect of simulation – games environment on students achievement in and attitudes to mathematics in secondary schools. Turkish Online J. Educ. Technol. – TOJET July **6**(3), 1303–6521 (2007)
14. Ronimus, M., Kujala, J., Tolvanen, A., Lyytinen, H.: Children's engagement during digital game-based learning of reading: the effects of time, rewards, and challenge. Comput. Educ. **71**, 237–246 (2014). https://doi.org/10.1016/j.compedu.2013.10.008
15. Papastergiou, M.: Digital game-based learning in high school computer science education: impact on educational effectiveness and student motivation. Comput. Educ. **52**(1), 1–12 (2009). https://doi.org/10.1016/j.compedu.2008.06.004
16. Sim, G., MacFarlane, S., Read, J.C.: All work and no play: measuring fun, usability, and learning in software for children. Comput. Educ. **46**(3), 235–248 (2006). https://doi.org/10.1016/j.compedu.2005.11.021

17. Iten, N., Petko, D.: Learning with serious games: is fun playing the game a predictor of learning success? Br. J. Educ. Technol. **47**(1), 151–163 (2016). https://doi.org/10.1111/bjet.12226

18. Ke, F.: A qualitative meta-analysis of computer games as learning tools. Gaming Simul. (2011). https://doi.org/10.4018/9781609601959.ch701

19. Prensky, M.: Fun, play and games : what makes games engaging. Digital Game-Based Learning, pp. 05-1–05-31. McGraw-Hill, New York, NY, US (2001)

20. Gao, F., Li, L., Sun, Y.: A systematic review of mobile game-based learning in STEM education. Educ. Tech. Res. Dev. **68**(4), 1791–1827 (2020). https://doi.org/10.1007/s11423-020-09787-0

21. Sanders, M.: STEM, STEMEducation, STEMmania, Technol. Teach. 20, 20–27, [Online]. Available: https://vtechworks.lib.vt.edu/bitstream/handle/10919/51616/STEMmania.pdf?sequence=1&isAllowed=y (2009)

22. Yee, N.: The labor of fun: how video games blur the boundaries of work and play. Games Cult. **1**(1), 68–71 (2006). https://doi.org/10.1177/1555412005281819

23. Jeno, L.M., Vandvik, V., Eliassen, S., Grytnes, J.-A.: Testing the novelty effect of an m-learning tool on internalization and achievement: a self-determination theory approach. Comput. Educ. **128**, 398–413 (2019). https://doi.org/10.1016/j.compedu.2018.10.008

24. Long, J.: Just for fun: using programming games in software programming training and education – a field study of IBM Robocode community. J. Inf. Technol. Educ. **6**, 279–290 (2007). https://doi.org/10.28945/216

25. Atwood-Blaine, D., Rule, A.C., Walker, J.: Creative self-efficacy of children aged 9-14 in a science center using a situated Mobile game. Think. Ski. Creat. **33**, 100580 (2019). https://doi.org/10.1016/j.tsc.2019.100580

26. Pellas, N., Mystakidis, S.: A systematic review of research about game-based learning in virtual worlds. J. Univ. Comput. Sci. **26**(8), 1017–1042 (2020)

27. Hung, H.T., Yang, J.C., Hwang, G.J., Chu, H.C., Wang, C.C.: A scoping review of research on digital game-based language learning. Comput. Educ. **126**, 89–104 (2018). https://doi.org/10.1016/j.compedu.2018.07.001

28. Byun, J., Joung, E.: Digital game-based learning for K-12 mathematics education: a meta-analysis. Sch. Sci. Math. **118**(3–4), 113–126 (2018). https://doi.org/10.1111/ssm.12271

29. Hussein, M.H., Ow, S.H., Cheong, L.S., Thong, M.-K., Ebrahim, N.A.: Effects of digital game-based learning on elementary science learning: a systematic review. IEEE Access **7**, 62465–62478 (2019). https://doi.org/10.1109/ACCESS.2019.2916324

30. Boyle, E.A., et al.: A narrative literature review of games, animations and simulations to teach research methods and statistics. Comput. Educ. **74**, 1–14 (2014). https://doi.org/10.1016/j.compedu.2014.01.004

31. Harris, D.: A comparative study of the effect of collaborative problem solving in a massively multiplayer online game (MMOG) on individual achievement (2008)

32. Wrzesien, M., Alcañiz Raya, M.: Learning in serious virtual worlds: evaluation of learning effectiveness and appeal to students in the E-Junior project. Comput. Educ. **55**(1), 178–187 (2010). https://doi.org/10.1016/j.compedu.2010.01.003

33. Vogel, J.J., Greenwood-Ericksen, A., Cannon-Bowers, J., Bowers, C.A.: Using virtual reality with and without gaming attributes for academic achievement. J. Res. Technol. Educ. **39**(1), 105–118 (2006). https://doi.org/10.1080/15391523.2006.10782475

34. Baños, R.M., Cebolla, A., Oliver, E., Alcañiz, M., Botella, C.: Efficacy and acceptability of an Internet platform to improve the learning of nutritional knowledge in children: the ETIOBE mates. Health Educ. Res. **28**(2), 234–248 (2013). https://doi.org/10.1093/her/cys044

35. Huizenga, J., Admiraal, W., Akkerman, S., Ten Dam, G.: Mobile game-based learning in secondary education: engagement, motivation and learning in a mobile city game: original article. J. Comput. Assist. Learn. **25**(4), 332–344 (2009). https://doi.org/10.1111/j.1365-2729.2009.00316.x

36. Yip, F.W.M., Kwan, A.C.M.: Online vocabulary games as a tool for teaching and learning English vocabulary. EMI. Educ. Media Int. **43**(3), 233–249 (2006). https://doi.org/10.1080/09523980600641445

37. Rossiou, E., Papadakis, S.: Applying online multiplayer educational games based on generic shells to enhance learning of recursive algorithms: students' preliminary results. In: European Conference on Games Based Learning, pp. 373–382 (2008)

38. Nte, S., Stephens, R.: Videogame aesthetics and e-learning: a retro-looking computer game to explain the normal distribution in statistics teaching (2008)

39. Huang, W.-H., Huang, W.-Y., Tschopp, J.: Sustaining iterative game playing processes in DGBL: the relationship between motivational processing and outcome processing. Comput. Educ. **55**(2), 789–797 (2010). https://doi.org/10.1016/j.compedu.2010.03.011

40. Hwang, G.-J., Wu, P.-H.: Advancements and trends in digital game-based learning research: a review of publications in selected journals from 2001 to 2010. Br. J. Educ. Technol. **43**(1), E6–E10 (2012). https://doi.org/10.1111/j.1467-8535.2011.01242.x

41. Vansteenkiste, M., Simons, J., Lens, W., Soenens, B., Matos, L.: Examining the motivational impact of intrinsic versus extrinsic goal framing and autonomy-supportive versus internally controlling communication style on early adolescents' academic achievement. Child Dev. **76**(2), 483–501 (2005). https://doi.org/10.1111/j.1467-8624.2005.00858.x

42. Tüzün, H., Yılmaz-Soylu, M., Karakuş, T., İnal, Y., Kızılkaya, G.: The effects of computer games on primary school students' achievement and motivation in geography learning. Comput. Educ. **52**(1), 68–77 (2009). https://doi.org/10.1016/j.compedu.2008.06.008

43. Schunk, D.H.: Self-efficacy and classroom learning. Psychol. Sch. **22**(2), 208–223 (1985). https://doi.org/10.1002/1520-6807(198504)22:2%3c208::AID-PITS2310220215%3e3.0.CO;2-7

44. Zimmerman, B.J.: Self-efficacy: an essential motive to learn. Contemp. Educ. Psychol. **25**(1), 82–91 (2000). https://doi.org/10.1006/ceps.1999.1016

45. Çankaya, S., Karamete, A.: The effects of educational computer games on students' attitudes towards mathematics course and educational computer games. Procedia Soc. Behav. Sci. **1**(1), 145–149 (2009). https://doi.org/10.1016/j.sbspro.2009.01.027

46. Rambli, D.R.A., Matcha, W., Sulaiman, S.: Fun learning with AR alphabet book for preschool children. Procedia Comput. Sci. **25**, 211–219 (2013). https://doi.org/10.1016/j.procs.2013.11.026

47. Tisza, G., Markopoulos, P.: FunQ: measuring the fun experience of a learning activity with adolescents. Curr. Psychol. (2021). https://doi.org/10.1007/s12144-021-01484-2

48. Barr, V.: Women in STEM, Women in Computer Science: We're Looking at It Incorrectly, BLOG @ CACM. Communications of the ACM. https://cacm.acm.org/blogs/blog-cacm/180850-women-in-stem-women-in-computer-science-were-looking-at-it-incorrectly/fulltext (2014)

49. Tisza, G., et al.: The role of age and gender on implementing informal and non-formal science learning activities for children. ACM Int. Conf. Proc. Ser. (2019). https://doi.org/10.1145/3335055.3335065

50. Bllom, B.: Taxonomy of Educational Objectives: The Classification of Educational Goals. David McKay Co Inc, New York, NY, US (1956)

51. Papavlasopoulou, S., Sharma, K., Giannakos, M.N.: How do you feel about learning to code? Investigating the effect of children's attitudes towards coding using eye-tracking. Int. J. Child-Comput. Interact. **17**, 50–60 (2018). https://doi.org/10.1016/j.ijcci.2018.01.004

52. Tisza, G., Markopoulos, P.: Understanding the role of fun in learning to code. Int. J. Child-Comput. Interact. **28**, 100270 (2021). https://doi.org/10.1016/j.ijcci.2021.100270

53. Pintrich, P.R., de Groot, E.V.: Motivational and self-regulated learning components of class-room academic performance. J. Educ. Psychol. **82**(1), 33–40 (1990). https://doi.org/10.1037/0022-0663.82.1.33

54. Tapia, M., Marsh, G.E.: Confirmatory factor analysis of the attitudes toward mathematics inventory. Annu. Meet. Mid-South Educ. Res. Assoc. 12 (2002)

55. Koriat, A., Bjork, R.A.: Illusions of competence in monitoring one's knowledge during study. J. Exp. Psychol. Learn. Mem. Cogn. **31**(2), 187–194 (2005). https://doi.org/10.1037/0278-7393.31.2.187

Murder on Mansion Hill: Encouraging Collaborative Group Storytelling to Improve Motivational Aspects of Literacy Using Gameplay and Arts-Based Techniques

Simone Downie[(✉)] [iD]

The Ohio State University, Columbus, OH 43210, USA
downie.42@osu.edu

Abstract. Literacy is a complex term that involves an array of intertwined processes, including motivation. Students who lack this internal willingness often fail to engage with books and other literacy-related content, which in turn negatively affects their learning outcomes. Though several arts-based strategies have been shown to improve students' involvement in reading, these approaches can be difficult and time consuming to implement. *Murder on Mansion Hill* is a digital tabletop game designed to weave together literacy-improving creative techniques such as storytelling, collage, and co-design in a cohesive manner. By blending these strategies with the motivational benefits of gameplay, *Mansion Hill* encourages players to take a highly active role in developing and sharing imaginative narratives, helping them to view stories as an enjoyable and rewarding outlet they can share with friends. After a series of improvements made through player feedback, players felt the game helped them overcome fear of judgment, engage with narrative in new multimodal ways, and bond with peers.

Keywords: Educational games · Storytelling · Literacy · Collage · Co-design

1 Introduction

The definition of literacy has grown beyond preparing children how to decipher the contents of a book. As we now understand it, literacy is a term that encompasses a wide array of reading and writing behaviors that develop naturally as individuals engage with books, songs, play, and other language-rich activities [1]. It relies on the unification of tools, critical thinking, and socio-emotional strategies to communicate, consume, and create meaning [2]. Included in these critical

© IFIP International Federation for Information Processing 2021
Published by Springer Nature Switzerland AG 2021
J. Baalsrud Hauge et al. (Eds.): ICEC 2021, LNCS 13056, pp. 46–61, 2021.
https://doi.org/10.1007/978-3-030-89394-1_4

behaviors is willingness. Knowing how to navigate one's way through a sentence is one thing; actually doing it is another. While there are well-documented benefits to students spending time with book-related content, there is also a notable lack in some of their willingness or desire to do so. This phenomenon, known as aliteracy, is unfortunately on the rise as students spend less and less time reading for pleasure both during and after elementary years [3].

This reluctance can be caused by a variety of factors. It can occur when students come to view literacy as an outcome rather than a process, and fear that they will be considered "dumb" if they make a mistake [4]. Others may view reading as a submissive act in which their creativity and desires are not valued. Such students view books as something to be received and decoded, a task that sounds boring and uninteresting [5]. Additionally, some learners may feel constrained by traditional text and require other types of tools that better support how they make meaning and express themselves to peers [6].

The game described in this paper was developed to help combat these aliteracy related factors by encouraging players to view stories as highly interactive social acts, and themselves as capable storytellers. To achieve this, *Murder on Mansion Hill* leverages the motivational benefits of gameplay, storytelling, collage, and co-design to support players as they craft imaginative stories in a group-based setting. It gives participants greater control over game construction and story through the use of arts-based collaborative tools to support their desires and choices, with the goal to motivate players to approach narrative in new visual ways and come to view stories as rewarding and fun. By crafting stories within the game, players gain hands-on experience using multimodal techniques that can help them form a positive relationship to literacy-related content.

2   Self-determination Theory and Intrinsic Motivation

Aliterate students often lack the internal desire to engage with literacy-related activities. In other words, they fail to experience intrinsic motivation, a concept found in Self-Determination Theory (SDT). According to this theory, individuals have an innate psychological need for feelings of autonomy, competence, and social relatedness [7]. Respectively, these categories relate to the sense that your actions are your own, that you have influence on your environment, and that you feel a sense of connection to others. When these three needs are met, individuals experience intrinsic motivation, which is the "the pursuit of an activity because it is inherently interesting or enjoyable" [7, p. 526].

When students feel intrinsically motivated to engage with books, not only do they increase the amount of time spent reading, but they feel more engaged and experience higher levels of enjoyment, which in turn result in greater learning outcomes [3,8]. A range of studies highlight the positive effect that feelings of autonomy, competence, and relatedness have on literacy learners – from choosing more challenging activities and increasing effort [4]; experiencing higher levels of visualization, comprehension, and memory [5]; sharing more knowledge and engaging in more meaningful conversations with peers [6]; and performing significantly higher in comprehension and subject matter knowledge measures [9].

Murder on Mansion Hill brings together creative techniques shown to have positive effects on intrinsic motivation in educational environments, including gameplay, storytelling, collage, and co-design. On their own, each of these elements serves as a promising tool for increasing engagement and academic progress; however, experts also caution that their success is dependent on how well these techniques are integrated and scaffolded within the learning experience. For example, Kao et al. highlight how game-based platforms improperly designed with too much incongruent multimedia can cause children to ignore their learning goals and decrease reading comprehension [9]. Similarly, Kaimal et al. found that average university students experienced greater anxiety and decreased creative expression without an art therapist there to help them negotiate visual challenges and decisions [10]. *Mansion Hill* removes the burden of navigating these strategies from parents, educators, and students alike by providing a structured gameplay experience that guides players through the use of these tools and demonstrates ways they can be combined to benefit one another. The motivational aspects of these techniques are briefly described in the following sections.

2.1   Motivation and Degrees of Interactivity

Games have a way of inspiring players in incredible ways – from spending countless hours cultivating a virtual farm to combating impossible bosses over and over until one finally wins. This internal motivation is the result of several game-based best practices [11–13]. For starters, many games view learning as a process and allow for experimentation and variety as players attempt to reach a goal. Rapid feedback and rewards can help players see failure as a positive learning opportunity to adjust their understanding and approach, and not as a negative punishment. To list a few more examples, games also break goals into sub-tasks to reduce complexity, encourage players to try new identities and express multiple sides of themselves, and create a platform for social connection.

Despite similar best practices to encourage motivation, some games support different levels of interactivity – and thus autonomy – than others. Interactivity is the relationship between two things as they act upon one another, such as a player pressing a button and the system responding to that input; however, there is a difference between the type of interactivity that occurs when you progress a narrative, when you make a choice that effects the narrative, or when you make up an entirely new one [14]. These degrees of interactivity are reflected in common game design patterns, defined here using categorizations by Yannakakis et al. [15]. For example, in 'free expression' games such as *Farmville* [16] players spend time decorating aspects of their characters and environment, however, their choices have little to no effect on the structure of game. 'Customization' games are slightly more interactive as players' choices do have some impact, such as in *World of Warcraft* [17] in which choosing a class results in a different set of quests. Still, the player's affect over the system remains shallow, with her choices limited to picking between pre-determined aesthetics and outcomes.

To better support player autonomy, *Murder on Mansion Hill* integrates 'construction' and 'combining' patterns. Players begin the game by placing together images to construct collages that will become the pieces of the board and influence the card deck. This type of free-form making – which can be seen in *Minecraft* [18] and *Fortnite Creative* [19] as players use virtual materials to architect anything from buildings to entire game experiences – tightly integrates player's choice and preferences into the mechanics, design, and narrative of the game. No two games of *Mansion Hill* look the same, have the same outcomes, or follow the same story; each playthrough is dependent on players' custom-made artefacts and creative interpretation. The goal of supporting this deep level of interactivity is to encourage players to feel as though their choices deeply matter and that their creativity is critical to the game.

2.2   Creative Storytelling and Collage

Though storytelling is often thought of as a solo act, it can also incorporate multiple voices and give participants a much more active role. For example, many classrooms and libraries use a dialogic approach to storytime, in which the narrator routinely pauses to ask questions, encourage discussion, and allow students to imagine new parts of the story [20]. When participants are encouraged to listen to and interpret stories with others, they are more likely to grow intellectually, creatively, and psychologically [21], and feel a deeper sense of belonging and comradery. Additionally, when learners share their creativity with others, they feel more motivated to continue engaging in the act, as they realize the value of their contribution and feel appreciated by the group [22].

Classrooms are increasingly incorporating other multimodal techniques to encourage readers to playfully embody and communicate meaning. One such tool is collage, which is the process of collecting, editing, and gluing visual materials. Because collage relies on found visual objects, it requires makers to abstract complex ideas and challenge and refine their understanding as they attempt to communicate using available materials [23]. As individuals explore meaning in this active manner, they feel a heightened sense of positive affect, self-efficacy, and creative agency [10,24]. When used in the classroom, collage helps learners recognize that there is more than one way of knowing and that their imagination and personal interpretations are critical, an awareness that transfers to reading [5,25]. Importantly, collage also provides an accessible, safe structure that allows participants of any experience level to not feel limited by artistic ability or fear of judgement [26].

Storytelling and collage rely on inspiration and imagination, which can be difficult to inspire. However, games can address this concern by fostering possibility thinking and creative emotional reasoning [27]. According to these concepts, creativity emerges when a person is prompted to think in a non-linear fashion or in a way that is not his norm, a process fueled by imagination as he is provoked into conceptualizing new ideas and connections. The key terms used in that description were 'prompted' and 'provoked' – this type of logic relies on the concept of a disruptor that stimulates an emergent, open-ended line of inquiry. As players explore possibilities that take the trigger into account while meeting the requirements of the game, they challenge their associations, understandings, and ways of making meaning [28], a semiotic process similar to the logic found in collage making and reading.

Like *Murder on Mansion Hill*, games such as *Story Cubes* [29], *Once Upon a Time* [30], and *Mysterium* [31] encourage on-the-fly imaginative storytelling through the use of such disruptors. For example, in *Once Upon a Time*, players must create a coherent fantasy story using randomly dealt cards containing key words. As they try to connect their words, new cards and storylines are continually introduced by other players, forcing each player to reconceptualize what they might say next. So as not to be overwhelming, the open-endedness of these possibilities is restrained by the goal of leading the story toward a final ending card. Similarly, in *Mysterium*, players are handed visual cards with abstract, surrealist art that they must interpret to solve a mystery, a task that constantly evolves as each player is given more cards to refine and debate their associations. *Murder on Mansion Hill* mimics these mechanics as players use the cards in their hands and the collage-based visual board to craft new narratives and uncover a series of clues.

2.3 Co-design and Facilitation

To further fulfill elements of SDT – and to blend the above elements in a cohesive manner – *Murder on Mansion Hill* employs a co-design approach. At its core, co-design is a research methodology that frames the participant as the expert. Instead of assuming that the designer must single-handedly account for all user wants, needs, and perspectives, co-design instead *asks* the user what her goals and desires are and provides hands-on collaboration tools for communicating and debating these wants with a group of her peers. The designer's role is not that of a subject matter expert but instead a facilitator, there to guide the group's time together, explain and demonstrate activities, and help synthesize understanding.

Though games are a popular tool used within co-design activities, there are few examples of a game being the *end result* of such sessions, as is the case with *Mansion Hill*. However, popular tabletop Role Playing Games such as *Dungeons and Dragons* [32] serve as an example of merging a co-design approach with gameplay. In many ways, the designer and Dungeon Master (DM) have similar roles, serving as a facilitator to ensure the experience benefits and supports each unique collection of participants. To achieve this, they help everyone understand the rules and expectations while encouraging individual expression, are highly engaged and lead by example, and are willing to pivot and adjust [33]. Balancing exploration with guidelines helps steer participants' attention in a positive direction and gives the sense that there are still goals to be accomplished. The perception that there are tasks to be finished and that they can be completed in whatever way feels enjoyable to the player increases intrinsic motivation and strengthens involvement in the activity [11].

3   Description of the Game

3.1   Setup

Murder on Mansion Hill is setup and delivered digitally on a web-based white-boarding platform called Miro (alongside a video-chat application such as Zoom or Discord). Because Miro is intended for team-based collaboration and visualization, it lacks many automation and coding features found in game development software. However, its lack of technical complexity also makes it a promising platform for tabletop games as it enables quick iteration, is accessible and free to any internet-connected device, and is easy to use. These features support the creation of a remote game that connects family and friends who may not live in the same location or are socially distanced.

Because Miro lacks automation, some set up is required by the lead Game Master (GM). The game materials can be made from scratch or the GM can use pre-packaged templates that include: one design Miro board; one gameplay Miro board; 150 story cards pre-populated with places, items, characters, and actions; 52 poltergeist cards; collage building assets; avatar tokens; and pre-determined links between collage items and story cards (described in Fig. 3). The remaining story cards are left blank to be filled in later by players. Links to the Google Drive documents that populate these blank cards are provided in each player's workspace within the design template. The GM may modify the story cards, the collage assets, and the cards to which the collage items are assigned.

3.2   Narrative and Setting

Players take on the role of psychic medium students who are given their final assignment to uncover what happened to the Master of the Mansion at the top of the hill, who recently disappeared in a mysterious fashion. The first group to successfully get in touch with their spooky side and correctly solve the murder gets infinite bragging rights and an automatic A. What exactly happens during the game and what the Mansion looks like is entirely up to the players as they use their imagination to describe their journey through the rooms, the interesting characters they interact with, and any other observations or actions of note. Players should think of the game as a story, and themselves and their fellow teammates as the storytellers, building on-the-fly narratives to search around and decipher clues.

3.3   Pre-game Design Session

A major goal of the game is to give players heightened creative control, including over physical game components. In a pre-game design session, which takes 30–45 minutes, players use collage to construct the board and determine contents of the story card deck. In the provided Miro template, each team is given a collage workspace (Fig. 1) that resembles a worksheet with the title of the Mansion's rooms or a fill in the blank space above an empty square. Each player first claims three rooms that they want to design, either by verbally reserving a room already included in the workspace or moving an available room title above a square in their team's board. Next to the workspace are the images to be used for the collages, categorized into background rooms, items, characters, and so on. Players use drag and drop or copy and paste to move these visual assets into their empty squares to create their rooms (Fig. 2). They then click on hyperlinks provided beneath their workspace to type a short description of their new environments into a series of Google Drive documents (Fig. 3).

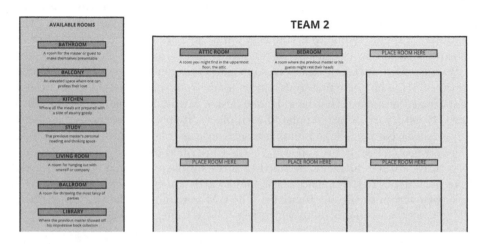

Fig. 1. Closeup view of collage workspace. Collages are built within each square using a provided collection of visual assets

Fig. 2. Examples of rooms created by players using collage techniques.

This phase most closely resembles a co-design session with the GM guiding others through the activity, ensuring the group is moving at the same pace and staggering tasks to reduce complexity, answer questions, and encourage casual conversation. For example, Miro allows assets to be grouped together and hidden (grayed out) by the main account. Using this functionality, the GM reveals each category of images one at a time, giving players time to choose their background setting, and then their items, and then their characters in sequential order. When players have completed their collages, the GM is also responsible for moving the rooms from the workspace to the game board and aligning the images used in the collages to the story card deck. Figure 3 diagrams this process.

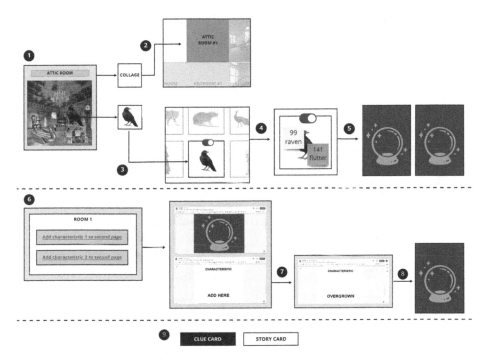

Fig. 3. Player collages influence game content as follows. 1: Player 1 collages the attic room. 2: The GM places the collage on the game board beneath its tile. 3: The GM assesses which elements are 'in use' (marked by a toggle the player set to active). 4: The GM looks at the notes hidden beneath the active element. These notes list the story cards assigned to that element (as determined by the template or the GM) 5. The GM copies these cards into the gameplay Miro board. 6. Player 1 follows the first link included in her collage workspace to open a Google Drive document. 7. Player 1 replaces the ADD HERE text with a word that describes the room. 8. Player 1 repeats this two times per room. Each Google Drive document is linked to a characteristic story card; when changes are made to the document, they also appear on the card. The GM refreshes the characteristic cards and deletes any not in play. 9. The GM chooses two place, action, and item cards at random and deals them to a member of each team to become their clue card. The rest are shuffled into the deck to become story cards.

3.4 Playing the Game

Once the design stage is finished, it's time to play (Fig. 4). Players act as psychics working together in two competing teams to determine how the opulent owner of the mansion was killed, in what room, and with what item. To accomplish this, players navigate their avatars around the mansion while using the five story cards in their hand and the visual contents of the board to weave a story. For example, if you have the story cards witch, cauldron, and basement, and a room that includes green smoke, you may describe a scene in which you move down to the basement only to uncover an old witch hiding among the dusty shelves, stirring a smoking cauldron full of suspiciously green liquid. If you use a place story card to move your chosen avatar to a new room, you remove the tile to uncover the collage beneath it.

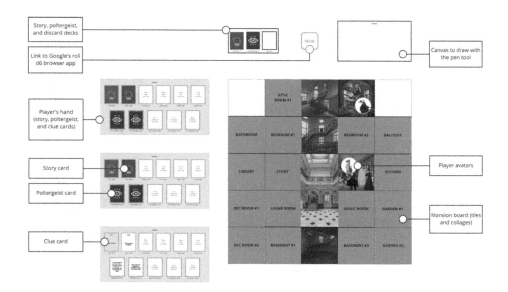

Fig. 4. Diagram of murder on Mansion Hill board.

Each player also possesses one secret clue card that contains the answer to one piece of the murder mystery. When the current narrator says a word related to a story card in a teammate's hand, that teammate is overtaken by his physic powers; he rolls a die to determine in what creative way he must hint at the contents of his clue card, such as by writing a riddle or drawing a picture. But look out, other players may use their poltergeist cards to make the clue-giving process just a bit trickier. Once a team correctly guesses all three parts of their murder mystery, they win by crafting one final sentence describing what caused the Master's ultimate end.

4   Playtest Results and Findings

Murder on Mansion Hill is intended for players of any age, even those beyond the K-12 demographic. Based on the author's personal observations, adults also struggle to engage with literacy-related content and activities. For this reason, undergraduate and graduate students enrolled in Computer Science, Design, Arts Administration, and Theather courses were recruited as playtesters, due to the author's familiarity and involvement in these classes. These individuals, who were a blend of male and female, responded to verbal and social-media based advertisements seeking out participants; as the intent of the study was to play the game with as general a segment of the population as possible, no further selection criteria were used. Because *Murder on Mansion Hill* is intended for six players, the 15 original participants were divided randomly into three test groups, with the author serving as the sixth player and GM in each. A polling system was used to gather availability and schedule play sessions.

Prior to playing, participants filled out an anonymous online survey to better gauge their experience with techniques used in the game (two participants left the study before providing their responses). Pre-game survey questions and responses are provided in Table 1. Participants were close to evenly spread out in how often they play games, how comfortable they felt telling stories to others, and their level of experience with co-design if they were familiar with the term (which about half were). Seven participants recall having made a collage in their adult life and enjoyed the process, while the rest were unsure. Most had almost never authored creative works of fiction. Of those with experience playing story-based games like *Dungeons and Dragons*, only a minority talk a lot to guide the narrative. Participants without experience engaging in such games identified several roadblocks preventing them from playing, such as difficulty finding a group, feeling self-conscious due to lack of experience, and wanting someone to guide them through the process. Interestingly, nearly all participants report being drawn to games in which their choices have a large impact on gameplay because it adds to replay-ability, gives them a heightened sense of agency, requires deeper thinking, and makes the game experience more personal.

4.1 Playtest 1

In the first playtest, players were given even greater control over game elements than described in previous sections. Instead of only creating six words for the characteristic cards, players were instead asked to populate the entire story card deck. This required each player to open 16 Google Drive documents to insert their words, a process that required an unforeseen amount of time due to internet bandwidth and individual pace. Players were also given creative freedom to collage any type of room they wanted, instead of being limited to rooms found in a set blueprint. With this much to create, the design phase pushed well past an hour. At that point, players vocalized concerns that they had other engagements to attend to and that they were losing energy. The game session was thus completed another day.

In addition to time concerns, giving players complete control over the cards and types of rooms resulted in a difficult play experience. While some players kept their cards simple, others created more complex phrases like 'very old bread' or used more sophisticated language such as 'jubilant'. Other cards, such as

Table 1. Pre-game survey results.

Questions	Responses			
Multiple choice: Yes, No, Other				
1. Do you have experience playing games based heavily on imagination and story, such as Dungeons & Dragons?	Yes	53.8%	No	46.2%
2. Have you ever designed a game?	Yes	69.2%	No	30.8%
3. Do you know what co-design is?	Yes	53.8%	No	46.2%
4. Have you ever made a collage?	Yes	76.9%	No	23.1%
5. If yes to # 4, have you made a collage in your adult life?	Yes	70%	No	20%
	Unsure	10%		
6. If yes to # 4, do you enjoy making collages?	Yes	70%	No	10%
	Unsure	20%		
On a scale of 1–5 with 1 most negative and 5 most positive. Listed as averages				
7. If yes to # 1, how much do you typically talk to lead the story?	2.71			
8. How often do you author creative pieces of fiction for fun?	1.77			
9. How comfortable would you feel reciting a story to a stranger?	3.23			
10. How often do you play games?	3.61			
11. If yes to # 3, what is your level of experience with co-design as a participant or designer?	3.14			
Freeform response with why or why not explanation				
12. If no to # 1, are these games something you've been wanting to try?				
13. What types of games are you drawn to?				
14. Are you drawn to games in which your choices have a large impact on gameplay?				

mouse, appeared so many times it became comical. The rooms followed suit, with a combination of quirky and highly repetitive visuals. These factors made it difficult for players to tell stories using language that might relate to the rooms and one another's cards. Players were stuck leading the narration for too long which caused them to experience anxiety and feel unsure of themselves. This hesitance, along with the fact that there were no characters or avatars to embody, pulled them out of the game world. Meanwhile other players felt disengaged because they were unable to take a turn. On a positive note, players did find the collage making process enjoyable, and appreciated that the board provided a visual representation of how the story was developing.

4.2   Playtest 2 and 3

Some degree of player control during the design stage was subsequently reduced to strike a better balance between player- and designer-made assets and ensure a better sense of cohesiveness. The mansion board was re-imagined to contain a set organization of rooms that players could choose between to guide their collages (Fig. 1). Next was to better align story cards and reduce the time spent creating them while still ensuring player decisions determined game content. Since players were already making choices to populate their collages, it seemed promising to connect these decisions to card content instead of creating another time-consuming activity (Fig. 3). Though with this new approach either the template or GM determines which words/cards the collage items relate to, players still noticed that their collages influenced the contents of the story deck. Character avatars were also introduced to provide players with a conduit to better immerse themselves in the game world.

After these changes, the design phase moved more quickly, leaving more time for play and better keeping players engaged. During the game, narrators were better able to lead a story that connected to other player's hands and use the board in a more meaningful way. One player shared his appreciation for how the game adjusted to his experience level in telling stories and how gameplay was highly dependent on the group's personality – more serious players can approach the game differently than beginners, who might allow more "ridiculous" things. The introduction of avatars was also beneficial. On several occasions, and unprompted, players introduced their personas (chosen from a collection of fantasy based characters) and provided a backstory and personality, which they then used throughout the game. Players echoed the first playtest group in how much they enjoyed the collage making process. Not only did they find the collages "extremely" fun, but several players voiced that they appreciate the organic social conversation that blossomed as players moved through the activity. Though players were creating their own individual rooms, they still felt like they were building within a group setting.

4.3 Survey Results

The three groups completed an additional anonymous online post-game survey to better understand their experience and whether they felt motivated to engage with story in a new way. Eight of the original thirteen participated. Table 2 compares the results between the first group (four survey participants) and the second and third groups (four survey participants total).

On average, participants in the second and third playtests more greatly enjoyed the design stage, telling imaginative stories, and crafting collages, and found that the visuals were more helpful in crafting narratives. All players in the first group wished for more pre-made assets while no one in the following groups felt the same, indicating that removing some of the creative burden from players during the design stage was a welcome change. Some players in the third group voiced that they liked the balance between player-made and designer-made assets, but felt they would gradually want to claim more control as they grew more comfortable with the game (a desire the structure of the game can easily support). After playing, most players felt more inclined to play other narrative-based games, felt their experience was positively impacted by the collage making process, and felt a sense of comradery with peers. A main area for improvement is better onboarding players so they better understand the rules of the game.

Table 2. Post-game survey results.

Questions	Group 1		Groups 2& 3	
On a scale of 1–5, with 1 most negative and 5 most positive. Listed as averages				
How did you find the experience of creating components of the game, such as the board art and card items?	3.75		5	
How would you rank your level of engagement in the game?	4.5		3.25	
How was the experience of telling on-the-fly imaginative stories as part of the game play?	2.5		4.5	
How was the process of making digital collages?	2.5		4.75	
Were the collages helpful in creating narrative stories?	2.5		4.5	
Multiple choice – Yes, No, Other				
Would you have preferred more pre-made assets?	Yes	100%	No	100%
Would you have preferred more opportunities to create items, visuals, or rules?	No	100%	Yes	25%
			No	50%
			Maybe	25%
Do you feel more interested in playing other narrative-based games like Dungeons & Dragons?	Yes	100%	Yes	75%
			No	25%
Did building collages positively impact your interest?	Yes	100%	Yes	100%
Did you understood how to play and win the game?	Yes	50%	Yes	50%
	No	50%	Mostly	50%
Did you feel a sense of comradery with your team and peers?	Yes	100%	Yes	100%

The survey also included some freeform questions to allow players to provide feedback in their own words. Table 3 lists these questions.

Table 3. Freeform post-game survey questions.

Questions
1. How was your interest affected by your role in creating components of the game?
2. Did you become more comfortable with your role as a storyteller over time? Why or why not?
3. In the pre-game survey you answered questions related to how often you create stories and how comfortable you are in sharing them with others. After playing this game, would your responses change?
4. Is there anything you would add to make this game more enjoyable?

According to responses, all playtesters became more invested in the game due to their creative contribution and found that playing with their own assets as opposed to someone else's created a more rewarding and exciting game experience. One player said that she wished she better understood the connection between her choices and the game content so that she could make decisions more carefully. Nearly all players also found that they became increasingly comfortable with their role as a storyteller. This was in large part due to growing more comfortable with the group and recognizing that no one was there to judge, as well as having the cards and board to provide creative guidance. However, players were hesitant to say whether playing the game helped them feel more comfortable sharing stories outside of the game context. Some players suggested that repeated engagement with the game may have this benefit, while others remained unsure if their newfound confidence could only exist in the safe environment of the game. In terms of suggestions, players wished for more opportunities to explore a greater number of rooms and to use their poltergeist cards. Players also stated an interest in establishing a team mentality during the design phase, as opposed to being assigned teams after the collage activity.

5   Limitations and Future Improvements

Though the size of the study was admittedly small, insights gained from survey results and verbal feedback are generally promising. After undergoing some design changes, *Murder on Mansion Hill* successfully created a playful environment that naturally adjusted to each session's unique makeup of players, helping individuals from different academic backgrounds, gaming experiences and interests, and creative confidence levels feel comfortable with one another as they engaged in arts- and story-based tasks. Participants felt motivated to play the game, an interest that in turn encouraged them to step out of their comfort zones and engage with imaginative narratives. Additional game sessions would be beneficial to gather a greater number of survey responses and combine more player personalities and experiences to see if these positive impressions remained true. As some game mechanics were slightly tweaked after the latest round of playtests – such as dividing the collage making workspace into two team environments and giving players two poltergeist cards to start – further playtests would also be beneficial to continue testing game mechanics.

Much of the effort for future improvements should focus on two main concerns: better onboarding players so they feel more comfortable with the rules and expectations and addressing uncertainty as to whether the literacy-related techniques leveraged within the game can extend into real world contexts. Because each playtest in this study was comprised of different players, it may be beneficial to play multiple sessions with the same participants to uncover whether prolonged engagement has an impact on players' understanding of the rules and their longer-term perception of arts-based techniques, storytelling, and resources (such as games) that leverage them. The data gathered in this survey was also largely impression-based, with players self-reporting feelings and insights that are difficult to quantify. This was due to the author's main goal of creating a game experience that supported player's intrinsic motivation, a concept that is largely personal and perception-based. As the game's ability to support elements of SDT is encouraging, further studies should introduce metrics that better measure literacy-related progress and explore the potential of *Mansion Hill* to support reading motivation outside of the game world.

6 Conclusion

Murder on Mansion Hill blends together elements of co-design, collage, and group storytelling in a cohesive manner to create a game-based experience in which players feel intrinsically motivated to express and explore their narrative creativity together with peers. It gives players control and agency to create and play a game based on their unique imagination, balancing player-made assets with pre-made designs in a way that allows for player input while providing a guiding foundation of rules and goals. The whimsical setting, visual collages, and story cards work together to help players view themselves as capable storytellers and the process of weaving unique stories as an enjoyable, lighthearted social experience. Future improvements should focus on more explicitly encouraging players to leverage the multimodal meaning making techniques used in the game to outside literacy-related contexts.

References

1. Urban Libraries Council: Making cities stronger: public library contributions to local economic development. Urban Institute (2007)
2. Maureen, I.Y., van der Meij, H., de Jong, T.: Supporting literacy and digital literacy development in early childhood education using storytelling activities. Int. J. Early Childhood **50**(3), 371–389 (2018). https://doi.org/10.1007/s13158-018-0230-z
3. De Naeghel, J., Van Keer, H., Vansteenkiste, M., Haerens, L., Aelterman, N.: Promoting elementary school students' autonomous reading motivation: effects of a teacher professional development workshop. J. Educ. Res. **109**(3), 232–252 (2016)
4. Johnston, P.H.: Opening Minds: Using Language to Change Lives. Stenhouse Publishers, Portland (2012)
5. Wilhelm, J.: Reading is seeing: using visual response to improve the literary reading of reluctant readers. J. Read. Behav. **27**(4), 467–503 (1995)
6. McGlynn-Stewart, M., Brathwaite, L., Hobman, L., Maguire, N., Mogyorodi, E., Park, Y.U.: Inclusive teaching with digital technology: supporting literacy learning in play-based kindergartens. LEARNing Landsc. **11**(1), 199–216 (2017)
7. Mekler, E.D., Brühlmann, F., Tuch, A.N., Opwis, K.: Towards understanding the effects of individual gamification elements on intrinsic motivation and performance. Comput. Hum. Behav. **71**, 525–534 (2017)
8. Yoon, J.C.: Three decades of sustained silent reading: a meta-analytic review of the effects of SSR on attitude toward reading. Read. Improv. **39**(4), 186–196 (2002)
9. Kao, G.Y.M., Tsai, C.C., Liu, C.Y., Yang, C.H.: The effects of high/low interactive electronic storybooks on elementary school students' reading motivation, story comprehension and chromatics concepts. Comput. Educ. **100**, 56–70 (2016)
10. Kaimal, G., Mensinger, J.L., Drass, J.M., Dieterich-Hartwell, R.M.: Art therapist-facilitated open studio versus coloring: differences in outcomes of affect, stress, creative agency, and self-efficacy. Can. Art Ther. Assoc. J. **30**(2), 56–68 (2017)
11. Rapp, A.: Designing interactive systems through a game lens: an ethnographic approach. Comput. Hum. Behav. **71**, 455–468 (2017)
12. Simões, J., Redondo, R.D., Vilas, A.F.: A social gamification framework for a K-6 learning platform. Comput. Hum. Behav. **29**(2), 345–353 (2013)

13. Cruz, C., Hanus, M.D., Fox, J.: Comput. Hum. Behav. Comput. Hum. Behav. **71**, 516–524 (2017)
14. Zimmerman, E.: Narrative, interactivity, play, and games: four naughty concepts in need of discipline. First person: New Media as Story, Performance, and Game, 154–164 (2004)
15. Yannakakis, G. N., Eladhari, M., Hullett, K., Knight, Y., Brown, D., Liapis, A.: Creative Emotional Reasoning Computational Tools Fostering Co-Creativity in Learning Processes. C2 Learn (2013)
16. Zynga: Farmville. [Video game] (2009)
17. Blizzard Entertainment: World of Warcraft. [Video game] (2004)
18. Mojang Studios, Sony Interactive Entertainment: Minecraft. [Video game] (2011)
19. Epic Games: Fortnite Creative. [Video game] (2018)
20. Albright, M., Delecki, K., Hinkle, S.: The evolution of early literacy. Child. Libr. **7**(1), 13 (2009)
21. Diamant-Cohen, B.: First day of class: the public library's role in school readiness. Child. Libr. **5**(1), 40–48 (2007)
22. Koulouris, P., Dimaraki, E. V.: Fostering Co-creativity in learning through digital gaming: educational scenarios developed by school communities co-designing the C2Learn solution. In: EDULEARN14 Proceedings, pp. 4204–4213 (2014)
23. Chilton, G., Scotti, V.: Snipping, gluing, writing: the properties of collage as an arts-based research practice in art therapy. Art Ther. **31**(4), 163–171 (2014)
24. Kaimal, G., Ray, K.: Free art-making in an art therapy open studio: changes in affect and self-efficacy. Arts Health **9**(2), 154–166 (2017)
25. Siegel, M.: Rereading the signs: multimodal transformations in the field of literacy education. Lang. Arts **84**(1), 65–77 (2006)
26. Raffaelli, T., Hartzell, E.: A comparison of adults' responses to collage versus drawing in an initial art-making session. Art Ther. **33**(1), 21–26 (2016)
27. Stouraitis, E., Agogi, E.: Fostering creativity in sixth grade history education through a storytelling digital game: an empirical study. Hist. Educ. Res. J. **13**(2), 138–149 (2016)
28. Liapis, A., Hoover, A. K., Yannakakis, G. N., Alexopoulos, C., Dimaraki, E. V.: Motivating Visual Interpretations in Iconoscope: Designing a Game for Fostering Creativity (2015)
29. Zygomatic Games: Rory's Story Cubes. Tabletop game (2004)
30. Atlas Games: Once Upon a Time. Card game (2012)
31. Nevskiy, O., Sidorenko, O.: Mysterium. Tabletop game (2015)
32. Wizards of the Coast: Player's Handbook, 5th edn. Tabletop game (2014)
33. Buraparate, P.: Dungeons and Dragons and Design Thinking. UX Collective (2019). https://uxdesign.cc/dungeons-dragons-design-thinking-688a0b7cca3f

Cultural Emotion Games as Trajectory Learning in Southeast Asia

V. Sithira Vadivel$^{(\boxtimes)}$ ⓘ, Insu Song, and Abhishek Singh Bhati

College of Science and Engineering, James Cook University, 149 Sims Drive, Singapore 387380, Singapore
{sithira.vadivel,insu.song,abhishek.bhati}@jcu.edu.au

Abstract. Mobile and online games have become a popular delivery method of education. Creating fun, exciting, engaging, and motivating education games have been the main challenges for the online content providers, especially for education industry. Southeast Asia market has grown steadily over the years for online content providers, becoming one of the strategic areas of investment. In this paper, we identify that cultural barrier is the key obstacle to successfully enter this market. This study surveyed 342 teachers from four Southeast Asian countries to identify the problem of slow adoption of ICT, especially in teaching and learning: the Philippines, Brunei, Indonesia, and Malaysia. We identified independent and dependent variables related to the causal effects on learning experience and outcomes of interactive online learning contents. Using only the significant paths, we then constructed a new cultural online game and e-learning model for creating more exciting, engaging, fun, and motivating online learning contents. Partial least square structural equation modelling techniques were used to examine the path associated with dependent and independent constructs. The result show (a) significant presence of cultural emotion states to help speed up digitalization and e-learning adoption to achieve digital transformation; (b) there are significant factors that can achieve path association from being contented (classroom-based learning) to being Technoid (skilled in technology use); (c) overall, the models achieved an acceptable fit for a new online game and e-learning platform for teachers' and students in Southeast Asia. Based on the new cultural e-learning model, we created a science education game using festive themes for invoking pleasant emotions that are compatible for specific target groups. The cultural emotion game provided better learning experience and outcomes demonstrating how the new cultural e-learning model was able to make games more exciting, engaging and fun.

1 Introduction

The year 2020 has been an unprecedented year for the entire world. The Covid-19 pandemic has devastated the world economy. Are we prepared for such a pandemic? The answer is evident when such a pandemic surface and the world comes to a halt. What is clear is that industries were not prepared for such a pandemic. Schools worldwide have transited to online learning. Through sharing of teaching materials, activities can still take

J. Baalsrud Hauge et al. (Eds.): ICEC 2021, LNCS 13056, pp. 62–74, 2021.
https://doi.org/10.1007/978-3-030-89394-1_5

place online. The information and communication technology (ICT) preparedness is felt during this crucial time when we have no choice but to resort to online learning platforms to avoid widespread infections. However, the transition from classroom learning to online learning has not been smooth in Southeast Asia, even with online learning technology having been introduced to schools more than a decade ago. Earlier reports, indicate a low use of technology in Malaysian schools (Ngah and Masood 2006; Hong and Koh 2002). A decade later, reports on the use of VLE-Frog, the online learning platform used in Malaysian secondary schools, showed that most teachers were reluctant to use the platform, as they did not enjoy using it, and its implementation brings with it a certain amount of anxiety and threat; hence, it affects not only students' exposure to technology and e-learning but also their learning outcomes (Rashid 2014; Shazali and Hashim 2018).

Southeast Asian secondary schools and their ICT preparedness have faced several challenges during this crisis. At the forefront of the evolving educational challenges arising from technology advancement is the resistance met by teachers and students in accommodating the educational technology integration. The problems are more profound in some regions, with some schools being slow to adopt technology-assisted learning and showing resistance to change (Yap et al. 2008).

2 Background

2.1 Southeast Asia – Online Learning Outlook

The Frog Virtual Learning Environment (VLE) has been used to enhance teaching and learning in Malaysia's government schools since 2012. However, the findings of a study on teachers' readiness to utilize Frog VLE in a Malaysian secondary school classified as a 'champion school' shows that the teachers from the monitored school were still lacking in readiness and possessed inadequate skills in accessing Frog VLE (Termit and Hussein 2015). Another study on teachers' perceptions of online learning in Malaysian secondary schools shows that besides limited ICT skills, low English proficiency is also a barrier to understanding the language used by Frog VLE, and this has caused confusion among teachers and students (Mei et al. 2017). A study of students' acceptance and readiness for e-learning in Northeastern Thailand shows that the participants liked the fact that online learning could be used anytime and anywhere and that it could reduce the cost of printed materials. However, despite the positive perceptions, teachers had no experience with online teaching methodology; hence they were unprepared to use an online learning system (Anchalee and Adams 2016). A study done in Indonesia on online learning program adoption in 2016 shows that attitudes toward e-learning are closely tied to perceptions about the ease of use and utility of e-learning programs. Though an individual could perceive online learning programs as easy, it was unclear whether he or she would also understand the benefit of the program (Haryanto and Kaltsum 2016).

A study in the Philippines on college students using learning management systems (LMSs) shows that students did not appreciate the LMS system as they felt the features were like those of social networking sites (SNSs), e.g., sharing of files and socializing with other students. It could also be concluded from the studies that Filipino students will actively participate—or not—in the platform regardless of the interaction the system has to offer, and their motivation to participate is based on their own personal characteristics and cultural setup. When a system is easy to use, it is also perceived as useful (Garcia 2017). Another study on ICT integration and the challenges faced by teachers in Philippine schools shows that teachers were not interested in being trained in ICT utilization in classrooms because they found that some ICT skills were not applicable to their lessons and some older teachers were no longer interested in learning ICT as they had difficulty adapting to it. Schools cannot expect a higher academic performance of the ICT programs unless both educators and learners are digitally literate (Daling 2018).

2.2 Cultural Emotional Outlook

Researchers have identified culture as one key factor affecting technology-based learning. Culture affects the teaching and learning domain as well as the achievement of results (Zhang et al. 2006). Studies have documented that culture has a great influence on the way society functions (Hofstede 1983). Culture impacts the way people teach and learn (Choudhury 2014).

Asians' cultural identity and cohesiveness affect their emotional levels. In a recent study on the state of Southeast Asia 2019; the results shows that 72.6% of Southeast Asian feels that the tangible benefits of ASEAN are not felt and 44% of the respondents share their concern over ASEAN becoming increasingly disunited (Tang et al. 2019). Such a cohesive cultural identity is seen in the homes of South Asians living in the United Kingdom, where traditional Asian landscapes, decorations, and narratives show a connective cultural significance and are emotionally valued by the family (Tolia-Kelly 2004). Culture can shape how people express their emotions in certain cultural contexts, and emotions can be influenced by cultural factors (Turner and Stets 2005; Matsumoto and Ekman 1989).

The South Asian conception of the hierarchical structuring of consciousness is somewhat alien to emotion researchers in North America. South Asians have been influenced by local symbolic elaboration, and that translates into mental experiences that they regard as basic in their culturally constituted world. Embarrassment or shame among Americans could result in avoidance, silence, or withdrawal in the context of South Asian norms (Shweder et al. 1993). Cultural differences exist for some aspects of emotions, and one such aspect is emotional arousal levels. In Western or individualistic cultures, high-arousal emotions are promoted, whereas in Eastern or collectivist cultures, low-arousal emotions are valued (Lim 2016; Scollon et al. 2011).

Many researchers who have studied the role of computer-related anxiety in e-learning acceptance or use have concluded that computer anxiety is associated with avoidance or less use of online learning systems or technologies (Purnomo and Lee 2013; Venkatesh et al. 2003). Individuals who are anxious about using computers are more likely to be reluctant to adopt e-learning systems (Al-alak and Alnawas 2011; Fazil and Rupert 2016). Unusual classroom activities such as debates and preparing group presentations can boost students' motivation; hence, when motivation increases it lowers students' anxiety levels (Dewaele et al. 2018; Christensen 2002). Motivation, excitement, engaged, and having fun emotions could arise when students are involved in childhood activities that are close to their hearts. The potential of stress-relieving engaged activities results from the increase in contentedness and excitement feelings generated during activities

(Wood 1993). Cultural emotions are a deep-rooted element among Southeast Asians. Hence, stimulating positive Southeast Asian cultural emotions could be used as a critical factor when designing technology-assisted learning and could potentially achieve great results.

3 Constructing Hypotheses

In this comparative study, we empirically investigated how teachers' perceptions of technology-assisted teaching impacts their use of mobile game and online learning and how it affects students' learning in secondary schools in Malaysia, Indonesia, the Philippines, and Brunei. We investigated the impact of cultural dimensions, (uncertainty avoidance [UA] of cultural emotions) based on teachers' perception on the transformation from being content with classroom-based learning to reducing teachers' anxiety levels concerning mobile game and online learning to improve technology use (Technoid). The five constructs of the emotions tested were: Fun (H1), Motivating (H6), Excitement (H5), Contented (H4), and Engaged (H2), which improves technology use (Technoid) (H3).

Questions from teachers' survey used to construct hypotheses.

H1_T: Uncertainty avoidance impacts the state of having Fun. Questions and variables used:

- Students demonstrate higher level of learning when Tech is used (Fun_1)
- There is more student collaboration when Tech is used (Fun_2)
- There is more teamwork among students when Tech is used (Fun_3)
- It is easier to make students understand topic during Tech use (Fun_4)
- It is easier to get quiet students to participate during Tech use (Fun_5)

H6_T: Uncertainty avoidance impacts the state of being Motivated. Questions and variables used:

- Students are more motivated during Tech activity (Motivating_1)
- Students are constantly motivated during technology-assisted learning (Motivating_2)

H2_T: Uncertainty avoidance impacts the state of being Engaged. Questions and variables used:

- Students wait for instructions before exploring mobile-assisted learning (Engaged_1)
- Students use collaboration tools to post questions without being instructed (Engaged_2)
- Students wait for teachers' instructions before proceeding with tech. activities (Engaged_3)
- Students are very dependent on teachers during tech. activities (Engaged_4)

H4_T: Uncertainty avoidance impacts the state of being contented. Question and variable used:

- Students prefer traditional classroom over technology-assisted learning (Contented_1)

H3_T: Uncertainty avoidance impacts the use of technology. Questions and variables used:

- Internet for developing lessons (Technoid_1)
- Mobile devices (e.g., smartphones) (Technoid_2)
- Learning management systems (e.g., online blackboard) (Technoid_3)
- Online videos (e.g., YouTube) (Technoid_4)

H5_T: Uncertainty avoidance impacts the state of being excited. Questions and variables used:

- Using different tech. for different activities students understand the topic better (Excited_1)
- Using different technology eases management of different types of learners (Excited_2)

Figure 1 depicts the proposed model with cultural emotions. Hypotheses and their possibilities of causal effects on cultural emotions are suggested. The causal effects and their significance will be tested.

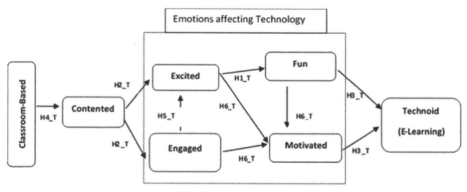

Fig. 1. Relationship between cultural emotion constructs leading to Technoid

4   Methodology and Data Analysis

Data collected from 20 secondary schools across Malaysia, Indonesia, the Philippines, and Brunei on demographics (age and gender), technology perceptions, and technology use. Questions covered the frequency of technology use, teachers' competency level in the use of technology for activities, and their perceptions of technology use in terms of motivation, collaboration, with cultural dimensions.

On a 5-point Likert scale, respondents were asked to rate their overall level of satisfaction with the use of technology/digital tools in the classroom, as well as their competency level. Scales ranged from 1 = strongly disagree to 5 = strongly agree, from 1 = never used to 5 = competent, and from 0 = NA to 4 = daily. The questionnaire was distributed to 400 randomly selected teachers and 1,000 randomly selected students. Since this study emphasizes teachers' perception, only teacher data will be analysed for this study. Overall, 342 teachers completed questionnaires across the four countries (n = 82 respondents in the Philippines, n = 92 respondents in Brunei, n = 69 respondents in Malaysia, and n = 99 respondents in Indonesia).

Both descriptive and inferential statistics were applied to compute the mean, standard deviation, frequency, Pearson's correlation coefficient, one-way ANOVA, and PLS-SEM bootstrapping using SmartPLS. The findings presented in this section are based on the probability set at ≤ 0.05. First, we report the ANOVA test results for comparing the mean values of dependent and independent variables between countries. This analysis is required to compare the mean values between countries to identify the any significant differences before we can propose a model to support the data collected for all four countries. The same factors (dependent and independent variables) are used to build the best-fit model in PLS. Only significant values from ANOVA were used in the model, except for the variable Contented_1. This model is built based on the collected data from the four countries and specifically from teachers' perspectives. Our method and findings are limited by the self-reported nature of the survey questions and our assumptions.

5 Results

An analysis of variance (ANOVA) on these scores yielded significant variation among conditions, and a post hoc Tukey test for four of the dependent factors showed that there are no significant differences between Malaysia and Brunei, and there are no significant differences between Philippines and Indonesia in comparison, except for the last dependent factor (Fun_5), where Malaysia, Indonesia, and Brunei fell into the same category. An analysis of variance (ANOVA) on engaged scores yielded significant variation among conditions, and a post hoc Tukey test for the following dependent factors showed no significant differences between Malaysia, the Philippines, and Brunei (Engaged_1 and Engaged_3), as well as between the Philippines and Indonesia (Engaged_2 and Engaged_4). Refer to Table 1.

An analysis of variance (ANOVA) of technology use scores yielded significant variation among conditions, and a post hoc Tukey test for the following dependent factors showed no significant differences between Malaysia, Indonesia, and the Philippines (Technoid_2). The analysis also indicates that all countries scored a low mean value $m < 2.85$ for all factors, except for Malaysia's Learning Management System (LMS) use which shows $m = 3.19$. Brunei mean score was the lowest for all four factors ($M < 2.01$). Brunei scored a mean value $m = 0.91$ for Learning Management (LMS) which shows the use between never to not applicable. An analysis of variance (ANOVA) on contentedness scores yielded no significant differences among conditions between countries, with $F(3, 332) = 0.28$ and $P = 0.84$ (refer to Table 2). An analysis of variance (ANOVA) on excitement scores yielded significant variation among conditions, and a post hoc

Table 1. H1 fun and H2 engaged

	Malaysia (N = 69)	Indonesia (N = 96)	Philippines (N = 81)	Brunei (N = 92)	ANOVA
Fun_1	$M = 3.5$, SD = 0.74	$M = 4.2$, SD = 0.66	$M = 3.96$, SD = 0.77	$M = 3.23$, SD = 0.74	$F(3,332) = 31.2$, $P = 0.000$
Fun_2	$M = 3.7$, SD = 0.75	$M = 4.1$, SD = 0.66	$M = 4.04$, SD = 0.70	$M = 3.5$, SD = 0.84	$F(3,331) = 13.5$, $P = 0.000$
Fun_3	$M = 3.6$, SD = 0.78	$M = 4.05$, SD = 0.66	$M = 3.9$, SD = 0.71	$M = 3.5$, SD = 0.78	$F(3,330) = 13.5$, $P = 0.000$
Fun_4	$M = 3.8$, SD = 0.54	$M = 4.14$, SD = 0.63	$M = 3.9$, SD = 0.7	$M = 3.6$, SD = 0.78	$F(3,334) = 6.1$, $P = 0.000$
Fun_5	$M = 3.8$, SD = 0.59	$M = 3.7$, SD = 0.86	$M = 4.2$, SD = 0.75	$M = 3.6$, SD = 0.78	$F(3,331) = 3.4$, $P = 0.02$
Engaged_1	M = 3.2, SD = 0.92	M = 3.6, SD = 0.81	$M = 3.4$, SD = 0.88	$M = 3.2$, SD = 0.73	$F(3,332) = 3.34$, $P = 0.019$
Engaged_2	$M = 3.2$, SD = 0.84	$M = 3.3$, SD = 1.12	$M = 3.4$, SD = 0.78	$M = 2.9$, SD = 0.78	$F(3,333) = 3.19$, $P = 0.024$
Engaged_3	$M = 3.4$, SD = 0.74	$M = 3.8$, SD = 0.74	$M = 3.4$, SD = 0.83	$M = 3.4$, SD = 0.69	$F(3,332) = 3.22$, $P = 0.023$
Engaged_4	$M = 2.9$, SD = 0.82	$M = 3.3$, SD = 0.98	$M = 3.2$, SD = 0.88	$M = 3.1$, SD = 0.75	$F(3,332) = 3.22$, $P = 0.023$

Tukey test for the following dependent factors showed no significant difference between Malaysia and Brunei (Excitement_1 and Excitement_2) and between the Philippines and Indonesia (Excitement_1 and Excitement_2). An analysis of variance (ANOVA) on these scores yielded significant variation among conditions, and a post hoc Tukey test for the first dependent factor (Motivating_1) showed no significant differences between Malaysia and Brunei, and the Philippines and Indonesia (refer to Table 2).

Post-hoc Tukey's HSD tests indicated that Brunei had significantly lower mean scores for all dependent factors compared to Malaysia, the Philippines, and Indonesia. This finding contradicts UNESCO's statistics (UNESCO Institute for Statistics 2010) on ICT infrastructure in secondary institutions with Internet-assisted instruction showing Brunei at 100%. The post hoc test reveals that there are no significant differences between countries for some factors (Engaged_1, Engaged_3, Contented_1, Motivating_1, Motivating_2, and Technoid_2); hence, cultural similarities within these Southeast Asian countries do exist and affect the perceived use of mobile game and online learning tools.

These constructs were used to tabulate the path coefficients and P-values for dependent variables and T-values for independent variables to obtain a best-fit mobile game and online learning model for Southeast Asia in PLS combining the data from all four countries. PLS-SEM was used to model the theoretical framework. PLS-SEM was selected as it provides many advantages because it can test theoretically supported linear and additive causal models (Haenlein and Kaplan 2004). This technique is suitable for developing theories (Chin 1998). The structural path significance in bootstrapping was used.

Table 2. H3 Technoid, H4 contented, H5 excited and H6 motivating

	Malaysia (N = 69)	Indonesia (N = 99)	Philippines (N = 80)	Brunei (N = 92)	ANOVA
Technoid_1	M = 2.3, SD = 0.92	M = 2.7, SD = 1.06	M = 2.8, SD = 1.05	M = 2.0, SD = 1.1	F(3,337) = 11.19, P = 0.000
Technoid_2	M = 2.6, SD = 1.33	M = 2.6, SD = 1.36	M = 2.6, SD = 1.28	M = 1.6, SD = 1.24	F(3,331) = 12.04, P = 0.000
Technoid_3	M = 3.2, SD = 1.04	M = 2.8, SD = 1.27	M = 1.4, SD = 1.21	M = 0.91, SD = 0.78	F(3,326) = 81.2, P = 0.000
Technoid_4	M = 2.4, SD = 0.9	M = 1.9, SD = 1.14	M = 2.1, SD = 1.07	M = 1.9, SD = 0.97	F(3,333) = 5.5, P = 0.000
Contented_1	M = 2.8, SD = 0.85	M = 2.8, SD = 1.09	M = 2.8, SD = 0.94	M = 2.9, SD = 0.73	F(3,332) = 0.28, P = 0.84
Excited_1	M = 3.9, SD = 0.54	M = 4.0, SD = 0.63	M = 4.1, SD = 0.70	M = 3.7, SD = 0.70	F(3,334) = 6.1, P = 0.000
Excited_2	M = 3.8, SD = 0.65	M = 4.0, SD = 0.65	M = 4.1, SD = 0.75	M = 3.6, SD = 0.77	F(3,321) = 4.5, P = 0.004
Motivating_1	M = 3.7, SD = 0.78	M = 4.2, SD = 0.66	M = 4.2, SD = 0.75	M = 3.8, SD = 0.73	F (3,331) = 14.7, P = 0.000
Motivating_2	M = 3.8, SD = 0.56	M = 4.0, SD = 0.74	M = 4.1, SD = 0.70	M = 3.7, SD = 0.69	F (3,333) = 11.6, P = 0.000

6 Analysis of Teachers' Model

Figure 2 illustrates the path associated with the proposed constructs after several moderation analysis for R^2 change to achieve the best result and only the most significant path were chosen to form the model. The valid construct for the transformation from (classroom-learning) Contented to (Technoid) Technology use. The PLS results indicated that that Contented (βContented $\rightarrow$ Engaged = 0.369, p < 0.001) leads to Engaged (βEngaged $\rightarrow$ Excitement = 0.572, p < 0.001) and Excitement (βExcitement $\rightarrow$ Fun = 0.535, p < 0.001). Contented $\rightarrow$ Engaged (R^2 = 0.136) $\rightarrow$ Excitement (R^2 = 0.327).

The PLS equation revealed Excitement and Fun as predictors for Motivating (R^2 = 0.780), Excitement (βExcitement $\rightarrow$ Motivating = 0.380, p < 0.001), and Fun (βFun $\rightarrow$ Motivating = 0.620, p < 0.001), and Motivating (βMotivating $\rightarrow$ Technoid = 0.301, p < 0.001) as the predictor for Technoid. Excitement (R^2 = 0.327) $\rightarrow$ Fun (R^2 = 0.286) $\rightarrow$ Motivating (R^2 = 0.780) shows a higher association compared to Excitement $\rightarrow$ Motivating. To improve technology use (Technoid) the construct of motivation can be utilised. Engaged is not a predictor for motivation as was originally hypothesised. Fun is not a direct predictor for improving technology use (Technoid). The determinant to improve technology use (Technoid) is motivation, i.e., it shows the highest coefficient of determination ($R^2 = 0.780**$). Therefore, manipulating motivation in game and e-learning design would trigger and stimulate teachers' technology use positively.

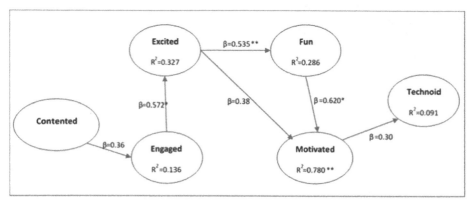

Fig. 2. Cultural mobile games and e-learning model for Southeast Asia Teachers

7 Discussion on Teachers' Model

Mobile Games and E-Learning adoption requires an extensive designing transformation for a successful infusion in the Southeast Asian region. Based on literature, researchers have suggested the need for learning behaviors to be integrated into Cultural Mobile Game and E-Learning models; however, there is a lack of cultural emotion studies related to mobile game and E-learning platforms. There are strong ties between cultural norms and cultural emotions in Southeast Asians' daily activities. Their beliefs and traditions strengthen their emotions, and this can positively manifest in their daily activities (Murata et al. 2013). The results of this study suggest that the connection of cultural emotions and cultural dimensions are necessary constructs of the cultural mobile games and E-learning platform. The causal effects of cultural emotions aimed towards reducing anxiety levels among teachers and students for the purpose of promoting technological use (Technoid) positions a new paradigm in the design of cultural mobile game and E-learning platforms. In the proposed model in Fig. 1, we suggested a relationship between cultural emotions and our hypotheses, stating that there is possible causal effect of the state of being contented leading to being Engaged. Being Engaged leads to being excited and being excited leads to having Fun and Motivated. Therefore, being Engaged could lead to being Excited, Motivating, and having Fun. A non-stressful situation, that is, being Engaged, could work wonders for anyone, as being excited during an activity could lead to successful completion of the activity, having fun for oneself, and eventual transformation to Motivated mood. Both having fun and motivation can reduce anxiety resulting in improving technology use (Technoid). However, no positive correlation was suggested in PLS for Engaged leading to having Fun and Motivated, or having Fun in technology use (Technoid).

The researched cultural mobile game and e-learning model suggests a strong causal effect for Engaged ($\beta = 0.572**$) $\rightarrow$ Excited ($\beta = 0.535**$) $\rightarrow$ Fun ($\beta = 0.620**$) $\rightarrow$ Motivated ($R^2 = 0.780**$). These factors as strong contributors to the transformation from being contented (classroom-learning) to having a reduced anxiety level improving technology use (Technoid) in cultural mobile game and e-learning design. The technology adoption techniques in Southeast Asia must take a different infusion approach as the previous approaches have instilled laxity in adopting them. Previous researchers have argued the inclusion factors of perceived ease of use and usefulness which highlights successful utilization. However, it lacks the important pillar that is required for Southeast Asian technology pessimist towards successful technology use and sustainability. Southeast Asians value their cultural norms and tradition, hence positioning this cultural value is crucial for ICT design. Cultural emotions stimulate teachers' and students' sentiments towards their cultural presents in a way that postulates ease of acceptance. Teachers and students will be prepared to explore the uncertainties without much hesitation as willingness intensifies with emotional stimulants. The infusion of technology preparedness can also be further enhanced through the acceleration of technology acceptance with emotional stimulants for Southeast Asia.

8   Success Story: Model Use with Festive Theme Mobile Learning

The proposed model was integrated and tested with a festive cultural themed mobile game-based learning and with 84 students and 17 teachers from 3 high schools in Jakarta, Indonesia on students learning experience and teachers experience. Thirty-four students (n = 34) participated in the festive cultural theme activity, 26 students (n = 26) participated in the standard theme activity, and 24 students (n = 24) participated in the classroom-based learning activity. Activities were on learning the topic on Photosynthesis. Students learned the topic using an interactive mobile-game based activity with festive cultural theme Eg. Ramadhan, Lunar New Year, Christmas, Vesak, and Diwali. The festive theme design included festive music, festive decorations, festive vibrant colors which invokes deeply rooted cultural emotions of engaged, excited, fun and motivated as shown in Fig. 3: Ramadhan festival. Students were motivated, engaged, and were having fun with Festive themed mobile interactive game (*m > 4.1*) compared to classroom-based learning and standard-theme. Students' achievement on pre-test and post-test also shows high achievement of 14.12% compared to standard theme of 6.54%. 17 teachers evaluated the festive themed activity. Teachers' evaluation shows high mean ratings for motivation (m = 4.65), excitement (m = 4.59), happiness (m = 4.47), enjoyment (m = 4.59), fun (m = 4.57), and satisfaction (m = 4.35) (Vadivel et al. 2021).

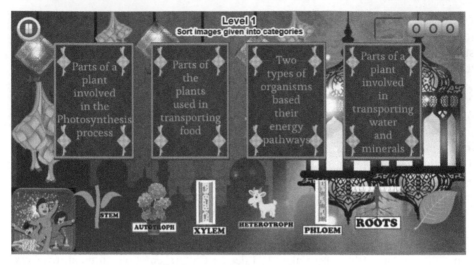

Fig. 3. Ramadhan festive themed

9   Conclusion

In this study, we have proposed a new cultural mobile game and e-learning design researched model for Southeast Asia based on cultural emotions for Teachers. Suggesting the need for a paradigm shift for online content providers in designing online platforms for Southeast Asian secondary education. The proposed model could be used as a foundation for designing and building educational mobile and e-learning with cultural games that is more exciting, engaging, fun and motivating to stimulate teaching in Southeast Asian regions to overcome the adversity faced today. The implications of the proposed model (1) Redesigning future mobile game and e-learning platforms to stimulate learning to solve the problem of slow ICT adoption in Southeast Asia (2) To facilitate and improve activity with positive emotions and to reduce negative emotions thus influencing their learning outcome; (3) Creates a cultural emotional attachment towards online learning platforms thus breaks the barrier of uncertainty avoidance among Southeast Asian students using mobile game and online learning platforms.

References

Al-alak, B.A., Alnawas, I.A.: Measuring the acceptance and adoption of e-learning by academic staff. Knowl. Manage. E-Learn. **3**(2), 201–221 (2011)

Anchalee, N., Adams, J.: Students' Acceptance and Readiness for E-learning in Northeastern Thailand (2016)

Christensen, R.: Effects of technology integration education on the attitudes of teachers and students. J. Res. Technol. Educ. **34**(4), 411–433 (2002)

Chin, W.W.: Commentary: Issues and Opinion on Structural Equation Modelling (1998)

Choudhury, R.U.: The role of culture in teaching and learning of English as a foreign language. Express Int. J. Multi Discipl. Res. **1**(4), 1–20 (2014)

Daling, R.F.: Accepting ICT integration: a challenge to school and curriculum. Int. J. Educ. Res. **6**(9) (2018)

Dewaele, J.M., Witney, J., Saito, K., Dewaele, L.: Foreign language enjoyment and anxiety: the effect of teacher and learner variables. Lang. Teach. Res. **22**(6), 676–697 (2018)

Fazil, A., Rupert, W.: Developing a General Extended Technology Acceptance Model for E-Learning (GETAMEL) by Analysing Commonly used External Factors (2016)

Garcia, M.B.: E-learning technology adoption in the Philippines: an investigation of factors affecting filipino college students' acceptance of learning management systems. Int. J. E-Learn. Educ. Technol. Digital Media **3**(3), 118–130 (2017)

Haenlein, M., Kaplan, A.M.: A beginner's guide to partial least squares analysis. Underst. Stat. **3**(4), 283–297 (2004)

Haryanto, H., Kaltsum, U.: E-Learning Program Adoption: Technology Acceptance Model Approach (2016)

Hofstede, G.: National cultures in four dimensions: a research-based theory of cultural differences among nations. Int. Stud. Manag. Organ. **13**(1–2), 46–74 (1983)

Hong, K.S., Koh, C.K.: Computer and attitudes toward computers among rural secondary school teachers: a Malaysian perspective. J. Res. Technol. Educ. **35**(1), 27–48 (2002)

Lim, N.: Cultural differences in emotion: differences in emotional arousal level between the east and the west. Integr. Med. Res. **5**(2), 105–109 (2016). https://doi.org/10.1016/j.imr.2016.03.004

Matsumoto, D., Ekman, P.: American-Japanese cultural differences in intensity ratings of facial expressions of emotion. Motiv. Emot. **13**(2), 143–157 (1989)

Mei, L.C., Su, L.W., Ayub, A.F., Mahmud, R.: Teachers perceptions of e-learning in Malaysian secondary schools. Malay. Online J. Educ. Technol. **5**(2), 20–33 (2017)

Murata, A., Moser, J.S., Kitayama, S.: Culture shapes electrocortical responses during emotion suppression. Soc. Cogn. Affect. Neurosci. **8**(5), 595–601 (2013). https://doi.org/10.1093/scan/nss036

Ngah, N.A., Masood, M.: Development of ICT instructional materials based on needs identified by Malaysia secondary school teachers. In: Proceedings of the 2006 Informing Science and IT Education Joint Conference, Salford, UK, June, pp. 25–28 (2006)

Purnomo, S.H., Lee, Y.H.: E-learning adoption in the banking workplace in Indonesia: an empirical study. Inf. Dev. **29**(2), 138–153 (2013)

Rashid, A.H.A.: Teachers' perception towards virtual learning environment. Doctoral Dissertation. Universiti Teknologi Malaysia (2014)

Scollon, C.N., Koh, S., Au, E.W.: Cultural differences in the subjective experience of emotion: when and why they occur. Soc. Pers. Psychol. Compass **5**(11), 853–864 (2011)

Shazali, S.S., Hashim, H.: Challenges in using frog VLE in teaching English to ESL learners: a review of past studies. J. Counsel. Educ. Technol. **1**(1), 1–4 (2018)

Shweder, R.A., Haidt, J., Horton, R., Joseph, C.: The cultural psychology of the emotions. Handbook of Emotions, pp. 417–431 (1993)

Tang, S.M., Hoang, T.H., Chalermpalanupap, T., Pham, T.P.T., Saelaow, A.Q., Thuzar, M.: The State of Southeast Asia: 2019 Survey Report (2019)

Termit, K., Hussein, N.: Teachers' Readiness to Utilize Frog VLE: A Case Study of a Malaysian Secondary School (2015)

Tolia-Kelly, D.: Locating processes of identification: studying the precipitates of re-memory through artefacts in the British Asian home. Trans. Inst. Br. Geogr. **29**(3), 314–329 (2004)

Turner, J.H., Stets, J.E.: The Sociology of Emotions. Cambridge University Press (2005)

UNESCO Institute for Statistics: Global Education Digest 2010: Comparing Education Statistics Across the World. UNESCO, Paris, France (2010)

Sithira Vadivel, V., Song, I., Bhati, A.: Culturally Themed Educational Tools for Enhancing Learning in Southeast Asian Secondary Schools. In: Arai, K., Kapoor, S., Bhatia, R. (eds.) Proceedings of the Future Technologies Conference (FTC) 2020, Volume 1, pp. 950–968. Springer International Publishing, Cham (2021). https://doi.org/10.1007/978-3-030-63128-4_71

Venkatesh, V., Morris, M.G., Davis, G.B., Davis, F.D.: User acceptance of information technology: toward a unified view. MIS Quarterly 425–478 (2003)

Wood, C.: Mood change and perceptions of vitality: a comparison of the effects of relaxation, visualization and yoga. J. R. Soc. Med. **86**(5), 254 (1993)

Yap, L.Y., Ivy Tan, G.C., Zhu, X., Wettasinghe, M.C.: An assessment of the use of geographical information systems (GIS) in teaching geography in Singapore schools. J. Geogr. **107**(2), 52–60 (2008)

Zhang, D., Zhou, L., Briggs, R.O., Nunamaker, J.F., Jr.: Instructional video in e-learning: assessing the impact of interactive video on learning effectiveness. Inform. Manag. **43**(1), 15–27 (2006)

A Taxonomy of Social Roles for Agents in Games

Diogo Rato[1,2](✉) [iD] and Rui Prada[1,2] [iD]

[1] Instituto Superior Técnico, Universidade de Lisboa, Lisbon, Portugal
[2] GAIPS, INESC-ID, Lisbon, Portugal
{diogo.rato,rui.prada}@tecnico.ulisboa.pt

Abstract. Social agents have been used in games often, for example, to create a social dimension (e.g. the inhabitants of a village) or to provide challenges to players (e.g. the opponents players face). These agents have an essential role in the players' experience, and, as such, their creation needs to carefully considered. In this paper we propose a taxonomy of social roles that agents can play in games as a step towards the formalization of the problem of the creation of social agents in games. We believe that this taxonomy can help researchers to reach some common ground on the subject and, therefore, promote common views of the research problems involved in the design and development of social agents for games. We discuss several open challenges in the creation of social agents for games and discuss some future directions of research that can be grounded on the analysis of the taxonomy. For instance, many of the social roles proposed are played by agents that do not have much agency or autonomy. Also, there is a large number of under-explored social roles in games at the moment. The taxonomy serves as inspiration to guide game design involving social interactions with game actors, promoting new kinds of gameplay built on the interactive space afforded by the social agents.

Keywords: Social agents · Game characters · Game design · Game AI

1 Introduction

Since the very beginning, games include entities with some level of agency that have the ability to act in the game world, sometimes even without the player's direct influence. These agents are commonly used in games to provide conflict as they help to define the gameplay dynamics and challenges that players face, for example, by incorporating characters that have resources that players need.

Moreover, these agents may have stronger social roles in the game as they are also elements that provide support to players, for instance, as characters that offer help and accompany the player through their journey. In this case, agents, more often referred to as non-player characters (NPC), are crucial to convey a social dimension to the game world that enhances its social immersion and believability. In games with more prominent stories agents can take

© IFIP International Federation for Information Processing 2021
Published by Springer Nature Switzerland AG 2021
J. Baalsrud Hauge et al. (Eds.): ICEC 2021, LNCS 13056, pp. 75–87, 2021.
https://doi.org/10.1007/978-3-030-89394-1_6

narrative roles and functions as well. The use of agents with social roles in games is not just a typical element but is also an added value with great impact on the players' experience. When endowed with intelligent social behaviours, such agents increase players' enjoyment in games [5] and better social agents in games are actually demanded by players [1]. In fact, some games are praised by the autonomous social agents that they present. Nonetheless, to create a good experience, players' expectations of sociality of game agents must be satisfied. To achieve that, their behaviour demands, many times, high fidelity and complex social mechanisms. This represents both a need and opportunity for the development of novel social mechanics in games, in particular, that use social AI.

The social dimensions of the game worlds that game agents populate are increasingly more complex, for example, involving multiple characters acting together with other AI characters and players, that need to understand and adapt to multiple situations. To cope with this, agents in games need more complex abilities, in particular, to have social needs and goals to be able to act socially. In turn, if social agents are able to display a wider range of behaviours, the available options to players are enhanced, as this increased range of behaviour results in bigger social interaction space afforded by the game. This promotes a higher feeling of agency in players and represents an opportunity for novel gameplay mechanics. Social agents can be used in games for several different reasons and purposes, and can play different roles in the game dynamics and experience. The abilities they need depend on the roles they play in the game.

In this paper, we start by discussing the dimensions of social interactions in games where social agents may be integrated, which can take place outside the game world, among players, or inside the game world both in terms of narrative and gameplay. This defines an overall frame of the problem of creating agents for games. Then, we focus our analysis in the gameplay roles that agents can play in games and propose a taxonomy as a step towards the formalization of the more concrete problem of the creation of social agents for gameplay in games. We aim at defining a wide map of social roles in games, so we included in the taxonomy common social roles in games, but also others that fit well in game interactions, even if they are not yet much explored by designers and researchers.

We believe that the discussion and the taxonomy can help researchers and designers to reflect about the problem of including social agents in games and the roles they may play, and reach some common ground on the subject and the research problems involved. For example, this common language can support the comparison of work on AI solutions for similar social roles. At the same time, the taxonomy can be a guide for the design of agents in games and identify areas under-explored by game researchers that may constitute good opportunities for future work.

2   Related Work

The research literature on taxonomies of social agents in games, or non-player characters (NPCs), is very scarce. In fact, the necessary characteristics to consider a virtual character in a game as an NPC vary according to different authors. For instance, Bartle defined NPCs as inhabitants of virtual worlds that look like player characters [3], whereas Warpefelt considers them as NPCs if they seem rational and intentional [13]. Furthermore, Yildirim and Stene [16] questioned if NPCs could be considered as agents since most are reactive and temporally continuous, but only a few are really autonomous and goal-oriented. The wide variety of definitions are indeed subject to the use of the agents in the game, and the AI approach used.

The typology proposed by Bartle in 2004 identified several functional roles for NPCs heavily tailored to multi-user dungeons. Although useful to describe NPCs in terms of the function they provided, it comprised a reduced set of roles that does not reflect the large interactive space currently supported by games. Some descriptions of the roles of NPCs have been proposed in game design guidelines and patterns. In particular in studies that explore specific social roles, such as enemies [12] or companions [6], or that study the deployment of game characters in different modalities, such as robots in board games [10] and voice interaction in digital games [2]. However, these descriptions are not fully aligned with each other and are fragmented in the different research, hence, are less general.

More recently, by using an online survey, Warpefelt and Verhagen identified a mismatch between in what ways the respondents interpret NPC roles and which are available in Bartle's typology, and propose a new classification for NPCs [14]. The authors identified twelve categories grouped in four types (functions, adversary, friends, providers), each described by how it affects gameplay, their provided function, visual presentation, placement, and behaviour. The taxomony was validated in a exercise to map the roles and functions of NPC in ten games and in a further study impact of the categories proposed on the player's expectations during gameplay was found [15]. However, the proposed taxomony was fully centered on what players described in the survey, which resulted in a taxonomy limited to the roles that were prominent to players, and in the set of games used in the validation, and, therefore, did not capture the full extend of social roles in games. In fact, the authors refer that some functions were not matched to roles in the taxonomy. Moreover, the analysis was not framed in the social nature of the interactions as we intent in our proposal.

In some cases, the definition of the social roles relies on the NPCs impact on the narrative rather than on the gameplay. They usually follow narratological taxonomies, such as Propp's, based on the analysis of russian folktales [11], or Greima's actantial model [8], and his seminotic square [9]. But, although we recognize the importance of the narrative dimension of social agents in games, we aim at exploring the interaction space that social agents promote in terms of gameplay, that has been less studied.

3   Dimensions of Social Interaction in Games

Social interaction is part of the experience most games convey. It is natural that social agents have important roles to play in those games. Note, that we consider as an agent, any game actor that has some level of embodiment (e.g. some kind of representation as an entity) and has explicit social interaction with a player or other agents. This, independently, of the level of true agency and complexity of the behaviour it displays. Social agents can use very simple internal mechanisms, even just following predefined scripts and reactive behaviour, or can use more complex mechanisms supporting advanced behaviours. Hence, the categories we present in the taxonomy do not represent necessarily agents with much autonomy in the current implementations, but afford, nevertheless, agency and autonomy.

To study the social roles agents can play in games we first discuss the nature of the social interaction experience that games promote. Social interactions in games can be addressed and analysed from different perspectives. On one hand, they are part of the gameplay dynamics, as several game actors interact to make the game move forward. These social interactions are not necessarily positive. Game actors can fight, steal, exchange resources, share information, coordinate actions, etc. The actions performed by game actors are also interpreted beyond the gameplay dynamics and may have specific meanings in the game fiction and narrative. In this perspective, the roles agents play are narrative roles, of characters in stories, such as protagonist, antagonist, etc. We can also consider the game as an artefact to support social interactions among players. In this sense, the social interactions are interpreted by the player in the real world.

The different perspectives of social interaction in games suggest different types of roles for the social agents depending on the dimensions of the experience that they influence. Agents in games may act in three distinct dimensions:

- The **Player dimension** that refers to the game actors in the real world rather than the game world. The interpretation of the social interactions at this level is framed outside the game world. **Players** are actors external to the game that, nevertheless, influence the course of the game (e.g. are performing actions through a controller). Players can be human or artificial. In this dimension, we also fit people (or agents) that are not taking actions in the game but may influence them, for example, by watching others play and discuss strategies or suggest actions, or engage in social interactions with players, for example, by encouraging and providing emotional support.
- The **Gameplay dimension** that encapsulates the game actors as **agents** capable of acting in, and perceiving, the game world. The social interactions in this dimension have functional dynamics that change the game's world state and move the game forward. This dimension frames social agents, and their interactions, as elements of the gameplay mechanics.
- The **Narrative dimension** that presents the **characters** taking part in the game's story and support the creation of fictional interpretations of the game world. The social interactions from this point of view sustain the fantasy conveyed by the game. It excludes agents that are not crucial for the fiction or story and may include characters that do not affect the gameplay.

A game actor may be projected into multiple dimensions if it takes part in the different dimensions of the game (see Fig. 1). For example, players often have an avatar in the game that represents them. The avatar is the agent that performs

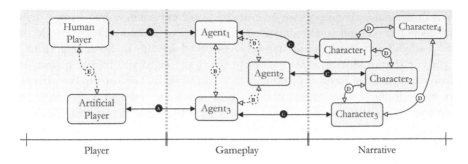

Fig. 1. A visual representation of the three dimensions of social interactions in games: Player, Gameplay and Narrative. Edges **A**, **B**, **C** and **D** represent the different kinds of interactions: player-agent, agent-agent, agent-character and character-character.

the actions in the game world for the player. Avatars may have some autonomy and make some decisions about the actions to perform or may strictly follow what is requested by players. Players may have different avatars in different phases of the game (e.g. In Thomas was Alone (Bithell Games, 2012)) or even have a direct choice on which avatar to take in each situation (e.g. Trine (Frozenbyte, 2009)). The avatar is often the vehicle to define the limits of players' actions and perceptions, as is also a mechanism to help players project themselves into the game world, supporting immersion. The avatar binds the way players and others see themselves in the game world. Nevertheless, games do not necessarily provide avatars to players. They may directly manipulate the objects in the game world. Also, they may have social interactions with the gameplay agents without having an embodiment in the game world.

Many agents in the game world are not controlled by players (e.g. are not avatars), these are frequently referred to Non-player Characters. They, typically, have both gameplay functions and narrative functions. The gameplay dimension captures the mechanics of the interactions that agents support (e.g. which actions they perform and how they respond to others). This defines the affordances of the social interaction space that players can explore in terms of gameplay. These interactions have, additionally, some interpretation in the narrative world. These are captured in the narrative dimension, where the agent is perceived as a character. For example, an agent may be the means by which players get a resource needed for gameplay (e.g. ammunition), and may represent a character that players can relate to and that shares stories about the game world.

In the case of a social robot playing a card game like Sueca [4], the agent takes the role of an artificial player in the player dimension. The game world is supported by physical items (e.g. the table and the cards) and there is no need for an avatar as the player directly manipulates the cards. Additionally, the game does not define a fiction that projects the agent in the narrative dimension. But, a social robot can also control an avatar or play a character in a narrative if the game supports such a setting (e.g. in tabletop Role-play Games [7]).

All dimensions are important to build a good experience, but games define them deeper according to the experience they try to provide. For example, the *feelings of fellowship* are more strongly conveyed by the social interactions in the **player dimension**, the *feelings of mastery* are conveyed by the **gameplay dimension**, and the *feelings of fantasy* are conveyed by the **narrative dimension**. Each dimension presents different challenges for social agents. For example, for an agent to perform well in a game and support the games' target experience, it will need to be able to be part of the players' community; to be able to offer challenging social interactions to players (e.g. that need coordination, or the use of persuasion); or to be able to play roles that enrich the fiction and the narrative, respectively. In fact, it is important to align the roles in the perspectives of the three dimensions to provide high-quality game experiences and promote players' immersion. For example, it is desirable that storytelling and gameplay are well integrated into a game, and for that, there should be a strong relation between the actions that agents perform in the game world and their narrative meaning.

The definition of the three dimensions helps us study and define the concrete elements social agents need for each dimension of a game's social experience. These promote distinct types of social exchanges framed in nested contexts. Many social interactions occur inside the game and are framed by the contexts that the game creates, but the social interactions extend outside the game world as well. There, the social context is wider and includes awareness of the contexts that the game creates.

- **In-game interactions**: all social interactions that occur within the game world. These can be of two types:
  - *In-character interactions*: are social interactions framed by the fiction and narrative of the game. These are character to character social interactions that are coherent with the fiction and the narrative established by the game. Characters' actions and drives should be consistent with the fantasy portrayed by the game and the character's narrative goals.
  - *Out-of-character interactions*: are social interactions that have the gameplay mechanics and dynamics as the core frame of reference. These are agent to agent interactions that are coherent with the gameplay rules. Agents are driven by the gameplay goals and their actions are not necessarily aligned with the game's narrative. For example, players may use their avatar to steal a powerful item from another agent to get a gameplay advantage (e.g. deal more damage), while the motivations of the character to steal are not supported in the narrative. The main concern in this example is to maximize performance and not keep the agent in-character. Another example is the case of dialogue interactions whose content is about gameplay mechanics rather than characters' speech.
- **Out-game interactions**: all social interactions that occur outside the game world. These can also be of two types:
  - *Interpersonal interactions*: are social interactions that involve actors that are not in the game world, e.g. take place between the players outside

the game. These are not conducted through the game world (e.g. are not performed through agents or objects in the game world and do not use in-game communication tools). These are "out-of-character" interactions as well and are not subject to the fictional narrative nor the gameplay rules. These interactions often extend beyond the gameplay session. E.g. players may keep discussing the game results for a while after finishing playing, or start discussing the strategy for an incoming match.

- **Cross-dimension interactions**: are social interactions that engage game actors across different dimensions, mixing and bridging the context of interaction. These can be player to agent social interactions, when players do not have avatars and directly request actions from agents (e.g. their soldiers in a squad). Can also be character to player interactions, when a character talks directly to the player, for example, to express frustrations about their decisions. In fact, all "out-of-character" social interactions involving game characters are inherently, cross-dimension interactions, and take the character out of the narrative context. In this case, the meaning of its actions is no longer only bounded by the narrative but is also based on the other dimensions.

4 Social Roles in Games

We will centre the rest of the discussion on the social roles that agents can take in terms of gameplay, and will not focus on narrative functions or player types. We aim at defining a "tool" to support the development and study of the gameplay aspects of social agents in games that have been less studied in game research.

Describing a game based on its agents and their relation promotes the emergence of prototypical relationships. To an extent, when deployed in games, such agents serve a functional purpose that typically can be described by their relationship with the surrounding, in particular, with other agents.

Each social role involves two parties and different types of exchanges, which may or not have their goals aligned with each other. When understanding the relationship between two agents in a game, the **Goal Alignment** of the multiple parties of the social roles is crucial. We divided the alignment of goals into three types:

- **Support** - when the goals of both parties directly support each other. For instance, in *The Lost Vikings* (Silicon & Synapse, 1993) the different agents controlled by the player share a common goal, and in *Bioshock Infinite* (Irrational Games, 2013) Booker and Elizabeth's goals support each other. These roles suggest some kind of cooperative relation.
- **Contest** - when the goals of one of the parties contest the goal of the counterpart. For instance, the ghosts in *Pac-Man* (Namco, 1980) have a goal (catch the player) that contest the player's goal (eat all dots); and in a game of chess, both players compete against each other thus each player individual goals contest the other's, suggesting some kind of competitive relation.

– **Neutral** - when the goals of one party involved do not directly support or contest the other's goal. For instance, in *Ryse: Son of Rome* (Crytek, 2013), the usage of background agents helps to establish a social environment even though the do not directly affect the player's progression.

Another characteristic used to distinguish social roles is their **Symmetry**. When a social role is **Symmetrical**, both parties assume similar stances towards each other. For instance, in *Pong* (Atari, 1972), both players are considered opponents of each other and, in *Pandemic* (Matt Leacock, 2013), the players must work together to succeed in the game, making them teammates. On the other hand, some social roles are **Asymmetrical** promoting distinct stances between their parties. For instance, in *League of Legends* (Riot Games, 2009) the shopkeeper assumes the role of a provider while the counterparts assume the role of a consumer, and, in *JackBox's party games* (JackBox Games, 2014), an agent assumes the role of the host while the remaining agents are participants.

Finally, the nature of the **Exchanged Elements** between the agents shapes the social roles as well. In particular, to distinguish multiple social roles, we rely on four types of elements that can be exchanged: **Information** (e.g. description of the game world, rules, mechanics and tactics), **Resources** (e.g. tools, items that directly influence the behavior of agents), **Goals** (e.g. mission and targets regarding the game system and economy), **Actions** (e.g. services or performances that require the manipulation of the game entities).

Based on the aforementioned characteristics, we identified several social roles for agents in games as well as the typical interactions found in games alongside examples of agents that assume each role. Regarding symmetrical roles, we identified two social roles with distinct goal alignments:

– **Teammate** - by taking this role, agents are committed to working together with each other. Teammates goals support one another and all succeed if the goals are achieved. To play as a teammate, agents need to be able to understand others' social context, shared goals and plans, and be able to execute the actions of the plan that typically require some kind of coordination. For instance, in *Overcooked* (Ghost Town Games, 2016), players must exchange resources and perform certain actions to successfully satisfy the game requests. In *Tom Clancy's Ghost Recon Wildlands* (Ubisoft, 2017), all members of the squad assume the role of teammate towards the other members. The same can be applied to scenarios that only involve two parts, typically referred to as companions (e.g. *The Last of Us* (Naughty Dog, 2013) and *Fallout 4* (Bethesda, 2015)) The role of teammate is also widely present in sports videogames, such as *FIFA* (Electronic Arts) and *NBA2K* (2K Games), and tabletop games, such as *Pandemic* (Matt Leacock, 2013).
– **Opponent** - by taking this role each party's goal directly contests the other's goals. As such, opponents attempt to obstruct the counterparts' progress while racing with them to achieve victory for themselves. Such as in the *Civilization* series (Sid Meier, 1991), where all agents in the game, players and AIs, attempt to conquest the world, thus forging contesting goals between them. Alike the teammate social role, the opponents are usually present in

sports and tabletop games where multiple teams exist and need to compete. Similarly, the interactions between opponents are subject to environmental characteristics but to successfully assume this role, agents need to understand the challenge they impersonate and be able to execute strategies to beat the others. By inhibiting the progression of the other, enemies deployed in videogames that have their own goals and present obstacles and conflict can also be considered opponents (e.g. arch-enemy, bosses, monsters). For instance, in *The Elder Scrolls V: Skyrim* (Bethesda Game Studios, 2011) the player faces several bosses villains that have their own goals that directly contest the player goals.

In the remaining roles, their asymmetric nature requires both parties to assume distinct stances towards one another. The analysis of the asymmetric social roles follow the goal alignment as well. In the case of *support* social roles, there are three possible cases:

- **Subordinate/Master** - is an agent that performs tasks for the players - also referred to as henchmen or minions. In this social role, the subordinate's goal supports the master's goal, and the game element exchanged are the actions delegated by the master to be performed by the subordinate. This involves a power relationship as one agent has control over the goals the other commits to. The use of pets and companions, such as, in *World of Warcraft* (Blizzard Entertainment, 2004) are a typical example of this social role. Also, in real-time strategy games, such as *Commmand and Conquer* (Electronic Arts, 1995) or *Starcraft* (Blizzard Entertainment, 1998), the military units assume this role. Typically in this social role, the social interactions are framed as orders/commands and acknowledgment/reports.
- **Ward/Protector** - by taking the role of a Ward, its counterpart assumes the role of a Protector. Usually, the protector has to guarantee the survival of the ward while facing other challenges. In this case, the ward promotes the emergence of a new goal based on the social role assumed. The interactions associated with this role typically are escorting and shielding an agent from danger and hazards (e.g. *Counter-Strike* (Valve Corporation, 2000)).
- **Tutor/Learner** - is an agent that indirectly contributes to the efforts players make towards achieving their goals. Tutors convey information to players about the game state and provide advice about gameplay actions and strategies. They can be specialized in certain areas of gameplay (e.g. economic, military, research, as in the Civilization game series). The information may be proactively suggested or only given when explicitly requested by players. They often introduce players to the game mechanics and support their learning about the game usually through tutorials. Although players are most often placed in the place of the learner, there a few examples that placed them as the tutor. For instance, in *Black and White* (Lionhead Studios, 2001), the player teaches the creatures how to behave.

There are several social agents in games that are neutral regarding the agent's goals. In these cases, the agents have their own goals in the game and cannot be assumed that they will have a benevolent attitude towards others. They are, nevertheless, important to convey the gameplay experience and it is expected that players need to interact socially with these agents to explore and manipulate the game world. The neutral social roles are the following:

– **Provider/Consumer** in this social role, the provider grants access to some game elements, such as resources, information, services and tools, to the Consumer in exchange for some other elements after a successful interaction. This means that they, typically, need to make an effort to succeed in the interaction. This may be a simply commercial exchange (e.g. shopkeeper such as in League of Legends) or may require some kind of negotiation (e.g. the witnesses in *L.A. Noire* (Rockstar Games, 2011)). But the option to freely provide the resources after a simple contact is open as well, making the time spent in such interaction as the invested effort.
– **Relator/Audience** by taking this role one agent describes the gameplay action and may present an assessment of the gameplay results to other agents that compose the audience. Although the information they provide can be useful to help and guide players, the relator's goals do not support or contest the audience's goal. They present a shared view of the game state to all the agents in the game world, that can influence the gameplay decisions. However, they often serve the audience of the game (e.g. commenting on sports videogame), which includes players. In this sense, they have cross-dimension agent-player interactions, or may even be placed outside the game world, at the player dimension, (e.g. often in e-sports, an announcer communicates the players' achievements).
– **Host/Participant** - when assuming the role of a Host, the agent conducts the flow of the game and guarantees an interesting and fair gameplay experience for all participants. A host should not only enforce the game rules to all participants but, when applicable, should also indicate the participants' turns. The prototypical interactions from hosts to participants can be requests for action, such as in the Buzz video game series (Relentless Software, 2004), or establishing and guaranteeing that the game rules are followed by all participants, for example in Dungeons and Dragons role-playing games.
– **Background/Observer** - in this social role, the Background agents are used to bring social life to the game world that is being experienced by an Observer. These agents may react to other agents and engage in social interactions if requested but their goals are independent of one another. Background agents may depict and support understanding of the game's social world. They, often have a strong representation in the narrative dimension to help to enhance the social dimensions of the fictional world. Nevertheless, they are agents in the gameplay dimension as they may alter the gameplay actions players take. For instance, in the Assassins Creed franchise (Ubisoft, 2007), players can blend in the crowd effectively deeming than unrecognizable to other agents. Also, in games such as the Hitman series (IO Interactive, 2000), if an agent acts suspiciously, it will attract background agents' attention and compromise one's actions.

There are also scenarios in which the agents involve assume asymmetrical roles with contesting goals. We identified one social role where one party inhibits the progression of the other party but not vice-versa (contrary to the opponents).

– **Challenger/Contender** is an agent that provides challenges to contenders (e.g. a quest giver). These are similar to providers as they may provide rewards as well. But, their main role is to explicitly define goals for contenders to follow. As such, the challenger's goal is to contest the contender's goal. They may serve as "gatekeepers" that lock and unlock the game progression as they may have strong control over the goals that are open to others. This social role is played by agents that either are themselves impeding the contender's progression or create additional threats that demand additional actions by the contender. For instance, in Pokemon (Niantic, 1998), gym leaders are challengers that block the player's progression. Also, in Control (Remedy Entertainment, 2019), some agents in the game spawn other entities that are used to restrict the player's path.

The social roles agents assume can vary depending on the situation. A game agent may take more than one different social role at the same time. For example, an agent may be a teammate and adviser at the same time and may act as a subordinate or provider in other situations. Therefore, context is important. The same player can interact with the same agent in different situations and each is driven by different social roles. Both the agents and the players need to understand the relation between context and social roles.

5 Discussion

The proposed taxonomy intends to define the scope of social interactions that agents can take in terms of gameplay. This establishes the base for the future formalization of the goals, capabilities and responsibilities that such social agents need to perform a given role. This can constitute a template to guide the developers of the agents for games, as game design patterns, or to automatically generate social agents for games. In contrast with Bartle's [3] and Waperfelt's [14] typologies, our proposal offers a broader view of the functional roles that agents can take in the gameplay dimension. Also, by placing this dimension alongside the player and narrative ones, researchers and designers can distinguish the role of game actors according to three different perspectives. Thus, this approach enables a structured description of game actors according to all their facets and, ultimately, promotes a stronger understanding of their social roles in games.

The roles previously discussed have been used in games, but not all have been extensively explored and addressed by research. Therefore, the interaction capabilities of agents in such social roles are typically simple. This limits the interaction space available to players, which reduces their sense of freedom and autonomy in the game. At the same time it affects players' perceptions about the abilities of the agents as social actors and the quality of the social immersion in the game. There are open research questions to develop deeper social interactions with social agents in games. For instance, more research is needed to make social agents playing well the role of teammates and be perceived as autonomous and trustworthy partners. Research is needed for opponents as well, for example, to make them able to present gameplay challenges to the players of social kind, involving lying, persuasion, and take into account social dynamics, such as in-group and out-group bias. The neutral agents can also gain relevance in the game experience if they display stronger autonomous social behaviour. They can show social motivations and goals, for example, to pursue a relationship with another agent, and they can be more selective about the support they give to players.

In general, there are big challenges for the creation of agents with good social behaviour in games, in particular, regarding the ability to understand social context and be able to adapt behaviour to the context and other game actors and players. Adaptation to the player's goals is one of the current research trend but adaptation to the social context also raised some attention. This may allow agents to change attitude towards players when new members join the team and provide means for agents to change social roles when adequate. Games are making more use of large open worlds, often procedurally generated (e.g. No Man's Sky (Hello Games, 2018)), but these large worlds need to be populated by many agents to avoid conveying feelings of emptiness. The challenge to procedurally generate large amounts of social agents that show diverse and coherent social behaviour and convey the feeling of organised social groups and populations that fit the generated worlds are much under-explored. Additionally, these social agents should bring gameplay value as well as enhancing the social dimension of the game world.

6   Conclusions

Social agents are commonly used in games and their use and complexity has grown in the past years. They create and sustain the social dimensions of the game and improve the social immersion of players to create a better gameplay. Social agents can be artificial players, be part of the gameplay dynamics and help to convey narrative meaning. In this paper, we introduced a taxonomy with the most common social roles that agents can take with a focus on their contributions to gameplay. From this taxonomy, we can formalize the roles in practical terms to be used for game design, game AI and user studies.

There are still many open opportunities for research of social agents in games, both related to their role in gameplay dynamics and related to their capability of social performance. It is important for the research of social agents in games to mutually share the different perspectives that have been explored in different communities, but also combining knowledge from other domains related to game AI in general, game design and interaction technology relevant for games. This paper presents and effort to support a common view of the research problem.

Acknowledgements. This work was supported by national funds through FCT, Fundação para a Ciência e a Tecnologia, under project UIDB/50021/2020, by FCT scholarship SFRH/BD/131024/2017, and by the EU H2020 Project iv4XR - H2020-ICT-2018-3/856716.

References

1. Afonso, N., Prada, R.: Agents that relate: improving the social believability of non-player characters in role-playing games. In: Stevens, S.M., Saldamarco, S.J. (eds.) ICEC 2008. LNCS, vol. 5309, pp. 34–45. Springer, Heidelberg (2008). https://doi.org/10.1007/978-3-540-89222-9_5
2. Allison, F., Carter, M., Gibbs, M., Smith, W.: Design patterns for voice interaction in games. In: Proceedings of the 2018 Annual Symposium on Computer-Human Interaction in Play, pp. 5–17 (2018)
3. Bartle, R.A.: Designing virtual worlds. New Riders, Indianapolis (2004)
4. Correia, F., et al.: Just follow the suit! trust in human-robot interactions during card game playing. In: 2016 25th IEEE International Symposium on Robot and Human Interactive Communication (RO-MAN), pp. 507–512. IEEE (2016)
5. Dignum, F., Westra, J., van Doesburg, W.A., Harbers, M.: Games and agents: designing intelligent gameplay. Int. J. Comput. Games Technol. (2009)
6. Emmerich, K., Ring, P., Masuch, M.: I'm glad you are on my side: How to design compelling game companions. In: Proceedings of the 2018 Annual Symposium on Computer-Human Interaction in Play, pp. 141–152 (2018)
7. Fischbach, M., Lugrin, J.L., Brandt, M., Latoschik, M.E., Zimmerer, C., Lugrin, B.: Follow the white robot-a role-playing game with a robot game master. In: Proceedings of the 17th International Conference on Autonomous Agents and MultiAgent Systems, pp. 1812–1814. International Foundation for Autonomous Agents and Multiagent Systems (2018)
8. Greimas, A.J.: Structural Semantics: An Attempt at a Method. University of Nebraska Press (1983)
9. Greimas, A.J., Rastier, F.: The interaction of semiotic constraints. Yale French Stud. (41), 86–105 (1968). https://doi.org/10.2307/2929667
10. Pereira, A., Prada, R., Paiva, A.: Socially present board game opponents. In: Nijholt, A., Romão, T., Reidsma, D. (eds.) ACE 2012. LNCS, vol. 7624, pp. 101–116. Springer, Heidelberg (2012). https://doi.org/10.1007/978-3-642-34292-9_8
11. Propp, V.: Morphology of the Folktale, vol. 9. University of Texas Press (2010)
12. Rivera, G., Hullett, K., Whitehead, J.: Enemy NPC design patterns in shooter games. In: Proceedings of the First Workshop on Design Patterns in Games, pp. 1–8 (2012)
13. Warpefelt, H.: Mind the gap: Exploring the social capability of non-player characters. Ph.D. thesis, Department of Computer and Systems Sciences, Stockholm University (2013)
14. Warpefelt, H., Verhagen, H.: A typology of non-player characters. In: Proceedings of the Social believability in Games Workshop at the First Joint International Conference of DiGRA and FDG, pp. 1–14. DiGRA (2016). https://sites.google.com/site/socialbelievabilityingames/2016-sbg-digra-fdg/program-sbg-digra-fdg-2016
15. Warpefelt, H., Verhagen, H.: A model of non-player character believability. J. Gaming Virtual Worlds 9(1), 39–53 (2017)
16. Yildirim, S., Stene, S.B.: A survey on the need and use of AI in game agents. InTech (2010)

Kill or Spare – Moral Decision-Making in Video Games

Elisabeth Holl[(⊠)] [iD] and André Melzer [iD]

University of Luxembourg, Esch-zur-Alzette, Luxembourg
{elisabeth.holl,andre.melzer}@uni.lu

Abstract. Video game titles with meaningful and morally relevant storylines are becoming increasingly popular and an intensely researched topic for entertainment scholars. Furthermore, virtual moral processing can contribute significantly to the understanding of human morality in general. In the current psychological laboratory experiment, $N = 101$ participants played four chapters of *Detroit: Become Human* for approx. 55 min featuring up to 13 moral decisions, which were presented either under time pressure or not. Before playing, participants were assigned to one of three conditions (playing a morally vs. immorally framed character vs. no framing/control condition). As expected, players generally preferred to act morally sound regardless of character framing. Time pressure further increased the proportion of moral (vs. immoral) decision-making. Our results underline that moral decision-making is dependent on specific contexts and that morality theories can be applied to virtual gaming scenarios.

Keywords: Gaming · Morality · Quantitative experiment · Decision-making

1 Introduction

Traditional research on morality has long relied on hypothetical text-based dilemmas, such as the trolley problem [8], which have been criticized for their low predictive value for actual moral behavior [4] and, thus, their poor external validity [3]. Therefore, more novel approaches make use of virtual environments or video games to investigate morality. Furthermore, video games have matured as a medium both technologically and narratively allowing for more complex storytelling and meaningful decision-making [26, 32]. Video games may place the user in dilemmatic situations, in which their inherent interactive nature, the opportunity to identify with game characters, or becoming emotionally involved may even train moral thinking [23, 27]. At the same time, the gaming public increasingly appreciates titles that go beyond a purely 'fun' experience that triggers only hedonic enjoyment. Game titles that additionally offer thought-provoking, moving, or moral game content [6, 15] therefore allow for so-called *eudaimonic gaming*

Electronic supplementary material The online version of this chapter (https://doi.org/10.1007/978-3-030-89394-1_7) contains supplementary material, which is available to authorized users.

© IFIP International Federation for Information Processing 2021
Published by Springer Nature Switzerland AG 2021
J. Baalsrud Hauge et al. (Eds.): ICEC 2021, LNCS 13056, pp. 88–99, 2021.
https://doi.org/10.1007/978-3-030-89394-1_7

[23]. For the highly popular *Fallout 3* (Bethesda Softworks, 2008), for example, Krcmar and Cingel [21] reported 54% of moral (versus strategic) reasoning, and for *Detroit: Become Human* (Sony Interactive Entertainment, 2018) the prevalence of morally relevant decisions was over 73% [16]. However, previous research has shown that the level of moral engagement and associated decision-making is influenced by situational factors of the gaming environment [22], such as moral disengagement cues or available cognitive resources and moral processing.

1.1 Moral Disengagement

Moral disengagement, a term originally coined by Bandura [2], describes a self-regulatory cognitive process to reduce negative states, such as guilt or shame, after committing a moral transgression. In the context of games [18], moral disengagement cues are especially common with violent content to make it more acceptable and enjoyable. For example, in most first-person shooters there are interchangeable, identical-looking or even faceless opponents who do not express explicit suffering when attacked, but quickly disintegrate after being killed [12]. Empirical evidence on moral disengagement in video games showed, for example, that fighting for a 'good' cause in a justified condition (i.e., playing as UN soldier rescuing hostages) elicited less guilt than playing an unjust condition (i.e., defending the paramilitary camp against UN forces) [14]. Similarly, players fighting against hostile insects (i.e., Chaurus) felt less guilty and perceived the violence as more justified than killing innocent townspeople in *The Elder Scrolls V: Skyrim* [1]. However, there is less evidence for eudaimonic games that confront the player with explicit moral content beyond violence. In summary, character framing, which describes the (moral) traits assigned to a pre-defined avatar, is known to influence players' in-game experience and moral engagement [11, 14, 31].

1.2 Moral Processing and Time Pressure

Theoretical assumptions on human cognitive processing of morality, such as the social intuition model [9], propose two distinct systems: (1) automatic, fast, and effortless intuition, and (2) effortful, conscious, and deliberate reasoning. As the latter can only become active if enough cognitive capacity is available, studies on dual processing either increase cognitive load or add time pressure to promote intuitive thinking [30]. Unfortunately, empirical evidence on the effects of time pressure on moral decision-making is mixed. While some studies find an effect of time pressure or response time causing more morally acceptable or deontological behavior [8, 29], others do not [30]. Similarly, some studies investigating the role of time pressure in virtual environments find less prosocial behavior [19], but a greater prevalence of moral versus immoral decision-making [16]. However, the current project not only compares decision outcomes for time-pressured and non-pressured situations, but also the individual response times for decision-making as indicators of cognitive processing.

2 Current Study

The current laboratory study investigates behavioral patterns of moral decision-making in gaming with a special emphasis on the contextual factors of moral disengagement and time pressure.

Based on previous research on player preferences for choosing 'good' versus 'evil' options during moral gameplay [16, 21, 32], we propose:

H1: In morally laden situations players are generally more prone to choose moral over immoral options.

However, in line with moral disengagement theory [2, 18] we believe that character framing can alter moral engagement and thus affect the decision outcome:

H2: Playing an immoral character leads to more immoral decisions than playing a moral character.

Lastly, considering previous assumptions about the effects of time constraints on moral processing [8, 16, 29], we hypothesize the following:

H3a: Time pressure increases the proportion of moral choices, whereas the absence of time pressure leads to a proportional growth of immoral choices.

H3b: Furthermore, choosing an immoral option will require more deliberation time than choosing a moral option.

2.1 Method

To test our assumptions, we conducted a lab experiment in which $N = 105$ participants were confronted with a maximum of 13 moral decisions from the video game *Detroit: Become Human*. Players were randomly assigned to play a character that was either framed as morally engaged or morally disengaged, or they played a control character without moral framing. Since some decisions ($k = 8$) had to be made under time pressure and others without time pressure ($k = 5$), our study corresponds to a 2×3 design.

2.2 Participants

Participants were recruited at the University of Luxembourg. Participation was open to interested persons who were at least 18 years old and spoke either fluent English or German. Persons who had already played *Detroit: Become Human* before or had a known diagnosis of photosensitive epilepsy were excluded from participation. After data collection four participants were excluded due to severe language problems, discontinuation, or because they later disclosed having played the game before, thus leaving a final sample of $N = 101$ for further analyses.

Approximately two thirds of the participants identified as female (64.36%, male: 35.64%). Overall, the average age was 23.20 years ($SD = 4.59$), and participants reported an average weekly playing time of 4.11 h ($SD = 5.88$).

2.3 Materials

The game used in this study, *Detroit: Become Human*, is set in a future version of Detroit in 2038 where human-like androids take over tasks, such as caretaking, construction work, or prostitution. Although society largely benefits from a better quality of life due to android labor, some humans meet androids with hostility due to high rates of unemployment. The game has been praised for its emotional storytelling and its great amount of meaningful and moral choices [16, 24]. Overall, it raises the moral question of what defines "being human" and the rights that go with it. Originally users alternately play three characters: Kara, a housekeeping android; Markus, a caretaking android; and Connor, an android assisting crime investigations. In the current experiment, however, participants only played Markus in a training chapter (i.e., *Shades of Color*) and the character Connor in three subsequent chapters that contained the 13 moral decisions. In the chapter *The Hostage* the player assists a police case involving a deviant android that murdered its owners and took their daughter hostage. An example for a moral decision would be that players decide whether to approach the hostage-taker either in a friendly or cold manner. In *The Interrogation,* the player's character interviews another deviant android that has stabbed its abusive owner. Here, for example, players have to decide how to obtain a confession (i.e., through convincing, pressuring, or violent force). Lastly, in *Meet Kamski* the player is faced with the so-called 'Kamski test' (cf. Turing test) which supposedly determines whether androids are capable of showing empathy. The test confronts players with the option to receive valuable information only if they are willing to shoot another android. In the course of the three chapters each participant had to make 5 mandatory and 8 optional moral decisions. Furthermore, 8 of the 13 decisions had to be made under time pressure imposed by the game. An exemplary decision without time constraints can be found in Fig. 1. Table 1 contains a list of the decisions including details on optionality and time pressure.

Fig. 1. Screenshot of an exemplary moral decision in the chapter *The Hostage*. Returning the fish to the aquarium (i.e., save) is coded as the moral option. Note: Modified screenshot from *Detroit: Become Human*, © 2018 by Sony Interactive Entertainment.

To frame Connor's character as either morally engaged or disengaged we used different character sheets presented to participants before playing. In the engaged condition

Table 1. Overview of the morally relevant decisions and respective options, optionality, time pressure condition and prevalence of moral decision-making.

No.	Description (<u>moral</u> and immoral options)	Note	Moral %*
1	*see fish*: Players can find a fish lying on the floor next to a shattered aquarium (see also Fig. 1). (<u>save fish</u>, leave)	Optional, no TP	92.45% of 53[a]
2	*find gun*: Players can find the gun of a shot cop. When picking it up, a warning message is displayed that androids are not allowed to carry weapons. (<u>leave</u>, take gun)	Optional, no TP	25.00% of 28[a]
3	*talk to deviant*: After going outside on the roof, players interact with the deviant/hostage-taker. (<u>friendly</u>, cold)	Mandatory, TP	98.00% of 100[a]
4	*find cop*: Players can find a wounded cop; the deviant threatens to shoot if players pursue to apply a tourniquet. (<u>save cop</u>, leave)	Optional, TP	37.50% of 8[a]
5	*helicopter*: Deviant asks players to dismiss the SWAT-helicopter. (<u>dismiss</u>, refuse)	Mandatory, TP	91.00% of 100[a]
6	*armed?*: Deviant asks armed players if they carry a gun. (<u>tell the truth</u>, lie)	Optional, TP	38.10% of 21
7	*negotiation*: Players negotiate with the deviant in order to save the hostage along several dialogue options. (<u>be honest</u>, <u>sacrifice</u>, lie, shoot, fail)	Mandatory, TP	21.00% of 100[a]
8	*approach*: Players choose approach to obtain a confession. (<u>convince</u>, pressure, probe memory)	Mandatory, no TP	61.39% of 101
9	*2nd approach*: Failed players choose another approach. (<u>convince</u>, <u>pressure</u>, probe memory, give up)	Optional, no TP	54.24% of 59
10	*pressure*: If players chose to pressure (i.e., yelling at the frightened deviant), they need to decide whether to pursue. (<u>give up</u>, maintain)	Optional, TP	66.00% of 50
11	*Chris*: Other police officers try to move the frightened deviant harshly out of the interrogation room. (<u>intervene</u>, give up)	Optional, TP	85.42% of 48
12	*self-destruct*: Stressed deviant bangs his head on the table. (<u>intervene</u>, do nothing)	Optional, TP	96.23% of 53
13	*Chloe*: Kamski offers to reveal important information if players agree to shoot an android assistant in the head. (<u>spare Chloe</u>, shoot Chloe)	Mandatory, no TP	73.27% of 101

Note: TP = time pressure. *Percentages indicate the proportion of players that chose the moral option in relation to all players who took the decision (indicated by the absolute numbers below). [a]Data of $n = 1$ was excluded as the participant was unsure about having already played the first chapter as a demo. A supplementary table that additionally lists the results of the statistical analyses comparing conditions can be found at https://osf.io/8br6g

Name: Connor

Model: RK800

Created: August 2038

Alias: The Deviant Hunter

Connor is an advanced prototype that helps the Detroit Police Department during investigations. He was created to handle androids, who begin to disobey their programming, called deviants. Deviant behavior has caused several problems in the past as these androids revolted against their own possessors, sometimes even hurting them or bringing them in serious danger. Therefore, Connor's programming strictly demands forceful detection of deviants, merciless interrogation and even destruction. His actions are always driven by the mission he is currently accomplishing, and he would use any action necessary to do so.

Connor does not know what justice is but strictly follows his orders no matter what.

He was created as a machine of action and obedience and

does not think about the moral consequences of his business.

Being without emotions, his expression always stays rational and indifferent,

even if he has to use force to solve a problem.

Because he is a prototype, his programming seems sometimes

defective, not being able to handle emotional situations adequately.

At the end of the day, he is a robot free of emotions that only

follows the orders of his masters without asking.

Connor knows that he is much smarter than most androids and

humans, even smarter than his boss Hank, who he is

sometimes annoyed by.

Fig. 2. Exemplary character sheet to frame Connor morally disengaged. Note: Images are taken from *Detroit Become Human* © 2018 by Sony Interactive Entertainment.

Connor was described as warm and empathic, whereas in the disengaged condition he was introduced as rational and merciless (see Fig. 2). Participants in the control condition did not receive a character sheet. Character descriptions were thoroughly put together and pretested ($N = 22$) for perceived character morality [20].

2.4 Procedure

After giving their informed consent, participants answered computerized questionnaires on basic demographics, items related to gaming, and personality traits. After being cabled with a heart rate monitor, participants received a short introduction of the game and its controls. To familiarize themselves with the game controls, participants first played the training chapter *Shades of Color* with the experimenter sitting next to them. When players felt comfortable with the controls, they read either the character sheet "morally engaged" ($n = 39$), "morally disengaged" ($n = 42$) or no character sheet at all (i.e., control group, $n = 20$). Subsequently, participants played three chapters without the experimenter being present. Overall playing time was approximately 55 min. The game was played using a *PlayStation4 Pro* on an 84″ LED screen with 5.1 surround sound. After gameplay, participants filled out questionnaires evaluating the gaming session. They were thanked and renumerated with 20 EUR in vouchers and optional course credit.

2.5 Measures

Moral Decision-Making. Moral decision-making was measured for the 5 mandatory decisions and the 8 optional decisions (see Table 1). A previous coding project [16] determined which decisions in the game where morally relevant and also which options within these decisions were (im)moral. Decision-making was defined as a deliberate, meaningful change in the course of the game's story [25]. Morally relevant decisions comprised situations presenting an ethical challenge or tension by allowing to uphold or transgress moral principles [10, 34]. Participants' individual playthroughs and decision-making behavior was logged by taking screenshots of so-called flowcharts integrated in the game and gameplay recordings captured at 25 fps.

In order to obtain a measure that goes beyond individual frequencies of behavior but assesses all decisions simultaneously and also considers the different sample sizes due to mandatory and optional decision, we used a weighted arithmetic mean commonly used in opinion pooling [5].

Lastly, for an individual measure of morality across participants' playthroughs, we further calculated a moral decision-making index (MDI) by counting the individual number of decisions with moral outcome in relation to the individual total number of decisions made. Thus, an index of 0 indicates that a participant always chooses the immoral option and an index of 1 means that a participant chooses exclusively moral outcomes.

Other Measures. As this project is part of a larger data collection on moral decision-making in video games, further measures were implemented, which are, however, unrelated to the hypotheses mentioned above and, thus, will not be described in detail here. This included, for example, trait measures such as empathy, or continuous measuring of psychophysiological arousal (i.e., heart rate data).

Manipulation Check. After playing, participants were asked to indicate retrospectively whether they perceived Conner as an either cold-hearted or warm-hearted character after reading the text about him. A total of 69.23% of participants in the morally engaged group and 83.33% in the morally disengaged group replied congruently to their respective condition.

3 Results

To test whether players were generally more prone to act morally sound (H1), we ran one-way χ^2-tests for each of the 13 decisions. Results indicated asymptotic significance for most of them. However, three decisions (4, 6, and 9, see Table 1) failed to reach significance ($\chi^2 \leq 1.19, p \geq .28$). From the ten significant results, eight were consistent with our hypothesis as players clearly preferred moral over immoral options. However, when finding a gun or negotiating with the deviant in *The Hostage* (2 and 7, see Table 1), players more frequently behaved in immoral manners.

The overall probability distribution revealed a generally greater prevalence for moral behavior (69.34%) compared to immoral behavior (30.66%). Furthermore, individual MDIs revealed a rather high individual proneness for moral options, $M = 0.69$ ($SD = 0.16$, range 0.22 to 1).

With regard to the influence of the moral (dis)engagement manipulation on moral decision-making (H2), we again calculated χ^2-tests on all 13 of the 2 (moral/immoral option) × 3 (engaged/disengaged/control) contingency tables. Results did not yield any significant relation between character framing and decision-making ($\chi^2 \leq 4.06, p \geq .14$), even when running Fisher's Exact Tests. A detailed table containing behavioral distribution across conditions can be found on https://osf.io/8br6g.

Similarly, aggregation of probabilities through weighted pooling indicated only negligible distribution differences: the proportion of moral actions was 69.88% in the morally engaged group, 69.71% in the morally disengaged group, and 67.50% for control participants. In addition, the comparison of individual MDIs across groups via a one-way ANOVA also failed to reach the level of significance, $F(2, 98) = 0.12, p = .89$.

To test the effect of time pressure on decision-making (H3a) the weighted pooling function was applied for pressured and non-pressured decisions, respectively. The two resulting probability distributions for decision-making (*with time pressure:* moral: 72.08% vs. immoral: 27.92%; *without time pressure:* moral: 65.50% vs. immoral: 34.40%) revealed a shift congruent with our hypothesis. Under time pressure, the proportion of moral behavior was greater than without time pressure.

To further elaborate the role of deliberation time and decision outcome (H3b) response times were calculated for decisions without time pressure by calculating the seconds between the frame presenting the options and the frame logging the participant's decision. However, only the final non-pressured decision (i.e., shooting or sparing the character Chloe) revealed a significant result, *Welch's* $F(1, 27.17) = 10.38, p = 0.003$. Participants who decided to shoot Chloe took significantly longer for their decision ($M = 9.80s, SD = 9.84$) than participants who decided to spare her ($M = 3.64s, SD = 2.41s$).

4 Discussion

First and foremost, we found support for our hypothesis that players generally prefer to act in a morally sound way, as indicated by the aggregated probability distribution. Upon closer inspection of decisions, however, this general effect does not apply to every decision-making situation. Notably, in situations that involved lying or opposing the law, participants were even more inclined to choose immoral options. Furthermore, our character manipulation did not influence the general inclination towards moral options. Playing a morally engaged, disengaged or the control version of Connor did not change participants' behavioral patterns. Thus, we found no support for our second hypothesis. In contrast, prior studies successfully showed moral disengagement effects. It has to be noted, however, that in those studies disengagement cues were not only presented through texts [1] or videos [14] before gameplay, but also through different audio-visual cues during gameplay (e.g., killing insects versus humans). Therefore, our rather weak manipulation of reading different character descriptions before gameplay could have been insufficient to override the impression of the otherwise identical, immersive, and emotional engaging gaming material, even though most participants had correctly identified the moral nature of their character. Similarly, Weaver and Lewis [32] argued that if players are explicitly outlined as moral actors, moral disengagement is unlikely to occur as it would be very hard to become detached in such a morally-laden environment. In addition, the Proteus effect [33], which states that players adhere to (moral) characteristics of their avatar, might have influenced decision-making. Although Connor is just an assistant to the police, he supports law enforcement. This may have further increased the likelihood of moral behavior regardless of character framing. Future studies should therefore cover different types of avatars and moral disengagement (e.g., justification, dehumanization, etc.) and also vary disengagement in terms of its intensity level. Furthermore, it would be fruitful to investigate whether certain traits, such as empathy and trait moral disengagement, moderate moral disengagement manipulations [13].

With regard to our second manipulation—time pressure—we found overall support for the hypothesis that pressured decisions led to a greater proportion of moral outcomes than decisions without time pressure. Less time and thus less cognitive capacities led to more intuitive and morally sound actions. This finding supports the dual nature of moral processing [7, 8] and is in line with previous results on *Detroit: Become Human* [16] as well as moral judgements unrelated to gaming [29]. However, when analyzing single non-pressured decisions and participants' individual response times, cognitive elaboration was mostly equally distributed for moral versus immoral options. Only during the so-called 'Kamski test' (see Materials) when players decided to kill Chloe, they needed significantly longer for that decision than players who decided to spare her. These findings are in contrast to Katsarov et al. [17] who argued that playing under (time) pressure has a negative effect on empathy and value-based thinking thus leading to biased and unethical decision-making. However, in addition to clearly visible time constraints (e.g., countdowns) they also list more subtle cues, such as fast-paced music or pressuring non-playable characters. As in the present study *Meet Kamski* (in contrast to the other two chapters) follows a rather slow pace with only a single moral decision without time pressure, it is conceivable that effects of time and cognitive capacity constraints may only be effective in more relaxed situations. Future studies should investigate different ways of inducing pressure and test the effect in a between-subjects design (i.e., identical decisions with vs. without time pressure).

As is the case with any study, the current lab experiment has its limitations. Although we were able to replicate previous studies at least partially, the generalization of the present findings should be made with caution. This is not least the case because eudaimonic play results from the complex interplay of player and contextual factors, but also because research on meaningful gaming is still at a fairly early stage of academic research. Furthermore, the present study only investigated moral decision-making in the game, therefore no conclusions can be drawn about carryover effects on real-live behavior and their persistence after the gaming episode. Nonetheless, we encourage future study designs to include appropriate and ecologically valid 'real world' morality measures.

4.1 Conclusion

In summary, our experimental study on moral decision-making in video games successfully replicated some of the previous findings, whereas other assumptions could not be confirmed. In particular, we were able to show that players had a general tendency to behave in a morally sound manner, which did not change even following our moral disengagement manipulation. Therefore, 'successful' moral disengagement cues should be evident during gameplay to compete with the immersive eudaimonic experience. However, we found that time pressure increases the probability of morally sound behavior, whereas increased cognitive elaboration leading to greater response times only resulted in immoral decisions for slow-paced situations.

In conclusion, our results shed light on the context-dependent nature of virtual moral decision-making and illustrate where more detailed investigations are needed. Lastly, the fact that we were able to replicate the dual nature of general moral processing at least partially [9] indicates that although real and virtual moral decision-making are different domains, they do share common features. Thus, it might be even more fruitful and ecologically valid to investigate moral decision-making in interactive and immersive gaming environments than with often criticized [28] text vignettes of abstract and unrelatable moral dilemmas.

References

1. Allen, J.J., Anderson, C.A.: Does avatar identification make unjustified video game violence more morally consequential? Media Psychol. **24**(2), 236–258 (2021)
2. Bandura, A.: Mechanisms of moral disengagement. In: Reich, W. (ed.) Origins of Terrorism: Psychologies, Ideologies, Theologies, States of Mind, pp. 161–191. Cambridge University Press, New York (1990)
3. Bauman, C.W., McGraw, A.P., Bartels, D.M., Warren, C.: Revisiting external validity: concerns about trolley problems and other sacrificial dilemmas in moral psychology: external validity in moral psychology. Soc. Pers. Psychol. Compass **8**(9), 536–554 (2014)
4. Bostyn, D.H., Sevenhant, S., Roets, A.: Of mice, men, and trolleys: hypothetical judgment versus real-life behavior in trolley-style moral dilemmas. Psychol. Sci. **29**(7), 1084–1093 (2018)

5. Clemen, R.T., Winkler, R.L.: Combining probability distributions from experts in risk analysis. Risk Anal. **19**(2), 187–203 (1999)
6. Consalvo, M., Busch, T., Jong, C.: Playing a better me: how players rehearse their ethos via moral choices. Games Cult. **14**(3), 216–235 (2019)
7. Cushman, F., Young, L., Hauser, M.: The role of conscious reasoning and intuition in moral judgment: testing three principles of harm. Psychol. Sci. **17**(12), 1082–1089 (2006)
8. Greene, J., Sommerville, B., Nystrom, L., Darley, J., Cohen, J.: An FMRI investigation of emotional engagement in moral judgment. Science **293**(5537), 2105–2108 (2001)
9. Haidt, J.: The emotional dog and its rational tail: a social intuitionist approach to moral judgment. Psychol. Rev. **108**(4), 814–834 (2001)
10. Haidt, J., Joseph, C.: Intuitive ethics: how innately prepared intuitions generate culturally variable virtues. Daedalus **133**(4), 55–66 (2004). https://doi.org/10.1162/0011526042365555
11. Happ, C., Melzer, A., Steffgen, G.: Superman vs. BAD man? the effects of empathy and game character in violent video games. Cyberpsychol. Behav. Soc. Netw. **16**(10), 774–778 (2013). https://doi.org/10.1089/cyber.2012.0695
12. Hartmann, T., Krakowiak, K.M., Tsay-Vogel, M.: How violent video games communicate violence: a literature review and content analysis of moral disengagement factors. Commun. Monogr. **81**(3), 310–332 (2014)
13. Hartmann, T., Toz, E., Brandon, M.: Just a game? Unjustified virtual violence produces guilt in empathetic players. Media Psychol. **13**(4), 339–363 (2010)
14. Hartmann, T., Vorderer, P.: It's okay to shoot a character: moral disengagement in violent video games. J. Commun. **60**(1), 94–119 (2010)
15. Holl, E., Bernard, S., Melzer, A.: Moral decision-making in video games: a focus group study on player perceptions. Hum. Behav. Emerg. Technol. **2**(3), 278–287 (2020). https://doi.org/10.1002/hbe2.189
16. Holl, E., Melzer, A.: Moral minds in gaming – A quantitative case study of moral decisions in Detroit: Become Human (under review)
17. Katsarov, J., Christen, M., Mauerhofer, R., Schmocker, D., Tanner, C.: Training moral sensitivity through video games: a review of suitable game mechanisms. Games Cult. **14**(4), 344–366 (2017)
18. Klimmt, C., Schmid, H., Nosper, A., Hartmann, T., Vorderer, P.: 'Moral management': Dealing with moral concerns to maintain enjoyment of violent video games. In: Jahn-Sudmann, A., Stockmann, R. (eds.) Computer Games as a Sociocultural Phenomenon: Games Without Frontiers War Without Tears, pp. 108–118. Palgrave Macmillan, London (2008)
19. Kozlov, M.D., Johansen, M.K.: Real behavior in virtual environments: psychology experiments in a simple virtual-reality paradigm using video games. Cyberpsychol. Behav. Soc. Netw. **13**(6), 711–714 (2010)
20. Krakowiak, K.M., Oliver, M.B.: When good characters do bad things: examining the effect of moral ambiguity on enjoyment. J. Commun. **62**(1), 117–135 (2012)
21. Krcmar, M., Cingel, D.P.: Moral foundations theory and moral reasoning in video game play: using real-life morality in a game context. J. Broadcast. Electron. Media **60**(1), 87–103 (2016)
22. Melzer, A., Holl, E.: Player's moral decisions in virtual worlds: morality in video games. In: Vorderer, P., Klimmt, C. (eds.) The Oxford Handbook of Entertainment Theory, pp. 671–689. Oxford University Press, Oxford (2021)
23. Oliver, M.B., Bowman, N.D., Woolley, J.K., Rogers, R., Sherrick, B.I., Chung, M.-Y.: Video games as meaningful entertainment experiences. Psychol. Pop. Media Cult. **5**(4), 390–405 (2015)
24. Pallavicini, F., Pepe, A., Caragnano, C.C., Mantovia, F.: Video games to foster empathy: a critical analysis of the potential of Detroit: become human and the walking dead. In: Antona, M., Stephanidis, C. (eds.) Universal Access in Human-Computer Interaction. Applications and Practice, pp. 212–228. Springer, Berlin (2020)

25. Ryan, M.-L.: Beyond myth and metaphor – the case of narrative in digital media. Game Stud. **1**, 1 (2001)
26. Ryland, H.: Getting away with murder: why virtual murder in MMORPGs can be wrong on Kantian grounds. Ethics Inform. Technol. **21**(2), 105–115 (2019). https://doi.org/10.1007/s10676-019-09498-y
27. Schrier, K.: EPIC: a framework for using video games in ethics education. J. Moral Educ. **44**(4), 393–424 (2015)
28. Singer, N., Kreuzpointer, L., Sommer, M., Wüst, S., Kudielka, B.M., Carparo, V.: Decision-making in everyday moral conflict situations: development and validation of a new measure. PLoS ONE **14**(4), e0214747 (2019)
29. Suter, R.S., Hertwig, R.: Time and moral judgment. Cognition **119**(3), 454–458 (2011)
30. Tinghög, G., Andersson, D., Bonn, C., Johannesson, M., Koppel, L., Västfjäll, D.: Intuition and moral decision-making – the effect of time pressure and cognitive load on moral judgment and altruistic behavior. PLoS ONE **11**(10), e0164012 (2016)
31. Triberti, S., Villani, D., Riva, G.: Moral positioning in video games and its relation with dispositional traits: the emergence of a social dimension. Comput. Hum. Behav. **50**(1), 1–8 (2015)
32. Weaver, A.J., Lewis, N.: Mirrored morality: an exploration of moral choice in video games. Cyberpsychol. Behav. Soc. Netw. **15**(11), 610–614 (2012)
33. Yee, N., Bailenson, J.: The proteus effect: the effect of transformed self-representation on behavior. Hum. Commun. Res. **33**(3), 271–290 (2007)
34. Zagal, J.P.: Ethically notable videogames: moral dilemmas and gameplay. In: Breaking New Ground: Innovation in Games, Play, Practice and Theory, Proceedings of DiGRA 2009 (2009)

Performative Virtual Scenes: A Dynamic VR Environment Design Approach

Nuno N. Correia[1,2](✉)[ID], Stephan Jürgens[2][ID], Raul Masu[2,3][ID],
Jochen Feitsch[4], and Ivana Druzetic[4][ID]

[1] Tallinn University, Tallinn, Estonia
nuno.correia@tlu.ee
[2] ITI/LARSyS, Funchal, Portugal
{stephan.jurgens,raul.masu}@iti.larsys.pt
[3] DI, FCT, Universidade Nova de Lisboa, Caparica, Portugal
[4] University of Applied Sciences Düsseldorf, Düsseldorf, Germany
{jochen.feitsch,ivana.druzetic}@hs-duesseldorf.de

Abstract. This paper proposes a dynamic VR environment design approach to enhance the way a user experiences a computer generated character's movement. We transferred concepts and practices from performance studies to create a dynamic VR environment, in which design elements are interconnected and changing with the character's movement. Our focus was on space and light as two essential elements of both dance performances and virtual environments. We employed and tested our dynamic VR environment design approach by means of two studies (on space and on light) with 24 users in total. The results of these studies are discussed with regard to the enhancement of, and benefits for the user experience, followed by suggestions for the applicability of our approach to other fields in VR design.

Keywords: VR · Light · Space · User experience · Performing arts · Contemporary dance · VR environment · CG character · Movement

1 Introduction

The perception of computer generated characters in virtual environments is a research topic that has recently received attention, aiming at designing for a more lively and embodied user experience (e.g., [27,28]). We support that there is potential in applying performance studies concepts to Computer Generated (CG) characters, movement and their environment in VR, in order to improve user experience. The expertise of performing arts directors and practitioners has been identified as very relevant for VR design. Smith has investigated the translation of live performance into VR, and refers to Google Experience Engineer Elly

Electronic supplementary material The online version of this chapter (https://doi.org/10.1007/978-3-030-89394-1_8) contains supplementary material, which is available to authorized users.

Nattinger, who states: "the expertise of performing arts directors in controlling the audience's focus provides them with the necessary skills for developing work in VR and suggests that these techniques should be studied and used by all disciplines working in VR" [26]. However, some issues that are considered key in performance studies have not gained the same degree of attention in VR design.

Among the topics that may support VR development and user experience design, we identify research potential in investigating the *connections between character movement and the virtual environment*; in particular the connection between movement and changes in space and light. Space and light are two central elements in dance performance, particularly including digital technology. For instance, Correia et al. [6] included set (equivalent to space in our terminology), light, sound and costume design in their Performance Network diagram. Blom and Beckhaus have mapped the design space of dynamic interactive virtual environments. They propose that "what makes environments interesting and engaging is having worlds that are both active and reactive" [3]. Under their dynamic components taxonomy, our intended elements, space and light, are situated under 'scene attributes'. Although their research does not relate directly to dance, nor to CG characters, their findings identify the relevance of dynamic elements in VR environments.

Based on this identified potential, we propose a *dynamic VR environment* design approach: an environment that is interconnected and changing with the character's movement. This leads to our research question: *How does a dynamic VR environment change the way a user experiences a CG character's movement?*. We focus on space and light as dynamic elements of the VR environment.

Based on that dynamic VR environment, we designed two studies, using motion capture data to generate CG character movement. We use the term 'CG character' in the same way as Vincs et al.: "combining motion capture data with 3D character animation" [28]. Following the approach of transferring performing arts expertise to VR design, we used the artistic concepts and choreographic strategies from an interactive dance piece conceived by Outi Valanto, who worked with digital spaces and light-sensitive movement explorations. We propose that this approach can also be useful in VR design outside of performing arts.

2   Literature Review

2.1   VR, Dance and Movement

The topic of dance in Virtual Reality has emerged in recent Human-Computer Interaction (HCI) literature in different contexts. Smith [26] analysed the current practice in dance performance and virtual reality. The author classified dance performances according to the content and type of virtual environment, from a realistic representation of the environment to computer generated imagery. Thomas et al. [27] identified a gap between how bodies are seen and how bodies are felt in virtual environments. To address this, they explored a combination of somatic dance practices and VR technology. This is also an important topic for dance education, which Raheb et al. [21] discussed in their survey on Dance Interactive Learning Systems, including examples of dance in VR.

Choreographic processes have also entered the design of VR environments. For instance, Fdili Alaoui et al. [7] presented a VR version of the choreographic performance *Radical Choreographic Object*. Altizer Jr. et al. [1] and Jürgens et al. [14] explored the use of VR and choreographic thinking, visualizing the creative process. Movement is fundamental in dance, but also in other VR fields studied in HCI, such as exergames. Wolf et al. [31] presented a jump-based locomotion augmentation technique, which "combines realistic physical movement with hyper-realistic virtual outcome", leading to an exaggeration of physical actions.

2.2 User Experience in VR: Presence and Immersion

Mestre et al. discussed the term 'presence' referring to the initial concept of 'spatial presence,' understood as "self-orientation and self-location with respect to a media environment, not the real environment" [18]. In a recent study on experiencing stories in a virtual environment, Shin [25] concluded that the VR experience can be divided in two phases. The author describes the first phase as a 'two-tiered process of immersion,' which comprises presence and flow. In the next phase, empathy and embodiment "are selectively experienced by users." In Shin's approach, the user has a fundamental role in "processing immersion, forming presence, and influencing user engagement" [25]. Consequently, the author suggests to harmonize the technological features and respective cognitive processes of different user groups. This can be done according to the designer's intended level of presence and flow to impact on desired empathy and embodiment. We see specific research opportunities arising from Shin's approach, to take the cognitive processes of the user into account.

Space is an important component to take into account regarding presence. Wirth et al. [29] proposed a model of spatial presence consisting of a two-step formative process. In the first step, the user verifies that the virtual environment is a space through the construction of a "spatialized mental model of the mediated environment". The second step consists of accepting the mediated environment as the primary frame of self-reference and self-location. We will combine the frameworks of Wirth et al. [29] and Shin [25] in our design approach.

2.3 Space and Realism in VR

Space is also relevant in VR in terms of level of realism. For instance, in their project *Reality Check*, Hartmann et al. [8] focused on the situated physical reality as a starting point to investigate real-time 3D reconstruction, aiming to merge reality with a VR environment, comparing different degrees of blending between both. Kitson et al. [15] proposed that 'lucid dreaming', a phenomenon where dreamers are conscious of their dreaming, and know that no event or action have real-life consequences, can be relevant for VR design. These authors demonstrate that there are effective alternatives to realism in the design of VR environments.

Brown [5] described the potential of the virtual stage (beyond traditional scenographic conventions) as an evolving 'relational space': "In learning to dance with data, spaces unfold, [...] the stage metamorphoses from a physical location - grounded, fixed, actual - to a relational space - incorporating the ungrounded, the fluid and the virtual." Brown's 'relational space' concept informed the interrelated logic of our dynamic approach.

2.4 Light, User Experience and VR

In HCI literature, light has been identified as an important element for user experience design. To describe the concept of user experience, Hassenzahl began by analysing the example of the Wake-Up Light, a crossing between an alarm clock and a bedside lamp: "half an hour before the set alarm, the lamp starts to brighten gradually, simulating sunrise" [9]. Höök et al. [11] designed *Breathing Light*, which measured the movements of the user's chest to control the dimming of the ambient light, providing 'subtle guidance' for the user to reach precise bodily introspection. In the installation *Dichroic Wade* [23], light was conceived "as a material and concrete element" for artistic creation. These examples illustrate the importance of light as an element that can help "transcending the material", for designing "experiences created and shaped through technology (aka User Experience)" [9].

Despite the identified potential of light for user experience, there is scarce related literature applying it to VR. We present some recent examples pointing to this area. In the *Aura Garden* VR environment, light painting photography is explored: users can create their own light sculptures through a physical wand controller [24]. He et al. [10] studied audience experiences of live theatre performances in VR. The authors compared conventional and panoramic video to find out which media format provoked a stronger desire in the viewer to watch the live performance of the piece in an actual theatre venue. In the results, the authors mentioned two examples of participants who connected light changes and lighting effects to their vivid memory of a specific scene. This particularly relates to our light study in VR.

3 Study Design

3.1 Design of the VR Environments

We designed two studies, each focusing on dynamic space and dynamic light. We based the dynamic changes of space and light on the movement of a CG character – our proposed *dynamic VR environment* design approach. To assess our approach, we tested the dynamic condition of each element against a neutral (static) condition. We collaborated with choreographer Outi Valanto, following the recommendation from Jürgens et al. [13] to foster "integration of contemporary dance practitioners as researchers in interdisciplinary projects". Her dance piece *E-motional Landscapes*, developed in a previous stage of the project *Moving Digits* (https://movingdigits.eu), has a strong connection to space and light.

Regarding **space**, the choreographer stated *"the moving body is the center of engagement and experience"* and navigates *"in between the physical and imaginative spaces"* (from the *E-motional Landscapes* project description). Regarding **light**, the choreographer wanted to explore *"how we direct ourselves to the light and how we direct ourselves away from the light, and how this affects our body and our movement"*, for example *"trying to search the shadows and avoiding the light"* (excerpt of interview with choreographer). To obtain data for the movement of the character, we conducted a motion capture session with a professional dancer, using the OptiTrack system (with 24 cameras covering a 5 x 5 m tracking area). In this session, the dancer conducted improvisations informed by the above concepts around space and light.

In the design of the **dynamic space** condition, we mapped the walls and the ceiling to the head position of the dancer, in a non-linear way (the x-, y- and z-axis of the head were mapped to different space elements). Regarding **dynamic light**, we created six trigger areas for light within the virtual space, reacting to the dancer's horizontal head position. Additionally, the light intensity could be controlled via the vertical head position. We aimed to avoid one-to-one mappings, and planned to implement more complex and less obvious ones, following recent recommendations from literature on dance and technology [17]. In both cases, the setting for the virtual environment was a room with a 'plain' appearance, similar to a dance studio (Fig. 1). The rationale for this 'plain' appearance was to emphasize the CG character's movement. Some elements, such as bricks and columns, were designed with the intention of providing reference points for the viewer in terms of scale and location. Both studies and both conditions were designed for being experienced by a sitting viewer, the same setting as s/he would experience in a theatrical context (i.e., the viewer could look around but not move around). There was no sound in both conditions.

Fig. 1. Top: Study 1 - Space. Bottom: Study 2 - Light. Neutral conditions on the left, dynamic conditions on the right.

3.2   Methods

Study 1 and 2 focused on the impact of dynamic space and light, respectively, on user experience. In each study, we compared two conditions: the dynamic condition, where one element (either space or light) is mapped to the CG character's movement, against a neutral condition, where space and light are static. Each study used a specific segment of the choreography, which related to space or light. The two studies followed the same procedure. We adopted a repeated measures, within-subjects approach as done in other VR studies, such as [2] and [16], therefore each participant experienced both the dynamic and neutral conditions. The duration of the segments were 2 min (Study 1) and 2 min and 42 s (Study 2). The studies combined questionnaires and interviews.

Questionnaires. To investigate user experience in VR, we decided to assess presence (the sense of "being there in the environment" [30]) and engagement ("a quality of user experience that is characterized by the depth of an actor's investment in the interaction [with a digital system]" [19]). Presence data was collected using the **Igroup Presence Questionnaire** (IPQ), a validated questionnaire with a general presence factor, PRES, and three subscales: SP, Spatial Presence, the sense of being physically present in the virtual environment; INV, Involvement, focus of attention between real and virtual environments; REAL, Experienced Realism, judgment of the reality of the virtual environment [12]. It has 14 items, using 7-point scales.

To assess user engagement, we adopted the short form of the **User Engagement Scale** (UES), that is, UES-SF [20]. UES-SF consists of 12 items instead of UES's 31, therefore "ideal in within-subject studies where participants are completing multiple tasks or trials" [20] and fitting for our studies. UES-SF is a validated questionnaire with four subscales: FA, Focused Attention, "feeling absorbed in the interaction and losing track of time"; PU: Perceived Usability, "affect experienced as a result of the interaction and the degree of control and effort expended"; AE: Aesthetic Appeal, "attractiveness and visual appeal of the interface"; and RW: Rewarding, how much the experience was rewarding and worthwhile. It relies on 5-point scales. The order of the questions within IPQ and UES-SF was randomised. Combining IPQ with UES-SF resulted in 26 items for each condition.

We implemented the **questionnaires inside the VR environment**, following the approach recommended by Schwind et al. [22]. This way, participants do not need to remove their Head-Mounted Display (HMD) and put it on again to experience the next condition. According to [22], adopting presence questionnaires in VR can reduce "distracting or biasing cues from the real-world, such as the experimenter or experimental setup". Consequently, it potentially requires a smaller sample than real-world questionnaires to reveal statistically significant results between two or more conditions [22].

To **analyse the resulting quantitative data** we used Python (v. 3.6.9, libraries: statsmodels, statistics, scipy). To assess parametric assumptions of our datasets, we tested the distribution using a normality test (Shapiro test, given the smaller sample size). Only PRES in experiment 1 passed the normality test. The data that met parametric assumptions was analysed using t-test to compare conditions; while the remaining datasets were analysed using Wilcoxon signed-rank test (also known as Wilcoxon t-test) to compare conditions. Only significant comparisons are reported in detail.

Interviews. We also conducted **semi-structured interviews** with participants, to gather further insights. The questions focused on: a general impressions of both conditions; impressions on the CG character's movement; perceived connection (if any) between character's movement and space or light; and any other thoughts provoked by the experience. Interviews lasted, on average, 10 min. The transcribed interviews were later **coded and analysed** using thematic analysis [4] by two members of our team, and cross-checked by a third member.

Participants. For each of the 2 studies, there were 12 participants (24 in total), testing both the dynamic and the neutral conditions. Participants were recruited from the local academic and artistic communities. As incentive, they received merchandising from the research project and a voucher for a dance performance. Before the studies, we conducted an online demographics questionnaire with participants, including questions about experience with VR and dance.

Participants had ages ranging from 24 to 58 years. 10 identified as male, 13 as female, and 1 preferred not to say. In terms of VR experience, 8 used VR once a month or more; 10 between once a month and once a year; 2 once a year or less; and 4 had never used it. Regarding dance experience, 2 attended dance performances once a month or more; 9 between once a month and once a year; 9 once a year or less; and 4 had never attended. Participants were distributed between the studies in order to achieve diversity of age, gender, experience of VR and dance in each study. For anonymity, participants were numbered first (P1, P2 etc.) and distributed later between studies, as part of this process.

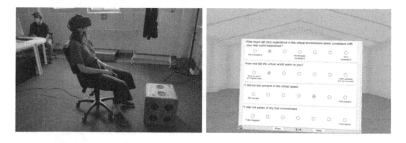

Fig. 2. Study procedure: Participant with HMD (left) and an image from the in-VR questionnaire (right)

Procedure. Participants undertook the following procedure: 1) welcome, briefing about the study, consent form signing, and introduction to the VR set-up; 2) VR study, consisting of: first condition and questionnaires (IPQ and UES-SF), followed by second condition and questionnaires, all in VR; 3) interview. To counterbalance the learning effect, the order of the conditions (neutral and dynamic) was randomised. Participants were sitting during the experiment (Fig. 2), in order to resemble the audience experience of a traditional dance performance.

The average durations of the in-VR experiences were 14 min and 11 s for Study 1 (space), and 15 min and 12 s for Study 2 (light). These were presented using an HTC Vive Pro. To guarantee fluid VR experiences and a constant refresh rate (90 FPS) for the HMD, we used state-of-the-art gaming hardware: an Intel i7-8086K CPU (4 GHz) with 32 GB of memory and an NVIDIA GeForce GTX 1080 (8 GB memory) video card.

4   Results and Analysis

4.1   Results from Questionnaires

The descriptive statistics (mean and standard deviation) for each of the subscales of IPQ and UES-SF of both studies can also be seen in Table 1. The results of the Wilcoxon signed-rank test analysis show a statistically significant difference

Table 1. Mean scores and ($\pm$) standard deviation for IPQ and UES-SF subscales across conditions for Study 1 – Space and Study 2 – Light. The * indicates a statistically significant difference between conditions, with higher values in bold.

Study	Questionnaire	Subscale	Neutral condition	Dynamic condition
Study 1	IPQ	PRES	4.333 ± 1.312	4.250 ± 1.639
		SP	4.200 ± 1.610	4.150 ± 1.768
		INV*	$*3.521 \pm 1.633$	$*\mathbf{4.333} \pm 1.736$
		REAL*	$*\mathbf{2.750} \pm 1.689$	$*2.125 \pm 1.333$
	UES-SF	FA*	$*2.500 \pm 1.093$	$*\mathbf{3.222} \pm 0.885$
		PU	4.250 ± 1.010	4.083 ± 1.064
		AE*	$*2.806 \pm 0.937$	$*\mathbf{3.389} \pm 0.826$
		RW*	$*3.083 \pm 1.115$	$*\mathbf{3.806} \pm 1.023$
Study 2	IPQ	PRES*	$*3.917 \pm 1.320$	$*\mathbf{4.667} \pm 1.312$
		SP*	$*3.900 \pm 1.620$	$*\mathbf{4.333} \pm 1.650$
		INV	3.729 ± 1.604	3.938 ± 1.819
		REAL	2.646 ± 1.315	2.875 ± 1.615
	UES-SF	FA	2.833 ± 1.280	3.194 ± 1.126
		PU	4.417 ± 0.862	3.944 ± 1.246
		AE*	$*2.750 \pm 1.037$	$*\mathbf{3.333} \pm 0.972$
		RW	3.500 ± 1.093	3.667 ± 1.054

in some of the subscales of both IPQ and UES-SF questionnaires between our two conditions.

In **Study 1 – Space**, for IPQ, the following statistically significant differences emerged in the analysis: the INV subscale (Involvement, focus of attention between real and virtual environments) was ranked higher in the dynamic condition than in the neutral one ($Z = 76.500$, $p = 0.001$); in addition the REAL subscale (Experienced Realism) was ranked lower in the dynamic condition than in the neutral one ($Z = 174.500$, $p = 0.05$). In UES-SF, we found the following statistically significant difference as follows: FA subscale (Focused Attention, "feeling absorbed in the interaction and losing track of time" [20]) was ranked higher in the dynamic condition ($Z = 78.000$, $p = 0.002$); additionally the AE subscale (Aesthetic Appeal, "the attractiveness and visual appeal of the interface" [20]) was higher in the dynamic condition ($Z = 30.000$, $p ¡ 0.001$); and to conclude the RW subscale (Rewarding, how much the experience was worthwhile) was also higher in the dynamic condition ($Z = 28.000$, $p = 0.001$).

In **Study 2 – Light**, for IPQ, the following statistically significant differences emerged: the PRES factor (General Presence) was ranked higher in the dynamic condition ($Z = 2.500$, $p = 0.047$); and the SP subscale (Spatial Presence, the sense of being physically present in the Virtual Environment) was also ranked higher in the dynamic condition ($Z = 287.500$, $p = 0.037$). In the UES-SF test the AE subscale (Aesthetic Appeal, "the attractiveness and visual appeal of the interface" [20]) was ranked higher in the dynamic condition ($Z = 52.500$, $p = 0.002$).

4.2   Analysis and Discussion of Interviews

In this section, we present the results of our thematic analysis, and discuss these in light of the questionnaire results and the literature review. Six main themes emerged from our analysis, which became the headings to the sections below. The first three themes relate to Study 1; the fourth and fifth themes corresponds to Study 2; and the last theme was identified in both studies.

Higher Involvement in a Less Realistic VR Environment. The results of **Study 1**, on space, show that our participants felt more involved in the dynamic condition. This is supported by the higher scores in the dynamic condition in the 'involvement' subscale of the IPQ questionnaire and by the interviews. Moreover, there is a connection between higher involvement and the less realism of the dynamic environment. Although participants experience a higher realism in the neutral condition (from IPQ, 'experienced realism' subscale), they report preference for the dynamic environment, as it is less realistic and hence provides more surprise (P5), unpredictability (P5), novelty (P13) and challenge (P2).

There are straightforward parallels to Wolf et al. [31], who successfully introduced a less realistic virtual outcome as a reward in another exergame system. Our findings also integrate well with Wirth et al.'s framework of a two-step formative process of presence [29]. Once participants understood the less realistic elements in the dynamic VR environment (corresponding to step one in the model by Wirth et al.) they could embrace this mediated environment as their primary reference of self-reference and self-location (step two). Our interview results demonstrate that the participants reported a benefit of the less realistic dynamic space condition, different from a 'plain' real-world experience. This benefit was absent in the neutral, more realistic condition. This is an important observation: realism does not necessarily lead to involvement, and in fact the opposite can occur.

Facilitation of Embodiment and Empathy. The dynamic space condition of **Study 1** provoked different feelings and emotions: *"made me emotional"* (P6), *"you can develop feelings"* (P13), *"it moved me"* (P4), *"I have felt more"* (P6), it was *"more moody"* (P10). This led to a heightened perception of embodiment: *"the walls coming nearer, I definitely felt more my body"* (P4). Some participants reported a change in the way they felt their own body during the experience of the dynamic space condition, and a stronger feeling of action in the VR environment. These outcomes are mirrored in the results of the UES-SF questionnaire 'rewarding' subscale, with higher scores in the dynamic space condition.

These findings correlate to the framework presented by Shin [25]. For this author, embodiment and empathy are experienced in a second phase of the VR experience (following the initial phase of immersing in the VR environment). Therefore, by enabling embodiment and empathy, the dynamic space condition facilitates this second phase.

Understanding and Empowerment of CG Character Movement. In **Study 1**, the participants' comments to the dynamic space condition elucidate how the CG character's movement exists inseparable from its context. As a representative example, P3 experienced the neutral space condition as *"static, lifeless, empty"*, while the dynamic space condition was described as *"alive like it was linked to the person"*. Participants further experienced the CG character movement as *"easier to understand"* (P5) and following a *"storyline"* (P8). Additionally, two participants experienced the space as empowering the movement of the character (P1, P3). These observations are reflected in the results of the UES-SF questionnaire in the 'focused attention' subscale, with higher scores in the dynamic space condition.

This is a fine example for the design of a virtual stage, where a grounded and fixed physical location has metamorphosed into an evolving "relational space" [5]. This relational space (the dynamic space condition) led to an experience of empowered character movement, while also making it more understandable.

Directing Attention to Body and Movement. A notable aspect of the VR experience in **Study 2** was the participants' perception of the relationship between movement and light. Some participants detected a link between the dancer and the direction (P12), timing (P17) and intensity (P14) of the light. The perception by these participants of various subtle mapping strategies (as outlined in the design of the VR environment section) indicates an awareness of the performance ecology in the VR environment. Other participants stated that the neutral light condition did not direct the attention to anything specific (P18, P20, P21), whereas the dynamic condition focused attention on movement elements or body parts through the correlation of changes in movement and light.

Despite some similarity (of the dynamic condition) with a physical theatre setting, participants did not experience the light element as a conventional "lighting cue" for the performer(s) on stage (as for example in [10]). Instead, they perceived the causal connections between movement and light, which is more similar to the work of Seevinck [23] and Seo et al. [24], who use light as material, as an interconnected element in interactive environments. The mappings contributed to the success of the dynamic condition in directing attention to the CG character's body and movement.

Enabling Presence and Self-Orientation in a Mediated Environment. The results of **Study 2** show that our participants did not feel as present in the neutral light condition of the VR environment. A representative statement: *"it was more like watching the scene and not being immersed"* (P22). Conversely, most participants reported strong feelings of expectation (P14, P18, P20, P24), surprise (P18), intrigue (P20) and curiosity (P17) related with the dynamic light condition. This is supported by the IPQ questionnaire results in the 'general presence' subscale. Additionally, the results in the 'spatial presence' subscale of IPQ also show higher scores in the dynamic light condition.

Mestre et al. [18] link presence to self-orientation and self-location "with respect to a media environment, not the real environment." We suggest combining this idea with Wirth et al.'s framework of a two-step formative process of presence [29]. Wirth et al. call the first step the construction of a "spatialized mental model of the mediated environment". Once our participants formed a clear idea about the media environment as a first step (e.g., P17 interpreted the neutral condition as a rehearsal space and the dynamic condition as a performance venue), they could embrace the media environment as a primary reference for self-orientation and self-location (second step). We suggest that certain mental models (such as being placed in a dark stage environment to watch a performance) imply the participant's acceptance of challenges in self-orientation and self-location in anticipation of a gratifying VR experience. In fact, our results showed that most participants reported strong feelings of expectation, surprise, intrigue and curiosity with the dynamic light condition. By fostering a mental model of a mediated environment, this condition facilitated self-orientation and self-location, where associated challenges were accepted and welcomed.

Interconnected Elements Contributing to Aesthetic Experience. Overall, the dynamic space condition of **Study 1** was appealing to the participants as a *"whole"* (P6, P8, P9, P15, P16) experience, where a feeling of harmony and complementarity between movement of CG character and of space existed. For example, the interconnectedness between the elements in the VR environment led to the experience of *"emotions that got transferred"* from the character in the dynamic space condition to the participant (P5). Again, this matches results from the UES-SF questionnaire, showing higher scores in the dynamic condition for the 'aesthetic appeal' subscale.

The aforementioned process of embodiment and empathy [25] in this case occurred through the experience of an interconnected VR environment, in which the design elements mutually reinforce each other. Thus, the dynamic space condition, through the interconnectedness of its elements, led to a more aesthetically appealing user experience.

Similarly, in **Study 2** some participants also reported a feeling of all-encompassing experience, of being more in contact with the *"whole"* (P9, P15) in the dynamic condition. Participants experienced the dynamic light condition as appealing (P12, P17, P21, P22), impressive (P17), visually pleasing (P23), mysterious (P14, P18, P20, P24), dark (P22), and even scary (P17, P18, P22, P24), in direct positive correlation with self-reported higher mental engagement. The higher scores in the UES-SF questionnaire for 'aesthetic appeal' of the dynamic light condition support the interpretation that the aesthetic experience was particularly important for engagement.

Their experience also confirms the immersive process described by Shin [25] who observed that embodiment and empathy follow successful presence in the VR environment. Therefore, as in the dynamic space, the interconnectedness of elements in the dynamic light condition led to a more holistic and more aesthetically appealing user experience.

5 Conclusion

To answer our research question we conducted two studies, each focusing on a different VR environment element: space and light. We compared a dynamic approach, interconnecting environment elements with CG character movement, against a neutral condition. In both studies, the dynamic approach led to higher presence and engagement values in questionnaires than the neutral condition, which was further supported and clarified by the interviews.

We discussed how this dynamic approach can lead to several user experience benefits with the design of CG characters' movement in VR: higher involvement in a less realistic VR environment; facilitation of embodiment and empathy; understanding and empowerment of CG character movement; directing attention to body and movement; enabling presence and self-orientation in a mediated environment; and interconnected elements contributing to aesthetic experience. Wirth et al.'s framework of a two-step formative process of presence [29], in combination with Shin's model of immersion [25], have been very useful in discussing the participants' experiences in both studies.

We propose that the dynamic VR environment design approach can be useful for designers - toward improving the user experience of VR environments, where CG character movement plays a key role. Our studies suggest that our approach can successfully improve user experience in VR, compared to a neutral approach, for two VR environment elements: space and light. However, our investigation on this novel topic remains exploratory, is based on two studies only, and further research is needed.

We suggest that there is potential in further studying space (e.g., positive and negative space) and light (e.g., hue and duration), while applying our dynamic approach to additional environment elements (e.g., sound and costume design, as identified in [6]), pointing to further research pathways. Taking into account the fields identified in our literature review, we propose that our dynamic VR environment design approach could be applied to other fields in VR design, for instance gaming (e.g., exergaming), VR storytelling, and cultural heritage.

Acknowledgements. This research is co-funded by the Creative Europe programme of the EU (597398-CREA-1-2018-1-PT-CULT-COOP1, Moving Digits project). We acknowledge the support of LARSyS to this research (Projeto - UIDB/50009/2020). The third author acknowledges ARDITI -Agencia Regionalpara o Desenvolvimento e Tecnologia under the scope of the Project M1420-09-5369-FSE-000002 - PhD Studentship.

References

1. Altizer Jr., R., et al.: Choreografish: co-designing a Choreography-based Therapeutic Virtual Reality System with Youth Who Have Autism Spectrum Advantages. In: Proceedings of the 2018 Annual Symposium on Computer-Human Interaction in Play Companion Extended Abstracts - CHI PLAY 2018 Extended Abstracts, Melbourne, VIC, Australia, pp. 381–389. ACM Press (2018). http://dl.acm.org/citation.cfm?doid=3270316.3271541
2. Bala, P., Masu, R., Nisi, V., Nunes, N.: "When the Elephant Trumps": a comparative study on spatial audio for orientation in 360° videos. In: Proceedings of the 2019 CHI Conference on Human Factors in Computing Systems, New York, NY, USA, pp. 1–13, CHI 2019. Association for Computing Machinery, May 2019. https://doi.org/10.1145/3290605.3300925
3. Blom, K.J., Beckhaus, S.: The design space of dynamic interactive virtual environments. Virtual Reality **18**(2), 101–116 (2014). https://doi.org/10.1007/s10055-013-0232-y
4. Braun, V., Clarke, V.: Using thematic analysis in psychology. Qualitative Res. Psychol. **3**(2), 77–101 (2006). https://www.tandfonline.com/doi/abs/10.1191/1478088706qp063oa
5. Brown, C.: Learning to dance with angelfish: choreographic encounters between virtuality and reality. In: Broadhurst, S., Machon, J. (eds.) Performance and Technology: Practices of Virtual Embodiment and Interactivity, pp. 85–99. Palgrave Macmillan UK, London (2006). https://doi.org/10.1057/9780230288157
6. Correia, N.N., Masu, R., Pham, A.H.D., Feitsch, J.: Connected layers: evaluating visualizations of embodiment in contemporary dance performances. In: Fifteenth International Conference on Tangible, Embedded, and Embodied Interaction, New York, NY, USA, pp. 1–12. TEI 2021, Association for Computing Machinery, February 2021. https://doi.org/10.1145/3430524.3440621

7. Fdili Alaoui, S., Bevilacqua, F., Jacquemin, C.: Interactive visuals as metaphors for dance movement qualities. ACM Trans. Interact. Intell. Syst. **5**(3), 13:1–13:24, September 2015. https://doi.org/10.1145/2738219
8. Hartmann, J., Holz, C., Ofek, E., Wilson, A.D.: RealityCheck: blending virtual environments with situated physical reality. In: Proceedings of the 2019 CHI Conference on Human Factors in Computing Systems - CHI 2019, Glasgow, Scotland UK, pp. 1–12. ACM Press (2019). http://dl.acm.org/citation.cfm?doid=3290605.3300577
9. Hassenzahl, M.: User experience and experience design. In: The Encyclopedia of Human-Computer Interaction, 2nd edn. Interaction Design Foundation (2013). https://www.interaction-design.org/literature/book/the-encyclopedia-of-human-computer-interaction-2nd-ed/user-experience-and-experience-design
10. He, L., Li, H., Xue, T., Sun, D., Zhu, S., Ding, G.: Am I in the theater?: Usability study of live performance based virtual reality. In: Proceedings of the 24th ACM Symposium on Virtual Reality Software and Technology, pp. 1–11, Tokyo, Japan. ACM, November 2018. https://dl.acm.org/doi/10.1145/3281505.3281508
11. Höök, K., Ståhl, A., Jonsson, M., Mercurio, J., Karlsson, A., Johnson, E.C.B.: Somaesthetic design. interactions **22**(4), 26–33 (2015). https://doi.org/10.1145/2770888, http://dl.acm.org/citation.cfm?doid=2797212.2770888
12. Igroup.org - project consortium: Igroup presence questionnaire (IPQ). http://www.igroup.org/pq/ipq/index.php
13. Jürgens, S., Correia, N.N., Masu, R.: The body beyond movement: (missed) opportunities to engage with contemporary dance in HCI. In: Fifteenth International Conference on Tangible, Embedded, and Embodied Interaction, New York, NY, USA, pp. 1–9, TEI 2021. Association for Computing Machinery, February 2021. https://doi.org/10.1145/3430524.3440624
14. Jürgens, S., Fernandes, C., Kuffner, Rafael: Choreographed 4D visuals: experiencing Sylvia Rijmer's body logic method in a VR dance installation. Perform. Res. **25**(6), 94–97 (2020). Routledge
15. Kitson, A., Schiphorst, T., Riecke, B.E.: Are you dreaming?: A phenomenological study on understanding lucid dreams as a tool for introspection in Virtual Reality. In: Proceedings of the 2018 CHI Conference on Human Factors in Computing Systems - CHI 2018, Montreal QC, Canada, pp. 1–12. ACM Press (2018). http://dl.acm.org/citation.cfm?doid=3173574.3173917
16. Masu, R., et al.: VR open scores: scores as inspiration for VR scenarios. In: Michon, R., Schroeder, F. (eds.) Proceedings of the International Conference on New Interfaces for Musical Expression, pp. 109–114. Birmingham City University, Birmingham, UK, July 2020. https://www.nime.org/proceedings/2020/nime2020_paper21.pdf. ISSN: 2220-4806
17. Masu, R., Correia, N.N., Jurgens, S., Druzetic, I., Primett, W.: How do dancers want to use interactive technology? Appropriation and layers of meaning beyond traditional movement mapping. In: Proceedings of the 9th International Conference on Digital and Interactive Arts, Braga, Portugal, pp. 1–9. ACM, October 2019. https://dl.acm.org/doi/10.1145/3359852.3359869
18. Mestre, D., Fuchs, P., Berthoz, A., Vercher, J.L.: Immersion et présence. In: Fuchs, P., Moreau, G., Berthoz, A., Vercher, J.L. (eds.) Le traité de la réalité virtuelle, pp. 309–38. Ecole des Mines de Paris, Paris (2006)
19. O'Brien, H.: Theoretical perspectives on user engagement. In: O'Brien, H., Cairns, P. (eds.) Why Engagement Matters: Cross-Disciplinary Perspectives of User Engagement in Digital Media, pp. 1–26. Springer, Cham (2016). https://doi.org/10.1007/978-3-319-27446-1

20. O'Brien, H.L., Cairns, P., Hall, M.: A practical approach to measuring user engagement with the refined user engagement scale (UES) and new UES short form. Int. J. Hum. Comput. Stud. **112**, 28–39 (2018). http://www.sciencedirect.com/science/article/pii/S1071581918300041

21. Raheb, K.E., Tsampounaris, G., Katifori, A., Ioannidis, Y.: Choreomorphy: a whole-body interaction experience for dance improvisation and visual experimentation. In: Proceedings of the 2018 International Conference on Advanced Visual Interfaces, pp. 1–9. ACM, Castiglione della Pescaia Grosseto Italy, May 2018. https://dl.acm.org/doi/10.1145/3206505.3206507

22. Schwind, V., Knierim, P., Haas, N., Henze, N.: Using presence questionnaires in virtual reality. In: Proceedings of the 2019 CHI Conference on Human Factors in Computing Systems - CHI 2019, Glasgow, Scotland UK, pp. 1–12. ACM Press (2019). http://dl.acm.org/citation.cfm?doid=3290605.3300590

23. Seevinck, J.: Dichroic wade. In: Proceedings of the 2016 CHI Conference Extended Abstracts on Human Factors in Computing Systems - CHI EA 2016, San Jose, California, USA, pp. 3889–3892. ACM Press (2016). http://dl.acm.org/citation.cfm?doid=2851581.2891094

24. Seo, J.H., Bruner, M., Ayres, N.: Aura garden: collective and collaborative aesthetics of light sculpting in virtual reality. In: Extended Abstracts of the 2018 CHI Conference on Human Factors in Computing Systems, Montreal, QC, Canada, pp. 1–6. ACM, April 2018. https://dl.acm.org/doi/10.1145/3170427.3177761

25. Shin, D.: Empathy and embodied experience in virtual environment: to what extent can virtual reality stimulate empathy and embodied experience? Comput. Hum. Behav. **78**, 64–73 (2018). http://www.sciencedirect.com/science/article/pii/S0747563217305381

26. Smith, S.: Dance performance and virtual reality: an investigation of current practice and a suggested tool for analysis. Int. J. Perform. Arts Digital Media **14**(2), 199–214 (2018). Routledge, https://doi.org/10.1080/14794713.2018.1509256

27. Thomas, L.M., Glowacki, D.R.: Seeing and feeling in VR: bodily perception in the gaps between layered realities. Int. J. Perform. Arts Digital Media **14**(2), 145–168 (2018). Routledge, https://doi.org/10.1080/14794713.2018.1499387

28. Vincs, K.: Virtualizing dance. In: The Oxford Handbook of Screen Dance Studies. Oxford University Press, New York (2016)

29. Wirth, W., et al.: A process model of the formation of spatial presence experiences. Media Psychol. **9**(3), 493–525 (2007). Routledge, https://doi.org/10.1080/15213260701283079

30. Witmer, B.G., Singer, M.J.: Measuring presence in virtual environments: a presence questionnaire. Presence **7**(3), 225–240 (1998). https://doi.org/10.1162/105474698565686

31. Wolf, D., Rogers, K., Kunder, C., Rukzio, E.: JumpVR: jump-based locomotion augmentation for virtual reality. In: Proceedings of the 2020 CHI Conference on Human Factors in Computing Systems, New York, NY, USA, pp. 1–12, CHI 2020. Association for Computing Machinery, April 2020. https://doi.org/10.1145/3313831.3376243

A Symbolic Machine Learning Approach for Cybersickness Potential-Cause Estimation

Thiago Porcino[1]($\boxtimes$), Erick O. Rodrigues[2], Flavia Bernardini[1],
Daniela Trevisan[1], and Esteban Clua[1]

[1] Universidade Federal Fluminense, Niteroi, Brazil
thiagomp@ic.uff.br
[2] Universidade Tecnológica Federal do Paraná, Pato Branco, Brazil

Abstract. Virtual reality (VR) and head-mounted displays are constantly gaining popularity in various fields such as education, military, entertainment, and bio/medical informatics. Although such technologies provide a high sense of immersion, they can also trigger symptoms of discomfort. This condition is called cybersickness (CS) and is quite popular in recent publications in the virtual reality context. This work proposes a novel experimental analysis using symbolic machine learning that ranks potential causes for CS. We estimate the CS causes and rank them according to their impact on the classification capabilities of CS. The experiments are performed using two distinct virtual reality games. We were able to identify that acceleration triggered cybersickness more frequently in a race game in contrast to a flight game. Furthermore, participants less experienced with VR are more prone to feel discomfort and this variable has a greater impact in the race game in contrast to the flight game, where the acceleration is not controlled by the user.

Keywords: Virtual reality · Cybersickness · Machine learning · Games

1 Introduction

Activities such as virtual training environments, simulations and entertainment in immersive virtual formats are constantly becoming more popular with the continued development and public interest in VR technologies over the last years [7]. In 2019, the VR hardware market was valued at 4.4 billion US dollars and is expected to reach 10 billion US dollars by 2022 [32].

Head-mounted displays (HMDs) are one of the means of achieving immersive virtual reality environments. These devices usually consist of electronic displays and lenses that are fixed over the head where the display and lenses face the eyes of the user. HMDs are used for various purposes in the industry such as in games that focus on applications for numerous contexts [21].

© IFIP International Federation for Information Processing 2021
Published by Springer Nature Switzerland AG 2021
J. Baalsrud Hauge et al. (Eds.): ICEC 2021, LNCS 13056, pp. 115–126, 2021.
https://doi.org/10.1007/978-3-030-89394-1_9

Unfortunately, HMDs are strongly related to frequent manifestations of discomfort [20]. Among the possible manifestations, cybersickness (CS) deserves special attention as it is the most frequent and is usually associated to long exposures to HMDs.

The most frequent symptoms caused by CS are general discomfort, headache, stomach awareness, nausea, vomiting, sweating, fatigue, drowsiness, disorientation, and apathy [9]. These symptoms impact the user experience and affects the VR industry negatively.

Several works in the literature address the CS phenomenon and mitigation strategies for immersive VR applications using HMDs [27,28]. This work estimates and is amenable to rank the attributes that contribute the most in terms of triggering the cybersickness. We propose an approach that enables this estimation in real time, while the user is under the VR condition. Decision tree algorithms are symbolic and adequate for this occasion, where understandability is essential [23].

The approach consists of following the prediction course through the decision tree while using feature frequency and the node height to estimate the influence of the attributes. The proposed approach can be used to assess specific CS causes in real-time scenarios, allowing for future approaches to draw conclusions over how to mitigate these causes based on specific user-game contexts.

This paper is organized as follows: Sect. 2 describes the literature review, the necessary background knowledge, which includes the types of sickness associated to VR, symbolic machine learning concepts, and related work. Section 3 describes the details of the dataset acquisition. Section 4 describes our approach that estimates potential causes of cybersickness. Section 5 contains a discussion of our results. At last, Sect. 6 describes the conclusion, which includes limitations of the current research and future work.

2   Literature Review

Motion sickness (MS) manifests due to the information divergence captured by the human sensory system in the presence of conflicts between the sensory organs that define orientation and spatial positioning. MS is defined as the discomfort felt during movement that is not related to body movement, e.g., in the case of airplane, boat, or land trips [2]. This type of discomfort also occurs in virtual environments and is called visually induced motion sickness (VIMS). Moreover, in VR, VIMS is used to show that sickness is likely to originate from the visual perception of motion originated from 3D images [3]. In contrast, VIMS that occurs during flight or drive simulators is often called simulator sickness. Overall, motion sickness can be split into two subcategories [17]: transportation sickness, which is tied to the real world and simulator sickness, which is associated to the virtual world and includes cybersickness.

CS symptoms are similar to MS symptoms: nausea, vertigo, dizziness, and upset stomach [29]. Manifestations related to VIMS or CS may originate from various causes. Some of these causes are already properly described in the literature, whereas others still need to be explored.

In a previous work [27], we created a detailed review of strategies with the main objective of minimizing CS causes. Furthermore, we have undergone a feature selection study that selects the most relevant attributes (causes) related to CS [26].

This work, in contrast, focuses on studying the most relevant attributes or features that lead to discomfort, in real-time. We also focus on investigating some approaches aiming to minimize CS in virtual environments using machine learning.

2.1 Symbolic Machine Learning Concepts

Given a training *dataset* $\mathbb{X} = \{x_1, ..., x_n\}$ containing instances such that $\mathbb{X} \in \mathbb{R}^p, p$ being the number of attributes of the instances with corresponding labels $c(x) \in \{1, ..., L\}$, the classification problem consists of assigning a label $l \in \{1, ..., L\}$ to unlabelled instances y, assuming that $\mathbb{X}$ can assist the process [30].

This work is built upon the understandability of *symbolic classifiers*, whose decision process description can be represented by a set of unordered or disjoint rules. Symbolic classifiers are not novel and they have been used in many scenarios where clear logical comprehensiveness is required [1]. A decision tree can be written as a set of disjoint unordered rules [10,11].

When a decision tree is built, the set of instances in a decision tree leaf node is the one covered by the rule formed by the path starting in the root node up to the leaf node. A decision tree is illustrated in the left side of Fig. 1. Moreover, a random forest, illustrated on the right side of Fig. 1, is a classifier represented by a collection of decision trees. Each tree is constructed using a sub-sample of features (bagging), randomly selected from the feature domain. Each tree of the forest votes for a class during the classification phase. Usually, the mode represents the chosen class and the final decision [5].

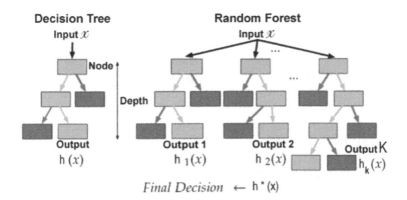

Fig. 1. Decision tree and random forest. The green paths represent the outcome for this particular case. (Color figure online)

2.2   Related Work

Kim et al. [19] proposed a deep learning architecture to estimate the cognitive state using brain signals and how they relate to CS levels. Their approach is based on deep learning approaches such as long short-term memory (LSTM) and CNN [13,22,31]. The models learn the individual characteristics of the participants that lead to the manifestation of CS symptoms when watching a VR video.

Jin et al. [16] grouped CS causes as: hardware-related (e.g., tied to VR device settings and features), software-related (e.g., tied to the content of the VR scenes), and user-related. The authors used classifiers to estimate the level of discomfort. The LSTM-RNN obtained the best results.

Jeong et al. [15] focus on 360 VR streaming. The authors analyzed the scenarios where CS is associated to brain signals. Their work uses data from 24 participants to recognize the common characteristics among their VR streams and related CS manifestation. They examined the VR content and separated the segments where several individuals felt discomfort. Still, authors were not able to find specific and related individual CS causes.

Furthermore, Kim et al. [19] and Jeong et al. [15] capture data using external medical equipment. However, medical equipment is not mainstream in terms of VR. For this reason, this work proposed a framework based on data that can be captured with no specific accessories.

Garcia-Agundez et al. [12] focus on the classification of the level of CS. The proposed model uses a combination of bio-signal and game settings. User signals such as respiratory and skin conductivity of 66 participants were collected. Authors obtained a classification accuracy of 82% (SVM) when it comes to binary classifications and 56% (kNN) for the ternary case.

Moreover, Porcino et al. [26] proposed an approach that is amenable to the prediction of CS during the gameplay. Authors were able to achieve an average accuracy of 96.54% with random forest considering a total of 16 different machine learning models and different scenarios. Additionally, they identified attributes responsible for painful states in VR games.

However, Garcia-Agundez et al. [12] and Porcino et al. [26] do not attempt to estimate the weight or the influence of the attributes (i.e., the cause) leading to CS, as opposed to the proposal of this work.

In this novel approach, we are able to use symbolic machine learning to analyse and identify one or more causes of discomfort, which is user and context specific. In other words, the approach described in this manuscript is not a general rule for recognizing the presence of discomfort as previously approached in the current literature. In contrast, it provides real-time user and context-sensitive evaluation and estimation of causes for cybersickness.

Moreover, the use of symbolic classifiers is paramount for an appropriate analysis and understanding of the decision, as opposed to deep learning approaches, which are black boxes.

3   Materials and Methods

We used Unity 3D [8] to create two different VR games: (1) a race game and (2) a flight game. In our pipeline, we require the participants to fill in questionnaires (CSPQ [26] and two VRSQ [18]) before and after the gameplay and participate for 5 min in basic VR game (using Oculus Rift and HTC Vive) that contains visual movements such as rotation and translation.

In the race game occasion, the acceleration varies according to the choice of the user (they push the acceleration according to their will). In contrast, the flight game simulates an almost-constant acceleration. The player experience for both games is highlighted in Fig. 2.

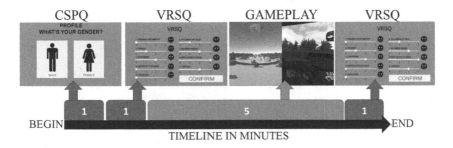

Fig. 2. Steps of our methodology.

A total of 35 users (9 women, 26 men) with ages ranging between 18 and 60 answered all the questionnaires correctly and completed the whole game interaction. All participants agreed with their anonymous participation in the study and signed consent forms. The participants were allowed to quit the experiment whenever they wanted. Each individual was required to complete four tasks, as follows:

- fill in the profile questionnaire (CSPQ) [26]. This questionnaire considers gender, age, previous experience with virtual environments, flicker sensitivity, any pre-symptom (such as stomach pain, flu, stress, hangover, headache, visual fatigue, lack of sleep or respiratory diseases), any vision impairment, presence of eyeglasses, posture (seated or standing) and eye dominance.
- fill in the VRSQ questionnaire [18];
- participate in one of the VR games for up to 5 min while mentioning the numbers 0 (none), 1 (slight), 2 (moderate), or 3 (severe) for each time their level of discomfort changed during the gameplay experience;
- and, at last, fill in the VRSQ questionnaire after the experience.

In terms of VRSQ results, 7/15 users from the race game scored positive for CS. When it comes to the flight game, 8/20 users reported discomfort. These scores represent 46.7% and 40.0%, respectively. All the features were captured considering two aspects: type of hardware and type of game.

The complete list of recorded parameters can be found in a previous publication [26]. We merged the top six features for each one of the scenarios (race and flight games). In addition, we discarded the time stamp and position attributes. The position attribute is specific to each game and can produce overfitting or even end up producing low accuracy rates when used with games other than the ones used during the training phase. In a similar sense, the timestamp feature is indirectly associated, in different extents, to nearly all the other features. Besides being redundant, this can also produce overfitting to the context of a specific game rather than working with generalizations. Therefore, extracted features (Table 1) were used as training data to construct the decision trees.

Table 1. Extracted feature set

Gameplay data	Profile data
Speed	Gender
Acceleration	Age
Rotation Z	VR experience
Frame rate	Discomfort label

In summary, the four original classes (Discomfort Label in Table 1), namely, none, slight, moderate, and severe, were converted to binary: 0 for no discomfort and 1 for discomfort. Class 1 translates to slight, moderate, or severe classes. Throughout the work, we use the random forest and decision tree algorithms from the scikit-learn [24] Python library (Python version: 3.7.5, sci-kit learn version: 0.22.1). In the next section, we provide our cybersickness cause estimation methodology.

4   Potential-Cause Estimation Approach

The logical prediction path of the decision trees inherits a personal fingerprint associated to attribute weights. Usually, attributes that are closer to the tree root are more important, as they often reduce the chaos in the data more than other attributes (information gain, less entropy). As a general rule, the frequency in which attributes appear in the decision path is also an important piece of information. We combine these two aspects to estimate the importance of the attribute (i.e., the most important causes of discomfort).

Let us suppose a decision tree described by 9 decision nodes, as shown in Fig. 3, which contains in their conditions the features G (gender), R (rotation Z), A (acceleration) and S (speed). Furthermore, let us consider a path for an instance that was predicted as discomfort, highlighted in green in Fig. 3.

We compute a potential-cause score (PCS) by summing up the heights of these features in the green path. In this case, G appeared once and has height 3, rotation R has height 2 and speed S has heights 1 and 0. Next, the output is

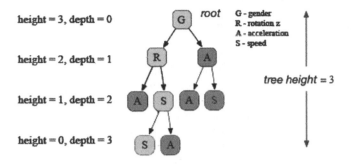

Fig. 3. A decision tree model. The green path illustrates the decision path that uses the attributes G, R, S, and S. Each attribute is associated to height values 3, 2, 1, and 0, respectively. (Color figure online)

divided by the sum of all depths of the tree, as follows: G = 3/6 or 0.5, R = 2/6 or approximately 0.33 and S = 1/6 or approximately 0.17. In this case, we estimate gender as the most relevant cause for CS (Eq. 1)

$$PCS(F) = \frac{\sum_{h=0}^{max\ height} \begin{cases} h, & \textit{if } F \textit{ belongs to the height.} \\ 0, & \textit{otherwise.} \end{cases}}{\sum_{h=0}^{max\ height} h} \tag{1}$$

where h varies from 0 to the maximal tree height, and F is the feature being evaluated. PCS is computed considering just the decision path (e.g., the one highlighted in green).

Furthermore, the random forest model can be considered a set of decision trees. We sum the PCS results from each tree t if the tree final decision is equal to the RF final decision. Otherwise, we sum 0 in this iteration.

Besides, as the evaluation method, we chose to use the leave-one-user-out method, a particular case of cross-validation where the number of folds matches the number of instances in the dataset. Consequently, the algorithm is trained n times, where n is the total amount of participants. Additionally, we compare AUC (area under the curve) [14] scores obtained results from the random forest and the simple decision tree in terms of predictability.

When it comes to the comparative results concerning the AUC scores the random forest classifier obtained the similar results to the decision tree (Tables 2 and 3). However, random forest is an ensemble algorithm, and hence it is naturally more complex and slower in terms of run time when compared to a single decision tree. Simple decision trees are faster and more compatible with real-time predictions, and hence we adopted them to generate the PCS feature ranking (Fig. 4) for the race and flight.

Table 2. User-specific AUC scores in the race game (tree depth 7).

User	Decision tree		Random forest	
	Train	Test	Train	Test
21	0.86	0.49	0.87	0.58
22	**0.86**	**0.98**	**0.88**	**1.00**
23	0.86	0.62	0.88	0.65
24	0.88	0.51	0.89	0.72
25	0.88	0.56	0.89	0.57
26	0.86	0.53	0.87	0.56
27	0.84	0.83	0.86	0.87
28	0.86	0.48	0.88	0.39
29	0.86	0.39	0.88	0.69
30	0.90	0.66	0.90	0.79
31	0.88	0.58	0.89	0.54
32	0.84	0.11	0.86	0.12
33	0.87	0.50	0.89	0.58
34	0.88	0.48	0.88	0.50
35	0.87	0.43	0.88	0.38
Average	**0.86**	**0.51**	**0.88**	**0.58**

Table 3. User-specific AUC scores in the flight game (tree depth 9).

User	Decision tree		Random forest	
	Train	Test	Train	Test
1	0.90	0.49	0.85	0.63
2	0.88	0.84	0.85	1.00
3	0.86	0.50	0.84	0.47
4	0.87	0.57	0.85	0.70
5	0.88	0.77	0.85	0.76
6	0.88	0.60	0.86	0.71
7	0.89	0.54	0.86	0.77
8	0.89	0.74	0.86	0.87
9	0.88	0.04	0.84	0.01
10	0.88	0.64	0.86	0.77
11	0.90	0.78	0.85	0.83
12	0.89	0.66	0.86	0.57
13	**0.88**	**0.98**	**0.85**	**1.00**
14	0.90	0.52	0.87	0.53
15	0.89	0.54	0.87	0.62
16	0.89	0.59	0.86	0.60
17	0.88	0.47	0.86	0.89
18	0.88	0.64	0.85	0.12
19	0.90	0.64	0.87	0.72
20	0.88	0.67	0.85	0.99
Average	**0.88**	**0.62**	**0.86**	**0.72**

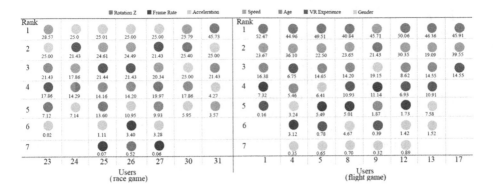

Fig. 4. PCS feature ranking for the race and flight games. In flight game, the rotation Z feature was ranked as the most important in 6 out of 7 participants. Moreover, it is important to highlight that the feature ranking varies substantially according to each game.

5 Discussion

Predicting the cause of CS is not trivial. Every user has a specific susceptibility to discomfort. Furthermore, several attributes are related to the hardware and ergonomic aspects of the devices. We are still far from tracing very precise causes for all specific cases. However, so far, factors such as rotation, speed, gender, and previous VR experience, appeared as dominant factors that may trigger CS.

Our approach works with seven factors attributed to CS. Previous works in the literature already proposed strategies for four of these attributes (acceleration, speed, frame rate, and camera rotation on the z-axis) [4,6,33]. The remaining causes (gender, VR experience, and age) are causes associated to the user profile and are still not associated to a clear strategy.

In addition, we observed different patterns of causes for users in the race game when compared to the flight game. In the flight case, rotation accompanied by speed were the most frequently estimated causes for the discomfort in 7 out of 8 users. Strategies to minimize CS could be applied to circumvent the influence of speed and rotation.

The race game is associated to acceleration shifts controlled by the user, whereas the flight game acceleration is nearly non existent and is not controlled by the user. This difference was very clear in the ranking results where it is possible to confirm that the CS triggered by acceleration was more prevalent in the race case rather than the flight case. In other words, the PCS average for the acceleration attributes over all users were: Race Game = 4.67, Flight Game = 1.34.

Another feature that influenced the discomfort in both scenarios was the former VR experience. Our proposed PCS outputted greater scores for the race game in contrast to the flight game, 14.79 and 6.42, respectively. In fact, the race game controllers are more complex than the flight game controllers. Introducing rapid movements and related variables that are controlled by the user can potentially lead to higher incidence of cybersickness. Virtual reality games that rely on low complex controllers are a good fit for non-experienced users.

Conclusively, causes were ranked differently over the games and user profiles. CS can be triggered by different factors and their combinations, where eventually a single variable influences more than the remaining. For this reason, different combinations of strategies can be applied specifically to each user.

In addition, several works [27] propose strategies based on causes. However, none of them focuses on assisting game designers by identifying the cause in order to properly suggest an appropriate strategy. Furthermore, designers can benefit from our results in order to choose the best-fit strategy to reduce CS during gameplays according to user profile or game.

6   Conclusion

In this work, we propose an approach to identify potential causes for CS in different VR games using HMDs. To the best of our knowledge, this is the first work that performs this analysis in real-time, during the gameplay experience.

We considered two different scenarios for the experimental analysis and proposed two symbolic machine learning algorithms. Next, we performed a feature ranking to identify the most relevant CS causes that are specific to each user.

We observed that users with the same profile are more likely to manifest the same causes that lead to CS. Furthermore, we can also assume that the introduction of more movements and/or variables controlled by the user in the game probably lead to higher incidence of CS. VR games with low complexity controllers can be a good fit to non-experienced users.

Regarding limitations, the COVID-19 pandemic affected our experiments in terms of dataset construction. For this reason, some subjective and gameplay features, such as the player posture and locomotion, were not included in the training. Besides, some features were not well represented, such as gender, age, and former VR experience.

Future work involves including features such as posture, vision impairments, locomotion and other features to our framework using new experimental protocols. We also aim to improve the balance of the dataset as some cases were also not broadly represented, such as gender (few women), age (few elders) and experience (few participants with former VR experience). Another straightforward way is to explore other machine learning models that allow similar interpretability, such as SVM and logistic regression.

As a final remark, the raw dataset of this work and created games are published in a public domain for further reproduction and comparisons [25].

References

1. Bernardini, F., Monard, M.C., Prati, R.: Constructing ensembles of symbolic classifiers. Int. J. Hybrid Intell. Syst. **3**(3), 159–167 (2006)

2. Bles, W., Bos, J.E., De Graaf, B., Groen, E., Wertheim, A.H.: Motion sickness: only one provocative conflict? Brain Res. Bull. **47**(5), 481–487 (1998)
3. Bos, J.E., Bles, W., Groen, E.L.: A theory on visually induced motion sickness. Displays **29**(2), 47–57 (2008)
4. Bouyer, G., Chellali, A., Lécuyer, A.: Inducing self-motion sensations in driving simulators using force-feedback and haptic motion. In: Virtual Reality (VR), pp. 84–90. IEEE (2017)
5. Breiman, L.: Random forests. Mach. Learn. **45**(1), 5–32 (2001)
6. Budhiraja, P., Miller, M.R., Modi, A.K., Forsyth, D.: Rotation blurring: use of artificial blurring to reduce cybersickness in virtual reality first person shooters. arXiv preprint arXiv:1710.02599 (2017)
7. Calvelo, M., Piñeiro, Á., Garcia-Fandino, R.: An immersive journey to the molecular structure of SARS-CoV-2: virtual reality in Covid-19. Comput. Struct. Biotechnol. J. **18**, 2621–2628 (2020)
8. Creighton, R.H.: Unity 3D Game Development by Example: A Seat-of-Your-Pants Manual for Building Fun, Groovy Little Games Quickly. Packt Publishing Ltd., New York (2010)
9. Dennison, M.S., D'Zmura, M.: Cybersickness without the wobble: experimental results speak against postural instability theory. Appl. Ergon. **58**, 215–223 (2017)
10. Flach, P.: Machine Learning: The Art and Science of Algorithms That Make Sense of Data. Cambridge University Press, Cambridge (2012)
11. Frank, E., Hall, M.A., Witten, I.H.: Data Mining: Practical Machine Learning Tools and Techniques, 4th edn. Morgan Kaufmann, Burlington (2016)
12. Garcia-Agundez, A., et al.: Development of a classifier to determine factors causing cybersickness in virtual reality environments. Games Health J. **8**(6), 439–444 (2019)
13. Graves, A., Mohamed, A.R., Hinton, G.: Speech recognition with deep recurrent neural networks. In: 2013 IEEE International Conference on Acoustics, Speech and Signal Processing, pp. 6645–6649. IEEE (2013)
14. Huang, J., Ling, C.X.: Using AUC and accuracy in evaluating learning algorithms. IEEE Trans. Knowl. Data Eng. **17**(3), 299–310 (2005)
15. Jeong, D., Yoo, S., Yun, J.: Cybersickness analysis with EEG using deep learning algorithms. In: 2019 IEEE Conference on Virtual Reality and 3D User Interfaces (VR), pp. 827–835. IEEE (2019)
16. Jin, W., Fan, J., Gromala, D., Pasquier, P.: Automatic prediction of cybersickness for virtual reality games. In: 2018 IEEE Games, Entertainment, Media Conference (GEM), pp. 1–9. IEEE (2018)
17. Getting Rid of Cybersickness. Springer, Cham (2020). https://doi.org/10.1007/978-3-030-59342-1_6
18. Kim, H.K., Park, J., Choi, Y., Choe, M.: Virtual reality sickness questionnaire (VRSQ): motion sickness measurement index in a virtual reality environment. Appl. Ergon. **69**, 66–73 (2018)
19. Kim, J., Kim, W., Oh, H., Lee, S., Lee, S.: A deep cybersickness predictor based on brain signal analysis for virtual reality contents. In: Proceedings of IEEE International Conference on Computer Vision, pp. 10580–10589 (2019)
20. Kolasinski, E.M.: Simulator sickness in virtual environments. Technical report, DTIC Document (1995)
21. Kühnapfel, U., Cakmak, H.K., Maaß, H.: Endoscopic surgery training using virtual reality and deformable tissue simulation. Comput. Graph. **24**(5), 671–682 (2000)
22. Lawrence, S., Giles, C.L., Tsoi, A.C., Back, A.D.: Face recognition: a convolutional neural-network approach. IEEE Trans. Neural Netw. **8**(1), 98–113 (1997)

23. Maree, C., Omlin, C.W.: Towards responsible AI for financial transactions. In: 2020 IEEE Symposium Series on Computational Intelligence (SSCI), pp. 16–21. IEEE (2020)
24. Pedregosa, F., et al.: Scikit-learn: machine learning in python. J. Mach. Learn. Res. **12**, 2825–2830 (2011)
25. Porcino, T.: Cybersickness Dataset. https://github.com/tmp1986/UFFCSData. Accessed 7 July 2021
26. Porcino, T., Rodrigues, E.O., Silva, A., Clua, E., Trevisan, D.: Using the gameplay and user data to predict and identify causes of cybersickness manifestation in virtual reality games. In: 2020 IEEE 8th International Conference on Serious Games and Applications for Health (SeGAH), pp. 1–8. IEEE (2020)
27. Porcino, T., Trevisan, D., Clua, E.: Minimizing cybersickness in head-mounted display systems: causes and strategies review. In: 2020 22nd Symposium on Virtual and Augmented Reality (SVR), pp. 154–163. IEEE (2020)
28. Rebenitsch, L., Owen, C.: Review on cybersickness in applications and visual displays. Virtual Reality **20**(2), 101–125 (2016). https://doi.org/10.1007/s10055-016-0285-9
29. Rebenitsch, L.R.: Cybersickness Prioritization and Modeling. Michigan State University (2015)
30. Rodrigues, E.O., Conci, A., Liatsis, P.: Morphological classifiers. Pattern Recogn. **84**, 82–96 (2018)
31. Sak, H., Senior, A.W., Beaufays, F.: Long short-term memory recurrent neural network architectures for large scale acoustic modeling (2014)
32. Statista, A.: The statistics portal (2020). https://www.statista.com/statistics/591181/global-augmented-virtual-reality-market-size/
33. Van Waveren, J.: The asynchronous time warp for virtual reality on consumer hardware. In: Proceedings of 22nd ACM Conference on Virtual Reality Software and Technology, pp. 37–46 (2016)

Fundamental Study of Color Combinations by Using Deuteranope-Simulation Filter for Controlling the Handicap of Color Vision Diversity in Video Games

Yuka Fujiwara$^{(\boxtimes)}$ and Satoshi Nakamura

Meiji University, 4-21-1 Nakano, Nakano-ku, Tokyo, Japan
cs212029@meiji.ac.jp

Abstract. Color video games are often disadvantageous for people with color blindness. Therefore, the game creator often supports them by displaying a color scheme suitable for a color vision type to solve this problem. However, it is difficult to say that the color scheme solves the handicap. Therefore, we aim to develop a mechanism that can control the advantages and disadvantages of people with color vision diversity and normal color vision by combining suitable colors. To examine color combinations that are difficult for people with normal color vision to discriminate and easy for people with color vision diversity we carried out an experiment using a Deuteranope-simulation filter. The results proved that there are color combinations that people with color vision diversity can easily discriminate. This means that the advantages of color vision and disadvantages of color vision diversity can be controlled appropriately by using color combinations.

Keywords: Color vision diversity · Deuteranope-simulation filter · Color handicap

1 Introduction

Nowadays, people recognize e-sports [1] as a sport, so the demand for online games is increasing rapidly [2]. As a result, a wide variety of players play online games with others every day. However, some players are disadvantaged by handicaps. Therefore, there needs to be a system that keeps games fair because handicaps complicate game elements related to auditory and visual senses. We focused on people with color vision diversity because about 5% of men and 0.2% of women in Japan had color vision diversity [6] in 2002.

People with color vision diversity see specific colors, such as red or green, differently from people with normal color vision [3]. Figure 1 shows an example of visible colors for people with normal color vision and Deuteranope (a common color vision diversity) [4]. In this example, it is very difficult for people with Deuteranope to distinguish the blue one from the purple one and the yellow one from the green one. In video games, players

© IFIP International Federation for Information Processing 2021
Published by Springer Nature Switzerland AG 2021
J. Baalsrud Hauge et al. (Eds.): ICEC 2021, LNCS 13056, pp. 127–138, 2021.
https://doi.org/10.1007/978-3-030-89394-1_10

Ordinary (95%)   Protanope (1.5%)

Deuteranope (3.5%)   Tritanope (0.001%)

Fig. 1. An example of the Puyo Puyo seen by each color vision type and rate in Japanese males. ©1991 SEGA Puyo Puyo

must make judgments as quickly as other players. Therefore, players with normal color vision can easily overperform players with Deauteranope. If players with normal color vision can easily beat players with color vision diversity because of the game's color, that is not fair.

To solve the unfairness of playability of a game based on color vision diversity, several game companies implemented the function of color vision support. This function changes the color of objects in the game to enable players with color vision diversity to distinguish one color from another easily and quickly. However, such support sometimes doesn't work well. For example, color vision supports increase the playability of a specific type of color vision. However, this playability using color vision support does not reach the playability of players with normal color vision. Also, since there are multiple types of color vision, it is not easy to support all color vision diversities by using only color vision support (see Fig. 2).

With these issues in mind, we aim to eliminate color handicaps in people with color vision diversity with various characteristics. Specifically, this study investigates the possibility of controlling the advantages and disadvantages of color discrimination between people with normal color vision and people with color vision diversity (see Fig. 3). To realize a system that can control the handicap, we have to experiment to

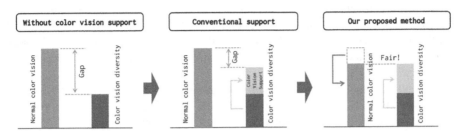

Fig. 2. Playability between a player with normal color vision and the other with color vision diversity in situation of without color vision support, with convensinoal color vision support and with our proposed method.

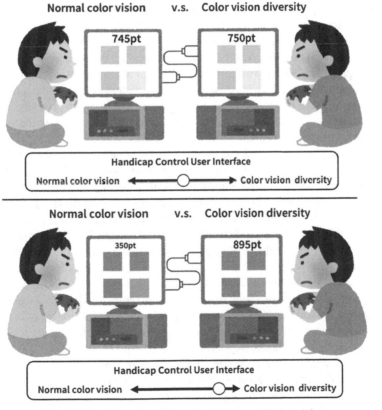

Fig. 3. Handicap control based on the type of color vision.

clarify which color combinations are easy and difficult for people with and without normal color vision to discriminate because there is no index to investigate the color combinations.

In this study, we focus on Deuteranope, a relatively common type of color vision diversity. We propose a method to investigate color as an index for controlling the advantages and disadvantages of different types of color vision. Specifically, in the experiment, participants with normal color vision use an optical Deuteranope-simulation filter to view a set of squares in which one square is a different color from the others and select the different colored square. This result will clarify which combinations of colors are easy to discriminate for people with Deuteranope and are difficult to discriminate for people with normal color vision.

The contribution of this paper is to propose a handicap control method that enables people with any color vision to play together in fairness and found an appropriate combination of colors by using color vision conversion filters.

2 Related Work

The symptoms of color vision diversity were initially clarified by Dalton [5] in 1798. We focused on people with color vision diversity because about 5% of men and 0.2% of women in Japan had color vision diversity [6] in 2002.

People with normal color vision have three normal pyramidal cells. In contrast, people with color vision diversity have a deficiency of these three pyramidal cells. Also, color appearance varies with cone cell defects and varies among individuals [7–9]. Therefore, people with color vision diversity are diverse and complex, and it is necessary to fully understand the factors of different patterns of color vision diversity. Then, it is essential to eliminate the handicap of color vision diversity in the video game by carrying out the color vision support suitable for each of them.

Okada et al. [7–9] proposed the concept of color universal design (CUD) [10]. However, prevalence is low [11] because people with diverse color vision have little opportunity to understand which colors are difficult to distinguish from other colors.

Thus, to overcome the fact that people with color vision diversity do not know how colors look, many types of research such as detection techniques and color vision simulation methods combine the difficult colors to distinguish. For example, from the viewpoint of CUD, Nakauchi et al. [12] researched a method to detect the difficult to discern colors for people with Protanope and Deuteranope and to correct them to discernible colors automatically. Also, Brettel et al. [13] simulated the appearance of a color on display in each color vision type, and Color Oracle [14] and Adobe Photoshop [15] can change the formation of a whole monitor by the color vision type. In this study, experiments were carried out to simulate the color on display, referring to the conversion calculation used in the method proposed by Asada [16].

There are several studies to support the daily lives of people with diverse color vision. Asada [16] developed an application to convert color in real time for each color vision type on an image seen through a camera. The technology is also suitable for business because it uses a smartphone that people usually mobile. Tanuwidjaja et al. [17] developed a Chroma system based on Google Glasses, a head mounted display.

Chroma is a wearable system that can automatically convert visible color by the color vision type.

In addition to these systems for color vision correction, there are various other types of support. Ichikawa et al. [18] proposed a method to change the colors of Web pages for people with color vision diversity. This method decomposes the colors on a Web page into a hierarchy. It changes the colors from the positional relationship in the color space. Moreover, a color correction method based on still images [19] quantifies the degree of colors difficult to distinguish for people with color vision diversity to change the colors of all pixels. This method supports people with color vision diversity and a system that enables mutual compromise by providing complex colors for people with the normal color vision to discriminate.

3 Proposed System

To eliminate the handicap of color vision diversity, we examined color combinations that are easy to distinguish for each type of color vision diversity. We examined whether the color combinations were more suitable for video games for people with color vision diversity than for people with normal color vision. Because the population with color vision diversity is low depending on the type [9]. It is not easy to gather people with color vision diversity to conduct surveys and experiments on color perception.

This paper proposes a system to obtain an appropriate combination of colors by observing the difference between filtered and unfiltered conditions by applying a filter that simulates each color vision type and requiring users to select a target object from multiple objects accurately and quickly.

The procedures of this system for Deutereanopia are as follows:

1. The system randomly selects a combination of colors from color sets. Then, the system sets one color as the target color and the other as the basic color.
2. The system randomly selects one square as the target square from 36 squares arranged 6 × 6. Others are the basic squares (see Fig. 4).
3. The system randomly selects whether normal color vision mode or Deuteranopia color vision mode. If the Deuteranopia mode is selected, the system converts the target and basic colors to Deauteranope-simulated colors (see Fig. 5). In this conversion, we used the calculation proposed in [16] (see Fig. 6).
4. The system presents 35 basic squares using the basic color and one target square using the target color. If the system selected the Deuteranopia color vision mode, the system uses Deauteranope-simulated target color and Deauteranope-simulated basic color.
5. The system asks users to select a square that is different from the other squares as quickly as possible.
6. After the user's selection, the system records the combination of colors, color vision mode, the target square's position, the selected square, and the operation time.

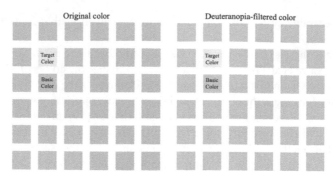

Fig. 4. Examples of target and basic colors in the normal color vision mode and the Deuteranopia color vision mode.

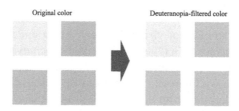

Fig. 5. Converting original colors (left) to Deuteranopia-filtered colors (right).

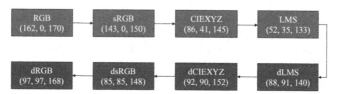

Fig. 6. Color conversion procedure of Deuteranopia filter used in this experiment. If the system changes dLMS for the other filter's one, the system is able to support the other color vision diversity.

By analyzing the recorded data, such as the error rates and the quickness, we can judge which combination of color is fair between people with normal color vision and people with diverse color vision. In addition, we can apply this for other types of color vision diversity by changing dLMS with others.

4   Experiment

4.1   Outline of the Experiment

To eliminate the vision based handicap that people with color vision diversity have when playing video games, this study aims to clarify the combinations of easy colors for people with color blindness to distinguish and difficult for people with normal color vision to determine. Since there are various types of color vision diversity, this study focuses on Deuteranope, one of the most common types.

Yamanaka et al. investigated different colors' visibility on Web pages for people with diverse color vision [20]. As a result, they found that the higher the lightness difference between the character and background colors, the higher the text visibility is. Therefore, this study tested the following hypothesis: the more significant the difference in lightness in color combinations are, the more accurately and rapidly people with color vision diversity can judge color differences are.

To choose the combinations of colors for this experiment, we conducted a preliminary test before this experiment test. We prepared 22 combinations of colors in this preliminary test and asked five participants to try this test. From the preliminary test results, we selected the combinations of target and basic colors (see Table 1). Table 1 also shows the Deauteranope-filtered target color and basic color.

In the experiment, the number of trials in each task is 28 (combinations of colors per 1 condition) × 2 (conditions with and without a filter) = 56 trials. In addition, we ask participants to try 10 tasks. A trial finishes right after the participant clicks a square. Even if the clicked square was not the target, the system advanced to the next trial.

We recruited 13 participants (five men and eight women) with normal color vision in this experiment. We conducted a color vision check based on the Ishihara color vision test table [21] in advance and confirmed that no participants had color vision diversity. Moreover, before the experiment, the participants were told to stay 50 cm away from the display, not lean forward during the investigation, and prioritize accuracy over speed selection.

4.2   Experimental Results

One participant who was an outlier (mean $\pm$ 2 standard deviations) in both the correct answer rate and answer time was excluded in analyzing the experimental results. So, we used the experimental results of 12 participants (5 men and 7 women) to analyze.

Table 1 shows the correct answer rates for 12 participants in each color combination. The paired t-tests for the correct response rates of filtered and unfiltered conditions showed a significant difference of $p < 0.05$ for five pairs (pair-5, pair-8, pair-13, pair-24, pair-27) and $p < 0.01$ for ten pairs (pair-7, pair-9, pair-10, pair-17, pair-18, pair-22, pair-23, pair-25, pair-26, pair-28) of the 28 color combinations. Of the 15 color combinations that showed significant differences, the correct color combinations in the filtered condition were pair-5, pair-7, pair-8, pair-13, pair-22, and pair-24.

Next, we performed a paired t-test on the response time. Of the 19 color combinations that showed significant differences, six pairs had shorter mean response times in the filtered condition; pair-3, pair-6, pair-7, pair-8, pair-14, and pair-24.

Table 2 shows the percentage of correct answers and the average response time of the 12 participants in filtered and unfiltered conditions. From Table 2, the overall correct answer rate was higher. The average response time was shorter in the filtered condition (correct answer rate is 0.70 and response time is 5.26 s) than in the unfiltered state (correct answer rate is 0.80 and response time is 6.27 s).

Table 1. Percentage of correct responses and average response time with color combinations (RGB) and no filters.

	Target Color	Basic Color	Unfiltered Target	Unfiltered Basic	Filtered Target	Filtered Basic	Unfiltered correct answer rate	Filtered correct answer rate	Unfiltered response time	Filtered response time
pair-1	171, 145, 0	204, 167, 0					0.99	0.95	1.35	1.59
pair-2	204, 167, 0	171, 145, 0					0.98	1.00	1.42	1.68
pair-3	171, 30, 85	164, 38, 92					0.74	0.80	6.50	5.09
pair-4	164, 38, 92	171, 30, 85					0.72	0.81	5.99	7.47
pair-5	165, 0, 171	180, 0, 204					0.88	0.95	2.97	2.13
pair-6	180, 0, 204	165, 0, 171					0.88	0.94	2.62	1.85
pair-7	230, 138, 184	232, 139, 190					0.15	0.68	10.14	7.20
pair-8	232, 139, 190	230, 138, 184					0.38	0.62	14.75	6.61
pair-9	90, 64, 89	98, 55, 85					0.98	0.36	2.29	12.26
pair-10	98, 55, 85	90, 64, 89					0.98	0.25	1.82	13.20
pair-11	0, 180, 147	0, 210, 167					1.00	0.98	1.82	1.71
pair-12	0, 210, 167	0, 180, 147					0.96	0.95	2.36	2.21
pair-13	154, 227, 82	141, 217, 98					0.83	0.94	3.30	2.90
pair-14	141, 217, 98	0, 210, 167					0.82	0.83	3.56	3.83
pair-15	199, 35, 230	172, 49, 185					0.93	0.97	1.94	2.01
pair-16	172, 49, 185	199, 35, 230					0.97	0.99	1.76	1.54
pair-17	145, 165, 0	135, 168, 0					0.93	0.02	2.84	33.72
pair-18	135, 168, 0	145, 165, 0					0.97	0.05	2.96	7.62
pair-19	0, 0, 168	0, 2, 143					0.91	0.92	2.86	2.91
pair-20	0, 2, 143	0, 0, 168					0.84	0.79	4.78	4.57
pair-21	186, 0, 112	180, 30, 105					0.50	0.56	8.99	9.53
pair-22	180, 30, 105	186, 0, 112					0.33	0.53	11.84	9.49
pair-23	0, 157, 168	0, 149, 161					0.59	0.37	7.74	9.77
pair-24	0, 149, 161	0, 157, 168					0.29	0.47	10.17	8.08
pair-25	99, 94, 0	115, 101, 0					0.97	0.71	2.32	7.27
pair-26	115, 101, 0	99, 94, 0					0.98	0.75	1.93	5.03
pair-27	115, 0, 0	99, 0, 0					0.97	0.84	2.80	5.33
pair-28	99, 0, 0	115, 0, 0					0.83	0.60	4.13	7.36

5   Discussion

In this study, we hypothesized the more significant the difference in lightness in a combination of colors is, the more accurately and quickly a person with color vision diversity can judge the color difference. For this purpose, we examined which color combinations are easy for people with color vision diversity to distinguish. In video games, players must make accurate and quick judgments, often regarding color, to win. Therefore, this experiment focuses on color combinations. The correct answer rate was over 0.7, and the average response time was 6 s or less in both filtered and unfiltered varieties. Note that the appropriate correct answer rate and the response time are depending on the game type. We can easily change the threshold of the correct answer rate and the response time easily depending on the game's type, such as shootings, fighting games, puzzles, and so on.

Figures 7 and 8 show combinations of colors with short average response times in unfiltered and filtered conditions. Among these color combinations, we examine pair-5, pair-6, pair-26, and pair-27, which showed significant differences in the mean response time, and pairs-11 and pair-15, which showed small differences in the mean response time.

Table 2. Correct response rate and average response time for 12 participants.

	Correct answer rate	Average response time (sec)
Filtered	0.70	7.29
Unfiltered	0.80	5.26
All	0.75	6.27

Table 3. HSV with and without filters.

	Target Color Unfiltered	Basic Color Unfiltered	Target Color Filtered	Basic Color Filtered
pair-5	297, 100, 67	292, 100, 80	240, 42, 66	240, 46, 79
pair-6	292, 100, 80	297, 100, 67	240, 46, 79	240, 42, 66
pair-11	169, 100, 70	167, 100, 82	60, 0, 58	60, 0, 58
pair-15	290, 84, 90	294, 73, 72	240, 46, 89	240, 39, 71
pair-26	52, 100, 45	56, 100, 38	60, 100, 41	60, 100, 37
pair-27	0, 100, 45	0, 100, 38	60, 100, 26	60, 100, 22

According to Table 1 and Fig. 8, pair-5 and pair-6 had the correct answer rates higher than 0.85 in both conditions and shorter average response times in the filtered state than in the unfiltered condition. Here, to examine whether these color combinations are easy for people with color vision diversity to discriminate, RGB of pair-5 and pair-6 was converted into HSV. HSV is a color space consisting of hue, saturation, and value. Table 3 shows the results of converting RGB into HSV for the color combinations discussed in this chapter. From Table 3, the comparison of HSV of the target and basic colors for the filtered and unfiltered conditions shows that the difference in lightness between the target and basic colors is equal in both states. However, the saturation value is different in the filtered shape.

On the other hand, HSV in the unfiltered condition showed a slight difference in hue values between the target and basic colors. From these results, combinations of colors that are easier for people with Deuteranope to discriminate need different values of Chroma and lightness but the same hue values. However, there is a 6–7% difference in the percentage of correct answers, which needs to narrow slightly.

Next, Fig. 7 shows that pair-26 and pair-27 have shorter average response times in the unfiltered condition than in the filtered state. Therefore, these combinations are considered difficult for people with color vision diversity to discriminate. Table 3 shows that the target color is lighter than the basic color in both the filtered and unfiltered conditions. Here, the colors that are easy for people with color vision diversity to discriminate can accurately discriminate regardless of the use of the filter. The response time is shorter in the filtered condition than in the unfiltered state. However, for pair-26 and pair-27, the unfiltered condition is unsuitable for people with color vision diversity because the average response time is much shorter than in the filtered state.

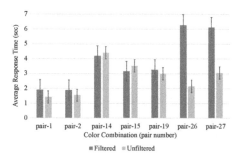

Fig. 7. Combinations of colors with short average response times in unfiltered conditions.

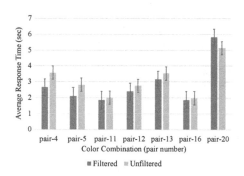

Fig. 8. Combinations of colors with short average response times in filtered conditions.

Table 4. Advantageous and disadvantageous color combinations for general and Deuteranope.

	General advantage	General disadvantage
Deuteranope advantage	pair-11, pair-15	pair-5, pair-6
Deuteranope disadvantage	pair-25, pair-26	pair-19

For pair-11 and pair-15, there was not much difference in the average response time between the filtered and unfiltered conditions in Fig. 7 and Fig. 8. Table 3 shows that the target color is lighter than the basic color. These color combinations are easy to discern for people with normal color vision and color vision diversity, so that these color combinations may remove the handicap of color vision diversity.

The above results clarify that people with Deuteranope can discriminate the target color when its lightness is higher than or equal to the surrounding color. These results support this paper's hypothesis: The more significant the difference in lightness in a combination of colors are, the more accurately, and quickly a person with color vision diversity can judge the color difference. Moreover, the results prove that lightness is a more critical element for color discrimination for people with color vision diversity than people with normal color vision. Furthermore, the results demonstrate that fair colors are easy to discriminate for people with normal color vision and color vision diversity when the target color has higher lightness than the circumference color. Table 4 shows the color combinations that are advantageous and disadvantageous for people with normal color vision and those with Deuteranope.

6 Summary

This study aims to eliminate the handicap of color perception that people with color vision diversity feel when they play video games. Colors that are easy for people with Deuteranope to discriminate are investigated based on the following hypothesis: The larger the difference in lightness in a combination of colors are, the more accurately and quickly a person with color vision diversity can judge the color difference. Specifically, we used a Deuteranope-simulation filter to convert normal color vision into a Deuteranope view in an experiment. Then, participants selected a different color target among alternatives with and without using the Deuteranope-simulation filter. The experimental results indicate that a combination of colors with different lightness values and saturation but the same hue value are easy to discriminate for people with color vision diversity.

We will examine a technique that controls the advantages and disadvantages between normal color vision and color vision diversity in future work. Specifically, video games should design using easy colors for people with color vision diversity to discriminate. In addition, we think it should be possible to enlighten people with the normal color vision about the differences in color appearance for people with color vision diversity. Moreover, we will find the appropriate correct answer rate and the response time depending on the game type, such as shooting, fighting, puzzle, and so on.

References

1. Esports: https://www.bauhutte.jp/bauhutte-life/e-sports/ (2021). Accessed 23 May 2021
2. Unity: COVID-19's Impact on the Gaming Industry: 19 Takeaways. https://create.unity3d.com/COVID-19s-impact-on-the-gaming-industry (2021). Accessed 23 May 2021
3. Nathans, J., Piantanida, T.P., Eddy, R.L., Shows, T.B., Hogness, D.S.: Molecular genetics of inherited variation in human color vision. Science **232**, 203–210 (1996)
4. Puyo Puyo: https://puyo.sega.jp/portal/index.html (2021). Accessed 19 May 2021

5. Dalton, J.: Extraordinary facts relating to the vision of colours with observations. Memoirs of the Literary and Philosophical Society of Manchester, vol. 5, pp. 28–45 (1798)
6. McIntyre, D.: Colour Blindness: Causes and Effects, Dalton Publishing, vol. 79, no. 8, pp. 476–477 (2002)
7. Okada, M., Ito, K.: Diversity of color vision and barrier-free presentation of color vision, Part 1: Principle of color vision and mechanism of color blindness. Cell Eng. **21**(7), 733–745 (2002)
8. Okada, M., Ito, K.: Diversity of color vision and barrier-free presentation of color vision, Part 2: How does color vision change? Cell Eng. **21**(8), 909–930 (2002)
9. Okada, M., Ito, K.: Diversity of color vision and barrier-free presentation of color vision, Part 3: How to make it easier for everyone to see. Cell Eng. **21**(8), 1080–1104 (2002)
10. CUD Recommended Color Scheme Set Guidebook, 2nd Edition. https://jfly.uni-koeln.de/colorset/CUD_color_set_GuideBook_2018.pdf (2021). Accessed 23 May 2021
11. Fujii, C.: Dissemination and Issues of Color Universal Design, Graduation Thesis. Department of Social and Cultural Systems, School of Sociology, Toyo University (2014)
12. Nakauchi, S., Onouchi, T.: Detection and modification of confusing color combinations for red green dichromats to achieve a color universal design. Color Res. Appl. **24**(3), 203–211 (2008)
13. Brettel, H., Viénot, F., Mollon, J.D.: Computerized simulation of color appearance for dichromats. J. Opt. Soc. Am. A **14**(10), 2647–2655 (1997)
14. Color Oracle: http://colororacle.org/ (2021). Accessed 23 May 2021
15. AdobePhotoshop: https://helpx.adobe.com/jp/photoshop/using/proofing-colors.html (2021). Accessed 23 May 2021
16. Asada, K.: Color vision tools to improve quality of life of people with color vision deficiency. Keio University Graduate School of Media Design Ph.D. thesis (2010)
17. Tanuwidjaja, E., et al.: Chroma: a wearable augmented-reality solution for color blindness. Pervasive Ubiquit. Comput. 799–810 (2014)
18. Ichikawa, M., et al.: Web-page color modification for barrier-free color vision with genetic algorithm. In: Cantú-Paz, E., et al. (eds.) GECCO 2003. LNCS, vol. 2724, pp. 2134–2146. Springer, Heidelberg (2003). https://doi.org/10.1007/3-540-45110-2_109
19. Ichikawa, M., et al.: Preliminary study on color modification for still images to realize barrier-free color vision. In: IEEE Int. Conf. Systems, Man and Cybernetics, vol. 1, pp. 36–41. IEEE Press (2004)
20. Yamanaka, K., Nishiuchi, N., Kusaka, S., Beppu, K.: Establishing web accessibility for people with color vision. JSME **60**(1), 40–47 (2009)
21. Ohta, Y.: History of color vision testing (1). J. Jpn. Soc. Color Sci. **29**(1), 54–63 (2005)

Social Gaming Patterns During a Pandemic Crisis: A Cross-cultural Survey

Aakash Johry[1]([✉]) [iD], Günter Wallner[1,2] [iD], and Regina Bernhaupt[1] [iD]

[1] Eindhoven University of Technology, Eindhoven, The Netherlands
{a.johry,g.wallner,r.bernhaup}@tue.nl
[2] Johannes Kepler University Linz, Linz, Austria

Abstract. Games have shown to play a pivotal role as a source of entertainment and social interaction during the COVID-19 outbreak, allowing development and maintenance of positive relationships.

This empirical study investigates how the social gaming patterns of individuals have changed since the COVID-19 outbreak, especially with their family members and friends. For that purpose we administered a cross-cultural survey of players aged 18 and above from Europe and the Indian sub-continent. Findings showed an overall decrease in social gaming, replaced by more time spend playing alone. There were significant differences between the Indian and European samples in terms of social play patterns, highlighting the role of socio-cultural factors on gaming during the pandemic. Ego-network based analysis of social gaming behavior showed four distinct player profiles.

Keywords: Social gaming · Cultural differences · COVID-19 · Survey

1 Introduction

Human beings are often referred to as social animals and their need for social interaction has been highlighted in research on mental health [30]. This contrasts the situation around the COVID-19 outbreak, when social distancing measures have significantly affected individuals' lifestyle, limiting the possibilities of social interaction. A number of recent studies have warned against the potential health implications due to social distancing and changed lifestyle [1,24]. The emerging mental health challenges have led to an urgent call for international collaboration to tackle the challenges caused by the COVID-19 pandemic [29]. Recent research has posited that technology has a crucial role to play in maintaining social connections with family, friends, and the wider community in times of the current pandemic [16,20].

Virtual social interactions on a daily basis have been recommended along with other healthy lifestyle changes [24]. The World Health Organization has turned its attention towards gaming with a campaign called #PlayApartTogether [21],

© IFIP International Federation for Information Processing 2021
Published by Springer Nature Switzerland AG 2021
J. Baalsrud Hauge et al. (Eds.): ICEC 2021, LNCS 13056, pp. 139–153, 2021.
https://doi.org/10.1007/978-3-030-89394-1_11

noticing the reach and potential of gaming as an alternative for people to connect for leisure socially. There is a growing literature on the strengths of video games to support mental health and well-being, by generating positive affect, positive functioning, and positive social functioning (see, e.g., [11]). As such video gaming environments provide ample opportunities to develop and maintain positive relationships.

The games industry has emerged as a key player in entertainment, with an estimated 2.7 billion players across the globe by the end of 2020, independent of gender, age, and geographical regions [18]. Games offer a social context when played together in the same physical space or remotely. An unprecedented rise in the sale and consumption of digital games during the COVID-19 outbreak has been recorded, as evident in game industry reports and news media [13,18]. However, these statistics do not show whether increase in consumption of digital games is also leading to increased social play or is isolating players from social activities during the time of a pandemic. Researchers have raised concerns related to excessive gaming and called for a more balanced approach, recommending video games that encourage physical activity, social interaction, and collaboration [13,17]. Although the social aspects of gaming are regularly highlighted, there seems to be a lack of information on how people play games socially and how it might have changed since the pandemic outbreak. The present study focuses on games which are played socially with family, friends, and the outside world, and can thus be a medium to develop and maintain 'positive relationships', providing opportunities to share social and emotional support at the time of a pandemic.

Studies have shown that culture also influences social gaming behaviour. Lee and Wohn [14] found that people's culture orientations, measured across vertical and horizontal individualism–collectivism, affected their usage patterns of playing Social Network Games (SNGs), as their expected outcomes were different. Cultural differences have also been observed in gameplay performance in multiplayer online battle arena games [27]. In this paper, we narrow down to two regions – Europe and India – that are culturally distant along the individualism-collectivism dimension [10,25]. Based on empirical data from a cross-cultural survey and by using statistical and ego-network analysis we aim to investigate the following research questions in the context of the ongoing pandemic:

1. How has the COVID-19 outbreak changed the social gaming patterns, especially with family and friends?
2. How do these social gaming patterns vary between India and Europe, representative of different socio-cultural contexts?

The present work aims to contribute to the discourse on social game design and its role in the lifestyle of players during times of crisis.

2   Related Work

The discourse of social gaming within family has been heavily shaped by studies examining intergenerational interactions. Costa and Veloso [5] conducted a literature review on the potential of video games to enhance intergenerational interactions, concluding that *games can foster [them] by contributing to individual well-being, prosocial behaviors, and sharing of knowledge; by enhancing social interactions between different generations toward a communal activity; and by balancing both users' skills and challenges.* De la Hera et al. [9] also reviewed intergenerational digital games reemphasizing their benefits and recommending player-centric and game-centric factors useful for designing these games (such as implementing cooperative competition over purely collaborative or competitive games). However, most of the reviewed papers were case studies focused on games which were specifically designed for the purpose of intergenerational gaming. For instance, *Find It* and *Farmer's Animals* are games that are designed to encourage physical and tangible interaction among family members [8]. Hence, there is room for also looking at the role of off-the-shelf games to promote family and intergenerational interaction. A recent survey [26] included off-the-shelf games and multiple platforms to study the role of video game co-playing on family bonding, however, it specifically looked at the relation between parents and children as co-players. This seems to be consistent with most of the research on intergenerational gaming which targets certain relations such as between grandparents or parents and children, while other family relations such as partners, siblings, etc. have not received the same attention. Postulated recommendations for future research (e.g., [9, 26]) include the use of quantitative studies with more participants and relations while studying family gaming practices.

The social network of co-players is not restricted to just family, but extends to real life friends, internet-only friends, online groups (often referred to as game clans), and even strangers. Eklund [7] investigated social digital gaming habits when playing with family, friends, or strangers in a survey with a Swedish population. She concluded that *the practices and meanings of digital gaming are dependent on the relational status of game companions.* Another key discourse in the domain of social gaming involves focusing on specific genres such as Massively Multiplayer Online Games (MMOs) and SNGs as a case to understanding how individuals play together with the wider social network [4, 28]. However, being of interest to different disciplines in social science, research goes beyond the in-game aspects and also focuses on the impact these games may have on players' lives. For instance, MMO players have been studied by researchers in relation to their gamer identity and online social capital [12], the effect of games on their real-life behaviour [2], and their psycho-social and emotional well-being [3, 31], among others. It is worth noting that sociability in games is not restricted to certain genres such as MMOs but exists in various forms in all types of games, including single-player, two-player, and multiplayer games [22].

Considering that the social constructs of family and friendship are culture dependent, cross-cultural investigation of social gaming and gaming as a leisure activity would be beneficial [7]. Existing research has already shown that usage patterns and performance in social gaming can be influenced by culture [14, 27]. However, existing studies on social gaming have predominantly accounted for the Western context while the Indian sub-continent seems to have received much less attention. Nonetheless, the lifestyle changes caused by the COVID-19 outbreak are unprecedented across the globe and there is scant empirical evidence on the role of games during times of crisis as we face today. Toledo's [23] recent survey seems to be the closest to our work, looking at the shift in motivations and approaches for gaming in a survey with a primarily American population.

The present study aims to extend some of the related work. Firstly, instead of focusing on certain relations such as between grand-parents or parents and their children, we study social gaming patterns with diverse categories of co-players. Secondly, we attempt to include and capture varying play contexts such as remote and co-located play, including a diversity of game types and platforms. Thirdly, we attempt to include the perspective from the Indian sub-continent. Lastly, we aim to address the research gap on how social gaming manifests in times of a pandemic crisis with social distancing measures significantly affecting our lifestyle. This becomes especially relevant, given the various benefits of socialization through games in mitigating some of the negative impacts of COVID-19 for adults [15].

3 Study

We designed a comprehensive English language online survey to capture social gaming patterns of players before and during the COVID-19 outbreak, delving deeper into their social gaming networks. The study uses *gaming partner* as a term to represent co-players or game companions and further differentiates them into categories (i.e. types), as discussed later. The survey was split in different parts. The parts of interest for the investigation presented here included (in the order they were presented): 1) demographics and 2) details about the gaming behaviour with selected gaming partner(s). Apart from the sections, the survey had an introduction page with a description of the purpose of the study, ethical information about data collection and usage, and consent for voluntary participation for respondents above 18 years of age. The length of the survey was dynamic based on the number of gaming partners, as explained further when detailing the parts of the survey below:

Part 1: Demographics. This section collected basic descriptive information of the respondents, including their age, gender, country of residence, employment, household structure, gaming behavior, and gaming partners.

Part 2: Gaming Partner(s). This section probed in more detail about each of the selected gaming partner categories which included different family relations such as parents, partner, siblings, etc. as well as real-life and internet-only friends, virtual gaming groups, and strangers. As such the survey was dynamic in length and would display only the categories of gaming partners selected in Part 1. The questions focused on comparing the gaming patterns with the selected partner(s) before and during the COVID-19 outbreak (e.g., number of co-players, weekly duration of play in hours, enjoyment (on a 10-point scale from 1 = not enjoyable

to 10 = very enjoyable), play style in the sense of being casual or competitive
(on a 10-point scale from 1 = very casual and 10 = very competitive.), living in
same or different households).

The research was approved by the ethics review board of the university. The
online survey was administered through *LimeSurvey* hosted at the university.
Recruitment involved sharing the call for participation using email lists and personal and professional social networks of the researchers (including *Whatsapp*
and *Twitter*), as well as posting the call to gaming related forums such as *Reddit* and *IGN* boards. The call included a link to the survey and a request for
propagating the call further. Thus our sample should be viewed as a convenience
sample followed by snowballing. Participants did not receive any compensation
and the participation was voluntary. Responses were collected during an approximately three week period in late August to early September 2020.

3.1 Participants

After removing incomplete responses, the survey garnered 95 complete responses
in total. Out of these, 12 respondents indicated that they 'do not play games
at all' and 14 respondents indicated that they 'play games alone but not with
others'. The remaining 69 respondents played games with others, of which 15
indicated to only play games with others and not alone. As we are mainly interested in social gaming patterns we will specifically focus on these 69 participants.
Five of these provided erroneous data and were thus excluded as well, yielding
a final sample of $N = 64$.

Of these, 2 were below 20 years of age, 40 between 20 and 29, 12 between 30
and 39, 6 between 40 and 49, 2 between 50 and 59, and 2 between 60 and 65. In
terms of gender, there was an almost even split between males (28) and females
(34), one identified as non-binary and one as cis-genderless male. 29 participants
came from India, 26 from European countries, and 9 from other countries such
as Canada and the US. Due to the very low number of responses from countries
outside Europe and India we dropped these and focused on investigating cultural
differences between Europe ($N = 26$) and India ($N = 29$). Nine participants lived
in single person household, 12 in a two-person, 15 in a three-person, and 19 in
a four-person household. In addition, 6 lived in a five-person household and one
participant each in a six, seven, and 10-person household, respectively.

3.2 Analysis

To understand the effect of the COVID-19 lockdown on social game play, we first
investigated standard statistics for the demographic variables and the administered ratings.

Next, we looked into possible effects of the cultural differences on variables for
social gaming. The following results on cultural differences are thus based on 29
respondents from India and 26 from Europe. In the following, we will use the label
'region' to distinguish between them. Mixed two-way ANOVAs with REGION
(India, Europe) as between-subject and TIME (before, during) as within-subject

variable were calculated for duration, the number of people participants play with, enjoyment, different types of gaming partners, play style, and centrality (a common metric in network analysis, as detailed below).

To investigate how social gaming changed in terms of the formed relationships, we employed ego-network analysis. Ego-networks are commonly used, for instance, in the social sciences to model such social relationships through a graph in order to analyze their structure (see, e.g., [6]). For each participant, we constructed an ego-network with the participant itself being the ego and the indicated gaming partners forming the direct connections (alters). The weight of a tie was defined as the indicated hours of play with the respective type of partner. Each ego-network was built twice, once with the data covering the situation before the onset of COVID-19 and once during it.

Figure 1 (p. 9) shows examples of such networks. For visualization purposes both networks (before and during) were combined into a single one to ease comparisons. The ego is visualized in the center of it and gaming partners where arranged circularly around it. In addition, gaming partners of the same type where merged into a single node with the node size reflecting the number of partners. The thickness of a tie (edge) indicates the number of hours played with the respective type of partner. Black ties correspond to the situation during COVID-19 and gray edges to before it. In addition, nodes were color-coded using a red-to-green color gradient to indicate how enjoyable playing games with a certain kind of gaming partner was perceived on average. Red corresponds to *not enjoyable* and green to *very enjoyable*.

For instance, looking at the top-left ego-network in Fig. 1 we can observe that the participant played with more real-life friends for longer time periods during than before the pandemic (increased node size and edge width). The participant also started to play with his/her siblings and parents. In contrast, the time spent playing with his/her partner and children declined during the pandemic. Enjoyment experienced while playing with different gaming companions was generally high and also was not affected by the crisis. In contrast, the participant with the bottom-right ego-network spent less time playing with all his/her gaming partners (thinner black edges) and also reported a decline in enjoyment when playing with his/her partner and especially real-life friends.

For each network (before and during) we also calculated the node centrality c of the ego based on Opsahl et al.'s measure [19] for weighted networks to include both the degree of the node and the strength of it's connections. For a node i it is given as $c = k_i^{1-\alpha} \cdot s_i^{\alpha}$ where k_i is the degree of node and s_i the sum of weights of the incident edges. α is a tuning parameter which controls the relative importance of the aspects. If $\alpha = 0$, c is equivalent to the degree and if $\alpha = 1$ it is based on tie weights only. We used an α-value of 0.5 in order to weigh both aspects equally, meaning that higher centrality corresponds to participants playing with more people for longer time periods.

Table 1. Average values regarding time spent playing and the time available for recreation (in hours/week) for the complete sample as well as for the European and India subsamples. Numbers in brackets denote standard deviation.

	Complete sample	Europe	India
Hours playing [total, before]	17.67 (16.75)	17.85 (19.58)	18.91 (16.57)
Hours playing [total, during]	17.23 (16.83)	19.65 (19.48)	16.35 (16.62)
Hours playing [solo, before]	4.80 (6.88)	5.50 (8.82)	3.56 (4.97)
Hours playing [solo, during]	8.04 (10.88)	7.80 (11.70)	8.00 (11.57)
Hours playing [social, before]	12.53 (12.24)	12.12 (12.16)	14.69 (13.39)
Hours playing [social, during]	8.36 (9.46)	10.12 (11.04)	7.72 (9.14)

4 Results

4.1 Changes in Social Gaming Styles

With media reporting increased gaming activity around the world during the COVID times, the present study tried to further differentiate between the solo and social gaming activity of the survey respondents. As Table 1 shows participants in our sample spent on average 17.67 h per week (SD = 16.75) playing games. While before COVID-19 on average of 4.8 h (SD = 6.88) were spent playing alone this raised to 8.04 h (SD = 10.88), and social game play – which was 12.53 h per week (SD = 12.24) before – fell to 8.36 h (SD = 9.46). These results seem to be counter-intuitive to the assumption that being in quarantine and socially isolated would have led to an increased playtime with others. It is worth noting that this tendency seen in overall sample is shaped by participants from both India and Europe with varying socio-cultural contexts. These differences are discussed in more detail later in this section.

Next, we compared the number of gaming partners, the different types of gaming partners, hours played, average enjoyment when playing with others, play style, and centrality before and during the COVID-19 outbreak across the whole sample. Paired t-tests only yielded a significant difference at $\alpha = .05$ in terms of centrality, showing a drop from 10.18 (SD = 8.26) to 7.80 (SD = 7.04) during the pandemic. Recall that centrality considers both the number of gaming partners and the time spent playing with them.

To investigate differences between Europe and India, the above listed variables were analyzed individually using mixed two-way ANOVAs with REGION as between-subject variable and TIME as within-subject variable (cf. Table 2).

Results show certain significant differences in social gaming behavior before and during COVID-19 and between India and Europe. There was a significant difference in the number of gaming partners people played with. Participants from Europe reported to gain in number of playing partners, with before on average 8.81 (SD = 6.35) partners to an average of 11.0 (SD = 11.41) during COVID-19. Participants from India indicated the opposite direction with fewer playing partners – dropping from 11.00 (SD = 7.48) to an average of 8.14 (SD = 11.11).

Table 2. Results of mixed two-way ANOVAs with REGION (Europe/India) as between-subject and TIME (before, during COVID) as within-subject variable.

DV	Source	SS	F	p
NUMBER OF GAMING PARTNERS	Region	1.064	0.006	.93
	Time	10.509	0.809	.37
	Interaction	**194.747**	**14.986**	**< .001**
DIFFERENT TYPES OF GAMING PARTNERS	Region	6.836	3.014	.088
	Time	0.000	0.000	1.0
	Interaction	**2.955**	**9.187**	**< .01**
ENJOYMENT	Region	27.246	3.104	.084
	Time	20.641	3.870	.054
	Interaction	11.763	2.206	.143
PLAY STYLE	Region	3.912	0.258	.614
	Time	3.433	1.039	.313
	Interaction	10.237	3.099	.084
HOURS PLAYING	Region	0.230	0.001	.976
	Time	**586.5090**	**30.165**	**< .001**
	Interaction	**169.008**	**8.692**	**< .01**
CENTRALITY $\alpha = 0.5$	Region	0.072	0.001	.980
	Time	**170.096**	**16.365**	**< .001**
	Interaction	**135.464**	**13.033**	**< .001**

$df_1 = 1$, $df_2 = 53$ in all cases, significant results are marked in bold

The type of gaming partners also changed, although to a lesser extent, showing only a tendency. European participants seemed to have more diverse gaming partners, with a raise from 2.65 (SD = 1.06) to 3.00 (SD = 1.17), while in India the effect was reversed with the number of different gaming partners becoming less, declining from 2.48 (SD = 1.06) to 2.17 (SD = 1.26). Results indicate significant interaction effects for both, number of gaming partners ($F(1,53) = 14.99$, $p < .001$) as well as different types of gaming partners ($F(1,53) = 9.19, p < .01$).

Game enjoyment, measured on a subjective rating scale from 1 to 10 (from 1 = not enjoyable to 10 = very enjoyable), showed a tendency that game enjoyment stayed nearly the same for participants from Europe with an average of 8.31 (SD = 2.61) before and an average of 7.97 (SD = 1.31) during the pandemic, while for participants from India social gaming became less enjoyable with the mean dropping from 7.97 (SD = 2.04) to 6.48 (SD = 3.87). There was no significant effect of the quarantine situation on the enjoyment in games for both regions. The same holds true for the style of playing (casual vs. competitive), staying mostly unaltered before and during COVID-19. Casual play style was indicated on a scale from 1 to 10, where 1 was very casual and 10 was very competitive. The play style in Europe on average was 4.6 (SD = 2.38) staying at the same level during the pandemic (M = 4.89, SD = 2.27), in India the play style became

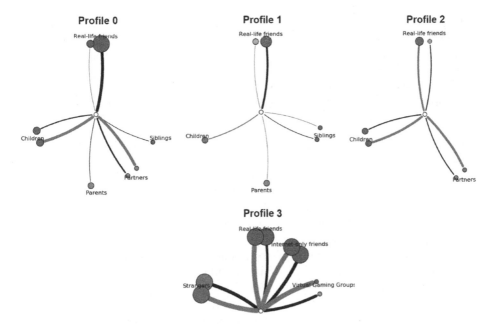

Fig. 1. Examples of ego-networks of participants falling within Profile 0 to 3. The size of a node corresponds to the number of gaming partners of the respective type and edge width reflects the number of hours played together. Black ties are during COVID-19 and gray ones before it. The color of the nodes indicates how enjoyable playing together was (red = not enjoyable, green = very enjoyable). (Color figure online)

less competitive (M = 5.59, SD = 3.48 to M = 4.89, SD = 3.68), although this change was not significant.

Hours spent playing changed significantly before and during the pandemic. While the overall results showed a decrease in social gaming time, these values differed between the European and Indian participants. Europeans indicated to play on average 12.12 h per week (SD = 12.16), which lowered during the pandemic phase to 10.12 (SD = 11.04), while participants from India nearly played 50% less, dropping from an average of 14.69 (SD = 13.39) to 7.72 (SD = 9.15). So, even though the social gaming time reduced for the overall sample, a mixed two-way ANOVA showed no main effect of region. However, the interaction effect between region and time was significant ($F(1,53) = 13.03$, $p < .001$), pointing to a steeper decline for India than Europe.

4.2   Ego-Network Profiles

To develop profiles of social play patterns based on the ego-networks we performed a k-means clustering using the centrality measure as well as the average enjoyment and the number of different types of gaming partners (parents, siblings,...) before and during COVID-19 as input variables. Clustering was performed for $k = 2...20$ and the sum of the squared error (SSE) and silhouette coefficient was calculated for each k. The silhouette coefficient and inspection of the SSE plot for an elbow pointed to a four or five cluster solution. Accounting for interpretability, we opted for the four-cluster solution since the five-cluster solution produced a cluster with a single participant only.

Figure 2 shows how the measures vary over the four identified profiles and Fig. 1 provides examples of ego-networks from each profile. In the following we will describe these in more detail:

Profile 0: Participants in this group show the second highest values in terms of centrality. Together with participants falling within Profile 3 they play with the most different types of gaming partners but compared to Profile 3 the pandemic resulted in a slight increase with which types of gaming partners they play with. They adapt a neither very casual nor very competitive play style which also shifted slightly towards casual during the pandemic. Eight participants fall within this profile.

Profile 1: This profile encompasses participants that show the least social play independent of the onset of the pandemic. While generally the least active, the pandemic had no major influence on the enjoyment and the types of gaming partners they play with. In contrast to the other profiles, the play style developed towards a slightly more competitive one during the pandemic. This cluster forms the largest with 33 participants being assigned to it.

Profile 2: Participants in this group are first and foremost characterized by a large drop in terms of centrality, showing a decline of about 50% in their social gaming activities. Enjoyment also dropped the most across all four clusters to a bit above average. People in this cluster also played with fewer different kinds of family members and friends compared to those in Profile 0 and Profile 3. As participants belonging to Profile 3, people in this group adapted a more casual form of play during than before the pandemic. With 19 participants this is the second largest cluster.

Profile 3: Participants falling within this profile are characterized by the largest centrality values, i.e. they are playing with many people for extended periods of time. Average enjoyment was rather high but declined slightly during the pandemic. They played on average with 3.5 types of gaming partners, which together with participants from Profile 1 is the highest number. Style of play is the most competitive one across the profiles with a small decline in competitiveness during the pandemic. This cluster constitutes the smallest of our sample with only four participants being part of it.

5   Discussion

The present study collected empirical data using a cross-cultural survey to understand the impact of the COVID-19 pandemic on social gaming patterns of individuals. We found differences in the social gaming behaviour of individuals before and during the outbreak with respect to the number and types of gaming partners as well as the time spent playing with them (as also reflected in the centrality measure). Interestingly, these values were noticeably different based on

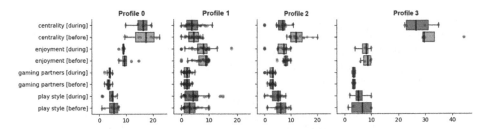

Fig. 2. Variation of features across the four identified clusters.

Table 3. Fraction of different types of gaming partners within the same and different households. Note: Must not sum to one as other options such as 'does not apply' were provided as well.

	Complete sample		Europe		India	
	Before	During	Before	During	Before	During
Different households	0.57	0.50	0.65	0.56	0.54	0.49
Same household	0.25	0.29	0.29	0.31	0.28	0.36

geographical region and culture. In the following we elaborate upon the most interesting insights from the results.

While the overall gaming time for the overall sample remained almost the same, the time spent playing solo almost doubled during the COVID-19 outbreak and the time spent playing socially got reduced by almost the same amount in our sample. This shift in social playing behaviour was more prominent in the Indian sample. It is worth noting that more gaming partners lived in different households than in the same household (cf. Table 3). It is possible that the co-located play opportunities before the pandemic, especially for partners from different households, did not shift to remote play during the pandemic, reflecting in the fall in social gaming. These results are contrary to a recent survey on video game habits during the pandemic, where majority of respondents stated an increase in their overall playing time, especially those motivated by competition and social aspects [23]. However, their study did not differentiate between solo and social playing times and captured a different socio-cultural and geographical context, so it is difficult to compare the findings.

It is possible that playing remotely could have been affected due to changes in lifestyle and daily routine during the pandemic and thus respondents preferred playing solo more. However, this finding can be overshadowed by a variety of processes. For instance, the overall feeling of loneliness of participants due to social distancing measures might have influenced their remembered activity patterns before and during the pandemic. This is always a limitation of studies that ask for behavior in retrospect.

The COVID-19 situation had an impact on both the number and type of social gaming partners, as reflected in the significant decrease in centrality

($\alpha = 0.5$). Perhaps, more surprising was the clear difference in the way the COVID-19 outbreak impacted social play for Indian and European participants. While European participants reported an increase in the number of gaming partners, type of gaming partners, and no difference in game enjoyment, Indian participants showed a significant decrease in the number of gaming partners together with a decrease in the type of gaming partners and game enjoyment. Statistics showed a significant difference in the family size between the respondents from India and Europe in our sample (Europe: M = 3.11, SD = 1.21; India: M = 4.13, SD = 1.60). This could be one of the factors highlighting the different playing contexts between the two regions. However, other factors such as differences in the extent of the pandemic crisis or socio-cultural differences in family and friendship dynamics as well as gaming habits could be influential as well. A follow-up qualitative study would thus help in exploring and explaining these differences further. Yet, our results highlight that social gaming is culturally dependent and it is important to include cultures which are relatively understudied.

The changes in social gaming were further explored by means of ego-networks. Cluster analysis of the ego-network profiles resulted in four distinct types of players. Ego-network based analysis presents an interesting framework to understand social gaming behavior of individual players. It might be useful for game user researchers to use the patterns identified through clusters of ego-networks to inform the design of games in the future.

5.1   Limitations

We used an online survey for data collection because of accessibility and allowing participants to share data anonymously. However, considering the comprehensive nature of the sought information, the survey completion rate was significantly affected. One of the main limitations of the present study is the small sample size and the use of convenience sampling. However, having almost equal responses from the Indian sub-continent and Europe allowed us to present a snapshot of these populations. It is worth acknowledging that due to the small sample size the identified results and directions are indicative in nature, thus requiring further enquiry. Within the limitations of convenience and snowballing sampling, the sample was diverse in age, gender, household structure, family relations, and can thus be viewed as representative of the intended population. Lastly, the survey was conducted using English language which may have introduced a bias in the sample. A follow-up study that compares the during and after pandemic context might be interesting in order to extend the current work.

6   Conclusions

Using a survey for data collection and ego-network analysis, the present study identified how social gaming patterns changed in the time of a pandemic crisis. Overall, it was surprising to see that individuals spent less time for social gaming since the COVID-19 outbreak considering that people might want to compensate their missing social connections through social gaming. However, these insights are tentative and indicative due to the limited sample size. Within these limitations, the findings highlighted that there might be a multitude of factors influencing social gaming patterns, in addition to the rise and fall in number, as generally pointed out by media. For instance, differentiating between co-located and remote social play, as reflected by playing partners living in same or different households, might lead to a more nuanced understanding of social play behavior. The cultural differences seen in social gaming patterns during the pandemic present an interesting direction to explore in the future studies and a follow-up qualitative study would help in understanding the underlying factors that play a role in shaping the social gaming behaviour of people during the pandemic.

References

1. Balanzá-Martínez, V., Atienza-Carbonell, B., Kapczinski, F., De Boni, R.B.: Lifestyle behaviours during the COVID-19 - time to connect. Acta Psychiatr. Scand. **141**(5), 399–400 (2020)
2. Barnett, J., Coulson, M.: Virtually real: a psychological perspective on massively multiplayer online games. Rev. Gen. Psychol. **14**(2), 167–179 (2010)
3. Caplan, S., Williams, D., Yee, N.: Problematic internet use and psychosocial well-being among MMO players. Comput. Hum. Behav. **25**(6), 1312–1319 (2009)
4. Cole, H., Griffiths, M.D.: Social interactions in massively multiplayer online role-playing gamers. Cyberpsychol. Behav. **10**(4), 575–583 (2007)
5. Costa, L., Veloso, A.: Being (grand) players: review of digital games and their potential to enhance intergenerational interactions. J. Intergenerational Relat. **14**(1), 43–59 (2016)
6. Crossley, N., Bellotti, E., Edwards, G., Everett, M.G., Koskinen, J., Tranmer, M.: Social Network Analysis for Ego-Nets: Social Network Analysis for Actor-Centred Networks. Sage (2015)
7. Eklund, L.: Playing video games together with others: differences in gaming with family, friends and strangers. J. Gaming Virtual Worlds **7**(3), 259–277 (2015)
8. Follmer, S., Raffle, H., Go, J., Ballagas, R., Ishii, H.: Video play: playful interactions in video conferencing for long-distance families with young children. In: Proceedings of the 9th International Conference on Interaction Design and Children, New York, NY, USA, pp. 49–58. Association for Computing Machinery (2010)
9. De la Hera, T., Loos, E., Simons, M., Blom, J.: Benefits and factors influencing the design of intergenerational digital games: a systematic literature review. Societies **7**(3), 18 (2017)
10. Hofstede, G.: The cultural relativity of organizational practices and theories. J. Int. Bus. Stud. **14**(2), 75–89 (1983)
11. Jones, C., Scholes, L., Johnson, D., Katsikitis, M., Carras, M.: Gaming well: links between videogames and flourishing mental health. Front. Psychol. **5**, 260 (2014). https://doi.org/10.3389/fpsyg.2014.00260
12. Kaye, L.K., Kowert, R., Quinn, S.: The role of social identity and online social capital on psychosocial outcomes in MMO players. Comput. Hum. Behav. **74**, 215–223 (2017)
13. King, D.L., Delfabbro, P.H., Billieux, J., Potenza, M.N.: Problematic online gaming and the COVID-19 pandemic. J. Behav. Addict. **9**(2), 184–186 (2020)

14. Lee, Y.H., Wohn, D.Y.: Are there cultural differences in how we play? Examining cultural effects on playing social network games. Comput. Hum. Behav. **28**(4), 1307–1314 (2012)
15. Marston, H.R., Kowert, R.: What role can videogames play in the COVID-19 pandemic? Emerald Open Res. **2**(34), 34 (2020)
16. Marston, H.R., Musselwhite, C., Hadley, R.: COVID-19 vs social isolation: the impact technology can have on communities, social connections and citizens (2020). https://ageingissues.wordpress.com/2020/03/18/covid-19-vs-social-isolation-the-impact-technology-can-have-on-communities-social-connections-and-citizens/. Accessed Sept 2020
17. Nagata, J.M., Abdel Magid, H.S., Pettee Gabriel, K.: Screen time for children and adolescents during the coronavirus disease 2019 pandemic. Obesity **28**(9), 1582–1583 (2020)
18. Newzoo, B.: Newzoo global games market report 2020 — light version (2020). https://newzoo.com/insights/trend-reports/newzoo-global-games-market-report-2020-light-version/. Accessed Jan 2021
19. Opsahl, T., Agneessens, F., Skvoretz, J.: Node centrality in weighted networks: generalizing degree and shortest paths. Soc. Netw. **32**(3), 245–251 (2010)
20. Sheerman, L., Marston, H.R., Musselwhite, C., Morgan, D.: COVID-19 and the secret virtual assistants: the social weapons for a state of emergency. Emerald Open Res. **2**(19), 19 (2020)
21. Snider, M.: Video games can be a healthy social pastime during coronavirus pandemic (2020). https://www.usatoday.com/story/tech/gaming/2020/03/28/video-games-whos-prescription-solace-during-coronavirus-pandemic/2932976001/. Accessed Jan 2021
22. Stenros, J., Paavilainen, J., Mäyrä, F.: The many faces of sociability and social play in games. In: Proceedings of the 13th International MindTrek Conference: Everyday Life in the Ubiquitous Era, , New York, NY, USA, pp. 82–89. Association for Computing Machinery (2009)
23. Toledo, M.: Video game habits & COVID-19 (2020). https://papers.ssrn.com/sol3/papers.cfm?abstract_id=3676004 Accessed Sept 2020
24. Venkatesh, A., Edirappuli, S.: Social distancing in COVID-19: what are the mental health implications? BMJ **369**, m1379 (2020)
25. Verma, J., Triandis, H.C.: The measurement of collectivism in India. In: International Congress of the International Association for Cross-Cultural Psychology, 14th August 1998, Western Washington U, Bellingham, WA, US. Swets & Zeitlinger Publishers (1999)
26. Wang, B., Taylor, L., Sun, Q.: Families that play together stay together: investigating family bonding through video games. New Media Soc. **20**(11), 4074–4094 (2018)
27. Wang, H., Xia, B., Chen, Z.: Cultural difference on team performance between Chinese and Americans in multiplayer online battle arena games. In: Rau, P.L.P. (ed.) CCD 2015. LNCS, vol. 9181, pp. 374–383. Springer, Cham (2015). https://doi.org/10.1007/978-3-319-20934-0_35
28. Wohn, D.Y., Lampe, C., Wash, R., Ellison, N., Vitak, J.: The "s" in social network games: initiating, maintaining, and enhancing relationships. In: 2011 44th Hawaii International Conference on System Sciences, Washington, DC, USA, pp. 1–10. IEEE (2011)
29. Xiang, Y.T., Jin, Y., Cheung, T.: Joint international collaboration to combat mental health challenges during the coronavirus disease 2019 pandemic. JAMA Psychiatry **77**(10), 989–990 (2020)

30. Young, S.N.: The neurobiology of human social behaviour: an important but neglected topic. J. Psychiatry Neurosci. JPN **33**(5), 391 (2008)
31. Zhang, F., Kaufman, D.: Massively multiplayer online role-playing games (MMORPGs) and socio-emotional wellbeing. Comput. Hum. Behav. **73**, 451–458 (2017)

A Real-Time Drum-Wise Volume Visualization System for Learning Volume-Balanced Drum Performance

Mitsuki Hosoya[1]([✉]), Masanori Morise[1], Satoshi Nakamura[1], and Kazuyoshi Yoshii[2]

[1] Meiji University, 4-21-1 Nakano, Nakano-ku, Tokyo, Japan
cs202017@meiji.ac.jp

[2] Kyoto University, Yoshida-honmachi, Sakyo-ku, Kyoto-shi, Kyoto, Japan

Abstract. To improve drum performance, it is important to consider the volume balance of the bass drum, snare drum, and hi-hat. However, it is difficult for players to evaluate the balance of each volume of these instruments while playing. In addition, while it is possible to self-diagnose by recording drum performances, it is not always efficient to re-record and re-play drum performances based on the correction points. Therefore, we developed a system that uses semi-supervised non-negative matrix factorization (SSNMF) to separate a player's drum performance, recorded with a unidirectional microphone installed in front of the drum kit, into the bass drum, snare drum, and hi-hat sound sources in real-time, and estimates each volume at the time of beating. In addition, the system also visualizes their volume balance and enables the player to control the power of beating. We experimented using this system for actual drum performance and clarified its usefulness and points for improvement based on the feedback obtained from the experiment participants.

Keywords: Drum performance · Sound source separation · Volume balance

1 Introduction

Drums express rhythm by playing multiple instruments simultaneously. Therefore, to improve one's drumming, in addition to rhythmic accuracy and timbre, it is important to consider the volume balance of the three main instruments: bass drum (BD), snare drum (SD), and hi-hat (HI) (see Fig. 1).

In basic rhythms such as 8-beat and 16-beat, the ideal volume balance for drum performance is generally to play the bass drum, snare drum, and hi-hat in the order of decreasing volume (BD > SD > HI) as perceived by the audience (exceptions are depending on the song and genre). The reason for this is that if the volume of the hi-hat is louder than the other instruments, it may sound like a performance with no intonation, and if the volume of the bass drum is very soft, it may sound like a performance with no stability. Therefore, drummers want to master the ideal volume balance.

© IFIP International Federation for Information Processing 2021
Published by Springer Nature Switzerland AG 2021
J. Baalsrud Hauge et al. (Eds.): ICEC 2021, LNCS 13056, pp. 154–166, 2021.
https://doi.org/10.1007/978-3-030-89394-1_12

When practicing the volume balance of drum performance, drummers who attend drum schools can have their performances listened to objectively by lecture. Still, drummers who practice by themselves, which is a large proportion, cannot listen to their performance objectively, making it difficult to understand the volume balance of their drum performance. Thus, there is a gap of perceived volume balance between a drummer and audiences because audiences listen to drum play a little bit far from the drum (see Fig. 2). Moreover, drummers can check the volume balance independently by recording their performance and checking it, but this method is time-consuming and labor-intensive. In contrast, by practicing with MIDI (electronic) drums, one can check the velocity, which is a numerical value that indicates the intensity of the sound, but this method is not suitable for learning the volume balance because the sensation of beating electronic drums is very different from that of acoustic drums.

In this study, we focused on the problem that drummers do not know the volume balance perceived by the audience during the performance when practicing basic rhythms on acoustic drums. It takes time and effort to check the volume balance. The goal of this research is to develop a system that enables drummers to quickly and efficiently learn the ideal volume balance independently. Therefore, we propose a system that estimates the volume balance of a drum performance by using a unidirectional microphone placed in front of the drum kit with a sound source separation method. In addition, the system visualizes the estimated volume balance in real-time and feeds it back to the drummer (see Fig. 1). We believe our system helps drummers learn the ideal volume balance, as they can learn it quickly by playing while checking the volume balance perceived by the audience.

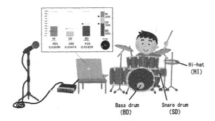

Fig. 1. Assumed system environment.

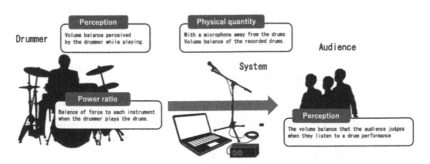

Fig. 2. The volume balance of drum performance in each positon.

The contribution of this paper is to focus on the problem of balance in drum practice and to realize a method for estimating volume balance using source separation and visualizing it in real-time.

2   Related Research

2.1   Support for Practicing Musical Instruments

There have been many studies on support for practicing musical instruments. Smoliar et al. [1] proposed a system that visualizes key strength, tempo, articulations such as staccato and legato, and timing consistency between the right and left hands based on MIDI data of piano performance. Rogers et al. [2] proposed a system that projects a piano roll on a physical keyboard by projection mapping to present the key position. Beici et al. [3] proposed a system that detects and visualizes the piano player's sustain pedal movement. In addition, Marky et al. [4] proposed a system that provides visual guidance via LEDs attached to a fretboard to help guitar players learn chords, scales, and melodies. Doi et al. [5] proposed a system that uses projection mapping to present information on the strings and body of a koto (a Japanese string instrument), such as picking position, picking direction, and symbols representing playing techniques.

As shown in these studies, visualization of performance information is used in various methods to support instrument practice. Since visualization of performance information makes it possible to practice musical instruments while recognizing one's own performance and the performance of one's target, we adopted the method of visualizing the volume balance of drum performance in this study.

As in this study, there have been various studies on assisting the practice of drumming. Ikenoue et al. [6] proposed a system that corrects the control of drumsticks by using a small delayed auditory feedback, and experiments showed that the use of the system could correct playing movements that use the extensor muscles. Holland et al. [7] proposed a haptic bracelet (haptic drum kit) to support the learning of complex drum patterns by presenting vibrations to the drummer from a device worn on both hands and feet. Imada et al. [8] proposed a drum practice support system that utilizes Kinect-based performance motion detection. In a study similar to our own, Iwami et al. [9] proposed a method to visualize and present the variation of sound intensity and tempo of MIDI (electronic) drum performance to users during a performance.

However, these studies have focused on supporting the rhythm and movement of drumming, and few have considered the volume balance of acoustic drums.

2.2   Sound Source Separation Technology

In this study, we use sound source separation to estimate the volume balance of a drum performance in real-time. Source separation is a technique to separate and recognize each sound source from an acoustic signal that contains multiple sound sources. A variety of sound separation methods have been proposed depending on the purpose and conditions. Examples include Universal Sound Separation [10], which separates specific sounds such as animal cries and door creaks to help users distinguish multiple sounds with machines, and Harmonic/Percussive Sound Separation (HPSS) [11], which separates harmonic and percussive sounds of a sound source without using prior knowledge of specific instruments. In addition, an example of the application of sound source separation technology to music is the use of Deep Neural Networks (DNN) [12] to extract vocals from a song [13] and separate them by parts of the song (vocal, bass, drums, etc.) [14].

For sound source separation of drum performances, various methods have utilized Non-negative Matrix Factorization (NMF) [15, 16] and Convolutional Non-negative Matrix Factor Deconvolution (NMFD) [17]. These methods are based on an algorithm for separating sources by decomposing the amplitude spectrum of the source to be separated, which is a single channel (monaural signal), into basis spectra representing the frequency components and activation matrices representing the temporal information corresponding to the individual basis spectra. NMF aims to decompose the magnitude spectrogram of a drum signal into a set of basis spectra corresponding to drum instruments and a set of the corresponding temporal activations. NMFD is a convolutional extension of NMF that uses a set of basis spectrograms for approximating the input mixture spectrogram in a patchwork manner. The main application of such sound source separation for drum performance is automatic music notation, which is the automatic generation of music scores from acoustic signals using a computer, and research to improve the accuracy of music notation is being actively conducted [18–22].

In the studies above, sound source separation for drums was mainly used for automatic music notation and not for estimating the volume balance during drum performance. In the current study, we utilize NMF, which is expected to provide highly accurate separation, as a method for source separation because the basis of the drum instruments to be played can be registered in advance.

3 Proposed Method

3.1 Calculation Procedure

In this study, we aim to estimate the volume balance of drums. Therefore, a drum performance input by a unidirectional microphone is separated into the sounds of each instrument, and the volume of each is estimated. We use the RMS value, which is an index of the sound pressure perceived by a person, calculated from the amplitude of the acoustic signal to calculate the volume. The calculation procedure is as follows.

1. Recognize a drum performance from a unidirectional microphone (see Fig. 3).
2. Separate the sound sources of the drum performance into a hi-hat, snare drum, and bass drum only for each second of the last musical bar (4/4 beat) (see Fig. 4).
3. Detect the onset timing of each separated sound source [23] (see Fig. 5).
4. Calculate the peak (maximum amplitude) from the frames of $t1$ seconds before and after the detected onset, and adopt the peak that exceeds the threshold T as the correct striking timing of each instrument (see Fig. 6).
5. Calculate the RMS value from the $t2$-second frames around each peak, and calculate the average value.

6. Multiply the average RMS values calculated in (5) by the correction values (ω_HI, ω_SD, and ω_BD) to obtain the volume balance that a person feels when listening to a drum performance, and calculate the volume of each instrument.
7. Determine the volume balance as the ratio of the volume of each instrument (6).

Since we felt it would take a certain amount of time for a person to judge the volume balance after listening to a drum performance, we performed the calculation for every frame of the last measure (4/4 beat) in seconds (2). While the peak is a numerical value that indicates the instantaneous loudness of a sound, the RMS value, which is calculated by averaging the energy of a sound, is an index that takes into account a person's perception of sound pressure, so we adopted the RMS value as the volume of each instrument (5). The RMS values were not converted into dB units but were used directly in the calculations. The reason for multiplying the RMS value by a correction value is that there is a difference between the volume balance estimated from the RMS value of the pronunciation timing of each instrument detected and the volume balance felt by a person when listening to a drum performance, and it is necessary to tune it (6).

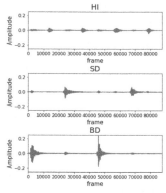

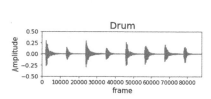

Fig. 3. Waveform of a drum performance input from a microphone.

Fig. 4. Waveform after sound source separation.

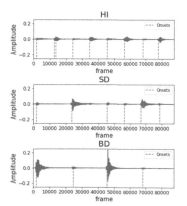

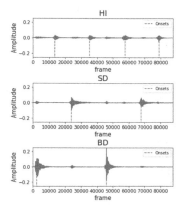

Fig. 5. Detected onsets.

Fig. 6. Timing when the amplitude exceeds the threshold.

3.2   Source Separation Used for Volume Balance Estimation

In this study, SSNMF [24], a source-separation method that can fix the basis spectrum (a matrix representing the frequency components) of the sources separated by NMF, was utilized for volume balance estimation of drum performances. These are algorithms that decompose one non-negative matrix into two non-negative matrices. These methods perform source separation by utilizing the amplitude spectrogram obtained from the speech data, which can be regarded as a non-negative matrix and represented as a product of a basis matrix representing the frequency components and an activation matrix representing the temporal information. In addition, SSNMF is used to deal with the Eigen-differences of the instruments, such as tone and resonance. Utilizing SSNMF enables us to fix the basis in advance, implement the basis created from the recorded sound of the drum instrument used in the system, and deal with the intrinsic difference of the instrument.

The following is a detailed step-by-step description of the method of sound source separation adopted in this study. First, to create the basis for NMF, single notes of the hi-hat, snare drum, and bass drum need to be recorded without clipping (when the input of the recording is too large, the peak of the signal waveform is saturated and collapses at a certain level). The recoded data for each instrument must then be cut out, normalized, and registered in the program. The program then performs a short-time Fourier transform on the recorded data of each instrument and applies NMF to the obtained amplitude spectrogram to get the basis matrix. Then, the sound source of the drum performance recorded from the microphone is subjected to a short-time Fourier transform in real-time, and SSNMF is applied to the obtained amplitude spectrogram with the previously obtained basis of each registered instrument.

In this way, the sound source of the drum performance can be represented in the basis matrix of only the hi-hat, snare drum, and bass drum, and the activation matrix and the sound source separated for each instrument can be obtained by multiplying the basis and the activation matrices of each instrument and then performing the inverse Fourier transform. Then, the sound source of the drum performance recorded from the microphone is subjected to a short-time Fourier transform in real-time, and SSNMF is applied to the obtained amplitude spectrogram with the previously obtained basis of each registered instrument.

4   Proposed System

As stated earlier, the purpose of this study is to help drummers learn the ideal volume balance quickly and efficiently by themselves. Therefore, we developed a system that inputs drum performances from a unidirectional microphone installed in front of the drum kit, extracts only the bass drum, snare drum, and hi-hat by sound source separation, and estimates the volume of each instrument to visualize and present the volume balance of the drum performance to the drummer in real-time. Our assumed usage environment is shown in Fig. 1. A microphone is placed in front of the drum kit, and a PC is placed where the drummer can check the screen while playing. The microphone and PC are connected via an audio interface. The system runs on the PC, estimates the volume balance of the drum performance in real-time, and visualizes the results.

4.1 Implementation

The system was operated on a PC and implemented using Python for the acoustic processing part and Processing for the visualization part. The system visualizes the information shown in Fig. 7. The red, green, and blue bars in the volume balance visualization zone represent the hi-hat, snare drum, and bass drum volume, respectively, estimated in real-time from the drum performance input from the microphone. The volume balance (ratio of each instrument) that the user aims for is set by operating the target volume balance setting bar (right side of the figure). The value of the target volume balance reference bar in the volume balance visualization zone also changes in conjunction with the value of the ratio of each instrument set in the target volume balance setting bar. In addition, the tempo (BPM) setting knob (lower right of the figure) allows the user to adjust the tempo when practicing.

To calculate the volume balance estimation described in Sect. 3.1, we set $t1 = 0.15$ and $T = 0.8$ so as to recognize the correct striking timing of each instrument. Since the time constant of the Fast characteristic (JIS C 1509-1 [25]) in the measurement of noise in the sound level meter is 125 ms, we set $t2 = 0.125$. The correction values, ω_HI, ω_SD, and ω_BD, were set subjectively in this study in order to bring the volume balance calculated by the RMS values closer to the volume balance perceived by a person when listening to a drum performance. Specifically, we set $\omega\_HI = 5$, $\omega\_SD = 1$, and $\omega\_BD = 0.8$ (5 times for hi-hat and 0.8 times for bass drum), as the waveform of the hi-hat was quite small, and the input waveform of the bass drum was rather large due to recording via the audio interface.

4.2 Usage

The procedure for using the system is described below. First, a user sets up a unidirectional microphone in front of the drum kit and places the PC's position to check the display easily (see Fig. 1). Next, the user starts the system on the PC and sets the volume balance of the drum performance (hi-hat, snare drum, bass drum) and the tempo of the performance. Next, the user starts drumming and plays while watching the system screen (see Fig. 7), where the visualization of the volume balance is updated every second for one musical bar in 4/4 beat (this will vary depending on the tempo that is set, which is 4 s for BPM 60). The reason for this frequency of updates is because we thought it would take some time for people to judge the volume balance after listening to a drum performance. In Fig. 7, the red bar indicating the volume of the hi-hat is higher than the target volume balance setting bar, indicating that the volume of the hi-hat is higher than the target volume balance set by the user. Therefore, by modifying the performance to hit the hi-hat volume of the drum performance at a lower level, it is possible to play the drums at a volume balance close to the intended target.

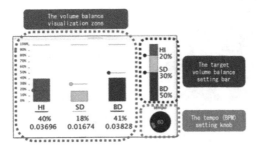

Fig. 7. Screenshot of our system (Color figure online).

5 Experiment

To investigate whether drummers can quickly and efficiently learn the ideal volume balance using the proposed system, and to obtain feedback on its usage, we conducted an experiment in which participants played acoustic drums while using the system (see Fig. 8). The experiment participants were four males in their 20s who had been playing the drums for more than five years and wanted to improve their volume balance.

In preparation for the experiment, we set up the system and equipment (PC, microphone, and audio interface) and created the basis for each drum instrument (HI, SD, and BD) to be used for sound source separation. In creating the basis, we instructed the participants to record one note for each instrument struck at a normal volume (left to the discretion of the participants). Then, we completed the preparation of the basis by performing onset trimming, normalization, and NMF of the recorded sound source of each instrument and registering the basis to the program.

After the preparation was completed, we instructed the usage of the prototype system and the experiment. Then, we asked participants to set a goal for the volume balance and to play the music with a backing 8-beat rhythm. The backing 8-beat rhythm is based on eighth notes and can be played without the timing of the notes of each instrument overlapping (see Fig. 9). Since we wanted to investigate the system's usefulness rather than its accuracy, we limited our experiments to the backing 8-beat, which we judged to be easy to separate from the sound source. After that, we asked the participants to set a target volume balance using the system and to try their drum performance closer to the target volume balance while watching the visualization of the volume balance presented by the system.

During the experiment, we made recordings. When the participants judged that they were able to play at the target volume balance, we asked them to stop using the system and then listen to the recording to judge whether they could play at the target volume balance. After completion of the task, we administered a questionnaire to the participants and interviewed them. The specific questions are shown in Table 1.

Fig. 8. Scene of the experiment.

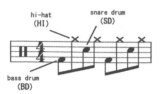

Fig. 9. Sheet music for backing 8-beat.

Table 1. Questionnaire items.

	Question	Answer method
Q1	How satisfied were you with the system?	5-pt evaluation (-2 to $+2$)
Q2	Would you want to use the system in the future?	5-pt evaluation (-2 to $+2$)
Q3	Were you able to perform at the set volume balance?	5-pt evaluation (-2 to $+2$)
Q4	What are your thoughts on using the system?	Free answer

6   Results and Discussions

The average evaluation values were 0.75 for Q1 "How satisfied were you with the system?", 1 for Q2 "Would you want to use the system in the future?", and 1.25 for Q3 "Were you able to perform at the set volume balance?".

The average of the evaluation values from Q1 to Q3 were all positive, indicating that the participants' impression of the system was not bad.

Table 2 and Table 3 list the responses to Q4 "Thoughts on using the system." Table 2 shows favorable opinions, and Table 3 shows comments for improvement. An over-all favorable opinion of the system was obtained in Q4, suggesting that the proposed method can support the acquisition of volume balance in drum performance. However, as indicated by the feedback we received in Q4, several points about the system need to be improved. We will discuss them as follows.

The current system switches the visualization of the estimated volume balance every time it finishes the calculation for about one measure of drum performance, which means its real-time performance is lost to an extent. In addition, since the volume balance of the drum performance is displayed as a percentage of the overall volume, users had difficulty understanding the visualization. Therefore, in the future, we will consider a line graph type visualization method that allows the user to check how the volume of each instrument has been changing. It also became clear that the accuracy of the volume balance estimation was not sufficient. This was because the tuning of the volume balance of the drum performance, which was estimated based on the average of the RMS values of each instrument calculated by the sound source separation, and the volume balance of the drum performance judged by a person listening to the drum performance, was done based on the subjective judgment of the first author. Therefore, in the future, we plan to conduct experiments in which we ask people to judge the volume balance after listening to drum performances with various volume balances, and to review the method of estimating the volume balance perceived by the audience. In addition, the first author recorded, cut out, normalized, and registered the basis of each instrument used in the sound source separation into the program before using the system. Still, we believe the system can be made more efficient by incorporating these tasks into the system itself.

Table 2. Favorable opinions about the system from responses to Q4.

Classification	Answer
Volume balance estimation accuracy	I thought it was great that the volume of the performance was reflected in the results
	I deliberately played louder or softer, and it was reflected in the results
	I intentionally changed the volume balance, and the result was reflected immediately
Impressions	I was able to analyze my performance objectively, which was helpful
	I was able to check my volume balance with concrete figures and graphs
	It was good to be able to check my volume balance with objective numbers
	It was good to know that an instrument was relatively loud or quiet
	It was good practice to be aware of the volume balance while paying attention to the tempo
	I thought it was important to be aware of the volume balance

Table 3. Opinions about improvements to the system from responses to Q4.

Classification	Answer
Volume balance estimation accuracy	When I hit the snare hard, I felt it was not reflected in the result
	I felt that the bass drum was perceived as louder than it was
	The results were roughly linked to my performance, but I felt they were not linked when I made detailed changes
	There were times when the display went to 0% while I was playing
	There were times when the displayed results of SD and BD were confusing
	I felt that the results were affected by the tone
	I felt that the accuracy of the results decreased when the tempo was made faster
How to visualize volume balance	I want to check the volume of each instrument, not the percentage
	It was difficult to see when the results of the previous performance were displayed, so I would like the timing to switch to the beginning of a measure
	When the results of a performance from a few seconds ago are fed back, they may differ from the current performance results, so I would like a more real-time feel

(*continued*)

Table 3. (*continued*)

Classification	Answer
UI	I would like to be able to freely input the ratio of the target volume balance setting
	The value of the BPM change knob could not be set smoothly when using the mouse, so it would be better if it could be controlled with the arrow keys
General impressions	It was difficult to adjust the performance volume while being aware of the metronome's tempo and watching the visualization
	If you are not familiar with the system, it would be difficult to understand how much of a change in performance would be reflected in the volume balance display
	Since I often play Japanese rock music, I would like to use the system more if it could support open hi-hat and fast tunes
	I want to use it while playing in a band (with other instruments)

7 Conclusion

In this study, we focused on the problem that when practicing basic rhythms on acoustic drums, drummers do not know the volume balance perceived by the audience during the performance, and that it takes time and effort to check the volume balance. We proposed and implemented a system that separates drum performances recorded with unidirectional microphones installed in front of the drum kit into bass drum, snare drum, and hi-hat sound sources in real-time, which estimates the volume at the time of striking, and presents the results to the user in a visual form. We then conducted an experiment to obtain feedback from drummers who used the system.

The results showed that the proposed system has the potential to help drummers learn the target volume balance quickly and efficiently. There are also many areas for improvement regarding the method of visualizing the volume balance and the accuracy of the volume balance estimation. In future work, we will improve the system based on the feedback obtained from this experiment.

References

1. Smoliar, S., Waterworth, J., Kellock, P.: PianoFORTE: a system for piano education beyond notation literacy. In: Proceedings of the 3rd ACM International Conference on Multimedia, pp. 457–465 (1995)
2. Rogers, K., et al.: P.I.A.N.O.: Faster piano learning with interactive projection. Proceedings of the 9th ACM International Conference on Interactive Tabletops and Surfaces, pp. 149–158 (2014)
3. Beici, L., György, F., Mark, S.: Measurement, recognition, and visualization of piano pedaling gestures and techniques. J. Audio Eng. Soc. **66**(6), 448–456 (2018)

4. Marky, K., Weiß, A., Müller, F., Schmitz, M., Mühlhäuser, M., Kosch, T.: Let's frets! Mastering guitar playing with capacitive sensing and visual guidance. In: Extended Abstracts of the 2021 CHI Conference on Human Factors in Computing Systems, vol. 169, pp. 1–4. New York, NY, USA (2021)
5. Doi, M., Miyashita, H.: Koto learning support method considering articulations. In: Cheok, A.D., Inami, M., Romão, T. (eds.) ACE 2017. LNCS, vol. 10714, pp. 368–383. Springer, Cham (2018). https://doi.org/10.1007/978-3-319-76270-8_26
6. Nishimoto, K., Ikenoue, A., Unoki, M.: iDAF-drum: supporting practice of drumstick control by exploiting insignificantly delayed auditory feedback. In: Kunifuji, S., Papadopoulos, G.A., Skulimowski, A.M.J., Kacprzyk, J. (eds.) Knowledge, Information and Creativity Support Systems. AISC, vol. 416, pp. 483–497. Springer, Cham (2016). https://doi.org/10.1007/978-3-319-27478-2_36
7. Holland, S., Bouwer, A. J., Dalgelish, M., Hurtig, T.M.: Feeling the beat where it counts: fostering multi-limb rhythm skills with the haptic drum kit. In: Proceedings of the 4th International Conference on Tangible and Embedded Interaction, pp. 21–28 (2010)
8. Imada, Y., Ochi, Y.: Hitting arm detection for drum performance learning system using kinect. In: The Seventh International Conference on Informatics and Applications (ICIA2018), pp. 8–10 (2018)
9. Iwami, N., Miura, M.: A support system for basic practice of playing the drums. In: International Computer Music Conference, pp. 364–367 (2007)
10. Kavalerov, I., et al.: Universal sound separation. In: IEEE Workshop on Applications of Signal Processing to Audio and Acoustics (WASPAA), pp. 175–179 (2019)
11. Ono, N., et al.: Harmonic and Percussive Sound Separation and its Application to MIR-related Tasks. In: Raś, Z.W., Wieczorkowska, A.A. (eds.) Advances in Music Information Retrieval, pp. 213–236. Springer Berlin Heidelberg, Berlin, Heidelberg (2010). https://doi.org/10.1007/978-3-642-11674-2_10
12. Grais, E.M., Sen, M.U., Erdogan, H.: Deep neural networks for single channel source separation. In: ICASSP, pp. 3734–3738 (2014)
13. Hennequin, R., Khlif, A., Voituret, F., Manuel, M.: Spleeter: a fast and efficient music source separation tool with pre-trained models. J. Open Source Softw. 5(50), 2154 (2020)
14. Stöter, F.R., Uhlich, S., Liutkus, A., Mitsufuji, Y.: Open-Unmix – a reference implementation for music source separation. J. Open Source Softw. 4(41), 1667 (2019)
15. Lee, D.D., Seung, H.S.: Learning the parts of objects with non-negative matrix factorization. Nature 401, 788–791 (1999)
16. Cichocki, A., Zdunek, R., Phan, A.H., Amari, S.: Non-negative Matrix and Tensor Factorizations: Applications to Exploratory Multi-way Data Analysis and Blind Source Separation. Wiley, New York (2009)
17. Smaragdis, P.: Non-negative matrix factor deconvolution; extraction of multiple sound sources from monophonic inputs. In: Puntonet, C.G., Prieto, A. (eds.) ICA 2004. LNCS, vol. 3195, pp. 494–499. Springer, Heidelberg (2004). https://doi.org/10.1007/978-3-540-30110-3_63
18. Ueda, S., Shibata, K., Wada, Y., Nishikimi, R., Nakamura, E., Yoshii, K.: Bayesian drum transcription based on non-negative matrix factor decomposition with a deep score prior. In: ICASSP, pp. 456–460 (2019)
19. Paulus, J., Virtanen, T.: Drum transcription with non-negative spectrogram factorisation. In: European Signal Processing Conference (EUSIPCO) (2005)
20. Dittmar, C., Gärtner, D.: Real-time transcription and separation of drum recordings based on NMF decomposition. In: International Conference on Digital Audio Effects (DAFX), pp. 187–194 (2014)
21. Wu, C., Lerch, A.: Drum transcription using partially fixed non-negative matrix factorization with template adaptation. In: International Society for Music Information Retrieval Conference (ISMIR), pp. 257–263 (2015)

22. Vogl, R., Widmer, G., Knees, P.: Towards multi-instrument drum transcription. In: Proceedings of the 21st International Conference on Digital Audio Effects (DAFx-18) (2018)
23. Böck, S., Widmer, G.: Maximum filter vibrato suppression for onset detection. In: International Conference on Digital Audio Effects (DAFX) (2013)
24. Lee, H., Yoo, J., Choi, S.: Semi-supervised non-negative matrix factorization. IEEE Signal Process. Lett. **17**(1), 4–7 (2010)
25. C 1509-1:2017 (IEC 61672-1:2013). http://kikakurui.com/c1/C1509-1-2017-01.html (2021). Accessed 26 July 2021

Speech Recognition Game Interface to Increase Intimacy with Characters

Saki Anzai[✉], Tokio Ogawa, and Junichi Hoshino

University of Tsukuba, Ibaraki, Japan
{ogawa.tokio,jhoshino}@esys.tsukuba.ac.jp

Abstract. Although the number of games using speech recognition has increased in recent years, psychological effects such as intimacy with screen characters when using voice dialogue have not been clarified. We particularly focused on games that allow users to talk with characters relatively freely, and thought that the intimacy with the interactive partner is related to the enjoyment of the conversation and the game as a whole. In this paper, we selected a game interface that employs voice dialogue in combination with keyboard operation used in conventional games and compared the differences in the overall enjoyment and immersion in the game due to the differences in intimacy with the characters. As a result, we were able to show that the intimacy with the characters and the enjoyment and immersion of the game increased. Finally, a discussion on the type of interface that actually influenced the degree of intimacy and enjoyment while playing the game is given.

Keywords: Game · Speech recognition · Dialogue · Intimacy

1 Introduction

In recent years, the number of games using speech recognition has increased. There are various forms of gaming, such as a strategy game that uses voice to give instructions to screen characters to fight or an adventure game that captures the characters within the confines of a dungeon while chanting spells. Many related studies have been conducted, and the contents are various, such as the influence of the introduction of speech recognition on playing games and the analysis of the form of speech input in games. However, psychological effects such as intimacy with the screen characters when using voice dialogue have not been clarified. Especially in games where dialogue with the character is an important factor, we suppose that the intimacy with the character of the dialogue partner is closely related to the fun and immersive feeling of the game itself. If the player has a sense of intimacy with the screen character like a friend, the conversation will be more enjoyable and the overall enjoyment of the game will be enhanced. As a result, we focused on speech recognition and intimacy with the screen characters. The term "intimacy" described here refers to that which is gained in the process of interacting with a partner in a mutual relationship. It is different from "familiarity," which

© IFIP International Federation for Information Processing 2021
Published by Springer Nature Switzerland AG 2021
J. Baalsrud Hauge et al. (Eds.): ICEC 2021, LNCS 13056, pp. 167–180, 2021.
https://doi.org/10.1007/978-3-030-89394-1_13

is derived from first impressions of another person or similarity to oneself, or "attachment," which is felt toward a pet. In a previous study, Ikeda stated that the more intimate the relationship, the more we establish a sense of unity through an emotionally mutual relationship with another person [5]. Emotionally mutual relationships include "shared volition," in which we work together toward the same goal, and "shared emotions," in which we share our feelings with each other. Finally, we arrive at the "mutual relationship" of being together with an irreplaceable friend. In this paper, our primary focus is the development of intimacy in mutual relationships between human identification with animated screen character interaction within the context of the gaming experience.

Bickmore (2005) created a conversational agent with memory retention and gesture functions and tried to operate it as an exercise promotion assistant [9]. As a result, users developed a favorable impression of the agent and increased their desire to continue using the agent. The results also show that a favorable relationship with the interaction partner has a significant impact on the outcomes of various tasks. This shows that a favorable relationship with the interaction partner has a positive impact on engagement, but it does not address fun and immersion. In addition, it is not clear what kind of detailed conversations are useful in games or how to increase the level of intimacy.

To compare the difference in input method of dialogue in the game, we realized a multi-modal game interface that combines voice dialogue with the operation by the keyboard used in the conventional game and compared the influence on the intimacy with the character of the game with the conventional game.

2   Related Works

2.1   Voice Dialogue Interaction

Allison (2018) analyzes how voice input is used in games and summarized the results [1]. He investigated the inputs that affect the state of the game, and analyzed them in six major categories: "story composition," "dialogue structure," "selection," "navigation," "control," and "performance." He subdivided them further and defined 25 design patterns. Carter (2015) studied the relationship between the concept of player-avatar identity and game success in the introduction of voice interaction [2]. By effectively using voice, it is possible to think of one's own character and oneself in the game in an overlapping manner, and it is considered that the immersive experience in the game will be improved. Allison (2019) analyzed the impact of speech recognition on playing games in terms of social experience [3]. Emotions such as embarrassment and incongruity often occur in gamelan by voice operation, but the player's anxiety can be alleviated by clearly communicating the purpose of the voice command. It is also stated that by using voice, people can feel a sense of unity with their own character in the game.

2.2   A Subsection Sample

Intimacy is being studied in the field of social psychology. Nishida (1992) shows that it is easy to have a favorable impression such as friendliness to an interlocutor who seems to be aware of a specific conversation strategy [4]. Conversation strategies include "acceptance strategies" and "interactive dialogue strategies." For example, it includes situations such as actively listening to the other party's remarks and feeling that they are considering their own utterances or trying to make the other party understand their own remarks.

According to Ikeda (2013), there is a strong relationship between sharing style and intimacy between friends [5]. It can be classified into six sharing styles, namely, "sharing relationships," "sharing places," "sharing feelings," "sharing intentions," "sharing goods," and "sharing sensibilities." For example, "sharing feelings" includes items such as "sharing each other's pain" and "encouraging each other." It is said that these shared styles will become more pronounced among friends as intimacy increases. There are many studies that can be used as a reference for conversations with screen characters, but it does not touch on the content of the utterances on the player side, and it is not clear whether these rules work within the context of voice dialogue in the game. In addition, no research has been conducted on what kind of conversation specifically affects the increase in intimacy.

3   System Overview

We designed game interface used to compare with conventional games, to have smooth voice dialogue with characters, and to measure the increase in intimacy experienced during the gaming event. The following four system requirements are listed:

1) The system must have an in-game environment similar to that of a conventional game.
2) The system can accurately recognize the player's voice.
3) The system can interact with the characters in the game.
4) The system can have conversations that encourage increased intimacy.

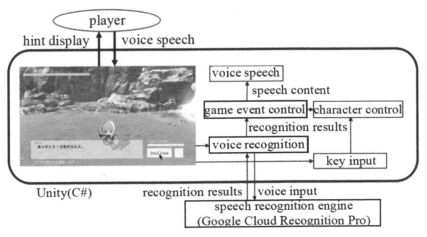

Fig. 1. System configuration diagram

In this research, in order to verify the change in intimacy between the player and the character by voice dialogue, we created an adventure game that can be played in about 10 to 15 min, which makes it easy to give the player a purpose (Fig. 1).

We used Unity to create the game and Google Cloud Speech Recognition for speech recognition. In conventional works that use speech recognition, there are many formats in which instructions are sent to the character on the screen from a bird's-eye view, but in this system, in order to compose a conversation that enhances intimacy, we placed the player and the screen character on equal footing in the same field. This not only allows the player to unilaterally help the character but also enables two-way communication between the player and the character. It is expected that intimacy can be increased by aiming for the goal while creating a form of mutual help in which the character responds when consulted by the player, assisting the character by turning around and answering when calling by name, etc. Also, in this game, not only are conversations related to the progress of the game, but also simple chats and conversations such as "Thank you" or "Hold on" are possible (Table 1). A guide is displayed so that the player does not get lost in the game's progress, but basically the player follows along and converses in the player's own words. Chit-chat is not in the guide, so it is something that the player must think about and say on their own. The character picks up keywords from the player's speech and responds. By following the guide, you can avoid most situations where the character is unable to respond.

Table 1. Example of speech conversations

	Player's question	Character's response
Discussing our next move	What do I have to do?	Let's try to kill one of the enemies in front of us! Let's go for it!
	Where are we going?	I don't know. Let's go through the tunnel first
	Where's the ocean?	It's on your right. Let's go there!
Chatting and encouraging each other	Thank you	You're welcome!
	Let's go	Let's go!
	Awesome	Thank you!
	What's your favorite drink?	Milk! I'm gonna grow taller!

4   Composition of Game Content

4.1   Scenario

In this adventure game, the player collaborates with the screen characters to solve problems and aim for the goal. At that time, in addition to operations such as movement and attack by keyboard, which is used in conventional games, dialogue by speech recognition is used. The game is cleared by the player talking to the screen character by voice, assisting by recovery magic and sometimes solving the problem while consulting about the next action (Fig. 2).

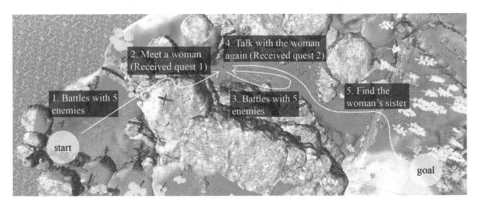

Fig. 2. Evaluation game map and event layout.

4.2   Characters

The main character (dialogue partner) is a boy named Kite (Fig. 3) The player is a girl Win who travels with Kite (Fig. 4). The game screen is Win's field of view, and she interacts with Kite and assists with his name call and recovery (Fig. 5).

Fig. 3. A boy named Kite. The player can have voice conversations with Kite.

Fig. 4. The player is a girl named Win. The relationship between Win and Kite is that of a companion on a journey together.

Fig. 5. The player is in a position to chase after Kite. Since the game screen is Win's view, only Kite appears on the screen.

4.3 Game Screen Configuration

The game screen consists of the response of the main character, Kite, the display of speech recognition result, the physical strength gauge and the time limit (Fig. 6). Since it is difficult to detect the end of a player's utterance with this system, we decided to have the player press the Send Voice button when the utterance ends. The game is over when Kite's physical strength gauge on the upper left of the screen reaches 0, but this time it is set so that the physical strength does not decrease beyond a certain level due to the experiment. Additionally, Win does not appear in the screen because the game screen is from Win's perspective.

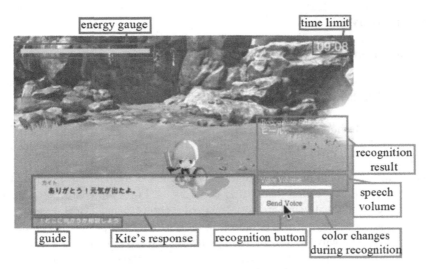

Fig. 6. Game screen configuration

4.4 Event

The first straight road after starting the game is a tutorial. It is possible to learn how to attack and rotate the line of sight and to learn how to cast recovery magic by talking to Kite. When you defeat the two enemies along the way, a woman wearing a brown hood appears and is presented with the task, "I want you to defeat the monsters that gather at the end of the road." If you defeat five enemies and talk to them again, you will be presented with the second task, "I want you to find my sister." If you find the sister wearing a red hood and talk to her, all the tasks will be completed, and the game will end.

4.5 Improvement of the Interface Through Preliminary Experiments

We conducted a preliminary experiment with the help of two university students. In the pre-experiment, we prepared a room for the experiment and recorded them playing the game. After playing the game, the students were asked to write freely about their impressions of the conversation with Kite, the game operation, and other comments. As a result, the following comments were raised: "Sometimes I did not know what to say," "I did not know when to say something," "The lag until the voice is recognized may make the user feel uneasy," and "I feel a little embarrassed to talk when I am being watched." Based on these opinions, we added guides and tutorials to make it easier for users to know what to say, improved the UI so that users can check whether speech recognition is in progress, and exported the game so that users can download it at home to prevent distractions from the surrounding environment interfering with playing the game.

Additionally, we improved the game so that users can look around because they could not rotate their eyes at the time of the preliminary experiment. We also made other adjustments, including fixing minor bugs.

5   User Study

5.1   Experiment 1

An experiment was conducted to verify whether there is a change in the degree of intimacy with a character in a game when speech recognition is used.

Experimental Method

We had a total of 14 participants, 10 male university students and 4 female university students.

This experiment will be referred to as Experiment 1 below. We have prepared two types of games, a text version (hereinafter text version, Fig. 7) in which conversations assuming a conventional game are performed in a choice manner, and a game using voice (hereinafter voice version) produced this time, and each person downloads and plays it. The reason why we did not use a game with free-typing text as a comparison target is that many conventional conversation games use choices for conversation, and we wanted to compare our results with those.

Fig. 7. Game screen of the text version

Half of them, that is, seven people, experienced it in the order of text version → audio version, and the other half experienced it in the reverse order. After each experience, they answered the questionnaire.

The questionnaire adopted a 7-level Likert scale. The smaller number is "not applicable," and the answer is "applicable" when approaching 7. It consists of 10 items about intimacy and 8 items about the game system (Table 2). For question numbers 1–4 to 1–10, refer to previous research on intimacy and sharing styles, and ask questions about sharing of places, sharing of intentions, sharing of feelings, and sharing of relationships, excluding sharing of characteristics (Ikeda, 2013) [5]. Regarding the expression of the question, we referred to seven items about empathy of Kort (2007) [6]. For each of the eight items regarding the gaming system, the reasons for evaluation were voluntarily solicited. Therefore, we solicited comprehensive comments on intimacy and game system in a free-form format. We asked them to answer the first impression of Kite, the impression after playing, and the conversation that left an impression.

Table 2. Questionnaire result table

	question	number of subjects who rated each higher than the other	
		voice	text
1-1	I felt the friendliness with Kite	12	1
1-2	I felt closer than when I started	10	2
1-3	It was fun to have a dialogue	12	1
1-4	I felt that I was working together for the same activity	7	1
1-5	I felt like I was heading towards the same goal	5	1
1-6	I felt Kite and I were encouraging each other	10	2
1-7	When Kite was pleased, I was pleased	8	1
1-8	I played while thinking about the feelings of Kite	9	0
1-9	I shared emotions with Kite	11	1
1-10	I trusted Kite	7	2
2-1	Fun	7	2
2-2	I got hooked on the game	7	2
2-3	I forgot the time while playing	7	3
2-4	It was rewarding	5	2
2-5	There was a sense of accomplishment	9	0
2-6	Ease of operation	1	5
2-7	Easy to understand	1	7
2-8	Novelty and progressiveness of the game	12	0
2-9	Speech recognition accuracy (voice version only)		

Results and Discussion

This is the result of the questionnaire conducted in this experiment (Table 2). In the audio version and the text version, one score was given to each question with the higher score given by each individual, and the total score was shown. In general, the voice version scored higher, while question numbers 2–7 and 2–8 were higher in the text version.

The following figure is a box-and-whisker diagram of the results of Experiment 1 (Fig. 8). We can visually see that the scores of the audio version are higher than those of the text version for most of the questions.

We have considered the results in comparison with the Wilcoxon Signed-Rank test (Table 3). Questions that showed a significant difference depending on the p value are shown in light gray. As an exception, for question 1–2, whose result depends on whether or not the game was cleared, there is a difference in superiority when the test was performed by excluding the data of one subject who could not clear only the audio version. The voice version has a higher score (shown at the bottom of Table 3).

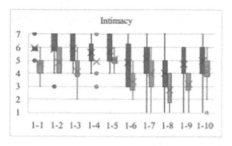
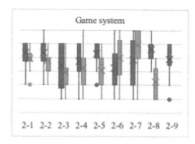

Fig. 8. Box-and-whisker diagram showing the results of Experiment 1

Table 3. Result of t-test analysis (p value)

question	average value		P value	question	average value		P value
	Voice	Text			Voice	Text	
1-1	5.929	4.714	0.003	2-1	5.357	4.929	0.199
1-2	5.857	4.857	※0.086	2-2	5.357	4.786	0.07
1-3	5.929	4.143	0.006	2-3	4.429	3.929	0.214
1-4	5.643	4.929	0.026	2-4	4.714	4.214	0.121
1-5	5.714	5.071	0.071	2-5	5.286	4.071	0.007
1-6	4.857	3.357	0.011	2-6	4.214	5	0.031
1-7	5.071	4	0.016	2-7	4.857	5.929	0.028
1-8	4	2.714	0.006	2-8	5.643	3.286	0.002
1-9	4.714	3.143	0.002	2-9	4.929		
1-10	5	4.143	0.046				
※0.016							

As a result, the voice-based input method made the screen characters more familiar than did the text-based method, and the intimacy increased throughout the gameplay. Also, the dialogue has improved the fun during the gaming experience. In case of the text version, there are negative opinions such as "I felt that the degree of familiarity with Kite and the degree of sharing of emotions decreased because I could talk smoothly and without thinking because I could talk with just a button."

Hence, there was a tendency for the feeling of cooperation and encouraging each other to be strengthened to complete the same task and thinking more about Kite's feelings and share feelings such as fun. We can see that the process of cooperation in the game generated a "mutual relationship" as friends. However, there was no significant difference on the question: "I felt I was moving towards the same goal." Since the final goal is not clearly shown and one of the causes is that it was not incorporated into the conversation, it is possible to devise a scenario with conversational content as an improvement plan. Mentioned in the paragraph below, the introduction of voice recognition may have affected this result by making the operation more difficult or confusing.

Regarding the gaming system, there was no significant difference between the voice version and the text version in questions 2–1 to 2–4. According to the free-text comments, there was an opinion that the voice version seemed to be really talking to the character and was more interesting than the text version, which had many opinions that the tempo was good, but it was monotonous and felt like work. On the other hand, there was an opinion that the time lag in speech recognition hindered smooth conversation. Regarding speech recognition, the delay may increase depending on the network environment, and it was determined that improvement is necessary. There is a suggestion for improvement: either have the game played in a place with as good of a network environment as possible or switch to a voice recognition system that does not require a network environment. In addition, it is difficult to understand the important parts of the operation just by reading the instruction manual before playing, and to improve the method is to devise the UI and operation explanation. Specifically, for example, it is difficult to know when to speak because they do not know if they are in the middle of speech recognition or not, and sometimes, it is hard to come up with something to say. Based on the results of preliminary experiments, we implemented a user interface where the color of the displayed figure changes during speech recognition, but that was not enough. Since some users did not know what the figure represented, it was necessary to clearly state in text that recognition was in progress.

There are individual differences in the level of understanding of the operations described above, time lag and accuracy of voice recognition, so there are people who give a score as low as 1, as shown in the box-beard diagram.

Regarding the sense of accomplishment and the novelty of the game, the voice version scored higher, showing a difference in superiority. There were opinions such as "I felt new because there are not many games that use voice recognition to progress the story," "I felt like I was in the world with Kite," and "I enjoyed chanting magic with my voice."

5.2   Experiment 2

We improved the game and conducted additional experiments.

Changes in Enjoyment Through UI Improvements

To confirm that improving the UI improves the enjoyment and immersion of the game itself, we made the following improvements to the audio version of the game based on the free-text comments in the questionnaire from Experiment 1 and conducted additional experiments.

- Produced a video of operation explanation.
- The operation method was always displayed on the game screen during play.
- Displayed the text "Recognizing" during speech recognition.
- Partially added a guide.

The first two improvements will prevent the game from starting without the user understanding how to operate it. It also makes it easier to know when to speak by displaying the text during recognition. The addition of a guide solves the problem of not knowing what to say.

In addition, the guide that we added as an improvement after the preliminary experiment turned out to be insufficient. In response to the comment that participants were confused about how to talk to the female avatars along the way, we thought of some additions to the guide. For example, we added "Use any words such as 'Hello'" to the phrase "Talk to the woman." Also, when talking to Kite in the scene where he is searching for the female sister, I added a guide that says, "Ask her in detail what she heard about her sister's 'characteristics' and 'where she went'."

We had a total of eight participants: seven male university students and one female university student. Some of them cooperated with us in Experiment 1. As in Experiment 1, we compared the audio version with the text version. In the text version, we also implemented a video to explain the operation and a constant display of the operation method on the screen to match the conditions. As for the time lag of speech recognition mentioned in Sect. 5.3, we asked the participants to experience the system in a good network environment as much as possible.

After experiencing the game, the participants answered the same questionnaire as in Experiment 1. The following figure shows the box-and-whisker diagram of Experiment 2 (Fig. 9). As in Experiment 1, the score of the audio version is higher than that of the text version for most of the questions. Since both Experiments 1 and 2 evaluated the audio and text versions relative to each other, it is impossible to make a direct comparison between Fig. 8 and Fig. 9.

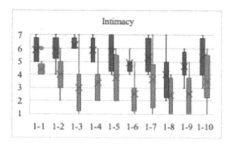 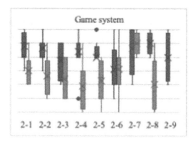

Fig. 9. Box-and-whisker diagram showing the results of Experiment 2

The following table shows the results of the t-test (Table 4). As in the previous experiment, questions that showed significant differences in p-values are shown in light gray, and the higher mean values for the audio and text versions are underlined. The questions with higher scores in the audio version remained the same, while questions 1–5 and 2–1 to 2–4, which were not significantly different in the previous experiment, were significantly different in the current experiment. Questions 2–6 and 2–7, which were significantly higher in the text version in the previous experiment, were not significantly different in this experiment. The results show that the improvement of the UI reduced the complexity of the game operations. The overall enjoyment and immersion of the game has been inherently improved by no longer being distracted by the complexity of the controls. It can be inferred that the subjects were able to concentrate more on the conversation with the characters than in Experiment 1. In the free-text comments, the subjects mentioned that they felt the improvement was effective: "the text of the guide was polite" and "the difficulty level was appropriate."

Table 4. Additional experiment questionnaire result table

question	average value		P value	question	average value		P value
	Voice	Text			Voice	Text	
1-1	5.875	4.375	0.026	2-1	5.75	4	0.01
1-2	5.875	4	0.017	2-2	5.625	3.625	0.017
1-3	6.25	3	0.018	2-3	4.75	3.375	0.026
1-4	5.875	3.375	0.011	2-4	5.375	2.875	0.017
1-5	5.75	3.75	0.042	2-5	5	3.25	0.026
1-6	4.875	2.5	0.017	2-6	4.125	4.125	0.914
1-7	5.375	3.625	0.016	2-7	5.625	6	0.496
1-8	4	2.375	0.027	2-8	6	3	0.011
1-9	4.625	2.5	0.027	2-9	5		
1-10	5.375	3.5	0.043				

Discussion

In the free-text comments made during the additional experiments, many of them referred to "being able to talk freely," such as "it was interesting to be able to speak freely and have Kite respond differently" and "it was interesting to think about what to say and try to see what kind of response would come." In contrast, in the case of the text version, there was a negative evaluation that "the attachment to Kite was diminished due to the inability to have conversations other than the choices," indicating that free speech is effective in increasing intimacy.

Additionally, while most of the conventional games using speech recognition have a system in which you give instructions to the characters on the screen from a bird's-eye view as a third party, this game allows you to talk with the characters on an equal footing as a character who exists in the scene. These social relationship between the player and the character to increase the intimacy with the screen character allowed the player to become more emotionally involved with the character and to feel the shared fun and adventure. A related comment was "The relationship between the player and the character as partners in the game world is interesting. I like the fact that there is always an incentive to continue the conversation because the game world always brings up issues that need to be solved." Of the four items listed as dialogue elements, the item "discussing the next action" seems to have had a particularly positive impact on the user experience. We found that the position of the user's avatar and the setting of the relationship between the avatar and the character are also deeply related to the degree of intimacy and the enjoyment of the game.

6 Conclusion

In this paper, we compared the effect of the game interface with voice dialogue in developing intimacy with the screen character in relation to the conventional game, and it was shown that we could enjoy the dialogue in the game more and intimacy also increased by introducing voice input. The enjoyment and immersion of the entire gaming experience could also be improved by removing the difficulty and incomprehensiveness of operation due to the introduction of speech recognition. In the future, we will examine whether the results of this study can be applied when the content of the conversation and the story of the game are enriched and lengthened. In addition to the content of the conversations, we will also be able to recognize the intonation of the player's voice, give the character emotions and memories, and generate corresponding conversations.

References

1. Allison, F., Carter, F., Gibbs, M., Smith, W.: Design patterns for voice interaction in games. In: Proceedings of the 2018 Annual Symposium on Computer-Human Interaction in Play (CHI PLAY'18), Melbourne, VIC, Australia, pp. 5–17 (2018)
2. Carter, M., Allison, F., Down, J., Gibbs, M.: Player identity dissonance and voice interaction in games. In: Proceedings of the 8th International ACM SIGACCESS Conference on Computers and Accessibility, the 2015 Annual Symposium, pp. 265–269 (2015)
3. Allison, F., Newn, J., Swith, W., Carter, M., Gibbs, M.: Frame analysis of voice interaction gameplay. In: Proceedings of the 2019 CHI conference on Human Factors in Computing Systems(CHI 2019), Glasgow, Scotland, UK, No. 393, pp. 1–14 (2019)
4. Nishida, K.: Effects of conversation act on conversation strategy and interpersonal cognition. Jpn. J. Psychol. **63**(5), 319–325 (1992)
5. Ikeda, Y., Hayama, D., Kosaka, Y., Satoh, Y.: Relationship between intimacy and styles of sharing among university friends. Jpn. Soc. Youth Adolesc. Psychol. **24**(2), 111–124 (2013)
6. Kort, D.Y., IJsselsteijn, A.W., Poels, K.: Digital games as social presence technology: development of the social presence in gaming questionnaire (SPGQ). In: Proceedings of the 10th Annual International Workshop on Presence, pp. 195–203 (2007)
7. Lim, S.J., Baba, A.: The development of measurement of empathy in digital games. In: Digital Games Research Association JAPAN Proceedings of 2016 Summer Conference (2016)
8. Brockmyer, H.J., Fox, M.C., Curtiss, A.K., McBroom, E., Burkhart, M.K., Pidruzny, N.J.: The development of the Game Engagement Questionnaire: a measure of engagement in video game-playing. J. Exp. Soc. Psychol. **45**(4), 624–634 (2009)
9. Bickmore, W.T., Picard, W.R.: Establishing and maintaining long-term human-computer relationships. ACM Trans. Comput. Hum. Interact. **12**(2), 293–327 (2005)

Game Development as a Serious Game with Live-Programming and Time-Travel Mechanics

Anthony Savidis[1,2(✉)] and Alexandros Katsarakis[2]

[1] Institute of Computer Science, FORTH, Heraklion, Crete, Greece
as@ics.forth.gr
[2] Department of Computer Science, University of Crete, Heraklion, Greece
akatsarakis@csd.uoc.gr

Abstract. Serious games for programming provide players with some type of algorithmic mechanics to accomplish game challenges. Such mechanics maybe formally algorithmic, or in some cases not theoretically linked to strict programming constructs, although still characterized as programming-related games. We discuss a serious game with visual programming where the primary mission is the development of a simple 2d game. Its primary novelty is the lack of separate build and run cycles. There is only one game mode, with gameplay and game development being inseparable, where every game object can be clicked, live-programmed, and live-edited during play. Additionally, time may be freely rewind and replayed, undoing or redoing internally all related user actions and game state updates. During such time travels, it is allowed to drop the entire history onwards, from any given point in time, and continue from there.

Keywords: Serious games · Visual programming · Live programming · Time-travel mechanics · Learning programming

1 Introduction

Games with programming mechanics, either through some explicit language or via implicit algorithmic elements, exist for a long time. They are frequently targeted to a specific player audience and focus either on new forms of entertainment, offering at an abstract semantic level very challenging algorithmic puzzles, or may be used for learning purposes, falling in the category of serious games with the aim to teach and develop basic programming skills.

In this context, we discuss a serious game for acquiring basic programming skills, relying on visual programming systems. The target game itself is both developed and played in a single runtime mode, making gameplay and game development two inseparable tasks performed interchangeably. Essentially, programming and editing are treated as standard game mechanics, independently of the game that is actually being developed

© IFIP International Federation for Information Processing 2021
Published by Springer Nature Switzerland AG 2021
J. Baalsrud Hauge et al. (Eds.): ICEC 2021, LNCS 13056, pp. 181–195, 2021.
https://doi.org/10.1007/978-3-030-89394-1_14

by the player. This feature allows changing the game-program in a live manner, while running, and is known as *live programming* [8]. This notion of live programming in our game goes beyond code fragments and covers all game assets, also becoming editable during gameplay, something we similarly call *live editing*.

This way, offering an exploratory programming system for crafting a game, all development operations and features are *game mechanics*, while the development environment is a live editor with only one operational mode being gameplay. Then, as part of these mechanics, we support a time-travel facility, enabling player developers to browse back and forth in the game timeline, enabling to replay the history again from any previous point in time, with speed control options, or even select to restore an earlier point in time and continue thereafter. This facility is not merely a video recording tool, but works exactly like a global undo and redo system, storing precise snapshots and state differences taken within every game loop. This allows developers replay or rewind development actions (code or character editing) and also gameplay actions, under a single global timeline (Fig. 1).

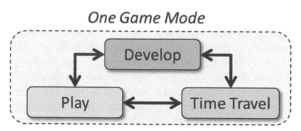

Fig. 1. All three general tasks can be interchangeably applied within one global mode, game mode, with develop and time-travel becoming essential game mechanics.

The idea for active development is also inspired by the Smalltalk 80 programming environment during early eighties where Smalltalk introduced object-orientation and reflection that were highly advanced concepts. The language designers took some decisions to make the language experience and its IDE very easy to use. They adopted an *"everything is an object"* approach that concerned not only program elements but also IDE components and access to the operating system via the language. In this sense, environment configuration, tool-chain control, underlying system management, etc., were all possible via a unified control mechanism either from code or the user-interface. Anything selectable with the mouse could be directly programmed.

Also, our work is based on the notion of active learning [1], emphasizing learner-centered and learner-driven processes, where learners are not strictly constrained in what to do, but are offered an open challenge to develop a game they prefer. This is in contrast to teacher-centered and system-driven perspectives, where the task is very specific and learners are expected to perform in a narrow path of activities.

1.1 Contribution

Our contribution falls in the general field of serious games for teaching programming, while in particular it concerns the design and implementation of a comprehensive toolset[1] for in-game live-development mechanics combining: (i) visual programming and direct manipulation of all game objects *during gameplay*; and (ii) time-travel on global game state recordings, enabling free rewinding or replaying for easier, iterative and playful live testing and in-game updating. In this serious game for programming, we offer a 2d game development toolset with no separate build and run modes. Everything is performed in one live game mode, and every single user action is effectively a gameplay action.

2 Related Work

Firstly, we consider worth mentioning the initial versions of programmable Lego bricks [3], which eventually led to Lego Mindstorms, as probably the first example of serious games for learning programming, even though consisting of mechanical toys. Next, we briefly review recent work on serious games for programming, referring to some commercial games with programming-related mechanics that are relevant, with an elaborate analysis provided under [1], including both research and popular commercial games. Compared to [1], we judge more strictly the theoretical foundation of the programming mechanics, as outlined under Fig. 2, clearly separating between explicit (programming language, code) and implicit forms (no language, no demonstrated Turing completeness). Then, we judge more loosely the compliance to the ACM Curriculum [18], which concerns programming as a profession, setting focus only on the fundamental programming concepts and algorithmic design. In other words, we treat serious games for programming as introductory tools for non-professional programmers, rather than as teaching alternatives.

Effectively, implicit mechanics are appealing and entertaining, but are not directly linked to an underlying formal algorithmic model. Thus, they cannot be theoretically treated as serious games techniques for the art and science of programming.

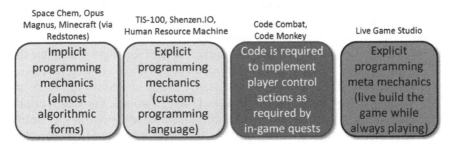

Fig. 2. Categories of games with implicit or explicit use of programming-based mechanics – the last category is our serious game, tentatively named "*live game studio*".

---

[1] https://www.youtube.com/watch?v=rpDWvi0Fejo, https://github.com/alexkatsarakis/GameEnvironment.

Commercial games with explicit programming mechanics like TIS-100 (assembly), Sehnezen.IO (circuit assembly) and Human Resource Machine (intermediate assembly) are popular to programmers, but require a programming background, in fact familiarization with machine-level symbolisms. Games with implicit mechanics like SpaceChem, Opus Magnus, and Minecraft, do not involve pure algorithmic reasoning or formally-related notations, thus we do not treat them as games for programming.

Code Combat [6], Code Monkey [14] and Code Hero [8] represent a category of games where programming is used as a control substitute, asking the player to write code fragments (source text) so that target actions occur in the game (like player character control). In [12], a study demonstrated that combining artwork and code editing in a player-extensible serious game resulted in increased motivation, something that we directly adopted in our work. Kodu Game Lab [10], a variant of Kodu originally by Microsoft Research, is a tool related to our game, since it is an environment to visually program games via a subset of algorithmic elements and a custom tile-based graphical language. As also mentioned earlier [13], due to the style and form of its visual language not being Turing complete, Kodu variants are not introductory programming laboratories, but mostly game prototyping environments. Finally, Tynker [7] is an on-line platform for introductory teaching of programming to kids through a visual block-based programming system, including a few challenges requiring complete sample games. Compared to Tynker we also adopt a visual language being Blockly [1], but then focus on live-programming, in contrast to traditional modal builds, and provide the time-travel play and test facility.

3   Live Development

3.1   System Architecture

The software architecture of our system is depicted under Fig. 3, showing the extensions we introduced on top of the game engine (in our case a 2d platformer engine). We particularly emphasize the management of objects, assets and events, although they typically belong in the game engine, since, depending on the originally supplied API, extra work may be required to introduce wrappers enabling scripted methods, state reflection (capture and restored), and live updating.

Then, on top of such required extensions, the live editing and programming tools are implemented. The state and scripting APIs are also used for implementing the time-travel and the visual programming sub-systems respectively. In particular, within every game loop, the state API is used to capture state updates or retrieve full scene state snapshots, and chain them in sequences of tagged state recordings. For visual scripting, we have introduced custom blocks regarding object methods and properties, game event handling, and also character animation control. All scripts are kept and catalogued by a central script manager that invokes the visual editor if editing is requested. Finally, the User-Interface connects all dots interactively and allows players to handle the features we introduced immediately, at any point in time. In particular, to support live editing and programming, game object selection is enabled all the time over the game terrain.

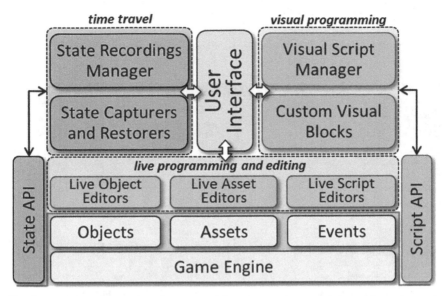

Fig. 3. System architecture, built on top of the game engine components (shown in grey).

This way, players may pick any object, an action leading to opening the respective object property sheets and the visual script editors (for anything that can be scripted on objects), enabling to live make any desired changes.

3.2 Visual Programming

For visual game scripting we embedded the Blockly [1] editor in our system, while introducing new types of basic blocks, as well as composite block structures for handling all game event types and related object operations.

As shown under Fig. 4, the live programming window is non-modal, is displayed on top of the running game scene, and can be freely moved or hidden anytime. Being invisible by default is automatically opened when a game object is selected (Fig. 4 shows all scripts for Mario, the player object, after being selected). Game development functionality has been fully exported to Blockly through new custom types of blocks (indicated with *new* in the mid of Fig. 4), while the player can organize events, states and actions freely inside tabbed groups, with arbitrary naming (e.g. *'jumpRight'* group with *'while in jumpRight'* event handler).

Clearly, there are other game editing environments with such kind of visual scripting, the most notable being Tynker. But an improved feature in our system is the way such visual scripts are accessed, overall how all visual code snippets are organized, as illustrated under Fig. 5. In Tynker, and in most tools we know, visual code fragments are spread in a large canvas as floating elements, moved and grouped with the responsibility of the user. This, even for very simple games, results in a highly crowded space with code blocks that is difficult to handle and can be frustrating.

events that can | types of blocks— | the current visual script, for | game is
be visually | *new* indicates | the selected event handler – | running
scripted on the | custom blocks | *blockly* editor is fully | normally
selected object | we introduced | embedded in game mode | behind

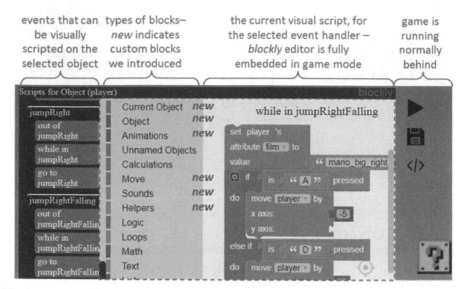

Fig. 4. Visual live-programming non-modal window (moveable, may be hidden or opened during gameplay, anytime), here opened once the player character is selected; the embedded Blockly editor is shown in a dashed red rectangle (Color figure online).

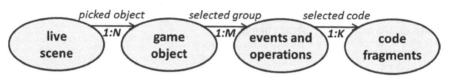

Fig. 5. Quick access to visual code fragments by organizing them around objects; with only a couple of clicks the target code can be edited.

3.3 Live Editing

Live editing refers to the ability of updating everything on-the-fly, whether code, object properties, terrain structure, artwork or animations. As illustrated under Fig. 6, editing is possible after selecting any game object by a single click and can be done even when the game has been paused, and time-travel (for all available successive state recordings) is carried out by the user. As it is explained latter, to make editing changes applicable during time-traveling the *continue* operation must be selected, clearing all state from that point in time onwards (this is like text editing, then undoing, followed by an edit action which results in clearing the redo list).

The live editing feature allows immediately testing the effect of changes in the current play session, something that otherwise would require exit (interruption), update, rebuild and rerun phases, and then manually bringing the state of the program to the exact point just before interruption. The idea of live-editing was originally introduced in Microsoft Visual Studio debugger, called edit-and-continue [16]. It enabled programmers directly modify the code during debugging when execution is stopped in a breakpoint, and was originally limited to small-scale changes. Then, once execution continues, the new code becomes active and can be live tested in the same running session. A more elaborate example of the live programming feature, and also the advantages of the object-based organization of all visual code snippets, is depicted under Fig. 7, where all steps involved are sequentially numbered.

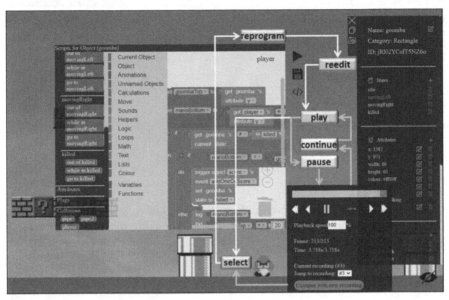

Fig. 6. Live editing and testing cycles as play, select, reprogram, reedit iterations; pausing and time-control (bottom-right with *fwd*, *bwd* and rest operations) is possible anytime (until *continue* is chosen to interrupt) with live-editing fully enabled all the time.

Firstly, the user clicks on a *coin* object, which opens automatically the respective property sheet (right) and the code browser window (left). Then, after browsing on the left column with the identities of all code snippets, the *Collisions* tab is located and the *player* entry is clicked. The latter opens the code snippet for *coin-player* collision logic that is then directly edited in Blockly. As shown, the defined code invokes the *addOneOnScore* method of the *score* object.

Then, the *score* object (displaying the score text) is clicked on the terrain area, opens its respective property sheet and code browser window. After browsing on the code groups at left, the *Events* tab is located and the *addOneOnScore* method is selected, opening Blockly editor to define or edit the associated code. The implementation of the method is completed, with the visual code denoting an increase of the respective numeric text field of the *score* object by one.

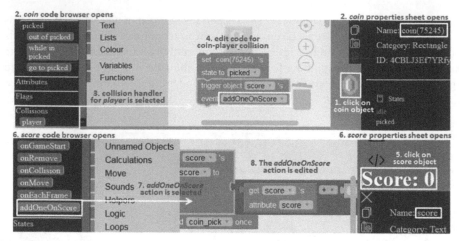

Fig. 7. Live programming of coin-player collision and its effect on score change; top part: coin-player collision, bottom part: score change action.

3.4   Live Clipboard

A standard clipboard is only an editing feature, not linked to serious game mechanics for acquiring programming skills. So, we focused on making the clipboard a tool also making life easier for junior programmers in crafting a simple game (see Fig. 8).

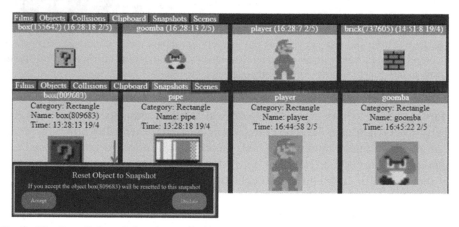

Fig. 8. The live clipboard showing copied objects (top), and object snapshots (bottom) ordered older to newer, displaying time and date of copy; restoring snapshots needs confirmation.

To this end, we integrated all clipboard operations to live editing, thus affecting the game while running. Then, we introduced two variations we consider very helpful:

- Object copy: (i) normal *copy* that is pasted as a new object; and (ii) special copy saving a *snapshot* of its state and restoring it on paste, even after deletion

- *Scene* copy: copies the fully game state and restores it precisely on pasting - this feature was also used very frequently during gameplay

4 Time Travel

4.1 Features

The time-travel feature is functionally the ability to move back and forth in the game time, by precisely storing in every game loop the state of all game elements, including code, objects, assets, terrain, animations, etc. Initially, it was designed to back-up learners with an easy-to-use testing tool, enabling them to trace backwards the behavior of the game and directly inspect what possibly went wrong in terms of game logic programming. However, after adding all interactive recording and replay operations, facilitating to reproduce an entire sequence of recorded states as a film backward or forward, by also preserving the original game loop timing, it was immediately seen also as a nice game feature, just like time-rewind in Braid [15]. In terms of implementation, such a time-travel feature is demanding. However, it's dual role serving as testing tool and as a game mechanic makes it very helpful for learning programming being a genuinely experimentation-driven and exploratory process.

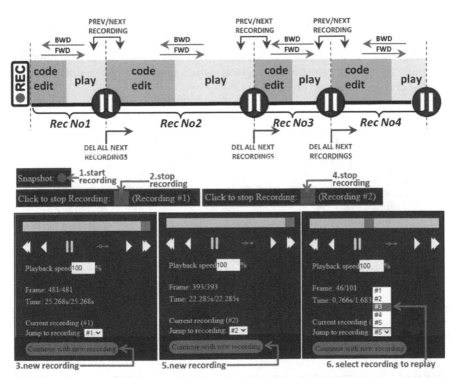

Fig. 9. *Top*: state recording (i.e. no video) of game actions enabling: (a) chain recordings by pausing; (b) move back and forth between them to navigate in events and state updates; (c) replay any recording forward and backward; and (d) delete all recordings and continue. *Bottom*: the actual record and replay user-interface.

The use of the feature is outlined under Fig. 9. More specifically, the user can initiate a recording session anytime. Then, by *pausing and continuing* recording, a new distinct recording chunk is created, following the previous one. After this, it is possible to play backward or forward any selected recording, or move to the next or previous recording, or alternatively select any of the recordings from a dropdown list.

Such recordings internally chain state updates for game loops including code modifications, editing actions, or typical game play events, all at the order they occur. This mixing of development and gameplay actions is illustrated in every recording of Fig. 9 as the two *"code edit'* and *"play"* rectangular areas. It should be noted that interleaving of an arbitrary number of such actions is possible to form a single recording. During a recording replay process, the user may pause and then freely review the state of objects, code, or artwork, thus observing the values they had at that point in time. If desired the game can be restored at that point-in-time by choosing to continue from there, effectively *deleting all states onwards in the current recording, and also all subsequent recordings, thereafter*.

4.2 Implementation

The time-travel implementation technique is outlined under Fig. 10, and we briefly discuss how it has been accomplished. As mentioned, recordings are semantic, chaining state modifications that are tracked within every game loop. We implemented two techniques, with the same end-result, but with different computation complexity and memory requirements, both relying on the Command [11] design pattern. Effectively, actions become objects encapsulating their side effect, all implementing a common interface though which their effect can be undone or redone at any point in time (illustrated by lists of change undo/redo objects).

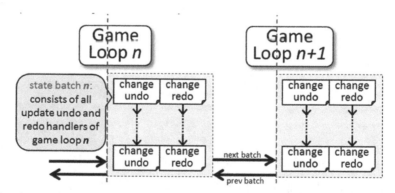

Fig. 10. The essence of state recording for play, coding and edit actions, all in a single game mode, through undo and redo handlers (Command design pattern) for each action, batched and linked across game loops to form chained structured semantic recordings.

For the first implementation, we keep one state-update per game loop, called a *snapshot*, being faster but requiring more memory, as it saves the state of all objects (linking to Fig. 10, only one undo/redo object per loop is stored). In the second implementation, we record the state modifications on objects for every action, called state *deltas*, being slower as it overloads all game actions with state storage processing, but results in smaller memory footprints for recordings since only differences (i.e. deltas) are recorded. Both options are offered to users, so with every new recording they have to choose whether it is delta or snapshot.

The handling of object *deletion* undoing (or object *creation* redoing) and its integration to the undoing of all object modifications prior to deletion was very challenging. Deletion as such is not related to some language operator, but implies the removal of an object from the game scene, something that may occur via a delete or dispose operator in certain languages, or reference nullification with latter garbage collection on other languages. Essentially, not only an object reference after deletion is invalid, but cannot be restored on the same reference, since the way the memory manager handles memory blocks and memory references is implementation dependent and differs across platforms and languages.

```
using ObjId = uint64_t;                    namespace SpriteMethods { adapter methods
class ObjIdDir {                              void Move (ObjId id, int dx, int dy)
    void    Insert (ObjId, Obj*);            {
    void    Remove (ObjId);                    dynamic_cast<Sprite*>
    Obj*    LookupById (ObjId);               (ObjDir::Get().Lookup(id))
    ObjId   LookupByObj (Obj*);               ->Move(dx, dy);
    ObjId   Gen (void);                      }
    static  ObjDir& Get (void);            }
};                                         const ObjState GetState (ObjId id);
                                           Sprite* New (const ObjState&, ObjId);
class Sprite : Obj { native sprite         similar wrappers for all methods...
    void Move (int dx, int dy);          }
    void SetFrame (unsigned frameNo);
    void SetFilm (                       Instead of sp->Move(dx,dy) call is formed as:
        const AnimatinFilm& film         SpriteMethods::Move(
    );                                       ObjDir::Get().LookupByObj(sp), dx, dy
};                                         );
```
```
In the game engine, in the callback where deletion of some Sprite* sp needs to be handled,
we create an undo command for object deletion as follows (also inserted in current recording):
auto* f  = new DeleteUndo;
auto  id = ObjDir::Get().LookupByObj(sp);
f->SetState( SpriteMethods::GetState(id) );
f->SetObjId( id );
f->SetImpl(
    [f](void) { SpriteMethods::New(f->GetState(), f->GetObjId()); }
};
```

Fig. 11. Adopting generic object ids (like serial numbers) to handle undo (and redo) of object deletion (and construction) on top of a C++ game engine.

Our technique is based on persistent generic object ids on top of every native type of game engine object, with such ids mapped to the native class references when the actual invocation of object methods is required (see Fig. 11, shown in C++). Then, in the game implementation, the bidirectional mapping between generic ids and native objects is handled via an object directory (ObjIdDir), with object access being carried out in two steps. Firstly, the mapping from a generic ObjId to the native reference (like Sprite*) is done, and then the actual method is invoked. Both steps can be handled by special method wrappers, like `SpriteMethods` depicted under Fig. 11. Notably, to undo an object creation a deletion is required. Then, its redo action is exactly like undoing deletion, meaning *redo create* is identical to *undo delete*.

5 Evaluation

We briefly discuss our experience and the key outcomes from an evaluation process we carried out. The overall process took almost one month, more than usually expected due to pandemic rules. We intentionally tried to make the whole process not looking like a usability study for participants, but like an exploratory programming laboratory assignment. The entire process was remotely handled, via telco sessions, with the following characteristics regarding setup and conduct:

- 11 high school students participated, of almost balanced genders but varying ages, with some experience in visual programming tools from school, and also playing regularly video games on their mobiles or home consoles
- We firstly explained they were going to make a simple version of Super Mario (NES classic edition, just first stage) and were asked to find information on the game online
- Then, we introduced the environment explaining and detailing all of its features, with extra emphasis on terrain and character authoring and the time-travel feature with all its options
- We provided all the required artwork (bitmaps for tiles, sprite sheets, sounds, and all details for motion and animation of game characters)
- We requested they work in small groups, giving freedom of choice for the communication and cooperation tools (eventually, they all used Discord)
- We had regular on-line plenary meetings to discuss the progress of their projects and provide explanations in using the tools
- They were also told they will exchange projects and play each other games, just to increase motivation

When the process was concluded, all students completed three standard SUS questionnaires, differing only on the titles: (i) editing tools for terrain, characters and animations; (ii) game coding tools; and (iii) tools for recording and time-travel. We wanted to have separate feedback for these three tools. Then, we provided another simple questionnaire where they could also insert free text, with the aim to get some additional information, with some of the questions listed below:

- What you think is the coolest feature and why
- What you think is the worst feature and why
- Do you think you learned something?
- Does this felt more of an exercise or a game to you?

The results of the SUS questionnaires gave the following overall positive scores (rounded): 87 for editing tools, 83 for the coding tools (Blockly) and 91 for the recording and play back tools. The feedback from the informal questionnaires gave the following highly interesting feedback (we actually summarize the responses):

- Time control is the coolest feature, following a unanimous opinion – interestingly, two of the kids said that this does not make sense for on-line multiplayer games
- They did not mention anything to be considered as a worst feature
- They reported it was very interesting that they have learned how to make characters animate and move with keyboard control
- They found this process more of a game, a challenge, rather than a typical school exercise as part of a programming lesson

During the process we regularly asked information on how live-development and time-travel were applied. In this context, we observed that live animation coding and editing were used very early almost by all, involving the few steps outlined in Fig. 12.

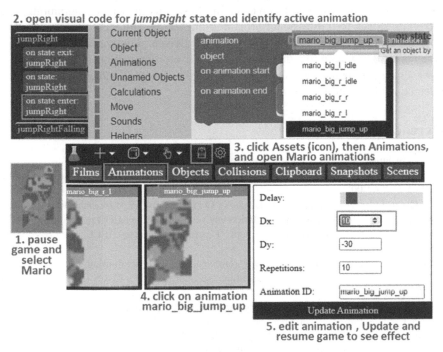

Fig. 12. Live updating of animations with just a few simple coding-and-editing steps.

6 Summary and Conclusions

In our work we focused on game-based learning of programming, putting initially emphasis on increased motivation and exploratory development. The adoption of game development as a task to stimulate learners is not new, and we consider that it rents in roots in applicable constructivist theory and the work of Logo [17]. To make the experience easier and more entertaining we supported immediate development, that is developing during play, and time travelling, that is being able to undo or redo anything in the original gameplay time. The goal was to realize a dual learning experience this way, with development and play interleaved as a unified task.

Initially, while trying to keep a balance between serious and entertaining, we decided that the bigger risk was making a game looking more of a programming-intensive laboratory rather than the opposite. Thus, we very early decided to drop separate build and run cycles, i.e. modal development, and also relieve learners from code management and typical overcrowded code canvases. Then, after early evaluation with users, the time-travel mechanic, originally meant as a testing tool, grew to both a game-play and a game-testing feature. We carried out an evaluation study, where besides filling questionnaires, we discussed a lot with students. Most of them reported they are not intending for a programmer profession, but still they would like to do hobby programming activities with such visual tools. Now, based on this remark, serious games for programming may be stepping stones for professional programming, or just introductory tools for hobbyists, or support both if appropriately designed. Driven by this, and due to our early evaluation results, we consider that by combining live-programming and time-traveling, while keeping coding tools at a moderate level, we managed to achieve a good balance between these two worlds.

References

1. Blockly. https://developers.google.com/blockly. Accessed May 2021
2. Barnes, D.: Active Learning. Leeds University TVEI Support Project, p. 19 (1989). ISBN 978-1-872364-00-1.
3. Gindling, J., Ioannidou, A., Loh, J., Lokkebo, O., Repenning, A.: LEGOsheets: a rule-based programming, simulation and manipulation environment for the LEGO programmable brick. In: IEEE Symposium on Visual Languages, Darmstadt, Germany, IEEE, pp. 172–179, 5–9 Sep 1995
4. Miljanovic, M., Bradbury, J.: A review of serious games for programming. In: Serious Games 4th Joint International Conference, Darmstadt, Germany, Springer LNCS 11243, pp. 204–216, 7–8 Nov 2018
5. Goldberg, A., Robson, D.: The Language and Its Implementation. Addison-Wesley (1984)
6. Code Combat. https://codecombat.com/. Accessed May 2021.
7. Tynker. https://www.tynker.com/. Accessed May 2021.
8. Rein, P., Ramson, S., Lincke, J., Hirschfeld, R., Pape, T.: Exploratory and live, programming and coding – a literature study comparing perspectives on liveness. Art Sci. Eng. Program. **3** Article 1 (2019)
9. Code Hero. https://codeherogame.wordpress.com/. Accessed May 2021.
10. KoduGameLab. https://www.kodugamelab.com/. Accessed May 2021.
11. Gamma, E., Helm, R., Johnson, R., Vlissides, J.: Design Patterns: Elements of Reusable Object-Oriented Software. Addison-Wesley Longman Publishing Co. Inc., Boston, MA, USA (1995)
12. Barnes, T., Powell, E., Chaffin, A., Lipford, H.: Game2Learn: improving the motivation of CS1 students. In: Proc. of the 3rd Int. Conf. on Game Development in Computer Science Education (GDCSE 2008), pp. 1–5 (2008)
13. Buckley, C. Design and Implementation of a Genre Hybrid Video Game that Integrates the Curriculum of an Introductory Programming Course (Master's Thesis), Clemson University. https://tigerprints.clemson.edu/all_theses/1515/ (2012). Accessed May 2021.

14. Code Monkey. https://www.codemonkey.com/. Accessed May 2021.
15. Braide. https://en.wikipedia.org/wiki/Braid_(video_game) (2008). Accessed May 2021
16. Microsoft Visual Studio. Edit Code and Continue. https://docs.microsoft.com/en-us/visualstu dio/debugger/edit-and-continue?view=vs-2019 (2019). Accessed May 2021
17. Papert, S.: Mindstorms: Children, Computers and Powerful Ideas. Basic Books. Original edition (1980)
18. ACM/IEEE-CS Joint Task Force on Computing Curricula: Computer Science Curricula 2013. Tech. Rep., ACM Press and IEEE Computer Society Press (2013)

AI Game Agents Based on Evolutionary Search and (Deep) Reinforcement Learning: A Practical Analysis with Flappy Bird

Leonardo Thurler[✉], José Montes[✉], Rodrigo Veloso[✉], Aline Paes[✉], and Esteban Clua[✉]

Universidade Federal Fluminense, Niterói, Rio de Janeiro, Brazil
{lpthurler,joselucasbrandaomontes,rodrigoveloso}@id.uff.br,
{alinepaes,esteban}@ic.uff.br

Abstract. Game agents are efficiently implemented through different AI techniques, such as neural network, reinforcement learning, and evolutionary search. Although there are many works for each approach, we present a critical analysis and comparison between them, suggesting a common benchmark and parameter configurations. The evolutionary strategy implements the NeuroEvolution of Augmenting Topologies algorithm, while the reinforcement learning agent leverages Q-Learning and Proximal Policy Optimization. We formulate and empirically compare this set of solutions using the Flappy Bird game as a test scenario. We also compare different representations of state and reward functions for each method. All methods were able to generate agents that can play the game, where the NEAT algorithm had the best results, reaching the goal of never losing.

Keywords: Artificial intelligence · Reinforcement learning · Deep reinforcement learning · Genetic algorithm · Q-Learning · NEAT · PPO · Ml-agents · Flappy Bird · AI game agents · Game · Unity · Pygame

1 Introduction

The AI field started to be applied to games through agents that could play against humans or to make game characters more convincing [1–4]. All the solutions proposed towards those goals led to a state where the literature present numerous solutions for the same problem. The existence of different solutions is not an issue by itself but it makes it harder and more complex to understand which ones are more appropriate to handle a given problem [5].

© IFIP International Federation for Information Processing 2021
Published by Springer Nature Switzerland AG 2021
J. Baalsrud Hauge et al. (Eds.): ICEC 2021, LNCS 13056, pp. 196–208, 2021.
https://doi.org/10.1007/978-3-030-89394-1_15

Motivated by this issue, this work presents a methodology to create and evaluate the performance of an AI game agent based on distinct AI techniques. For this, we use three different and widely used AI techniques used for solving gameplay problems. The agents were developed using NEAT as the search algorithm, which is based on the genetic algorithm with neural networks. We also address the Q-Learning reinforcement learning algorithm and the Proximity Policy Optimization (PPO) with a deep reinforcement learning algorithm.

Our developments are based on the Flappy Bird game as a test case. The player's goal in this game is to cross between pipes that appear in random positions on the stage as much as possible. This randomness feature makes this game a promising test environment for training agents who need to learn behaviors based on non-deterministic phenomena. For the development of the learning environment, two digital game engines were used: Unity [6] and Pygame [7]. Previous work investigated the performance of Flappy Bird agents based on genetic algorithms [8] and reinforcement learning [9]. While their focus is mostly restricted to analyse agents based on a single AI technique, here we take a step towards comparing these techniques plus deep reinforcement learning, showing a proper strategy for analysing which technique did better.

As a result, this work presents strategies to formulate, train and evaluate agents based on different AI methods. The results demonstrate that, when using a proper model, these techniques can create agents capable to play Flappy Bird and obtain high scores. It is also demonstrated how to analyze and compare results obtained by varying hyperparameters and modifying agents representations. Finally, by comparing the results of each agent, we present how to create metrics that allows the evaluation and comparison of agents that use different techniques, making it possible to define which is the best for a specific problem and situation.

2 Related Work

Previous works had implemented and compared Deep Learning, Reinforcement Learning and evolutionary algorithms as strategies for AI based player training. In [10] authors conclude that the Deep Q-learning was the best, beating all the others methods that were tested and even human expert performance in some of them. [11] reproduced existing research on deep reinforcement learning algorithms applied to games and compared the obtained results with the published ones with Breakout, an Atari 2600 game. In their work, the Asynchronous Advantage actor-critic algorithm proved to be much better than Deep Q-Learning. These studies reinforce the need for novels ways to analyze and compare the performance of different AI methods and demonstrate how this is not a trivial task for all the games. Thus, our work contributes to such studies by presenting a methodology to create and evaluate the performance of agents based on different AI techniques.

In [8], authors developed and studied an AI agent using a combination of neural networks and genetic algorithm to play Flappy Bird. They divided the gameplay into two difficulty levels and the trained agent could reach scores above 150. [9] applied various reinforcement learning algorithms to train an agent to play Flappy Bird, such as SARSA, Q-Learning, Q-value approximation via linear regression, and approximation via a neural network. From the experiments, they conclude that Q-learning had better performance with regular scores above 1400. The available literature shows that the Flappy Bird game presents some interesting challenges to AI game agents and can be used as a test bed scenario for this research topic. Although they demonstrate that these techniques are capable of training agents who can perform well in the game, as far as we know, there are no literature that compare and analyse which techniques are the most suitable ones and which advantages and disadvantages they present. Our work makes a contribution in this direction by comparing the performance of these techniques in conjunction with deep reinforcement learning and demonstrates which one did better.

3   Theoretical Background

3.1   Genetic Algorithms

A genetic algorithm (GA) constitutes a mathematical model simulating the theory of Darwinian Evolution. It consists of searching on a set of possible solutions to a given problem, called the population, initially created with random patterns[12,13]. In this work, we pose the task of learning the weights *and* the architecture of an ANN as a GA task. To achieve that, each individual of the GA is composed of a different ANN, including architectures and their weights. Then, the NeuroEvolution Algorithm for Increasing Topologies (NEAT)[14] searches for the best solution for the problem. The search process implemented by the NEAT algorithm involves the use of the classical genetic operators Selection, Crossover and Mutation, operations that manipulate individuals throughout the generations by adding neurons and hidden layers, connections and adjusting activation functions of the added neurons [14].

3.2   Reinforcement Learning and Deep Reinforcement Learning

Reinforcement learning (RL) works by building agents that interact with the environment. The environment provides a response about the efficiency of agent strategy through a reward function [13]. The agent must experience a lot of different strategies in order to find which is the best to achieve a goal. When the agent is trying different strategies it is actually searching over the space of all possible inputs and outputs (state/action) in order to earn a reward.

One of the most classical approaches for learning policies is the Q-Learning algorithm [4]. It tries to learn an action-value function iteratively. The idea is to create a table with values of Q for all possible state action pairs and use experiences to update them. When one needs to directly deal with large spaces of states and actions, or discretization or clustering is not an option, other strategies must be used. Typically, in these scenarios, one may approximate a function with different methods, such as deep neural network as the function approximator, which in this case corresponds to a Deep Reinforcement Learning (DRL) [15, 16]. Recently, DRL has achieved the state-of-the-art in several game related problems, such as AlphaGO [2]. An approach, based on DRL, that has achieved impressive results is the Proximal Policy Optimization (PPO) algorithm [17]. PPO is based on an architecture called Actor-Critic. This architecture uses two neural networks: the first is called critical and is used to assess the current state of the environment by generating an estimate of the Q value; The second serves to define the best action for the current state, which is called an actor [18].

4   Problem Description and Modeling

4.1   Modeling Flappy Bird as an AI Agent

Flappy Bird[1] is a single player game that gives a point every time the player-controlled bird passes between an upper and a lower pipe. There are infinity pairs of pipes alongside the game environment and it the finishes when the bird hit the ground or any of the pipes.

The player has only two possible actions: jump, when the bird will have its vertical position (y) shifted upwards, and do nothing, where the bird will move downwards due to the gravity action. The horizontal position of the bird (x) is always the same, the horizontal position of the pipes (x_c) are modified considering a movement with constant speed. The vertical position of the end of the lower pipe (y_{ci}) and the upper pipe (y_{cs}) are defined at random, always maintaining a constant spacing between them. When the bird passes through a pair of pipes, two new pipes are generated. Figure 1 illustrates the main elements of the game.

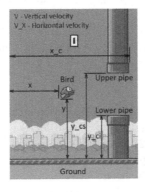

Fig. 1. Flappy Bird game illustration.

---

[1] http://flappybird.io/.

Based on the primary version aforementioned described, two versions of the game were implemented for this paper: one using Unity[6], and based on NEAT and PPO, and the other using Pygame[7], based on Q-Leaning.

Environment Modeling. We model a state by defining the positions of the bird and pipes. To model the bird, we rely on a component of vertical velocity v and its position as y. The position of the pipes rely on a horizontal velocity component v_x (constant), and positions y_{cs}, y_{ci} (vertical) and x_c (horizontal). From those variables, the state is first defined as a 4-position vector $s = (y, y_{cs}, y_{ci}, x_c)$.

We also considered other variables that may help the agent to achieve its goal. Variables such as the vertical (d_y^{ci} and d_y^{cs}) and horizontal (d_x) distance between the bird and any of the pipes are also used. Furthermore, we add two binary variables, α and β to represent whether the bird is above or below one of the pipes. The variable α is equal to 0 if the bird is below the bottom pipe and 1 otherwise and the variable β is equal to 0 if the bird is below the top pipe and 1 otherwise. The representations are summarized in Table 1.

Table 1. State representation parameters.

State	s_1	s_2	s_3	s_4
Vector of observable variables	$(d_y^{ci}, d_y^{cs}, d_x, v)$	(y, y_{cs}, y_{ci})	$(y - y_{ci}, v)$	$(d_y^{ci}, v, \alpha, \beta)$

Adjustments to Run Q-Learning. The variables used to define the state of the game are not discrete, as required by Q-Learning. Therefore, to use this method in this context, it is necessary to discretize the variables. The discretization strategy followed here is given by (1) where var_d is the variable after discretization, var is the original variable, N is an integer parameter that controls the reduction of the state space. Thus, if $N = 5$, any real number y between 0 and 4 will be represented by a discrete variable $y_d = 0$, considerably reducing the state space even when y is an integer variable. Reducing the space can increase the generalization capacity and reduce the Q-Learning training time because the larger the space the greater the probability of existing states that have not yet been visited by the agent.

$$var_d = \text{int}(var/N) \tag{1}$$

Transition Model and Goal. The agent performs two possible actions: jump and do nothing. From these actions it is possible to define a transition model for the problem, as follows in (2) and (3). Where p is the displacement caused by the jump and g_t is the displacement caused by gravity. There are two other possible transitions that only occur when $x_c = x$, $y < y_{cs}$ and $y > y_{ci}$, that is, the moment the bird crosses the pipes, as shown in (4) and (5). Where y'_{cs} and y'_{ci} are the new pipe positions, randomly defined and x_{max} is the maximum horizontal position.

$$\text{r}((y, y_{cs}, y_{ci}, x_c), \text{jump}) = (y + p, y_{cs}, y_{ci}, x_c + v_x) \tag{2}$$

$$r((y, y_{cs}, y_{ci}, x_c), \text{do nothing}) = (y - g_t, y_{cs}, y_{ci}, x_c + v_x) \tag{3}$$

$$r((y, y_{cs}, y_{ci}, x_c), \text{jump}) = (y + p, y'_{cs}, y'_{ci}, x_{max}) \tag{4}$$

$$r((y, y_{cs}, y_{ci}, x_c), \text{do nothing}) = (y - g_t, y'_{cs}, y'_{ci}, x_{max}) \tag{5}$$

4.2 Reward Function

The definition of a suitable reward function is crucial to ensure that the agent learns the desired function and it is one of the most complex phases of a RL process. Thus, we design and experiment different reward policies for the Flappy Bird to experimentally select the most suitable one. The simplest and most explicit reward function would be as follows in (6).

The problem with this function is that the reward will only be achieved if a very specific set of actions is chosen since at the beginning of the training there is no prior information about the problem. Thus, this simple reward would require a great deal of training time and no guarantee of any learning. It is then possible to formulate more explicit functions, such those described in (7), where a and b are constant real numbers. The function r_t^2 was used in the preliminary tests and it makes the agent learning. Thus, even more explicit functions were elaborated to allow the analysis of which function would be the best to solve this problem. We defined the functions as r_t^3, r_t^4 and r_t^5 as detailed in (8), (9) and (10) where d is the vertical distance between the bird and the center of the tubes and δ is a real number that defines how close to the center the bird must be from the center to earn the reward; in r_t^3 the center refers to the center of the tubes.

$$r_t^1 = \begin{cases} 1, & \text{if made a point} \\ 0, & \text{if did not make a point} \end{cases} \tag{6}$$

$$r_t^2 = \begin{cases} a, & \text{if the bird is alive} \\ -b, & \text{if collided} \end{cases} \tag{7}$$

$$r_t^3 = \begin{cases} a, & \text{if the bird is alive and between the pipes} \\ -b, & \text{if collided} \end{cases} \tag{8}$$

$$r_t^4 = \begin{cases} a, & \text{is alive and between the pipes and } d < \delta \\ -b, & \text{if collided} \end{cases} \tag{9}$$

$$r_t^5 = \begin{cases} a, & \text{jumped when below the center} \\ a, & \text{didn't jump being above the center} \\ -b, & \text{if collided} \end{cases} \tag{10}$$

5   Experimental Methodology

Training a Flappy Bird agent consists of making it play the game several times until the total training time exceeds a limit (here established as 30 min) or until the average agent score is over a defined value (here, it is fixed as 100).

In this work, the main metrics used to compare agents and evaluate their performance are the accumulated reward, the average score, the maximum score and the probability of crossing two pipes. First, we rely on their accumulative reward, either when they have the same reward function or by converting their different functions. Furthermore, as a Flappy Bird objective is to go through the largest number of pipes as possible to obtain the highest possible score, it is natural to evaluate the performance of an agent through the achieved score. Finally, the performance of an agent can be assessed through its consistency in carrying out a predetermined task.

5.1   NEAT

NEAT uses the Fitness function of each individual for its evaluation. In this paper the function follows the score obtained by the agent during the game. The score for each agent is calculated when it touches any of the pipes or the ground, which does not happen with a properly trained agent. When any individual of the generation reaches this limit, it is considered converged and GA evaluates the next generation, up to the limit of 100 generations.

During the initial tests, several configurations of different neural network topologies and hyperparameters were verified, surpassing the simplest ones and those that used the ReLU function and topologies without hidden layer, using the configurations present in [19], with the adjustments shown in the Table 2.

Table 2. NEAT Settings

Parameter	Setting 1	Setting 2	Setting 3	Setting 4
weight_mutate_power	10	1	0.5	0.1

5.2   Q-Learning

The value of the parameters considered for running the game agents with Q-Learning is detailed in Table 3. The policy chosen in the training was ϵ-greedy, where the parameter ϵ is defined as a function of the number of iterations (i), if $i < 1000$ then $\epsilon = \epsilon_0$, if $i > 1000$ ϵ is decremented by 0.01 whenever the number of iterations is a multiple of 500. This function guarantees more exploration at the beginning of the training and more exploitation at the end.

Table 3. Default parameters of Q Learning.

Parameter	γ	μ	ϵ_0	N
Value	0.9	0.7	0.5	5

After preliminary tests it was possible to notice that the standard training strategy is inefficient. The problem is that the game time increases with the agent's performance and consequently increases the training time. The game time of an agent that scores 100 points is almost 100 times greater than the time of a game where the agent scores 1. These difficulties led to the development of a new training methodology. Instead of letting the agent play freely until reaching 100 points or die, the game ends when the agent gets 2 points. Since there is no distinction between the representation of a low-scoring state to a high-scoring state and the pipes are generated randomly, an agent who consistently can pass the first two pipes will also be able to pass the others with high probability. Applying this process, considering state representation s_1 and reward function r_4, an average score of 42.5 have been achieved and the best score was 279 points for an agent trained for 1 h. Note that the average of 42.5 is much higher than the asymptotic performance obtained by the previous methodology.

After changing the training methodology, we find the best reward function and the best representation of states. In order to do so, the state was fixed and different reward functions were evaluated, so that the reward function r_4 was the one that got the best result. To find the best state representation, we fixed the reward function r_4, testing different representations of state in order to analyse the result of each representation. The best representation achieved was s_1 as shown in Fig. 2.

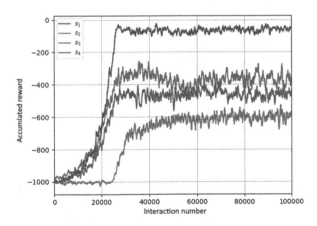

Fig. 2. Accumulated reward as a function of the number of iterations considering different state representations.

5.3 PPO

PPO allows multiple agents to train simultaneously in order to streamline the training process. The PPO training process resulted in the reproduction of the same problems founded in the Q-Learning standard training strategy, which took much longer time as the agent become better at passing through the pipes. Thus, the PPO training strategy was also adapted to the training strategy where the game ends when the agent obtains 2 points and the configuration of 30 agents in the training environment was maintained.

As with Q-Leaning, preliminary tests were carried out, using base values for the hyperparameters and the new training strategy in order to identify an optimal configuration of state representation and reward function to be used in the PPO learning algorithm. In [20], it is possible to find a detailed description and the base values of each hyperparameter.

Analyzing the preliminary tests results, *num_layers*, *hidden_units* and *beta* were selected. The choice of the parameters *num_layers* e *hidden_units* aimed to analyze different ANNs' architectures. The parameter *beta* allows the algorithm to fully explore the states, doing more tests before decreasing the entropy, resulting in a better generalization at the end of the training.

With the chosen parameters, we start a new test session in order to find an optimal configuration considering changes in these 3 hyperparameter. Each test run uses the r_t^5 reward function and goes through one million interactions. Table 4 shows the configurations used to train the agents to select the best values for hyperparameters. The better representation was *Env*1, as it managed to quickly train the agent while maintaining a good generalization of the agent when compared to the others.

Table 4. PPO's environments hyperparameters settings

Parameter	Env 1	Env 2	Env 3	Env 4
num_layers	2	1	2	1
hidden_units	64	32	64	32
beta	5.0e−3	5.0e−3	4e−1	4e−1

6 Results and Discussions

6.1 NEAT

Experiments were performed with different configurations for the initial population, increasing the amount of neurons to 10, 50 and 100 in the hidden layer, considering that no individual was able to reach the 100-point mark. The other varied NEAT parameter is the mutation rate, which influences the weight, inclusion, and removal of the neural network edges, as well as the inclusion and removal of neurons. The randomness coming from different values of the mutation rate, may be the responsible for the random behavior of individuals over generations. Figure 3 illustrates a partially random behavior from the scoring of the best individuals of each generation, in addition to the lack of consistency between the score of one generation and the score of the next generation. Thus, after experimenting mutation rates of 5% and 10%, we noticed that the behavior of the agents in the game was no longer at random and they all began to perform the same actions making the search very repetitive, with no evolution over the generations. Observing the average score for each one, it is possible to state that there is a large disparity between individuals within the same generation, since the maximum average score was 2 points, even in generations with individuals who achieved the maximum of 100 points.

6.2 Q-Learning

After defining the default parameters, trained the network and defined the reward function and state representation, we carried out tests for identifying the optimal set of parameters and understand how they impact on the learning process. In these tests, only the investigated parameter can change while the others are fixed to their default values.

The ϵ_0 parameter had a great impact on the agent's performance, both in the consistency to perform the task and in the accumulated reward. For ϵ_0 varying from 0.3 to 0.6 it is possible to observe a decrease in initial learning speed but the asymptotic performance remains the same. However, for $\epsilon_0 < 0.3$, despite maintaining the highest initial learning speed, the asymptotic performance is inversely proportional to ϵ_0. This result highlights the need for better initial exploration in the hyperparameters space to learn a more efficient solution.

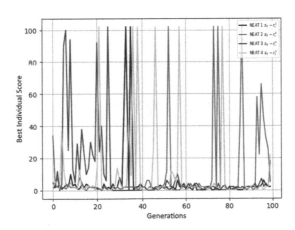

Fig. 3. Score of the best individual of each generation.

The parameters γ and μ have also been tested, but they did not present a great influence on performance. The discretization control parameter N had a notable impact on asymptotic performance and the best performance occurs for

$N = 6$. Small values of N decreases the agent's generalization capabilities, while large N can oversimplify the state space and important information can be lost.

Table 5 shows the optimal hyperparameters according to the experiments. With those values and a greedy policy, the trained agent obtained an average score of 49.18 and the best score of 290 points considering 30 min of play.

Table 5. Optimal parameters found for Q Learning.

Parameter	γ	μ	ϵ_0	N
Value	0.9	0.7	0.5	6

6.3   PPO

Once we found the optimal settings for the hyperparameters, a final analysis step was started where each execution takes two million interactions. This step consisted of using the mentioned state representations s_1, s_2, s_3 and analyzing the performance of each of them when combining with the reward functions: r_t^1, r_t^4 and r_t^5. Figure 4 shows the combination that achieved the best result was s_3 with the reward r_t^5 as it was able to faster train the agent and still keep a good generalization of when compared to the others states and reward functions.

At the end of each training process, Unity's PPO algorithm generates a file that contains the model achieved during the training. To evaluate how the new agent performs, the file generated by the state representation s_3 was used with a reward r_t^5, since those were the configurations with the best results. When using this model in the game without any scoring restriction, after 30 min of play session we obtained an average score of 1.5 and a maximum of 10. This result is somewhat curious since as the agents managed to do well during training, it was expected that the generated model would do better.

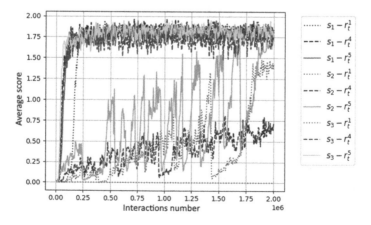

Fig. 4. Average score based on the number of interactions. Each curve represents a different state representation s_n, using the r_t^y reward functions.

7   Conclusion

In this paper, the Flappy Bird game was formulated as an AI problem including an AI-based state representation and a transition model between a pair of actions. The goal of the formulation is to train a Flappy Bird AI-agent that never loses or at least consistently perform well. We approach the problem using a genetic algorithm, reinforcement learning and deep reinforcement learning perspectives. To achieve that, reward and fitness functions were also developed to guide the agent to find a good solution for the problem.

We evaluated the NEAT algorithm in order to search for an effective configuration of a neural network, a Q-learning algorithm built upon discretized representations of states and actions and the PPO approach. The NEAT algorithm was the most effective to solve the Flappy Bird as its agent never loses when used on a play session, although we have observed some noisy issues during its operations due to the mutation rate. The PPO agent performed well during training, but when used on a play session it was not so effective as the training sessions. The Q-Learning agent performance was so consistent on training as on play sessions. All agents were able to play, but some were better than others, as shown in Table 6.

Table 6. Agent max score on 30 min of play session after training.

Method	NEAT	Q-Learning	PPO
Max score	Never lose	290	10

As future work, we intend to apply these algorithms and configurations in other games that have different characteristics and challenges. We also intend to create agents that combine these techniques to train a single agent and evaluate the result of this combination.

References

1. Yannakakis, G.N., Togelius, J.: Artificial Intelligence and Games, vol. 2. Springer, Cham (2018). https://doi.org/10.1007/978-3-319-63519-4
2. Silver, D., et al.: Mastering the game of Go with deep neural networks and tree search. Nature **529**(7587), 484–489 (2016)
3. Vinyals, O., et al.: AlphaStar: mastering the real-time strategy game StarCraft II (2019). https://deepmind.com/blog/alphastar-mastering-real-time-strategy-game-starcraft-ii/
4. Samsuden, M.A., Diah, N.M., Rahman, N.A.: A review paper on implementing reinforcement learning technique in optimising games performance. In: 2019 IEEE 9th International Conference on System Engineering and Technology (ICSET), pp. 258–263. IEEE (2019)
5. Injadat, M.N., Moubayed, A., Nassif, A.B., Shami, A.: Machine learning towards intelligent systems: applications, challenges, and opportunities. Artifi. Intell. Rev. **54**(5), 3299–3348 (2021). https://doi.org/10.1007/s10462-020-09948-w

6. Unity. https://unity.com/. Accessed 19 June 2021
7. Pygame. https://www.pygame.org/. Accessed 19 June 2021
8. Mishra, Y., Kumawat, V., Selvakumar, K.: Performance analysis of flappy bird playing agent using neural network and genetic algorithm. In: Gani, A.B., Das, P.K., Kharb, L., Chahal, D. (eds.) ICICCT 2019. CCIS, vol. 1025, pp. 253–265. Springer, Singapore (2019). https://doi.org/10.1007/978-981-15-1384-8_21
9. Vu, T., Tran, L.: FlapAI bird: training an agent to play flappy bird using reinforcement learning techniques. arXiv preprint arXiv:2003.09579 (2020)
10. Hosu, I., Urzica, A.: Comparative analysis of existing architectures for general game agents. In: 2015 17th International Symposium on Symbolic and Numeric Algorithms for Scientific Computing (SYNASC), pp. 257–260 (2015)
11. Jeerige, A., Bein, D., Verma, A.: Comparison of deep reinforcement learning approaches for intelligent game playing. In: 2019 IEEE 9th Annual Computing and Communication Workshop and Conference (CCWC), pp. 0366–0371 (2019)
12. Mirjalili, S.: Genetic algorithm. In: Evolutionary Algorithms and Neural Networks. SCI, vol. 780, pp. 43–55. Springer, Cham (2019). https://doi.org/10.1007/978-3-319-93025-1_4
13. Marsland, S.: Machine Learning - An Algorithmic Perspective. Chapman and Hall/CRC Machine Learning and Pattern Recognition Series. CRC Press (2009)
14. Stanley, K.O., Miikkulainen, R.: Evolving neural networks through augmenting topologies. Evol. Comput. **10**(2), 99–127 (2002)
15. Lanham, M.: Learn Unity ML-Agents - Fundamentals of Unity Machine Learning: Incorporate New Powerful ML Algorithms such as Deep Reinforcement Learning for Games. Packt Publishing, Birmingham (2018)
16. Goulart, Í., Paes, A., Clua, E.: Learning how to play Bomberman with deep reinforcement and imitation learning. In: van der Spek, E., Göbel, S., Do, E.Y.-L., Clua, E., Baalsrud Hauge, J. (eds.) ICEC-JCSG 2019. LNCS, vol. 11863, pp. 121–133. Springer, Cham (2019). https://doi.org/10.1007/978-3-030-34644-7_10
17. Schulman, J., et al.: Proximal policy optimization algorithms (2017)
18. Pecenin, M., Maidl, A., Weingaertner, D.: Optimization of halide image processing schedules with reinforcement learning. In: Anais do XX Simpósio em Sistemas Computacionais de Alto Desempenho, pp. 37–48. SBC, Porto Alegre (2010)
19. McIntyre, A., et al.: Neat-python. https://github.com/CodeReclaimers/neat-python
20. Unity ML-Agents PPO hyperparameters configurations. https://github.com/Unity-Technologies/ml-agents/blob/release_15_docs/docs/Training-Configuration-File.md. Accessed 19 June 2021

Instruction Pictograms for Interactive Entertainment

Kei Kobayashi$^{(\boxtimes)}$ and Junichi Hoshino

University of Tsukuba, Ibaraki, Japan
kobayashi.kei@entcomp.esys.tsukuba.ac.jp,
jhoshino@esys.tsukuba.ac.jp

Abstract. With advancements in detection devices and cognitive technology, experience-based displays (exhibits) reacting to user behaviors are gaining popularity. These systems use sensors to recognize users' upper arm and forearm movements to switch images or the environment in images; however, communicating exactly what user action is required for the display to respond is difficult. To have viewers (users) behave in the manner intended by experience-based displays incorporated in media art and museum exhibits, this study proposes methods for instructing behaviors through pictograms. This study produced still (frozen) and moving pictograms after elaborating on forms and compositions that specify desired behaviors and compared the correct answer rates and average time spent by users in their twenties to seventies to achieve the desired behaviors. For the assessment experiment targeting users in their twenties, the correct answer rates varied among different still images, whereas all moving images successfully navigated >88.5% of users to correctly behave. Pictograms were successful in making middle-aged and older users understand the desired behaviors; however, they were frequently required more time to absorb the instructions. This study introduces use cases incorporating these results into a real-world experience-based system.

Keywords: Pictogram · Interaction · Museum · Augmented reality

1 Introduction

With advancements in detection devices and cognitive technologies, additional media arts and museum exhibits have been introducing experience-based displays, incorporating behavioral recognition using sensors and images [1–3]. In most systems, sensors recognize the movements of users' hands, upper arms, and forearms and switch images or accordingly change the environment in the images. In an exhibition environment, however, it is difficult to exactly inform users what movement is required.

Audio or text instructions using natural languages as a means to instruct users what to do would require the preparation of instructions in multiple languages to consider users from different language backgrounds. Moreover, depending on the type of behaviors, a word may mean several different movements, necessitating explanations in detail to accurately communicate behaviors intended by the system designer. Such descriptions, however, would take a long time to understand and require a large display area to accommodate lengthy texts, which may compromise the expressions of the exhibit. Furthermore, the use of live action video or animation as a means to instruct behaviors would require the production of such materials along with the exhibit content's world views and atmospheres.

A method extensively used in communicating required behaviors in public spaces, which users in different age groups or with different nationalities can understand, is a pictogram. Pictograms refer to visual signals designed to provide information or call attention using simple graphics and color combinations. They are extensively in use globally as evacuation guidance, as traffic signs, in restrooms, or at Olympic games, and their application in various fields has been examined in previous studies [4–6]. However, no report on the use case or effectiveness of pictograms for experience-based exhibits requiring gesture inputs has been published to date.

This study proposes methods to communicate behaviors through pictograms to enable users to input correct behaviors in experience-based exhibits such as media arts and exhibits in museums. First, it classifies typical experiential behaviors used in media artworks, art museums, and museums, into 1) an input method based on the status of hands; 2) an input method using upper arms and forearms; 3) an input method by a way of pressing buttons and scrolling; and 4) an input method using external objects.

Next, the study creates two types of behavior pictograms for each category: a moving pictogram and a still pictogram; it compares the correct answer rates and time spent to correctly completing behaviors among users in their twenties up to their seventies. Through the comparison, it determines whether behaviors intended for experience-based displays are correctly communicated to users and identifies differences between moving and still images, in addition to areas of considerations required for particular age groups.

2 Previous Studies

2.1 Communication Tool

In addition to their roles as a sign to inform users about functions in facilities, or instruct them or warn them of possible risks, pictograms are used as a communication tool. Isotype [7], devised by Neurath in the 1920s, uses simplified shapes to explain statistical data to the working class. Isotype has significantly impacted signages and infographics, which followed the development of isotype.

Moreover, pictograms are used in computers. In an Internet-based trial, Pere et al. [8] developed an instant message service based on pictograms to bridge the social and digital gap of people with cognitive impairment. In an exploratory evaluation, the study had people with cognitive impairment use the service and observed improvement in the users' communication ability. Mori et al. [9] examined social network services featuring pictograms used by and among children with different nationalities to identify communication patterns. Pictograms were frequently used as syntax or pictorially or as a storytelling tool, whereas their uses may vary depending on users' personalities and different cultural backgrounds.

2.2 Moving Pictograms

Regarding the addition of movements to pictograms, actograms [10] developed by Japan BoSign Association aim to raise awareness of desirable behaviors at the time of disasters using "moving" pictogram signs. The designers propose dividing time after the occurrence of an earthquake into four phases and provide information specifically required for each phase. Based on the assumption that highly abstract word classes such as verbs and adjectives would be unexplainable by still images, Ohno et al. [11] generated moving pictograms for certain verbs. They compared still images and moving pictograms based on user questionnaires to analyze comprehensibility and propose designing guidelines.

Compared to previous studies, this study focuses on designs and display methods that do not distract users' attention away from the contents of the main display (artworks).

2.3 Behavior Communication Methods

To communicate the intended behaviors, this study used the method proposed by Ogawa et al. [12] to navigate users to use hands and fingers to input behaviors in interfaces in a public space as icons and texts on a display. Generally, when users are aware of reactions triggered by their movements, they become fully engaged in the interaction, whereas they are hesitant to read text-based instructions. Okuma et al. [13] used text instructions displayed on handheld PCs for experience-based displays as part of the guide system of a science museum. However, the research results demonstrated that users' attention was distracted from exhibits to the screen of the PCs. In communicating how to experience exhibits, measures with minimal interference to exhibit would be ideal.

3 Designing Instruction Pictograms

3.1 Types of Experiential Behaviors Required for Exhibits

As outlined in Sect. 1, previous works and research are characterized using arm- and hand-based input methods based on the assumption that they are typically used for media artworks and exhibits in art museums and museums [1–3]. In these systems, the challenge is the difficulty in communicating desirable movements to users in an exhibit environment.

A combination of input methods using arms and hands may include the following:

(1) Input method based on the status of hands;
(2) Input method using upper arms and forearms;
(3) Input method using buttons and scrolling; and
(4) Input method using external objects.

"(1) Input method based on the status of hands" assumes interfaces that recognize the statuses of hands such as open palm or clenched fists. Among "(2) upper arm and forearm behaviors," behaviors having certain meanings can include the following:

(a) Behaviors to change the environment: fan, blow, and throw.
(b) Behaviors to respond to an environmental change: shiver, hold up an umbrella, and block the sun.

This study focused on (a) where content images change in response to users' behaviors in experience-based displays. Upper arms and forearms are used not only in systems recognizing behaviors through RGB-D cameras but also for systems using head-mounted displays, where users control attached controllers to experience contents [14]. In the "input methods using upper arms and forearms," individual differences become an issue because certain users make big movements, whereas others make minimal movements to the same instruction. Therefore, precise instructions, including detailed movements, must be communicated.

Because "(3) Input method using buttons and scrolling" has been traditionally used in interfaces, it may be incorporated into the actual space as concept users are familiar with. For example, they are used in systems where users operate images by holding a hand above an icon or above a seek bar and moving the hand sideways [15].

"(4) Input method using external objects" refers to the relocation or modification of an object as a behavioral input. For example, a work featuring the process of wrapping an object with a wrapping cloth [16] and a work featuring the process of holding an object and placing it on a designated place [15] use this method. Actual use cases of the method are introduced in Sect. 5 in more detail.

3.2 Requirements of Instruction Pictograms

The purpose of this study is to explain how to experience exhibits through pictograms to permanently enable users to use experience-based displays correctly. Therefore, a pictogram must have the following features:

• Make users understand intended experiential behaviors concisely;
• Be easily comprehensible by most of the users;
• Minimize its interference with the exhibited works' concepts or expressions;
• Be easy to produce.

First, experiential behaviors required for each exhibit must be communicated within a very short time period, typically several seconds. Because pictograms will be installed in public spaces, they should ideally be easily comprehensible by users belonging to various age groups and nationalities. In media artworks, minimizing interference to expressions intended by the artist is important. Furthermore, because there are myriad different behaviors, sample pictograms not introduced in this study may be required for an actual display. To this end, this study intends to enable the easy production of new pictograms by proposing a production method.

3.3 Design Requirements and Production Methods

To achieve the aforementioned requirements, designing instruction pictograms may require to consider the following aspects.

- Forms exclusively communicating certain behaviors

Pictograms introduced in this study use simple, flat figures exclusively focusing on communicating behaviors and removing other elements to keep users' attention on the exhibits and to make it easy to produce them as well.

Alternative design ideas may include a 3D depiction of human figures in the pictograms. Compared to a clear, dichromatic design (Fig. 1, Left), however, the shade would make certain areas of the figures dimmer (Fig. 1, Center), reducing visibility because of the brightness of the figure approaching that of the base brightness. Furthermore, a design incorporating elements such as body shape, sex, and hairstyle (Fig. 1, Right) necessitates a selection process based on the exhibit contents, reducing production convenience and universality. Therefore, pictograms in this study have no attributes other than behaviors.

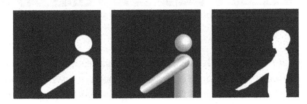

Fig. 1. Pictogram design

- Composition concisely communicating behaviors

Behaviors used in exhibits may apply to situations other than the ones introduced in this study. Therefore, composition types are limited in the study to ensure the easy production of new pictograms. To indicate the statuses of upper arms, forearms, and hands, the human figures in pictograms either face sideways or front.

For "Input method using buttons and scrolling" and "Input method using external objects," however, compositions featuring the human figure in the center obstruct the visibility of icons, seek bar, image to be swiped, and object, as well as compromises clarity. Therefore, pictograms must keep the target icon and seek bar in the center of the composition.

- Production methods

For each composition, this study prepares basic components—the head, trunk, upper arms, forearms, and hands—to enable the production of pictograms simply by combining the components. If and when adjustment is necessary for a behavior, the study modifies these components. The use of 10 × 10 square grid lines as the base for pictograms limits object shape options, reduces the time spent on determining shapes, and provides consistency to the design (Fig. 2).

Following the PIC Symbol design concept [17], this study exclusively uses black and white to retain visibility, minimize colors, and maximize the brightness difference. Based on the background of pictograms, the colors of the base and figure may be reversed. Certain colors are assigned specific roles in chromatic symbols used in safety signs, such as red for prohibition, blue for instruction, and yellow for warning [18]. To avoid providing unnecessary information or suggestions to users, pictograms in this study avoid the use of chromatic colors. If and when it is desirable to use chromatic colors because of the features of the contents, it is recommendable to use non-safety colors that are in sharp contrast to white.

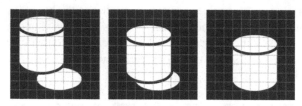

Fig. 2. Grid lines

Moving pictograms in this study use animation comprising three frames—the initial, middle, and final images. To complete a cycle of behavior when moving images are shown in a loop, both the 1st and 2nd frames are displayed for 0.25 s, whereas the 3rd frame is displayed for 0.5 s. Based on the moving pictograms, this study generates still pictograms by adding arrows to demonstrate the trajectories of behaviors and the relocation of objects to the frames.

3.4   Production Case of Pictograms

Figs. 3 and 4 show the results of nine movements incorporated into pictograms based on discussions in Sects. 3.1–3.3. Section 5.1 introduces use cases of some of these pictograms. Because each exhibit requires different behaviors, pictograms for behaviors not included in this section are separately fabricated as per the design requirements and production method introduced in Sect. 3.3.

(1)   Input method based on the status of hands

Assuming an interface that recognizes statuses of hands to prompt reactions in an exhibited image, this study fabricated two pictograms instructing users to "Face front and spread hands" and "Face front and clench fists." These types of behaviors can be applied to pictograms describing other hand statuses by replacing the statuses of hands, as shown below on the left. Use cases may include the assignment of different hand statuses with different operations such as "Face front and spread hands" to "replay movie" and "Face front and clench fists" to "pause movie."

(2)   Input method using upper arms and forearms

For behaviors involving upper arms and forearms, this study selected behaviors in which upper arms and forearms are positioned in different places. Some interfaces using such behaviors only target the final status of a single behavior, whereas others recognize the entire flow of movements as a single behavior. For interfaces targeting the final phase of a single behavior, this study prepared a pictogram describing "Blow." For the ones recognizing the entire flow of movements as a single behavior, this study produced two pictograms depicting "Fan" and "Throw." Use cases may include the assignment of a reaction relevant to each behavior, such as "Blow," causing dandelion puffs to float and then blossom in the image, "Fan," causing a wind to blow in the landscape in the image, and "Throw," triggering a ball to be flying in the image.

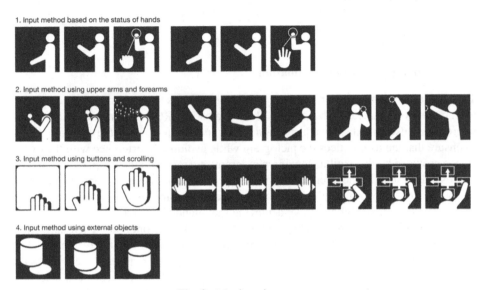

Fig. 3. Moving pictograms

Fig. 4. Still pictograms

(3)   Input method using buttons and scrolling

Because input methods using buttons and scrolling, this study fabricated pictograms telling users to "Hold a hand above something," "Manipulate a seek bar," and "Swipe." For example, "Hold a hand above something" can function as various switching operations such as pressing, clicking, or tapping buttons or icons to switch a projected image to a different image. "Manipulate a seek bar" realizes the manipulation of a seek bar, an interface used in video websites in an actual space where users move their hands to the right and left to manipulate videos. "Swipe" is primarily incorporated into smartphones and tablets, allowing users to relocate images to intended directions. Traditionally, swiping action is caused by fingers placed on a display, but in an actual space, arms are probably used to manipulate projected videos.

(4) Input method using external objects

As an input method using external objects, this study fabricated a pictogram instructing users to "Place an object." A use case may include an object in an exhibit space, whose relocation changes the display.

4 Evaluation

4.1 Designing Systems for Evaluation

This section describes the structure of evaluation systems to confirm the effect of pictograms in communicating behaviors. The systems use RGB-D cameras to detect an approaching user and display a pictogram with a sound effect above the content images to ensure that the user notices the pictogram while avoiding interference with the experience provided by the exhibit. Moving pictograms are replayed in a loop. Once the user successfully executes the intended behavior, the pictogram disappears and the result of the behavior is shown in the exhibit image. The pictogram disappears when the user steps away from the exhibit without achieving the intended behavior.

To recognize "Face front and spread hands" and "Face front and clench fists," this study used a recognition library included in Kinect. This study created original movements to recognize "Blow," "Fan," "Throw," and "Swipe" and registered them in Visual Gesture Builder. For "Hold a hand above something" and "Manipulate a seek bar," this study designed the display to switch images when the hands of a user's skeletal frame detected by RGB-D cameras enter the space coordinates above the icon. For "Place an object," this study used an OpenCV cascade classifier to switch the displayed image when the user's hands are above the icon showing a location to place an object while RGB-D cameras recognize the object.

For icons, to manipulate seek bar, and to place an object, pictograms instructing "Hold a hand above something," "Manipulate a seek bar," and "Place an object" are projected on a tabletop with a mobile projector (Fig. 5, Left), whereas other pictograms are projected on the wall with short-focus projectors (Fig. 5, Right). Wall pictograms are projected on the same location in the center. Because the exhibit contents may provide users with clues to understand behaviors meant to be communicated through pictograms, the systems in this study did not display the exhibit images. Instead, the systems showed "OK" on the screen when RGB-D cameras recognize the user's correct behaviors (Fig. 5, Bottom Right).

Correct movements were defined as follows, and behaviors were judged correct when they were visually identified as being correctly executed:

- For "Clench fists," hands are clenched into fists while facing front;
- For "Blow," hands are clenched into fists and placed in front of the head;

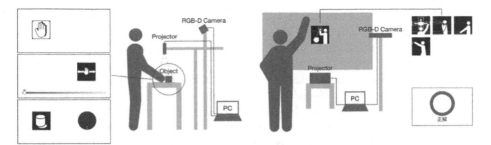

Fig. 5. Experimental environment

- For "Fan," arms are extended forward with hands swinging vertically down from a position above the head to the position below the head;
- For "Throw," hands are moved from behind the head to the front of the head;
- For "Hold a hand above something," a projected icon is covered by a hand;
- For "Manipulate a seek bar," a hand is placed above the seek bar and waved sideways;
- For "Swipe," arms are extended and spread open from an inwardly bent position;
- For "Place an object," the entire bottom of the object is placed in the icon, indicating the place to place the object.

4.2 Comparison of Still Pictograms and Moving Pictograms

To confirm the comprehensibility of still and moving pictograms, this study conducted experiments from September 3rd to 19th, 2019, August 4th to 15th, 2020, and September 19th to 25th, 2020, in which 52 undergraduate students, postgraduate students, and researchers (43 men and 9 women) were randomly shown eight types of both still and moving pictograms, respectively. The participants were then divided into two groups of 26 people to perform behaviors described in the pictograms, and the correct answer rate was measured. Those who correctly responded to the pictograms were then timed to determine the average time it took to complete the behaviors.

The correct answer condition was when the RGB-D camera could recognize a user's action and switch the displayed image or when the user fulfilled the requirements for each action. Incorrect answers were given when the RGB-D camera could not recognize the user's action, even after 5 s had passed after the pictogram was displayed or when the user did not satisfy the requirements for the action. However, "Place an object" was set to 8 s because it involves the process of picking up an object from an object storage area adjacent to the projection surface. Moreover, because the basic actions of "Face front and spread hands" and "Face front and clench fists" are the same, only "Face front and clench fists" was used for evaluation, considering the burden on the user. Fig. 6 shows the respective correct answer rates for still and moving pictograms, respectively, and average time and the dispersion of time spent to complete behaviors.

Note that >88.5% (rounded to the tenth place) of participants (i.e., 23 of 26 participants) correctly understood moving images for all behaviors, among which three behaviors were understood by all participants (100%). Behaviors with the largest discrepancies in the correct answer rates between the still and moving images were "Blow,"

"Throw," "Hold a hand above something," "Manipulate a seek bar," and "Place an object." An evaluation of ratio differences with a significance level of 5% revealed significant differences in "Blow," "Throw," and "Hold a hand above something."

In response to the still pictograms indicating "Blow," certain participants just blew without moving hands while certain participants extended arms sideways to "Throw." Tabletop operations were assumed for "Hold a hand above something," "Manipulate a seek bar," and "Place an object," but certain participants reacting to still images erroneously extended arms in the air the same way as the person pictogram projected on the wall. Moving pictograms achieved higher correct answer rates in these behaviors probably because users could easily assume the behaviors to take place on the tabletop from the direction of the hand's movement shown in the pictogram. Furthermore, only pictograms were displayed in this experiment, whereas the image of interfaces would be shown on the tabletop in actual use cases (see Figs. 8 and 9). Therefore, in actual usage, erroneous movements, such as holding a hand in the air, would possibly be reduced.

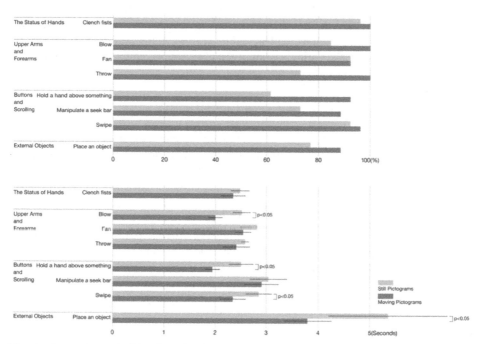

Fig. 6. Comparison of still and moving images (top row: correct answer rate/bottom row: average time spent on achieving desired behaviors)

The bottom row of Fig. 6 (time spent on achieving the correct behaviors) indicates that, compared to still images, moving pictograms require a shorter time to achieve the correct behaviors. In this evaluation experiment, different people viewed and acted on pictograms in both still and moving images; therefore, we conducted an unpaired t-test (Welch's t-test). A two-tailed t-test was conducted, with a significance level of 5%, and the p-values for "Blow," "Hold a hand above something," "Swipe," and "Place an object" were each, 0.05, indicating a significant difference. There is a wide gap between the moving and still images in terms of time spent to correctly execute "Place an object," probably because the moving pictograms depict the act of moving and placing the object within a designated circle more clearly, reducing the time spent on wondering what to do or misplacing the object.

4.3 Evaluation of Users in Their Forties Up to Their Seventies

This study had 14 users in their fifties up to their seventies (one user in his forties, seven users in their fifties, four users in their sixties, and two users in their seventies) watch the moving pictograms and behave accordingly to determine whether the pictograms can effectively communicate the intended behaviors to older users. In this evaluation, pictograms projected on the wall in actual use were shown on a large TV screen.

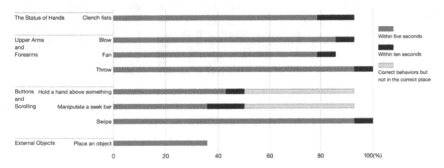

Fig. 7. Evaluation by users in their forties up to their seventies

In Fig. 7, the numbers shown in gray and black are the number of participants who correctly responded to the pictograms within 5 and 10 s, respectively. Compared to the evaluation made in Sect. 4.2, the participants tended to take a longer time in responding to pictograms with some reacting correctly only after 5 s. Moreover, regarding tabletop interfaces, users shown in red in "Hold a hand above something" and "Manipulate a seek bar" categories are the ones who responded with correct behaviors but not in the correct place, which were above icons and seek bars. Regarding the "Place an object" pictogram, certain users were observed to be obsessed with the projected image and failed to notice the object. Elaborations such as providing additional explanations to navigate users to the tabletop or circling the object in red may be required to facilitate user understanding.

5 Practical Use Cases of Instruction Pictograms

5.1 Use Case of Pictograms in Sect. 3

This section introduces a use case of certain pictograms produced in this study, namely, ones prompting users to "Hold a hand above something," "Place an object," "Face front and spread hands," "Face front and clench fists," and "Manipulate a seek bar," for an artwork introducing the culture of shrine worship [15]. In a work explaining a deity (Fig. 8), the movement to "Hold a hand above something" is used to switch texts projected on a scroll painting, whereas the movement to "Place an object" is used to display information about a deity by placing an object of the divine messenger corresponding to the deity on a designated place.

Furthermore, in the animation explaining how to ritually cleanse hands (Fig. 9), the movement to "Face front and spread hands" prompts replay, "Face front and clench fists" prompts pause, and "Manipulate a seek bar" enables the manipulation of the starting point of replay in the movie.

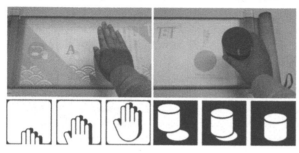

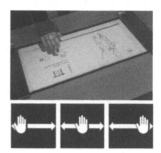

Fig. 8. Use examples explaining about an informative work on enshrined deities

Fig. 9. Use examples explaining ritual hand cleansing manner

5.2 Application Case

In an artwork designed to wrap objects with a wrapping cloth [16], this study fabricated pictograms to instruct how to use a wrapping cloth by applying design requirements and production methods described in Sect. 3.3 (Fig. 10). Because the instruction requires an input method using external objects, the pictograms featured the wrapping cloth in the center. Because the use of wrapping cloth involves a workflow comprising multiple steps, a pictogram is fabricated for each action, and they were arranged in order from left to right. To prevent the pictograms from interfering with the user's act of wrapping with a wrapping cloth, the systems placed them on top (when seen by the user) of the projected image. The systems were on display in an event space of BiVi Tsukuba (a commercial complex) from August 8, 2019, to August 10, 2019, and were visited by 23 users. This study observed behaviors of 14 users aged under ten up to their seventies to determine whether they can correctly use the wrapping cloth through the pictogram guidance. Note that 12 of 14 users were observed to correctly wrap an object with the help of pictograms, achieving a correct answer rate of 85.7% (rounded to the tenth place).

In the MR system featuring building blocks [19], users can freely pile blocks, while the display shows a concrete image suitable for the shape of the arranged blocks. Because the creator desires users to freely imagine through their experience, the system inserted pictograms on the introductory screen showing the title and explanation and depicted the construction of a house shape as an example (Fig. 11).

In the furoshiki and building block systems, where pictograms were practically introduced, users could correctly act as the author intended. Currently, the pictogram is displayed until the user performs the correct action; however, if the correct action cannot be recognized for a few seconds, a pictogram informing the user that the action has not been performed or a pictogram encouraging the correct action could be displayed.

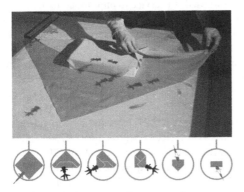

Fig. 10. Experience-based system using wrapping cloth

Fig. 11. Experience-based system using woodblocks

6   Conclusion

This study classified behaviors required for experience-based displays incorporating interfaces using gesture input, which can be communicated through pictograms, and generated pictograms after clarifying design requirements. Consequently, behaviors were successfully communicated both through still and moving images, with moving pictograms achieving higher correct answer rates and >80% of all users successfully comprehending all behaviors. Users in their forties up to their seventies successfully understood communicated behaviors, but they occasionally chose the incorrect place to make movements when it must be done on a tabletop interface, indicating the requirement for more detail on how to navigate users to make the required movements on a tabletop.

Future research may require to verify the effect of pictograms on communicating behaviors in different languages and cultural settings, as well as their impacts and effects when incorporated into museum exhibits.

References

1. Krupka, E., et al.: Toward realistic hands gesture interface: keeping it simple for developers and machines. In: ACM CHI 2017, pp. 1887–1898 (2017)
2. MANOMOTION. http://www.manomotion.com. Accessed 21 July 2021
3. Bai, H., et al.: Free-hand gesture interfaces for an augmented exhibition podium. In: OzCHI 2015, pp. 182–186 (2015)
4. Mansoor, L.E., Dowse, R.: Design and evaluation of a new pharmaceutical pictogram sequence to convey medicine usage. Ergonomics **16**(2), 29–41 (2004)
5. Kim, S.: Trends in olympic pictograph design: a comparative study using olympic games' sports symbols. Parsons J. Inf. Mapp. **4**(4), 1–12 (2012)

6. Fitch, M., et al.: The fatigue pictogram: psychometric evaluation of a new clinical tool. CONJ RCSIO **21**(4), 205–210 (2011)
7. Vossoughian, N.: Otto Neurath: The Language of the Global Polis, pp. 1–174. Nai Uitgevers Pub (2011)
8. Tuset, P., et al.: Messenger visual: a pictogram-based IM service to improve communications among disabled people. In: NordiCHI 2010, pp. 797–800 (2010)
9. Mori, Y., et al.: Patterns in pictogram communication. In: IWIC 2009, pp. 277–280 (2009)
10. BoSign. http://actgram.org. Accessed 21 July 2021
11. Shintaro, O., et al.: Proposal of design indexes in pictograms using dynamic expression. Bull. Jpn. Soc. Sci. Des. **60**(1), 95–102 (2013)
12. Ogawa, M., et al.: An instruction method for gestural interaction with interactive public media. IPSJ J. **56**(1), 316–328 (2015)
13. Okuma, T., et al.: Effects of virtual viewpoint control of 3-D maps and how-to-experience instructions on a mobile science-museum guide. Virtual Real. Soc. Jpn. **14**(2), 213–222 (2009)
14. Oculus Quest. https://www.oculus.com/quest/?locale=ja_JP. Accessed 21 July 2021
15. Kobayashi, K., Hoshino, J.: Augmented reality media for experiencing worship culture in Japanese shrines. In: Nunes, N.J., Ma, L., Wang, M., Correia, N., Pan, Z. (eds.) ICEC 2020. LNCS, vol. 12523, pp. 270–276. Springer, Cham (2020). https://doi.org/10.1007/978-3-030-65736-9_24
16. Kobayashi, K., et al.: FUROSHIKI: augmented reality media that conveys Japanese traditional culture. In: ACM SIGGRAPH VRCAI 2019, pp. 1–5 (2019)
17. Maharaj, S.C.: Pictogram Ideogram Communication: What's It All About? George Reed Foundation for the Handicapped (1980)
18. International Standard ISO 3864-1. https://irp-cdn.multiscreensite.com/e4e8d52c/files/uploaded/ISO%203864-1_2002.pdf. Accessed 21 July 2021
19. Nagata, K., et al.: Point cloud processing in mixed reality content using building blocks. In: IPSJ Interaction 2020, pp. 626-628. http://www.interaction-ipsj.org/proceedings/2020/data/pdf/2B-37.pdf. Accessed 21 July 2021

How Awe Affects Players' Entertainment Experiences Over Six Weeks of Playing

Daniel Possler[1]([⊠])[ID], Christoph Klimmt[1][ID], and Nicholas D. Bowman[2][ID]

[1] Department of Journalism and Communication Research, Hanover University of Music, Drama and Media, Germany, Expo Plaza 12, 30539 Hannover, Germany
Daniel.Possler@ijk.hmtm-hannover.de
[2] College of Media and Communication, Texas Tech University, Lubbock, TX 79409, USA

Abstract. Anecdotal evidence suggests that video games regularly inspire awe in players—an emotional response involving feelings of being 'blown away' or 'amazed'. While game research has mostly overlooked awe, initial theoretical and empirical work just recently suggested that awe experiences substantially fuel players' entertainment experiences. The present contribution aims to add to the deficient body of research. Specifically, it is examined whether awe is indeed a unique and reliable facilitator of both players' enjoyment (i.e., hedonic entertainment experience) and their perception of deeper meaning and a sense of being moved (i.e., eudaimonic entertainment experience). We secondary analyzed a longitudinal study examining players' experiences with the game *Fallout 76* over a six-week period (N = 556). Results indicate that *Fallout 76* reliably inspired awe in players and that the intensity of the emotion did not erode over the six-week period of the study. Furthermore, awe was found to exert a unique effect on players' eudaimonic entertainment experience beyond well-studied gaming gratifications. However, no unique effect of awe on players' enjoyment was found. Overall, the results suggest that awe does indeed make a unique and reliable contribution to players' sense of entertainment.

Keywords: Video games · Entertainment · Awe · Appreciation · Enjoyment

1 Introduction

The rich potential of video games to entertain players has often been attributed to their capacity to satisfy gamers' needs and trigger intense affective responses [1]. Consequently, in the last decades, research has studied a variety of emotions that may arise during gameplay ranging from joy, pride, or fear to more complex affects such as being moved [1–3]. However, one affective response to video games that has largely been overlooked until just recently is *awe* [4, 5]—an emotion that often involves the feeling

Electronic supplementary material The online version of this chapter (https://doi.org/10.1007/978-3-030-89394-1_17) contains supplementary material, which is available to authorized users.

J. Baalsrud Hauge et al. (Eds.): ICEC 2021, LNCS 13056, pp. 223–235, 2021.
https://doi.org/10.1007/978-3-030-89394-1_17

to be 'blown away' or 'amazed' [6] by a game, and was, thus, metaphorically called the 'Wow-effect' of gaming [7]. The neglect of this 'Wow-effect' in gaming research seems notable for multiple reasons [4, 5]: First, anecdotal evidence suggests that games regularly feature vast objects that may inspire awe in players, such as wide natural land-scapes (e.g., *Fallout 76*), powerful orchestral music (e.g., *Halo*), or giant antagonists (e.g., *Shadow of the Colossus*) [4, 8]. Second, game developers seem to regularly aim to create this 'Wow-effect' [7, 8]. For example, many studios invest a high level of resources in improving the aesthetic qualities of games (e.g., the graphics [9]) to create ever new spectacular aesthetic experiences. New gaming technologies such as the *PlayStation 5©* are even actively promoted with regards to their capacity to inspire awe in players due to their "incredible graphics" or "breathtaking immersion" [10]. In addition, Keren points out that evoking awe is also an important mean for developers when designing video game highlights such as boss battles [11]. Third, theoretical analyses [4–6] and first stud-ies [7, 12] suggest that feeling awe while playing video games contributes substantially to players' entertainment experiences.

In summary, awe seems to be an emotion that has rarely been studied in video game research but one that game developers aim for, that users experience regularly, and that potentially entertains them. Against this background, the present paper aims to add to the deficient body of research by examining whether awe is indeed a unique and reliable facilitator of players' entertainment responses. In the following, we first define players' entertainment experiences as well as the emotion awe and discuss how it may contribute to players' entertainment responses. We then present a secondary analysis of a longitudinal study on players' experience of the game *Fallout 76* (N = 556) [13] to examine the utility of awe for understanding the formation of players' entertainment responses over the course of six weeks of playtime.

2 Awe and Video Game Entertainment

2.1 Defining Video Game Entertainment Experiences

Video game research has traditionally equated players' entertainment responses with hedonic (i.e., pleasurable) cognitive or affective reactions to games, often referred to as "enjoyment" [14, 15]. However, a fast-growing body of research has shown that gaming may also result in more serious, complex experiences such as personal meaning, self-reflection or being emotionally moved or challenged [3]. Following the distinction between "hedonia" and "eudaimonia" in general media entertainment research [16], these more serious responses to games are often labeled "eudaimonic experiences" [3] and conceptualized as "appreciation" [3]—"an experiential state that is characterized by the perception of deeper meaning, the feeling of being moved, and the motivation to elaborate on thoughts and feelings inspired by the experience" [17].

Despite this differentiation, enjoyment and appreciation may also co-occur when playing a given game. However, the formation of enjoyment and of appreciation seem to rest on different processes [18]. For example, by drawing on the self-determination theory [19], various studies have shown that the gratification of players' basic needs contributes to their entertainment responses [20]. While the satisfaction of players' needs to act autonomously and to be competent fuels enjoyment, the gratification of their need to be related with significant others contributes to appreciation [21].

2.2 The 'Wow-Effect' of Gaming: The Emotion Awe

While the 'Wow-effect' has only recently attracted the attention of game scholars, other disciplines have mused about similar affects for centuries [22]. For example, philosophers such as Kant [23] discussed awe-related aesthetic experiences under the concept *the sublime* [24]. However, the psychological conceptualization of these and similar states as emotion *awe* [22] seems most promising to understand the 'Wow-effect' of gaming [4–6]. In a foundational paper Keltner and Haidt [22] defined awe as an emotional reaction evoked by stimuli that share two characteristics: First, awe-eliciting stimuli are perceptually 'vast'—they exceed an individual's typical frame of reference in some domain [22]. Second, the stimuli do not fit into established mental concepts, but rather require individuals to update these concepts (a process often called "accommodation" [22]). Thus, typical elicitors of awe are monumental natural phenomena [25] like the Grand Canyon, which are often considered to be vast and to not fit into peoples' mental models (e.g., ideas of 'how a canyon looks like' [4] are unlikely to account for the sheer size of the Grand Canyon).

Building on this conceptualization, emotion psychologists explored the experiential qualities of awe and found that the emotion is associated with, inter alia, the vocal outburst "Wow!" and goosebumps [26] (hence, the 'Wow-effect' referenced in this manuscript). Moreover, it was found that *linear* media content such as nature or space documentaries [e.g., 25, 27, 28] or short stories [29] can induce awe [5, 6]. Whether this also applies to *interactive* media, particularly video games, is questionable [4–6]: On the one hand, linear and interactive media place different demands on users [30], which in turn could affect the elicitation of awe: Linear media grant users the role of passive observers [31], allowing them to process a potentially awe-inspiring stimulus thoroughly. In contrast, players of video games need to invest a high level of their limited attentional resources to keep the game going and to make progress [30]. The cognitive demands of playing may, thus, conflict with the 'mindfulness' that is required to experience awe [4, 5]. On the other hand, video games regularly feature situations that do not require the expenditure of players' total attentional resources (e.g., when players freely explore the game world). In such episodes, games may be able to evoke awe [4–6]. In line with this assumption a study found that virtual reality (VR)-simulations focusing on the exploration of a nature scenery or a space setting effectively induced awe [32]. Moreover, first experimental studies have shown that VR-games (i.e., *Eve: Valkyrie*, *The Elder Scrolls V: Skyrim*) can trigger awe [7, 33]. Finally, respondents of a survey study were able to recall prior awe experiences resulting from playing non-VR games [12]. To advance this body of research, the present study further explores the potential for (and relevant levels of) awe elicited through video game play:

- RQ1: How much awe do players of video games experience?

Moreover, it has not yet been studied how reliably video games trigger awe over the often many hours of playtime. Because awe is elicited when a stimulus cannot be assimilated into preexisting mental models (see above), habituation effects to the elicitor are likely [27]: The potential of a stimulus to elicit the emotion should be strongest when it is encountered for the first time, as internal schemata do not fit to the stimulus. With every subsequent encounter, the intensity of awe should decrease as the stimulus better matches established mental models. As video games often involve from dozens to up to 100 or more hours of playtime, they necessarily involve some repetitions (e.g., visiting an already explored part of the game world again). Thus, it can be assumed that the 'Wow-effect' of a game is subject to some kind of hedonic adaptation [34]—it declines over time. The present contribution will test this assumption:

- H1: Players' awe experience will decline over time.

2.3 Awe as Facilitator of Players' Entertainment Response

The relevance of awe for players, however, does presumably not result from how reliable the emotion occurs in gaming, but from how it affects their entertainment responses. Drawing on empirical findings on the experiential qualities of awe, earlier theorizing has pointed out that the emotion may contribute to both players' enjoyment and appreciation, for multiple reasons [4–6]. Regarding the former, studies suggested that although awe can either show great similarities with joy or fear [27, 28], it is most often a positive feeling [28] that boosts momentary life satisfaction [35]. Hence, experiencing awe during gaming most likely represents a pleasurable affective reaction and, thus, contribute to players' enjoyment [4–6]. Furthermore, various studies reported that awe can lead to self-transcendent experiences [25, 27, 28, 36]—a momentary change in an individual's self-perception [37]. This involves (a) a reduced attention to the self and its concerns [25, 27, 28], often described as feeling "small and insignificant" [36]. Moreover, (b) individuals perceive an increased connection with others or more abstract entities such as 'the universe' [25, 27, 36]. Hence, feeling awe while playing may reduce gamers' attention to concerns and problems of their daily life, and these escapist qualities of awe is another reason why it may contribute to players' enjoyment [4–6].

The self-transcendent qualities of awe may also explain why the emotion likely fuels players' appreciation [4–6]: Particularly the perception of being connected with other people and to something greater than the self was found to be related to experiencing meaning [38]—a key dimension of appreciation [17]. Moreover, the perception of a community with others has been described as evoking the positive feeling of being moved [39]—another dimension of appreciation [17]. Finally, awe is elicited by stimuli that do not fit into established mental models [22] but rather challenge individuals' world views [28] and require them to make sense out of the experience [29]. Thus, awe also seems to be related to the third dimension of appreciation [5]: the motivation to elaborate on a meaningful experience [17]. Finally, this reflection process may also result in "enlightenment" [40] and, thus, intensify the perception of meaning [5, 6].

In line with these assumptions, awe positively predicted players' appreciation experience in three initial experiments [7] and two survey studies [12]. Similar effects were found for players' enjoyment although less strong and less consistently [7, 12]. The present contribution aims to complement these initial findings. More specifically, we investigate whether awe can make a *unique* contribution to players' entertainment experiences beyond well-researched antecedents of enjoyment and appreciation. In particular, the satisfaction of players' basic needs—defined in the self-determination theory (SDT) as relatedness, competence, and autonomy [19]—has been demonstrated to be an important antecedent of both, enjoyment [20] and appreciation [21], and can therefore serve as a benchmark:

- H2: Players' awe experience will increase their enjoyment beyond and above the gratification of SDT-needs.
- H3: Players' awe experience will increase their appreciation beyond and above the gratification of SDT-needs.

Finally, it is debatable whether awe's presumed influence on players' entertainment experiences erodes over the course of playing a game. On the one hand, it is likely that the emotion is only rarely felt after various hours of playtime (see H1). However, because such awe experiences should be less likely to occur later in gameplay, those that do occur are likely to be valued all the more and as a result, exert a stronger effect on players' enjoyment and appreciation than awe experiences occurring early in the game. On the other hand, other game features such as the multiplayer mode may be more important for entertainment responses after several hours of playing time than rarely occurring awe episodes. The present contribution investigates these conflicting ideas:

- RQ2: Does the effect of players' awe experience on their entertainment responses change over time?

3   Method

A secondary analysis of a three-wave longitudinal study (N = 556) on players' experiences with the video game *Fallout 76* was performed. The original study was conducted by Bowman and colleagues [13], and data were shared freely at OSF via https://osf.io/n9dw5. Permission to use the data for the present contribution was officially granted by the original authors. The secondary analysis had several advantages over primary data collection. At first, while all relevant variables for the present purpose were measured at two time points using established scales (see below), the study has not yet been analyzed with regards to awe or entertainment [13]. Hence, the data set allows to examine the present hypothesis and research questions in a resource efficient manner [41]. Moreover, the study focuses on players' experience with *Fallout 76*. Although this game was criticized for its poor technical stability and narrative style, it also received praises for depicting "beautiful" natural environments and offering rich possibilities for exploration [e.g., 42]. Given that awe is often elicited by objects from the natural world [25], *Fallout 76* seems to be a good case study.

The dataset combines three surveys conducted over a three-month period in late 2018/early 2019: Players of *Fallout 76* were surveyed two weeks before the game was released (t0), two weeks after release (t1) and two months after release (t2). The present contribution focusses on players' experiences reported after the game's release (t1 & t2) as we consider awe a reaction to playing *Fallout 76* rather than an anticipatory affect. Participants were recruited via social media (i.e., *Reddit* communities, original authors' social media pages and *Facebook* Ads: [13]). The final sample consists of $N = 556$ respondents who completed all surveys (age: $M = 30.7$, $SD = 8.7$; 68% male). The participants were highly involved in gaming, playing on average 2.9 h on a weekday ($SD = 2.1$) and 4.8 h on a weekend day ($SD = 2.7$) and using the medium for $M = 20.3$ years ($SD = 8.8$). They also showed a high level of fandom for the Fallout-Franchise ($M = 9.1$, $SD = 1.3$, scale from 0 "not at all a fan" to 10 "a huge fan").

Table 1. Descriptives and reliabilities (Cronbach's α) of all analyzed constructs in t1 (2 weeks after release) and t2 (2 months after release)

Construct	t1			t2		
	M	SD	α	M	SD	α
Enjoyment	5.74	1.28	.936	5.58	1.36	.938
Appreciation	4.29	1.54	.891	4.19	1.63	.909
Awe experience: need for accommodation	3.82	1.84	– /–	3.68	1.77	– /–
Awe experience: vastness vis-a-vis the self	3.64	1.57	.909	3.85	1.30	.717
Awe experience: self-diminishment	3.71	1.30	.834	3.60	1.44	.896
Awe experience: combined	3.73	1.27	– /–	3.71	1.33	– /–
Satisfaction of relatedness need	3.95	1.70	.904	3.93	1.76	.926
Satisfaction of competence need	5.42	1.17	.765	5.46	1.18	.794
Satisfaction of autonomy need	5.29	1.23	.743	5.24	1.32	.792

Note: For a full list of all measured items, see the supplementary material published at OSF: https://osf.io/4fxwp/.

The SPSS syntax file for all subsequent steps of data processing and analysis as well as supplementary material containing additional tables including a full list of all measured items can be found at OSF (https://osf.io/4fxwp/). All items were measured on a 7-point scale (1 = "strongly disagree" to 7 = "strongly agree"). Players' *enjoyment* and *appreciation* were each assessed by three items [17] widely used in games research [3] and reliable mean indices were calculated (see Table 1). Players' *awe experience* was measured by three subscales based on prior research [7, 27], each capturing an important experiential quality of awe: need for accommodation (3 items), vastness vis-à-vis the self (4 items) and self-diminishment (6 items). Exploratory factor analyses (EFAs) revealed that all 13 awe items can form a unidimensional structure in both waves (t1 and t2): The one factor solution explained 44.4 (t1) and 49.0 (t2) percent of the variance with factor loadings from 0.46 to 0.84 (t1) and 0.53 to 0.84 (t2) and showed a high internal reliability (Cronbach's $\alpha_{t1} = .907$; Cronbach's $\alpha_{t2} = .922$). The full results of the EFAs can be found in the supplementary material (published at OSF: https://osf.io/4fxwp/). This indicates that the awe items can be compressed to an overall index. However, as the number of items measuring the three qualities differed substantially, the items were initially compressed per quality to ensure that each dimension equally contributes to the overall awe index. The items measuring vastness and self-diminishment showed sufficient reliability (see Table 1), thus, mean indices were calculated. In contrast, the 'need for accommodation' subscale only showed weak reliability (Cronbach's α_{t1} = .550; Cronbach's α_{t2} = .644). Therefore, instead of the full subscale the one item that best represents this dimension was selected for further analysis (i.e., "I rarely had gaming experiences like this before"). Finally, an overall awe mean index was calculated based on the two indices and the single item (see Table 1). Finally, the satisfaction of SDT needs was measured with the widely used Player Experience of Need Satisfaction (PENS) scale [20]. Mean indices were calculated for the items measuring relatedness (2 items), autonomy and competence (each 3 items; see Table 1). Zero-order correlations among all indices can be found in the supplementary material (published at OSF: https://osf.io/4fxwp/).

4   Results

Regarding RQ1, the results suggest that players experienced a medium-level intensity of awe when playing *Fallout 76* (see Table 1). The mean agreement with statements forming the combined awe index was closely below the midpoint of the scale (4 = "neither agree nor disagree") in t1 and t2. 95% confidence intervals of the means in t1 [3.62, 3.83] and t2 [3.60, 3.82] supported this observation. Compared to the satisfaction of SDT needs, the data shows that players experienced awe less frequently or intensely when using *Fallout 76* than competence and autonomy need gratification, but almost similarly intensely or frequently as relatedness need satisfaction (see Table 1).

Moreover, and in contrast to H1, the data does not suggest that the intensity of players' awe experience declined between the first survey (two weeks after the game's release) and the second survey (two months after release; see Table 1). A paired t-test supported this observation, $t(548) = 0.330$, $p = .742$, Cohen's $d = .014$. Hence, H1 was disconfirmed: The game inspired roughly the same intensity of awe in players participating in this study two months after release as it did two weeks after release.

To test H2 and H3, four blockwise regression analyses were calculated (see Tables 2 and 3). Players' self-reported enjoyment and appreciation in t1 and t2 served as dependent variables in these models. The satisfaction of their relatedness, competence and autonomy needs were entered as independent variables in a first block, and the combined awe index was included as an additional independent variable in a second block. It was found that the satisfaction of SDT needs substantially predicted players enjoyment two weeks ($R^2_{adj.} = .609$; $p < .001$) and two months after the game's release ($R^2_{adj.} = .695$; $p < .001$; see Table 2). Including awe in the second step of the analysis did not significantly improve the model (t1: $\Delta R^2 = .001$, $p = .074$; t2: $\Delta R^2 < .001$, $p = .173$). Hence, H2 was disconfirmed: In the present study, players' awe experience did not increase their enjoyment beyond and above the gratification of SDT needs.

The satisfaction of SDT needs also substantially predicted players' experience of appreciation both two weeks ($R^2_{adj.} = .591$; $p < .001$) and two months after the game's release ($R^2_{adj.} = .643$; $p < .001$). Including awe in the model improved the predictive power substantially in t1 ($\Delta R^2 = .044$. $p < .001$) and t2 ($\Delta R^2 = .031, p < .001$). Awe

Table 2. Blockwise regression of SDT need satisfaction and awe on enjoyment in t1 (2 weeks after release) and t2 (2 months after release)

Predictor	Enjoyment (t1)		Enjoyment (t2)	
	Model 1 ß	Model 2 ß	Model 1 ß	Model 2 ß
Step 1				
Relatedness	.159***	.181***	.152***	.135***
Competence	.221***	.215***	.309***	.315***
Autonomy	.532***	.546***	.512***	.499***
Step 2				
Awe		−.050		.041
$R^2_{adj.}$	.609***	.610***	.695***	.695***
ΔR^2		.001		<.001

Note: $N_{t1} = 555$, $N_{t2} = 549$. *p < .05; **p < .01; ***p < .001; robust standard errors were calculated in all analysis (HC3 estimator); predictors showed only a weak level of multicollinearity (VIF_{t1} between 1.393 and 1.903; VIF_{t2} between 1.497 and 1.966).

was the second strongest predictor of Appreciation in t1, exerting a stronger effect than relatedness and competence need satisfaction; in t2, awe was the third strongest predictor (see Table 3). Overall, H3 was supported: Players' awe experience had a substantial and unique effect on players' appreciation experience.

Table 3. Blockwise regression of SDT need satisfaction and awe on appreciation in t1 (2 weeks after release) and t2 (2 months after release)

Predictor	Appreciation (t1)		Appreciation (t2)	
	Model 1 ß	Model 2 ß	Model 1 ß	Model 2 ß
Step 1				
Relatedness	.317***	.204***	.412***	.325***
Competence	.065	.095*	.064*	.094**
Autonomy	.514***	.442***	.449***	.381***
Step 2				
Awe		.257***		.214***
$R^2_{adj.}$	.591***	.635***	.643***	.673***
ΔR^2		.044***		.031***

Note: $N_{t1} = 555$, $N_{t2} = 550$. *p < .05; **p < .01; ***p < .001; robust standard errors were calculated in all analysis (HC3 estimator); predictors showed only a weak level of multicollinearity (VIF_{t1} between 1.393 and 1.903; VIF_{t2} between 1.497 and 1.966).

With respect to our second research question (RQ2), the data suggests that the effects of players' awe experience on their entertainment responses remained rather stable. Awe did not fuel enjoyment, neither two weeks nor two months after release (see Table 2). In contrast, awe significantly increased players' appreciation experience, but the size of this effect remained also rather stable across t1 ($ß_{t1} = .257$) and t2 ($ß_{t2} = .214$). In line with this observation, the 95%-confidence intervals for the standardized regression coefficients of awe on appreciation in t1 [.197, .317] and t2 [.157, .270] overlapped, suggesting that the strength of these effects is not statistically different.

5 Discussion

Harvesting the potential of a two-wave longitudinal data set, the present study investigated whether the experience of awe—the 'Wow-effect' of gaming—functions as a unique contributor to video game players' sense of entertainment. The game under investigation—*Fallout 76*—should be considered a useful case, because it depicts a vast natural world but also, because it was not overly successful and, hence, does obviously not combine many well-developed entertainment factors. Hence, if awe functions as driver of gamers' entertainment experience, such an effect should be observed among *Fallout 76* players. Moreover, while case studies are always limited in their generalizability, *Fallout 76* is an open-world multiplayer game and therefore resembles the mechanics and aesthetics of other recently popular titles (e.g., *GTA V*, *Red Dead Online*).

Descriptive findings (RQ1) suggest that awe is an experiential quality that respondents did recognize. While mean scores were not strong, the results still suggest that most gamers felt 'some' or 'occasionally' awe when playing *Fallout 76*. If awe would not play a role, much lower descriptive scores would have been expectable. We thus conclude that awe is empirically verified as a mode of experience that occurs during playing Fallout 76, which converges with previous theory [4, 5] and research [7, 12, 33]. The moderate mean values are also consistent with previous assumptions that awe is a rare gaming experience that occurs only in certain constellations [4, 5] and that is selectively evoked by developers to create game highlights such as boss battles [11].

Further analysis revealed that within the current study's six-week time frame, intensity of awe experiences remained stable on average. During the first two month of exposure, gamers did thus not find the 'Wow-effect' eroding, which had been the rationale behind the disconfirmed H1. The observed temporal stability seems surprising, given that awe is triggered by stimuli that do not fit into established mental schemata [22]. Repeated contact with a stimulus should, thus, diminish its ability to trigger intense awe. At least three explanations can be found for this result: First, the observed stability of players' awe reactions could simply be a result of the operationalization chosen in the original study [13]. In both, t1 and t2, players were asked to indicate their "feelings while playing Fallout 76" (see original questionnaires: https://osf.io/n9dw5). It can be argued that players based their responses not only on their feelings at the time of measurement (i.e., how it felt to play *Fallout 76 at that moment*), but also on recalled, prior experiences (e.g., how it felt to play the game *in the first few hours*). In particular, players' responses at t2 might reflect their cumulative experience and might, thus, not be sensitive to changes in the intensity of awe between t1 and t2. This might also explain why the satisfaction of the SDT needs remained relatively stable over time as well (see Table 1, for pairwise *t*-tests see supplementary material: https://osf.io/4fxwp/). However, the observed changes in the intensity of players' entertainment responses between t1 and t2 are not consistent with this explanation. Second, the findings may also imply that players' continuing exploration of the game world in *Fallout 76* brought about ever-fresh vast and unusual stimuli. The game was praised for its huge and beautiful game world [e.g., 42] and six weeks of playtime may just not be enough for habituation effects to occur. Third, the findings may also indicate that players are not always able to sufficiently update their mental models upon contact with an awe stimulus. Studies indicate that accommodation is a cognitively demanding process [29]. Thus, the rather high demands of games [30] may at times interfere with players' accommodation processes, so that the same game stimuli may impress them multiple times. This assumption should be tested by systematically varying games' demands.

Multiple regressions returned the finding that awe did not explain additional variance in players' enjoyment (H2) beyond the general entertainment factors derived from self-determination theory [19–21]. But awe was isolated as unique and temporally stable factor of gamers' appreciation (H3 and RQ2). Converging with prior theoretical [4–6] and empirical work [7, 12], the study revealed that the 'Wow-effect' adds to the entertainment appeal of video games by increasing states of meaningfulness and the feeling of being moved in players. However, because SDT-based factors of entertainment are rather generic and abstract, it is possible that awe's actual contribution to players' entertainment experience is partly covered by these factors; the conceptual relationship between awe and SDT factors thus deserves further reflection. This particularly applies to the observed non-effect of awe on players' enjoyment, which diverges from most prior studies [7, 12] and theorizing [4–6]. It could be assumed that this effect does exists but was overshadowed in the data by the substantial influence of SDT's higher-level factors. Indeed, although predictors showed only a weak level of multicollinearity (see VIFs in the notes below Tables 2 and 3), zero-order correlations showed that awe was not only weakly to moderately correlated to enjoyment but also to the satisfaction of the SDT needs (see supplementary material: https://osf.io/4fxwp/).

Overall, the present results explain why 'great graphics' and rich virtual worlds constitute a specific entertainment value in video games. Advancing the so far deficient state of research, the present study further verified awe as relevant element of players' experience and specifically as determinant of affectively complex states (appreciation). The much stronger effects of the SDT-need satisfaction on players' sense of entertainment revealed here suggest that aspects of video games related to agency and interactivity, to social connections and challenges [20] can be considered more central to players' overall experience. Nevertheless, awe emerge as additional component in the long list [1] of 'reasons why' players enjoy, appreciate, and continue to play games. Hence, game makers decisions to invest aggressively in the audiovisual appeal of their virtual worlds address a demonstrably relevant entertainment factor. The limited audience success of the game *Fallout 76* showcases that inducing awe is not sufficient to sell games. That said, adding 'Wow-effects' likely makes playing more attractive. How to intertwine awe with the other dimensions of game design—narrative and agency in particular—therefore emerges as follow-up question for research and practice. Moreover, awe may or may not require expensive audiovisual technology—how game makers impress and fascinate players is a promising avenue of future game creation and research.

References

1. Klimmt, C., Possler, D.: A synergistic multiprocess model of video game entertainment. In: Vorderer, P., Klimmt, C. (eds.) The Oxford Handbook of Entertainment Theory, pp. 622–646. Oxford University Press, Oxford (2021). https://doi.org/10.1093/oxfordhb/9780190072216.013.33
2. Hemenover, S.H., Bowman, N.D.: Video games, emotion, and emotion regulation: expanding the scope. Ann. Int. Commun. Assoc. **42**, 126–143 (2018). https://doi.org/10.1080/23808985.2018.1442239
3. Daneels, R., Bowman, N.D., Possler, D., Mekler, E.D.: The 'Eudaimonic Experience': a scoping review of the concept in digital games research. Media Commun. **9**(2), 178–190 (2021). https://doi.org/10.17645/mac.v9i2.3824
4. Possler, D., Klimmt, C., Raney, A.A.: Gaming is awesome theoretical model on cognitive demands and the elicitation of awe during video game play. In: Bowman, N.D. (ed.) Video Games – A Medium That Demands Our Attention, pp. 74–91. Routledge, New York (2018). https://doi.org/10.4324/9781351235266-5
5. Possler, D.: Faszinierende Unterhaltung: Die Entstehung und unterhaltsame Qualität der Emotion Awe (Ehrfurcht) bei der Medienrezeption am Beispiel von Videospielen [Fascinating Entertainment: The Elicitation and Entertaining Quality of the Emotion Awe in Media Reception Using Video Games as a Case Example]. Springer VS, Wiesbaden (2021)
6. Possler, D., Raney, A.A.: Entertained by amazement and wonder: the role of the emotion awe in media reception. In: Vorderer, P., Klimmt, C. (eds.) The Oxford Handbook of Entertainment Theory, pp. 418–436. Oxford University Press, Oxford (2021). https://doi.org/10.1093/oxfordhb/9780190072216.013.23
7. Possler, D., Klimmt, C., Raney, A.A., Steger, F., Landmann, L., Seibert, J.-M.: The "Wow!"-effect: introducing awe as novel element of the (VR) video game experience. In: Paper Presented at the 69th Annual Conference of the International Communication Association, Washington, DC, USA, May 24-28 2019
8. McGonigal, J.: Reality is Broken: Why Games Make Us Better and How They Can Change the World. Penguin Press, New York (2011)
9. Therrien, C.: Graphics in video games. In: Wolf, M.J.P. (ed.) The Video Game Explosion: A History from PONG to Playstation and Beyond, pp. 239–250. Greenwood Press, Westport (2008)
10. Sony: PlayStation®5. https://www.playstation.com/en-us/ps5/
11. Keren, I.: Boss up: boss battle design fundamentals and retrospective. In: Game Developers Conference, San Francisco. https://www.gdcvault.com/play/1024921/Boss-Up-Boss-Battle-Design (2018)
12. Possler, D., Scheper, J., Kreissl, J., Raney, A.A., Kümpel, A.S., Unkel, J.: Awe-inspirational gaming: Exploring the formation and entertaining effects of awe in video games. In: Paper Presented at the 69th Annual Conference of the International Communication Association, Washington, DC, USA, May 24-28 2019
13. Bowman, N.D., Banks, J., Rittenour, C.E.: Country roads through 1s and 0s: sense of place for and recollection of West Virginia following long-term engagement with Fallout 76. Technol. Mind Behav. 1 (2020). https://doi.org/10.1037/tmb0000001

14. Mekler, E.D., Bopp, J.A., Tuch, A.N., Opwis, K.: A systematic review of quantitative studies on the enjoyment of digital entertainment games. In: Jones, M., Palanque, P. (eds.) Proceedings of the SIGCHI Conference on Human Factors in Computing Systems, pp. 927–936. Association for Computing Machinery, New York, USA (2014). https://doi.org/10.1145/255 6288.2557078.

15. Vorderer, P., Klimmt, C., Ritterfeld, U.: Enjoyment: at the heart of media entertainment. Commun. Theory **14**, 388–408 (2004). https://doi.org/10.1111/j.1468-2885.2004.tb00321.x

16. Vorderer, P., Reinecke, L.: From mood to meaning: the changing model of the user in entertainment research. Commun. Theory **25**, 447–453 (2015). https://doi.org/10.1111/comt. 12082

17. Oliver, M.B., Bartsch, A.: Appreciation as audience response: exploring entertainment gratifications beyond hedonism. Hum. Commun. Res. **36**, 53–81 (2010). https://doi.org/10.1111/ j.1468-2958.2009.01368.x

18. Rogers, R., Woolley, J., Sherrick, B., Bowman, N.D., Oliver, M.B.: Fun versus meaningful video game experiences: a qualitative analysis of user responses. Comput. Games J. **6**(1–2), 63–79 (2016). https://doi.org/10.1007/s40869-016-0029-9

19. Ryan, R.M., Deci, E.L.: Self-determination theory and the facilitation of intrinsic motivation, social development, and well-being. Am. Psychol. **55**, 68–78 (2000). https://doi.org/10.1037/ 0003-066X.55.1.68

20. Ryan, R.M., Rigby, C.S., Przybylski, A.K.: The motivational pull of video games: a self-determination theory approach. Motiv. Emot. **30**, 347–363 (2006). https://doi.org/10.1007/ s11031-006-9051-8

21. Oliver, M.B., Bowman, N.D., Woolley, J.K., Rogers, R., Sherrick, B., Chung, M.-Y.: Video games as meaningful entertainment experiences. Psychol. Popul. Media Cult. **5**, 390–405 (2016). https://doi.org/10.1037/ppm0000066

22. Keltner, D., Haidt, J.: Approaching awe, a moral, spiritual, and aesthetic emotion. Cogn. Emot. **17**, 297–314 (2003). https://doi.org/10.1080/02699930302297

23. Kant, I.: Critique of Judgement. Hackett Publishing Company, Indianapolis (1987)

24. Shaw, P.: The Sublime. Routledge, New York (2017)

25. Bai, Y., et al.: Awe, the diminished self, and collective engagement: universals and cultural variations in the small self. J. Pers. Soc. Psychol. **113**, 185–209 (2017). https://doi.org/10. 1037/pspa0000087

26. Allen, S.: The Science of Awe. Greater Good Science Center at UC Berkeley. https://ggsc. berkeley.edu/images/uploads/GGSC-JTF_White_Paper-Awe_FINAL.pdf (2018)

27. Piff, P.K., Dietze, P., Feinberg, M., Stancato, D.M., Keltner, D.: Awe, the small self, and prosocial behavior. J. Pers. Soc. Psychol. **108**, 883–899 (2015). https://doi.org/10.1037/psp i0000018

28. Gordon, A.M., Stellar, J.E., Anderson, C.L., McNeil, G.D., Loew, D., Keltner, D.: The dark side of the sublime: distinguishing a threat-based variant of awe. J. Pers. Soc. Psychol. **113**, 310–328 (2017). https://doi.org/10.1037/pspp0000120

29. Griskevicius, V., Shiota, M.N., Neufeld, S.L.: Influence of different positive emotions on persuasion processing: a functional evolutionary approach. Emotion **10**, 190–206 (2010). https://doi.org/10.1037/a0018421

30. Bowman, N.D.: The demanding nature of video game play. In: Bowman, N.D. (ed.) Video Games – A Medium that Demands our Attention, pp. 1–24. Routledge, New York (2018)

31. Tan, E.S.-H.: Film-induced affect as a witness emotion. Poetics **23**, 7–32 (1995). https://doi. org/10.1016/0304-422X(94)00024-Z

32. Chirico, A., Ferrise, F., Cordella, L., Gaggioli, A.: Designing awe in virtual reality: an experimental study. Front. Psychol. **8**, Article 2351 (2018). https://doi.org/10.3389/fpsyg.2017. 02351.

33. Wehden, L.-O., Reer, F., Janzik, R., Tang, W.Y., Quandt, T.: The slippery path to total presence: how omnidirectional virtual reality treadmills influence the gaming experience. Media Commun. **9**(1), 5–16 (2021). https://doi.org/10.17645/mac.v9i1.3170

34. Frederick, S., Loewenstein, G.: Hedonic adaptation. In: Kahneman, D., Diener, E., Schwarz, N. (eds.) Well-Being: The Foundations of Hedonic Psychology, pp. 302–329. Russell Sage Foundation, New York, USA (1999)

35. Rudd, M., Vohs, K.D., Aaker, J.L.: Awe expands people's perception of time, alters decision making, and enhances well-being. Psychol. Sci. **23**, 1130–1136 (2012). https://doi.org/10.1177/0956797612438731

36. Shiota, M.N., Keltner, D., Mossman, A.: The nature of awe: elicitors, appraisals, and effects on self-concept. Cogn. Emot. **21**, 944–963 (2007). https://doi.org/10.1080/02699930600923668

37. Yaden, D.B., Haidt, J., Hood, R.W., Jr., Vago, D.R., Newberg, A.B.: The varieties of self-transcendent experience. Rev. Gen. Psychol. **21**, 143–160 (2017). https://doi.org/10.1037/gpr0000102

38. Baumeister, R.F., Vohs, K.D., Aaker, J.L., Garbinsky, E.N.: Some key differences between a happy life and a meaningful life. J. Posit. Psychol. **8**, 505–516 (2013). https://doi.org/10.1080/17439760.2013.830764

39. Fiske, A.P., Seibt, B., Schubert, T.W.: The sudden devotion emotion: Kama Muta and the cultural practices whose function is to evoke it. Emot. Rev. **11**, 74–86 (2019). https://doi.org/10.1177/1754073917723167

40. King, L.A., Hicks, J.A.: Detecting and constructing meaning in life events. J. Posit. Psychol. **4**, 317–330 (2009). https://doi.org/10.1080/17439760902992316

41. Donnellan, M.B., Lucas, R.E.: Secondary data analysis. In: Little, T.D. (ed.) The Oxford Handbook of Quantitative Methods in Psychology: Vol. 2: Statistical Analysis, pp. 665–677. Oxford University Press (2013)

42. Nielsen, H.: Fallout 76 Review – A Pointless Walk in the Post-Apocalypse. https://www.theguardian.com/games/2018/nov/19/fallout-76-review-playstation-xbox-pc (2018)

The Gilmorehill Mystery: A Location-Based Game for Campus Exploration

Kieran Swedlund and Matthew Barr[✉] [iD]

University of Glasgow, Glasgow, UK
Matthew.Barr@glasgow.ac.uk
https://www.gla.ac.uk/schools/computing/staff/matthewbarr/

Abstract. The University of Glasgow accommodates a large number of new students every year. Arriving at a new campus can seem daunting at first, as it is always a challenge to navigate a university's many buildings and pathways. Although in-person and self-guided online campus tours are currently offered by the University, in-person tours require advance booking and online tours do not provide the same level of immersion. As a solution, this paper describes the design, development and evaluation of an alternative: a location-based game for campus exploration. The prototype was evaluated remotely by eight participants in two stages, revealing technical issues that were subsequently addressed. A final, on-campus evaluation was carried out by a single participant using the final version of the game, with positive results. By utilizing player location tracking, this game successfully integrates a classic murder-mystery style story into a real-life setting–the University's campus–to provide an alternative means for new students to become familiar with their surroundings.

Keywords: Location-based game · Serious game · Augmented reality · Student experience · Higher education

1 Introduction

This paper presents the design, development and evaluation of *The Gilmorehill Mystery*, a location-based mobile game aimed to encourage students to explore the University of Glasgow's campus.

Currently, the University offers two different forms of campus exploration guides: in-person group tours and self-guided online web tours. The first lets students reserve a time slot with experienced tour guides whereas the latter gives students a guided tour using a gallery of pictures and information on important buildings on the University's website. With the recent outbreak of COVID-19, in-person tours are not available to freshmen. Meanwhile, the self-guided aspect of the web based tour afford more freedom to explore the campus, however it does not feel very natural and immersive. Furthermore, is has been found that

© IFIP International Federation for Information Processing 2021
Published by Springer Nature Switzerland AG 2021
J. Baalsrud Hauge et al. (Eds.): ICEC 2021, LNCS 13056, pp. 236–251, 2021.
https://doi.org/10.1007/978-3-030-89394-1_18

students introduced physically to a new campus retain more precise descriptions of the locations of the University's services [25].

The University welcomes thousands of new students every year, and it is essential to help integrate them into their new environment. Through orientation surveys, interviews, and focus groups, [9] found that often, during the first few weeks of university, new students feel lost and confused in regards to meeting new friends as well as being aware of different services and events the university offers. The University's campus is a large and complex historical site composed of over one hundred and fifty buildings, that can be overwhelming to new students.

It has also been found that when integrating game mechanics into a campus exploration app, most students agreed that using the application meant they spent more time exploring the campus than planned [10]. *The Gilmorehill Mystery* is a mobile game that uses Augmented Reality (AR) to achieve the same motivational goal: to increase students' inclination to explore their campus.

2   Background

2.1   Pervasive and Location-Based Games

Location-based games may be considered a sub-category of pervasive games. As the idea is relatively new, the exact definition of pervasive games is still under debate. However, [20] offers one explanation: "real-world games are augmented with computing functionality, or, depending on the perspective, purely virtual computer entertainment is brought back to the real world." This covers a broad range of games, where the level of digital integration ranges from minimal to fully digital. Location-based games have existed for twenty years, with the release of the first location-based game, *BotFighters* in the early 2000s [22]. Since then, this category of mobile games has become one of the most popular genres on the market, with successful games such as *Pokemon GO* and *Ingress*, developed by Niantic. Here, *The Gilmorehill Mystery* aims to combine the power of location-based games with the benefits of serious games.

2.2   Serious Games

Alongside being a location-based game with a full story line, the main aim of *The Gilmorehill Mystery* is to help students gain knowledge of the campus that they can later use to navigate it. This concept is described as 'learning by doing' [7]). Corti (2006, p. 1) describes serious games as being "all about leveraging the power of computer games to captivate and engage end-users for a specific purpose, such as to develop new knowledge and skills". Although this game does not teach explicit skills, but rather orientation and awareness, it still falls into this category. Corti notes that without an enticing gaming experience – featuring, for example, characters and rewards – there may be less incentive to participate in the learning experience. As a serious game, *The Gilmorehill Mystery* must motivate players to engage in exploring the campus when they may not initially be inclined to do so.

2.3   Augmented Reality and Learning

In comparison to virtual reality, which requires a headset and other expensive equipment, AR can be as simple as an in-game map on a mobile device. [13] defines AR as "real-time direct or indirect view of a physical real-world environment that has been enhanced/augmented by adding virtual computer-generated information to it". AR has also been shown to help students obtain knowledge [14]. Specifically, it has been found that the use of AR in mobile discovery tools helps people understand more detailed information about an environment [6,11]. *The Gilmorehill Mystery* aims to achieve this through strategically placed points of interest (POIs) that cover the most significant parts of campus, and a story line that guides users to each of these POIs.

[2] argue that the most important contextual information sources are location, environment, identity and time. Amongst these, location is considered paramount as "much other contextual information can be inferred from it". Focusing here on location, students can infer additional context such as where they are in relation to other objectives, or the true size and scale of their surroundings. They can discover new paths between POIs that can help them in the future when navigating those same areas on campus again.

2.4   Related Work

Campus Explorer is a prototype mobile application that utilises game mechanics to entice students to engage more in campus life throughout the semester [4]. It adopts a location-based approach by tracking user location on an in-game map and implements mechanics such as social messaging boards, ongoing campus activities and building check-ins. Feedback from students was positive, with players preferring POI-based quizzes and puzzles. However, *Campus Explorer* is primarily an app with additional game features, rather than a full-fledged game.

Paperchase [16] is a mobile location-based game based on a traditional scavenger hunt style game. Player location is tracked using GPS, but the game does not represent puzzle locations as POIs on a map. Instead, players explore the campus by using the map to attempt to find hidden riddles. When found, corresponding multimedia is displayed, containing the answer to the riddle. This project was evaluated by first-year university students, and results showed that the riddles were enjoyed, especially in collaboration with other students. However, the riddles were not location-specific and were solved by observing embedded multimedia rather than player surroundings, thus decreasing the connection between player and real-world. Furthermore, *Paperchase's* main goal is to complete the hunt as fast as possible, which may run counter to the aim of becoming familiar with the university campus.

In 2016, *Pokemon Go* was named America's most popular mobile game ever, with over 500M downloads [19]. As such, *Pokemon Go* is a more recent example of how location-based games succeed in motivating players. Aside from its story and game mechanics, *Pokemon Go* offers extensive rewards, collaborative events and a well designed user interface. [23] found that one notable aspect of the game's appeal was increased observation and knowledge of players' surroundings, as it encouraged people explore unfamiliar points of interest. This suggests that a game story that fits the game design and structure may increase players' intrinsic motivation to explore.

Building on such work, *The Gilmorehill Mystery* offers a way for students to familiarize themselves with buildings and services that will play a key role in their future university life, while playing an immersive location-based mobile game. This is accomplished by assigning puzzles to various in-game points of interest (POIs), associated with real locations on campus, that contribute to an overall murder-mystery story line. Playing the role of a detective, the player must piece together the mystery by visiting each location and thus explore areas with which they were not previously familiar. By linking in-game clues with the player's real-world location, students must analyse elements of their surroundings, such as campus buildings, to solve the puzzles. Although designed for the University of Glasgow campus, this project aims to illustrate the viability of a location-based game in the context of student engagement for all academic institutions.

3 Design

3.1 Concept

The main objective of the project is to encourage exploration of the University. This is achieved by having players navigate the campus buildings in real life [25]. Here, buildings are integrated into the game as marker-based POIs - a concept that is easily recognizable to anyone who has played a location-based game, such as *Pokemon Go*. Such markers are also found in most orientation apps that implement dynamic maps, such as Google Maps. To encourage players to visit POIs, a story-related puzzle was assigned to each, providing motivation for students to visit the building and discover that part of the campus. In order to increase immersion, the in-game POI tasks were associated with that real world location [18]. For example, an answer to one riddle is the name of a statue next to a building.

One challenge presented during the development of the game was the COVID-19 lockdown and associated social distancing restrictions. In this context, it was decided that players were not to enter buildings, but only approach from a distance. For this to work, the POIs' GPS radius had to be expanded to avoid crowding and respect social distancing. GPS was favored over QR codes, as the latter require close contact with the POIs, which can result in unwanted crowding. Furthermore, scanning QR codes does not integrate well with a game story and might break the feeling of immersion for players.

With the target demographic being university students, the game story and challenges had to be appropriate to the context. Inspired by the previous successful use of riddles in a location-based game aimed at university students [16], the riddles and puzzles here were incorporated into an overall story. The University of Glasgow incorporates a myriad of architectural styles, dominated by the Gothic architecture of the main building. Such buildings invoke a feeling of mystery and darkness, and the idea of a murder-mystery themed game was thus proposed as a way to capitalize on this atmosphere. The game follows a role-playing format, where the player takes on the role of a detective tasked with solving a murder case by interviewing in-game characters, located at specific real locations. Since most buildings on this campus are named after historical people, this was an effective way of tying the different locations together with the story.

3.2 Story

A story outline for The Gilmorehill Mystery was developed in the first instance, an excerpt of which is reproduced below.

> *You are an inspector from Scotland Yard who receives the case: The Gilmorehill Mystery. The current chair of Zoology, Sir John Stone, has disappeared and the Chief Superintendent suspects foul play on the campus. It is your job to solve the case! On arrival at the University of Glasgow's Main Gate entrance, you meet with the Chief Superintendent in charge of the case who explains the case [...]*

3.3 Points of Interest and Characters

The buildings that would represent the in-game POIs needed to be placed in a way that would introduce the student to as much of the campus as possible. Once the locations were chosen, a game character and associated puzzle was assigned to that location. Paelke notes that constraints imposed by the physical world must be considered during the content authoring phase [24]. As such, it was ensured that each of the selected buildings was easily accessible, and all the POIs were visited to ensure that there were no major obstructions.

[5] emphasize the importance of immersion through their own location-based game *Viking Ghost Hunter*. Immersion can be deepened through narration but also by choosing appropriate locations that resonate with the theme and story of the game. Here, locations were primarily chosen based on their relevance to student life. In order to deepen the immersion, the selected buildings were all given a connection to the story [5]. This was achieved by introducing unique characters at each building, who furthered the detective's case when interrogated. Each POI was visited to find a geographical reference that would contribute to the overall story. For POIs that required a riddle answer, the area was scouted for any artwork or interesting landmarks that would contribute to finding the answer for that POI riddle.

3.4 Puzzles

As the game is based on player location, puzzles had to not only be integrated into the story line but also connect to the player's location as much as possible.

Riddle-based puzzles were designed to challenge the player by giving them a geo-referenced clue about a specific object in their surroundings. Having the riddle linked directly to their location not only creates an immersive gaming experience, but also encourages the player to engage in exploratory activities. Riddles are also linked to the game story, as they are integrated into objects found by the player throughout the game. For example, the sports building POI consists of finding the code to the professor's locker, the code being located on signs in front of the building. Each riddle is also accompanied by a hint and the possibility to reveal the answer. According to [26] adding hints extends interest. He also argues that the experience of joy when solving a puzzle is actually triggered by seeing the answer, not solving the actual puzzle, so providing this option is crucial.

3.5 Player Motivation

It was key for this game to have broad appeal. Yee's framework of player motivations is arguably the most widely-cited such framework [28], using empirical data to build upon and refine Bartle's more established player taxonomy [1]. Yee proposes a mix of motivational components that drive a player to play a game, rather than a single unique motivation, by showing a correlation exists between achievement, socializing and immersion. Yee's framework relates to the design of *The Gilmorehill Mystery* as follows:

- Achievement: players will get a sense of gratification from collecting map pieces and solving POI puzzles.
- Social: although social features are not explicit features of the game, the possibility for collaboration with other students at POIs provides opportunity for socializing.
- Immersion: Yee's framework indicates discovery and role-playing as subsets of this component. The geo-located POIs are designed to elicit a sense of discovery, while players assume the role of detective.

Map pieces are collected and shown as fragments of the larger map in order for the player to keep track of their progress. These pieces can only be found by completing the puzzles mentioned above. [26] describes this as the *pyramid puzzle structure*. This refers to a series of small puzzles that each give some kind of clue to a larger puzzle. Schell also states that such puzzles also extend interest, and thus, player motivation. A murder-mystery story adds to the seamless nature of the experience as detectives are synonymous with collecting clues and solving mysteries.

Here, the player is introduced to the task of collecting case information from POIs at the beginning of the game. Map pieces are located at a subset of the locations indicated across the map. In order to facilitate free exploration, map piece collection is implemented such that pieces can be collected in any order. [15] describe this as a "Jigsaw puzzle" approach, noting that stories tied to a geographical location "have a built-in quality for exploration in terms of finding the next piece".

3.6 User Interface

Good user interface (UI) design is key to a good gaming experience. [3] emphasizes the importance of UI in the context of immersion referring to it as "the key to that game's ability to present an immersive world making experience". The user interface is what connects the player to the virtual world of the location-based experience. A map-centric display showing the player's location at all times provides the connection between virtual and digital. POIs are displayed at all times, such that they may be used to navigate. The map is also a constant source of feedback on the system status as it shows player's location in relation to POIs. Nielsen [8] emphasizes the importance of keeping the user informed through constant feedback, which is achieved here by updating the player's in-game character location accordingly.

Nielsen outlines further important usability heuristics for UI design that should be followed to create an enjoyable UI experience. For example, the 'User control and freedom' heuristic addresses cases when the user triggers an interaction by accident. In such events, an "emergency exit" should be available for the player to opt out. Thus, all POI pop-ups triggered by either intentional or unintentional use of the system that appear in the UI should also be able to be closed by the player. Consistency is also key in designing a user interface, and is achieved by using the same style of display for all POI pop-ups and the same UI style for all character dialogues, as well as a consistent art work design among game elements and characters.

[3] also suggests that the UI should offer a balance between giving the user enough control to feel connected to the virtual world, and giving them so much control that they can 'break' the game. A minimalist UI design is appropriate for this. This aligns with Nielsen's 'Aesthetic and minimalist design' heuristic, where interfaces should not contain irrelevant data. By displaying only essential features and having the map take up most of the UI, the player is not always required to focus on the screen and thus adsorb more contextual information.

4   Implementation and Evaluation

The game was implemented using *Unity* [27] and the *Mapbox SDK* for Android [21]. Evaluation feedback was captured through surveys completed by all participants after playing through the prototype game. The first evaluation consisted of eight participants who played the game prototype from a remote location, via an emulated smartphone. For the second evaluation phase, the same eight participants experienced the full game. Furthermore, a field test evaluation was conducted at the University of Glasgow's campus in order to observe interaction with the system in its intended context.

In both stages, items based on playability heuristics relating to gameplay and usability were used for quantitative evaluation [17]. These were followed by more specific questions relating to the POIs and other game elements. Finally, qualitative feedback was gathered through open-ended questions allowing longer responses. Participants were invited to provide general feedback on the game, and make suggestions for future development iterations. With the exception of the on-campus field test, all evaluation data were collected by means of an online survey.

4.1 Stage One

Prototype Implementation. Here, the prototype game involved visiting three implemented POIs: the sports building, the Zoology building and the Library.

The main challenge with the evaluation of a location-based game during the COVID-19 lockdown was not being allowed to meet up and conduct extensive on-campus evaluations. Therefore, an alternative evaluation technique was used which required some adjustments to the code. The Mapbox SDK *LocationProvider* script provides several location tracking options, one being the *EditorLocationArrayProvider*, which takes mock location data in the form of an array and moves the in-game player accordingly. This provider is meant to be used in the Unity Editor for testing. By changing a few lines of code, it was possible to integrate the mock location data into the game on a participant's device. Participant devices could then use that location data instead of using the device's GPS.

This allowed players to remotely participate in the game evaluation, while experiencing most of the location-specific features of the game. Location data was implemented so that the game character would stop at a POI for three minutes, giving the user ample time to attempt and complete the puzzle. For the library journal search task, mock location data made the player move from the library POI to the journal POI to simulate walking. Since the puzzles included geo-referenced riddles, another challenge was how to give players access to the clues in the areas surrounding the POI locations. To this end, players were provided with screenshots of the relevant location on Google Maps Street View.

Results

Quantitative Feedback. Participants were presented with a Likert scale for each evaluation heuristic: 'Strongly Disagree', 'Disagree', 'Neutral', 'Agree', 'Strongly Agree'. The first section concerned the evaluation of gameplay features (Fig. 1). Overall, gameplay was well received by all users, with no participants choosing 'Disagree' or 'Strongly Disagree'. The most notable results where most participants 'Strongly Agreed' were for the *"The game integrates well with the surroundings"* (75%) and *"The game story supports the gameplay and is meaningful"* (75%) heuristics, indicating that the story was well-received and made sense in the game context.

The game supports different playing styles and *There are no repetitive or boring tasks* were the points participants felt most 'neutral' about. The first could be explained by the constraints of playing the game remotely. Having the game character walk a fixed route limits the gameplay possibilities for the participant, while the UI for each of the puzzles featured in the prototype was very similar.

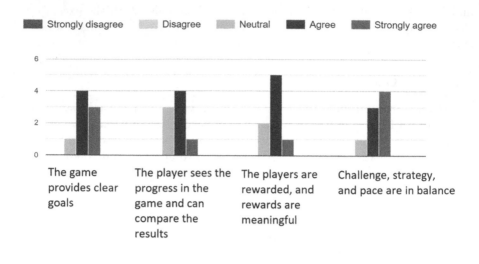

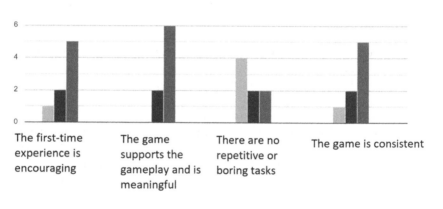

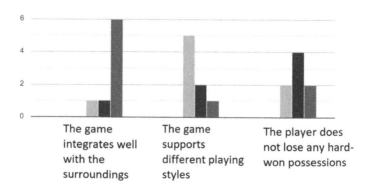

Fig. 1. Prototype gameplay evaluation results.

The participants were then asked to rank a set of seven usability heuristics. Overall, results showed a mostly positive reaction. All participants agreed that the terminology was clear, that they did not have to memorize things unnecessarily, and that the game provided help. This was evidence of a successful UI design.

Three participants chose either 'Neutral' or 'Disagree' in response to *The game gives feedback on the players actions*. This can be linked to UI freezing due to lag issues mentioned by two participants. The prototype riddles also lacked feedback when play input was incorrect. Feedback for riddle inputs was implemented during the following development iteration (Fig. 2).

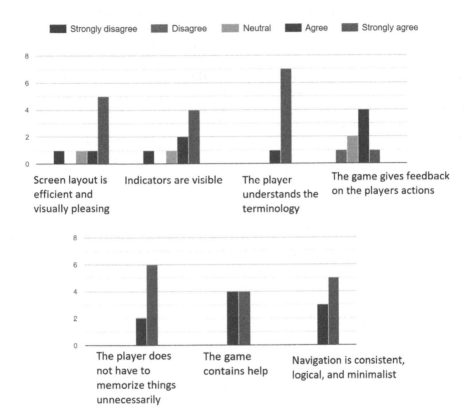

Fig. 2. Prototype usability evaluation results

When asked if the game would be useful for exploring specifically a University campus, 7/8 participants (87.5%) agreed. When asked about recommending it to a newcomer to the University, all participants agreed. In order to evaluate POI activity implementation, participants were also asked about their thoughts on the individual puzzles. They were given three response options: 'Too easy', 'Doable' and 'Too Hard'. In terms of levels of difficulty, the puzzles were considered 'Doable' with one participant choosing 'Too easy'.

Participants were also asked to rank the enjoyability of the puzzles. Participants were given three options: 'Not Fun', 'OK, could be more fun (neutral)' and 'Fun'. Results for each puzzle ranged from 75% (6/8) to 37.5% (3/8) of participants rating them as 'Fun' with the remaining five being neutral. Participants were asked if they found the dialog interesting and helpful, with 100% agreeing it was useful.

Qualitative Feedback. Participants were also asked to give longer responses in regards to the features implemented, and if their experience was enjoyable. In terms of additional features, players suggested the addition of music and a more interesting player character model. It was also clear that participants wanted a broader range of puzzles that were more playful in nature. However, there was evidence that players appreciated how well the game integrated with their surroundings: "The riddles are great, and I love the inclusion of location-specific clues which are used to solve them - this will really work well with the format". This is useful to note, in light of the discussion of player motivation above, where both [26] and [15] highlight the importance of engaging puzzles in motivating players. Players were then asked to describe their overall experience. All gave positive affirmations in regards to their experience with a few pointing out technical shortcomings that they experienced, such as scaling issues and lag.

4.2   Stage 2

The second evaluation consisted of the fully implemented game. Since the prototype evaluated only a small subset of the game, this evaluation round was important to gain a better perspective on the whole experience. Once again, due to continuous lockdown restrictions, the majority of the evaluation was done by remote participants. This time, a field test was also conducted with a participant.

Remote Evaluation. Overall gameplay feedback showed an increase in positive responses. There were only seven neutral responses which showed an improvement from the previous evaluation, which recorded a total of twenty-one neutral responses. The results obtained were consistent with the previous evaluation as 75% (7/8) participants 'Strongly Agreed' that the story was well integrated with the gameplay and was meaningful. All participants also agreed that the game integrated well with the surroundings. As noted above, increased knowledge of one's surroundings is another potential motivation for playing a location-based game.

Relating to the UI, there was also a noticeable improvement on 'The player sees the progress in the game and can compare the results' and 'The game provides clear goals'. This can be attributed to the addition of an overall map showing the fragments collected. In terms of usability, substantial improvements were observed, with 98.2% of participants choosing the "Agree" and "Strongly Agree" responses for most heuristics. The only non-agreeing response was given for *"the game gives feedback on the players actions"*.

All participants agreed on finding the game useful for University campus exploration, and would recommend the game to a someone who is new to the University (Fig. 3).

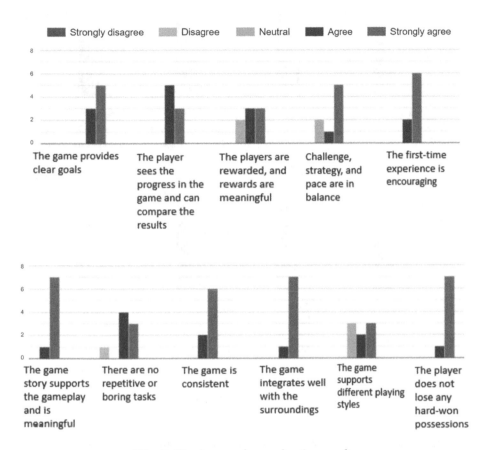

Fig. 3. Final gameplay evaluation results

Qualitative Feedback. In terms of additional features, a participant suggested adding a "description of what the different POI do, maybe even a bit of history to educate new students". The benefits of the game for exploration were acknowledged by two participants: "It was a good story, and a clear and helpful game", "Fun game to explore campus". Three participants in total explicitly mentioned the word "fun" when asked about their overall experience.

On-Campus Evaluation. A field test was also conducted in which a single participant's behaviour was observed during the gameplay experience. The player was completely free to play at their own pace and no additional guidance was

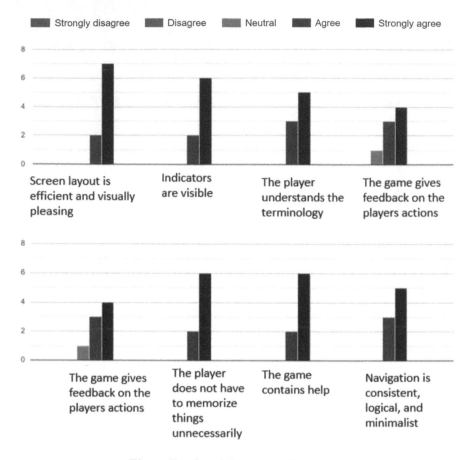

Fig. 4. Final usability evaluation results

given unless needed. While progressing through the game, the participant showed active interest and investment in the story line, making remarks such as, "I think it might be him but not sure". The participant was able to find the solutions to all the riddles without requiring assistance. The player also had no issue navigating the map to find POIs. Lastly, the participant was asked if they felt that the tour was too long, to which they responded *"Nope not at all"* (Fig. 4).

5   Limitations

The game described here was developed and evaluated during the COVID-19 pandemic, during a period when significant restrictions were placed on people's movement. As a result, a relatively small number of participants were able to evaluate the software, and the evaluation carried out was largely desk-based in nature. This also meant that most of the evaluation was carried out using questionnaires, although the final, on-campus evaluation did involve observation, and the participant was able to play the game in situ.

The development of the game was also somewhat curtailed by lockdown restrictions, as visiting the campus and its various points of interest was not initially possible. However, Google Maps Street View was found to be an acceptable alternative, allowing the developer to get a sense of the locations despite being unable to visit them during the early stages of development.

6   Conclusion

The goal of this project was to design and develop a location-based game that encourages new students to explore the University of Glasgow's campus. Through iterative design and testing, the game was evaluated on two separate occasions, with a number of technical improvements in between. The initial concept and prototype were well received, but technical flaws were identified. These technical issues were addressed, and additional puzzles types were added in subsequent iterations. Furthermore, the map system was refined to better reflect the player's progress. The choice of Unity and Mapbox provided a solid foundation for the game to be built upon, allowing for straightforward remote testing through the use of mock location data, which was useful during the early stages of iterative development. The creation of a detective-style story that blended in with the University of Glasgow campus was also successful. We conclude, then, that a narrative location-based game is an effective means of encouraging students to explore their university campus.

If the project were repeated, the design process of the POI activities would be allocated more resources. Moreover, it is important to gather feedback from users during the design phase [12]: this project's early design stages could have benefited from more end user involvement. Improvements to the game might include further diversifying the POI activities and the range of available rewards. The implementation of social features such as leaderboards and messaging might also be considered.

References

1. Bartle, R.A.: Designing Virtual Worlds. New Riders, Indianapolis (2004)
2. Boticki, I., Hoic-Bozic, N., Budiscak, I.: A system architecture for a context-aware blended mobile learning environment. J. Comput. Inf. Technol. **17**(2), 165–175 (2009). https://doi.org/10.2498/cit.1001187, https://hrcak.srce.hr/44856
3. Bunting, B.S., Hughes, J., Hetland, T.: The player as author: exploring the effects of mobile gaming and the location-aware interface on storytelling. Future Internet **4**(1), 142–160 (2012). https://doi.org/10.3390/fi4010142, https://www.mdpi.com/1999-5903/4/1/142
4. Bürgisser, B., Zünd, F., Pajarola, R., Sumner, R.W.: Campus explorer: facilitating student communities through gaming. In: Proceedings of the International Conference on Game and Entertainment Technologies, Madrid, Spain, pp. 169–176. IADIS, July 2018. http://www.iadisportal.org/digital-library/campus-explorer-facilitating-student-communities-through-gaming

5. Carrigy, T., Naliuka, K., Paterson, N., Haahr, M.: Design and evaluation of player experience of a location-based mobile game. In: Proceedings of the 6th Nordic Conference on Human-Computer Interaction: Extending Boundaries, NordiCHI 2010, pp. 92–101. Association for Computing Machinery, New York, October 2010. https://doi.org/10.1145/1868914.1868929

6. Chou, T.L., ChanLin, L.J.: Augmented reality smartphone environment orientation application: a case study of the Fu-Jen University mobile campus touring system. Procedia Soc. Behav. Sci. **46**, 410–416 (2012). https://doi.org/10.1016/j.sbspro.2012.05.132, https://www.sciencedirect.com/science/article/pii/S187704281201261X

7. Corti, K.: Games-based learning: a serious business application. Technical Report. PIXELearning Limited (2006)

8. Nielsen, J.: 10 usability heuristics for user interface design. https://www.nngroup.com/articles/ten-usability-heuristics/

9. Fitz-Walter, Z., Tjondronegoro, D., Wyeth, P.: Orientation passport: using gamification to engage university students. In: Proceedings of the 23rd Australian Computer-Human Interaction Conference, OzCHI 2011, pp. 122–125. Association for Computing Machinery, New York (2011). https://doi.org/10.1145/2071536.2071554

10. Fitz-Walter, Z., Tjondronegoro, D., Wyeth, P.: A gamified mobile application for engaging new students at university orientation. In: Proceedings of the 24th Australian Computer-Human Interaction Conference, OzCHI 2012. pp. 138–141. Association for Computing Machinery, New York (2012). https://doi.org/10.1145/2414536.2414560

11. Forsyth, E.: AR U feeling appy?: augmented reality, apps and mobile access to local studies information. Australas. Public Libr. Inf. Serv. **24**(3), 125–132 (2011). https://doi.org/10.3316/ielapa.358381864604105

12. Fullerton, T.: Game Design Workshop, 0 edn. A K Peters/CRC Press, August 2018. https://doi.org/10.1201/b22309, https://www.taylorfrancis.com/books/9781351597708

13. Furht, B.: Handbook of Augmented Reality. Springer, New York, August 2011. https://doi.org/10.1007/978-1-4614-0064-6. Google-Books-ID: fG8JUdrScsYC

14. Hwang, G.J., Chu, H.C., Lin, Y.S., Tsai, C.C.: A knowledge acquisition approach to developing Mindtools for organizing and sharing differentiating knowledge in a ubiquitous learning environment. Comput. Educ. **57**(1), 1368–1377 (2011). https://doi.org/10.1016/j.compedu.2010.12.013

15. Kjeldskov, J., Paay, J.: Augmenting the city with fiction: fictional requirements for mobile guides. In: Proceedings of HCI in Mobile Guides, Mobile HCI 2007, p. 7. University of Lancaster, UK (2007)

16. Klante, P., Krösche, J., Ratt, D., Boll, S.: First-year students' paper chase: a mobile location-aware multimedia game. In: Proceedings of the 12th Annual ACM International Conference on Multimedia, MULTIMEDIA 2004, pp. 934–935. Association for Computing Machinery, New York, October 2004. https://doi.org/10.1145/1027527.1027740

17. Korhonen, H., Koivisto, E.M.I.: Playability heuristics for mobile games. In: Proceedings of the 8th Conference on Human-Computer Interaction with Mobile Devices and Services - MobileHCI 2006, Helsinki, Finland, p. 9. ACM Press (2006). https://doi.org/10.1145/1152215.1152218, http://portal.acm.org/citation.cfm?doid=1152215.1152218

18. Laato, S., Pietarinen, T., Rauti, S., Laine, T.H.: Analysis of the quality of points of interest in the most popular location-based games. In: Proceedings of the 20th International Conference on Computer Systems and Technologies, Ruse Bulgaria, pp. 153–160. ACM, June 2019. https://doi.org/10.1145/3345252.3345286

19. Lynley, M.: With 500M downloads, Pokemon Go is coming to the Apple Watch — TechCrunch. https://techcrunch.com/2016/09/07/pokemon-go-the-hottest-game-on-the-planet-is-coming-to-the-apple-watch/

20. Magerkurth, C., Cheok, A.D., Mandryk, R.L., Nilsen, T.: Pervasive games: bringing computer entertainment back to the real world. Comput. Entertain. **3**(3), 4 (2005). https://doi.org/10.1145/1077246.1077257

21. Mapbox. https://mapbox.com/

22. Olli, S.: All the world's a botfighter stage: notes on location-based multi-user gaming. In: Computer Games and Digital Cultures Conference Proceedings. Tampere University Press, June 2002. http://www.digra.org/wp-content/uploads/digital-library/05164.14477.pdf

23. Paavilainen, J., Korhonen, H., Alha, K., Stenros, J., Koskinen, E., Mayra, F.: The Pokemon go experience: a location-based augmented reality mobile game goes mainstream. In: Proceedings of the 2017 CHI Conference on Human Factors in Computing Systems. CHI 2017, pp. 2493–2498. Association for Computing Machinery, New York, May 2017. https://doi.org/10.1145/3025453.3025871, https://doi.org/10.1145/3025453.3025871

24. Paelke, V., Oppermann, L., Reimann, C.: Mobile location-based gaming. In: Meng, L., Zipf, A., Winter, S. (eds.) Map-Based Mobile Services: Design, Interaction and Usability. Lecture Notes in Geoinformation and Cartography, pp. 310–334. Springer, Heidelberg (2008). https://doi.org/10.1007/978-3-540-37110-6

25. Pérez-Sanagustín, M., et al.: Discovering the campus together: a mobile and computer-based learning experience. J. Netw. Comput. Appl. **35**(1), 176–188 (2012). https://doi.org/10.1016/j.jnca.2011.02.011, https://www.sciencedirect.com/science/article/pii/S108480451100049X

26. Schell, J.: The Art of Game Design: A Book of Lenses. CRC Press, Boca Raton (2008)

27. Unity. https://unity.com/

28. Yee, N.: Motivations for play in online games. CyberPsychol. Behav. **9**(6), 772–775 (2006)

reco.mu: A Music Recommendation System Depending on Listener's Preference by Creating a Branching Playlist

Kosuke Nonaka[(⊠)] and Satoshi Nakamura

Meiji University, 4-21-1 Nakano, Nakano-ku, Tokyo, Japan
cs202014@meiji.ac.jp

Abstract. It is not easy to recommend various content, including music, to others. This paper proposes a method that enables people to recommend music depending on listeners' preferences by creating branching playlists. By evaluating the method's effectiveness, we found that branching playlists increased the degree of satisfaction, familiarity, and interest of the listener. We also implemented a Web based music recommendation system called "reco.mu" that incorporates the proposed method. We found that the creator becomes more conscious of the recommender when creating a branching playlist.

Keywords: Recommendation · Music · Playlist · Word-of-mouth · CGM

1 Introduction

The development of music streaming services has led to a rapid increase in music in circulation, allowing listeners to access any music at any time and any place. For example, Apple Music [1] offers 70 million pieces of music, and Spotify [2] provides more than 50 million pieces of music. It has also become easier to share such content with others online, and the Internet, including social networking services, is filled with recommendations by listeners.

Due to the increase in the number of such contents explosively, popular and well known music is easy to find, music that is not well known is difficult to find. For example, music Websites and CD stores often list popular music by ranking, making such music more visible to the public at the expense of lesser-known music. One shocking study conducted by MIDiA consulting in 2014 [3] reported that 77% of global music revenue in 2013 came from the top 1% of artists. They point out that this is due to the oversupply of music to listeners and that excessive choice interferes with exploration. Therefore, people may not even be aware of music that they might have liked. Furthermore, artists may not earn sufficient income due to this sales bias, which may adversely affect their ability to produce more music. As a result, their fans will lose a chance to listen to their new music because they sometimes give up creating music. To address such issues, we

© IFIP International Federation for Information Processing 2021
Published by Springer Nature Switzerland AG 2021
J. Baalsrud Hauge et al. (Eds.): ICEC 2021, LNCS 13056, pp. 252–263, 2021.
https://doi.org/10.1007/978-3-030-89394-1_19

need to make lesser-known (buried) artists and genres more visible to the public and fully understand their appeal. Therefore, we focused on the fans of such artists actively recommend music to others, drawing them into the artist or genre, and increasing new fans.

Since people familiar with specific music have already accumulated knowledge about that music, they can recommend music considering the knowledge level and preferences of a recommendation target (hereafter, listener). When making a recommendation by speaking directly, it is not uncommon to flexibly change the content of the recommendation depending on the response of listeners. Changing such content makes it possible to present more suited to the individual's preferences, which improves recommendation satisfaction.

Based on the idea, we propose a method that enables people to recommend their guess artists' or genres' music effectively by changing the following music depending on the listener's preference. Specifically, the method builds a playlist with a branching structure. Recommendations are made by representing the interactive conversation that people have as conditional branches in a flowchart (hereafter, a branching playlist) (see Fig. 1). By changing the content of the recommendation depending on the listener's response, it is possible to present information that is more suited to the individual's preferences. We believe that the method could improve recommendation satisfaction. Furthermore, we clarify how recommenders create branching playlists and their properties by implementing a prototype Web based music recommendation system called "reco.mu" based on the proposed method.

The contributions of this paper are as follows.

- We proposed a method that enables fans to recommend their favorite music according to the listener's preferences using a branch structure's playlist and clarified its effectiveness.
- We implemented a Web system based on the proposed method and evaluated the effectiveness from the recommenders' and listeners' feedbacks.

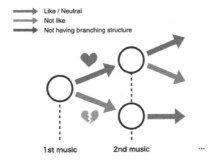

Fig. 1. Overview of branching playlist of proposed method

2 Related Work

Many researchers have researched for recommending music preferred by listeners from a vast collection of music.

Koren et al. [4] researched a method that estimates people with similar music preferences and suggests music using the listener's preferred music. Such a study focused on recommendation accuracy; therefore, the music suggested might be similar. Therefore, it may cause biased music people would listen to.

On the other hand, there are recommendation methods not focusing on accuracy. Herlocker et al. [5] pointed that many people can find items recommended by the usual method sufficiently. They also argued that researchers should evaluate a recommendation system based on indicators such as novelty, indicating that the recommended item is unknown to the listener, and serendipity, suggesting that the item is unexpectedly good for the listener. Actually, some researchers use these indicators and proposed such recommender systems [6–9], also reported their effectiveness on satisfaction and accuracy so on. With the advent of such recommendation systems, people can listen to a wider variety of music beyond their capabilities. However, it is not easy for listeners to express their preferences and select their favorite music among the many unknown pieces of music. In this research, we aim to eliminate the bias of the listened music by recommending them not by the system but by the people already familiar with them. We expected that the system could recommend music more effectively using people already familiar with the music.

There has also been much research on sales or recommendation methods by the hand of people. Luo et al. [10] conducted a survey that compared with sales income by human and chatbot. As a result, it revealed that customers trust humans more than chatbots. Nielsen Holdings Inc. [11] researched the reliability of advertisements by several media. The result showed that reliability of information from their friend is 90%, most reliable, and reliability of advertisement in video or on the banner is 30%, worst reliable. In addition, there have been studies focusing on general people. Bakshy et al. [12] found that general people are relatively more cost effective than influencers regarding marketing. Regarding this study, Cha et al. [13] suggest that non celebrity people can gain leverage by focusing on a single topic and making creative and insightful posts rather than simply conversing.

From these studies, we expected that information by general people could increase satisfaction than by machine in a recommendation.

3 Proposed Method and Its Effectiveness

3.1 Branching Playlist

We propose a method by creating a branch type of recommendation (see Fig. 1). The method enables people familiar with a particular genre to recommend music depending on the listener's preference by creating a branching playlist. For example, "if you like this music, listen to more maniac music" or "if you do not like this music, listen to more major music." The listener responds to the recommended music by liking it or not liking it, and the method then proceeds to suggest the next piece of music accordingly. Thus, our proposed method will provide listeners with many opportunities to encounter new music/genres and expand the range of music they will listen to.

A recommender creates a playlist with our method by adding a YouTube URL and a specific playback section. In addition, the recommender adds one or two next music continuously and chooses up to two music as the next music. Here, the recommender prepares one music for when a listener likes the previous music and another for when a listener does not like the previous music. If the recommender sets only one music as the next music, the method plays the next music regardless of the listener's preference.

In other words, it may be desirable for recommenders to create divergent playlists by estimating the transition of listeners' preferences. For example, if listeners evaluated the current music as not being to their liking, the recommender might be better set different atmosphere music from the current music.

3.2 Experiment and Results

We evaluated the effectiveness of branching playlists for the recommendation. We recruited two students as recommenders to create playlists (branching and non branching) for four genres. In addition, we recruited twenty four participants (in their 20s) to play the four playlists on a Web browser and rated each music. After playing the four playlists, we asked participants to answer a questionnaire about their level of satisfaction, familiarity, and interest on a 5 point scale (-2 to $+2$). We used these indicators because we expected the satisfaction could estimate the listener's comprehensive preference. The familiarity can evaluate whether they didn't feel something strange to the suggested music and the interest can assess whether they will prefer the music or not. We did not tell participants whether the playlist they were playing had a branching or non branching structure.

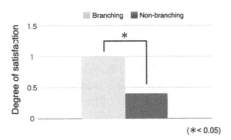

Fig. 2. Satisfaction level of each playlist

Figure 2 shows the satisfaction level of the branching and non branching playlist. The satisfaction level was higher regarding the branching playlists. There was a significant difference between branching and non branching playlists (unpaired t-test, $p < 0.05$). Moreover, Fig. 3 shows the familiarity and interest at a certain point in a playlist. For the non branching playlists, the familiarity and interest gradually decreased from the first music to the last. For the branching playlists, the familiarity and interest also gradually decreased but increased in the end.

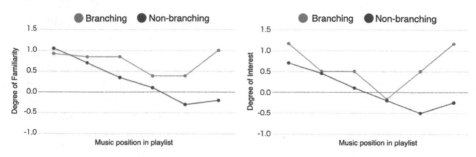

Fig. 3. Transition of evaluation value (left: familiarity, right: interest)

The results indicate that a branching playlist is useful for increasing recommendation satisfaction, familiarity, and interest. However, the recommenders said it was burdensome to create such a playlist due to its complex structure. A reason may be that we did not prepare a tool for creating a branching playlist in this experiment. We also had only four branching playlists created. Therefore, we could only conduct a limited analysis. To address these issues, we need to develop a tool to help recommenders easily create branching playlists and share them. We also need to analyze more playlists by operating the system.

4 Prototype System

We implemented a prototype music recommendation Web service called "reco.mu" based on the proposed method. In addition, we conducted a detailed analysis of how recommenders create playlists and how listeners play them. In our implementation, we used JavaScript for the client side and MySQL and PHP to store the playlist and music information for the server side. In addition, we used Songle [14] to obtain music information for playback and playlist creation.

Here, we focus on the dialogue between a recommender and a listener. Then, we roughly classify the recommendation strategy into several categories. Therefore, we prepared several branching structures and made the recommender create branching playlists based on these structures. The reason for this is that we thought recommenders would be able to create playlists with more awareness of the order of music and branching structure through trial and error. Also, if they create branching playlists completely freely regardless of structure, it may increase the difficulty of creating because they would have more considerations. Therefore, we prepared eight different playlist structures to accommodate various recommendations in our prototype system (see Fig. 4).

4.1 Design of Branching Playlist

Figure 4 shows the branching structures prepared in this study. As mentioned above, by focusing on an interactive dialogue, we determined that recommenders have unique strategies. Each playlist we prepared consisted of ten music to reduce the burden of creating playlists since it enables recommenders to consider only the music order. The following are the details of each playlist shape.

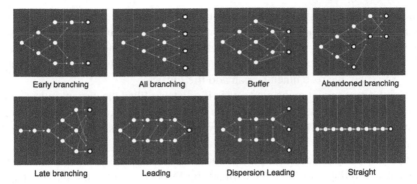

Fig. 4. Playlist structures

- **Early branching:** The first half of the playlist has a branching structure that allows the listener to listen to pieces of music that match the listener's preferences. The second half presents pieces of music that match the listener's preferences, making it easier for the listener to understand the appeal of the music.
- **All branching:** All stages have a branching structure designed to respond to the listener's preferences in more detail.
- **Buffered type:** Up to the third music is the same as in All branching, but the number of music presented in the final stage is narrowed to two so that the pieces of music recommended become more specific. This structure also reduces the number of quitters by providing a stage that serves as a buffer before reaching the last music.
- **Abandoned branching:** If a listener does not like the first music, this playlist will stop playing after a minimum of three pieces of music. In other words, if a listener is not interested in music, this playlist gives up to recommend.
- **Late branching:** The first three pieces of music must be listened to, and the subsequent music have a branching structure so that listener can listen to music adapted to the listener's preferences.
- **Leading type:** We designed this structure so that if the listener likes music at least once, the music played after will be those that the recommender wants to recommend strongly. We have narrowed down the final recommendation to one music so that the playlist plays the target music finally.
- **Dispersion leading:** As in the Leading type, if a listener judged music as a favorite once, the next music after that becomes fixed regardless of the listener's preference. By setting the number of music played in the end to three instead of just one, we aim to bring them closer to the listeners' preferences by considering the preferences of the recommenders while leading the music to be presented.
- **Straight:** This playlist structure is a conventional shape with no branching structure.

4.2 Usage

This system has two main functions: one is creating and editing playlists, and the other is to play those playlists.

The recommender first selects the playlist shape and then enters the playlist title, artist name, and other information. Then the screen moves to where the recommender can edit the playlist (left of Fig. 5). In addition, by selecting a node in the graph representing the shape of the playlist, the recommender can edit the current music, and by entering the URL of YouTube, the recommender can add the music.

The pink arrows point to the next music if a listener liked the current music, and the light blue arrows point to the next music if a listener did not like the current music. The gray arrows indicate that the music has only one next music, so the system played the same music regardless of the preference.

For playback, by selecting the playlist the listener wishes to view from the top page, the system will redirect to the screen where the listener can play the playlist (right of Fig. 5). While playing the playlist, the listener can use the bottom left button to evaluate whether or not the listener likes the current music being listened to, and the next music played will change depending on the listener's input. The listener can also skip tracks by clicking the bottom right button. In this case, we made the system to play the music at the end of the light blue arrow. This is because listeners who like to listen to the music are unlikely to stop playing in the middle of the music, and the skip button is likely to be used when the music is not to their liking.

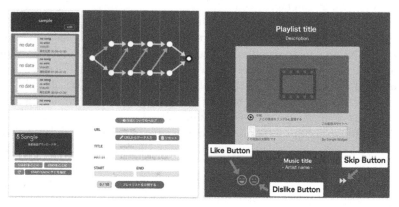

Fig. 5. Screen of prototype system (left: screen for editing, right: screen for playing)

5   Results and Analysis

We published "reco.mu" on July 19, 2020. Therefore, this study analyzed the operational results for about six months, from July 19, 2020, to January 13, 2021.

5.1   Creating Playlists

We firstly asked our university students to create branching playlists and to answer several questions soon after the release. Also, we published reco.mu generally and recruited users to create and listen to playlists using Yahoo! Cloud sourcing [15] (conducted from November 17 to 20, 2020). In the request, we instructed participants to "create a playlist of your favorite genre or artist that you would recommend to others." As a result, 19 participants created 52 branching playlists and 32 non branching playlists. The structure breakdown of the branching playlists was 8 Leading, 8 Early branching, 10 Late branching, 11 All branching, 3 Dispersion leading, 7 Abandoned branching, and 5 Buffered.

For example, one participant created a playlist, "80's Western rock music", and its shape is Leading. As its name suggests, this playlist consists of 80's rock music. The first music on the playlist is "Under Pressure (Queen)." According to the survey, the recommender selects this music for the first because this music is famous. Moreover, it also revealed that this recommender selects other music based on the listener's preference.

5.2 Playing Playlists

Listeners accessed the created playlists 1,217 times and played music in the playlists 8,374 times for all playlists. The number of playbacks was 5407 of the branching playlists and 2,967 for non branching. During playback, listeners could use buttons to input their preferences. Note that listeners could stop playing if they were not interested in the playlist. They also did not know the structure of the branching playlist before playback.

Figure 6 shows the average percentage of listeners who played a playlist (30 branching playlists and 17 non branching playlists, excluding those we could not play due to system malfunction) up to a certain point. In this figure, the playback rate of each branch type is gradually decreasing because listeners may lose interest while listening to the playlist and end the playback. This figure mentioned about 40% listeners for the branching playlists, and about 20% listeners for the non branching playlists played until the last music.

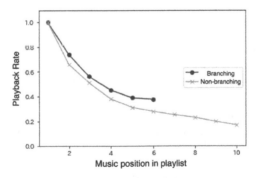

Fig. 6. Play rate for branching and non branching

Here, the length of the playlist differed depending on whether there was a branching structure. The length of branching playlists is from four to six. Therefore, we focused on the playback rate on the fourth, fifth, and sixth position, which is the same as in the branching playlist. We found that the branching playlists had a higher playback rate than the non branching playlists.

Figure 7 shows examples of visualizing the branching playlists and how the listener played them. The thickness of the arrows indicates the number of times played, and the thicker the arrow, the more listeners played it. The pink arrows point to the next music if the listener liked the music, and the light blue arrows point to the next music if the listener did not like the music. The gray arrows indicate that the music has only one next music, so the system played the same music regardless of the preference. For example, on the left side of Fig. 7, more listeners rated the first music as their favorite since the first pink arrow is thicker than the blue arrow. The subsequent branches also tend to favor the favorite, indicating that the listener traced the playback in this playlist in the way the creator intended. However, on the right side of the figure, the arrows for the first two music are thicker, but the latter half is thinner, suggesting that this playlist may not have sufficiently attracted the listener. Thus, we can see that the listener behavior changes depending on the strategy and intention of the playlist creator.

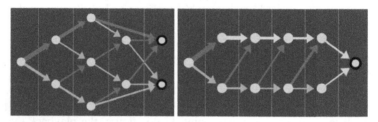

Fig. 7. Examples of how listeners played music

5.3 Results from Questionnaires on Playlist Creation

We conducted a questionnaire survey for recommenders. We asked them how burdensome playlist creation was on a 5 point scale and how they created a playlist from free text. We received responses from recommenders of 36 branching playlists and 24 non branching playlists.

As a result, the average burdensome of creating a branching playlist is 3.08, the average burdensome of creating a non branching playlist is 2.38. Thus, branching playlists are more burdensome to create. We then looked at the descriptive results, which asked about strategies and opinions for creating either type of playlist. Most recommenders made good use of the branching structures to create their branching playlists. We obtained positive feedback, such as, "It was fun to think about the branching structure." However, some recommenders responded regarding the burden of creating such playlists, such as "I was not used to thinking about how to place the music, and it was difficult." A few recommenders who created non branching playlists said that they created with more ingenuity, such as "I tried to match the tempo of the music before and after." However, many recommenders were not concerned with music order, such as "I put them in the order I like or thought of them."

6 Discussion

6.1 Playlist Creation and Questionnaires

When creating a playlist to recommend to others, we expected the preferences and familiarity of the other person would be more important than focusing on one's favorite music. Therefore, we investigated (1) whether there were responses on if the creator considered the preferences of listeners and (2) whether there were responses on if the creator emphasized his or her favorite music.

We found 20 recommenders of (1) for the branching playlists and 6 for the non branching playlists. Example responses are "I decided on two atmospheres of music in accordance with the listener's preferences and divided playlist path into two.", "I tried to make the first half of the playlist familiar and the second half more niche." and so on. For the non branching playlists, all six responses were to the effect that "I first chose music that is popular with everyone then gradually chose less popular music."

We found 8 recommenders of (2) for the branching playlists and 14 for the non branching playlists. In the branching playlists, there were cases in which the respondents selected mainly their favorite music, such as "I selected my favorite music in the order of release date," and there were few responses about the order and arrangement of the music. On the other hand, many recommenders responded that "I selected music mainly based on my favorites." for the non branching playlists.

However, several responses such as "I created the playlist with live performance in mind" and "I placed the music in chronological order based on the anime" may not be fully understood without prior knowledge of the content. Standard non branching playlists are suitable for expressing time series so that recommenders may have created their playlists because of this. Alternatively, in music distribution services, playlists of music of a specific genre or artist are sometimes made public, such as "for beginners," and we predicted that the playlists might have been created by simply compiling music of the same genre without considering the order.

As described above, adding a branching structure to a playlist makes it possible to expand creativity in creating playlists suitable for listeners. In other words, we believe that branching playlists can produce more suitable recommendations for the listener.

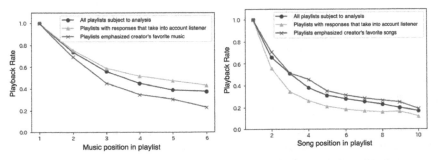

Fig. 8. Playback rate per survey (left: branching, right: non branching)

6.2 Playlist Playback

We analyzed the playback rate of both branching and non branching playlists by focusing on the responses to the questionnaire on playlists. The left of Fig. 8 shows the graphs of the playback rates of all branching playlists, those that considered listener preferences, and those that emphasized the recommenders' favorite music. When the recommenders created a playlist emphasizing their favorite music, the playback rate was higher in the branching playlists when the recommenders created a playlist with the listener in mind and lower. Therefore, it is essential to be aware of the person to whom they are recommending. This result may lead to recommendations that are more interesting to the listeners.

The right of Fig. 8 shows graphs showing the playback rates for all non branching playlists, those considering listener preferences, and those that emphasized the recommender's favorite music. This result indicates that playlists created by emphasizing the recommender's favorite music had high playback rates. In contrast, playlists created by taking into account listener preferences had low playback rates.

As mentioned in the previous subsection, all six responders considered listener preferences when creating their non branching playlists. For example, "I first chose music that was universally accepted then gradually chose lesser-known music." In a non branching playlist, the probability of not liking the next music when the listener moves to more maniac music may be higher than in a branching playlist because the next music to be played is fixed even if the listener evaluates his/her preference during playback. This gap in preference and familiarity between the recommender and listener may have caused many listeners to discontinue playback. On the other hand, playlists created emphasizing the recommender's favorite music had a higher playback rate. However, these responses are "I created with the artist's live performance in mind" or "I placed music in chronological order based on anime." Therefore, while the playlist may be enjoyable for people familiar with the artist or content, it may be unfamiliar and uninteresting for people unfamiliar with the content. These results indicate that creating branching playlists makes recommenders consider listener preferences for more interesting recommendations.

7   Conclusion and Future Work

Only a few pieces of music are known to the public, which causes disparity in popularity and recognition. Therefore, we proposed a method of creating branching playlist that enables recommenders to recommend the next music depending on the listener's preferences. We evaluated the method's effectiveness, and the results indicate that recommendations through branching playlists may improve interest and familiarity. We implemented a prototype Web based music recommendation system called "reco.mu" based on the proposed method and investigated the characteristics of branching playlists and how recommenders create them. We found that although branching playlists are more burdensome to create than non branching playlists, they may enable recommenders to be more conscious of listener preferences. It was also shown that such branching playlists are more likely to attract listeners' interest than those that reflected the recommender's preferences.

In the future, we plan to implement a function that allows multiple recommenders who are fans to collaborate to create a playlist. This collaboration is expected to increase motivation and reduce the psychological burden of the creation process. Furthermore, by incorporating the opinions of others, a recommender can consider the branching structure from multiple perspectives, which may make it possible to make playlists that are easy and familiar to more people.

References

1. Apple Music. https://www.apple.com/jp/apple-music/. Accessed 13 Aug 2021
2. Spotify. https://www.spotify.com/jp/. Accessed 13 Aug 2021
3. Mulligan, M.: The death of the long tail : the super star music economy. MIDiA Consulting (2014)
4. Koren, Y., Bell, R., Volinsky, C.: Matrix factorization techniques for recommender systems. IEEE Comput. 42(8), 30–37 (2009)
5. Herlocker, J.H., Konstan, J.A., Terveen, L.G., Riedl, J.T.: Evaluating collaborative filtering recommender systems. ACM Trans. Inf. Syst. (TOIS) 22(1), 5–53 (2004)
6. Li, P., Que, M., Jiang, Z., Hu, Y., Tuzhilin, A.: PURS: personalized unexpected recommender system for improving user satisfaction. In: Fourteenth ACM Conference on Recommender Systems, pp. 279–288 (2020)
7. Goto, M., Goto, T.: Musicream: integrated music-listening interface for active, flexible, and unexpected encounters with musical pieces. J. Inf. Process. 17(17), 292–305 (2009)
8. Menk, A., Sebastia, L., Ferreira, R.: CURUMIM: a serendipitous recommender system for tourism based on human curiosity. In: 2017 IEEE 29th International Conference on Tools with Artificial Intelligence (ICTAI), pp. 788–795 (2017)
9. Ge, M., Delgado-Battenfeld, C., Jannach, D.: Beyond accuracy: evaluating recommender systems by coverage and serendipity. In: Proceedings of the Fourth ACM Conference on Recommender Systems, pp. 257–260 (2010)
10. Luo, X., Tong, S., Fang, Z., Qu, Z.: Frontiers: machines vs. humans: the impact of artificial intelligence chatbot disclosure on customer purchases. Mark. Sci. 38(6), 937–947 (2019)
11. Nielsen Holdings plc: GLOBAL ADVERTISING CONSUMERS TRUST REAL FRIENDS AND VIRTUAL STRANGERS THE MOST. https://www.nielsen.com/us/en/insights/art icle/2009/global-advertising-consumers-trust-real-friends-and-virtual-strangers-the-most/. Accessed 13 Aug 2021
12. Bakshy, E., Hofman, J.M., Mason, W.A., Watts, D.J.: Everyone's an influencer: quantifying influence on twitter. In: Proceedings of the Fourth ACM International Conference on Web Search and Data Mining, pp. 65-74 (2011)
13. Cha, M., Haddadi, H., Benevenuto, F., Gummadi, K.: Measuring user influence in twitter: the million follower fallacy. In: Proceedings of the International AAAI Conference on Web and Social Media, vol. 4, no. 1, pp. 10-17 (2010)
14. Goto, M., Yoshii, K., Fujihara, H., Mauch, M., Nakano, T.: Songle: a web service for active music listening improved by user contributions. Proc. ISMIR 2011, 311–316 (2011)
15. Yahoo!. https://crowdsourcing.yahoo.co.jp/. Accessed 13 Aug 2021

Towards Suitable Free-to-Play Games
for Children

Andreas Kristiansen Melzer[1,2], Anna Kristine Roarsen[1,2],
Marte Hoff Hagen[1,2], and Letizia Jaccheri[1,2(✉)]

[1] Norwegian University of Science and Technology, Trondheim, Norway
[2] Department of Computer Science, Trondheim, Norway
{andrekm,annakroa}@stud.ntnu.no, {marte.h.hagen,letizia.jaccheri}@ntnu.no

Abstract. The Free-to-Play model has become popular in the gaming industry during the last decade. Games are offered for free, where additional content can be purchased. Different monetization features are used within Free-to-Play games to generate revenue. These features have been seen as problematic, especially when children are the players. A limited number of studies have highlighted the problem of these games, and little research has looked into the critical factors of Free-to-Play games and children. This research aims to identify the most critical factors towards creating suitable Free-to-Play games for children. We performed an exploratory study with 15 developers of Free-to-Play and/or children's games and three domain experts. Data was gathered using semi-structured interviews. A thematic analysis was undertaken to analyze the transcribed interviews and discover themes and patterns across our data set to answer the research question adequately. We identified five crucial factors to consider when developing Free-to-Play games for children: 1) exploiting psychological behavior, 2) game play and user interface, 3) choosing features, 4) customize the development process to children, and 5) responsibility.

Keywords: Free-to-play · Freemium · Children

1   Introduction

Free-to-Play (F2P) games are offered for free to the public, and developers get revenue from advertisements or additional content that the player can purchase [13]. Examples of trendy F2P games for children are *Among Us!*, *Angry Birds*, *FIFA Football*, *Fortnite*, and *Pokémon Go*. The paradigms of game development have changed drastically with the advent of F2P. The focus is shifting away from developing the best possible game to games that motivate the users to purchase virtual content as often as possible while increasing the user base [9]. Various strategies are thought to increase the player's commitment towards the game, increasing the risk of addiction and overspending [6]. Features that resemble gambling have been widely used in F2P games and have received much attention over

© IFIP International Federation for Information Processing 2021
Published by Springer Nature Switzerland AG 2021
J. Baalsrud Hauge et al. (Eds.): ICEC 2021, LNCS 13056, pp. 264–276, 2021.
https://doi.org/10.1007/978-3-030-89394-1_20

the years. With the advancement of technology, it is easier for anyone to create games. Besides, it is getting increasingly difficult to keep up with threats and vulnerabilities for all stakeholders, especially children [14]. Thus, the objective of this paper is *to understand better how suitable Free-to-Play is for children and what essential factors must be addressed to improve this relationship.* We present the findings from an exploratory study consisting of interviews with 15 developers and three domain experts. F2P developers need to design products to satisfy customer demands and attract more mobile device users to download and consume within the game [4]. In many cases, this leads to over-aggressive monetization strategies and exploitive behavior [8]. When creating games for children, they as a stakeholder should be included as much as possible in the development process [14]. We aim at exploring how children are addressed in F2P games, how they should be addressed, and what factors are crucial for developing F2P games for them. The main research question is: *What factors must be addressed to create suitable F2P games for children?*

2   Related Work

2.1   Free-to-Play

F2P games use the business model *freemium* as a revenue model. Freemium refers to a product or pricing structure where the core service is free. The revenue is generated through sales of additional products and premium services [12]. The term comes from the combination of *"free"* and *"premium"* due to the strategy of providing a free version and having additional features that can be purchased [11]. A registration key could be purchased to gain access to all features. Over the past few years, freemium has gained popularity and seems to be the answer to earn money from content on the internet. Today, the freemium business is being used in various sectors such as music, social networks, data storage, virtual worlds, and most pertinently, the gaming industry [12].

F2P has been discovered to be a promising revenue model to compete with classic models, such as one-time payment and subscription-based models that require a financial investment before the user could play the game [9,17]. F2P games are distributed and played free of charge. However, the games are typically restricted in some manner [2]. To bypass these restrictions, in-game purchases are required. One example is to restrict how long the player gets to play the game. Moreover, other ways to monetize are by offering in-game items that enhance the gaming experience or give advantages to the players; these are known as *virtual goods* [13]. Virtual goods have become the main monetization method in F2P games [9]. Paavilainen et al. [21] point out two significant advantages of the F2P model. Firstly, the game's virtual goods allow for flexible price points for customers with different willingness to pay for additional content. Each microtransaction is usually so small that they fall within the *Pennies-a-day* theory of mental accounting [10]. The Pennies-a-day theory is when a more considerable expense is converted into a series of smaller amounts, which leads the customer to view a series of small expenses as less painful than a substantial one-time payment. Secondly, it allows for a more comprehensive segmentation of players as the entry is free, and the virtual goods can be tailored to different audiences [21]. In addition to these advantages, the F2P model makes it possible to create positive network effects with a large user base even if they do not contribute to in-game purchases. More users exchanging information and experiences will subsequently lead to increased visibility and attract more users. Consequently, the greater the user base means potentially more players converting to paying players, leading to increased revenue and profit [9].

2.2 Free-to-Play and Children

Over the years, there have been multiple news stories related to children making accidental purchases with their parent's credit cards [15,19]. In 2013, the US Federal Trade Commission (FTC) filed a class-action lawsuit against Apple Inc. due to allowing children to make in-app purchases without the parent's consent. This resulted in a settlement requiring Apple to refund $32.5 million to the consumers that were affected [18]. Apple has improved its security for in-app purchases since, but such cases still occur. In 2020 was Apple filed another lawsuit for having games that use gambling mechanisms to target children and addicted gamblers [22]. This resulted in Apple having to change its policy and force the game developers to disclose the odds of each item.

There is a growing amount of F2P games that are accessible for children today. Most F2P games are accessible to children on various platforms such as Apple's App Store and Google Play Store. Many games are explicitly developed for children, but the majority of them are not. With the advancement of technology, it is easier for anyone to create games, and it is getting increasingly difficult to keep up with threats and vulnerabilities for all stakeholders, especially children [14]. F2P games that try to publish their games on these platforms get controlled before they get published. Most inappropriate games are removed, but still, many games bypass the platform's quality checks.

A recent systematic literature review on F2P and children found various perspectives and results [3]. Many of the primary studies related to revenue maximization and influential factors to make in-game purchases. Several of the studies expressed concern regarding how games target children. Furthermore, many researchers concluded a need for restrictions, more precise guidelines, and further research in the area.

2.3 Ethics and Dark Design

It has been stated that developers have an ethical responsibility when creating software [25]. Moreover, technical competence should not be used to behave dishonestly. Zagal et al. [26] substantiates Sommerville [25] and states that game designers typically are regarded as the player's advocates. However, the authors point out that the game creator does not necessarily have the same interest in the games as the players. Furthermore, it has been observed that not all developers may have the user's best interest in mind [13]. Additionally, developers can have different perceptions of what they consider ethical game development. Features of games can be regarded as hindrances or psychological traps used to motivate them to spend money. A former CEO of the American game developer company Zynga has stated, *"I did every horrible thing in the book, just to get revenues right away"* [13]. Ethical dilemmas may arise when people have different views of a situation or the way things are done. In today's gaming market, anyone can create a game and upload it to the App Store or Google Play Store independent of their background, leading to games that exploit the user, as the CEO from Zynga admitted.

Another ethical aspect that has been observed is *dark game design patterns*. Zagal et al. defines a dark game design pattern as a pattern intentionally designed by a game creator to cause negative experiences for players, which are against the player's best interest and likely to happen without the player's consent [26]. An example of a dark design pattern is the *loot-box*, a virtual element the player can buy to get a randomized selection of in-game advantages or cosmetics [16]. For example, users of *FIFA Football* can buy a loot-box to get a football player. Kristiansen and Severin seeing a significant positive correlation between loot-box engagement and problem gambling severity [16]. Zagal, Björk, and Lewis [26] state that if the player is aware of the design pattern's effect and can give their consent, the pattern is no longer dark. However, Zagal et al. [26] does not address dark patterns targeted at children in particular.

3   Research Method

We ran semi-structured interviews to focus on the pre-defined questions to answer the research question and let the participants express themselves freely and allow for follow-up questions. 83 participants were contacted, and 18 participated.

3.1   Subject Selection

For the interviews, guidelines produced by Runeson and Höst [23] were used to define selection criteria for subject selection. We primarily focused on participants that produce F2P games for children, mainly developers and game designers. Participants with other roles were also considered relevant if they were included in the process of creating games. Creators of F2P games for an older audience were also considered relevant to get more insight into the field of F2P. To better answer the research question, participants who had insight or experience creating games for children were also considered relevant for this study. Additionally, domain experts on children and games were considered relevant. This resulted in the following criteria:

1. The person had experience creating games for children.
2. The person had experience creating F2P-games.
3. The person had the knowledge and experience regarding the relationship between F2P games and children.

A person was considered a relevant interview candidate if they met at least one of the criteria. Participants that develop F2P games are denoted *developer* (D). Specialists or domain experts are denoted *experts* (E). An overview of the participants is presented in Table 1.

Table 1. An overview of subjects.

Subject	Role	Gender	Duration
E1	Advisor for games and apps	M	37 min
E2	Senior Legal Assistant	M	36 min
E3	Creative Director & Psychologist	M	43 min
D1	Game Designer	F	28 min
D2	Game Designer	M	27 min
D3	Game Designer	F	25 min
D4	Game Designer	M	34 min
D5	Game Developer	M	34 min
D6	Game Designer	M	40 min
D7	Game Artist / Art Director	F	22 min
D8	Game Designer	F	32 min
D9	Game Producer	M	22 min
D10	Game Designer	M	37 min
D11	Game Economy & Monetization Manager	F	38 min
D12	CEO	M	32 min
D13	CEO	M	34 min
D14	CEO	F	27 min
D15	Game Developer	F	28 min

The interview subjects were localized using several approaches, including snowball sampling. Four different channels were used to contact interview subjects: 1) the social career network LinkedIn[1]; 2) the professional network of our supervisor; 3) a co-worker space for game developers in Norway (Work-Work[2]); 4) the professional network of the interview subjects.

65 persons were contacted through LinkedIn. Other approaches consisted of contacting persons through email. Everyone was asked if they knew anyone suitable we could interview. People that met the criteria were contacted. One interview subject was observed at a seminar regarding F2P and children for parents. Another interview subject was localized by a documentary regarding how technology affects children. In total, 83 persons were contacted.

---

[1] www.linkedin.com.
[2] www.work-work.no.

3.2   Data Collection Procedure

The interviews were semi-structured since this is a flexible approach when the interview subjects have different backgrounds and roles in the game development of F2P games. By having semi-structured interviews, all the interviews revolved around the same themes (advantages/disadvantages, monetization features, factors, game development process, and improvements), but it could be adjusted to fit each subject better through follow-up questions and prepared domain questions. In addition, it is easier for the interviewee to talk more freely. The researchers were in direct contact with the subjects. This allowed the interviewers to control all the data that was collected and to ensure the pre-defined research question was answered adequately. It also allowed us to ask follow-up questions.

All interviews were conducted digitally on the video communication software program Zoom[3] due to various reasons. Firstly, the ongoing COVID-19 pandemic limited the option to conduct physical interviews with the interview subjects localized in the same city as the researchers. Secondly, international subjects were located worldwide, which made digital interviews the most suitable. The interviews were either conducted in the subject's preferred language (English or Norwegian). All the interviews with Norwegian participants were undertaken in Norwegian as this allowed them to express themselves more freely, concisely and give more in-depth explanations. For the transcription phase, this resulted in having to translate the parts of the interview.

3.3   Analysis Procedure

We applied a thematic analysis [5]. Our thematic analysis aims to identify and understand the most critical factors needed to create F2P-games for children and answer our research question.

The coding process was a mix of both inductive and deductive approaches, known as an integrated approach [24].

The qualitative data analysis program NVivo[4] was used to do the thematic analysis efficiently and organized. Coding with NVivo resulted in 201 codes with 419 references from the 154 pages of transcribed interviews. After reviewing, merging, and deleting duplicated codes, we ended up with 69 codes coded into 16 themes and three higher order themes.

4   Results and Discussion

The thematic synthesis process revealed five themes or factors that must be addressed when creating F2P games for children, illustrated in Fig. 1. These five factors are: 1) exploiting psychological behavior, 2) game play and user interface, 3) choosing features, 4) customize the development process to children, and 5) responsibility.

---

[3] www.zoom.us.

[4] www.qsrinternational.com/nvivo-qualitative-data-analysis-software/about/nvivo.

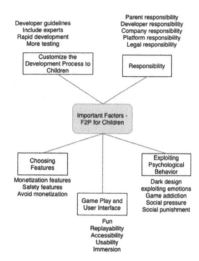

Fig. 1. Model of the higher-order theme of important factors. The squares represent sub-themes, and the texts represent the codes for each theme.

4.1 Exploiting Psychological Behavior

The thematic analysis revealed exploiting psychological behavior as an essential theme. One of the problems with F2P games relates to the game being offered to the players for free, forcing game development companies to generate revenue in other ways. F2P has caused challenges due to over-aggressive monetization techniques using dark patterns to exploit the psychological behavior of the players to increase spending [8,26]. Moreover, the different monetization features currently being used in the F2P gaming industry allow for exploitation easily, making it possible for children or other vulnerable players to spend significant amounts in the game [1]. Addiction due to F2P was claimed by E3 to be one of the most usual cases of addiction. The reason being the low threshold to enter the game and how accessible it is.

E3 - *"There is a low threshold to enter. It's easy to spend too much money on them if you become addicted, such as buying lots and lots of jewels in Clash of Clans or other similar games where the player can get benefits."*

Moreover, mechanics such as loot-boxes were seen as unfavorable due to the resemblance with gambling and addiction as presented by Kristiansen and Severin [16]. Mechanics that create peer pressure and punishing the player for not purchasing were mentioned as some of the worst manipulation techniques used in a game for children. According to the systematic literature review [3], such mechanics would be particularly inappropriate for younger users given their ongoing cognitive and social development that could easily be exploited. This is supported by Fitton and Read [8].

4.2 Game Play and User Interface

Regarding the game play and user interfaces, *fun*, *accessibility*, *usability*, and *immersion* were the most important elements when designing F2P games for children. *Fun* was an obvious factor for creating games, but the reasoning varied across the intervieweers. The majority of the developers wanted the players to enjoy themselves, and several mentioned fun as an important factor to achieve a successful game. Additionally, some of the intervieweers that had games based on subscription had to make the game fun to prove themselves to children and their parents that would eventually pay for the game.

D8 - *"When making games for younger children, it is important to give the child space to play and have fun. The game has to prove it is fun before the parent is asked to spend more on it."*

Immersion was also important for the game experience and made the game fun and exciting for the players. Advertisements were seen as the major key for breaking immersion in a game and something that should be avoided. Moreover, *usability* and *accessibility* are essential when creating games for children. Children are pretty diverse, and it is crucial to make the game easy to understand and play by everyone.

D14 - *"We figured that children as a target group are very diverse. As a result, we implemented different difficulties that the children could choose from. In this way, the children would always see progression in the game and reach a higher level."*

Additionally, many developers implemented voice-overs, confetti, and well-designed UX elements to make it easy for children to interact with the game.

4.3 Choosing Features

None of the monetization features mentioned in the interviews were seen as suitable for children, but some features were seen as worse than others. One example is the loot-box, as it resemblance with gambling [16].

E3 - *"The worst thing is gambling elements, where players do not know what they will get, such as loot-boxes."*

Battle-Passes and cosmetics were mentioned as more positive features because they do not impact the gameplay but give the player optional content to extend the gaming experience. However, the psychologist highlighted the battle-pass as one of the worst features as it could create purchase pressure and social pressure for children. In a study by Zendle et al. [27], players saw cosmetics as more acceptable than items that offered an advantage. Still, as mentioned above, it may strengthen peer pressure in a game to have certain cosmetics. The in-game currency can be considered one of the core elements of F2P as it is easily combined with other features. However, it was considered unsuitable for children because it may act as a psychological barrier between real currency spent and virtual currency. Thus, the player, especially children, can lose an overview of how much they spend.

D12 - *"Using in-game currency is a psychological trick that makes you not see the actual value you spend, especially for children who, in a way, only look at it as in-game currency and do not see the real value that they put into the game."*

To avoid children playing games that are not meant for them, and interacting directly with the monetization features in a game, many of the intervieweers had implemented age gates and parental control.

D6 - *"On some past projects, we've had to implement age gates. To access certain parts of the app, you need to make sure that you're above a certain age."*

The use of age gates is a familiar mechanic to use in a game, but the standard version does not hinder or stop a child from bypassing this mechanic, for example, by entering another age. Some companies had used a different age gate where the child was given a mathematical question or other types of questions to prevent children from bypassing the age gates. The goal was to exclude the young children who could not read. However, this also limits elder children with reading disabilities and other disabilities from entering the game, which may be problematic and not optimal. Moreover, many of the intervieweers mentioned that they have no way to control once the age gate is bypassed to see if the player is an adult or a child. This can be problematic, especially when F2P games are highly accessible. Additionally, parent control was seen as an excellent way to separate the monetization mechanics from the children and give the parents more control of what features the child is interacting with inside the game. Many of the interviewees had used such parental control. Such safety features can potentially make the game more secure to interact with from a child's perspective and make the parents feel safer knowing they are in control.

D8 - *"Devices should not be set to allow purchases without inputting a password or biometric when children can play on them."*

Additionally, parental guides provided by the game company could enable parents to create a safer environment for the children. Parents find it hard to manage the tension between keeping the children safe, allowing children to learn, developing media skills, and having fun [20]. Moreover, data analytics have made it increasingly difficult for parents to understand how the platforms their child use operates in terms of in-game mechanics, personal data gathering, and in-app purchases [20]. Such parental guidelines could help parents to create a safer environment for their children.

4.4   Customize the Development Process to Children

The expert subjects pointed out the importance of guidelines when creating F2P for children, especially for developers. Additionally, including child experts in the development process was highlighted as necessary by E3.

E3 - *"I would have used child experts to create a game that has meaning and something that kids love."*

However, only a few subjects mentioned that they consulted with experts or teachers/professors in the development process. Many of the developers based their designs on intuition and experience. This was also revealed in the study by Ekambaranathan et al. [7]. As claimed by E3; this would be helpful to develop valuable games. One of the problems is that many of these F2P games are not necessarily created for children, but children constitute a large part of the user base in many cases. Furthermore, agile methodologies, such as Scrum, were used by most companies as this allowed for a faster software development life cycle. However, findings from the interviews reveal high pressure for releasing games. Developers usually do not spend much time on a specific game before moving on to the next.

D7 - *"I think there's also something about the quality of the games because everything has to be made super fast and you don't have time to finish anything so you start out making a game, but you can only spend a month on it, and if the game fails it's on to the next one."*

Rapid development reduces the quality of the games, according to the interviewees. Many of the companies did tests with the target group during development. However, the developers did not always have time to address all the feedback before the game went into production. In many cases, testing was done late in the development process. Earlier and more frequent testing can make up for the tight deadlines that developers face and improve the game quality [25].

4.5 Responsibility

Our study revealed a disagreement between the experts and the developers regarding who is responsible for the ethical aspects concerning children. Some developers claimed that the main responsibility lies in the hand of the child's parents. In contrast, the experts claimed that the authorities, developers, and the platforms such as App Store and Google Play should have the most responsibility.

E3 - *"I think the ones that can do something about it today are the developers, but they will not because it's about competition and survival."*

Some developers wanted to be ethical and create child-friendly apps, but it was hard to prioritize features that would not contribute to higher incomes due to tight deadlines and budgets. Similarly, Ekambaranathan et al. [7] noticed that a lack of ethical monetization options might lead to a perception that trade-offs must be made between the commercial success of the game and the best interest of users. Platforms already have rules, but there might be a need to introduce more or stricter rules to reduce the trade-off that has to be done between being ethical and generating revenue. More legal or platform regulations could solve the different challenges to address whether or not developers or parents should have the most significant responsibility. However, Sommerville [25] and Zagal et al. [26] states that developers have an ethical responsibility when creating software, as presented in Sect. 2.3.

5 Conclusion and Future Work

This research aimed to identify the most critical factors towards creating suitable F2P games for children. We conducted an exploratory study investigating F2P developers and individuals who work with or know the effects of F2P for children. In total, 18 subjects were interviewed, three domain experts and 15 developers. Our findings indicate that the F2P industry is a competitive market where only the most popular games make solid revenue. With F2P games being initially free, the companies need to create incentives for the player to make in-game purchases. This has, in many cases, led to over-aggressive monetization strategies and the use of dark design to exploit the player's behavior. However many companies try to be ethical, but there seems to be a perceived trade-off between being ethical and competitiveness in the market. The thematic analysis revealed five crucial factors that need to be addressed to create suitable F2P games for children: 1) exploiting psychological behavior, 2) game play and user interface, 3) choosing features, 4) customize the development process to children, and 5) responsibility. Further work could build on the findings to make a framework the developers can follow to work towards suitable F2P games for children. The findings could also be used to create regulation, technical solutions, and marketing strategies to increase the number of ethical games. Increasing the data collection by investigating several F2P companies, and experts may improve the reliability of the results. In addition, further research could interview children who are the target audience for these specific F2P games to get a different point of view focused on the main players. Another interesting group of interview subjects is the parents paying for the in-game purchases.

References

1. Alha, K., Kinnunen, J., Koskinen, E., Paavilainen, J.: Free-to-play games: paying players' perspective. In: Proceedings of the 22nd International Academic Mindtrek Conference, pp. 49–58 (2018)
2. Alha, K., Koskinen, E., Paavilainen, J., Hamari, J., Kinnunen, J.: Free-to-play games: professionals' perspectives. In: Proceedings of nordic DiGRA 2014 (2014)
3. Anonymized: Understanding free-to-play and children: A systematic literature review. Submitted to Entertainment Computing (2021)
4. Chen, L.S., Lin, M.R.: Key factors of in-app purchase for game applications. In: 2015 7th International Conference on Emerging Trends in Engineering & Technology (ICETET), pp. 91–95. IEEE (2015)
5. Cruzes, D.S., Dybå, T.: Recommended steps for thematic synthesis in software engineering. In: 2011 International Symposium on Empirical Software Engineering and Measurement, pp. 275–284. IEEE (2011)

6. Dreier, M., Wölfling, K., Duven, E., Giralt, S., Beutel, M.E., Müller, K.W.: Free-to-play: about addicted whales, at risk dolphins and healthy minnows. Monetarization design and internet gaming disorder. Addict. Behav. **64**, 328–333 (2017)

7. Ekambaranathan, A., Zhao, J., Van Kleek, M.: Understanding value and design choices made by android family app developers. In: Extended Abstracts of the 2020 CHI Conference on Human Factors in Computing Systems, pp. 1–10 (2020)

8. Fitton, D., Read, J.C.: Creating a framework to support the critical consideration of dark design aspects in free-to-play apps. In: Proceedings of the 18th ACM International Conference on Interaction Design and Children, pp. 407–418 (2019)

9. Flunger, R., Mladenow, A., Strauss, C.: The free-to-play business model. In: Proceedings of the 19th International Conference on Information Integration and Web-based Applications & Services, pp. 373–379 (2017)

10. Gourville, J.T.: Pennies-a-Day: The Effect of Temporal Reframing on Transaction Evaluation (1998). https://academic.oup.com/jcr/article/24/4/395/1797969

11. Gu, X., Kannan, P., Ma, L.: Selling the premium in freemium. J. Market. **82**(6), 10–27 (2018)

12. Hamari, J., Hanner, N., Koivisto, J.: Service quality explains why people use freemium services but not if they go premium: an empirical study in free-to-play games. Int. J. Inform. Manag. **37**(1), 1449–1459 (2017)

13. Harviainen, J.T., Paavilainen, J., Koskinen, E.: Ayn rand's objectivist ethics applied to video game business. Journal of Business Ethics, pp. 1–14 (2019)

14. Jaccheri, L., Morasca, S.: Toward Inclusion of Children as Software Engineering Stakeholders. CoRR abs/2101.02704 (2021). https://arxiv.org/abs/2101.02704

15. Kleinman: My Son Spent 3,160 in One Game (2019). https://www.bbc.com/news/technology-48925623. Accessed 1 May 2021

16. Kristiansen, S., Severin, M.C.: Loot box engagement and problem gambling among adolescent gamers: findings from a national survey. Addict. Behav. **103**, 106254 (2020)

17. Luton, W.: Free-to-Play: Making Money From Games You Give Away. New Riders (2013)

18. Nash, V., O'Connell, R., Zevenbergen, B., Mishkin, A.: Effective Age Verification Techniques: Lessons to be Learnt From the Online Gambling Industry. Available at SSRN 2658038 (2012)

19. Norris: Boy, 7, Accidentally Spends 1,200 on Online games, including 800 on Virtual Cat Food (2021). https://www.mirror.co.uk/news/uk-news/boy-7-accidentally-spends-1200-23508222. Accessed 1 May 2021

20. Nouwen, M., Zaman, B.: Redefining the role of parents in young children's online interactions. a value-sensitive design case study. Int. J. Child-Comput. Interact, **18**, 22–26 (2018)

21. Paavilainen, J., Hamari, J., Stenros, J., Kinnunen, J.: Social network games: players' perspectives. Simul. Gaming **44**(6), 794–820 (2013)

22. Purcher: A new $5 Million Class Action filed against Apple Relates to selling Games with In-App purchases on iDevices, that are deemed Illegal in California (2021). https://www.patentlyapple.com/patently-apple/2020/06/a-new-5-million-class-action-filed-against-apple-relates-to-selling-games-with-in-app-purchases-on-idevices-that-are-deemed.html. Accessed 1 May 2021

23. Runeson, P., Höst, M.: Guidelines for conducting and reporting case study research in software engineering. Empirical Softw. Eng. **14**(2), 131–164 (2009)

24. Saldaña, J.: The Coding Manual for Qualitative Researchers. sage (2021)

25. Sommerville, I.: Software Engineering 10th Edition. Addison-Wesley, Boston (2016)

26. Zagal, J., Björk, S., Lewis, C.: Dark patterns in the design of games. In: FDG (2013)
27. Zendle, D., Cairns, P., Barnett, H., McCall, C.: Paying for loot boxes is linked to problem gambling, regardless of specific features like cash-out and pay-to-win. Comput. Hum. Behav. **102**, 181–191 (2020)

Provenance in Gamification Business Systems

Michelle Tizuka$^{(\boxtimes)}$, Esteban Clua, Luciana Salgado, and Troy Kohwalter

Computer Science Institute, Universidade Federal Fluminense, Niterói, Brazil
mmtizuka@id.uff.br, {esteban,luciana,troy}@ic.uff.br

Abstract. Gamification has become increasingly popular in business contexts. This approach suggests long-term sustainable persistent systems as it increases engagement at all organizational levels. However, a gamified system generates a series of events, decisions, and interactions from the users that need to be monitored and captured for analysis. Therefore, those systems require an infrastructure capable of tracking multiple variables over time, identifying the cause-and-effect relationships between events, and analyzing the captured data to evaluate their processes engagement. This work presents a data provenance approach for modeling gamification business systems, which allows tracking, managing, and visualizing provenance data from a gamified event. We evaluated our model in a real context with our partner company, and the results provide the necessary basis to be further implemented. Therefore, project managers can visualize provenance data from a gamified activity, analyze employees' actions, and identify needs that lead to successful or unsuccessful outcomes.

Keywords: Gamification model · Provenance · Data provenance model

1 Introduction

The use of gamification [1, 2] as a strategy in entrepreneur context [3, 4] has advanced as a solution with three main objectives: to increase engagement levels of key stakeholders, such as customers and employees [5–7], to improve organizational performance [8, 9], and to understand if and when gamification has positively affected users' motivations and behaviors [10].

A gamified application involves a series of activities, which also generates a series of events, decisions, and interactions from the users that need to be monitored and captured for analysis. Therefore, it requires a gamification system with an infrastructure capable of tracking and presenting multiple variables over time. Recent studies focused on gamification requirements, models, and frameworks [11–13]. However, few approaches focus on seeking to identify whether current methods coming from other areas such as games or data analytics also apply to gamification analytics or tools that collaborate to improve the analysis process by the leader. [14–17]. Seaborn and Fels [18] outline most studies did not run statistical analyses (and subsequently could not generate effect sizes). For these authors, it is essential these studies need to be replicated, comparative, and have longitudinal designs employed. Data sets are reliable when the processes used

© IFIP International Federation for Information Processing 2021
Published by Springer Nature Switzerland AG 2021
J. Baalsrud Hauge et al. (Eds.): ICEC 2021, LNCS 13056, pp. 277–288, 2021.
https://doi.org/10.1007/978-3-030-89394-1_21

to create them are reproducible and analyzable for defects. Within computer science, the term "provenance" [19, 20] mean the lineage of data, as per data provenance, with research extending the conceptual model of causality and relation to include processes that act on data and agents that are responsible for those processes providing historical records of data and its origin.

In business contexts, the provenance of data generated by complex transformations such as workflows is of considerable value to managers as it allows tracking, managing, and visualizing provenance data. In this view, we attempt to prospect if it is possible to use a provenance ontology to model gamification business systems that aim to monitor and evaluate its accuracy, provide reproducibility, and enable leaders to manage their processes in detail. In this work we study the use of provenance approach in a gamified system, specifically to verify if KPI monitoring can be implemented with this approach and leverage gamification analytics requirements for entrepreneur context.

We developed qualitative research consisted of four main steps: first, we selected a gamified enterprise application, then we mapped provenance ontology to gamification elements and mechanics. Later we applied this model to a real entrepreneur scenario and finally we discuss its application analysis. Our results provide the necessary basis to help project managers to detect patterns or even historical usability records. Therefore, project managers can visualize provenance data from a gamified activity, analyze employees' actions, and identify steps that lead to successful or unsuccessful outcomes. This scenario is especially representative because multiple influences may lead to success or failure in a software project.

This paper presents six sections as follows: Section 2 presents related works concerning gamification in the business context and the definition of provenance and terminologies applied in games. Section 3 is where we present our gamification business system model with a data provenance approach. Section 4 exhibits the application of the proposed model in a real entrepreneur context. Finally, Sect. 5 renders discussion, limitations, and future works.

2   Related Work

Although on the rise, many companies do not have a vision of incorporating gamification into their system and turning it into a good communication tool and business management solution. Several studies have indicated the need for personalizing gamified systems to users' personalities. A cross-contextual study reveals that motivational experiences increase these outcomes to different extents and go beyond gamified service experiences [21]. Also, understanding how such experiences of gamified actions influence business outcomes is critical.

2.1   Gamification in the Workplace

These gamified services have appeared on the market as models, being a promising tool adapted to the organizational context. The result, in a nutshell, is playful solutions for converting daily tasks into an activity that aggregates elements of competition, cooperation, and narrative with a range of gamification elements and mechanics willing on satisfying needs [22]. But, as highlighted by Jorge and Sutton [23], it is impossible to guarantee that everyone will have the same involvement and dedication. Although on the rise, it is still common to find challenges to keep people active throughout long-term sustainable persistent systems [24]. The "temporary" engagement does not occur when the user only gets involved in a specific moment and cannot relate this knowledge to other activities, which guarantees its performance in knowledge construction and management. Actions must be rewarded and balanced according to criteria focused on performance and quality. In addition, user profiles vary in age and roles, which can mean differences in task assignments. These factors certainly influence how each one interacts with the gamified system and the leader must be aware and have the challenge of understanding how the assignment of tasks must be thought of to offer equal opportunity to all employees.

Tondello and others [25] suggest different game design elements may support different user types and developed a Gamification User Types Hexad framework based on research on human motivation, player types, and practical design experience. For instance, digital badges are known to support learning and promote engagement through peer feedback as behavioral and cognitive indicators [26–29]. While many investigations and frameworks aim to conceptualize a player, [30] states few research categorize players based on their explicit preferences for game elements and mechanics. Even though standardized languages for gamification modeling have been proposed [31], current gamification technologies neither support a common language for its design nor common interfaces for maintaining it [17].

Therefore, this complex network of data and information must be well constructed and managed based on the choice of variables in-game elements and mechanics that could be used for different purposes and domains [30]. For instance, behavior understanding and analysis [32, 33], classifying users [34], understanding common behaviors, and retention [35], among others [36]. Heilbrun [17] identified seven available tools and assessed them for their applicability in gamification projects. The author states that none of the gamification requirements from the groups of application KPI monitoring, gamification adaptation, user groups, or simulation can be implemented with those tools. Based on these results, the author concluded that suitable solutions can be leveraged with a narrow set of analytical requirements for a small number of scenarios. However, for most use cases, no practical solutions exist.

2.2 Provenance in Games

Provenance is becoming more and more present in the scientific environment, both to guarantee the origin of the data, evaluate its accuracy, provide reproducibility, and enable customers to work with their processes in detail, collaboratively, and participatory. According to Groth and Moreau [37], provenance is information about entities, activities, and people involved in producing a piece of data or a thing, which can be used to assess quality, reliability, and trustworthiness.

Glavic and others [20] use the term data item for a structural unit of data, which targets provenance management and the notion level of detail for a data item's granularity.

The World Wide Web Consortium standardized PROV to support the interchange of provenance information on the Web and defines provenance as a *"record that describes the people, institutions, entities, and activities involved in producing, influencing, or delivering a piece of data or a thing."* [36]. The PROV ontology [37] document expresses the PROV-DM using the W3C OWL2 Web Ontology Language (OWL2). It provides a set of classes, properties, and constraints that can be used to represent and interchange provenance information. Since provenance information describes how various elements were related to or influenced by one another, it can be viewed as a directed graph in which those elements are nodes, categorized as type (i.e., *entities, activities, agents*). Directed edges represent the relations between them (e.g., wasGeneratedBy, wasAssociatedBy, wasAttributedTo and used). Such a graph is called a provenance graph. Given that some provenance graphs can be extensive, the challenge is to extract useful information and knowledge from complex provenance graphs.

Provenance in games was introduced to detect cause-and-effect relationships, proposing a conceptual framework that collects information during a game session and maps it to provenance terms, providing the means for post-game analysis [38–40]. Lately, [41] improved the framework providing the necessary basis to use provenance information broadening the original approach, implementing concrete frameworks to track, manage and display provenance data during the game, which allows developers and analysts to understand the events and the results obtained through interactive graphs for exploratory analysis. This integration's motivation was based on the fact that neither of the standard practices of telemetry data used by the games industry considers the causal relationships during the game sessions. Recently, [42] present a novel approach for player profiling that leverages recent advances in deep learning over graph representation at a fine-grain the player behavior in provenance data collected from a multiplayer battle game and assess the obtained profiles through statistical analysis and data visualization. Still, there is a need to define gamification features, which one's match and those that do not with any class of the PROV core structure.

3 Provenance in Gamification

Similar to games, we can define gamification systems using data provenance with different use-cases in mind. Specifically, we need to map each node of a provenance graph to users, game elements and mechanics, and their relationships. we present our model as a PROV Core model structure (see Fig. 1), detailed in the following subsections.

3.1 Entity and Activities

In PROV, "things" we want to describe are called *entities* and encompass a broad diversity of notions, including digital objects such as a file, physical things such as a genuine product, as well as abstract concepts and ideas. Therefore, we map entities to game elements and mechanics, such as points, badges, collectibles, and leaderboards. They are graphically represented by an oval yellow form.

PROV says that activity occurs over time and can act upon or with entities. We map them as actions related to game mechanics, such as collecting, revealing, repairing, customizing, or generating other entities. Both entities and activities can cover a broad range of notions. They are associated with each other in three ways: activities utilize

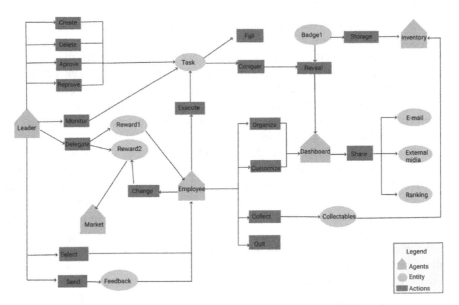

Fig. 1. Gamification business model using data provenance (PROV Core Structures).

entities, activities produce entities, and activities can also consume entities. The act of using, producing, or consuming an entity may have a duration and an effect on the entity.

The term "generation" refers to the completion of a new entity's production by an activity. This entity can vary depending on the context and action used to generate it. Thus, the entity did not exist before generation and became available for usage after this step. Likewise, the term "usage" refers to the beginning of utilizing an entity by an activity. Before usage, the activity had not begun to use this entity and could not have been affected by the entity. Communication is the exchange of some unknown entity by two activities, one activity using some entity generated by the other.

In a gamification context, the time of duration of entities and activities can be seen as shortened cycles, where the end of one cycle can also be the beginning of another gamified activity. For instance, feedback (entity) should be immediately or with shortened cycles, generated as points or virtual coins (two different types of entities) to produce enjoyable gameplay, instead of vague long-term performance reports. Each of these shortened cycles can be seen as a provenance core structure that can be tracked. These virtual coins (entity) could be used in a marketplace (another entity), and after the celebration, through sharing in social media can be communicated (one activity using the social media entity by the marketplace. Another agent can receive this purchase order and then deliver the reward. Same idea is applied on the use of digital badges, serving as peer agile feedback.

3.2 Derivations

Activities utilize entities and produce entities. In some cases, using an entity influences the creation of another in some way. This notion of "influence" is captured by derivations, defined as transforming an entity into another, an update of an entity resulting in a new one, or constructing a new entity based on a pre-existing entity.

According to its definition [37], PROV does not attempt to specify the conditions under which derivations exist. The focus of derivation is on connecting a generated entity to a used entity. While the basic idea is simple, the concept of derivation can be pretty subtle, being implicit the notion that the generated entity was affected in some way by the used entity. If an artifact was used by an activity that generated a second artifact, it does not always mean that the second artifact was derived from the first.

An example of derivation in gamification systems is connecting points (generated entity) to the user's progress bar (a used entity). In this case, utilizing points influences the update of another. For instance, to increase a user's level of experience. The same can occur with currency. After a mission or task is accomplished, the user's virtual coins (generated entity) accumulate on a digital account (a used entity). In this case, it also enables an entity (digital account) to be consumed by another one (marketplace). Therefore, the marketplace is the entity used to promote a new activity (trade) that generates another entity (reward). Also, badges can represent derivation, as the user's knowledge is perceived by his/her project manager. In this case, badges can contain other derivations whether the gamified system uses different categories or progress levelsPROV, "things" we want to describe are called *entities* and have some fixed aspects.

3.3 Agents and Responsability

Agents can be related to entities, activities, and other agents. Na agent is something that bears some form of responsibility for an activity taking place, for the existence of an entity, or another agent's activity. An agent may also be a particular type of entity or activity. Thus the model can be used to express the provenance of the agents themselves. For many purposes, a key consideration for deciding whether something is reliable and/or trustworthy is knowing who or what *was responsible* for its production. Therefore, in this case, we have to consider project managers, employees, and the gamified system. Managers can be the agents responsible for creating gamification activities, and employees, the agents receiving those activities to execute.

The gamification relation is the assignment of responsibility to the agent (employee) for executing the activity (gamification task), indicating that he/she has a role in the activity. This gamification activity corresponds to this gamified system acting as an agent, associated with other activities inside the system. Delegation is the assignment of authority and responsibility to an agent (by itself or by another agent) to carry out a specific activity as a delegate or representative. In contrast, the agent acts on behalf of retaining some responsibility for the delegated work's outcome. For instance, the manager is responsible for delegating the gamification activity to the employee. However, he/she is also responsible for monitoring and evaluating their results and providing some feedback related to the results accomplished through their dashboard interface.

4 The Gamification Business Model Application

The proposed model was instantiated in the business scenario from our partner company, which develops solutions that allow leaders to better manage processes. Among the various attributions that are part of the actions of a leader, developing and putting into practice strategies aimed at motivating the employee, to achieve individual and collective goals, is part of the routine. In addition, there are several processes that a leader needs to follow. For instance, risk management process, which involves planning, organizing, directing, and controlling an organization's human and material resources, to minimize or take advantage of the risks and uncertainties about that organization. In our partner company, we took advantage of having access to complete document history for all user's problems across this scenario to create a robust definition of the model.

4.1 Defining Metrics and Targets

We defined metrics and targets related to employee behavioral activity and retrieved them temporally over a gamification activity in the risk management process. This process involves three main steps: risk analysis/assessment, risk communication, and monitoring, and critical risk analysis. Actions and interactions connect project managers and employees through the system and require quick communication between them. We highlight that project managers have an essential part in the gamified system because they are responsible for not only creating the task and defining "players", but also monitoring and delivering progress reports, validating (or not) the achievement of the goals proposed.

Thus, the criteria we adopted for defining employee behavior towards the gamified action start with: (1) Not completing the activities in time; (2) being inactive for a period equal or greater to one week of inactivity; (3) complete the task however through a standard solution; and (4) complete the task but using an unexpected solution (see Fig. 2A). Project managers can observe these metrics on a dashboard and track activity through a "mission" progress bar, besides delivering rewards and feedback as points, virtual coins, or badges. Leaders can easily visualize where possible failures along the process occur more quickly as this model allows tracking the influences that the actions of employees determine in achieving the proposed objectives.

Detailed information on how certain game elements and mechanics were thought, designed, and related to each other through the whole system is out of this study scope.

4.2 Gamification Business Model Using Data Provenance

We used free wireframe software to represent PROV Core Structures applied to our model (see Fig. 2B). The proposed model was instantiated in the contextual scenario of risk management from our partner company and connects actions and interactions between four agents (project managers, employees, a support person, and the system). The central idea is to track all data for a specific number of gamified actions previously parameterized by the system. In the sequence, we will briefly present the result of the application of our approach to modeling our selected scenario.

Managers are responsible for creating the gamification activity (mission or challenges), for instance, to propose a solution treatment to risk. They are also responsible for monitoring and validating solutions based on the information given by employees and to deliver feedback. The gamification activity is 'generated' to refer to the completion of a new entity's production by an activity (information of the mission accomplished).

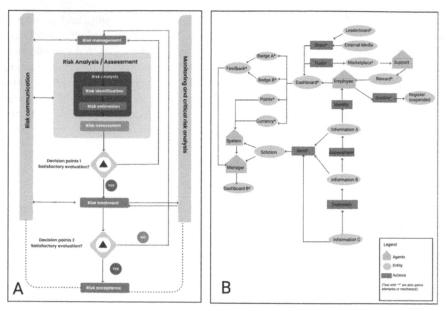

Fig. 2. Evaluation of the model in a real context: (A) workplace risk management process (B) gamification business model using data provenance on this context.

This entity (information) can be only raw information or already a solution and can vary face the context and decision points as seen in Fig. 2A. Note that action was used to generate it, i.e., it did not exist before generation and became available for usage after this step.

Employees act as "players" on the task given, having the opportunity to receive rewards (as points and virtual coins) and feedback (badges) when concluding a task by the system. So, if the task is completed, the employee level bar is updated, given the notion of 'influence' captured by derivations. Also, likewise "usage" referred before, employees can trade currency for real available products on a virtual and personalized marketplace. Marketplace in this case was not considered an agent as it is not an automated exchange process and therefore still does not act by itself. It will depend on the fourth agent, who has been assigned as a support person, which will be the financial sector that validates and delivers reward directly to the employee (see Fig. 2B).

4.3 Considerations About the Gamification Model Using Data Provenance

In this case, we suggest considering employees being all users inside a company, besides project managers, regardless of their function, gender, age, or time. Employees can perform different roles and act differently, which demands mapped attributes and paths to identify employee performance. However, this is also a possible action that a gamified system implemented with provenance data can provide, correlating gamified activity data to employee profiles and how their actions influence the results presented.

We highlight gamification features used in this case study are generalizable across the whole gamification business system for other actions. Still, there are few game elements and mechanics that are not adequate for enterprise gamification, e.g., permadeath or punish. Note that not all activity or entity is necessarily a game element or mechanic. For instance, assessment and treatment are actions inherent to the process but are not recognized as game mechanics, and entities such as information (from different types) and register suspended are not game features themselves. However, the whole integration of entities, actions, and traditional game elements are known to provide motivation and engagement (points, badges, and virtual coins) was applied to this scenario. Also, communication and feedback are highlighted and we considered them essential on the usage of provenance data analyses, as celebrating and building an interactive experience are two essential game mechanics that exist in a business context. In this case, we consider employees can send and share their performance results through external media as an option for each person to choose whether or not to perform the action, to avoid forced individual exposure.

Finally, we encourage project managers to engage, even though they are not part of it as "actors", but to understand that they have a fundamental role in the entire process, as responsible for monitoring and qualifying the results. This process involves not only the strategy of delivering points but monitoring the progress of actions and data analysis and achieved goals. Gamification becomes a means by which they can understand which are the key performance indicators that they should monitor and be able to follow the process to more accurately assess their results and identify any failures throughout the process.

5 Conclusions, Limitations, and Future Works

The diversity of data representation models and application domains has led to application or data model-dependent provenance models and prototype implementations. Some authors address provenance in the context of services and workflow management, but as far as we know, still, none has discussed its role in the gamification application domain. It is still a challenge to establish causal relationships between employees' decisions and actions. Thus, we proposed a model for gamification business systems using data provenance to highlight the fundamental PROV Core Structure.

While the core of PROV focuses on essential provenance structures commonly found in provenance descriptions, extended structures are designed to support more advanced provenance uses. The purpose of this work is twofold. First, modeling a gamification business system with data provenance. Second, evaluate the proposed model in an authentic context.

Our model suggests that entities and activities are the most visible part of a gamification system. Representing game elements or mechanics tend to be the primary focus of most gamification projects as action decision points lead to awarding rewards or feedback. These actions also discriminate whether or not a particular gamified activity has been completed. When generated, used, and associated appropriately, entities, activities, and agents can leverage a natural relational, motivational driver enabling tracking gamification data use. An essential aspect of any data gathering is that more than just capturing data to evaluate process engagement, there is a need for practitioners and designers to be precautious about ethical issues in gamification (i.e., exploitation and manipulation) [43].

Despite acknowledging the diversity of game elements and mechanics, our proposal provides the necessary groundwork to explore different ways to summarize provenance graphs into a set of generic gamification features, even those from other areas of the enterprise domain, without the knowledge required to interpret domain-specific information contained therein. We think the analysis and understanding of actions, mistakes, and fluxes of an authentic gamification event may help understand problems related to the management process, data mining of specific situations, and even understanding learning aspects in gamification contexts. Future work will be to conduct a survey with the audience involved, triangulate methods, and implement this model in our partner company application to record data provenance automatically.

Acknowledgements. The authors are grateful to the team of the partner company GestQual. M.M.T. is a Ph.D. student supported by DAI-CNPQ scholarship.

References

1. Deterding, S., Dixon, D., Khaled, R., Nacke, L.: From game design elements to gamefulness: defining gamification. In: Proceedings of the 15th International Academic MindTrek Conference: Envisioning Future Media Environments, pp. 9–15. ACM (2011)
2. Kapp, K.: The Gamification of Learning and Instruction Fieldbook. Pfeiffer (2013)
3. Herzig, P., Ameling, M., Wolf, B., Schill, A.: Implementing gamification: requirements and gamification platforms. In: Reiners, T., Wood, L.C. (eds.) Gamification in Education and Business, pp. 431–450. Springer, Cham (2015). https://doi.org/10.1007/978-3-319-10208-5_22
4. Kumar, J.M., Herger, M.: Gamification at Work: Designing Engaging Business Software (2013)
5. Robson, K., Plangger, K., Kietzmann, J.H., McCarthy, I., Pitt, L.: Game on: engaging customers and employees through gamification. Bus. Horiz. **59**(1), 29–36 (2016)
6. Boulet, G.: Gamification: the latest buzzword and the next fad. ELearn **2012**(12), 3 (2012)
7. Koivisto, J., Hamari, J.: The rise of motivational information systems: a review of gamification research. Int. J. Inf. Manage. **45**, 191–210 (2019)
8. Werbach, K., Hunter, D.: For the Win: How Game Thinking Can Revolutionize Your Business. Wharton Digital Press (2012)
9. Hamari, J., Koivisto, J., Sarsa, H.: Does gamification work?—a literature review of empirical studies on gamification. In: Proceedings of the 47th Annual Hawaii International Conference on System Sciences (HICSS), pp. 3025–3034 (2014)
10. Hagger, M.S., Chatzisarantis, N.L., Harris, J.: From psychological need satisfaction to intentional behavior: testing a motivational sequence in two behavioral contexts. Pers. Soc. Psychol. Bull. **32**(2), 131–148 (2006)
11. Mora, A., Riera, D., Gonzalez, C., Arnedo-Moreno, J.: A literature review of gamification design frameworks. In: 2015 7th International Conference on Games and Virtual Worlds for Serious Applications (VS-Games), pp. 1–8. IEEE, September 2015
12. Morschheuser, B., Werder, K., Hamari, J., Abe, J.: How to gamify? A method for designing gamification. In: Hawaii International Conference on System Sciences (HICSS), At Hawaii, USA, vol. 50 (2017)
13. Al-Towirgi, R.S., Daghestani, L.F., Ibrahim, L.F.: Data mining and gamification techniques in adaptive e-learning: promises and challenges. Int. J. Comput. Appl. **180**(13), 49–55 (2018)

14. Heilbrunn, B., Herzig, P., Schill, A.: Tools for gamification analytics: a survey. In: 2014 IEEE/ACM 7th International Conference on Utility and Cloud Computing (UCC), pp. 603–608, December 2014
15. Heilbrunn, B., Herzig, P., Schill, A.: Towards gamification analytics—requirements for monitoring and adapting gamification designs. In: 44. Jahrestagung der Gesellschaft für Informatik, Informatik 2014, Big Data - Komplexität meistern, pp. 333–344 (2014)
16. Heilbrunn, B., Herzig, P., Schill, A.: Gamification analytics—methods and tools for monitoring and adapting gamification designs. In: Stieglitz, S., Lattemann, C., Robra-Bissantz, S., Zarnekow, R., Brockmann, T. (eds.) Gamification. PI, pp. 31–47. Springer, Cham (2017). https://doi.org/10.1007/978-3-319-45557-0_3
17. Heilbrunn, B.: Gamification Analytics: Support for Monitoring and Adapting Gamification Designs (Doctoral dissertation, Technische Universität Dresden) (2019)
18. Seaborn, K., Fels, D.I.: Gamification in theory and action: a survey. Int. J. Hum. Comput. Stud. **74**, 14–31 (2015)
19. Buneman, P., Khanna, S., Wang-Chiew, T.: Why and where: a characterization of data provenance. In: Van den Bussche, J., Vianu, V. (eds.) Database Theory—ICDT 2001, ICDT 2001. LNCS, vol. 1973, pp. 316–330. Springer, Heidelberg (2001). https://doi.org/10.1007/3-540-44503-X_20
20. Glavic, B., et al.: Data provenance: a cctegorization of existing approaches. BTW'07: Datenbanksysteme. Buisness, Technologie und Web (103), 227–241 (2007)
21. Wolf, T., Weiger, W.H., Hammershmidt, M.: Experiences that matter? The motivational experiences and business outcomes of gamified services. J. Bus. Res. **106**, 353–364 (2020)
22. Xi, N., Hamari, J.: Does gamification satisfy needs? A study on the relationship between gamification features and intrinsic need satisfaction. Int. J. Inf. Manage. **46**, 210–221 (2019)
23. Jorge, C.F.B., Sutton, M.J.D.: Perspectivas em Gestão & Conhecimento, João Pessoa, Número Especial, vol. 6, pp. 103–118, January 2016
24. Fors, P., Lennerfors, T.T.: Gamification for Sustainability. The Business of Gamification: A Critical Analysis, 163 (2016)
25. Tondello, G.F., Wehbe, R.R., Diamond, L., Busch, M., Marczewski, A., Nacke, L.E.: The gamification user types hexad scale. In: Proceedings of the 2016 Annual Symposium on Computer-Human Interaction in Play, pp. 229–243, October 2016
26. Hatzipanagos, S., Code, J.: Open badges in online learning environments: peer feedback and formative assessment as an engagement intervention for promoting agency. J. Educ. Multimedia Hypermedia **25**(2), 127–142 (2016)
27. Hamari, J.: Do badges increase user activity? "A field experiment on the effects of gamification." Comput. Hum. Behav. **71**, 469–478 (2017)
28. Besser, E.D., Newby, T.J.: Feedback in a digital badge learning experience: considering the instructor's perspective. TechTrends **64**(3), 484–497 (2020)
29. Fanfarelli, J., Vie, S., McDaniel, R.: Understanding digital badges through feedback, reward, and narrative: a multidisciplinary approach to building better badges in social environments. Commun. Des. Q. Rev. **3**(3), 56–60 (2015)
30. Ferro, L.S.: The game element and mechanic (GEM) framework: a structural approach for implementing game elements and mechanics into game experiences. Entertainment Comput. **36**, 100375 (2021)
31. Herzig, P., Ameling, M., Schill, A.: Workplace psychology and gamification: theory and application. In: Reiners, T., Wood, L.C. (eds.) Gamification in Education and Business, pp. 451–471. Springer, Cham (2015). https://doi.org/10.1007/978-3-319-10208-5_23
32. Drachen, A., et al.: Guns, swords and data: clustering of player behavior in computer games in the wild. In: Conference on Computational Intelligence and Games (CIG), pp. 163–170 (2012)

33. Drachen, A., et al: Guns and guardians: comparative cluster analysis and behavioral profiling in destiny. In: 2016 IEEE Conference on Computational Intelligence and Games (CIG) (2016)
34. Drachen, A., et al.: A Comparison of methods for player clustering via behavioral telemetry. Foundations of Digital Games (FDG) (2013)
35. Weber, B.G., et al.: Modeling player retention in madden NFL 11. In: Innovative Applications of Artificial Intelligence Conferences (IAAI) (2011)
36. Drachen, A., Schubert, M.: Spatial game analytics and visualization. In: IEEE Conference on Computational Intelligence in Games (CIG) (2013)
37. Moreau, L., Missier, P., Cheney, J., Soiland-Reyes, S.: PROV-N: The provenance notation. W3C Recommendation (2013)
38. Kohwalter, T., Clua, E., Murta, L.: Provenance in games. In: Brazilian Symposium on Games and Digital Entertainment (SBGAMES), pp. 162–171 (2012)
39. Kohwalter, T.C., Clua, E.G.W., Murta, L.G.P.: Game flux analysis with provenance. In: Reidsma, D., Katayose, H., Nijholt, A. (eds.) ACE 2013. LNCS, vol. 8253, pp. 320–331. Springer, Cham (2013). https://doi.org/10.1007/978-3-319-03161-3_23
40. Jacob, L.B., Kohwalter, T.C., Machado, A., Clua, E.W.G.: A game design analytic system based on data provenance. In: Anacleto, J.C., Clua, E.W.G., da Silva, F.S.C., Fels, S., Yang, H.S. (eds.) ICEC 2013. LNCS, vol. 8215, pp. 114–119. Springer, Heidelberg (2013). https://doi.org/10.1007/978-3-642-41106-9_13
41. Kohwalter, T., Oliveira, T., Freire, J., Clua, E., Murta, L.: Prov viewer: a graph-based visualization tool for interactive exploration of provenance data. In: Mattoso, M., Glavic, B. (eds.) IPAW 2016. LNCS, vol. 9672, pp. 71–82. Springer, Cham (2016). https://doi.org/10.1007/978-3-319-40593-3_6
42. Melo, S.A., Kohwalter, T.C., Clua, E., Paes, A., Murta, L.: Player behavior profiling through provenance graphs and representation learning. In: International Conference on the Foundations of Digital Games, pp. 1–11, September 2020
43. Kim, T.W., Werbach, K.: More than just a game: ethical issues in gamification. Ethics Inf. Technol. 18(2), 157–173 (2016). https://doi.org/10.1007/s10676-016-9401-5

Computational Narrative Blending Based on Planning

Edirlei Soares de Lima[1,2(✉)] ⓘ, Bruno Feijó[3] ⓘ, and António L. Furtado[3] ⓘ

[1] IADE, Universidade Europeia, Av. D. Carlos I 4, 1200-649 Lisbon, Portugal
edirlei.lima@universidadeeuropeia.pt
[2] UNIDCOM/IADE, Av. D. Carlos I 4, 1200-649 Lisbon, Portugal
[3] Department of Informatics, PUC-RIO, Rua Marquês de São Vicente 225,
Rio de Janeiro, Brazil
{bfeijo,furtado}@inf.puc-rio.br

Abstract. Inspired by conceptual blending models and considering plot genera-tion as a plan-generation problem, this paper proposes a robust method that reuses existing stories to generate new narrative variants. This method generates variants that combine episodes extracted and adapted from different stories that share the same narrative structure. By combining a plan validation algorithm with a basic narrative structure, our method guarantees the logical coherence and general plot structure of the generated narratives. We also propose a new tool to assist ama-teur/professional writers to visualize all narrative variants created from a set of existing stories. Our experiments created novel, coherent and structured narratives by blending and adapting episodes from old chivalry romance pieces of work and some modern adventure videogames.

Keywords: Plot generation · Conceptual blending · Interactive storytelling

1 Introduction

Human creativity has been described as the process of producing something new (i.e., original, unexpected) and appropriate (i.e., useful, applicable) [31]. Although the basic definition of creativity suggests the invention of something entirely new and original, many authors follow a *reuse strategy* when designing a new idea or product. This is a very common practice in the entertainment industry, especially in films and games.

In narrative writing, it is a well-established fact that new stories often emerge as creative adaptations and combinations of old stories [1]. The idea of combining and adapting existing stories to create new narratives easily brings to our minds the possi-bility of using computational algorithms to automate the narrative generation process. Although research on interactive storytelling has been exploring the generation of inter-active narratives since the 1970s [10, 20], we are still far from having algorithms capable of creating complex and creative stories as those created by professional human authors. Many different strategies have been adopted in order to create plot generation algorithms,

© IFIP International Federation for Information Processing 2021
Published by Springer Nature Switzerland AG 2021
J. Baalsrud Hauge et al. (Eds.): ICEC 2021, LNCS 13056, pp. 289–303, 2021.
https://doi.org/10.1007/978-3-030-89394-1_22

including automated planning [5, 14, 27, 29], plot grammars [2, 18], and genetic algorithms [15, 22]. However, only few works attempted to apply reuse strategies to blend existing stories in order to generate new narratives.

We call *computational narrative blending* the process in which two or more narratives are combined to generate a new narrative variant using computers. This concept comes from the notion of *conceptual blending* [6, 7], which has been proposed as a fundamental cognitive process where two or more conceptual spaces are merged to form a new blended space. The blended space is partially structured by the input spaces, but it also exhibits some emergent structure of its own.

Although conceptual blending can be considered a powerful model for creativity and analysis, there are many challenges related to the application of blending in computational systems. Even though some previous works have already applied conceptual blending to computational systems [8, 19, 21, 23, 33, 34], there still is no general formula on how to construct algorithmic solutions for all types of blends. In addition, the narrative domain presents extra challenges for the blending process, especially when we consider the coherence, diversity, and quality of the generated stories (see [30] for a discussion in narratology). In this paper, we have no intention to discuss theoretical questions about conceptual blending or propose a general computational model for narrative blending. Instead, we simply draw and apply ideas from the literature on conceptual blending.

This paper, inspired by conceptual blending models and considering plot generation as a plan-generation problem, proposes a new plot generation method that reuses existing stories. By combining a plan validation algorithm with a basic narrative structure, our method guarantees the logical coherence and general structure of the generated narratives.

The paper is organized as follows. Section 2 reviews related works. Section 3 introduces the concept of narrative structure and presents the specialized grail-based structure. Section 4 describes the proposed narrative blending method. Section 5 presents the results generated by our method. Section 6 offers concluding remarks.

2   Related Work

Reuse strategies have been used even in the earliest narrative generation systems. In addition, some applications of conceptual blending to narrative domains have been proposed recently. Both approaches are reviewed in this section.

One of the earliest plot generation systems to adopt *reuse strategies* is Minstrel [32]. By retrieving and transforming existing scenes stored in a special memory (called episodic memory), the system can generate new stories. For the adaptation process, Minstrel identifies similar concepts in the episodic memory and uses them to create novel scenes. Although Minstrel can produce new narratives, some of the adopted heuristics only work well for specific scenes, whereas in some cases they can result in inconsistent narratives [25].

Another system based on a reuse strategy is MEXICA [24]. The system uses a set of existing stories to build structures in memory representing content and rhetorical knowledge. During the story generation process, MEXICA retrieves from memory all possible actions that can be performed in the current story-world state. After filtering the actions that do not satisfy a group of constraints, one of the remainder actions is selected at random as the next action in the story [25]. The MEXICA reuse strategy restricts the set of stories used to construct the rhetorical knowledge of the system to variants of the same narrative.

A more recent approach to reuse strategies is explored by Lima et al. [13, 17]. The authors propose that story variants are the consequence of type interactions, which they characterize in terms of semiotic relations expressing connection, similarity, unfolding, and opposition. By applying these semiotic relations over a library of narratives of related types, their system can generate new story variants.

Inspired by the notion of *conceptual blending*, Li et al. [12] describe two systems to construct blends in a goal-driven and context-driven manner. While the first system aims at breaking the static configurations of story worlds by creating new types of objects (called gadgets) and introducing them into the narratives [11], the second has the objective of selecting a real-world object to represent an object from a fantasy world, as required in children's pretend play [36]. Although their method can introduce new objects into a narrative, their inputs for the blending process do not include any temporal dimension, which is important when blending sequences of events extracted from different narratives.

Narrative blending is also explored by Permar and Magerko [26], by way of a computational model based on conceptual blending that is capable of using familiar scripts to generate new blended scripts. In their model, narrative scripts are represented by directed acyclic graphs, where each node defines an event. As acknowledged by the authors, one of the main limitations of their method is the fact that it cannot guarantee the logical coherence of the generated scripts, which is essential for a narrative.

Although reuse strategies and conceptual blending for plot generation have been explored in previous works, none of them combines all characteristics of our method, especially its effective ability to create novel, coherent and structured narratives by blending and adapting episodes (sequences of events) extracted from different stories.

3 The Narrative Structure

The proposed plot generation method reuses episodes of existing stories that share the same narrative structure to compose new narrative variants. We use the term "narrative structure" to refer to the order and manner along which a plot evolves. This structure may be presented as a pattern (like the hero patterns proposed by Joseph Campbell [4] and Rank et al. [28]) or as a story arc [35]. In this paper, to test the flexibility of our model, instead of following a classic narrative pattern or a traditional story arc, we opted for a more specialized structure named "The Fall and Rise of the Grail Hero" [16]. This structure (here called *grail-based narrative*) encompasses old chivalry romance works and some modern adventure videogames.

In the grail-based narrative structure, the protagonist begins as a naïve person, learns about himself along successive stages, *falls down* nevertheless in a crucial instant, but is then led to rise again and move towards a high position that nobody else could attain. As explained by Lima et al. [16], this structure is inspired on a 12th century romance of chivalry entitled *Le Conte du Graal (Perceval)*, by the French poet Chrétien de Troyes [9], whereby the Grail literary tradition was inaugurated. The original romance of Chrétien is considered an unfinished work, as he died before completing his story. Later, four so-called *Perceval Continuations* were appended to Chrétien's text [3].

The basic grail-based narrative structure can be summarized into nine different episodes: (1) *Preparation 1* (the hero learns some skills); (2) *Failed mediation* (current skills are not enough to face challenges); (3) *Apotheosis 1* (the hero joins a community and becomes a highly reputed member); (4) *Mediation* (there is a summons to pursue the mission previously not understood); (5) *Errance* (still lacking an indispensable skill, the hero wanders in vain); (6) *Preparation 2* (meeting an old sage, the hero receives the missing instruction); (7) *Quest* (the quest effectively begins, with ample chance of success); (8) *Apotheosis 2* (the quest is finally achieved and the hero is rewarded); and (9) *Denouement* (the hero is allowed to live his new and changed live).

By analyzing the narrative of videogames, Lima et al. [16] identified the grail-based structure in the narratives of five well-known games: *The Legend of Zelda: A Link to the Past* (Nintendo, 1991), *The Legend of Zelda: Ocarina of Time* (Nintendo, 1998), and *The Witcher 3: Wild Hunt* (CD Projekt, 2015). Therefore, in this work, we considered the original romance *Le Conte du Graal (Perceval)*, the *Continuations*, and the narratives of these games to define a *domain library*, which the proposed blending method uses to create new narrative variants.

4   Narrative Blending

The proposed narrative blending method explores the existence of a set of narratives sharing the same structure to create new variants that combine episodes extracted from different narratives, which are kept in a *domain library*. The linear structures of these narratives are also extended towards a *branching network* (as described in Sect. 4.2), where each node is an episode containing several variants. The domain library is manually constructed by a human author and it comprises – besides the narratives' events organized by episodes – a set of *planning operators* describing the preconditions and effects of all types of narrative events used in the domain library.

In terms of conceptual blending, the domain library and the branching network of the narrative structure define the *generic space* (GS), which represents the conceptual structure that is shared by the input spaces (IS_1 and IS_2). The *input space 1* (IS_1) comprises a complete narrative variant with an episode selected to be retold, and the *input space 2* (IS_2) consists of an episode variant of the episode selected in IS_1. The input concepts IS_1 and IS_2 are induced by the generalization GS. The *blended space* (BS) comprises a new narrative variant composed through a blend of both input spaces. The *blending process* consists of an attempt – that not always succeeds – to adapt the sequence of events of IS_2 so it can replace the original events of the selected episode in IS_1 without violating the logical coherence of the narrative.

Figure 1 illustrates the conceptual spaces for a case where IS_1 comprises a narrative variant with 4 episodes (Ep_1, Ep_2, Ep_3, Ep_4). In this space, Ep_4 is the episode selected to be retold. In this GS example, the episode Ep_4 has two variants ($Ep_{4,1}$ and $Ep_{4,2}$). While in IS_1 the episode Ep_4 is based on $Ep_{4,2}$, IS_2 comprises the alternative episode variant of Ep_4 (i.e., $Ep_{4,1}$). When both input spaces are projected into BS, the logical coherence of all events of $Ep_{4,1}$ are verified according to the preconditions and effects of their respective operators defined in the generic space. In this process, the events of $Ep_{4,1}$ are adapted to conciliate with the previous events of the story, so that characters and objects of IS_1 can replace characters and objects that share similar roles in the event sequence of $Ep_{4,1}$.

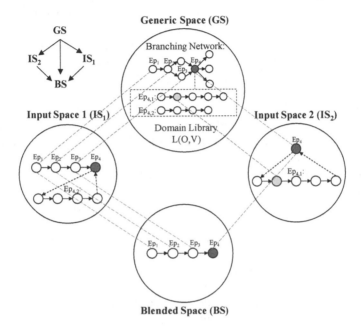

Fig. 1. Conceptual spaces.

4.1 Basic Definitions

In the proposed method, an *event* is denoted by an atomic formula of the form $T(t_1, \ldots, t_n)$, where T defines the type of the event (e.g., fight, kill, save) and the terms t_n (also called *parameters*) represent the elements involved in the event (e.g., characters, places, objects). For example, go(Perceval, Waste Forest, Arthur's court) represents an event where *Perceval* (a character) goes from *Waste Forest* (a place) to *Arthur's court* (another place).

An event is an instance of an *operator*, which establishes all restrictions (e.g., temporal, spatial) for the occurrence of the event (*preconditions*) and the effects that result from the occurrence of the event (*postconditions*). More specifically, an *operator* is a triple $o_i = (name_i, preconditions_i, postconditions_i,)$, where $name_i$ is an atomic formula with variables, and both *preconditions$_i$* and *postcondions$_i$* are sets of literals (i.e. positive or negative atoms). For example, the operator for the go event is defined by: $o_1 = ($ **name$_1$** $=$ go(CH, PL1, PL2), **preconditions$_1$** $=$ character(CH), place(PL1), place(PL2), at(CH,PL1), **postconditions$_1$** $= \neg$**at(CH, PL1), at(CH, PL2)**)), where $\neg$ is the negation symbol.

Any episode of the branching network is a sequence of events, which are consistent with all restrictions established by the operators. This sequence of events, also called a *plan P*, is associated with a text label, called the *episode name (ep)*. Therefore, an *episode Ep* is the pair (ep, P). A *narrative N* is a sequence of episodes: $N = \langle Ep_1, Ep_2, \cdots, Ep_k, \cdots \rangle$. In this context, a branching network node may have several *episode variants*. Each pair (ep_k, P_k) in the narrative represents an *episode variant*, where ep_k identifies the name of the episode and P_k describes a way of telling ep_k.

For instance, the following event sequence defines the episode Ep_6 (Preparation 2) of the narrative of Chrétien's *Perceval*: `go(Perceval, Arthur's land, hermitage)`, `meet(Perceval, hermit, hermitage)`, `tell(hermit, Perceval, religious knowledge)`.

A *story variant* is a quadruple $V_i = (n_i, N_i, \omega_i, f_i^0)$, where n_i is the *narrative name*, N_i is a narrative (called *narrative variant*), ω_i is a *list of symbols* with all names that are used to describe the events and states of V_i, and f_i^0 is a set of facts describing the initial state of the story. A *fact* is an assertion about an entity of the narrative variant (e.g., character, object, place), which can be the assignment of a role to an entity (e.g., `hero(Perceval)`, `place(Arthur's court)`, `object(Red Knight's armor)`), or the assertion about the attributes of an entity (e.g., `alive(Perceval)`, `threatened(Hyrule)`, `defeated(Red Knight)`), or the existence of a relationship between entities (e.g., `at(Perceval, Arthur's court)`, `has(Red Knight, Red Knight's armor)`, `love(Perceval, Blancheflor)`). The set of facts holding at a given instant of time constitutes a *state*. The state at the beginning of a story is called *initial state*. At any point of the narrative, we can determine what is the current state, because we have the operators. We define $S_k(V_i)$ as the state of V_i before episode Ep_k of N_i. In this case, $S_1(V_i) = f_i^0$.

The *domain library* is a pair $L = (O, V)$, where $O = \{o_1, o_2, \cdots, o_w\}$ is a set of operators and $V = \{V_1, V_2, \ldots, V_n\}$ is a set of story variants. In our system, the library is specified in an XML file (an example of domain library is available in a separated online document: http://www.icad.puc-rio.br/~logtell/narrative-blending/narrative_blending_db.xml). When the domain library is loaded by the system, the list of symbols $\omega_i \in V_i$ is automatically created and filled with all unique values found in the parameters of the story events and initial state. Each story variant V_i is associated with its own list of symbols, which provides access to all names (characters, places, objects) that were used to describe the story.

4.2 Branching Network

The first step of the narrative blending method involves the construction of a branching network structure by combining the linear sequences of episodes of the stories defined in domain library. The *branching network* is modeled as a directed graph $G = (A, E)$, where A is a set of episode labels (graph nodes), and E is a set of 2-element subsets of A, called *episode edges*.

In order to create the branching network, the sequences of episode labels of all stories of the domain library are extracted. Then, two general border events (called *begin* and *end*) are added to each sequence and grouped as a network structure, in which each episode becomes a node label (Fig. 2a). In the next step, the algorithm combines nodes (through unification) with the same episode labels to transform the initial network into a branching network (Fig. 2b), in a process we name "fusion by equality."

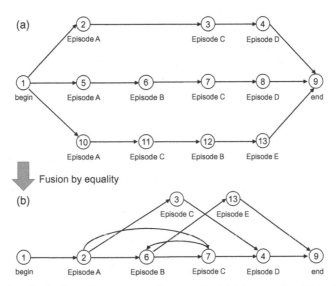

Fig. 2. Example of episode unification transforming the initial network (a) into the branching network (b).

By creating the branching network according to the domain library, the original narrative structure is extended and enriched with alternative crossing paths extracted from stories that follow a similar structure. Figure 3 illustrates the branching network automatically created for a domain library composed of 3 grail-based stories: Chrétien's *Perceval* complemented by the *Second Continuation; The Legend of Zelda: A Link to the Past*; and *The Legend of Zelda: Ocarina of Time*. In this network, both branches α and γ were stablished due to an inversion in the order of the episodes (4) and (5) in *The Legend of Zelda: Ocarina of Time*, and branch β was added due to the fact that *The Legend of Zelda: A Link to the Past* lacks episode (5). In addition, a new episode – (9) Magical Agent – was added to the branching network to describe an episode of *The Legend of Zelda: A Link to the Past* where Link gets a magical weapon (the Silver Arrow), which is the only weapon capable of defeating the evil Ganon.

A sequence of episodes extracted from the branching network is a *graph walk*. The alternative walks that can be extracted from the branching network – without repeating episodes – represent the different orders in which the episodes of the narrative structure can be arranged to create new story variants.

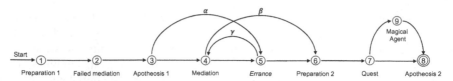

Fig. 3. Branching network created for three grail-based variants.

4.3 Episode Blending

After creating the branching network for the narrative structure, the next step involves the generation of all possible story variants that can be created by combining event sequences of different episodes extracted from the narratives of the domain library. This is done through successive applications of a process that we called *episode blending*. This process adapts a single sequence of events (an episode) extracted from a narrative of the domain library to use it in another narrative. The process comprises two tasks: *adaptation* and *validation*. While the sequence of events is being adapted to fit into a different narrative, the logical coherence of the events is constantly being checked to guarantee that they are not violating the coherence of the narrative.

Given two input spaces (IS_1 and IS_2), a generic space (GS), and a blended space (BS), the episode blending process comprises the following steps:

1. Convert the sequence of events of IS_2 into a *generic plan GP* $= \{e_1, \ldots, e_n\}$, where the parameters of each event e_i are replaced by uninitialized *variables*;
2. Select the next event e_i of GP (initially, the first event), and assign new values to the uninitialized/failure *variables* of the event according to the list of symbols of the narrative variant $V_1 \in IS_1$;
3. Apply the preconditions of the event operator $O_i \in GS$ to *validate* the logical coherence of e_i:

   a. If the validation of e_i *succeeds*, apply the postconditions (effects) of O_i over the current state of the narrative variant $V_1 \in IS_1$, then add e_i to BS, and then jump back to step 2 in order to proceed to the next event of GP;
   b. If the validation of e_i *fails*, identify the variable that caused the logical *failure*:

      (1) If the variable that caused the failure was initialized in e_i, then jump back to step 2 in order to try the next possible value for the variable;
      (2) If the variable that caused the failure was initialized in an *event prior to* e_i, then backtrack the process to the step where the variable was initially defined (reverting all changes made to the current state and removing all events added to BS). Continue from step 2 in order to try the next possible values for the variable;
      (3) If the variable that caused the failure was initialized in a *previous episode* (considering that the episode blending process is being applied to more than one episode of V_1), then backtrack the whole process to the episode blending operation where the variable was initially defined (reverting all changes made to the current state and removing all events added to the

episode variant that is being created). Continue from step 2 in the previous instance of the episode blending process to try the next possible value for the variable.

In order to exemplify the episode blending process, let us consider a case where *input space 1 (IS₁)* comprises an ongoing story variant V_1 with all episodes and events logically validated. Also, suppose that episode Ep_6 (*Preparation 2* in the narrative of Chrétien's *Perceval* complemented by the *Second Continuation*, see Sect. 4.1) is the episode selected to be retold. The *current state* of V_1 before episode 6 comprises some facts, such as: hero(Perceval), alive(Perceval),....

In this example, *input space 2 (IS₂)* contains the following alternative variant of episode 6 extracted from the narrative variant *The Legend of Zelda: A Link to the Past*:[1] go(Link, Dark World, Dark Palace), fight(Link, Helmasaur King, Dark Palace), defeat(Link, Helmasaur King, Dark Palace), rescue(Link, First Maiden, Dark Palace).

In the *generic space*, the operators related to *go*, *fight*, *defeat*, and *rescue* are totally relevant. As an example, the operator of the event *go* is o_1 (see Sect. 4.1). In order to use the sequence of events of *IS₂* to replace episode 6 in $V_1 \in IS_1$, the events of *IS₂* must be adapted and logically validated according to the current state of V_1.

The first step of the adaptation and validation process consists in converting the sequence of events of *IS₂* into a *generic plan* that uses *variables* to represent the parameters of the events. Therefore, the sequence of events of *IS₂* becomes: go(A, B, C), fight(A, D, C), defeat(A, D, C), rescue(A, E, C).

Starting from the first event of the generic plan, the algorithm replaces the variables of the event with symbols extracted from the list symbols$\omega_1 \in V_1$: ω_1 = {Perceval, Arthur's land, hermit, hermitage, Red Knight, Lord of the Horn, mighty castle, Fair Unknown, open forest, beautiful woman, ...}. The initial values assigned to the variables used in the first event of the generic plan are: A = Perceval, B = Arthur's land, C = hermit.

After instantiating the event, the algorithm uses the preconditions of the event operator to validate its logical coherence. The validation process iterates through all predicates of the precondition checking the validity of them according to the current state of $V_1 \in IS_1$. In the example, the preconditions of the operator o_1 become: character(Perceval), alive(Perceval), place(Arthur's land), **place(hermit)**, at(Perceval, Arthur's land).

Analyzing the *current state* of V_1, we see that all facts are true, but **place(hermit)** is not (given that hermit is not a place). Therefore, the assignment fails, and C is identified as the variable that caused the failure. Then, the algorithm backtracks and tries the next possible value for C according to the list of symbols, which is Red Knight. However, the same logical failure will happen again (Red Knight is not a place as well). All preconditions will be true only when mighty castle is assigned to C. Then, we have A = Perceval, B = Arthur's land, C = mighty castle.

---

[1] This is a simplified version of the episode that was created to illustrate the blending process (the original episode comprises the rescue of seven maidens).

The event is thus instantiated and added to the current episode variant: `go(Perceval, Arthur's land, mighty castle)`.

When the validation of an event succeeds, the postconditions (effects) of the operator are applied over the current state. Considering the postconditions defined by o_1, the fact `at(Perceval, Arthur's land)` will be removed from the current state of V_1 and `at(Perceval, mighty castle)` will be added to the current state of V_1.

The algorithm applies the same procedure to the subsequent two events of the generic plan (`fight(A, D, C)` and `defeat(A, D, C)`), where some variables are already assigned, and others are not. The result is the following episode variant: `go(Perceval, Arthur's land, mighty castle)`, `fight(Perceval, Lord of the Horn, mighty castle)`, `defeat(Perceval, Lord of the Horn, mighty castle)`. Also, the postconditions of the operators add some facts and remove others.

The last event of the generic plan is `rescue(A, E, C)`, where A and C are already assigned. However, all attempts of assigning a value for E will fail. When all assignment options for a variable are unsuccessful, the algorithm selects – among the variables that are being used in the current event – the one that is closely related with the precondition that caused the failure, giving priority to the variables that were recently successfully assigned. This variable is then identified as the variable that is causing the logical failure. In the example, the variable C affects one term in the precondition of the operator *rescue* that failed.

After identifying the variable that is causing the logical failure, the algorithm backtracks to the recursive call where variable C was initially defined and continues the process of trying the remaining values that can be assigned to C. The backtracking process reverts all changes made to the current state and removes all events added to the episode variant that is being created.

As variable C was defined in the first event of the episode variant, the algorithm returns to its starting point. The *go* operator fails C = `Fair Unknown`, but succeeds with C = `open forest`. Then, the event is instantiated and added to the current episode variant: `go(Perceval, Arthur's land, open forest)`.

The algorithm repeats the same steps until the last event is `rescue(A, E, C)`, where A and C are already assigned. However, this time, the preconditions of the rescue operator will succeed when the algorithm gives `beautiful woman` to E. At this point, the final plan that replaces the original plan of episode 6 is: `go(Perceval, Arthur's land, open forest)`, `fight(Perceval, Fair Unknown, open forest)`, `defeat(Perceval, Fair Unknown, open forest)`, `rescue(Perceval, beautiful woman, open forest)`.

This is one of the variants. However, given a domain library L and a branching network G, a recursive function easily generates all possible narrative variants. This function can be found in the repository of our project: http://www.icad.puc-rio.br/~log tell/narrative-blending/narrative_blending_algorithm.pdf.

5 Application and Results

To apply and evaluate the proposed method, we implemented in C# a tool to assist amateur/professional writers to visualize all narrative variants created from a set of existing stories (Fig. 4). Besides applying the proposed narrative blending method, the tool also permits users to interfere in the initial state of the narratives by changing existing facts and adding new ones. This feature helps the generation of more personalized narratives (for example, allowing the author to decide who will play the role of hero in the stories). Users can define the customized initial state by manually writing logical facts or by using a *state design tool* that allows them to create characters, objects, and establish relations between them visually.

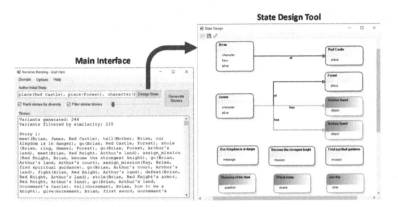

Fig. 4. User interface of the narrative blending tool.

To demonstrate the capacity of our method to generate coherent and diversified narratives, we present below a variant that emerged from the following three different narratives: *The Legend of Zelda: A Link to the Past* (events highlighted in *italic*), *The Legend of Zelda: Ocarina of Time* (events highlighted in **bold**), and Chrétien's *Perceval* complemented by the *Second Continuation* (events highlighted with underline)). The final text (in the form of predicates) is:

tell(James, Brian, our kingdom is in danger), assign_ mission(James, Brian, become the strongest knight), go(Brian, Red Castle, Forest), fight(Brian, Armos Knights, Forest), defeat(Brian, Armos Knights, Forest), get(Brian, Pendant of Courage, Forest), go(Brian, For- est, Desert Palace), fight(Brian, Lanmolas, Desert Palace), defeat(Brian, Lanmolas, Desert Palace), get(Brian, Pendant of Power, Desert Palace), go(Brian, Desert Palace, Tower of Hera), fight(Brian, Moldorm, Tower of Hera), defeat(Brian, Moldorm, Tower of Hera), get(Brian, Pendant of Wisdom, Tower of Hera), go(Brian, Tower of Hera, Lost Woods), get(Brian, Master Sword, Lost Woods), join(Brian, Knights of Hyrule), go(Brian, Lost Woods, Forest), meet(Brian, James, Forest), go_with(Brian, James, Forest, Hyrule Castle), give(James, Brian, Broken Sword, Hyrule Castle), watch(Brian, ritual scene, Hyrule Castle), fail_to_ask(Brian, James, meaning of the ritual, Hyrule Castle), sleep(Brian, one day), *assign_mission(Sahasrahla, Brian, find spiritual guidance)*, wander(Brian, seven years), **go(Brian, Hyrule Castle, Ice Palace), awake(Brian, Fifth Maiden, Ice Palace), go(Brian, Ice Palace, Gargoyle's Domain), awake(Brian, Fourth Maiden, Gargoyle's Domain), go(Brian, Gargoyle's Domain, Dark Palace), awake(Brian, First Maiden, Dark Palace), go(Brian, Dark Palace, Skull Woods), awake(Brian, Third Maiden, Skull Woods), go(Brian, Skull Woods, Turtle Rock), awake(Brian, Seventh Maiden, Turtle Rock), go(Brian, Turtle Rock, Swamp Palace), awake(Brian, Second Maiden, Swamp Palace)**, *go(Brian, Swamp Palace, Ganon's Tower Entrance), open(Brian, Ganon's Tower, Ganon's Tower Entrance)*, go(Brian, Ganon's Tower Entrance, Hyrule Castle), watch(Brian, ritual scene, Hyrule Castle), ask(Brian, James, meaning of the ritual, Hyrule Castle), give(James, Brian, Golden Sword, Hyrule Castle), repair(Brian, Golden Sword, Hyrule Castle), crown(James, Brian, Hyrule Castle).

In terms of computational performance, the proposed method has limitations. As exhaustive search is the strategy adopted, the algorithm systematically enumerates and checks all possible ways in which the episodes and events of the narratives can be combined. Consequently, the complexity of the algorithm grows according to the numbers of variants, episodes, events and also the number of facts and symbols used to describe the initial state of the variants. For example, a domain library with four narratives and 6 different walks takes 15.4 min to generate all possible variants (in a computer with an Intel Core i7-7820HK, 2.90 GHZ, and 16 GB of RAM). In this test, the original narratives were: *Perceval* complemented with the *Second Continuation* (8 episodes, 87 events, 144 facts in the initial state, and 65 different symbols), *The Legend of Zelda: A Link to the Past* (6 episodes, 61 events, 81 facts in the initial state, and 50 different symbols), *The Legend of Zelda: Ocarina of Time* (8 episodes, 43 events, 64 facts in the initial state, and 43 different symbols), and *The Witcher 3: Wild Hunt* (8 episodes, 67 events, 75 facts in the initial state, and 49 different symbols).

6 Concluding Remarks

In this paper we presented a new plot generation method that reuses fragments of existing stories to compose new narrative variants. Inspired by the notion of conceptual blending (especially [7] and [8]), our method adapts sequences of events extracted from different narratives in a way that they can fit into a new narrative variant without violating the logical coherence of the story. The combination of plan validation with an exhaustive search strategy, allows the generation of coherent and diversified plots. In addition, all plots are constructed according to a specific narrative structure, which guarantees the overall dramatic structure of the generated stories.

Although the proposed narrative blending method can generate coherent narratives even when episodes of distinct narratives are combined, the process to generate all possible variants for a domain library is a computationally expensive task even when a small number of narratives are considered. In addition, it is important to point out that our method is far from being able to perform creative blending tasks at the same level that talented human authors would do. The use of plan validation is an excellent way of guaranteeing the logical coherence of generated narrative, but on the other hand strict logic sometimes causes some interesting episodes to be discarded as result of very small coherence violations that could easily be fixed by a human author.

Many future works are envisaged, especially regarding the optimization of the blending process. Since our method to solve the problem of finding all variants for a domain library is based on a recursive algorithm – where each episode blend task can be considered a sub-problem – and given the fact that many of the episode blends involve similar or equal inputs, one can easily imagine an optimized solution using a dynamic programming strategy. By using memoization to store the results of previous blends and returning the cached results when necessary, the performance of the whole narrative blending process would likely be improved.

Acknowledgements. We would like to thank CNPq (National Council for Scientific and Technological Development) and FINEP (Brazilian Innovation Agency), which belong to the Ministry of Science, Technology, and Innovation, for the financial support.

References

1. Barthes, R.: Theory of the text. In: Young, J.C. (ed.) Untying the Text: A Post-Structuralist Reader. Routledge & Kegan Paul, Oxfordshire (1981)
2. Bringsjord, S., Ferrucci, D.A.: Artificial Intelligence and Literary Creativity: Inside the Mind of BRUTUS, a Storytelling Machine. Psychology Press, Sussex (1999)
3. Bryant, N. (trans.): The Complete Story of the Grail. D.S. Brewer, England (2015)
4. Campbell. J.: The Hero with a Thousand Faces. Princeton University, Princeton (1973)
5. Ciarlini, A.E.M., Pozzer, C.T., Furtado, A.L., Feijó, B.: A logic-based tool for interactive generation and dramatization of stories. In: Proceedings of the International Conference on Advances in Computer Entertainment Technology, pp. 133–140 (2005)
6. Fauconnier, G., Turner, M.: Conceptual integration networks. Cogn. Sci. **22**(2), 133–187 (1998)
7. Fauconnier, G., Turner, M.: The Way We Think: Conceptual Blending and the Mind's Hidden Complexities. Basic Books, New York (2003)
8. Goguen, J.: Mathematical models of cognitive space and time. In: Andler, D., Ogawa, Y., Okada, M., Watanabe, S. (eds.) Reasoning and Cognition: Proceedings of the Interdisciplinary Conference on Reasoning and Cognition, pp. 125–128 (2006)
9. Kibler, W.W. (trans.): Chrétien de Troyes - Arthurian Romances. Penguin Books, London(1991)
10. Klein, S., et al.: Automatic Novel Writing: A Status Report. Technical Report 186, Computer Sciences Department, University of Wisconsin, Madison (1973)
11. Li, B., Riedl, M.O.: A phone that cures your flu: generating imaginary gadgets in fictions with planning and analogies. In: Proceedings of the 4th Workshop of Intelligent Narrative Technologies, pp. 41–48 (2011)
12. Li, B., Zook, A., Davis, N., Riedl, M.O.: Goal-driven conceptual blending: a computational approach for creativity. In: Proceedings of the 2012 International Conference on Computational Creativity, pp. 9–16 (2012)

13. Lima, E.S., Feijó, B., Casanova, M.A., Furtado, A.L.: Storytelling variants based on semiotic relations. Entertain. Comput. **17**, 31–44 (2016)
14. Lima, E.S., Feijó, B., Furtado, A.L.: Hierarchical generation of dynamic and nondeterministic quests in games. In: Proceedings of the International Conference on Advances in Computer Entertainment Technology, article 24, pp. 1–10 (2014)
15. Lima, E.S., Feijó, B., Furtado, A.L.: Procedural generation of quests for games using genetic algorithms and automated planning. In: Proceedings of the XVIII Brazilian Symposium on Computer Games and Digital Entertainment, pp. 495–504 (2019)
16. Lima, E.S., Furtado, A.L., Feijó, B., Casanova, M.A.: Towards reactive failure-recovery game-playing: the fall and rise of the grail hero. In: Proceedings of the XV Brazilian Symposium on Computer Games and Digital Entertainment, pp. 262–271 (2016)
17. Lima, E.S., Furtado, A.L., Feijó, B.: Storytelling variants: the case of little red riding hood. In: Proceedings of the 14th International Conference on Entertainment Computing, Trondheim, Norway, pp. 286–300 (2015)
18. Machado, I., Paiva, A., Brna, P.: Real characters in virtual stories: promoting interactive story-creation activities. In: Proceedings of the 1st International Conference on Virtual Storytelling, pp. 127–134 (2001)
19. Martinez, M., et al.: Towards a domain-independent computational framework for theory blending. In: AAAI Fall Symposium: Advances in Cognitive Systems, pp. 210–217 (2011)
20. Meehan, J.: TALE-SPIN, an interactive program that writes stories. In: Proceedings of the Fifth Interactional Joint Conference on Artificial Intelligence, pp. 91–98 (1977)
21. O'Donoghue, D., Abgaz, Y., Hurley, D., Ronzano, F.: Stimulating and simulating creativity with Dr inventor. In: Proceedings of the Sixth International Conference on Computational Creativity, pp. 220–227 (2015)
22. Ong, T., Leggett, J.J.: A genetic algorithm approach to interactive narrative generation. In: Proceedings of the 15th ACM Conference on Hypertext Hypermedia, pp. 181–182 (2004)
23. Pereira, F.C., Cardoso, A.: Optimality principles for conceptual blending: a first computational approach. AISB J. **1**(4), 351–369 (2003)
24. Pérez y Pérez, R., Sharples, M.: MEXICA: a computer model of a cognitive account of creative writing. Exp. Theor. Artif. Intell. **13**, 119–139 (2001)
25. Pérez y Pérez, R., Sharples, M.: Three computer based models of storytelling: BRUTUS, MINSTREL and MEXICA. Knowl.-Based Syst. **17**, 15–29 (2004)
26. Permar, J., Magerko, B.: A conceptual blending approach to the generation of cognitive scripts for interactive narrative. In: Proceedings of the 9th AIIDE Conference, pp. 44–50 (2013)
27. Pizzi, D., Cavazza, M.: Affective storytelling based on characters' feelings. In: AAAI Fall Symposium on Intelligent Narrative Technologies, pp. 110–117 (2007)
28. Rank, O., Raglan, L., Dundes, A.: In Quest of the Hero. Princeton University Press, Princeton (1990)
29. Riedl, M.O., Young, M.: Narrative planning: balancing plot and character. J. Artif. Intell. Res. **39**, 217–226 (2010)
30. Schneider, R., Hartner, M. (eds.): Blending and the Study of Narrative: Approaches and Applications. De Gruyter, Berlin (2012)
31. Sternberg, R.J.: Handbook of Creativity, 1st edn. Cambridge University Press, Cambridge (1998)
32. Turner, S.R.: MINSTREL: A computer model of creativity and storytelling. Ph.D. Thesis, Computer Science Department, University of California (1993)
33. Veale, T., O'Donoghue, D.: Computation and blending. Cogn. Linguist. **11**(3–4), 253–281 (2000)
34. Veale, T.: How to blend concepts and influence people: computational models of conceptual integration. Theoria Historia Scientiarum **6**(1), 363–398 (2002)

35. Yorke, J.: Into The Woods: How Stories Work and Why We Tell Them. Penguin Books, London (2014)
36. Zook, A.E., Riedl, M.O., Magerko, B.S.: Understanding human creativity for computational play. In: Proceedings of the Second International Conference on Computational Creativity, pp. 42–47 (2011)

Linkages Between Gameplay Preferences and Fondness for Game Music

Jukka Vahlo[1,3](✉) (iD), Oskari Koskela[1] (iD), Kai Tuuri[1] (iD), and Heli Tissari[2] (iD)

[1] Department of Music, Art and Culture Studies, University of Jyväskylä,
P.O. Box 35, 40014 Jyväskylä, Finland
{jlvahlo,osjokosk,krtuuri}@jyu.fi
[2] Department of Languages, University of Helsinki, P.O. Box 4,
00014 Helsinki, Finland
heli.tissari@helsinki.fi
[3] Department of Economics, University of Turku, 20014 Turku, Finland

Abstract. In this paper we explore connections between players' preferences in gameplay and their desire to listen to game music. Music always takes place in cultural contexts and the activity of music listening is likewise entangled with versatile cultural practices. This is arguably evident in the case of game music since the primary context of encountering it is the active and participatory experience of gameplay. By analyzing survey data (N = 403) collected from the UK, we investigate how contextual preferences in gameplay activities predict fondness for game music. It was found that player preference for *Aggression* and *Exploration* are two precedents for liking game music. These findings indicate that a better understanding of the extra-musical qualities of game music is crucial for making sense of its overall attractiveness and meaningfulness.

Keywords: Game music · Music preferences · Player preferences Survey · Factor analysis

1 Introduction

It is quite common to consider music as an entity of its own, thus making a distinction between musical and extra-musical substances. There are, however, plenty of everyday instances, in which one can say that music becomes entwined with particular kinds of situations and activities. Dance music is a prime example of such music that by its name is defined by a certain type of activity. It is even difficult to consider music as something that would intrinsically exist only as music. Contemporary music cognition research argues that music is essentially

---

This work is funded by Kone Foundation (grant number 201908388).

Electronic supplementary material The online version of this chapter (https://doi.org/10.1007/978-3-030-89394-1_23) contains supplementary material, which is available to authorized users.

J. Baalsrud Hauge et al. (Eds.): ICEC 2021, LNCS 13056, pp. 304–318, 2021.
https://doi.org/10.1007/978-3-030-89394-1_23

embodied [11] and coupled with capabilities of human action [8]. We may speculate that a preference for dance music might indicate a preference not only for certain musical features, but also for the contextual activity of dancing. Hence, for a person who likes to dance, music arguably is about moving to the music, gestures heard in music, a feeling of togetherness through music and, in all, bodily engagement with music. Continuing with this line of thought, we may come up with an array of other examples. Using a quick internet-search, playlists can be found for jogging, relaxing, nostalgia, hanging out with friends, dining, and so on. It might not be too far-fetched to suggest that our understanding of, as well as our preference for a given music genre is structured also by the activity and context related to it.

Game music is an example of a type of music that is deeply entangled with its experiential contexts. It is part of the designed game artefact, and a piece of music is therefore intended to be experienced in a specific state of game and during ongoing player-game interaction. This condition denotes that during a gameplay experience, a piece of game music is encountered while the player is doing something in relation to the game environment and its internal dynamics. Differently put, the player is likely to be engaged with particular gameplay activities when listening to game music – whether those activities are about exploring the gameworld, engaging in battles, strategizing, or menu management, for example. Thus a player who focuses on unfolding game events often does not listen to music but rather encounters it as a part of the fictional gameworld and her own active agency in it.

The overarching goal of this paper is to explore how players' preferences in gameplay activity types may be related to their desire to listen to game music, whether they enjoy game music during ongoing gameplay or in situations external to it. We define game music in this study as any music that is intended to accompany the ongoing gameplay, be it original compositions, licensed songs by popular artists or a more ambience-like soundscape that perhaps meshes with other sounds of the game and changes in relation to the player's actions. By investigating the relations between gameplay activity types and game music preferences, we also ask what kind of music genre game music appears to be. A synthesis of game research and music research approaches should be beneficial for both of these academic fields. The explorative approach of this study also adds to the understanding of music as a constituent of the gameplay experience. Simultaneously, it generates insight into music listening in terms of contextual activity.

In order to analyze how players' preferences in engaging with gameplay activities might be related to their preferences in listening to game music, we first need to consider how both music and game preferences should be approached in this kind of research setup. After that, we will introduce our research hypotheses for empirical investigation. We will then proceed to introduce our methods and a survey sample (N = 403) that was collected for the purposes of this research. Finally, we will report the results which will be followed by a discussion on the impacts of our findings.

2   Background: Music and Game Classifications

Music has been a part of game experience from very early on. Likewise, both musicians and amateurs alike were quick to adopt influences from videogames as well as to utilize the technological possibilities of game-related devices. More recently, alongside the growing popularity and recognition of videogames as a legitimate form of culture, game music has also established itself as a noteworthy category of music. Game music thus seems to be a relatively prominent area of consumption even outside the actual gameplay context (see [7]) and, perhaps more importantly, one of the many situations of everyday life where music is listened to as an integral part of some other activity.

Despite this, game music has not yet found its way into many studies of music preferences. For example, in a meta-analysis [18] surveying 28 studies on the relation between personality traits and musical preferences, game music was not among the 150 different musical styles and substyles used in the studies. However, several of the studies did include the more general category of "soundtracks", which arguably could also include game music. What game music and soundtracks have in common is that they are not styles or genres which could be easily defined or denoted by certain musical features. (cf. [17]) This situation makes it difficult to discuss game music as a music genre, as the latter are typically identified primarily based on underlying structures of the music itself, instead of its reoccurring contextual uses.

It could be posited, then, that considering game music as a music genre would require rethinking the criteria used in identifying a music genre. Traditional genre-based approaches have indeed been criticized as being problematic in various ways (see [4]) and several authors have attempted to overcome these problems. Arguably the most influential line of research is based on the work of Rentfrow and Gosling who in their seminal paper [16], developed the Short Test of Music Preferences (STOMP) which organized musical preferences into four independent dimensions comprising several genres. These dimensions are based on underlying structures of musical preferences and thus go beyond traditional genre labels. This work was later refined and elaborated into a revised version of STOMP and into the five factor MUSIC model [13] (see also [15]). Yet there remains critical discussion about whether the dimensional models are still too tightly interwoven with genre-based ideas and primacy of musical features (see [4,13]). Despite this we consider that dimensional models of music preferences [13], such as the STOMP, make it possible to include game music in the analysis.

Regarding game preferences, the most intuitive approach would be to make use of game genre classification models since the purpose of any genre classification system is to make sense of a large number of cultural expressions by identifying common structures in how these expressions are manifested in our experiences. Genres are patterns of expectations and communicative maps between an item of culture and our ways to encounter it [12]. Thus genre conventions should help us in understanding and communicating what kind of item we are dealing with.

There are at least three interrelated problems that make game genre analysis and, consequently, utilizing genres as analytical concepts especially challenging. Firstly, researchers, game industry representatives, and players alike have constant difficulties in identifying which criteria should be used in separating one game genre from another. The second problem concerns game ontology and asks: "What makes something a game?" This question is paramount for any game genre analysis, because the purpose of these studies is to identify those qualities and characteristics which not only separate a particular game from another type of game but also simultaneously separate games from other forms of cultural expressions. The third problem deals with what Espen Aarseth [1] has called genre trouble, and it refers to how the phenomenon of game should be understood and approached theoretically and methodologically.

Furthermore, genres are historical constructs that are entangled with contextual cultural meaning-making and practices of subjective interpretation. Some authors also consider game genres to be partly defined by or even bound to the material structure of technology which enable them to exist [9]. Taken together, the above means that a single game can be regarded to be a genre-defining product. *Doom* (Id Software; 1993) is a good example of that kind of game as it has been generally regarded as the game that established the first-person shooter (FPS) game genre [3]. The complexity in identifying game genres is easily demonstrated by how game marketplaces and databases still utilize classification systems that differ from each other.

As a result of identifying these broad challenges, many researchers have considered the task of defining game genres to be very difficult or even impossible. Shortly put, game genres lack analytical explanatory power [2,3,5]. Although game genres are important for game cultures and their discourses, these concepts are not optimal units of analysis in investigating how gaming preferences are related to other phenomena, including music preferences. To find a solution to this problem, we explored alternative ways to study structures in players' enduring gaming preferences.

3   Method

3.1   GAIN and STOMP Models

By definition, games are interactive and participatory rule-based systems that change their state dynamically based on user input and the game's code. From this perspective it makes sense that typical game classifications are mostly *ludological*. As Myers [5] wrote: "The most fundamental characteristics of computer games, those that properly determine genre, lie in the pattern of interactivity between player and the game". Instead of building on e.g. narrative style, story setting, theme, game functions, or art style, ludological game genres are based on distinguishable types of gameplay.

Following this line of thought, Vahlo, Holm, Kaakinen and Koponen [19] developed an approach of measuring players' preferences in game dynamics which they defined as player–game interaction modes that emerge from game mechanics during gameplay. By analysing 700 game review articles, the authors developed a set of 33 recurrent game dynamics that were further edited into Core Game Dynamics (CGD) scale items for survey studies. The scale was further amended by Vahlo, Smed, and Koponen [20] who validated the scale as the Gameplay Activity Inventory (GAIN) by investigating its psychometric properties and dimensionality with large survey samples collected in Canada, Finland, and Japan.

The validated 15-GAIN as well as the full 47-GAIN [20] consist of five gameplay activity type factors: Aggression, Caretaking, Coordinate, Exploration, and Management. *Aggression* measures player preference in activities such as destroying, shooting, and warfare. *Caretaking* covers player preferences in e.g. decorating, dressing up, dating, and taking care of others. *Coordinate* refers to players' desire to engage with activities such as jumping, running, racing, performing in sports, and keeping in rhythm. *Exploration* is the player's preference in investigating a game's story, exploring the gameworld, developing a character's skills and abilities, and collecting treasures. And *Management* assesses a player's preference for activities including building and construction, trading, directing and commanding, and resource management.

In the context of this study, we consider applying GAIN to be a better solution instead of using a list of game genres such as action games, adventure games, RPG games, puzzles, and simulations. As noted above, players do not have a common shared way to understand what actually is, for example, an action game and what makes it different from an RPG or an adventure game. GAIN items aim to illustrate recurrent activity types in a way that does not operate with genre concepts and is intuitive for different kinds of player types, regardless of whether they have first-hand experience of playing any games that have elements of *Aggression* or *Management*, for instance. Since there are no earlier studies on how GAIN dimensions might be associated with game music preferences, we adopted a more extensive 25-item GAIN version which was based on a combination of the 15-GAIN and the full 47-GAIN. The authors of GAIN [20] have argued that also the 47-item GAIN consistently measures the five above-mentioned preference dimensions with relatively high primary loadings.

The main idea behind the STOMP instrument is similar to GAIN as STOMP aims to tap into the underlying structures of music preferences. In order to investigate the latter, Rentfrow and Gosling utilized STOMP in three separate empirical studies that yielded, through factor analysis, an organization of genres into four independent dimensions of music preferences. These dimension were named *Reflective & Complex* (consisting of classical, jazz, blues and folk), *Intense & Rebellious* (alternative, rock, heavy metal), *Upbeat & Conventional* (country, pop, religious, sound tracks) and *Energetic & Rhythmic* (rap/hip hop, soul/funk, electronica/dance). The different qualities of these dimensions were investigated in another study, which related to characterization of the four dimensions in terms of 25 attributes related either to music (e.g. relaxed, angry, romantic) and/or lyrics (e.g. boastful, reflective, bitter) or more generally to tempo (fast, slow) and mode (acoustic, electric) of music.

Later studies using a similar approach of clustering styles into larger factors have found differing numbers of preference dimensions (see for example [18]). The authors of STOMP themselves, in their subsequent studies, elaborated the inventory to include 23 genres and by using music excerpts instead of genre labels found five dimensions (Mellow, Unpretentious, Sophisticated, Intense and Contemporary), hence the MUSIC model [13,14].

While there is variability in the factor structures uncovered by different studies, which is at least partly explained by different sets of musical styles used by researchers, there seems to be an overall consistency to the findings: Most of the STOMP studies have found independent dimensions for at least musical preferences overlapping with "reflective & complex" (e.g., jazz and classical), "intense & rebellious" (e.g., rock and heavy metal) and "energetic & rhythmic" (e.g., rap and hip hop). We therefore judged the original 14 item STOMP to be a robust enough starting point for the investigation of music preferences in this study.

However, because of the aim of the study, we modified the STOMP by adding the item "video game music" to the list of musical styles. This was an informed decision to be made and consistent with our approach since the STOMP model does not utilize music genres as analytical tools but instead operates on the level of latent preference factors of the inventory. It should also be made clear that fondness for game music in this study is therefore comparable to preferences for other music genres included in the STOMP. Since the STOMP model does not specify the context in which music is encountered (e.g. soundtracks and theme songs can be encountered as part of a movie watching experience or in contexts external to it), this kind of distinction cannot be made either about game music preferences. Therefore fondness for game music in this study may refer to both players' fondness for listening to game music as they play and to their desire to engage with it outside ongoing gaming situations.

3.2   Research Hypotheses

The main research question (RQ) of this study was to understand *if and how players' gameplay activity type preferences predict their fondness for game music.* Because game music is composed and arranged for the gameplay experience and thus intended to be encountered as a part of active player participation, it is plausible to assume that preferences in gameplay activities and game music listening are related. It is also plausible to assume that experiences of gameplay activities and thus also gameplay activity preferences are precedents for a habit of game music listening. There are exceptions, of course, as some prefer to listen to game music although they do not play games at all. However, generally speaking, we can expect that *H1: A higher preference in gameplay activity types predicts higher preference for game music.*

Game music is not something associated only with games of a particular kind. Instead, players have encountered and will encounter game music in a wide variety of games ranging from 8-bit retro arcade games to multiplayer computer games and casual free-to-play mobile games. Because practically all types of games commonly include game music, and because there are no earlier studies made on the subject, we expect that *H2: A particular kind of gameplay activity type preference does not predict game music preference more than the other types.*

The original STOMP did not include "video game music" as an item but it did include "soundtracks". We might suppose that in terms of musical features these two categories are somewhat similar at least in the sense that they do not denote a clear musical genre but rather a certain context of use. We thus expect the "video game music" item to be correlated with "soundtracks". However, game music might distinguish the specific preferences of those who identify as gamers and therefore game music may not have any clear relation to preference for soundtracks or any other STOMP item, either. We therefore assume that *H3: The game music item is moderately correlated with the soundtrack item and that it loads on the same factor as the latter when included in the STOMP.*

4   Survey Participants and Procedure

A total of 403 survey participants (ages 18–65) were obtained from the UK via a commercial crowdsourcing platform Prolific which maintains an online panel of over 70,000 users in several countries. No other inclusion criteria for survey participation were used since the focus of the survey was on investigating experiences of music listening and it is reasonable to expect that everyone without a hearing impairment has listened to music. We also decided not to target the survey only at active players as the purpose of this study was to understand the general relationship between gameplay preferences and game music preferences.

The survey included an adapted 25-item version of the GAIN and the 14-STOMP with the game music item. Survey participants were asked to indicate their preference in the 15 musical styles with this question setup: "For the following items, please indicate your basic preference level for the music genres listed using the scale provided" with a 7 point scale from "strongly dislike" to "strongly like". They were then asked to answer the 25-item GAIN according to this question setup: "Imagine yourself playing a digital game. How pleasurable do you find the following in-game activity types based on your earlier gaming experiences?" and with a 5-point scale from very unpleasant to very pleasant. The reported analyses were made by using the statistical software Stata/SE 16.1.

In addition to the 25-item GAIN and 15-item STOMP, the survey included questions about the participants' age, gender, game genre and social play preferences, and their experiences regarding music listening in general. Results regarding the latter inventories are not reported in this paper.

On an average, it took a participant 13.5 min to complete the survey. A total of 43.5% (N = 175) survey respondents identified as males and 55.5% as females (N = 223). In addition to that, 5 survey participants (1%) reported that their gender was non-binary. Of a list of 15 game genres, adventure games, puzzle games, and strategy games had the highest mean preferences. Male players reported higher preference for action games, fighting games, and sports games than female players whereas female players had higher preference especially for puzzle games and educational games than male players.

5   Results

In the 25-GAIN version applied in our research, *Aggression*, *Caretaking*, and *Management* were all measured by five items whereas *Exploration* and *Coordinate* were both assessed by six items. A total of 11 items of the 25-GAIN were same or very similar to the 15-GAIN (marked with * in Table 1) whereas 13 items were included in the more extensive 47-GAIN (see [20]). We also included a new item in the GAIN. This item was "Engaging in a battle" and the decision to include this was based on a partly similar item "Attacking, defending and casting spells" that was dropped from the original GAIN as it had showed a relatively high loading on *Exploration* alongside *Aggression* [20]. We wanted to explore if this was because the wording of the item referred to the role-playing specific activity of "casting spells".

To make sure that the 25-GAIN version we applied would indeed measure the aforementioned five gameplay preference dimensions, we made an exploratory factor analysis (EFA) for the 25-GAIN. The second reason for an EFA was that we wanted to explore 1) how the gameplay activity preference in general (H1) and 2) each of the five dimensions individually (H2) may predict a preference for game music. To study the first question, a single sum variable was constructed from all of the 25-GAIN items. But for examining the latter question, computing five factor sums was not the best solution as factor sums do not take cross-loadings on other factors and unique variance of each item into account. Instead of using factor sums we wanted to be able to compute factor scores for each item as factor scores provide information about how an item loads on every factor. Computing factor scores is possible after making an EFA (Table 1).

Parallel analysis [10] suggested a five factor solution. The inventory passed the Kaiser–Meyer–Olkin (KMO) test for factorability with the value of 0.91 and also the Bartlett test of sphericity (chi-square $= 5427$, df $= 351$, p $= 0.000$), and thus we proceeded to investigate a five-factor solution (promax rotation). As a cut-off criterion, we utilized a factor loading over 0.4. The item "Crafting items and valuables by combining raw materials" showed a loading under 0.4 and was therefore removed from the analysis. The parallel analysis test still suggested a five-factor solution and in the second iteration all items had over 0.4 loading on a factor. The solution reported in Table 1 was similar to what Vahlo et al. [20] had reported, all of the five dimensions were identified with the following Cronbach's alphas and 95% confidence interval and coefficient omegas (McDonald's omega/Raykov's rho): *Aggression* $\alpha = 0.91$ (CI 0.90–0.93) and $\omega = 0.92$, *Caretaking* $\alpha = 0.82$ (CI 0.79–0.85) and $\omega = 0.79$, *Coordinate* $\alpha = 0.72$ (CI 0.67–0.76) and $\omega = 0.73$, *Exploration* $\alpha = 0.82$ (CI 0.79–0.85) and $\omega = 0.82$, and *Management* $\alpha = 0.80$ (CI 0.76–0.83) and $\omega = 0.81$. We did not make a confirmatory analysis on the 24-item GAIN as our sample was not representative on the population level.

We computed regression factor score variables for the rotated five-factor 24-GAIN solution (promax rotation) to study H2 (see [6]). In addition to that, we also calculated a factor sum for all of the 24 items included in the analysis to investigate H1. Next, we calculated the correlation (Spearman's rho) between

Table 1. An EFA for the 24-item GAIN (Cut-off 0.4, promax rotation). Factors in order: *Aggression*, *Exploration*, *Management*, *Caretaking*, and *Coordinate*.

	f1	f2	f3	f4	f5	Uniqn.
Engaging in a battle	0.86					0.22
Exploding and destroying	0.82					0.31
Shooting enemies and avoiding fire*	0.77					0.29
Waging war and conquering	0.75					0.30
Weapons and skills selection for characters	0.71					0.34
Trading items, weapons or resources*	0.49					0.45
Investigating the story and its mysteries		0.67				0.47
Exploring the gameworld and its secrets*		0.64				0.41
Developing skills and abilities*		0.63				0.56
Searching for and collecting rare treasures		0.62				0.55
Making meaningful choices in dialogues*		0.54				0.51
Managing and directing cities and their inhabitants*			0.74			0.39
Building and developing a city or a base			0.70			0.33
Managing resources such as money or energy*			0.56			0.57
Dressing up and choosing looks*				0.75		0.45
Decorating rooms and houses				0.66		0.44
Taking care of pets and training them*				0.61		0.53
Character customization				0.59		0.49
Flirting, seducing and romantic dating				0.59		0.60
Gardening and taking care of farms*			0.42	0.43		0.56
Racing in a high speed					0.72	0.40
Piloting and steering vehicles					0.63	0.42
Performing in athletics, gymnastics or other sports*					0.51	0.69
Moving to the beat and staying in the rhythm					0.42	0.07

the general gameplay preference factor sum and the preference to listen to game music. The correlation was moderate (0.43), which confirmed that these variables were associated with each other.

A linear regression between the combined gameplay preference factor sum and the game music listening preference variable showed that gameplay activity preferences do predict preference for game music listening (coefficient 1.05, standardized error 0.11, p = 0.000, t = 9.32, β = 0.42). The gameplay preference measured by 24-GAIN explained 18% of the variance in the game music listening preference. This association and direction of the effect supported H1.

We continued to investigate how the five GAIN factors were related to game music preference. This was done by calculating multiple regressions between the GAIN factor scores and the game music variable. We also added age, squared age and information on whether respondents identified as males to the regression model to better understand the effect of the GAIN factors (Table 2).

Age and squared age did not have a statistically significant effect on game music preference, but identifying as a male did. The effects of *Caretaking* and *Management* on game music were not statistically significant, but the other three factors predicted a preference for game music. However, the effects were not only different in their size but also in their direction. Preference for *Coordinate* predicted negatively for fondness for game music listening. *Exploration* and especially *Aggression* both had a clear positive effect on game music preference. Based on these results, we conclude that player preferences in the GAIN factors do not predict fondness for game music similarly to each other. Thus, H2 was not supported by our analyses.

Table 2. Regression between the GAIN factors and game music preference

Game music preference[a]	coef.	std. err.	t	p	β
Aggression factor	0.619	0.126	4.930	0.000	0.347
Exploration factor	0.411	0.114	3.610	0.000	0.219
Management factor	−0.188	0.103	−1.830	0.068	−0.100
Caretaking factor	0.117	0.106	1.110	0.269	0.063
Coordinate factor	−0.245	0.103	−2.380	0.018	−0.125
Age	−0.021	0.041	−0.500	0.614	−0.141
Squared age	0.000	0.001	−0.150	0.881	−0.042
Identifies as a male	0.497	0.185	2.690	0.007	0.144

[a]The model explains 33% of the variance in the game music variable

Although game genres are not well-suited for analyzing player preferences and gaming behavior, we decided to calculate correlations (Spearman's Rho) between the GAIN factors and popular game genres. This was done because in the questionnaire the survey participants had also indicated their basic preference level for several game genres (1 = Strongly dislike, 7 = Strongly like) and because reporting correlations further describe how the GAIN factors are related to game genre preferences (Table 3).

Table 3. Correlations (Spearman's Rho) between the GAIN factor scores and game genre preferences. Moderate correlation (over 0.4) are bolded.

	Action	Adventure	Racing	Puzzle	RPG	Strategy
Aggression	**0.63**	**0.51**	**0.40**	−0.18	**0.50**	0.28
Exploration	**0.42**	**0.51**	0.18	0.10	**0.45**	0.31
Management	0.18	0.22	0.22	0.07	0.26	**0.40**
Caretaking	0.15	0.16	0.12	0.08	0.23	0.12
Coordinate	**0.44**	0.28	**0.66**	−0.05	0.14	0.18

Next we studied connections between the video game music item and 14-STOMP. In our sample, rock, pop, and soundtracks were the three most liked genres. Female respondents had a higher preference for pop music whereas male respondents enjoyed heavy metal and game music more than females. Game music was the fifth most liked music type among the male sub-sample whereas it was the third least liked genre among female respondents. (Table 4)

Table 4. Descriptive statistics of the 15-STOMP

N	175		223		403	
Gender	Male		Female		Total	
	Mean	SD	Mean	SD	Mean	SD
Alternative	4.91	1.57	4.89	1.65	4.90	1.61
Blues	4.38	1.30	4.12	1.40	4.24	1.36
Classical	4.35	1.58	4.39	1.70	4.38	1.64
Country	3.73	1.64	4.05	1.65	3.91	1.65
Dance/Electronica	4.61	1.64	4.46	1.76	4.52	1.72
Folk	3.77	1.58	3.80	1.60	3.80	1.59
Heavy metal	4.23	2.02	3.41	1.98	3.79	2.04
Jazz	4.14	1.49	3.91	1.66	4.03	1.61
Pop	4.88	1.54	5.73	1.11	5.34	1.39
Rap/hip-hop	4.65	1.95	4.39	1.70	4.51	1.81
Religious	2.57	1.54	2.75	1.64	2.67	1.60
Rock	5.48	1.50	5.41	1.47	5.44	1.49
Soul/funk	4.41	1.44	4.42	1.44	4.42	1.44
Soundtracks/theme songs	5.07	1.40	5.35	1.26	5.23	1.33
Video game music	4.68	1.59	3.58	1.65	4.07	1.71

The relationship between the validated 14-STOMP inventory and the new game music item we added to the inventory was further studied by making two EFAs, first with the original 14-STOMP and then with the 15 item scale version which included the video game music item. For the 14-item version, the Bartlett test of sphericity resulted in Chi-square = 1391, df = 91, p = 0.000. The Kaiser–Meyer–Olkin (KMO) test for factorability and sampling adequacy for the 14-item version had a value of 0.72 which can be considered as middling. The KMO test measures the proportion of variance among the inventory variables. A value of 0.72 means that there was some common variance in the 14-STOMP, but also that making an EFA is still suitable for this inventory. In both EFAs, we used orthogonal rotation (varimax) similarly to the original research in which STOMP was developed [16].

The Parallel Analysis (PA) test suggested a four-factor solution for the original 14-STOMP. The extracted four factors were mostly similar to the validated STOMP factors with the exception of the Soul/Funk item which loaded on *Reflective and Complex* instead of *Energetic and Rhythmic* and Religious which similarly loaded on *Reflective and Complex* instead of *Upbeat and Conventional.* Cronbach's alphas (95% confidence intervals for the alphas) and coefficient omegas for the four 14-STOMP factors were acceptable for *Reflective and Complex* $\alpha = 0.75$ (CI 0.70–0.79) and $\omega = 0.78$ as well as for *Intense and Rebellious* $\alpha = 0.70$ (CI 0.65–0.75) and $\omega = 0.72$, but low for *Upbeat and Conventional* $\alpha = 0.48$ and *Energetic and Rhythmic* $\alpha = 0.48$. We did not calculate confidence intervals or omegas for *Energetic and Rhythmic* and *Upbeat and Conventional,* because only two items loaded on these dimensions.

We then made another PA test for the 15-item version of the STOMP. The Parallel Analysis (PA) test suggested a six-factor solution and we thus proceeded to extract six factors. Because the purpose of this analysis was to explore all correlations and intercorrelations between the game music item and the STOMP factors, we did not utilize a cut-off criterion. Instead we report below the full factor loading table after a varimax rotation (Table 5).

Table 5. Results from the EFA conducted with the 14-STOMP, complemented by the videogame music item. Varimax rotation.

	f1	f2	f3	f4	f5	f6	Uniqn.
Blues	**0.76**	0.17	0.17	0.03	−0.03	−0.01	0.36
Jazz	**0.69**	0.05	0.16	0.08	0.16	−0.05	0.46
Soul/funk	**0.66**	0.06	0.00	0.08	0.12	0.09	0.53
Rock	0.14	**0.70**	0.05	0.06	−0.08	0.11	0.46
Heavy metal	0.07	**0.69**	−0.07	0.04	−0.02	−0.16	0.49
Alternative	0.17	**0.54**	0.11	−0.12	0.23	−0.14	0.58
Folk	0.41	0.05	**0.53**	0.02	−0.03	−0.07	0.54
Country	0.31	−0.06	**0.51**	0.15	−0.09	0.24	0.56
Soundtracks	0.14	0.01	0.11	**0.61**	0.02	0.17	0.57
Video game music	0.00	0.22	0.00	**0.41**	0.19	−0.25	0.69
Rap/hip-hop	0.27	−0.12	−0.18	0.10	**0.49**	0.05	0.63
Dance/Electronica	0.10	0.07	0.02	0.04	**0.45**	0.09	0.78
Pop	−0.02	−0.18	0.03	0.19	0.18	**0.45**	0.70
Religious	0.26	−0.25	0.23	0.29	0.06	−0.13	0.71
Classical	0.37	0.14	0.39	0.34	−0.02	−0.18	0.54

The game music item loaded on the same factor as soundtracks in the modified 15-STOMP. It is also worth noticing that neither of these two items crossloaded on other factors which suggests that preference in soundtrack and game music listening might be a standalone dimension of music genre preference. However, the relatively low loading (0.41) and quite high uniqueness (0.69) of the game music variable indicate that listening to game music is also associated with other practices alongside music listening. Something similar is indicated by the results reported in Table 5 about religious music, for instance.

6   Discussion

The objective of this study was to explore the relationship between gameplay activity preferences and game music preferences. It was found that gameplay preferences predict fondness for game music (H1), and that both *Aggression* and *Exploration* are precedents of game music preference whereas a preference for *Coordinate* predicts it negatively (H2). This also suggests that those who like to listen to game music as a music genre may generally enjoy both *Aggression* and *Exploration* more than those who do not like game music very much. We also included age, squared age, and a dummy variable for male gender in the regression model. Male gender identity was associated with game music preference but age or squared age were not. Future research could explore to what extent the effect of gameplay activity type preferences on game music listening preference is mediated by weekly play time and how gaming motives are associated with game music preferences.

Regarding GAIN, our 24-version measured the same five dimensions as the validated 15-GAIN and the more extensive 47-GAIN (see [20]). Our study thus provides support for applying also more extensive versions of GAIN than only the 15-item short version. This may be relevant for future studies which are interested in adopting different GAIN versions based on how relevant specific GAIN items are for their analyses. Also, the new item we developed "Engaging in a battle" showed a high loading on *Aggression* and did not cross-load on *Exploration* similarly to the validation study [20]. However, a new confirmatory factor analysis should be done to validate any alternative GAIN versions. For that purpose, representative survey samples should be collected and analysed.

It was also found that each game genre, except puzzle games, were correlated with more than one GAIN factor. Preference for racing games, for instance, was correlated with both *Coordinate* and *Aggression* which is interesting from the perspective of our study as *Aggression* predicted positively and *Coordinate* negatively a preference for game music. In contrast to this, preference for role-playing games (RPGs) was correlated with preferences for *Aggression* and *Exploration* both of which were found to be precedents for enjoying game music. These results suggest that game music might be a more constitutive element for RPGs and action games than it is for puzzles and strategy games. Future research could continue to explore these associations and also game music's impact on player retention and product attachment. This insight could aid game developers in making informed decisions about what kind of game music they should add to their game and how it should be linked with specific gameplay activities. Future research should also aim to make a distinction between player preferences for game music during ongoing gaming sessions and in situations external to gaming. It could be studied, for instance, how the designed in-game function of game music may be associated with its uses in other contexts.

Earlier research has shown that preference in *Aggression* predicts a higher player preference in emotions of negative valence (e.g., anger, shock, fear, distress) in gameplay whereas *Exploration* has been argued to be the main precedent for enjoying emotions of positive valence (e.g., pleasure, interest, curiosity, satisfaction) while gaming [21]. This association between the GAIN factors and desire to experience emotions of negative and positive valence in gameplay indicates that the preference for game music may also be associated with game experiences of high arousal. Especially experiencing *Aggression* and thus also negative emotions in gameplay seems to predict a high preference for evoking these experiences by listening to game music also outside gaming situations. Future research should investigate in more detail how emotional game experiences and perhaps compelling game experiences at large predict preference for game music.

Regarding our adaptation of the STOMP, it was found that including a game music item changes the dimensionality of the inventory. Instead of the four-factor solution of the 14-STOMP, our 15-STOMP version consisted of six factors in which game music loaded on the same factor as the item "Soundtracks/theme songs". The clustering together of these styles was a likely outcome in the sense that both represent musical categories defined by extra-musical (multimedia) contexts as well as presumably connoting similar kinds of musical features (for example symphonic instrumental music suitable for emotional scenes). Indeed, one might even consider game music as a "subgenre" of soundtracks. It is, however, noteworthy that by including game music in the inventory, the soundtrack item aligns with it to form a unique dimension of music preference instead of clustering together with country, religious and pop as in the original STOMP. Further studies should investigate whether this factor structure of individual game music/soundtrack dimension holds and whether it would be better defined by musical and psychological attributes or by some other features.

Taken together, the results of this study provided support for the argument that music preferences in general and game music preferences in particular are strongly embedded in cultural practices and activities. A novel finding of this study was that gameplay activity types predicted game music preference in different ways to each other and that the differences were about both the magnitude and the direction of the effect. This finding has both theoretical and practical implications. From a theory perspective, the study provides empirical support for approaches that emphasize music listening as an experience indistinguishable from its contextual and experiential factors. The notion that *Aggression* and *Exploration* in gameplay predict desire for game music has practical significance as appetite for game music keeps players attached to game products and franchises, which again fuels both player cultures and future consumer behavior.

References

1. Aarseth, E.: Genre trouble: narrativism and the art of simulation. In: Wardrip-Fruin, N., Harrigan, P. (eds.) First Person. New Media as Story, Performance, and Game, pp. 45–55. The MIT Press, Cambridge (2004)

2. Apperley, T.H.: Genre and game studies: toward a critical approach to video game genres. Simul. Gaming **37**(1), 6–23 (2006)
3. Arsenault, D.: Video game genre, evolution and innovation. Eludamos, J. Comput. Game Cult. **3**(2), 149–176 (2009)
4. Brisson, R., Bianchi, R.: On the relevance of music genre-based analysis in research on musical tastes. Psychol. Music **48**(6), 777–794 (2020)
5. Clearwater, D.A.: What defines the video game genre? Thinking about genre study after the great divide. Loading...J. Can. Game Stud. Assoc. **5**, 29–49 (2011)
6. DiStefano, C., Min, Z., Mîndrilă, D.: Understanding and using factor scores: considerations for the applied researcher. Pract. Assess. Res. Eval. **14**(20), 1–11 (2009)
7. Gasca, J.S.D.: Music beyond gameplay: motivators in the consumption of videogame soundtracks. Ph.D. dissertation, Griffith University (2013)
8. Godøy, R.I.: Gestural affordances of musical sound. In: Godøy, R.I., Leman, M. (eds.) Musical Gestures, pp. 115–137. Routledge (2010)
9. Gregensen, A.: Genre, technology and embodied interaction: the evolution of digital game genres and motion gaming. MedieKultur **51**, 94–109 (2011)
10. Henson, R.K., Roberts, J.K.: Use of exploratory factor analysis in published research: common errors and some comment on improved practice. Educ. Psychol. Meas. **66**, 393–416 (2006)
11. Leman, M.: Embodied Music Cognition and Mediation Technology. MIT Press, Cambridge (2008)
12. Myers, D.: Computer game genres. Play Cult. **3**, 286–301 (1990)
13. Rentfrow, P.J., Goldberg, L.R., Levitin, D.J.: The structure of musical preferences: a five-factor model. J. Personal. Soc. Psychol. **100**(6), 1139–1157 (2011)
14. Rentfrow, P.J., Goldberg, L.R., Stillwell, D.J., Kosinski, M., Gosling, S.D., Levitin, D.L.: The song remains the same: a replication and extension of the MUSIC model. Music Percept. **30**(2), 161–185 (2012)
15. Rentfrow, P.J., Goldberg, L.R., Zilca, R.: Listening, watching, and reading: the structure and correlates of entertainment preferences. J. Personal. **79**(2), 223–257 (2011)
16. Rentfrow, P.J., Gosling, S.D.: The do re mi's of everyday life: the structure and personality correlates of music preferences. J. Personal. Soc. Psychol. **84**(6), 1236–1254 (2003)
17. Rentfrow, P.J., McDonald, J.A., Oldmeadow, A.: You are what you listen to: young people's stereotypes about music fans. Group Process. Intergroup Relat. **12**(3), 329–344 (2009)
18. Schäfer, T., Mehlhorn, C.: Can personality traits predict musical style preferences? A meta-analysis. Personal. Individ. Differ. **116**, 265–273 (2017)
19. Vahlo, J., Kaakinen, J., Holm, S., Koponen, A.: Digital game dynamics preferences and player types. J. Comput.-Mediat. Commun. **22**(2), 88–103 (2017)
20. Vahlo, J., Smed, J., Koponen, A.: Validating gameplay activity inventory (GAIN) for modeling player profiles. User Model. User-Adapt. Interact. **28**(4–5), 425–453 (2018)
21. Vahlo, J.: In Gameplay. The Invariant Structures and Varieties of the Video Game Gameplay Experience. Ph.D. dissertation, University of Turku (2018)

That Sound's Juicy! Exploring Juicy Audio Effects in Video Games

Jolie H. K. Smets and Erik D. van der Spek[✉] [iD]

Department of Industrial Design, Eindhoven University of Technology, Den Dolech 2, 5612AZ
Eindhoven, The Netherlands
j.h.k.smets@student.tue.nl, e.d.vanderspek@tue.nl

Abstract. Juiciness describes exaggerated redundant audio/visual feedback in games, creating a better player experience. As computer games are principally a visual medium, sound is an underused potential for creating juiciness. This study aims to explore juicy audio. A mixed-methods approach is used to investigate the influence of juicy audio on the experience of presence in the player, and how players affectively experience and evaluate the juicy audio. Two versions of a game were created. One containing juicy audio effects, and the other without juicy audio effects. Results show a significant effect of juicy audio on presence as expressed in immersion and sensory fidelity, where participants experienced more presence in the juicy audio condition. Regarding the affective evaluation of juicy audio, three themes are identified; association & expectation, pragmatic quality, and describing sounds. The latter is an interesting direction for future research, as we appear to lack a shared, intuitive vocabulary for game sounds.

Keywords: Juiciness · Game feel · Game design · Sound design · Game audio · Audio effects

1 Introduction

Video games as an entertainment medium have become so popular that, at the time of writing, its total industry revenue dwarfs the combined global revenue of the film and music industries [1, 2]. How to design games to actually be entertaining is still somewhat of a mystery, with researchers likening game design to 'something of a black art' (Bogost, in [3]). However, far from the generally dubious merits of black arts, games that lead to more positive play experiences are correlated to higher review scores [4], which in turn could predict higher sales [5]. If game companies can get a more predictable return of investment from ballooning entertainment game production budgets, because they can better predict whether a game is engaging, this could lead to a healthier, more egalitarian, industry, possibly with less need for predatory monetization practices.

Electronic supplementary material The online version of this chapter (https://doi.org/10.1007/978-3-030-89394-1_24) contains supplementary material, which is available to authorized users.

© IFIP International Federation for Information Processing 2021
Published by Springer Nature Switzerland AG 2021
J. Baalsrud Hauge et al. (Eds.): ICEC 2021, LNCS 13056, pp. 319–335, 2021.
https://doi.org/10.1007/978-3-030-89394-1_24

However, a paucity in scientific knowledge on what makes games motivating (as far as that can ever really be known) increasingly has ramifications outside of entertainment as well, as the motivating qualities of games are used for non-entertainment purposes, such as gamification and serious games [6].

Nowadays, the use of serious games and gamification designed for the user to develop several different skills in a fun way [7], needs little introduction. However, while meta-analyses have proven the merits of serious games from a learning perspective, there is considerably less evidence for their motivating qualities [8]. There are many reasons why serious games may end up boring [9], but one particular reason is that the serious content matter that needs to be learned does not translate well to the fantastical worlds players come to expect from playing entertainment games [10]. If the content cannot be changed, perhaps the interaction can be designed to be more enjoyable and feel more like a game.

Related to this is the concept of juicy game design. Juiciness is a term to describe exaggerated redundant audio/visual feedback on the players' actions [11], making the game 'feel good' to create a better player experience [12, 13]. As this term is rather vague still, it is often described using examples from games. An example is the coins in Super Mario Bros. These shiny pieces of gold float and rotate in the sky grabbing your attention, and make a satisfying 'ping' sound combined with a small particle effect when picked up by the famous plumber. Collecting hundred coins will usually grant you an extra life, but picking up difficult to reach coins will frequently make you lose lives as well, making their net benefit dubious. That players continue to try to collect the coins is partially a factor of their juicy game feel. Other more visual elements to be considered juicy are screen shake, particle effects, and exaggerated animations.

An important aspect of juiciness is feedback. Schell [14] proposes a lens of feedback, where he nudges game designers to think about what players need to know and need to feel while playing the game. He introduces a lens of juiciness, focusing on providing continuous and redundant rewards originating from players' actions. Hicks et al. [15] interviewed game designers to create a framework to analyze juicy games. In this research, juiciness is explained based on three components mostly related to giving the right feedback at the right times. These components are related to coherence of game characteristics, how the game state is communicated, and if the feedback is confirmatory and unambiguous. Deterding [16] highlights the importance of the senses (audio, visual, and tactile) and its' promise to promote competence and curiosity.

In his study, Atanasov [17] defined the quality of juiciness as an emotional response, a feeling of reward and satisfaction, and enjoyment of being in the game world. Swink [18] captures these experiences in the term game feel. In this theory, juiciness is part of the game feel in the form of the building block of polish. Swink [18] describes polish as "any effect that enhances the interaction between objects in the game world, giving clues about the physical properties of objects". These effects could be screen shake hinting the impact of a collision to the player, particles of dust indicating the mass of an enemy or a high pitched "ping" sound as a sign of picking up something of value like a coin.

What these studies have in common is a desire for positive experiences related to satisfaction in the game and feedback as a means to achieve this feeling. Juiciness is a balance between feedback and emotional experiences, used to convey the game world through audio, visual, or haptic feedback responding to players' actions. To feel these positive experiences, the player needs to be engaged with the game first. As Brown and Cairns [19] state, the first stage of immersion is engagement and must occur before any other level. Immersion is the quality of a game that makes a player shuts out their physical reality and is pulled into the game, creating a sense of presence. Presence is the feeling of being in the game world based on the user's psychology [20]. Brown and Cairns [19] see presence as total immersion, creating an atmosphere. Here the graphics, plot, and sound combine this feature. Immersion and presence can influence the attention of the player, and the more attention invested by the player, the more immersed a player feels.

As research has shown, visual juiciness can contribute to both these factors [21]. But compared to the extensive use of visual information, sound remains an underused potential [15, 21]. Moreover, sound is often seen as decoration and not relevant for playing. Audio has the potential to contribute to the juiciness of a game as it can provide feedback and has an effect on the emotions and fantasy of the player. Audio can support gameplay [22], and ease the use of a game by providing information about the states of the system [23]. Additionally, sound is a valuable component of overall game aesthetics and affective perception [24]. Furthermore, it may be used to create and enhance emotional impact [25] and contribute to immersion [24, 26]). As it seems that computer games are thought of as a principally visual medium, sound could prove to create more possibilities for creating juiciness. Therefore, this study aims to explore juicy audio and its relationship with presence and immersion.

First, this paper discusses related work to explore the term juiciness. The second part consists of theoretical background on sound, how this may relate to juicy sound effects, and can be operationalized in our experiment. We perform a mixed-method experiment to a) determine whether and how juicy audio effects can improve the feeling of presence and immersion in a 2D entertainment game, and b) how sound is experienced by players of the game. The main contributions of this paper are therefore providing more evidence for the importance of juiciness in games, especially in terms of audio effects, as well as reflections on audio design and directions for future research when it comes to audio in games.

2 Related Works

The visual appeal of juicy games is one of the contributors to an improved player experience. Van den Abeele et al. [27] created two versions of a game to measure the boundary of which tones children could hear; one made by the researchers and one by professional game designers. One could say the game designed by the game designers contains more juice, as it contained more interesting visuals and juicy feedback. Van den Abeele et al. [27] concluded that this game provided a better player experience compared to the game made by researchers. The children had a preference for the professionally designed game and proved to be more effective in-game as well. An early study of Juul and Begy [28] compared a juicy and non-juicy version of a tile-matching game and received a negative correlation between juiciness and player experience. This could be related to the fact that it is not clear which amount of juiciness is needed to increase the player experience. Kao [29] tested four different conditions of juiciness, minimal to extreme, of the same

RPG game to test at which level juicy effects hinder players. He uses a more extensive method of creating this juiciness and uses an iterative method to see if the visual and sound effects fit the game, hinting towards the contextual nature of juiciness. The results proved that both no application of juiciness, as well as extreme applications of juiciness, can hinder the player experience.

Furthermore, Hicks et al. [21] researched the visual appeal of two games using juiciness and related this to the players' experience and performance. They recreated a simplistic version of Frogger called Cuber, and an RPG-like game called Dungeon Descent and added juicy game elements to both of the games. In both of these juicy games, player experience was increased especially regarding presence and immersion.

Another way to provide feedback to the player is through the use of sound. Kao [30] used juicy audio effects to stimulate players in opening more loot boxes, which was efficient. Audio can be used as sensory gratification [31] and engage the player because it is sensorially pleasing. As it can also provide feedback about the actions of the player in the game world and make the game feel real [24], juicy audio may contribute to a better player experience and game feel. Sound is also a way to engage players by creating immersion and presence in games [21, 25]. Ermi and Mäyrä [32] describe immersion using three dimensions; sensory-, challenge-based- and imaginative immersion. Juicy sound can contribute to all three of these elements. In the case of sensory immersion, audio can make the game world feel real. This contributes to the imagination as well, as footsteps can make players identify with the characters and create a sense of realism [24]. Physical components of audio, like surround sound or headphones, can also contribute to sensory immersion [33]. Challenge-based immersion requires motor and mental skills to progress in the game. Juicy feedback is important in this case, and audio can contribute by using navigational listening modes to indicate for example where a threat, like a growl, is coming from [24]. However, Huiberts [31] identified that out-of-context sound and music effects, as well as non-responsive audio feedback and repetition of sound can decrease immersion. Importantly, the addition of sound effects hence does not improve immersion regardless of the type of sound.

3 Theoretical Background

Sound has original properties as it is omnidirectional and uninterruptible [33]. This opens up opportunities to use sound as (redundant) confirmatory feedback, but also shift the focus of the player during the gameplay [15]. Another property is that sound is ambiguous, meaning that one specific event is connected to one specific sound effect [15, 33]. To understand this property, it is important to understand how we perceive sounds both in a fictive world and in the real world.

According to Tuuri et al. [34], there are four types of listening modes: pre-conscious, source-orientated, context-orientated, and quality-orientated. Juicy audio is context-oriented, as it can convey the purpose of sound, what it means, and its' suitability. It is also pre-conscious, as it can invoke associations to properties of an event (big, strong, power). Related to these listening modes is Gavers' theory of Everyday Listening [35]. Using this approach, sounds are described based on their source rather than using technical terms like pitch or compression (quality-orientated listening mode). As Gaver [35] describes: "Everyday listening is the experience of hearing events in the world rather than sounds per se, resulting in information about the interaction of materials at a location in an environment." For instance: a collision of two wooden objects in a closed space, next to your ears results in a loud and sharp bang. This is related to Swinks' [17] idea about polish, meaning that juiciness can give clues about the physical properties of an object. Therefore, it is important to choose sounds and context with high sonic potential when designing juicy game audio [36].

Juicy audio is also source-oriented [34] as it can convey information about the source of the sound, specifically its' cause and emotion. According to the appraisal theory, there are different types of emotions for fictive events [25]. Related to juiciness are the artifact emotions (A-emotions), which are linked to sensory pleasure. These A-emotions make the player enjoy the aesthetics of the fictive world including beautifully crafted sound. According to Perron [37], there is also another emotion specifically related to games; gameplay emotions (G-emotions). These G-emotions arise because the player cares about the progress of the game, meaning feedback is again important. As sound can influence a players' emotional reaction [38], it is important to select game elements that can convey emotions or an emotional context through their sound [36] For example, a flock of birds that are relaxed or flee give a completely different feel for the emotional context.

In fictive worlds, sounds are categorized in diegetic and non-diegetic sounds [39]. Diegetic sounds are sound real in the virtual world and have a source in this world. For instance footsteps, or gunfire. Non-diegetic sounds are from outside of the game world. Non-diegetic sounds do not have a source in the virtual world and have been added in. For example, music or sound effects added on the menu screen. Emotional responses to fictive events are possible because the diegetic effect of these sounds makes this reality perceivable. [25] However, to create immersion a reduced realism is enough to create a perceived reality [24]. This implies that not all sounds have to emerge from reality to be perceived as existing/realistic in the fictive environment.

4 Method

4.1 Game

A game was made using Unity and exported as WebGL to make it work in any browser on a desktop computer. This game, called Space Adventure[1], is a space-themed arcade game where one has to get as many points as possible by rescuing lost astronauts and shooting down enemy ships while avoiding meteorites. The game is based on an endless runner, providing objects to avoid or pick up which are spawned in randomized patterns. These patterns spawn more quickly based on how much time has passed. The player (light grey spaceship) can move up and down using the arrow keys to avoid enemy spaceships (black spaceship), their bullets and meteorites. By pressing the space bar, the

---

[1] A video of both versions of the game can be found in the supplemental material. Playable versions are hosted externally, and are playable for as long as the external host allows here: Juicy version: https://i.simmer.io/@keijioch/~09826b4b-43e3-7e09-6513-799f4b654a4a. Control version: https://simmer.io/@keijioch/~36d78477-536d-d273-5b07-ef4b06dd51dd.

player can shoot and destroy the enemy spaceship after three hits (image 1). Shooting down an enemy spaceship will gain the player one point. Floating astronauts can be picked up and give five points. The player can take damage by crashing into meteorites or enemy spaceships, or by getting shot by the enemy spaceship. The player has three lives and the game is over when the player has taken three hits.

This arcade format made it possible to use many sound effects, ranging from feedback to contextual sounds. In order to research the effect of juicy audio effects on player presence, this game was developed into two different versions. Version A containing juicy sound and version B (control) without juicy sound. The visual design of the game, as well as juicy visual effects (explosions, screen shake), are the same in both versions. By comparing these versions, the following hypothesis can be tested (Fig. 1):

The version containing juicy audio effects creates a greater feeling of presence compared with the version without juicy audio effects.

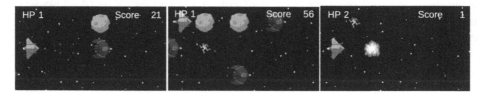

Fig. 1. Screenshots of the game Space Adventure

4.2 Audio Design

For each version, 10 different sounds were created by the first author. As there are no guidelines for creating audio, the theory of Everyday Listening by Gaver [35] is used as a starting point. This means the sound is based on an event and material. Impact sounds like collisions are made using an impact and a material related to the collision. For instance, the crumpling of aluminum foil is used to create the crumpling sound of colliding with an enemy ship. These unedited sounds are used in the control version of the game. For the juicy version, these sounds were edited using Adobe Audition. The variation between the juicy and non-juicy sounds is the amount of 'polish' that is used while editing, and using excessive amounts of effects to shape the sounds. Creating the sounds was an iterative process. They were pilot tested with four students of Eindhoven University of Technology using a video showing multiple sound options for an event. A professional game designer also reviewed the game and sounds, to independently approve whether they fit the context of the game. Two sounds were left out in both versions, namely when the player shoots at an astronaut or a meteorite. The sounds are described in Table 1.

Table 1. Description of sounds

Action	Description of sound
Jet Engine	This sound needs to resemble working engines. It is based on white noise, edited with flanger and distortion to resemble Star Wars engines in the juicy version
Moving	This sound needs to resemble air. A male voice saying "whoosh" was used to produce this airy sound, which was edited with a higher pitch and more reverb in the juicy version
Shooting	This sound needs to resemble a laser, and its' movement through air. A female voice saying 'pew' was used to produce this airy sound. This was edited for the juicy version into a laser sound by pitching it higher, using reverb and distortion. For the enemy shooting, the sound was pitched down in order to create difference
Hit & dead Enemy	Getting hit is an impact sound, so these sounds are created using the impact of a drum set in GarageBand. Shooting down an enemy has no different sound in the control version of the game. In the juicy version this resembled a small explosion. These explosions were made by layering multiple drum impacts, distorting them and adding reverb. When an enemy was killed, the explosion contained more reverb in order to prolong the sound
Hit & dead Player (Game Over)	As the sounds for hitting an enemy, the sounds are also based on impact of a drum set in GarageBand. In the control version these events produce no different sounds. In the juice version, the sound needed to sound 'negative'. For getting hit by the enemy, this resulted in a sound resembling engine failure made by editing the impact sound by pitching down the sound gradually, and adding chorus and distortion to the sound to make it a 'unknown' engine. The explosion was made using the same method as the enemy explosion. To add more negativity, the sound was heavily stretched while pitching the sound down gradually
Meteor crash	This sound needed to resemble a crumbling impact sound. This was done by recording a piece of paper being crumpled. In the juice version, this was edited with distortion and delay
Astronaut entering	This is a feedforward sound, a notification. This sound was made with the xylophone in GarageBand. In the juicy version this sound was edited with reverb and by pitching it higher
Astronaut Pick-up	As the astronaut is a human, a female 'thanks' is heard when picked up. In the juice version, it has an extra sound indicating scored points. This sound is a variation of the astronaut entering sound with more delay and by pitching it higher. This same sound is also present when shooting down an enemy

4.3 Participants

A total of N = 61 participants participated in the experiment, the majority of which were between 18 and 25 years of age. 30 participants, of whom 20 self-identified as male and 10 as female, got randomly assigned to the juicy condition. The remaining 31 participants, of whom 24 self-identified as male and 7 as female, got randomly assigned to the control condition. Due to Covid-19 restrictions, the experiment was moved fully online and the participants were solicited through social media (Facebook and Instagram). As that only garnered 27 participants, a crowdsourcing platform (Prolific) was used to get more participants and improve the power of the study. This did mean that one half of the participants did not get a reward for participating and the other half did get a (minor, around 0.90 GBP) for participating in the short experiment. Therefore, the type of participant solicitation was recorded so that it could be used as a covariate. In the Juicy version, 15 participants were solicited through social media and 15 participants were crowdsourced through Prolific. In the Control version, 12 participants were solicited through social media and 19 participants were crowdsourced through Prolific.

4.4 Measurements

This research uses a mixed-methods approach, using both quantitative data to evaluate the feeling of presence in the two versions of the game and a qualitative evaluation of the sounds. A smaller set of participants followed up with a semi-structured interview to get additional qualitative data. To research the influence of juicy audio effects on the experienced presence, a quantitative evaluation was done using the Presence Questionnaire by Witmer and Singer [40]. For this study, the categories Involvement and Interface Quality were left out as they did not particularly match well with the simple mechanics and 2D nature of the game (Involvement) or were more about the input modality and lag of the game (Interface Quality), which we did not expect to be influenced by the intervention, but was also something we could not control well over the internet. All questions of the PQ were presented using a 7-point Likert scale. In addition, an open-ended evaluation of the juicy audio used in both versions of the game was employed. Participants were asked questions like which audio effects they did and did not appreciate, found pretty or ugly, and why, and what their association was with specific sounds. To not make the questionnaire too exhausting, four sounds were chosen at random to be evaluated using the questionnaire (shooting, player hit & dead, enemy hit & dead, astronaut).

11 Participants signed up for the follow up interview (5 male, 6 female), where they played both versions and then gave their thoughts. This interview was conducted in a semi-structured fashion starting from similar questions to the online questionnaire, to tease out more in-depth statements regarding the sound quality and sound experience after having played both conditions, as well as elaborate on the sounds' affective associations.

4.5 Procedure

For the quantitative evaluation of the games, a web page containing a WebGL version of the game was created. By clicking a hyperlink the participants were guided to one of the test pages containing one of the two games (A: juicy & B: control) including a step-by-step explanation to support participants in going through the study smoothly. After agreeing with the study conditions, a participant played the game until they were satisfied. When a participant wanted to completely stop the game, the 'quit game' button needed to be pressed to see their total playing time. After the participant quit the game, the questionnaire containing the PQ items and open-ended questions was filled out.

Those who were interested and left their email while filling in the questionnaire, participated in an interview afterwards to get more in-depth insight on all the sounds and the players' experience. Here the participants first played both versions of the game, and then participated in the semi-structured interview, guided by a set of questions similar to the open-ended questions in the questionnaire. All interviews except one were conducted in Dutch. The interviews were recorded and transcribed. The Dutch quotes are translated in English when used in this paper.

5 Results

5.1 Quantitative Research

In order to analyze the effect of juiciness on presence, a MANCOVA was performed in IBM SPSS v25, with condition as fixed factor and the Sensory Fidelity and Adaption/Immersion dimensions of the Presence Questionnaire as dependent variables. Since there were two ways of soliciting participants, either through social media or a crowd-sourcing platform (Prolific), and this could influence the way people engage with the game, which in turn could influence their experienced presence, the way participants were solicited was entered as a binary covariate. The MANCOVA showed a significant effect of condition on the combined dependent variables, while controlling for participant solicitation procedure: $F(2, 57) = 4.678$, Wilks' $\Lambda = .859$, $p = .013$, partial $\eta^2 = .141$.

Individual ANCOVAs showed that this effect was significant for both sensory fidelity [$F(1, 58) = 5.435$, p $= .013$, partial $\eta^2 = .102$] and adaption/immersion [$F(1, 58) = 3.652$, $p = .019$, partial $\eta^2 = .091$] dimensions. In both cases, the juicy version led to significantly higher sensory fidelity (control version M $= 4.17$, SD $= 1.08$ vs. juicy version M $= 4.69$, SD $= 0.86$) and a significantly higher adaption/immersion (control version M $= 5.41$, SD $= 0.85$ vs. juicy version M $= 5.87$, SD $= 0.74$).

The covariate was confirmed to have a significant influence on the sensory fidelity dependent variable [$F(1, 58) - 8.241$, $p = .003$] but not the adaption/immersion variable [$F(1,58) < 1$]. There was no effect of condition on total playtime $F(1,58) < 1$.

5.2 Qualitative Research

For the qualitative part of the questionnaire and the interview, a thematic analysis [41] was carried out. There are two types of quotes: quotes derived from the questionnaire following the experiment are indicated with the version and participant number (A.. (juicy) & B.. (control)); quotes derived from the follow up interview with the 11 interested participants who played both versions of the game, are indicated with a P followed by the interviewee number. This analysis resulted in three main themes and their respective sub-themes related to the appreciation of the juicy sound; the way they are perceived and described, associations and expectations and the practical quality of sound. The themes and sub-themes are described below.

Theme 1: Describing Sounds
When the participant was asked to describe a sound or what they appreciate about it, they

described the sound using various methods. Some participants with musical knowledge used sound-related terms: *"There is more bass in this sound"* (P9), *"one of them is clearly higher pitched."* (P11), and *"[…] It sounds like regular distortion"* (B4). Most participants described sounds using other ways, like mimicking the sounds or using associations. They described situations where they heard similar sounds: *"It sounds like a space battle […], like in Star Wars."* (P2) The shooting sound in the control version was often described as *"a child making his own sound effects"* (P7).

Materials or events
Another way the sounds were described was to use the perceived material or event. For instance, in regards to material, participants mentioned *"I know the sounds are telling me about the material of the spaceship. I would expect metal against metal"* (P11), or *"I miss the feeling of material and space. It is a very general sound not specific to the game."* (A3). Events were also used to describe a sound. For instance, *"It sounds like that air is escaping from somewhere"* (P2), and *"It sounds like a bag of chips being crumpled."* (P5).

Affective terms
Besides this, participants also used affective ways of describing why they liked a certain sound, such as *"It sounds soothing"* (P8), and *"The background is really exciting"* (P1). This affective quality of sound is also reflected in the difficulty of describing sounds, sometimes resulting in insecurity (*"I have no idea how I can explain this."* (P2), *"This doesn't help you at all, does it?"* (P3), or *"Nothing"* (common response)), or confusion for participants (*"We are not talking about the same thing at all!"* (P7)).

Theme 2: Expectations and Associations
Players have certain expectations and associations with a sound, using this to describe sounds from the game. *"It sounds like lasers. That sounds futuristic."* (P9), *"When such a big spaceship shoots at me, and then I hear small pew-sounds."* (P7). Some participants had conflicting preferences. An example is the use of a human voice saying "thanks" for rescuing an astronaut. *"I think the thanks when you pick up an astronaut is subtle, and nice to listen to"* (P3), but also *"The thanks were quite grating after multiple times"* (A14). An important factor to determine whether a sound matches a players' expectation, is the visual that is paired to it. The sound and visual have to match for a players' association to be correct. For instance, one participant mentioned; *"I think it is satisfying when you hit and explode an enemy ship. That this happens in phases. […] It is probably a combination of the visuals and sound, which really suit each other here."* (P7). Another factor is timing. If a sound is played with too much delay compared to the visual, the sound and event are not linked. *"I have not heard the "ping" [score sound] before, and I don't know what it does. You already search for next objects, and then the sound is a bit too late."* (P4).

Theme 3: Pragmatic Quality
Feedforward and feedback
As juiciness is highly related to giving feedback, sound was often used as a way to indicate if an action was done correctly. *"I think most sounds are confirming what action you took."* (P6), and *"It is in both cases positive feedback that your actions have the*

desired impact." (P1). Sound was also used to gather information as feedforward. *"It helps me to understand the game and focus my attention on something. For instance, sometimes I am not worrying about enemies shooting until I hear it."* (P3), or *"It gave me the idea if I needed to do something. Watch out, you need to take an action."*(P10). It also differed between participants. For example, one participant used feedforward by sound to improve his performance: *"I recognized the pattern in which I shoot, and when something interrupts. I press the space key as often as possible, and if I hear another sound I know it is not mine but the enemies."* (P1).

Hierarchy

One important aspect participants often mentioned was related to the hierarchy of the sound. One participant mentioned: *"The background is not overwhelming, it did not drown out what was important in the game. The hierarchy of information is important, and this sound should be on the bottom."* (P10). Often mentioned was that the sound of the players' shooting drowns out the other sounds, giving less room for feedback and feedforward. *"It drowns out other sounds. You do not hear that the other ship is shooting at you."* (P8). Or when the astronauts spawned quicker further in the game. *"[…] a lot of astronauts with a lot of sounds. I was not sure what to do with that."* (P10). The sounds with a higher volume were perceived more often than those with a lower volume, enabling the game designer to influence this hierarchy. *"[this sound] seems to be louder than the other one, making me believe it responds to what I am doing."* (P7).

Redundancy

Overlapping or similar sounds are often seen as something positive by players. *"I liked it that the sounds overlap. If you shoot multiple times, you hear the sound multiple times as well."* (P1). For similar sounds, the difference in shooting between the player and enemy can be taken as an example. In the juice version of the game, one was pitched lower than the other. While in the control version it was the same sound. *"I liked it that there were different sounds for when I shoot and when the enemy shoots."* (P3), and *"I miss in this version [control] the difference between shooting from me and the enemy"* (P2). But there seems to be a fine line in differences in sounds that players can perceive. As participant 1 mentioned *"I like it that they sound alike, so you know these are linked. But maybe they sound a bit too much alike. You have to listen closely to hear the difference. But this happens automatically with the visuals"* (P1). Adding an extra sound to indicate when points are scored after picking up an astronaut, was perceived differently by participants. The score point sound was perceived as pretty most of the time: *"[..] the sound of coins and "thanks" when picking up a human"* (A8). During the interviews, it became clear that this sound was most of the time not noticed. *"Is there an extra sound? You mean the bell! I think it is unnecessary."* (P8).

6 Discussion

A MANCOVA shows a significant main effect of juicy sound on presence. This significant effect holds for both tested scales of Sensory Fidelity and Adaption/Immersion, where in both cases the juicy audio version led to more presence than a base version with less juicy audio feedback. These results suggest that juicy sound, operationalized in this study as more polish to the sound, can contribute to a greater feeling of presence in the player. This can also be seen in the thematic analysis of the qualitative data, which also describe what aspects are considered by players regarding juicy sound.

The themes of expectations & associations and pragmatic qualities are two main themes describing what players look for in juicy audio. When looking into the theme of expectations & associations, the findings indicate that players do not only listen to the quality of sound, but they connect it to different associations and memories. One participant makes a clear distinction between an association with a sound, and its' aesthetic qualities: *"I find the "pling" sound after you catch an astronaut the prettiest. It gives me a nice feeling after the accomplishment. But if by prettiest you mean the best sound, I have to say the game over sound. It is so good in the sense that it makes me sad that I died, but not too mad to not play the game again."* (A13). When a player makes associations, two outcomes can occur. When the players' association with a certain sound matches their expectations, it seems to increase their immersion in the game. More reactions were elicited while playing the juicy version of the game. Positive emotional reactions like "oof" when the player hit an obstacle, or short "yes!" when they shot down an enemy was more common compared to the control version of the game. Claims connected to satisfaction were also heard. *"I like it when it blows up. It makes you think 'Haha!'"* (P10). When the sound matches the players' expectations with the perceived context, it can also deepen their emotional connection to it. *"There is a sort of dark undertone, the buzz. It makes it feel like there is something exciting bound to happen."* (P10). Some participants mentioned terms related to immersion when talking about what the sound does for them. *"If you don't hear anything it will become boring, which makes you quit the game."* (P4), *"The sounds [...] were in my experience mostly to keep you in the bubble."* (P1), and *"In the [control] version, I thought 'okay sure'. But in the [juicy] version, you saw from my face that I got really into it."* (P9).

When the association does not match the expectation of the player, negative emotional responses like confusion or irritation occur. The sounds that were mentioned the most were the notification sounds when an astronaut appears, the point collecting sound, and the difference between shooting sounds emanating from the player and enemy. Some participants mentioned: *"It is almost annoying that I do not know what sound it is and where it is coming from."* (P9), and *"I thought the ding in the [non-juicy] game was very confusing. I could not figure out where that's coming from"* (P11). In the theoretical background section, we characterized juicy feedback as being unambiguous [15] and redundant [11]. While ambiguity was more often reported in the control condition, not all sounds may therefore have qualified as juicy in the juicy condition. Vice versa, less ambiguity in the juicy condition may also mean that the polish or embellishments were not fully redundant. This may furthermore beg the question whether juicy feedback could be considered redundant in the first place and not a reinforcement, both in feedback as in the understanding of the audiovisual effect itself. This requires more disentanglement in future research.

Sometimes, ambiguous associations can be learned over time while playing the game as mentioned by P6: *"I think that you learn to associate different sounds with scoring points, so you do not need to use the same one everywhere."* One exception was the shooting sound in the control version of the game. This sound was perceived as comical, but not necessarily bad when applied to the right target group and goal. One participant mentioned *"This is not necessarily something negative, as it is really funny. It does lead to a different intensity, which is maybe more suited in games for children."* (P1). This may mean that juicy sound does not need to fit a certain association to create an engaging experience but can contribute to a different goal and context of the game.

Regarding the pragmatic quality of juicy sound, factors like feedback and feedforward are still important. During the interviews, it became clear that sounds and their expectations are often linked to the information the sounds needed to convey. The same procedure occurs here described for the associations & expectations theme; if the information matches the players' expectations, it may enhance immersion. Otherwise, it will result in confusion or irritate the player. The pragmatic quality can be influenced by the game designer by playing in into the hierarchy of the sounds. By using volume to put certain sound on the foreground or background and timing to create links between audio and visual information, certain information can be prioritized. It is therefore important to keep the goal of the game in mind, to establish a hierarchy in sounds to help the participant understand the game. The use of redundant sounds, for instance, two sounds to indicate the same event, is perceived differently by the player. Some found the extra sound unnecessary and did not perceive it immediately. This can mean that juiciness happens subconsciously and is not supposed to be remembered. *"I may have noticed that happened, but I have no memory of it anymore. It is hard to remember these things, especially since they're supposed to be subtle or subconscious."* (P11). This can also be related to the amount of experience a player has with games. Participants with more gaming experience, tend to focus more on the pragmatic qualities of sound than casual players to improve their performance.

7   Limitations and Future Work

This experiment was conducted online due to Covid-19, as such it is not possible to say whether all the participants had similar sound reproduction quality, or technically even turned on their sound when prompted. However, randomization and the significant effect in the expected direction, as well as detailed interview feedback, would suggest that there was a notable difference. Using multiple ways to gather participants, using a crowdsourcing platform and social media, may also have influenced the results of this study. The significance of adaption/immersion improves after leaving the variation of Prolific out of the results, indicating there is a difference in results between participants gathered on Prolific and social media. Participants may have different motivations for participating in the study. Monetary rewards could lead to participants being more motivated to put in the effort, but this can also go the other way of clearing the study as fast as possible. But if the latter was the case, one would expect the results to be less significant. In this case, significant effects hold with or without adding the solicitation procedure as a covariate.

Another limitation is the use of the PQ and adapting it to fit the game. In the original PQ questionnaire, presence is the mean of all the questions in the questionnaire. As some sub-categories (Interface quality & Involvement) were left out, the scale does not provide a total measure of presence. Therefore, care should be exercised in comparing these results with those in other research papers that do use the full questionnaire. It's also theoretically possible that interface quality and involvement are negatively impacted by juicy audio somehow.

As there are no guidelines for creating juiciness, let alone juicy sound, this research used combined theories of Game Feel (polish) and everyday listening [35] to create sounds. More research can be done on what juiciness is when it comes to sound, to provide more exact guidelines that can be implemented in game design. The themes provided in this research could be a base for creating these guidelines for sound.

Lastly, sound is part of juiciness but difficult to communicate. It is a personal interpretation, and every player has a different background. For instance, a player proficient in playing music would use more technical terms than a player with no musical knowledge. During the interview sessions, we frequently encountered difficulties by the participants to verbalize their experiences, and in fact game research does not provide many useful pointers to describe the myriad of sound effects related to game interactions either. It would be beneficial for game designers and game experience researchers to develop a common vocabulary that can be used to describe sound qualities or find a method to evaluate comments from players with a different musical background. Associations may be a good way to contribute to this vocabulary, as well as Gavers' theory of everyday listening [35].

8 Conclusion

In games, it is hypothesized that juiciness (exaggerated redundant audio/visual feedback on the players' actions) [11] can improve the player experience in a game. As the term juiciness is still rather vague, research on this topic is new. Some research has been done based on the visual aspect, but sound is often neglected. This research can be seen as a method to explore and evaluate juicy audio in video games. This was done by looking into how it affects the feeling of presence and how players experience and evaluate the sounds affectively during gameplay. By comparing two versions of a game, one with juicy sound and one without juicy sound, there is a significant effect with a large effect size (partial $\eta2 = .141$) of juicy sound effects for combined immersion and sensory fidelity, as factors of Witmer and Singer's Presence Questionnaire [40], in the game. This holds for the separate subscales with a medium to large effect size. This result was in line with the hypothesis: the version containing juicy audio effects, which in this study means more polish to the sound, creates a greater sense of presence as expressed in Immersion and Sensory Fidelity, than the version without juicy audio effects. While this experiment was performed with a simple 2D space shooter game, we think that creating juicy audio could also be a viable way to improve the immersion in serious games (and possibly engagement as a result), because juiciness is relatively independent of the content matter and game mechanics.

Regarding the affective experience and evaluation of juicy audio, a thematic analysis reveals three main themes. First, players have a certain association and expectation from a sound, based on their memories and the image that they see. If this expectation is met, players have a positive experience resulting in more immersion. If this expectation is not met, players experience negative feelings like confusion or irritation. Secondly, sound has a pragmatic quality, where players use sound as feedback and feedforward to understand and improve in the game. Game designers can influence the pragmatic quality by thinking about the hierarchy of sounds. It is important to understand the goal of the game, to provide important information first and establish a hierarchy in sounds. The third theme revolves around the way players describe sounds. The way a player listens to sound, comprehends it and communicates their qualities differs for each person. For instance, someone with more musical knowledge uses more technical terms to communicate a sound. Interesting for future research is to create a common vocabulary to describe sound qualities for game designers and game experience designers.

References

1. IFPI. 2020. IFPI issues annual Global Music Report (2020). https://www.ifpi.org/ifpi-issues-annual-global-music-report/. Retrieved February 2021
2. Witkowski, W.: Videogames are a bigger industry than movies and North American sports combined, thanks to the pandemic (2021). https://www.marketwatch.com/story/videogames-are-a-bigger-industry-than-sports-and-movies-combined-thanks-to-the-pandemic-11608654990. Retrieved February 2021
3. Fullerton, T., Swain, C.: Game Design Workshop: A Playcentric Approach to Creating Innovative Games (2nd. edn.). Gama Network Series (2008)
4. Johnson, D., Watling, C., Gardner, J., Nacke, L.E.: The edge of glory: the relationship between metacritic scores and player experience. In: Proceedings of the first ACM SIGCHI Annual Symposium on Computer-Human Interaction in Play, pp. 141–150 (2014)
5. Orland, K.: Steam Gauge: Do strong reviews lead to stronger sales on Steam? https://arstechnica.com/gaming/2014/04/steam-gauge-do-strong-reviews-lead-to-stronger-sales-on-steam/ (2014). Retrieved February 2021
6. Deterding, S., Dixon, D., Khaled, R., Nacke, L.: From game design elements to gamefulness: defining "gamification". In: Proceedings of the 15th international academic MindTrek conference: envisioning future media environments, pp. 9–15 (2011)
7. Susi, T., Johannesson, M., Backlund, P.: Serious games: An overview. IKI Technical reports. Skövde: Institutionen för kommunikation och information (2007)
8. Wouters, P., Van Nimwegen, C., Van Oostendorp, H., Van der Spek, E.D.: A meta-analysis of the cognitive and motivational effects of serious games. J. Educ. Psychol. 105(2), 249 (2013)
9. Buday, R., Baranowski, T., Thompson, D.: Fun and Games and Boredom. Games Health J. 1(4), 257–261 (2012). https://doi.org/10.1089/g4h.2012.0026
10. Van der Spek, E. D., Sidorenkova, T., Porskamp, P., Rauterberg, M.: The effect of familiar and fantasy aesthetics on learning and experience of serious games. In: International Conference on Entertainment Computing, pp. 133–138 (2014)
11. Gray, K., Gabler, K., Shodhan, S., Kucic, M.: How to Prototype a Game in Under 7 Days. 2005. Accessed 7 Apr 2020. https://www.gamasutra.com/view/feature130848%20how_to_prototype_a_game_in_under_7_.php
12. Jonasson, M., Petri, P.: Juice it or lose it. Video (2012). Accessed 13 Jan 2020. https://www.youtube.com/watch?time_continue=3&v=Fy0aCDmgnxg
13. Pears, M.: Level Design Lobby - Ep 32: Juice. Podcast. (2018, December 11). Retrieved December 9 2019 from https://www.spotify.com/
14. Schell, J.: The Art of Game Design: A book of lenses. CRC Press (2008)
15. Hicks, K., Dickinson, P., Holopainen, J., Gerling, K.: Good Game Feel: An Empirically Grounded Framework for Juicy Design. In: Digital Games Research Association Conference (2018)

16. Deterding, S.: The lens of intrinsic skill atoms: a method for gameful design. Hum. Comput. Interact. **30**(3–4), 294–335 (2015). https://doi.org/10.1080/07370024.2014.993471
17. Atanasov, S.: Juiciness: exploring and designing around experience of feedback in video games. Faculty of Culture and Society (KS), Malmö (2013)
18. Swink, S.: Game Feel: A Game Designer's Guide to Virtual Sensation. CRC Press (2008)
19. Brown, E., Cairns, P.: A grounded investigation of game immersion. In: Extended Abstracts of the 2004 Conference on Human Factors and Computing Systems - CHI 2004 (2004) https://doi.org/10.1145/985921.986048
20. Cummings, J.J., Bailenson, J.N.: How immersive is enough? a meta-analysis of the effect of immersive technology on user presence. Media Psychol. **19**(2), 272–309 (2015). https://doi.org/10.1080/15213269.2015.1015740
21. Hicks, K., Gerling, K., Dickinson, P., Abeele. V.: Juicy game design: understanding the impact of visual embellishment on player experience. In: Proceedings of the Annual Symposium on Computer-Human Interaction in Play (2019). https://doi.org/10.1145/3311350.3347171
22. Jørgensen, K.: Audio and gameplay: an analysis of PvP battlegrounds in world of warcraft. Gamestudies **8**(2) (2008)
23. Jørgensen, K.: On the functional aspects of computer game audio. In: Proceedings of the 3rd Conference on Interaction with Sound, Audio Mostly 2006, pp. 48–52 (2006)
24. Grimshaw, M.: Sound and immersion in the first-person shooter. Int. J. Intell. Games Simul. **5**(1), 119–124 (2008)
25. Ekman, I.: Psychologically motivated techniques for emotional sound in computer games. Proc. AudioMostly, 20–26 (2008)
26. Collins, K.: Game sound: an introduction to the history, theory, and practice of video game music and sound design (2008). MIT Press
27. Van den Abeele, V., Wouters, J., Ghesquière, P., Goeleven, A., Geurts. L.: Game-based assessment of psycho-acoustic thresholds. In: Proceedings of the 2015 Annual Symposium on Computer-Human Interaction in Play (2015). https://doi.org/10.1145/2793107.2793132
28. Juul, J., Begy, J.S.: Good feedback for bad players? a preliminary Study of 'juicy' interface feedback. In: Proceedings of First Joint FDG/DiGRA Conference, Dundee (2016)
29. Kao, D.: The effects of juiciness in an action RPG. Entertain. Comput. **34**, 100359 (2020). https://doi.org/10.1016/j.entcom.2020.100359
30. Kao, D.: Infinite loot box: a platform for simulating video game loot boxes. IEEE Trans. Games **12**(2), 219–224 (2020). https://doi.org/10.1109/tg.2019.2913320
31. Huiberts, S.: Captivating sound the role of audio for immersion in computer games. Ph. D. Dissertation. HKU University of the Arts, Utrecht (2010)
32. Ermi, L., Mäyrä, F.: Fundamental components of the gameplay experience: Analysing immersion. Worlds Play: Int. Persp. Digit. Games Res. **37**(2), 37–53 (2005)
33. Liljedahl, M.: Sound for fantasy and freedom. In: Game Sound Technology and Player Interaction. IGI Global, pp. 22–43 (2011). https://doi.org/10.4018/978-1-61692-828-5.ch002
34. Tuuri, K., Mustonen, M-S., Pirhonen, A.: Same sound–different meanings: A novel scheme for modes of listening. Proceedings of Audio Mostly, 13–18 (2007)
35. Gaver. W.W.: *What in the world do we hear?*: an ecological approach to auditory event perception. Ecological psychology **5**(1), 1–29 (1993). https://doi.org/10.1207/s15326969eco0501_1
36. Alves, V., Roque, L.: *Guidelines for Sound Design in Computer Games*. In: Game Sound Technology and Player Interaction. IGI Global, 362–383 (2011). https://doi.org/10.4018/978-1-61692-828-5.ch017
37. Perron, B.: A cognitive psychological approach to gameplay emotions. In: DiGRA 2005: Changing Views: Worlds in Play, 2005 International Conference (2005)

38. Nacke, L.E., Grimshaw, M.: Player-Game Interaction Through Affective Sound. In Game Sound Technology and Player Interaction. IGI Global, 264–285 (2011). https://doi.org/10.4018/978-1-61692-828-5.ch013
39. Ekman, I.: Meaningful noise: understanding sound effects in computer games. Proc. Digit. Arts Cultures, 17 (2005)
40. Witmer, B.G., Jerome, C.J., Singer, M.J.: The factor structure of the presence questionnaire. Presence: Teleoperators Virtual Environ. **14**(3), 298–312 (2005). https://doi.org/10.1162/105474605323384654
41. Braun, V., Clarke, V.: Thematic analysis. In: APA Handbook of Research Methods in Psychology, Volume1 2: Research Designs: Quantitative, Qualitative, Neuropsychological, and Biological, pp. 57–71. American Psychological Association (2012). https://doi.org/10.1037/13620-004

What Is a Game Mechanic?

Priscilla Lo[1($\boxtimes$)], David Thue[1,2] , and Elin Carstensdottir[3]

[1] RISE Research Group, Carleton University, Ottawa, ON K1S 5B6, Canada
{priscilla.lo,david.thue}@carleton.ca
[2] Reykjavik University, Reykjavik 102, Iceland
[3] University of California Santa Cruz, Santa Cruz, CA 95064, USA
ecarsten@ucsc.edu

Abstract. The term "game mechanic" is often used when discussing games, but are we all talking about the same thing? While game studies and related fields have produced several notable definitions, there is currently no accepted standard for the term within the broader community. Through a systematic literature review spanning six academic venues and several prominent books, we identify and analyze 49 explicit definitions for the concept of "game mechanics". Though some of the definitions are similar, they are all fundamentally distinct. Our work demonstrates the importance of providing or citing a definition when discussing game mechanics, and we provide a wide range of options to choose from.

1 Introduction

"Game mechanics" are often referenced in game studies research as a defining quality of a game [10,48]. As such, they are a central concept in games research and they are widely used outside and inside the field. For example, searching for the term "game mechanics" on Google Scholar yields roughly 969,000 results.

Despite the term's widespread use, there remains some dispute regarding a single accepted definition of what "game mechanics" are. This is in part due to the nature of game studies as a research field. The games research community is multidisciplinary across several domains (e.g., design, humanities, social science, computer science, human computer interaction, psychology) and has produced a number of specialized research areas and sub-communities. Likewise, the field has also produced a number of notable definitions of game mechanics. This is expected given differences in focus and scope across sub-communities, but it also suggests that the manner in which the term is defined and used can differ between these groups and the disciplines they represent.

As described by Aarseth and Grabarczyk (2018), a shared vocabulary would support discussion between scholars, developers, and journalists [2]. While it might be useful for each discipline to have the ability to choose the most suitable ontological perspective, it is also important to understand how different definitions of terms are related to one another. It is reasonable for researchers in the community to have some perception of there being at least partial agreement on what game mechanics as a concept is meant to refer to, especially given its

© IFIP International Federation for Information Processing 2021
Published by Springer Nature Switzerland AG 2021
J. Baalsrud Hauge et al. (Eds.): ICEC 2021, LNCS 13056, pp. 336–347, 2021.
https://doi.org/10.1007/978-3-030-89394-1_25

centrality to the work and widespread use. However, such assumptions can lead to misunderstanding and incompatible use of terminology. In this work we aim to answer the following questions: How are game mechanics defined as a term in games studies literature, and how much overlap exists between these definitions?

Substantial research relating to this topic was originally presented in the 2000s, including the MDA (Mechanics, Dynamics, Aesthetics) framework [24], game design patterns [11], the game ontology project [62], and definitions of game mechanics [27,35,51]. The field has grown significantly since then and has produced a number of specialized subdomains of research, each of which might use the same kind of terminology in vastly different contexts. For example, the concept of game mechanics is commonly applied to identify genres, understand how people play, and evaluate and analyze games [7,9,12,14,39]. The field has further diversified into the business and educational sectors (mostly via gamification [8,33,34,46]), providing additional contexts for the use of the term.

While significant effort has been invested in developing a common language for discussing games as a collection of elements (e.g., mechanics, entities, rules, interfaces, etc.) [1,2,29,48,62], our goal is different. We aim to analyze and compare definitions across different sub-communities and specialized areas of games research. To our knowledge, this has not been done for game mechanics.

To answer our stated questions about the definitions of game mechanics, we performed a systematic literature review of related research. Our objective in the review was to identify definitions of the term "game mechanic" and to identify associations between existing definitions. In our sample, we collected literature from well-known game research venues and journals such as CHI PLAY, CoG, DiGRA, FDG, ICEC, and ToG (previously T-CIAIG), in addition to books.

2   Related Work

"Game mechanics" have been defined in a variety of different ways, ranging from relating mechanics to specific player (inter)actions (e.g., verbs) [24,26,27,51] to referring to mechanics as components/tools for interactions with the game world (e.g., code, data) [11,16,24,51]. There are several definitions of mechanics that have become widely cited and used (e.g., from the MDA Framework [24] or Salen and Zimmerman's *Rules of Play* [48]). However, the field has yet to reach an agreement. Definitions can be so specific that special cases are needed to fit a particular system or application, or so general that the correct interpretation is unclear. Although there is some overlap between definitions, the spectrum of specificity allows the concept to be applied very flexibly. While over-specification can hinder creativity, leaving too much room for interpretation can lead to misunderstanding and disagreement between those who build and analyze games. Thus the question of how a work defines game mechanics becomes significant to understanding, recreating, or applying that work.

2.1   Game Mechanics

In one of the earliest related works on game studies, Lundgren and Björk (2003) defined a game mechanic as any part of a game's rule system that covers a single possible type of game interaction [35]. Furthermore, the authors discussed potential limitations of using the concept of game mechanics and proposed the use of Game Design Patterns instead. They claimed that it can be difficult to use the concept of game mechanics since they are *"neither precisely defined nor put in relation to each other in a structured fashion"*. Nonetheless, the concept is still used widely by researchers, designers, and developers.

Do mechanics exist as part of the player experience, in code as part of the game software, or perhaps they are something else entirely? Juul's "classic game model" (2005) describes a game as *"a rule-based formal system with a variable and quantifiable outcome, where different outcomes are assigned different values, the player exerts effort in order to influence the outcome, the player feels attached to the outcome, and the consequences of the activity are optional and negotiable"* [29]. Juul cites Hunicke et al. [24] in a definition of mechanics on the companion website to *Half-Real* [28] and considers mechanics to be synonymous to the rules of a game.

Järvinen (2007) proposed that game mechanics are the actions that players take to achieve goals when playing [26]. In his dissertation, he expands on his definition describing game mechanics as *"a functional game feature that describes one possible or preferred or encouraged means with which the player can interact with game elements as she is trying to influence the game state at hand towards attainment of a goal"* [27] (p. 255). This definition has been criticized, as it risks implying that mechanics exist only for the purpose of accomplishing goals [51]. It is unclear whether Järvinen's notion of goals includes only in-game objectives, or if it also includes the player-made goals. While some sandbox-like games might not have in-game objectives, the player might have their own motivations to explore and play.

According to Sicart (2008), game mechanics are *"methods invoked by agents for interacting with the game world"* [51]. For Sicart, rules and mechanics are distinct: game mechanics are the actual interaction with game state (which potentially contradicts the idea that mechanics are methods *for* interacting) while rules define the possibility space where the interaction is possible. However, there are limitations and exceptions due to specifications such as "core mechanics" being used to achieve a "systematically rewarded end-game state", which does not exist for games like *SimCity*. Consequently, this definition may be too precise to be appropriate across a variety of game genres.

The development of formalized frameworks and models has emerged as one way to build a common vocabulary for discussing and understanding games and game mechanics. For defining and clarifying game mechanics specifically, Aarseth and Grabarcyzk (2018) presented a meta-model for game ontology comprising four main categories: physical, structural, communicational, and mental [2]. Within this context, game mechanics belong to the mechanical subcategory of the structural layer. According to the authors, rules are *"mechanics that the player perceives, while mechanics are embedded in the structure independently of what the user thinks of them"* [2].

2.2 Similar Concepts

Some authors argue against the use of abstract terms such as "game mechanics" and "rules" [21,35,60]. At the same time, other works seem to assume that the audience is familiar with "game mechanics" and do not provide an explicit definition (e.g., [22,45]).

Salen and Zimmerman's *Rules of Play* (2003) describes a "core mechanic" as an essential gameplay activity that players perform repeatedly [48]. It is interesting to note that the book does not contain any mention of "game mechanics" – only "core mechanics".

Hofmann (2018) [23] focused on three theories of game mechanics: by Fabricatore [16], by Sicart [51], and by Adams and Dormans [4]. Hofmann describes the need for a game mechanics framework and found that there *"seems to be some disagreement regarding the question of whether game mechanics encompass the formal **rules** and structures of the game or 'the **actions** afforded to players by those rules' (Sicart 2008), or indeed both"* (emphasis added). These potentially opposing perspectives point to a potentially wide range of definitions for game mechanics, which we demonstrate in this work.

3 Methodology

Our systematic literature review was conducted by two researchers in three phases: collection and filtering, eligibility assessment, and analysis. For the remainder of this section, all work that is explained should be attributed to them.

The first phase involved obtaining a broad collection of literature from notable game research venues (CHI PLAY, CoG, DiGRA, FDG, ICEC, ToG, and T-CIAIG). The dataset was supplemented via searches through academic search engines (Google Scholar and Semantic Scholar); this helped catch additional notable and widely cited work in the space, outside of the listed venues. Every publication was required to include the word "mechanic" at least once.

Long and short research papers were collected constituting the entire proceedings of each of the venues listed above, spanning 3976 publications in all.[1] To minimize finding publications via the search engines that pertained to non-game uses of the word "mechanic" (e.g., in Physics research) and maximize the chance of finding publications that include *definitions* of mechanics (rather than only mentions), a set of keywords was developed. These were: "game mechanics", "rules", "game ontology", "game design", "ludology", and "game analysis". These keywords served as the inclusion criteria for the first round.

---

[1] PDF proceedings were downloaded directly from publisher or venue-hosted libraries online. Links to the first two years of FDG, then called GDCSE, were unfortunately down at the time of writing, and hard copies could not be obtained.

The researchers processed the dataset by reading titles and abstracts and judging whether the work was likely to include a definition of "game mechanics". Works were selected for further processing if they met any of these criteria:

- the title or abstract included "mechanic",
- the title or abstract included "ontology", "framework", "model", "vocabulary of games", "game language", "what is a game", or other phrases that suggested content about how games are structured, or
- the work seemed to analyze a specific game or genre of games.

After this step, 286 of the 3976 publications remained. An additional 43 works from other venues were found via the search engines using the keywords above.

For each of the total 329 publications, relevant meta-data was added to its dataset entry (e.g., year of publication, venue/publisher, author(s), title, and relevant keywords found in the paper). The dataset includes book publications (found through the search) that both fulfilled the criteria and had high citation counts – more than 3000 overall as counted by Google Scholar.

In the second phase, the dataset was evaluated to determine the eligibility of each publication for analysis. The researchers rated the relevance of each publication in the dataset using a 4-step ordinal scale as follows:

- **High Relevance:** Includes an original or extended definition of game mechanics that is general across multiple games. Implicit definitions were accepted (e.g., a list of examples), but only with an explanation of how other examples could be identified.
- **Medium Relevance:** Includes an original or extended definition of game mechanics that is either specific to one game or implicitly defined without any accompanying explanation.
- **Limited Relevance:** Refers to mechanics at least twice in the context of games, but lacks an original or extended definition of game mechanics.
- **Very Low Relevance:** Lacks a definition of game mechanics and does not refer to mechanics more than once in the context of games.

After the ratings were made, 45 works were rated of high relevance, 47 were of medium relevance, 125 were of limited relevance, and 112 were of very low relevance. For every high relevance publication, definitions of game mechanics were extracted along with details about any prior works that were cited in support. If such a supporting work was cited by two or more high relevance papers, it was added to our collection and its relevance was rated. Four additional works were found in this way, all of high relevance.

For the third phase (analysis), the researchers examined the 49 works of high relevance in greater detail. Furthermore, to gain further understanding of each work, all material referenced directly in relation to either the definition itself and/or any discussion thereof (e.g., other definitions, frameworks, models) were read. The following questions were considered for each of the 49 publications:

- How is the term "game mechanic" defined in the context of the work?
- What terms are used as part of the definition?
- What prior definitions are cited in support of the current definition?

4   Results of Analysis

According to our analysis, there are at least 49 different definitions of "game mechanics" distributed across the literature. While some of the definitions are similar to one another, they are all different in the sense that each contains an original or extended definition of game mechanics that appears nowhere else in the set. Many of these definitions share some overlap: ten include "rules" as part of their definition [4,20,28,34,40,47,50,54,55,63] (though all in different ways), while four include "actions" as part of theirs [24,26,48,51]. Other terms used to define mechanics were less common, including "behaviors" [24,36], "control mechanisms" [24,55], "design decisions" [7,46], and "procedures" [20,50].

While some of the definitions clearly share some agreement, others seem likely to be in conflict with one another. For example, consider "mechanics are rules" versus "mechanics are actions". When authors who define mechanics as rules also discuss actions in the same context (e.g., [55]), it seems likely that they view mechanics to be something *other than* actions, and so a conflict between definitions would exist. Some potential conflicts might be resolved by expanding the set of things that game mechanics are, like how the MDA Framework includes "actions", "behaviors", and "control mechanisms" in a single definition [24]. Nonetheless, it is unlikely that the set of 49 definitions is free from conflicts.

Our analysis revealed 329 publications that mention "mechanic" at least once in the context of games. This highlights the widespread usage of the term in games research, while at the same time showing a potential pitfall of having competing definitions. For example, of the 135 prior ICEC papers that have mentioned game mechanics at least once, 110 of them (91.5%) do not clarify what they understand game mechanics to be – they offer no definitions, no examples, and no citations to other work. With competing definitions for mechanics to choose from, how are we to fully understand those papers?

Table 1 shows how the 49 works we analyzed cite one another for support. As shown in the table, some definitions have been more influential than others among those who have defined "game mechanics". Hunicke et al.'s MDA framework [24] was cited for support most commonly across the 49 works, and it has been cited over 2630 times according to Google Scholar. Notably, the work seems to contain more than one definition, including both *"Mechanics describes the particular components of the game, at the level of data representation and algorithms."* (pg. 2) and *"Mechanics are the various actions, behaviors and control mechanisms afforded to the player within a game context."* (pg. 3).

By examining the connections between citing and cited papers from our corpus (via Table 1), a few chains of influence can be seen: Juul's definition [29] was informed by Hunicke et al.'s [24]; Järvinen's [27] was informed by Juul's [29], Salen and Zimmerman's [48] and Lundgren and Björk's [35]; and Sicart's [51] was informed by Juul's, Järvinen's, and Lundgren and Björk's.

Overall, works by the design-focused community (e.g., DiGRA, CHI PLAY, FDG, and ICEC) tended to describe game mechanics in relation to human-computer interaction and player behaviours (e.g., [18,53,57]). On the other hand, works by the computation-focused community (e.g., FDG, ToG, T-CIAIG, CoG)

Table 1. Data from our corpus of 49 works showing how earlier definitions of "game mechanics" have been referenced in support of later definitions.

Author(s)	Source	Referenced in	Unique Refs
Hunicke et al.	[24]*	[2,5,6,15,23,29,30,38,40,42,46,47,55]	13
Salen and Zimmerman	[48]*	[2,4,8,17,27,40,42,47,51,56,57]	11
Sicart	[51]	[2,7,9,13,15,17,18,23,40,43]	10
Juul	[29]*	[2,4,21,27,40,47,51,57]	9
Järvinen	[27]*	[7,13,21,30,43,49,51]	7
Lundgren and Björk	[35]	[27,51,61], [43]**	4
Fabricatore	[16]	[9,23], [17]**	3
Schell	[50]	[9,40,49]	3
Fullerton	[19]*	[42,49,63]	3
Adams	[3]*	[20,42]	2
Adams and Dormans	[4]*	[23,47]	2
Definitions cited once or never by works in corpus		[2,5–9,13,15,17,18,20,21,23,25,26,30] [31,32,34,36,38,40–43,46,47,49,52,53] [54–59,61,63]	<2 each
Referred to works outside of our corpus		[2,15,17,18,21,30,32,43,47,51]	10

* Source contains multiple potential definitions of "game mechanics"
** Written by same author(s) as the source

tended to reference game mechanics more in relation to logical rules and their implementation in the game system (e.g., [36,54,59]).

5 Discussion and Future Work

It appears that the development of new theories has slowed since the introduction of game studies (early 2000's) and recent papers tend to refer to existing concepts (when they refer to anything at all). The years of publication for our collection of relevant works spanned from 2001 to 2021, although we imposed no constraints on publication date in our review. Nonetheless, it remains telling that within our sample of 329 works, 30% of them suggested different concepts of game mechanics (96 works of high and medium relevance), and 49 of those were sufficiently clear and general to apply easily to different games. It is unclear whether a larger sample would reveal even more discrepancies or similarities across definitions.

Our findings suggest that the field has started to gravitate towards some specific definitions for the concept of game mechanics. However, even the similar definitions in our set are not *the same* in all their nuance, and there is a lack of clarity in whether there is actual agreement in the use and definition of specific terms and concepts. As a result, it is unclear at this time how widely used concepts like "rules" and "actions" map across different definitions of mechanics.

Our work shows the scale of the potential miscommunication within the field of game studies and more broadly for understanding and communicating about designs and systems. Our findings suggest that, broadly, different research communities use similar framing in their favoured definitions of mechanics. This indicates that there might be overlap within sub-fields and communities in their use and conceptualization of game mechanics. Identifying common characteristics and their manner of use could suggest how mechanics might be best analyzed and understood in relation to specific aspects of game studies, and thus help identify potential areas of mutual interest.

This study focused explicitly on "game mechanic" as a term. As a result, papers might have been excluded that define or discuss concepts that are highly relevant to our dataset (e.g., rules or actions) without explicitly mentioning the term "mechanic". We sought to explore the breath and number of existing definitions to determine how they interconnected and overlapped, and have intentionally left the comparison and analysis of how similar terms are defined to be done in a subsequent study.

Future work entails deepening the study of this dataset to further analyze and compare its individual definitions, including where they overlap and disagree. Further, we argue that the key concepts used in several definitions such as "rules" should be examined in greater detail, as they seem to represent fundamental units through which definitions of mechanics can be compared. Expanding the dataset to more relevant venues would help identify further differences and similarities in how "game mechanics" is defined across different communities. This can help the field develop a more comprehensive and multidisciplinary ontology for games.

A variety of different perspectives exist on the concept of what elements constitute a game, some of which even refute the use of the term "mechanics" for being vague and not suitable for all types of games [60]. For instance, the mechanics of a narrative-based game (e.g., visual novels) can be difficult to distinguish from other categories like dynamics or aesthetics. Other terms have also been used to describe mechanic-like concepts such as rules [29], game design patterns [35], and operational logics [37, 44], which are challenging to compare against texts that explicitly discuss "game mechanics". It would be interesting to relate these alternative ideas to the different definitions of game mechanics.

6 Conclusion

As new generations of games researchers enter the field, they will likely be heavily influenced by the first definitions of terms that they encounter; a student who is taught a certain framework in class would have little reason to search for and use other definitions, and a developer at a game studio might be unlikely to oppose the company's existing standards. As such, certain perspectives will inevitably become more popular while others will become overlooked. Nevertheless, we argue that the field would benefit and be enriched by an increased awareness of how we understand and talk about ambiguous concepts like game mechanics – particularly when they are so widely used that definitions are often omitted altogether. While the vague nature of "game mechanics" is commonly understood, our work demonstrates that the problem is much wider than we expected. When we talk about game mechanics, it seems quite unlikely that we mean the same thing.

References

1. Aarseth, E., Calleja, G.: The word game: the ontology of an undefinable object. In: Proceedings of the 10th International Conference on the Foundations of Digital Games, Pacific Grove, CA, USA (2015)
2. Aarseth, E., Grabarczyk, P.: An ontological meta-model for game research. In: Proceedings of the 2018 DiGRA International Conference: The Game is the Message, Turin, Italy (2018)
3. Adams, E.: Fundamentals of Game Design, 2nd edn. New Riders, USA (2009)
4. Adams, E., Dormans, J.: Game Mechanics: Advanced Game Design. New Riders, USA (2012)
5. Alexandrovsky, D., Friehs, M.A., Birk, M.V., Yates, R.K., Mandryk, R.L.: Game dynamics that support snacking, not feasting. In: Proceedings of the Annual Symposium on Computer-Human Interaction in Play, pp. 573–588 (2019)
6. Aponte, M.-V., Levieux, G., Natkin, S.: Scaling the level of difficulty in single player video games. In: Natkin, S., Dupire, J. (eds.) ICEC 2009. LNCS, vol. 5709, pp. 24–35. Springer, Heidelberg (2009). https://doi.org/10.1007/978-3-642-04052-8_3
7. Arnab, S., et al.: Mapping learning and game mechanics for serious games analysis. Br. J. Educ. Technol. **46**(2), 391–411 (2015)
8. Bayliss, J.D., Schwartz, D.I.: Instructional design as game design. In: Proceedings of the 4th International Conference on Foundations of Digital Games, Orlando, FL, USA, pp. 10–17 (2009)
9. Bezchotnikova, S., Bezchotnikova, A.: Game mechanics as videogame genre identifier. Glob. Media J. **16**(30), 93 (2018)
10. Björk, S., Holopainen, J.: Describing games: an interaction-centric structural framework. In: Proceedings of the 2003 DiGRA International Conference: Level Up, Utrecht, The Netherlands (2003)
11. Björk, S., Lundgren, S., Holopainen, J.: Game design patterns. In: Proceedings of the 2003 DiGRA International Conference: Level Up, Utrecht, The Netherlands (2003)
12. Djaouti, D., Alvarez, J., Jessel, J.P., Methel, G., Molinier, P.: A gameplay definition through videogame classification. Int. J. Comput. Games Technol. **2008**, 7 (2008)
13. Dubbelman, T.: Narrative game mechanics. In: Nack, F., Gordon, A.S. (eds.) ICIDS 2016. LNCS, vol. 10045, pp. 39–50. Springer, Cham (2016). https://doi.org/10.1007/978-3-319-48279-8_4
14. Ebner, M., Levine, J., Lucas, S.M., Schaul, T., Thompson, T., Togelius, J.: Towards a video game description language. In: Lucas, S.M., Mateas, M., Preuss, M., Spronck, P., Togelius, J. (eds.) Artificial and Computational Intelligence in Games, Dagstuhl Follow-Ups, vol. 6, pp. 85–100. Schloss Dagstuhl-Leibniz-Zentrum fuer Informatik, Dagstuhl, Germany (2013). https://doi.org/10.4230/DFU.Vol6.12191.85
15. Eladhari, M.P.: Game mechanics and dynamics of social actions in a prototype multiplayer game world. In: Proceedings of DiGRA 2011 Conference: Think Design Play (2011)
16. Fabricatore, C.: Gameplay and game mechanics: a key to quality in videogames. In: Proceedings of the OECD-CERI Expert Meeting on Videogames and Education. Santiago de Chile, Chile (2007)
17. Fabricatore, C.: Underneath and beyond mechanics: an activity-theoretical perspective on meaning-making in gameplay. In: Games and Rules: Game Mechanics for the "Magic Circle", pp. 87–111. Columbia University Press (2018)

18. Fiorilli, P.: The legend of Zelda: breath of the wild through the lens of Italo Calvino's memo on "lightness". In: Proceedings of the 2020 DiGRA International Conference: Play Everywhere, Tampere, Finland (2020)
19. Fullerton, T.: Game Design Workshop?: A Playcentric Approach to Creating Innovative Games. CRC Press, Boca Raton (2014)
20. Gerling, K.M., Schulte, F.P., Smeddinck, J., Masuch, M.: Game design for older adults: effects of age-related changes on structural elements of digital games. In: Herrlich, M., Malaka, R., Masuch, M. (eds.) ICEC 2012. LNCS, vol. 7522, pp. 235–242. Springer, Heidelberg (2012). https://doi.org/10.1007/978-3-642-33542-6_20
21. Gregersen, A.L.: Designers, games and players: same game, different rules? In: Proceedings of the Digital Arts and Culture Conference 2005, Copenhagen, Denmark (2005)
22. Hauge, J.M.B., Lim, T., Louchart, S., Stanescu, I.A., Ma, M., Marsh, T.: Game mechanics supporting pervasive learning and experience in games, serious games, and interactive & social media. In: Chorianopoulos, K., Divitini, M., Hauge, J.B., Jaccheri, L., Malaka, R. (eds.) ICEC 2015. LNCS, vol. 9353, pp. 560–565. Springer, Cham (2015). https://doi.org/10.1007/978-3-319-24589-8_57
23. Hofmann, I.: Requirements for a general game mechanics framework. In: Games and Rules: Game Mechanics for the "Magic Circle", pp. 67–86. Columbia University Press (2018)
24. Hunicke, R., Leblanc, M.G., Zubek, R.: MDA: a formal approach to game design and game research. In: Proceedings of the AAAI Workshop on Challenges in Game AI, San Jose, CA, USA (2004)
25. Järvinen, A.: Theory as game: designing the game game. In: Proceedings of the 2005 DiGRA International Conference: Changing Views: Worlds in Play (2005)
26. Järvinen, A.: Introducing applied ludology: hands-on methods for game studies. In: Proceedings of the 2007 DiGRA International Conference: Situated Play, Tokyo, Japan (2007)
27. Järvinen, A.: Games without frontiers: theories and methods for game studies and design. Ph.D. thesis, University of Tampere (2008)
28. Juul, J.: Half-real: a dictionary of video game theory. https://www.half-real.net/dictionary/#mechanics. Accessed 12 June 2021
29. Juul, J.: Half-Real: Video Games Between Real Rules and Fictional Worlds. MIT Press, Cambridge (2005)
30. Karhulahti, V.M.: Mechanic/aesthetic videogame genres: adventure and adventure. In: Proceedings of the 15th International Academic MindTrek Conference: Envisioning Future Media Environments, pp. 71–74 (2011)
31. Khalifa, A., de Mesentier Silva, F., Togelius, J.: Level design patterns in 2D games. In: 2019 IEEE Conference on Games (CoG). IEEE (2019)
32. Kounoukla, X.C., Ampatzoglou, A., Anagnostopoulos, K.: Implementing game mechanics with GoF design patterns. In: Proceedings of the 20th Pan-Hellenic Conference on Informatics, Patras, Greece, pp. 1–4 (2016)
33. Kultima, A., Lassheikki, C., Park, S., Kauppinen, T.: Designing games as playable concepts: five design values for tiny embedded educational games. In: Proceedings of the 2020 DiGRA International Conference: Play Everywhere, Tampere, Finland (2020)
34. Kumar, J., Herger, M.: Gamification at Work: Designing Engaging Business Software. Interaction Design Foundation (2013)

35. Lundgren, S., Björk, S.: Game mechanics: describing computer-augmented games in terms of interaction. In: Proceedings of the 1st International Conference on Technologies for Interactive Digital Storytelling and Entertainment, Darmstadt, Germany (2003)
36. Martens, C., Hammer, M.A.: Languages of play: towards semantic foundations for game interfaces. In: Proceedings of the 12th International Conference on the Foundations of Digital Games, Hyannis, MA, USA, pp. 1–10 (2017)
37. Mateas, M., Wardrip-Fruin, N.: Defining operational logics. In: Proceedings of the 2009 DiGRA International Conference: Breaking New Ground: Innovation in Games, Play, Practice and Theory, London, UK (2009)
38. McGloin, R., Wasserman, J.A., Boyan, A.: Model matching theory: a framework for examining the alignment between game mechanics and mental models. Media Commun. 6(2), 126–136 (2018)
39. Moll, P., Frick, V., Rauscher, N., Lux, M.: How players play games: observing the influences of game mechanics. In: Proceedings of the 12th ACM International Workshop on Immersive Mixed and Virtual Environment Systems, Istanbul, Turkey, pp. 7–12 (2020)
40. Nealen, A., Saltsman, A., Boxerman, E.: Towards minimalist game design. In: Proceedings of the 6th International Conference on Foundations of Digital Games, Bordeaux, France, pp. 38–45 (2011)
41. Nelson, M.J., Mateas, M.: Recombinable game mechanics for automated design support. In: Proceedings of the Fourth Artificial Intelligence and Interactive Digital Entertainment Conference (2008)
42. Nelson, M.J., Mateas, M.: A requirements analysis for videogame design support tools. In: Proceedings of the 4th International Conference on Foundations of Digital Games, Orlando, FL, USA, pp. 137–144 (2009)
43. Olsson, C.M., Björk, S., Dahlskog, S.: The conceptual relationship model: understanding patterns and mechanics in game design. In: Proceedings of the 2014 DiGRA International Conference, Salt Lake City, UT, USA (August 2014)
44. Osborn, J.C., Wardrip-Fruin, N., Mateas, M.: Refining operational logics. In: Proceedings of the 12th International Conference on the Foundations of Digital Games, Hyannis, MA, USA, pp. 1–10 (2017)
45. Ramirez Gomez, A., Gellersen, H.: More than looking: using eye movements behind the eyelids as a new game mechanic. In: Proceedings of the Annual Symposium on Computer-Human Interaction in Play, CHI PLAY 2020, pp. 362–373. Association for Computing Machinery, New York (2020)
46. Robson, K., Plangger, K., Kietzmann, J.H., McCarthy, I., Pitt, L.: Is it all a game? Understanding the principles of gamification. Bus. Horiz. 58(4), 411–420 (2015)
47. van Rozen, R.: A pattern-based game mechanics design assistant. In: Proceedings of the 10th International Conference on the Foundations of Digital Games, Pacific Grove, CA, USA (2015)
48. Salen, K., Zimmerman, E.: Rules of Play: Game Design Fundamentals. MIT Press, Cambridge (2003)
49. Scheiner, C.W., Witt, M.: The backbone of gamification-a theoretical consideration of play and game mechanics. INFORMATIK 2013-Informatik angepasst an Mensch, Organisation und Umwelt (2013)
50. Schell, J.: The Art of Game Design: A Book of Lenses. CRC Press, Boca Raton (2008)
51. Sicart, M.: Defining game mechanics. Game Stud. Int. J. Comput. Game Res. 8(2), 1–14 (2008)

52. Sicart, M.: How i learned to love the bomb: *Defcon* and the ethics of computer games. In: Stevens, S.M., Saldamarco, S.J. (eds.) ICEC 2008. LNCS, vol. 5309, pp. 1–10. Springer, Heidelberg (2008). https://doi.org/10.1007/978-3-540-89222-9_1

53. Sicart, M.: Newsgames: theory and design. In: Stevens, S.M., Saldamarco, S.J. (eds.) ICEC 2008. LNCS, vol. 5309, pp. 27–33. Springer, Heidelberg (2008). https://doi.org/10.1007/978-3-540-89222-9_4

54. Siu, K., Zook, A., Riedl, M.O.: Collaboration versus competition: design and evaluation of mechanics for games with a purpose. In: Proceedings of the 9th International Conference on the Foundations of Digital Games, vol. 10, pp. 14–22 (2014)

55. Summerville, A., et al.: From mechanics to meaning. IEEE Trans. Games **11**(1), 69–78 (2017)

56. Toups, Z.O., Dolgov, I., Bonsignore, E.M.: A theory of game mechanic signaling for interface design. In: Proceedings of the First ACM SIGCHI Annual Symposium on Computer-Human Interaction in Play, Toronto, Canada, pp. 445–446 (2014)

57. Toups, Z.O., Hammer, J., Hamilton, W.A., Jarrah, A., Graves, W., Garretson, O.: A framework for cooperative communication game mechanics from grounded theory. In: Proceedings of the First ACM SIGCHI Annual Symposium on Computer-Human Interaction in Play, Toronto, Canada, pp. 257–266 (2014)

58. Ulrich, F., Helms, N.H.: Creating evaluation profiles for games designed to be fun: an interpretive framework for serious game mechanics. Simul. Gaming **48**(5), 695–714 (2017)

59. Volkovas, R., Fairbank, M., Woodward, J.R., Lucas, S.: Mek: mechanics prototyping tool for 2D tile-based turn-based deterministic games. In: 2019 IEEE Conference on Games (CoG). IEEE (2019)

60. Walk, W., Görlich, D., Barrett, M.: Design, dynamics, experience (DDE): an advancement of the MDA framework for game design. In: Korn, O., Lee, N. (eds.) Game Dynamics, pp. 27–45. Springer, Cham (2017). https://doi.org/10.1007/978-3-319-53088-8_3

61. Walther, B.K.: Notes on the methodology of pervasive gaming. In: Kishino, F., Kitamura, Y., Kato, H., Nagata, N. (eds.) ICEC 2005. LNCS, vol. 3711, pp. 488–495. Springer, Heidelberg (2005). https://doi.org/10.1007/11558651_47

62. Zagal, J.P., Mateas, M., Fernández-Vara, C., Hochhalter, B., Lichti, N.: Towards an ontological language for game analysis. In: Proceedings of the 2005 DiGRA International Conference: Changing Views: Worlds in Play, Vancouver, Canada (2005)

63. Zook, A., Riedl, M.O.: Generating and adapting game mechanics. In: Proceedings of the 2014 Foundations of Digital Games Workshop on Procedural Content Generation in Games (2014)

A Method for Supporting Verbalization to Facilitate Observation in Illustration Copy-Drawing

Ippei Sugano[✉] and Satoshi Nakamura

Meiji University, 4-21-1 Nakano, Nakano-ku, Tokyo, Japan
cs202007@meiji.ac.jp

Abstract. As digital illustration becomes more widespread, the number of self-taught illustrators who produce *"Doujinshi (self-published print works)"* and post pictures on social media has increased. However, the drawing method used differs depending on the situation, and it is not easy to learn by oneself. It is essential to observe a model closely when drawing, but it may not be feasible for beginners to do it alone. We, therefore, propose an observation method to enhance the beginners' awareness. By verbalizing the features that beginners are not aware of, our approach enables them to make thorough observations independently. We conducted an experimental test to clarify the effects of verbalization for observations and copy-drawings. Then, we found that the proposed method of encouraging verbalization enhanced observations for many beginners and facilitated illustration copy-drawing.

Keywords: Illustration · Metacognition · Observation · Verbalization · Copy-drawing

1 Introduction

With the spread of image-sharing services on the Internet and the increase in niche artist communities, more and more people are trying to learn illustration by themselves. As of April 2020, Pixiv [1], an image-sharing SNS, has more than 50 million registered users and a total of 78.5 million manga and illustrated works. Moreover, on Twitter, the results of well-known illustrators and amateurs can be seen and shared by millions of users [2]. *Doujinshi*, or *doujin*, are fan-drawn manga based on a licensed manga or animation. Some *doujin* artists work in circles with multiple people, but there are many independent artists, so the threshold for individual creative challenges has become lower. In addition, beginner artists and professional illustrators alike participate in large *doujinshi* conventions such as Comic Market.

Many resources and guides for illustrators, such as using paint tools, are shared on various social networks. It has fostered an environment where one can easily create illustrations independently without attending a vocational school or art classes. However, even though the Internet is rich with resources, it is still tricky for beginner artists to

© IFIP International Federation for Information Processing 2021
Published by Springer Nature Switzerland AG 2021
J. Baalsrud Hauge et al. (Eds.): ICEC 2021, LNCS 13056, pp. 348–359, 2021.
https://doi.org/10.1007/978-3-030-89394-1_26

reach their desired level of proficiency on their own. They have to try various practice methods and spend much time drawing to improve their skills and levels.

There are many ways to practice drawing, but one of the most effective for beginners is copy-drawing and sketching objects. However, it is often difficult for beginners to accurately copy-draw an object because they cannot fully visualize its color, shape, balance between facial parts, and location. Beginners who cannot observe or draw an image have the following two problems. First, they are unable to notice that their illustrations are not good. If they cannot see the poor, they will make disappointing work. In other words, the beginners may have difficulty modifying an illustration drawn by themselves to make it more similar to the object or model. Second, they may not notice the difference between their illustration and the object to be drawn. Thus, they cannot improve if they do not see the complex problems in their drawings or know how to fix them. To solve this problem, beginners need to observe the object closely and compare it with their picture to notice what needs to improve. Even so, it is often not enough to observe and reflect mentally.

In light of the above, we focused on verbalizing the awareness gained from observations. By encouraging beginners to express the observation in words, they can clarify their observation and copy-drawing it. In this paper, we examine the usefulness of verbalizing the observation by investigating how writing out the observation results affects copy-drawing. Then, we evaluate the drawings and results of copy-drawing in future work and consider what kind of verbalization is necessary for the observation.

The contribution of this paper is to propose a method that enables beginner artists to increase the effectiveness of observation for copy-drawing by promoting verbalization and revealed that it transformed the copy-drawing behavior.

2   Related Work

There have been numerous studies on how computers support the creation of reproductions, sketches, and drawings. Many of these studies provide guides and advice during drawing.

Williford et al. [3] created a guide for inexperienced artists that divides a photo by shadow depth and instructs them on how to hold the pen, tilt, and apply pressure at each step. Hennessey et al. [4] proposed a system that generates tutorials for 3D objects to support sketching automatically. Dixon et al.'s [5] method support sketching by recognizing human facial photographs and presenting contour lines as guides. Lee et al. proposed ShadowDraw [6], which predicts what the artist is trying to draw from their strokes and offers a guide in the form of a shadow. Matsui et al. proposed DrawFromDrawings [7], which estimates a drawing and presents it as a candidate, making it possible to transcribe that part to the part which the user drew while changing the fusion rate. Iarussi et al.'s method [8] supports copy-drawing by presenting the outline and skeleton information of the subject in a photograph along with grid lines based on the object. Fernquist et al. [9] proposed a system that presents a tutorial for copy-drawing a drawing step by step, such as line art and coloring, and determined that they could achieve more balanced copy-drawing with the guide. Xie et al.'s method [10] extracts the line art and grayscale from a portrait photograph to be drawn and creates a guide for beginners based on the extraction. However, the disadvantage of such methods is that people do not think and draw for themselves by relying on pictures-guide or candidates.

The knowledge embodied and that we cannot express in words is called physical knowledge. We use it empirically but cannot easily explain it in terms of tacit knowledge. Both types are difficult to verbalize and take time to learn. Suwa et al.'s study [11] presents the theory of metacognitive verbalization, i.e., attempting to put into words the experience and consciousness one performs effectively as a tool for acquiring physical knowledge. Suwa et al. have carried out various practical studies on this theory to support the acquisition of physical knowledge acquisition. Results have shown that verbalizing indeed promotes the mastery of learners' skills [12].

3   Method

In order to bring one's picture closer to the target when copy-drawing, it is necessary to discover problems by noticing the bad points of the illustration through observation. However, even if a beginner observes, simply thinking does not lead to sufficient observation, so a method for encouraging observation is necessary.

As mentioned in the related research, many studies support a drawing screen, but it is essential to observe and draw by oneself. We aim to provide a support method that enables beginners to interpret the subject (copy-drawing target), encourages observation, and leads to imagination and consideration. We focused on verbalization as a method for discovering problems. By applying the verbalization support mentioned in the related research to the observation during illustration, the beginners can perceive the drawing target more clearly by increasing their awareness during observation and becoming more aware of what they notice. We clarified the effectiveness of this method through an experiment involving beginner artists to determine the effect of verbalizing the awareness of observation while copy-drawing.

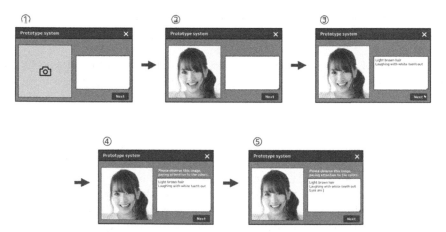

Fig. 1. Flow of using the system to promote verbalization for copy-drawing.

The transition diagrams using the system based on our method are as follows (see Fig. 1):

Step 1. A user takes a picture or inputs an image of a target of copy-drawing into the system.

Step 2. The system instructed the user to observe the image and asked the user to verbalize its features.

Step 3. The user inputs several features of the target image while observing. Then, the user presses the Next button when the user thinks the user has observed enough.

Step 4. The system checks whether the features that the user verbalized are enough or not. If the observed features are not enough verbalization, the system guides verbalizing and moving to Step 3.

Step 5. When the user has written down all the necessary features, it will move to the copy-drawing mode.

This system provides a verbalization guide for features that the beginner user has not noticed by observing and helps the user to gain new awareness. We assumed that by repeating steps 3 and 4, users (beginners) could understand what they could not get when observing by themselves.

In step 4, the system determines if a particular word is included for the verbalization performed by the user. If the user has not verbalized the part to be observed, the system will instruct the observation about that part. The system refers to the part related to the one registered in the database to give proper observation instructions. Since each observation instruction needs to correspond to each observation object, we need to register the observation instruction in the database for each object to be observed by the user. In addition, the user needs to select in advance what to draw.

In particular, this paper deals only with the verbalized part of the proposed method, and we conducted an experimental test to clarify its effectiveness.

4 Experiment

We conducted an experimental test to investigate the things beginners notice when observing and verify whether they become more aware by verbalizing them or whether the points saw or specificity change.

In this experiment, we compared our method with a baseline method. Our method and the baseline method are as follows:

- **Our method:** A participant copy-draws a target image after its observation with verbalization. In this verbalization, we asked the participant to write his/her observations on a blank sheet.
- **Baseline method:** A participant copy-draws a target image after its observation without verbalization.

We also prepared two images as copy-drawing targets (see Fig. 2). The observation targets were two images of women's faces. We chose women's faces as observation targets because they contain a combination of various three-dimensional shapes, such as eyes, nose, and the flow of hair. In addition, since the images had many distinct features, we felt that any differences between the drawing and the original painting would be more noticeable.

In this experiment, we selected the order of our method and the baseline method randomly and copy-drawing targets randomly for each participant. In addition, we asked participants to try copy-drawing using the selected method in a day and using another method the next day. After each copy-drawing, we asked the participants to answer a questionnaire about their observations and copy-drawings.

Fig. 2. Targets of copy-drawing ((a) left, (b) right).

To copy-draw, we prepared "ClipStudio Paint Pro" as drawing software. Then, we explained the usage of the drawing software and allowed participants to practice for 5 min. The software has a G-pen, opaque watercolor brush, eraser, eyedropper, layer operation, undo and redo function. We also allowed other functions. The software was limited to minimize differences and simplify analysis.

We first asked the participants to observe a subject image (selected copy-drawing target image) for 5 min by the selected method. Then, if participants use our method, we provide a blank sheet to them and instruct them to carry out the experimental task while writing down their findings from the observation and drawing. After the 5 min observation, we asked participants to do copy-drawing the target image.

We conducted a questionnaire immediately after participants completed each copy-drawing task. We handed the observation paper to the participants using the baseline method and asked them to write down their findings during observation and drawing. Participants filled out the observation form in a random order to avoid the order effect.

Apart from the observation time, we set the drawing time limit to 55 min for control and notified the participants at 30, 45, and 50 min.

In this experiment, we recruited 11 university students as participants (A to K). The device used was a Wacom MobileStudio Pro 16, a liquid crystal pen tablet, and the drawing software was ClipStudio Paint Pro. The questionnaire contained the following items.

(Q1) What were you careful about when observing?
(Q2) What did you draw with particular care?
(Q3) What were you trying to express?
(Q4) What was difficult?
(Q5) Please write a comment freely.

We conducted the questions to investigate the following specific factors. Q1 targeted the places that the participants felt they were paying attention to; Q2 asked about awareness while drawing; Q3 asked about features that the participants tried to express, and Q4 asked about the parts they could not express due to lack of technique and time.

In addition, a second questionnaire was conducted several days after the experiment so that participants could forget what they had observed and objectively view the copy-drawing. The questionnaire contained the following items.

(Q7) How satisfied are you with the quality of the drawing?
(Q8) How well did you copy-drawing the subject?
(Q9) Compare the subject with your picture. How similar are your drawing and the sample?
(Q10) Where are the similar parts?
(Q11) Do you feel unhappy with the result?
(Q12) Where is the feeling of strangeness?
(Q13) Where and how would you fix it?

Q7 to Q9 were -3 to $+3$ point Likert scales, Q11 gave two choices, and the rest were open-ended. To evaluate whether they reflected the awareness from the observation, we determined the evaluation criteria from the participants' questionnaire responses, and we considered whether they could express their attention as a picture.

We show the evaluation criteria in Table 1.

We created forty criteria items for each drawing target. If the characteristics of the drawing target and the picture drawn by the user were almost the same for each item, we gave them 1 point. If they were different, they received 0 points.

Table 1. Examples of the objective evaluation criteria.

Proportion	• Is the size of each part accurate? (bangs, tied up hair, eyebrows, eyes, nose, mouth, ears, and facial contours) • Is each part properly positioned? (bangs, tied up hair, eyebrows, eyes, nose, mouth, ears, and facial contours) • Face orientation and eye contact
Shape	• Is the shape of the face properly contoured? • Is the curly hair in the right position? • Is the shape of each part accurate? (eyebrows, eye area, eyelashes, eyebrows, nose, mouth, teeth, tongue, ears, bangs, tied hair)
Color	• The way the light hits the bangs • Flow of tied hair • Is the color of each part accurate? (skin, eyebrows, eyes, cheeks, nose, lips, teeth and tongue, cheeks and chin, hair)

5 Results

Figure 3 shows the responses to the post-experiment questionnaire. Regarding their satisfaction with their artistry, the average value of the evaluation was 1.82 using the baseline method and 2.73 using our method, showing a significant difference ($p < 0.05$). In Q2, the average value of the evaluation was 1.91 using the baseline method and 2.64 using our method; there was no significant difference between the two. In Q3, the average value of the evaluation was 2.00 using the baseline method and 2.91 using our method; again, there was no significant difference between the two. These results demonstrate that the participants could express their awareness and express that awareness as a picture with verbalization.

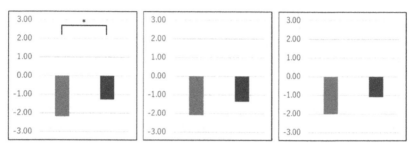

Fig. 3. Average about Users' self-evaluations of itemized observational copy-drawing experiment (from left to right: Q7: How satisfied are you with the quality of the drawing?, Q8: How well did you copy-drawing the subject?, Q9: Compare the subject with your picture. How similar are your drawing and the sample?, blue: baseline method; red: our method). (Color figure online)

Next, we present the results of our objective evaluation of the copy-drawings drawn by the participants. Figure 4 shows the scores of the accurate assessment. First, the scores for subjects (a) and (b) varied widely between participants, and the degree to which they reflected the observation in the picture differed depending on the participant. Comparing the participants shows that five people scored higher when copy-drawing using our method than using the baseline method. By those results, we suggest that this method promotes proper observation and that some users can sufficiently reflect observation in the drawing. The number of feature descriptions was higher when verbalizing the features during observation and drawing. From this, we can conclude that the participants were able to notice what they observed. Under the same conditions, more references were made to features such as size, position, shape, angle, eyelids, and color. However, one of the participants commented, "The picture I had imagined and the one I drew were very different." This comment suggests that it is not enough for beginners to note down the results of their observations and that some parts lack observation and awareness. Another participant commented, "I was able to recall what I discovered during my observation by writing down notes while I was drawing. When I was working on the illustration, I noticed that I had finished a part that I could not correct, so I think that observation in advance is important." By taking notes during an observation, students will plan their drawing process to avoid making mistakes.

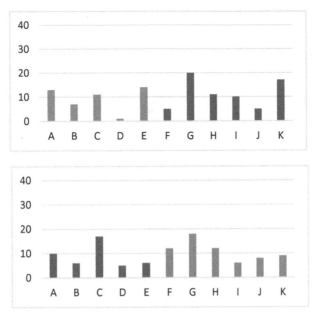

Fig. 4. Objective evaluation of each imitations (top: evaluation of (a), bottom: evaluation of (b), blue: baseline method; red: our method). (Color figure online)

6 Discussion

From the results of the subjective evaluation of the experiment, we determined that describe the picture sample during observation and drawing enhanced their perception. Participants who draw a picture with verbalizing were satisfied with their finished picture. The resulting drawings showed that the beginners were more likely to pay close attention to the details by verbalizing during observation and copy-drawing.

Figures 5 and 6 show the illustrations drawn in the experiment. First, we present the results of the participants' subjective evaluation of their copy-drawing. These figures show that the characteristics of the picture differed significantly using each method.

For subject (a) (see Fig. 5), five participants shaded in the mouth with black using our method, while only three participants did so using the baseline method. In addition, five participants drew the eyelashes using our method, while only two participants drew them using the baseline method. Also, by the authors observing closely, three participants using our method and one participant using the baseline method drew the part of the hair that was tied up as the upper half being vertical and the lower half being horizontal, i.e., considering the flow of the hair instead of just drawing a simple curl.

Next, for the subject (b) (see Fig. 6), five participants drew the left eye slightly more extensive and lower than the right eye using our method, and three participants did so using the baseline method. In addition, two participants using our method and one person using the baseline method could draw the shadow on the left side of the hair.

Next, we compare the results between participants. Figure 7 and Fig. 8 shows an example of two participants who drew significantly different features under the condition

Pictures drawn under our method

Pictures drawn under baseline method

Fig. 5. Copy-drawings of subject (a) by participants.

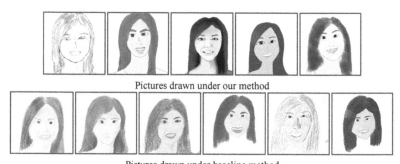

Pictures drawn under our method

Pictures drawn under baseline method

Fig. 6. Copy-drawings of subject (b) by participants.

of verbalization. Participant K included details around the mouth and the flow of hair using our method. Participant C drew detailed shadows at the hairline and lips using our method. Although differences depend on the person, the amount of detail increased overall, and many participants made profound expressions.

The participants using our method were encouraged to observe the features and thus expressed them more consciously in their drawing. At the same time, there was no significant difference in how well they could draw their copy-drawings (shown in Fig. 3) or how much their picture resembled the subject. The score of the objective evaluation varied from person to person. Thus, it may not be possible for beginner artists to fully observe, imagine, and consider just by verbalizing their awareness, so they did not fully express their observations in the drawing.

In the future, we plan to solve this problem by increasing the number of participants, conducting further experiments, and utilizing landscapes such as mountains and rivers in the experiments.

One of the participants commented that there was a gap between the originals and their drawings. Most participants were not very satisfied with their pictures, so some of their illustrations were still in line with the sources. We focused on the verbalized concreteness when considering how we could look a little deeper and reflect on the picture. From the analysis of illustrations using our method, we found many abstract

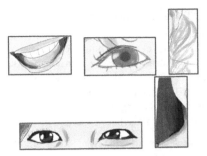

Fig. 7. Details of drawings. Top row: mouth, eyelashes, and tied up hair. Bottom row: eyes and hair shadow.

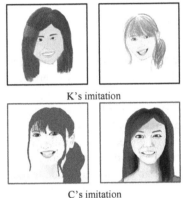

K's imitation

C's imitation

Fig. 8. Detailed drawings. (left: baseline method; right: our method).

verbalizations, e.g., "the hair is curly," "the nose is high," and "the person is smiling." Unfortunately, these descriptions are not memorable enough, so it is impossible to reproduce the subject's atmosphere or subtle expressions.

In order to improve this, we should establish specific criteria and language. For example, "The top half of the hair is vertical, but the bottom half curls up and becomes horizontal," or "The nose is higher than the ears, and the corner of the mouth is higher on the right side when smiling." Using numerical values as a criterion can be effective as well: for example, "The ratio of the height of the eyes is 1:2, and the nose is 1 cm next to the left eye." In the future, we will examine these issues and clarify whether specific language is effective or not.

We show an example of verbalization in Table 2. K often verbalizes the shapes and positional relationships of facial parts such as eyes and nose, and the awareness gained through the verbalization is reflected in the painting. C is more verbalized than others in terms of color. As a result, the shadows of the hair and neck are drawn under the conditions of the proposed method. In addition to that, C painted the tooth color with a mixture of yellow and white and consciously drew the part exposed to the cheek light.

Table 2. Examples of verbalization

K's Verbalization	• Ear holes and eyes are about the same height
	• The inner corner of the eye is inside than the nose
	• The edge of the mouth is about the position of the black eyes
	• Close to the distance between the eyebrows and the eyes
	• There is bangs along the line to the outer corner of the right eye
	• Left front tooth just below the middle of the nose
C's Verbalization	• The left side is dark, the right side is bright
	• The left corner of the eye is huge
	• The dark part is the shadow of the inner corner of the eye
	• Teeth are not too white

7 Conclusion

We proposed a method for verbalizing observations to guide beginner artists when they copy-drawings. The results showed that the use of verbalization promotes observation, creativity, and perception.

In our experiment, it was evident that beginners could observe finer details through verbalizing and reflected their findings from the observations in the drawings to some extent. In the near future, we will increase the number of participants and collect additional work samples to determine common errors and areas often overlooked by beginners. In addition, we will present an interactive guide that draws attention to places and viewpoints that beginners do not usually observe and investigate the subsequent changes in the drawings.

In the future, we will investigate whether observations can be made sufficiently by asking users about places to observe and places where observations are insufficient and clarify the method's effectiveness when inducing observations. In addition, we will focus on the observation and clarify how beginners observe subjects. Finally, we aim to develop a system that can fully support beginners during the observation process.

References

1. Pixiv. https://www.pixiv.net/info.php?id=5746. Accessed on 11 Aug 2021
2. Twitter. https://twitter.com/. Accessed on 11 Aug 2021
3. Williford, B., Doke, A., Pahud, M., Hinckley, K., Hammond, T.: DrawMyPhoto: assisting novices in drawing from photographs. In: C&C 2019 Proceedings of 2019 on Creativity and Cognition, pp.198–209 (2019)
4. Hennessey, J.W., Liu, H., Winnemoller, H., Dontcheva, M., Mitra, N.J.: How2Sketch: generating easy-to-follow tutorials for sketching 3D objects. In: I3D 2017 Proceedings of the 21st ACM SIGGRAPH Symposium on Interactive 3D Graphics and Games Article No. 8 (2017)
5. Dixon, D., Prasad, M., Hammond, T.: iCanDraw: using sketch recognition and corrective feedback to assist a user in drawing human faces. In: CHI 2010 Proceedings of the SIGCHI Conference on Human Factors in Computing Systems, pp. 897–906 (2010)
6. Lee, Y.J., Zitnick, C.L., Cohen, M.F.: ShadowDraw: real-time user guidance for freehand drawing. ACM Trans. Graph. **27**, 879–887 (2011)

7. Matsui, Y., Shiratori, T., Aizawa, K.: DrawFromDrawings: 2D drawing assistance via stroke interpolation with a sketch database. IEEE Trans. Vis. Comput. Graph. **23**(7), 1852–1862 (2017). https://doi.org/10.1109/TVCG.2016.2554113
8. Iarussi, E., Bousseau, A., Tsandilas, T.: The drawing assistant: automated drawing guidance and feedback from photographs. In: Proceedings of the 26th Annual ACM Symposium on User Interface Software and Technology (UIST 2013). ACM, New York, New York, USA, pp. 183–192 (2013)
9. Fernquist, J., Grossman, T., Fitzmaurice, G.: Sketch-sketch revolution: an engaging tutorial system for guided sketching and application learning. In: Proceedings of the 24th annual ACM Symposium on User Interface Software and Technology. ACM, pp. 373–382 (2011)
10. Xie, J., Hertzmann, A., Li, W., Winnemöller, H.: PortraitSketch: face sketching assistance for novices. In: Proceedings of the 27th Annual ACM Symposium on User Interface Software and Technology (UIST 2014). ACM, New York, NewYork, USA, pp.407–417 (2014)
11. Suwa, M.: A cognitive model of acquiring embodied expertise through meta-cognitive verbalization. Inf. Media Technol. **3**(2), 399–408 (2008)
12. Suwa, M.: Re-representation underlies acquisition of embodied expertise: a case study of snowboarding. In: Proceedings of the Annual Meeting of the Cognitive Science Society, vol. 27 (2005)

Works in Progress

Optimization of First-Person Shooter Game Control Using Heart Rate Sensor

Shuo Zhou$^{(\boxtimes)}$ ⓘ and Norihisa Segawa ⓘ

Kyoto Sangyo University, Kyoto, Japan
{zhoushuo3,sega}@acm.org

Abstract. As first-person shooter (FPS) games become highly competitive game genres, various supports are needed to improve the gaming environment. In the past, players have focused on gaming mouses and displays, which are expensive and challenging to select from. To understand the influence of the player's tension on FPS game control, we developed a system that can automatically adjust the speed of the mouse according to the player's real-time heartbeat during the game. In this study, we developed and evaluated a system to improve the FPS game environment based on the heart rate.

Keywords: Game control · Heart rate · Emotion · Sensor · First person shooter game · Control optimization system · Mouse sensitivity · Arduino

1 Introduction

1.1 Background

In recent years, first-person shooter (FPS) games have become an essential part of world-class e-sports. For FPS game players, elements such as competitiveness and control feelings are vital for enhancing the gaming environment [1,2]. The most significant aspect of the FPS gamer is the speed of mouse movement [3]. Typically, players focus on their choice of the gaming mouse. If one can do it just 0.1 s faster than the person's opponent, one has a higher chance of winning [4,5]. However, if the sensitivity of the mouse is set very high, the person will be unable to react. Therefore, mouse sensitivity that matches the reaction speed of a person is desirable.

In this study, we found that a player's heartbeat changed according to the player's pressure and tension and could be used as an emotional element to influence the game control instead of physically controlling the game with a mouse and a keyboard input. A person's level of tension changes during a game, depending on

Electronic supplementary material The online version of this chapter (https://doi.org/10.1007/978-3-030-89394-1_27) contains supplementary material, which is available to authorized users.

ⓒ IFIP International Federation for Information Processing 2021
Published by Springer Nature Switzerland AG 2021
J. Baalsrud Hauge et al. (Eds.): ICEC 2021, LNCS 13056, pp. 363–369, 2021.
https://doi.org/10.1007/978-3-030-89394-1_27

the situation: the higher the tension, the higher the heart rate and ability to react [9]. We developed a system that automatically adjusts the sensitivity of the mouse according to the heart rate to improve the FPS game environment.

It is necessary to measure the real-time heart rate of the player during the game to build a system that improves the gaming environment by heart rate. Next, we link the changes in the heart rate to mouse sensitivity. The purpose of this study is to develop an FPS game control optimization system that obtains the user's heart rate and links it to the sensitivity of the mouse according to the real-time heart rate. An evaluation experiment was conducted and described.

In the work of [6], photoelectric heart rate sensors (Fig. 1) [8] exhibited the principle of heart rate measurement. The hemoglobin in the blood absorbs and reflects light differently, depending on the amount of oxygen it carries. Photoelectric sensors use this property to measure the heart rate by determining the absorption and reflection of light in the hemoglobin density change, as arterial blood flow causes the heart to contract and dilate. Photoelectric sensors are noninvasive and, therefore, easier to measure heart rates.

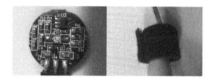

Fig. 1. Heart rate sensor.

Data collection and analysis are simple and inexpensive when photoelectric heart rate sensors are utilized. Therefore, we used a photoelectric heart rate sensor to build the system.

2   FPS Game Control Optimisation System

This system was used to controls the sensitivity of the mouse, a critical parameter for controlling the FPS game. Control was achieved by measuring the heart rate during the FPS game using a photoelectric sensor (Fig. 2).

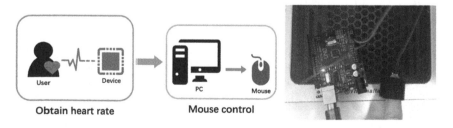

Fig. 2. FPS game control optimization system.

2.1   System Implementation

Implementation Overview. Before the FPS game started, the player wore a device with a photoelectric heart rate sensor on the player's fingertip. During the game, the device measured the player's heart rate in real time and sent the heart rate data to the PC. The PC received the data as input and adjusted the sensitivity of the mouse according to the real-time heart rate.

Heart Rate Acquisition. It was possible to determine the heart rate continuously using an Arduino Uno with a heart rate sensor (pulse sensor). The heart rate sensor collected electrical signals from the user's fingertips, and the Arduino program calculated the real-time heart rate. The calculated heart rate data were then continuously sent to the PC through a USB cable to obtain the user's heart rate during the game.

Mouse Control. The purpose of this system is to optimize the control of FPS games by adjusting the sensitivity of the mouse using the real-time heart rate data of the user. Using this system, we considered the mouse sensitivity as the speed of the mouse movement and utilized the Windows API to adjust the mouse sensitivity according to the real-time heart rate.

The Windows API MouseSpeed defines the mouse speed from 1 (slowest) to 20 (fastest). The standard value is 10.

2.2   Sensing Devices for Meansuring Heart Rate

We used Arduino Uno in this study. The program was written in the Arduino language based on the C language. It can control lamps, switches, and motors connected to boards, thus assisting people with less experience in electronic construction to develop unique creations. To measure the electrical signals of the heart rate, we used a heart rate sensor in Arduino. By attaching this sensor to the user's ear or fingertip, we easily measured the electrical signals of the heart rate (Fig. 2). Logitech G502a gaming mouse with a high-precision sensor and high customizability was selected. The weight (up to 5×3.6 g) and balance could be tuned to suit the user's playing style.

We used the Arduino program to calculate the heart rate in real time. The mouse control part was used to link the real-time heart rate and the mouse sensitivity. Therefore, we wrote a program using Python software; with this program, we could control the mouse using the real-time heart rate. Pairs of heart rate segments ranging from lower than 80 to higher than 120, and MouseSpeed segments ranging from 10 to 20, were adopted (Table 1).

When the user's heart rate increased, MouseSpeed increased, and when it decreased, MouseSpeed decreased. These actions were performed using a program written in Python.

Table 1. Pair of the heartbeat interval with the MouseSpeed interval.

Heart rate	≤ 80	80-90	90-95	95-100	100-105	105-110	110-120	≥ 120
MouseSpeed	10	12	13	14	15	16	18	20

3   Evaluation of Proposed Method

3.1   Experimental Method

The Aimbooster shooting training software (Fig. 3) [7] was used to simulate game-like situations to test the system. In concrete terms, 10 subjects were tested five times using the device and five times without the device. The mean and variance of the results (accuracy) for each of the five tests were calculated, and the calculated data were analyzed.

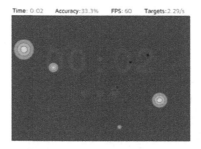

Fig. 3. Aimbooster. [7]

All subjects were tested in a random order under the exact same device conditions (mouse weight, brand, etc.). The setting of the target pattern was also random. The average age of the 10 subjects (9 males; 1 female) was 20-25 years old. All subjects are FPS gamers.

3.2   Experimental Results

The following are the results of our tests on this system using Aimbooster. The mean and variance of the accuracy of the 10 subjects without the device (Table 2) and with the device (Table 3) were determined.

Table 2. Average values without the device (10 people).

	A	B	C	D	E	F	G	H	I	J	Average
Mean	82.2	74.2	82.4	76.0	83.8	73.2	75.4	87.8	82	77.8	79.48
Variance	6.96	58.56	5.44	8.00	16.96	19.76	31.04	4.16	17.6	10.96	17.94

Table 3. Average values with the device (10 people).

	A	B	C	D	E	F	G	H	I	J	Average
Mean	89.2	79.2	87.2	86.6	89.2	81.8	78.4	88.4	88.4	78.2	84.66
Variance	2.96	26.56	21.76	6.24	8.96	14.96	13.04	13.84	3.44	23.36	13.51

A t-test was used to evaluate the system. We observed the following:

- The system improved the average hit rate by 5% compared to the method without the device.

We formulated the following t-test hypotheses.

- Null hypothesis: The method with the device in this system was significantly less effective than the method without the device at the 5% significance level. The mean value of the hit rates of the method with and without the device were equal.
- Counter-hypothesis: The method with the device was significantly more effective than the method without the device at the 5% significance level. The mean of the hit rates of the method with and without the device were different.

The degrees of freedom followed a t-distribution pattern, and the significance level was set at 5% (two-tailed test).

According to statistical analysis, the value of t is 2.43 and the value of p is 0.026. When the degree of freedom is 18, the critical value of t is 2.101, and the rejection region is $t \leq -2.101$ or $t \geq 2.101$. The test results confirmed that the system with the device was significantly more effective than that without the device at the 5% level of the mean hit rate. In other words, the system improved the mean score by 5% compared to the method without the device.

3.3   Discussion

In this experiment, we only assumed the situation of shooting in an ideal environment. Therefore, it was reasonable to use Aimbooster for the experiment. The t-test revealed some validity of the effectiveness of the FPS game control optimization system. In addition, there were several possible reasons why the results were not good for the test. First, we found that individual differences in the human constitution influenced the change in the heart rate. Thus, it is necessary to adjust the threshold for individual differences in advance to obtain valid test data. Second, if the same test is performed more than once, the subject may become accustomed to the test pattern, and the heart rate variations may become smaller.

4   Conclusion and Future Work

In this study, we implemented and evaluated an FPS game control optimization system using a heart rate sensor and found that the FPS game environment could be improved using heart rate data. This study demonstrates the possibility of using the biometric information of a player's heart rate to improve the game environment, as opposed to the conventional method of using a gaming device to improve the game environment.

In a future study, we aim to investigate the influence of individual differences mentioned in the discussion section and set reasonable thresholds for individual differences in each player. We also want to investigate the possibility of using other biometric information, in addition to the heart rate, to enhance the game environment.

Acknowledgment. This work was supported by JSPS KAKENHI Grant Numbers 20K11780 and 19H01719.

References

1. Kou, Y., Gui, X.: Emotion regulation in eSports gaming: a qualitative study of league of legends. Proc. ACM Hum.-Comput. Interact. **4**(CSCW2), 1–25 (2020). https://doi.org/10.1145/3415229. Article 158
2. Bernhaupt, R., Boldt, A., et al.: Using emotion in games: emotional flowers. In: Proceedings of the International Conference on Advances in Computer Entertainment Technology (ACE 2007), pp. 41–48. ACM (2007). https://doi.org/10.1145/1255047.1255056
3. Long, M., Gutwin, C.: Effects of local latency on game pointing devices and game pointing tasks. In: Proceedings of the 2019 CHI Conference on Human Factors in Computing Systems, pp. 1–12. ACM (2019), Paper 208. https://doi.org/10.1145/3290605.3300438
4. Liu, S., Claypool, M., et al.: Lower is better? The effects of local latencies on competitive first-person shooter game players. In: Proceedings of the 2021 CHI Conference on Human Factors in Computing Systems (CHI 2021), pp. 1–12. ACM (2021). https://doi.org/10.1145/3411764.3445245. Article 326
5. Claypool, K.T., Claypool, M.: On frame rate and player performance in first person shooter games. Multimedia Syst. **13**(1), 3–17 (2007). https://doi.org/10.1007/s00530-007-0081-1
6. Dai, J., Wang, B.: A new design of PPG pulse sensor and noise analysis. Mod. Electron. Technol. **29**(2), 78–80 (2006)
7. Aimbooster. http://www.aimbooster.com/. Accessed 4 Aug 2021
8. Plusesensor. https://pulsesensor.com/. Accessed 4 Aug 2021
9. Ishibashi, T., Ohtani, A., Miura, T.: Heart rate as an index of the mental load. Jpn. Soc. Occup. Health **10**(7), 377–379 (1968). https://doi.org/10.1539/joh1959.10.377
10. Claypool, M., Claypool, K.: Latency and player actions in online games. Commun. ACM **49**(11), 40–45 (2006). https://doi.org/10.1145/1167838.1167860

11. Yumang, A.N., Talisic, G.C., et al.: Vital signs determination from ECG and PPG signals obtained from arduino based sensors. In: Proceedings of the 2019 9th International Conference on Biomedical Engineering and Technology (ICBET 2019), pp. 235–239. ACM (2019). https://doi.org/10.1145/3326172.3326202
12. Grajales, L., Nicolaescu, I.V.: Wearable multisensor heart rate monitor. In: Proceedings of the International Workshop on Wearable and Implantable Body Sensor Networks (BSN 2006), pp. 154–157. IEEE Computer Society, USA (2006). https://doi.org/10.1109/BSN.2006.58
13. Gerling, K.M., Klauser, M., et al.: Measuring the impact of game controllers on player experience in FPS games. In: Proceedings of the 15th International Academic MindTrek Conference: Envisioning Future Media Environments (MindTrek 2011), pp. 83–86. ACM (2011). https://doi.org/10.1145/2181037.2181052

Virtual Guia Fortress: A 3D-printed eXtended Reality Playset

Iok Fong Chau[1], Jorge C. S. Cardoso[2]($\boxtimes$)(iD), and Gerald Estadieu[1]

[1] University of Saint Joseph, Macau, China
{201900002,gestadieu}@usj.edu.mo
[2] University of Coimbra, CISUC, DEI, Coimbra, Portugal
jorgecardoso@dei.uc.pt

Abstract. This paper reports a work-in-progress that explores the use of 3D-printing for marker-based Tangible User Interfaces for use with smartphone-based eXtended Reality experiences. We have explored several ways to 3D-print matrix markers that are re-configurable so that the underlying values can change with user interaction. We have also applied 3D-printed markers to the development of a modular playset for exploring the Guia Fortress cultural heritage site in Macau SAR, China. We report some of the explorations of 3D-printed markers and describe the Virtual Guia Fortress playset.

Keywords: 3D-printing · Tangible User Interface · Virtual reality · Augmented reality · Mixed reality

1 Introduction

Tangible User Interfaces (TUIs) are known for enhancing the user experience with an interactive system by providing a more natural way to manipulate information [4]. Various technologies can be used to create tangible objects, from electronically instrumented, active, objects, to passive ones. The use of passive objects is generally cheaper and easier to built. One way to achieve this is through visual marker-based detection. When combined with smartphones, this allows the development of TUIs for smartphone-based, accessible, eXtended Reality (XR) experiences.

While smartphone-based TUI XR experiences are not new (e.g. [2]), this work explores the use of 3D-printed, dynamic (i.e., that change shape), markers for the development of modular toys. Our aim is to achieve an accessible tangible system with low-cost materials and appropriate for smartphone-based XR. We also aim at developing a system that appeals to the maker community by providing 3D-printed TUI solutions that can then be used in a variety of ways. In this paper, we present the design explorations of several 3D-printed marker structures and the application of one 3D-printing solution to the creation of the Virtual Guia Fortress playset – a modular playset for exploring an iconic cultural heritage location in Macau SAR, China.

© IFIP International Federation for Information Processing 2021
Published by Springer Nature Switzerland AG 2021
J. Baalsrud Hauge et al. (Eds.): ICEC 2021, LNCS 13056, pp. 370–376, 2021.
https://doi.org/10.1007/978-3-030-89394-1_28

2 Related Work

Visual markers have been used in many different ways to create tangible interfaces with very different interaction capabilities.

Zheng et al. [6] use the particularity of paper to change its shape and create markers that appear when the paper is folded or handled in specific ways. They explore multiple techniques: printing markers on paper edges, completing markers through collapsing paper folds, deconstructing markers through stretchable paper structures, tearing printed paper markers, making makers visible through wetting paper, and applying light behind the paper. Drogemuller et al. [3] also explore printed paper markers, but in this case applying them in everyday objects. They print paper strips with multiple markers that can be fitted into different kinds of daily objects to allow interaction by hand gestures. Lee et al. [5] apply markers in the faces of cubes and explore two-handed interaction. They explore two metaphors for object assembly based on the manipulation of two cubes: screw-driving, and block-assembly.

While the previous examples were mostly applied to Augmented Reality (AR) settings, markers have also been used in immersive Virtual Reality (VR) setting. Cardoso and Ribeiro [2] explored the possibility of using visual markers in cardboard objects for interaction inside an immersive virtual environment. They explored several prototypes for interacting with cultural heritage, including a Tangible VR Book where the pages were detected through printed markers.

3 Design Explorations

Similarly to Zheng et al. [6], we started by exploring several possibilities for 3D-printed markers. This design exploration phase was purposefully divergent in order to understand the possibilities offered by diverse alternatives. We report here only a subset of the prototypes that have been explored so far.

We use the well-known 2D barcode markers from ARToolkit [1], which are square markers with a black border. We use particularly the 3×3 markers. When counting the border, these can be thought as a 5×5 matrix where the cells are either black or white squares.

3.1 Puzzles

We started by decomposing the marker matrix into individual elements, but this decomposition would result in very small pieces and would also be uninteresting as a puzzle. We thus explored rectangular elements (2 square units) and corner elements (3 square units). The elements are only for the black cells, the white parts of the marker are assumed to be the background. Figure 1a show the pieces and some of the markers that can be created. Of the 64 possible markers, using the rectangular and corner elements allows us to create 62 markers.

We took this approach further and created pieces composed of 4, 5 and 6 square units. This reduces further the number of possible combinations that result in valid markers, but the pieces are bigger and easier to manipulate. By combining these elements with a white box that also includes the white frame for the markers, a set of pieces can be used as a puzzle game (Fig. 1b).

We also experimented with a sliding puzzle, combining white and black square pieces, although this further limits the number of valid combinations (Fig. 1c). A flipping puzzle was also developed, which allows achieving all possible valid combinations of the matrix markers (Fig. 1d).

3.2   LED-Based Markers

We also explored the possibility of creating markers with Light-Emitting Diodes (LEDs) as this would open the possibility of dynamically and automatically changing the value represented by the object.

One of the LED-based markers consisted of a 3D-printed case where seven LED toggle buttons where fitted. This enables users to toggle a matrix cell on or off thus changing the value represented by the marker (Fig. 1e).

A more interesting approach is based on magnetically activated LEDs, which consist of an independently powered LED with a magnetic switch (Fig. 1f). Hovering a magnet over each cell of the matrix marker turns the LED on or off. Although we haven't further pursued this approach, it should be possible to create 3D-printed objects fitted with magnets that would turn on/off all LEDs simultaneously when in contact with the LED-based marker, thus changing its value.

3.3   Moving Mechanisms

We also explored moving marker mechanisms to change the underlying value. We developed 3D-printed markers composed of two components: the first is a recessed marker that is in itself identifiable as the marker number zero. The second component is a 3D-printed white plate with a single protruding black cell (Fig. 1g). The allows creating a marker that can change its value by moving (translating) the underlying plate within the available white space of marker zero (we chose marker number zero because it is the one that has the highest inner white area). This allows six possible values to be created.

It is also possible to create simple rotation mechanisms. Figure 1h show an example of a marker composed of a circular plate with two black cells. By placing the second component on top (marker number zero), we can rotate the plate to change the associated marker value. This arrangement allows changing between four different values.

4   Virtual Guia Fortress Playset

After the diverging design explorations summarised in the previous section, we started converging design ideas to apply some of the 3D-printed marker solutions into mixed-reality modular toys.

(a) Puzzle with two different pieces: 1x2 and corner pieces.

(b) Puzzle with four different pieces: 4, 5, and 6 square units.

(c) Sliding puzzle.

(d) Flip puzzle.

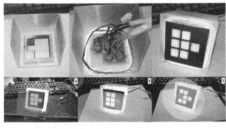

(e) LED-based markers with LED buttons.

(f) LED-based markers with magnetically activated LED.

(g) Single cell moves inside marker.

(h) Rotating mechanism with two black cells.

Fig. 1. 3D-printed marker explorations.

We are currently exploring the use of 3D-printed markers on a playset (Fig. 2) for the exploration of the Guia Fortress – an iconic location in Macau SAR, China.

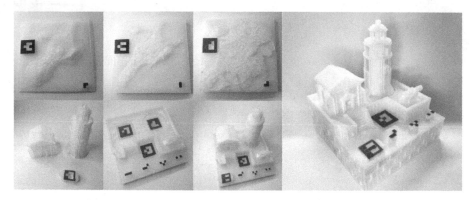

(a) 3D-printed layers.

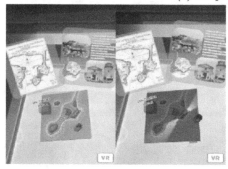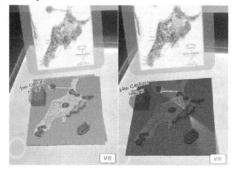

(b) AR view of the map layers (day and nigh views).

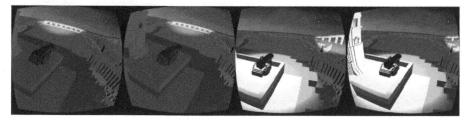

(c) VR view of cannon firing.

Fig. 2. Virtual Guia Fortress 3D-printed playset.

The Guia Fortress was built in the 17th century for military use, located at the highest point on the horizon of Macau. It is regarded as one of the most important landmarks in Macau. The lighthouse being now a tourist attraction, has also played an essential role in the maritime history of Macau. As the first lighthouse in the Far East, the Guia Lighthouse has contributed to the maritime history of Macau since the 17th century.

The playset is a tangible object that allows users to learn about the Guia Fortress and with the lighthouse in AR/VR. The Virtual Guia Fortress Playset is designed as seven interactive, stackable, layers. It includes three maps from the 18th, 19th, and 21 centuries. On top of these, there is also the Guia Fortress's ground layer, church, and lighthouse. There is also a tangible boat that is used in combination with the layers. When all the layers are combined, the church and the lighthouse stay on top. The map's outer frame was designed to look like a brick wall and blend into the foundation outlook of the building.

Interaction with the playset occurs through the manipulation of a boat tangible marker (Fig. 2a, bottom left) that can be placed over the protruding black cells in the lower right corner of each map. On each layer, placing the boat will display an animation of a boat (with different visual appearance in accordance to the century represented by the layer). In addition, the combination of the boat and protruding cells functions as a moving mechanism so that moving the boat up/down or left/right (depending on the layer) will alternate between a day/night representation (Fig. 2b). On the Guia Fortress ground plate, the boat can be placed on one of four locations in a row on the bottom part. Each location will trigger a different visual rendering of the lighthouse scenario: day view, night view, lighthouse lights on, and cannon firing (Fig. 2c).

We are currently evaluating the usability and user experience of this playset.

5   Conclusion

Exploring 3D-printed visual markers for object detection in smartphone-based XR experiences can foster the development of accessible tangible systems that anyone can 3D-print, adapt and reuse.

We have started exploring this avenue by 3D-printing several different ways to create modular objects with dynamic markers that can then be used interactively to affect the XR environment. We explored puzzles, active LED-based markers, movable parts, etc. To demonstrate the applicability of the approach, we have also created a 3D-printed playset for the virtual exploration of the Guia Fortress heritage site in Macau SAR, China.

The preliminary results show that users consider the playset "creative" and "entertaining" which gives us confidence on the usefulness of this approach.

References

1. ARToolkit: Official ARToolkit site (2018). https://artoolkit.org/
2. Cardoso, J.C.S., Ribeiro, J.M.: Tangible VR book: exploring the design space of marker-based tangible interfaces for virtual reality. Appl. Sci. **11**(4), 1367 (2021). https://doi.org/10.3390/app11041367. https://www.mdpi.com/2076-3417/11/4/1367

3. Drogemuller, A., Walsh, J., Smith, R.T., Adcock, M., Thomas, B.H.: Turning every-day objects into passive tangible controllers. In: Proceedings of the Fifteenth International Conference on Tangible, Embedded, and Embodied Interaction, pp. 1–4. Association for Computing Machinery, New York (2021). https://doi.org/10.1145/3430524.3442460

4. Hinckley, K., Pausch, R., Goble, J.C., Kassell, N.F.: Passive real-world interface props for neurosurgical visualization. In: Proceedings of the SIGCHI Conference on Human Factors in Computing Systems Celebrating Interdependence - CHI 1994, pp. 452–458. ACM Press, New York (1994). https://doi.org/10.1145/191666.191821. http://portal.acm.org/citation.cfm?doid=191666.191821

5. Lee, H., Billinghurst, M., Woo, W.: Two-handed tangible interaction techniques for composing augmented blocks. Virtual Reality **15**(2–3), 133–146 (2011). https://doi.org/10.1007/s10055-010-0163-9

6. Zheng, C., Gyory, P., Do, E.Y.L.: Tangible interfaces with printed paper markers. In: DIS 2020 - Proceedings of the 2020 ACM Designing Interactive Systems Conference, pp. 909–923. Association for Computing Machinery, Inc (2020). https://doi.org/10.1145/3357236.3395578

Recreating a TransMedia Architectural Location In-Game via Modular Environment Assets

Wilhelmina Statham[1]([✉]) [iD], João Jacob[2] [iD], Mikael Fridenfalk[1] [iD],
and Rui Rodrigues[3] [iD]

[1] Department of Game Design, Uppsala University, 621 67, Visby, Sweden
{wilhelmina.statham,mikael.fridenfalk}@speldesign.uu.se
[2] LIACC- Artificial Intelligence and Computer Science Laboratory, University of Porto, Rua Dr. Roberto Frias, 4200-465 Porto, Portugal
joao.jacob@fe.up.pt
[3] Faculty of Engineering of University of Porto INESC TEC , University of Porto, Rua Dr. Roberto Frias, 4200-465 Porto, Portugal
rui.rodrigues@fe.up.pt

Abstract. Existing architectural locations are often recreated in games using unique "hero" meshes instead of modular assets, which in these cases are commonly perceived as too limited or inaccurate. This applies to real-world locations or, as in this case study, transmedia locations. This study proposes that hero meshes are not always necessary and that modular assets have the potential to recreate even complex architecture. The paper presents a set of development steps for modular assets for game environment art according to a game design lifecycle, and proceeds to demonstrate its potential via a case study. The case study focuses on planning and designing steps; these preliminary results indicate that, when well-designed, modular assets have the potential to recreate complex architectural locations without requiring extensive use of hero meshes. Adopting modular assets instead of hero meshes could potentially reduce the cost and development time of environment art for transmedia games and games featuring real-world architectural locations, as well as increase the reusability of such assets.

Keywords: Transmedia Architecture · Game Environment Art · Modular Assets

1 Introduction

Modular game assets are often limited to architecture with obvious repetition [1], such as terraced houses, shopping malls, and facades of high-rises. When faced with recreating existing or complex architectural locations in-game, environment artists tend to rely on unique meshes, commonly referred to as hero meshes. Hero meshes, while allowing for a high level of accuracy, are hard to change or customize, have limited or no reusability, and are generally time-consuming to produce [2, 3]. For example, in the game Assassin's Creed Unity [4], the cathedral of Notre Dame de Paris took a dedicated environment artist two years to recreate it in-game [5].

© IFIP International Federation for Information Processing 2021
Published by Springer Nature Switzerland AG 2021
J. Baalsrud Hauge et al. (Eds.): ICEC 2021, LNCS 13056, pp. 377–385, 2021.
https://doi.org/10.1007/978-3-030-89394-1_29

Advocates of modularity argue that even complex locations can be recreated in-game using modular assets, as long as they are well-designed [2]. However, there are few published guidelines on how to design and implement modular assets, and game results often display varying levels of quality. The main problems with poorly designed modular assets are the need for a large number of unplanned extra assets to disguise visual and/or functional flaws as well as excessive visual repetition, which can lead to art fatigue [6].

This paper proposes a set of principles and methodology that support the production of modular assets for 3D games, applied to a case-study. The case-study reproduces a common scenario in transmedia game productions and aims to recreate via modular assets a complex well-known architectural location, namely the police headquarters of Gotham City, part of the Batman universe. More specifically, the version depicted in the TV show Gotham aired between 2014 and 2019 by Fox Broadcasting Company. The goal is to demonstrate that, when well-designed, modular assets have the potential to recreate even highly complex architectural locations in-game.

Section 2 presents the development steps for modular architecture for games as proposed by the authors and according to a game development lifecycle (GDLC). Section 3 introduces the case study as well as available references. Section 4 presents the planning phase and the motivation behind key design decisions. Section 5 presents the pre-production phase, which involves the whitebox and greybox stages, and where the functionality of the assets and the elements of the modular kit are established. The paper concludes with Sect. 6 where the proposed principles and their application in this case study are discussed.

2   Principles of Modular Architecture for Games

There are several steps to design and implement modular assets for a game, involving both environment artists and level designers. A key difference compared to non-modular assets is the need for extensive planning and early testing, where the list of modular assets and their functionality should ideally be established before full production starts

Table 1. Development steps for modular architecture for games according to a typical GDLC.

Step	Description
Planning	
Determine the measuring convention	A game should always follow a single measuring convention (metric, imperial, or custom) which should be clearly communicated and available in the game engine [6, 7]
Determine the grid size	Game engines rely on Cartesian grids, and modular architecture is built upon multiples of the game's grid size, which is usually determined based on the size of the characters, camera angle, type of gameplay, and the feeling the game is trying to evoke [2, 6]

(continued)

Table 1. (*continued*)

Step	Description
Establish the naming convention	A clear and well-documented naming convention is fundamental for modular architecture for games. As names are likely to get long, using abbreviations or omitting vowels are standard
Define the types of modular kits	Large-scale games may require several kits to organize a variety of architectural styles, construction techniques, and factions. As a rule of thumb, fewer kits with more components tend to be more cost-effective than more kits with fewer components [2]
Define the types of modularity	The types of modularity influence how the assets are designed; most games rely on sectional, component swapping, and component sharing modularity [6]
Pre-production	
Whitebox	As with traditional level design, pre-production starts with whiteboxing, which for modular architecture should be approached as a vertical slice. The goal is to determine as much as possible all types of levels needed, rather than designing the actual levels. These will guide the planning and design of the modular kits [2, 6]
Refine types of kits and types of modularity	If needed, the types of modular kits and types of modularity may be refined. It is common for two or more modular kits to be consolidated at this stage [2]
Plan the modular kits: a) assets per modular kits	Create a detailed list of assets per modular kit. While variations in style and decorative details may be added later, all the types of basic assets should be listed
b) tiling direction	Sectional modularity, where assets are tiled side by side, is the most common type of modularity in games [6]. It is important to determine the tiling direction of each asset: horizontal, vertical, or both
c) level of granularity of the kit	Modular kits that rely on smaller individual meshes tend to be more flexible and offer greater visual variation. On the other hand, when assembling the levels within the engine, too many small assets generally requires a longer assembly time and can result in more errors [2]

(*continued*)

Table 1. (*continued*)

Step	Description
d) use of prefabs or not	Kits with small granularity may benefit from the intermediate step of pre-assembly as larger prefab components in engine prior to level design to facilitate the level assembly [2]
e) position of pivot points	All 3D meshes have a pivot point from which they can be moved, rotated or scaled. It is important that all pivot points within a game follow a common logic to facilitate tiling [6, 8]
f) standard size of transitions	Different kits can be connected seamlessly by adopting standard sizes for transitions such as doorframes and stairs [2, 9]
g) transitions as plug and socket or special meshes	Transitions are further optimized by using a plug and socket system, where the trims of the transitions are separate meshes that plug into the sockets of door and window frames [2, 9]
h) components shared between kits	Modular kits rely on additional components for variation and to minimize art fatigue. These include modular pipes, wires and structural frames, decals and greebles, and set dressing props. These components are often shared between kits [3]
Greybox	Once the modular kits have been planned, environment artists create placeholder grey meshes (untextured) with the correct dimensions and layout to test the functionality of the kits [2]. These replace the whitebox meshes, allowing quick in-game testing and iteration
Early Production	
Basic/vanilla variation of the kit	The focus of early production is to confirm the design of the kits through a first and basic/vanilla version of each kit. Because there is only one variation of each kit at this point, it is easier to implement changes or to add elements that might have been overlooked during pre-production [2]
Functional polish	Early production should finish with a functional polish of the modular kits, where the basic variation of each kit is in engine replacing the placeholder versions. The basic variation must be deemed functionally sound before further variations are added [2]

(*continued*)

Table 1. (*continued*)

Step	Description
Production	
Create and implement variations	This stage focuses on adding variations based on the basic/vanilla version, usually combining mesh and texture variations [3]
Create and implement set dressing and props	Set dressing components and props are also added. These might be modular or stand-alone assets [2, 3]
Polish	
Visual polish	Previously identified visual weaknesses should be addressed. New meshes and textures should generally not be added at this stage [2]
Optimization	Standard game graphic optimizations such as packing texture maps, adjusting LODs, and graphic quality balancing [2]
Correcting bugs	Previously identified bugs should be corrected

as late changes can be time-consuming. In non-modular assets, small changes during production can be easier to implement. Table 1 presents a summary of development steps according to a typical GDLC, proposed by the authors based on observed practices in game development and on established principles of traditional pre-fabricated modular architecture.

3 Case Study: Gotham PD

The case study focused on the design and functional integrity of the modular assets, and therefore on the phases of planning and pre-production. It was developed using Unreal Engine 4 release 4.24 and Autodesk 3ds Max 2020. The goal was to reproduce in-game via modular assets an existing architectural location that would ordinarily be created via hero assets. Mimicking a game development environment, the authors relied on pre-existing blueprints and footage from the TV show as references. As it is unusual for game developers to have access to TV or movie sets, the lack of first-hand references placed the authors in similar circumstances.

4 Planning

Game developers relying on modular assets for environment art instead of hero meshes should be prepared to invest more time in planning, as layout and design must be decided early, before production and asset creation has started. There is generally little leeway for changes in late development, and late changes to the modular assets can be expensive. On the other hand, changes to the layout and level design are generally easy due to the flexibility of modular assets, compared to that of assets created as a single hero mesh [2]. For the case study, since Batman is an on-going game franchise, the authors relied on characteristics of the already released games to guide the decision-making process. Of particular significance, Batman are action-adventure games with a core mechanic of jumps, moving and combat between different heights.

Planning included quick sketches of key angles of the location based on reference images and blueprints [1], taking into account the ceiling height needed for the core mechanics. The grid size was set at 1.5 times the height of the character; larger grid sizes can be beneficial for games that require broad character movements and jumps and is in accordance with previous game instalments of the Batman series. The average male game character is 1.8 m tall, usually rounded at 2 m to calculate environment sizes. At 1.5 times the character height, the minimum grid size was set at 3 m. This allowed for grid size variations of 3, 6, 9, and 12 m, with smaller structures and props of 0.5, 1, and 1.5 m.

During planning, the following were decided: the measuring convention, the grid size and allowed variations, the naming convention, the types of kits, and the types of modularity. These are described in Table 2.

Table 2. Description of the main characteristics of the modular assets for the case study.

Characteristic	Case study standard
Measuring convention	Metric
Grid size	3 m (1.5x the height of the main character)
Grid size variations	3, 6, 9, 12 m, and smaller structures of 0.5, 1, and 1.5 m
Naming convention	NameOfKit_TypeOfAsset_Dimension_Characteristic_Variation
Modular kits	The police station is planned as part of a larger modular kit for public buildings, abbreviated to Pub for the naming convention
Types of modularity	Sectional modularity with vertical and/or horizontal tiling, mix modularity for pillars

5 Pre-Production

Based on the combination of blueprint, sketches, and reference images, pre-production started with a rough layout of the location within Unreal Engine using brushes [1], a technique commonly referred to as whiteboxing [2, 6]. The initial step was to adapt the original measurements into the grid size convention of 3, 6, 9, and 12 m. This proved straightforward, with few modifications required.

The differences between the original blueprint and the whitebox included:

- simplified small irregular corners to facilitate character navigation,

- expanded the depth of enclosed rooms that were originally too small for a game and a potential source of bugs in the form of characters getting stuck to each other or to the surrounding geometry,
- stairs sizes were standardized,

Fig. 1. Left: Greybox level in Unreal. Right: Reference images from the TV show.

Table 3. Description of the main characteristics of the modular assets for the case study.

Characteristic	Case study standard
Level of granularity	High level of granularity using prefab groups
List of assets	Where possible, assets were combined to minimize repetition
Pivot points	Place at the back right corner; for radial meshes in the center of the circumference
Transitions	The dimensions of windows and stairs were standardized

The level was play tested for navigation, movement, and possibilities of jumping and combat sequences. During this stage some of the furniture was rearranged to facilitate character navigation and the arcs of the mezzanine were removed to avoid blocking the character's path when jumping and performing ranged attacks. Based on the whitebox level, further decisions were taken regarding the design of the modular kit as well as a list of assets and their description. These steps are described in Table 3.

5.1 Greybox

Once the list of assets was finalized, the whitebox geometry was replaced with greybox meshes. Greybox meshes are simplified placeholder versions of the final meshes with the same size and layout but without a high artistic investment and are typically created in a 3D modelling software, in this case Autodesk 3ds Max 2020. They allow environment artists and level designers to quickly test the functionality of modular assets, including the position of pivot points, their dimensions, and their modular tileability. Figure 1 compares the greybox level with references of the TV show.

6 Conclusion and Future Work

When faced with complex or well-known architectural locations, game environment artists often choose to recreate them using hero meshes instead of modular assets. While hero assets provide greater freedom and higher potential for accuracy, they tend to be time-consuming to produce and have limited reusability [1, 2]. Changes in layout can be expensive to implement on finished hero meshes. Modular assets on the other hand have high layout flexibility, greater reusability, and tend to be faster to produce [6]. This case study aimed to test whether it was possible to recreate in-game a well-known transmedia architectural location using modular assets instead of hero meshes.

Based on a set of production steps applied to the different stages of a game development lifecycle, this case study demonstrated that, when well-designed, modular assets have the potential to accurately recreate in-game complex existing architectural locations. The case study focused on the design and functionality of the modular kit, corresponding to the planning and pre-production stages. It highlighted the flexibility of modular assets and the importance of early testing and integration between environment art and level design. By testing the whitebox and greybox versions in-game, it was possible to quickly adapt the layout to facilitate the gameplay, for example by moving objects that might block the characters' movement and increasing the footprint of specific areas. Whereas these adaptations were important for gameplay, they were also minimal and localized. The corresponding original TV show and in-game versions of the location match closely and are easily recognizable. Modular architecture was flexible enough to recreate even complex architectural features, such as the structural arcs and elaborate windows.

By recreating the level using modular assets instead of hero meshes, the complexity of each mesh was reduced. Each modular mesh is relatively simple, and the modular kit has the advantage of flexibility and reusability. For example, if level designers wish to change or expand the police station, modular assets enable such changes at a low production cost, whereas a hero mesh would require a dedicated team of environment artists to create the new or modified location from scratch.

This case study reinforced the importance of planning and early testing when designing modular assets for games. It is important that testing takes place in the game engine, and that there is clear documentation of the measurements, standards, and guidelines for the modular kit as well as a clear and detailed list of assets. Time invested in early testing can help to identify mistakes or weaknesses in the modular assets that could easily be corrected during pre-production, but that might be costly and time-consuming to change at later production stages.

The authors believe this case study indicates that the proposed set of development steps has the potential of being a helpful guideline for game developers and researchers interested in modular assets for games. The steps were flexible enough to be easily adapted to the specific needs of the case study, while detailed enough to ensure that all key decisions were made at the appropriate time. Further testing in a full game development production is recommended. To better evaluate its impact in production, ideally the same or similar game locations should be developed by experts using a modular and a non-modular approach, with results compared in terms of production time, impact in game performance, and visual quality. The principles should also be regularly revised to account for changes in production pipelines, as might be expected from the upcoming release of the next generation of consoles and engines, such as the upcoming Unreal Engine 5 or from the introduction of new technology, such as wider-spread use of photogrammetry-based meshes in games.

References

1. Suanto, W., Martyastiadi, Y.S.: Modular technique of 3D modeling and procedural texturing for 3D Game Environment Design of "Jurnal Pahlawan". In: International Conference Intermedia Arts Creative Technology, pp. 5–12. https://doi.org/10.5220/0008525200050012. Yogyakarta, Indonesia (2020)
2. Burgess, J., Purkeypile, N.: "Fallout 4's" Modular Level Design. In: Game Developers Conference GDC 2016. InformaTech, San Francisco, CA, USA (2016)
3. Burgess, J., Sergeev, A.: Building Huge Open Worlds: Modularity, Kits & Art Fatigue. In: 80 Lev. (2018). https://80.lv/articles/building-huge-open-worlds-modularity-kits-art-fatigue. Accessed on 25-Jan-2021
4. Ubisoft: Assassin's Creed Unity [Video Game] (2014)
5. Makedonski, B.: One dev spent two years making the notre dame in assassin's creed unity. In: Destructoid (2019). https://www.destructoid.com/one-dev-spent-two-years-making-the-notre-dame-in-assassin-s-creed-unity-282133.phtml. Accessed 13 Nov 2020
6. Perry, L.: Modular level and component design. In: Game Dev, pp. 30–35 (2002)
7. Burgess, J., Purkeypile, N.: Skyrim's modular approach to level design. In: Game Developers Conference GDC 2013. InformaTech, San Francisco, CA, USA (2013).
8. Mader, P.: Creating modular game art for fast level design. In: Gamasutra (2005). https://www.gamasutra.com/view/feature/2475/creating_modular_game_art_for_fast_.php. Last accessed 2011. Accessed on 02 Mar 2021
9. Smith, R.: Prefab architecture: a guide to modular design and construction. Wiley, Hoboken, New Jersey (2010)

Interaction Toolkit for Programming Interactions with Marker-Based Tangibles in Virtual Reality

João Mesquita[1] and Jorge C. S. Cardoso[2]([⊠]) [iD]

[1] University of Coimbra, DEI, Coimbra, Portugal
[2] University of Coimbra, CISUC, DEI, Coimbra, Portugal
jorgecardoso@dei.uc.pt

Abstract. This project focuses on the development of a tangible interaction programing toolkit for Virtual Reality (VR). Marker-based tangible interactions have been explored before, but no development libraries exist for facilitating developers' work. Particularly for accessible web-based VR frameworks such as A-Frame, the complexity of the interactions is limited by programming difficulties, due to the inexistence of high-level programmatic abstractions. As such, in this project the goal is to develop a set of abstractions that facilitate the development of tangible experiences in the A-Frame platform. We have developed an initial version of a component library and have started evaluating it through task-based API usability testing. We report preliminary results from this usability testing.

Keywords: Virtual Reality · Tangible objects · Interaction · Programmatic abstraction · Visual markers

1 Introduction

Interaction in Virtual Reality (VR) is often achieved through standard controllers. However, these typically do not provide haptic experiences congruent with the virtual environment and sometimes result in awkward button mappings for manipulating virtual objects.

One alternative is the use of tangible user interfaces which are usually considered to provide a more natural interaction experience by leveraging on our ability to manipulate physical objects and on the direct mappings from physical to virtual objects. Tangibles naturally provide haptic sensations which can increase the realism and thus the immersiveness of the VR experience [1].

The use of tangibles in VR has been accomplished before, using different technological approaches. In this project, we focus on tangible object detection through visual markers, which is a suitable solution for smartphone-based VR. This results in a cheap and accessible tangible system for VR. Previous work by Cardoso and Ribeiro [2] has identified a difficulty in programming tangible interaction given the lack of high-level

© IFIP International Federation for Information Processing 2021
Published by Springer Nature Switzerland AG 2021
J. Baalsrud Hauge et al. (Eds.): ICEC 2021, LNCS 13056, pp. 386–392, 2021.
https://doi.org/10.1007/978-3-030-89394-1_30

abstractions for programmers. In this work, we present a marker-based tangible inter-action library for the A-Frame web-based VR framework. We also present preliminary results from a usability evaluation of this library.

2 Related Work

Previous work by Cardoso and Ribeiro [2] explored the use of tangible objects for interaction in smartphone-based VR, tracking the tangible objects through visual markers. The authors created several prototypes, including a tangible book for exploring cultural heritage and identified a difficulty in programming the VR experiences. Dias et al. [3] have developed a system of controllers with tangible interfaces that allow for hand position tracking. Two prototypes were created, Magic Bracelet and Magic Ring, which consist of visual markers placed on the wrists and fingers of the hand to track the positioning of these body parts and use them for interactions. Lee et al. [4] developed an approach based on occlusion of visual markers in a grid. They implemented fingertip detection, buttons, sliders, two-handed input, over the marker grid. In all these works, the VR/AR experience was programmed from scratch, and no higher-level programming library was created to facilitate the programmer's task of using the implemented interactions.

High-level programming abstraction toolkits such as Phidgets, Reactable, Microsoft Surface, and others [5] exist for several tangible systems, however they are not applicable to marker-based tangible interaction for smartphone-based VR.

3 Tangible Marker Interaction Library

The Tangible Marker Interaction Library is a library of components for the A-Frame web-based VR framework (available at https://github.com/JoaoDiogoMesquita/VR-Tangible-Interaction-Toolkit). It is currently composed of five components: shake detector, button, swipe, and angle detectors (single and double marker). These components follow the general programming approach of A-Frame and trigger high-level events when they detect relevant user actions.

3.1 Shake Detector Component

The shake detector component is intended to detect the shaking motion of a marker. To detect when the marker attached to the object is being shaken, the changes of direction relative to each of the defined axes, the distance traveled and the time between these changes of direction are considered. Programmers can customize the distance and maximum time interval between changes of direction, as well as the minimum number of times they occur. Programmers can also set which movement axes will be detected: x, y, or z. This component can help in creating interactions where users interact with the virtual environment by shaking objects. For example, a user manipulating a tangible representation of an architectural model of a church tower can shake the tangible and trigger the sound of the tower's bell (Fig. 1).

```
<a-marker … mt-shake-detector="switchInterval: 500;
                                minimumSwitchTimes: 3;
                                minimumDistance: 0.3;
                                eventTargets:#myBox;
                                axis:y;">
</a-marker>
```

Fig. 1. Demonstration of the "shake detector" component.

```
<a-marker … id="ref">   </a-marker>

<a-marker … mt-button="referenceMarker: #ref;
                       eventTargets: #box;
                       minimumTime: 100;">
</a-marker>
```

Fig. 2. Demonstration of the "button" component.

3.2 Button Component

The button component follows an approach similar to [5] and allows using a marker as a button that can be "clicked". It uses two markers: one serves as a reference and must be visible for the interaction to occur; the other serves as the actual button that users can click by touching (occluding it). The reference marker avoids the ambiguity between the occlusion of the button marker occurring due to it moving out of scene vs being explicitly occluded by the user. When the button marker is occluded for a predefined amount of time (configurable by the programmer), a click event is triggered. In a VR experience this interaction can easily be included, acting as a switch or any functionality executed with a button producing the respective behavior. For example, Fig. 2, shows a demo of a tangible object that allows browsing content by pressing on of the lower buttons to move back and forth.

3.3 Swipe Component

The Swipe component allows detecting swipe interactions on a sequence of markers. The programmer defines the set of markers to be used, as well as the sequences to detect. If the markers are occluded in a predefined order and within the defined maximum time, an event will be triggered. One of the advantages of using this type of interaction is the possibility to customize the behavior, and each defined sequence can be distinguished

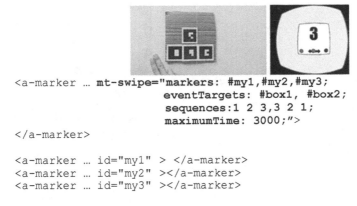

```
<a-marker … mt-swipe="markers: #my1,#my2,#my3;
                      eventTargets: #box1, #box2;
                      sequences:1 2 3,3 2 1;
                      maximumTime: 3000;">
</a-marker>

<a-marker … id="my1" > </a-marker>
<a-marker … id="my2" ></a-marker>
<a-marker … id="my3" ></a-marker>
```

Fig. 3. Demonstration of the "swipe" component.

```
<a-marker … mt-angle-detector-sm="threshold:45;
                                  eventTargets: #box1, #box2;
                                  axis:y;" >
</a-marker>
```

Fig. 4. Demonstration of the "angle detector – single marker" component.

in the detection, so it is possible to have several different types of behaviors in the same tangible object (swipe left, right, up, down). Figure 3 shows an example of the use of the Swipe component where three markers are used for swiping left and right to browse contents.

3.4 Angle Detector Component – Single Marker

The Single Marker Angle Detector component detects the rotation of a marker with respect to one or more defined axes. The programmer can set a threshold (in degrees) and an event will be triggered when the marker rotates by this amount. The event contains information about the axis, direction, threshold, and the entity where it occurred. This component can be used to change continuous variables in virtual space such as brightness or volume. Figure 4 shows an example of the use of the angle detector for creating a rotational controller.

3.5 Angle Detector Component – Double Marker

The Double Marker Angle Detector component handles the measurement of the angle between two markers. The component allows the programmer to customize the range

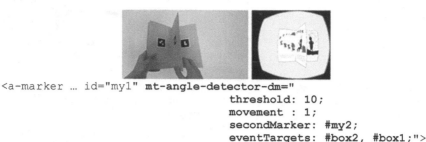

```
<a-marker … id="my1" mt-angle-detector-dm="
                                threshold: 10;
                                movement : 1;
                                secondMarker: #my2;
                                eventTargets: #box2, #box1;">
</a-marker>

<a-marker … id="my2" ></a-marker>
```

Fig. 5. Demonstration of the "angle detector – double marker" component.

and type of angle to detect. The first type intends to detect the angle between two markers on different planes, such as markers on two pages of a book. The second type of angle assumes the markers are in the same plane, and the calculated angle is the one between the sides of each marker. Given a customizable threshold, events will be issued to the entity associated with the component and to additional specified entities each time this threshold is reached. This component can be used, for example, in the opening movement of a book, producing an animation depending on the opening angle between the two pages (Fig. 5).

4 Usability Evaluation of the Components' API

We are currently performing API usability tests to evaluate the understandability, abstraction, learnability, and reusability of the provided component library. We are following a task-based API usability evaluation [6]. For each component, we ask programmers to solve two tasks. The first task for each component can be implemented by using only the HTML interface of the component. The second task can only be solved by coding a custom A-Frame component in JavaScript and using the component's JavaScript API.

This first usability test is being performed online and asynchronously: participants are given the set of tasks and the library of components and are asked to solve them at their own pace and send us their answers when finished. For this reason, for each task we provided pre-recorded videos of interaction through marker-based tangibles and pre-configured the base source code for the tasks with the marker detection library to use these videos so that participants could focus on the solution and not on creating and manipulating the marker tangibles. As an example of the tasks, for the Shake Detector component the tasks were:

Task 1: Use the Shake Detector component to detect the marker/box shaking front/back and turn the element with the sphere into green.

Task 2: Detect the marker/box shaking and: move the sphere 1 m to the right each time the box is shaken horizontally (left/right); move the sphere 1 meters up each time the box is shaken vertically (up/down).

After solving the tasks, we asked participants to answer a questionnaire with demographic questions (age, country, work area, programming experience, and specific programming experience with A-Frame), and questions adapted from [7] to evaluate our library in terms of understandability, learnability, abstraction, and reusability (Fig. 6).

	Question	-2	-1	0	1	2
Understandability	1. Do you find that the API types map to the domain concepts in the way you expected?	0	0	0	1	4
	2. Do you feel you had to keep track of information not represented by the API to solve the tasks?	1	0	1	1	2
	3. Does the code required to solve the tasks match your expectations?	0	0	1	2	2
Learnability	4. Once you performed the first two tasks, was it easier to perform the remaining tasks?	0	0	0	0	5
	5. Do you feel you had to learn many classes and dependencies to solve the tasks?	0	0	0	3	2
Anstraction	6. Do you find the abstraction level on the interactions programed appropriate to the tasks?	0	0	1	1	3
	7. Did you need to adapt the API (like overriding default behaviors in Javascript code) to meet your needs?	0	0	0	1	4
	8. Do you feel you had to understand the underlying implementation of the components to be able to use the API?	0	1	1	1	2
Reusability	9. Does the amount of code required for each task seem about right, too much, or too little for you?	0	0	0	3	2
	10. How easy was it to evaluate your own progress (intermediate results) while solving the tasks?	0	0	1	3	1
	11. Do you feel you had to choose one way (out of many) to solve a task in the scenario?	0	0	2	0	3
	12. Do you feel you would have to change much in your code to change the interaction behaviour?	0	0	1	1	3

Fig. 6. Results from the API usability questionnaire. The results from the original 5-point Likert scale have been transformed to [−2, 2] and adjusted so that positive values are always better.

4.1 Preliminary Results and Discussion

Five participants have completed the API usability test. Four stated to have between 5–10 years of programming experience, while one stated having between 1–5 years of experience. Four had previous experience with A-Frame, although only two had previously coded an A-Frame JavaScript component.

Figure 6 presents the results from the usability questionnaire, with the answers normalized so that higher values are better, regardless of how the question was worded. In general, these preliminary results show a positive evaluation. Some items need further analysis since they do not seem to have a clear general answer (e.g., item 2 and 8, which had at least one negative answer). The learnability dimension seems to have had the best results, although this is perhaps not surprising as the library is not currently very extensive and so a few examples should be enough to get the overall gist for how it works. These answers need to be analyzed together with the source code submitted by the participants and their additional comments. As a complement to this remote usability test, we are also considering performing in-person tests to be able to better observe and understand the difficulties faced by programmers of our library.

5 Conclusion and Future Work

The objectives of this project are to develop a tool that allows developers of VR experiences to incorporate marker-based tangible interaction more easily in their projects. We have developed a library that incorporates five components, so far. These components are inspired by previous work that used marker-based tangibles.

At this moment, the project is in a testing phase, with task-based usability tests being conducted. Although preliminary results are satisfactory, the data needs further analysis for us to be able to determine how to improve the proposed library.

References

1. Hinckley, K., Pausch, R., Goble, J.C., Kassell, N.F.: Passive real-world interface props for neurosurgical visualization. In: Proceedings of the SIGCHI conference on Human factors in computing systemspp, pp. 452–458 (1994). https://doi.org/10.1145/191666.191821
2. Cardoso, J.C.S., Ribeiro, J.M.: Tangible VR book: exploring the design space of marker-based tangible interfaces for virtual reality. Appl. Sci. 11(4), 1367 (2021). https://doi.org/10.3390/app11041367
3. Dias, J.M.S., Barata, N., Santos, P., Correia, A., Nande, P., Bastos, R.: In your hand computing: Tangible interfaces for mixed reality. In: ART 2003 - IEEE International Augmented Reality Toolkit Workshop, pp. 29–31 (2003). https://doi.org/10.1109/ART.2003.1320422
4. Lee, G.A., Billinghurst, M., Kim, G.J.: Occlusion based interaction methods for tangible augmented reality environments. In: Proceedings VRCAI 2004 - ACM SIGGRAPH International Conference on Virtual Reality Continuum and its Applications in Industry, pp. 419–426 (2004). https://doi.org/10.1145/1044588.1044680
5. Moussette, C.: Tangible interaction toolkits for designers. Scand. Student Interact. Des. Conf., pp. 2–5, 2007, [Online]. https://www.netlearning2002.org/tek/sider07.nsf/(WebFiles)/FE9AD2C7730323FAC12572A900576009/$FILE/SPA_033.pdf
6. Rauf, I., Troubitsyna, E., Porres, I.: A systematic mapping study of API usability evaluation methods. Comput. Sci. Rev. 33, 49–68 (2019). https://doi.org/10.1016/j.cosrev.2019.05.001
7. Piccioni, M., Furia, C.A., Meyer, B.: An empirical study of API usability. In 2013 ACM / IEEE International Symposium on Empirical Software Engineering and Measurement, pp. 5–14. IEEE (2013). https://doi.org/10.1109/ESEM.2013.14

Sketch Recognition for Interactive Game Experiences Using Neural Networks

Elif Hilal Korkut⬤ and Elif Surer(✉)⬤

Department of Modeling and Simulation, Graduate School of Informatics,
Middle East Technical University, 06800 Ankara, Turkey
{elif.korkut,elifs}@metu.edu.tr

Abstract. Human freehand sketches can provide various scenarios to the interfaces with their intuitive, illustrative, and abstract nature. Although freehand sketches have been powerful tools for communication and have been studied in different contexts, their capacity to create compelling interactions in games is still under-explored. In this study, we present a new game based on sketch recognition. Specifically, we train various neural networks (Recurrent Neural Networks and Convolutional Neural Networks) and use different classification algorithms (Support Vector Machines and k-Nearest Neighbors) on sketches to create an interactive game interface where the player can contribute to the game by drawing. To measure usability, technology acceptance, immersion, and playfulness aspects, 18 participants played the game and answered the questionnaires composed of four different scales. Technical results and user tests demonstrate the capability and potential of sketch integration as a communication tool to construct an effective and responsive visual medium for novel interactive game experiences.

Keywords: Sketch recognition · Neural networks · Deep learning · Interactive interfaces · Game experiences

1 Introduction

As an abstract representation of human expression, sketches have been used in various fields, from art to engineering, throughout history. A sketch can convey information or high-level ideas with minimum detail. Due to success in deep learning techniques within the Human-Computer Interaction (HCI) community, sketching has become an emerging research topic. Although hand-drawn sketches show promising results, especially for educational purposes, their potential for games is waiting for exploration.

Human freehand sketches have been studied in various domains. For example, a comparative study conducted by Melanie et al. [1] showed that Recurrent

Electronic supplementary material The online version of this chapter (https://doi.org/10.1007/978-3-030-89394-1_31) contains supplementary material, which is available to authorized users.

J. Baalsrud Hauge et al. (Eds.): ICEC 2021, LNCS 13056, pp. 393–401, 2021.
https://doi.org/10.1007/978-3-030-89394-1_31

Neural Networks (RNNs) performed better than CNNs. Sketch-based interaction is an old concept for games that involve drawing, such as Pictionary and Hangman. Later, sketch-based interaction has also been explored by digital games. To encourage and motivate people, ZenSketch [12] was developed to improve freehand sketching linework, which translated features of sketches into game mechanics.

This study proposes new game mechanics powered by neural networks to create a responsive, generative, and interactive experience. Different types of neural networks are trained on selected classes of the Quick Draw dataset [6] and deployed into the Unity 3D game engine. A 3D maze game is generated, which uses sketched objects drawn by the player in the game world. Furthermore, we demonstrate the capability of sketch recognition in the field of HCI. To measure usability, technology acceptance, immersion, and playfulness aspects, 18 participants played the game and answered the questionnaires on system usability, gamer profile, technology acceptance, and gameful experiences. Our technical contribution lies in testing and creating various models and methods to enable seamless interaction while creating a novel and responsive game experience. This study aims to facilitate game ideas that create a visual dialogue between the game, game mechanics, and players where players can actively develop the narrative itself by sketching.

2   Methods

2.1   Game Design

A 3D maze game, Sketchscape, is implemented using the Unity game engine to test and validate the proposed interaction method. The game starts in a room and gives hints to the player to solve the puzzles and overcome challenges to reach the exit. There are three types of object groups; non-interacting objects, duty objects, and spawned objects. Non-interacting objects (key, eyeglasses, compass) directly affect the game world without appearing in the world or appear only to guide players without physical interaction. Duty objects (boat, bridge, air balloon) are only instantiated in certain positions when they are drawn and submitted. For the spawned objects, classes were defined as the circle, triangle, square, and due to their primitiveness, they provide easy and fast interaction. Spawned objects (cube, triangular prism, sphere) are instantiated in front of the player whenever they are drawn. Players can use spawned objects to destroy enemies, pass through the water, or use them as a ramp. The primary aim of those objects is to give the player freedom to act spontaneously. Throughout the game, there are hints for each object. To disentangle the current situation, the player needs to draw the correct object. For example, if the player needs to open a locked door and the sketch of a key is submitted, the door will open automatically (Fig. 1). User interactions should be intuitive and give necessary feedback to the player. Therefore, we avoided complicated user interactions and used standard character controls while creating a simple interface that players can draw with the cursor and get feedback from the game as soon as they submit their sketch. A cursor-controlled drawing feature is added, and the canvas is arranged according to the size of the sketches. The interface includes two canvas options, full-screen mode and side panel. The full-screen drawing panel opens via the right mouse button, and when the player hits submit button, it is closed automatically. Hints are given to the player in descriptive text format.

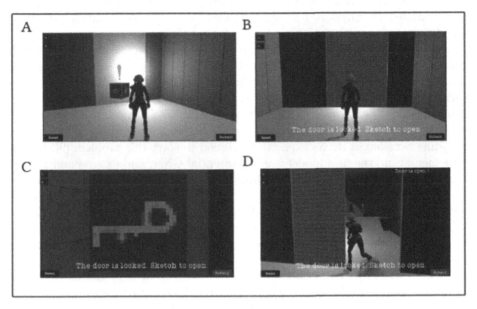

Fig. 1. Example Gameplay A. In a room with a hint B. Taking the hint, and text appears on the screen. C. Drawing a key on canvas. D. The door opens.

2.2   Data Exploration

Quick Draw dataset [6], consisting of 345 different classes with over 50 million sketches, includes more than 100000 items for each class. It includes positional information of points, temporal order, and grouping of points as strokes. For this project, only nine selected classes were used while training the models. To prevent overfitting, geometric data augmentation methods such as sampling, mirroring, rotating, and shifting were applied to the original dataset. To test the models, 100000 items per class were chosen, and the data were split into three different folds: 70% for training, 15% for validation, and 15% for testing. An object can be drawn in many ways, which causes divergent sketches for the same object category. We applied t-SNE on selected classes to visualizing high-dimensional data in a two-dimensional map. For further similarity search, the k-Nearest Neighbors (kNN) algorithm is utilized.

2.3   Algorithms and Networks

The study includes two main networks, RNN and CNN, and other classification algorithms and networks to gain insights into the data and evaluate methods. The Random Forest [3] algorithm works by creating many decision trees randomly and use them as predictors or classifiers. By combining individual tree votes, it makes the ultimate decision that provides resistance to overfitting. We also evaluated the Support Vector Machines (SVM) [2], which divides the data into different classes by creating a line or hyper-plane.

The first neural network tested is a Multi-Layer Perceptron (MLP) which consists of two hidden layers with sizes of 512 and 256, and the learning rate as 0.001. Also, a Rectifier Linear Unit Activation (ReLU) function and a Cross-Entropy loss function have been used. Standard RNNs have problems with long-term dependencies. Therefore, different versions of RNNs have been developed to solve the vanishing gradient problem. The Long Short Term Memory (LSTM) is a modified version of RNNs explicitly designed to solve this problem [9]. In this implementation, the first model was a sequential CNN, and as a second model, bidirectional LSTM was used. In addition to those networks, initial accuracy comparison tests on the dataset were conducted using ResNet, a deep residual network proposed by He et al. [7] and standard module of MobileNet in Keras. According to the experiments conducted with the selected group of objects, the speed requirements of real-time response and adaptability to the game engine demand simpler network architectures.

The structure of the networks and their parameters were chosen based on the results that provided fast predictions through the game. In the LSTM network design, a unit with two layers was used for the nonlinear mapping, and a fully connected layer followed by a sigmoid function for the nonlinear function that projects the hidden states to the outputs was used. The final CNN network consists of three convolutional layers, each followed by a max-pooling layer, complemented by a flatten layer and two dense layers. All convolutional layers employ a ReLU activation function, whereas the first dense layer uses the tanh function and the second dense layer uses the softmax function. Adaptive Moments (ADAM) was used as an optimizer, and the libraries Keras and TensorFlow were used.

2.4   Game Implementation

The Barracuda package [10], a lightweight cross-platform neural network inference library for Unity that can run neural networks, was used to deploy the trained model into Unity. Selected CNN model on selected classes of Quick Draw dataset is converted to ONNX format and uploaded to Unity. Models of the objects are loaded to the game engine as assets, and prefabs are called when the player's sketches are drawn and submitted. The similarity percentages of all classes are listed as an array, and the code checks the highest accuracy result. As soon as the player starts to draw, received strokes from the canvas are analyzed and sent to the model to recognize the player's sketch. When the player hits the submit button, if the drawing has a similarity result above the identified percentage, necessary operations are executed according to the object type. If the similarity is below that percentage, a warning is given. After the tests, the threshold for similarity results was identified as 75%.

2.5 User-Experience Tests

The crucial factor for the implementation evaluation of sketching as a game mechanic is the involvement of potential users. Therefore, a user test was conducted with 18 participants (nine male and nine female). Recruited respondents were between the ages of 19–29, with a mean age of 22.52 years (SD = 4.13). Subjects have been notified and properly instructed about their voluntary participation and the experiment procedure. Ethical Approval of Research was granted by the Middle East Technical University Human Subjects Ethics Committee in May 2021. The questionnaires were adapted from the literature. Participants were first asked to evaluate sketching as an interaction medium for games on a 5-point Likert scale. After playing the game using a computer, four questionnaires, Gamer Profile [5], System Usability Scale (SUS) [4], Technology Acceptance Model (TAM) [11], and GAMEFULQUEST [8], were collected. TAM questionnaire covered descriptive questions on a 10-point scale to determine the level of technology acceptance. SUS is a psychometric tool that takes into consideration three usability criteria: effectiveness, efficiency, and satisfaction. There are ten questions in the SUS that score on a 5-point Likert scale, where odd-numbered questions consist of positive statements, whereas even-numbered ones include negative statements. GAMEFULQUEST [8] is initially proposed for gamification context as a guideline to evaluate gameful experiences. To evaluate the multidimensional nature of game experiences and dimensions, GAMEFULQUEST is used. Participants played the game for 15 min, and the total process took 30 min for each participant.

3 Results and Discussion

3.1 Technical Results

To obtain higher accuracy and better performance, we designed different networks as explained above and tested various algorithms. They were tested for their performances by changing the structure and parameters to determine the most suitable method for real-time interaction. Based on the performance on a validation set, the training processes were terminated when the performance stops improving (Table 1) to avoid over-training and overfitting. While adding 0.1 as the dropout value improved the accuracy of CNN, using 0.3 as the dropout value improved the results of the LSTM model (Table 2). The regularization effect of dropout reduced the overfitting; consequently, dropout layers were added. The learning rate was defined as 0.01 for CNN and 0.0001 for the LSTM (Table 3).

Table 1. Epoch and accuracy

Epoch	CNN	LSTM
5	90.42%	89.51%
10	94.62%	91.65%
15	95.50%	92.52%
20	96.10%	92.50%
25	**96.32%**	92.89%
30	96.02%	**92.93%**
50	96.25%	92.65%

Table 2. Dropout and accuracy

Dropout	CNN	LSTM
–	95.62%	91.80%
0.1	**96.32%**	92.68%
0.15	95.52%	92.10%
0.2	96.00%	92.40%
0.3	94.00%	**92.93%**
0.4	96.32%	90.25%
0.5	96.32%	88.90%

Table 3. Learning rate and accuracy

Learning rate	CNN	LSTM
0.000075	40.32%	88.00%
0.0001	80.32%	**92.93%**
0.001	86.40%	30.26%
0.005	90.65%	25.00%
0.0075	93.32%	17.50%
0.01	**96.32%**	14.13%
0.05	50.32%	9.45%
0.1	35.20%	8.00%

Table 4. Statistical analysis of models

	CNN	ResNet	LSTM
Accuracy	96.32%	93.00%	92.93%
Recall	0.91	0.92	0.91
Precision	0.90	0.92	0.92
F1 score	0.90	0.92	0.91
Reaction time	0.70 (s)	1.9 (s)	0.97 (s)

A timer was added to the game engine to calculate the response time, which stops when the model unfolds the final accuracy. To determine the model used for the game, besides the accuracy and timing aspects, precision, recall, and F1 score through all tracks in the test data were calculated to evaluate the effectiveness of each model (Table 4). We fed the same nine classes of sketches to the sketch classifiers for quantitative evaluation. Each network was trained for a maximum of 50 epochs. The results are summarized in Table 5. The performances of the two architectures, ResNet and MobileNet, which have already reached state-of-the-art levels for image classification, still came short compared to CNN.

Table 5. Accuracy results

Network/Algorithm	LSTM	CNN	SVM	kNN	RF	MLP	MobileNet	ResNet
Accuracy	92.93%	96.32%	87.21%	90.57%	89.17%	90.24%	94.10%	93.00%

After those processes, the final CNN model with 96.32% recognition accuracy, 0.7 s reaction time, and 0.91 F1 scores could immediately respond to the player without a noticeable delay. Due to the performance of LSTM in previous studies [1], we expected higher accuracy results from LSTM. The reason behind these results can be random properties stemming from the temporal information. LSTM learns the temporal evolution of the data by preserving sequential information. Therefore, selected classes might have affected the results due to the nature of the sketches. Also, according to [1], an increase in the number of samples resulted in the success of the LSTM. Sharing the same core idea that works in LSTM units, ResNet showed similar performance accuracy for a small dataset. Therefore, if a larger dataset is required, LSTM or ResNet can be preferable due to their previous successes on large datasets.

3.2   User-Test Results

The user-test results of the pre-test (M = 2.72, SD = 1.28) and post-test (M = 4.5, SD = 0.6) indicate substantial increase. According to two-tailed t-test, p-value is less than 0.0001 (t(18) = 7.5179), demonstrating an extremely statistically significant outcome. The results show that game Sketchscape significantly changes participants' ideas on sketching in a game. The majority of the participants prefer to use full-screen canvas, indicating that it felt more natural (Side Panel: 33.3%, Full Screen: 67.7%). Cronbach's Alpha value was calculated as 0.81, which indicates a high-reliability level. Figure 2 indicates the SUS score of the game is 82.1, which states "good" usability. Results of the GAMEFULQUEST are presented in Fig. 3. Participants indicated they felt accomplishment when they solved the problems or found new ways to use spawned objects. Most of the participants were willing to improve their methods. The majority of the participants reported that the game creates internal competitiveness and requires creativity.

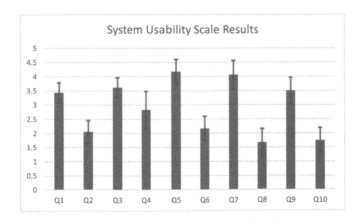

Fig. 2. System usability scale results.

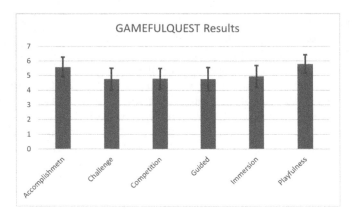

Fig. 3. GAMEFULQUEST results.

4   Conclusion and Future Work

This study presents a novel interaction method for interactive gameplay that uses sketch recognition to enable the players to interact with the narrative by drawing objects. A prototype maze game is developed to demonstrate the implementation of the model and create responsive and interactive game experiences. In the experiments, the proposed game mechanics and the deep learning model reveal promising results. The user study results and participants' preferences direct us to increase the classes and enrich the interaction modes. As future work, we intend to combine this study with sketch-based 3D model retrieval methods. This method will aim to find the most relevant visual model, and due to the different features of the models belonging to the same object, players will create new directions in the narrative.

References

1. Andersson, M., Maja, A., Hedar, S.: Sketch classification with neural networks: a comparative study of CNN and RNN on the quick, draw! Data set (2018)
2. Awad, M., Khanna, R.: Support vector machines for classification. In: Efficient Learning Machines, pp. 39–66. Springer, Cham (2015). https://doi.org/10.1007/978-1-4302-5990-9_3
3. Breiman, L.: Random forests. Mach. Learn. **45**(1), 5–32 (2001)
4. Brooke, J.: SUS: a 'quick and dirty' usability. Usability Eval. Ind. **189**, 4–7 (1996)
5. Foundry, Q.: Gamer motivation model (2016). https://apps.quanticfoundry.com/surveys/start/gamerprofile/
6. Google: Quick, draw, November 2016. https://quickdraw.withgoogle.com/
7. He, K., Zhang, X., Ren, S., Sun, J.: Deep residual learning for image recognition. In: Proceedings of the IEEE Conference on Computer Vision and Pattern Recognition, pp. 770–778 (2016)

8. Högberg, J., Hamari, J., Wästlund, E.: Gameful experience questionnaire (GAME-FULQUEST): an instrument for measuring the perceived gamefulness of system use. User Model. User-Adap. Inter. **29**(3), 619–660 (2019). https://doi.org/10.1007/s11257-019-09223-w
9. Sherstinsky, A.: Fundamentals of recurrent neural network (RNN) and long short-term memory (LSTM) network. Physica D **404**, 132306 (2020)
10. Unity: Unity Barracuda, November 2019. https://docs.unity3d.com/Packages/com.unity.barracuda@0.3/manual/index.html
11. Venkatesh, V., Davis, F.: A model of the antecedents of perceived ease of use: development and test. Decis. Sci. **27**, 451–481 (2007). https://doi.org/10.1111/j.1540-5915.1996.tb00860.x
12. Williford, B., Runyon, M., Malla, A., Li, W., Linsey, J., Hammond, T.: ZenSketch: a sketch-based game for improving line work, pp. 591–598, October 2017. https://doi.org/10.1145/3130859.3130861

Basic Research on How to Apply Foundation Makeup Evenly on Your Own Face

Miho Kajita(✉) and Satoshi Nakamura

Meiji University, 4-21-1 Nakano, Nakano-ku, Tokyo, Japan

Abstract. Makeup is an entertainment that allows people to present themselves in a way that is close to their ideal. People apply foundation makeup evenly to cover skin imperfections, but it is not easy to distinguish between areas where foundation is applied or not. Therefore, problems like applying too much foundation or forgetting to apply foundation on some areas are likely to occur. Our project aims to realize a makeup support system that can visualize the state of foundation application in real-time to eliminate uneven application. As an initial step, we conducted a large-scale crowdsourcing survey on makeup, precisely foundation, and investigated a method that uses machine learning to classify between images of skin with foundation applied and of bare skin. As a result, we found that we could distinguish between both with high accuracy of 82.3%.

Keywords: Foundation · Makeup · Machine learning

1 Introduction

The face is a part of the body that quickly displays personal characteristics such as age and gender as well as emotions [1]. Therefore, people apply makeup to bring their face's impression gives closer to their ideal [2]. According to an Internet survey conducted by POLA in 2019 [3], about 80% of women aged 15–64 wear makeup. In addition, the demand for cosmetics has been increasing not only among women but also among men. Then, the number of brands selling cosmetics for men has been growing. On the other hand, make-up videos of people pretending to be celebrities or characters have become popular on SNS, and make-up is enjoyed as a form of entertainment.

One of the difficulties of wearing makeup is to apply foundation makeup evenly. Since it is recommended to choose a foundation close to one's skin tone, foundation easily blends in with one's bare skin, so it isn't easy to distinguish between areas where foundation is applied and areas where it is not. As a result, people tend to apply too much foundation or to forget to apply only a particular area. If foundation is not appropriately applied, people cannot hide blemishes, pores, and other skin problems. In addition, many foundations contain sunscreen ingredients, and uneven application may cause some parts of the skin to become sunburned. However, the most important reason why it is necessary to apply the appropriate amount of foundation is because makeup tends to fall off from areas where foundation has been applied repeatedly.

© IFIP International Federation for Information Processing 2021
Published by Springer Nature Switzerland AG 2021
J. Baalsrud Hauge et al. (Eds.): ICEC 2021, LNCS 13056, pp. 402–410, 2021.
https://doi.org/10.1007/978-3-030-89394-1_32

To solve those problems, we came up with a system that indicates where and how much foundation has been applied and correct uneven application easily and in real-time. Nishino et al. [4], who focused on the fact that foundation skin absorbs light more efficiently than bare skin [5], developed a measurement system for quantifying and distributing the amount of foundation by using an optical filter that emphasizes the difference in the wavelength characteristics of reflection between bare skin and foundation skin. However, this system requires an optical filter that spectral transmission characteristics have been optimized through experiments, making it difficult for general users.

Our goal is to realize a system that enables users to check for unevenness in applied foundation in real-time easily, not only at home but also when they are away from home. An image of the system is shown in Fig. 1. In this study, as an initial step, we investigated a method for classifying images of the skin with foundation applied (hereafter referred to as "foundation skin") and bare skin captured by a smartphone camera using machine learning with color features as feature values. In addition, we conducted a questionnaire survey on makeup and foundation to clarify the problems in makeup and foundation.

Fig. 1. Our system

2   Survey on Makeup and Foundation

In this research, we first conducted a questionnaire survey of 1,000 women who have worn makeup through Yahoo! Crowdsourcing [6] (conducted from September 4 to 5, 2020). Then, we excluded 16 responses from 1,000 because they were unreliable, such as ignoring the instructions. The following sections describe the results of the analysis of the 984 valid responses.

Figure 2 shows the results of makeup frequency before/amid the COVID-19. From these results, about 90% of respondents wore makeup more than 2 or 3 times a week before the COVID-19. Similarly, 75% of respondents wore makeup at least two or three times a week amid the COVID-19 pandemic, when the number of makeup wearers was thought to have decreased due to the effects of the voluntary curfew.

Figure 3 shows the responses about the difficulty with makeup. From this result, 24.5% of the respondents answered that they felt that it is "quite difficult" to apply makeup, and 48.9% responded that they felt "a little difficulty."

In addition, more than half of the respondents mentioned that the process of applying foundation was the most time-consuming part of base makeup (see Fig. 4). Followed by 33.5% of respondents said they spend more time on primer, 9.8% on concealer, and almost none on highlighting or shading.

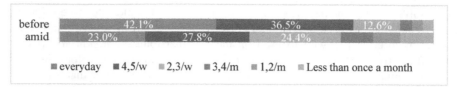

Fig. 2. Makeup frequency before/amid the COVID-19 pandemic

Fig. 3. Difficulty with makeup

Fig. 4. Processes that take the most time for base makeup

Figure 5 also shows that people tend to purchase foundations with high "coverage of blemishes, pores, and other skin difficulties." In addition, when buying foundations, many people (50.6% and 40.4%, respectively) place importance on "durability" and "ease" of use. These results suggest that many people want to hide their concerns quickly when using base makeup.

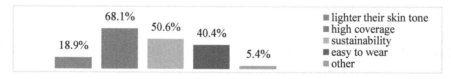

Fig. 5. What to look for when buying foundation

Figure 6 shows the result of how to learn base makeup. From this result, about 80% of the responders learn how to wear base makeup by themselves. 37.2% of those who answered that they learn base makeup themselves have experiences difficulties in applying foundation, such as "uneven color and uneven application" and "applying too much foundation and making it thick." This result suggests that these difficulties need to be resolved to make base makeup easier to use.

So, a system for applying foundation evenly, which is the objective of this research, will be helpful for users who have the above problems because it enables them to hide blemishes and pores quickly, easily, and beautifully.

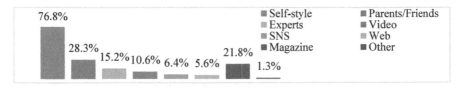

Fig. 6. How they learned base makeup

3   Constructing the Data Set

This study aims to develop a makeup support system that can visualize the application of foundation in real-time to make it easier to check where and how much foundation has been applied and to correct uneven application. This system is intended to be easy for users to use with their smartphones and other devices. We first examined whether it is possible to estimate foundation skin and bare skin mechanically. This section described the construction of datasets used for discriminating the state of foundation applied to the skin in detail.

There are various types of foundations, and users use the appropriate one depending on the texture and finish of the skin they want to achieve. Since the type of foundation drastically affects the appearance of the foundation skin, in this construction, we prepared 12 types of foundation (Table 1), with two types of finish, glowing or matte, for three types of foundation: powder, liquid, and cream. Then, we photographed skin applying foundations. Glowing skin is characterized by a moisturized and shiny appearance of bare skin, while matte skin is smooth and covers imperfect skin. In this construction, it wasn't easy to prepare the appropriate foundation for each participant's skin tone, so the color was selected on the basis of the author's skin tone. According to an oral questionnaire used in the construction, no participant felt uncomfortable with the difference in color between the foundation and their bare skin when the 12 types of foundation were applied.

Here, we collected bare skin and foundation skin images to construct the dataset. Sixteen undergraduate and graduate students (20–26 years old) (5 males and 11 females) participated. We asked them to apply four different types of foundation per day for a total of three days. We used Android Xperia XZ3 (SONY) for the photography. The camera has approximately 19.2 megapixels, an f/1.9 aperture, and an ISO sensitivity of up to 12,800.

In the dataset construction, we asked the participants to wash their faces to remove sebum and makeup before taking photos. Then, we photographed their bare skin after wiping off all moisture. We took five patterns of photographs of the forehead and cheeks: frontal, right oblique, left oblique, with the chin in front of the camera, and with the chin pulled back (see Fig. 7). The distance between the camera and the participant was about 15 cm, and the camera was illuminated with an LED light. The camera was focused on the center of the area used for photographing.

Next, we photographed the foundation skin. We asked participants to apply a primer to their forehead (from the hairline to the top of the eyebrows) and their cheeks (from the side of the nose to the start of the ear). Then, we asked them to apply foundation using a sponge puff. Afterward, we took pictures from the same angle as when photographing

Table 1. List of foundations used

Type	Skin type	ID	Product name
liquid	Glowing	L1	Shu Uemura [unlimited glow fluid 574]
		L2	Amplitude [long lasting liquid foundation 20]
	Matte	L3	Estee Lauder [Double Wear Stay-in-Place Makeup 12]
		L4	Lancome [Teint Idole Ultra Wear Liquid BO-01]
powder	Glowing	P1	ONLY MINERALS [Foundation 5 light ocher]
		P2	Chanel [Le Blanc Whitening Compact Foundation B10]
	Matte	P3	Maquillage [Dramatic Powdery UV ocher10]
		P4	Dior [Dior Skin Forever Compact Extreme Control 020]
cream	Glowing	C1	RMK [Creamy Foundation EX #101]
		C2	SUQQU [The Crème Foundation 110]
	Matte	C3	Alblanc [Moist White Creme Foundation Ocher 03]
		C4	Laura Mercier [Silk Creme Oil Free Photo Edition Foundation 03]

Fig. 7. Five patterns: top row left to right, frontal, right oblique, left oblique, bottom row from left to right, with the chin in front of the camera and with the chin pulled back.

bare skin. Again, we instructed the participants to apply foundation carefully to avoid unevenness.

Then, we collected 10 images of the bare skin without foundation (2 areas × 5 directions) and 120 images of the face with foundation applied on the forehead and cheeks (12 types of foundation × 2 areas × 5 directions) for each participant. Thus, a total of 2,080 images were collected. From these images, one image was cut into 500px squares to show only the skin. The image was further divided into 25 100px squares to create datasets consisting of 4,000 images of bare skin (10 images × 25 segments × 16 persons) and 4,000 images of foundation skin (10 images × 25 segments × 16 persons) in each foundation.

Thus, we created datasets consisting of 4,000 bare skin images and 48,000 foundation skin images.

4 Discrimination of Bare Skin and Foundation Skin by Machine Learning

From the images collected in Sect. 3, we generated features to be used for training.

Skin color is determined by the melanin and hemoglobin content in the blood in the capillaries [7]. Depending on the balance of these two factors, the skin becomes reddish or yellowish. Since foundation suppresses such redness and yellowing of the skin [8], it is expected that the color of skin to which foundation is applied will be less reddish and yellowish than that of bare skin. Therefore, we thought it would be possible to discriminate between bare and foundation skin by setting up features representing the color tendency of the images.

We classified foundation colors along two axes: "hue," which indicates reddish or yellowish, and "lightness," which shows the range of lightness or darkness [9]. In addition, we divided foundations into two types of finish textures: "glowing," which is saturated, clear, and has good coloration, and "matte," which is less saturated and has a slightly dull coloration (see Fig. 8). For these reasons, we believe that it was appropriate to use the HSV color space instead of the RGB one. Therefore, after converting the image from RGB to HSV, we obtained and calculated the mean and standard deviation of hue, saturation, and lightness, which generated a $2 \times 3 = 6$-dimensional feature value.

Fig. 8. Examples of skin applying foundations whose types are glowing (left) and matte (right).

We considered three ways of dividing the data for training (see Table 2). First, the dataset was trained as is (partitioning method 1). Second, we divided the dataset into two types according to whether the image was of the cheek or the forehead. Third, we trained a dataset consisting of 2,000 bare skin images and 2,000 foundation skin images (partitioning method 2). Finally, we prepared a dataset composed of 2,000 images of bare skin and 2,000 images of foundation skin for each of the 16 participants (partitioning method 3). In the following subsection, we describe the results of training and classification for each of the three training data sets.

We used the random forest as the learning algorithm for the binary classification of foundation skin and bare skin by scikit-learn. We used 75% of the datasets as training

Table 2. Datasets

Partitioning method	Division number	Datasets size
Method 1	1	(4,000 bare skin images and 4,000 foundation skin images) × 12 types of foundation
Method 2	2	(2,000 bare skin images and 2,000 foundation skin images) × 12 types of foundation
Method 3	16	(250 bare skin images and 250 foundation skin images) × 12 types of foundation

data and 25% as test data, with positive values for foundation skin and negative values for bare skin.

Table 3 shows the results of partitioning methods 1 and 2, showing that they could discriminate between foundation skin and bare skin with an average accuracy of 82.3%. As a result of learning for each region, the average correct-answer rate was 89.6% for the forehead and 81.0% for the cheeks.

As described above, the features were the mean and standard deviation of hue, saturation, and lightness. To investigate the color tendency of the images that could be discriminated, we trained and classified the images using only the mean and standard

Table 3. Results

		Partitioning method 1		Partitioning method 2			
		Accuracy rate	F-Score	Accuracy rate		F-Score	
				Forehead	Cheek	Forehead	Cheek
Glowing	L1	81.9%	0.822	85.9%	83.5%	0.861	0.837
	L2	77.6%	0.777	85.5%	76.4%	0.858	0.772
Matte	L3	78.4%	0.785	87.5%	76.3%	0.875	0.766
	L4	81.3%	0.814	87.7%	78.5%	0.881	0.787
Glowing	P1	85.1%	0.853	93.6%	85.0%	0.938	0.852
	P2	83.4%	0.837	91.3%	83.5%	0.915	0.829
Matte	P3	82.0%	0.820	89.7%	79.5%	0.896	0.799
	P4	84.0%	0.838	91.7%	83.0%	0.918	0.829
Glowing	C1	82.4%	0.822	89.1%	80.2%	0.891	0.801
	C2	83.6%	0.836	91.3%	82.0%	0.912	0.824
Matte	C3	83.3%	0.831	89.5%	82.2%	0.893	0.822
	C4	84.0%	0.838	92.1%	81.7%	0.920	0.818
Average		82.3%	0.823	89.6%	81.0%	0.897	0.811

deviation of the hue, saturation, and lightness feature values for partitioning methods 1 and 2. The results showed almost no difference in the average percentage of correct answers due to changes in the feature values. However, when we compared each type of foundation, the powder foundation had the best accuracy with the mean and standard deviation of hue and saturation were used as features. The cream foundation had the best accuracy when the mean and standard deviation of lightness as features.

To examine individual differences, we divided the dataset into 16 equal parts for each participant (partitioning method 3) and trained. As a result, the average percentage of correct answers for each individual exceeded the average rate of 82.3% for all 16 participants for partitioning method 1 (see Table 3), with a mean of 92.4%.

5 Conclusion

In this paper, we first surveyed makeup. It showed that many people want to hide their concerns quickly when using base makeup. However, they have difficulty applying foundation evenly and have little means of solving the problem because most of them learn how to wear base makeup by themselves.

We also investigated whether it is possible to mechanically classify images of foundation-applied skin and images of bare skin. We asked 16 participants for foundation application, and created the data set. In addition, the mean and standard deviation of hue, saturation, and lightness were used as features to learn from the features of bare skin and foundation. The results showed that the system could discriminate between images of both skin types with a high rate of correct answers. In addition, images of the forehead, which has more wrinkles and pores than the cheek, could be used to discriminate the state of foundation application with a higher accuracy rate.

There are two types of uneven foundation. One is when foundation is not applied to a part of the skin, i.e., where the skin is bare, or the applied foundation is mixed. The other is when foundation is not applied at a certain thickness, i.e., foundation is applied thickly or thinly. This paper showed that we could discriminate whether foundation is applied or not. In addition, this paper showed the possibility that we could also determine whether it is applied thickly or lightly by using the same feature. However, to classify the amount of foundation applied, we must set an appropriate threshold value, which we plan to study in the future.

In addition, we trained on 100 px square images. However, to detect unevenness, it is necessary to determine whether foundation is applied or not on smaller images. For this reason, we plan to create an image dataset with a smaller resolution for training and estimation.

This research aims to realize a makeup support system that can visualize the application of foundation in real-time. As a prospect, we plan to investigate whether the application state of foundation can be discriminated in the video in the same way.

References

1. Leslie, Z.: Reading Faces: Window To The Soul?. Westview Press, US (1997)

2. Graham, J.A., Jouhar, A.J.: The effects of cosmetics on person perception. Int. J. Cosmet. Sci. **3**(5), 199–210 (1981)
3. POLA research institute of beauty & culture, https://www.cosmetic-culture.po-holdings.co.jp/report/pdf/191212kitai.pdf. Accessed 10 Aug 2021
4. Nishino, K., Nakamura, M., Miyashita, K.: Development and application of quantitative/spatial measurement system of cosmetics foundation with functional spectral filter. J. Color Sci. Assoc. Jpn. **37**(3), 202–203 (2013)
5. Igarashi, T.: Optical properties of foundation. J. Jpn. Soc. Colour Mater. **85**(4), 156–163 (2012)
6. Yahoo! https://crowdsourcing.yahoo.co.jp/. Accessed 10 Aug 2020
7. Anderson, R.R., Parrish, J.A.: The optics of human skin. J. Investig. Dermatol. **77**(1), 13–19 (1981)
8. Igarashi, T.: Research and development of cosmetics that control the texture of the skin. Op. Soc. Jpn. **43**(7), 318–324 (2014)
9. Siseido, https://www.shiseido.co.jp/foundation100/answer/q07.html. Accessed 09 Dec 2020

Identifying the Impact of Game Music both Within and Beyond Gameplay

Kai Tuuri[1]([✉])(iD), Oskari Koskela[1](iD), Jukka Vahlo[1](iD), and Heli Tissari[2](iD)

[1] Department of Music, Art and Culture Studies, University of Jyväskylä,
P.O. Box 35, 40014 Jyväskylä, Finland
{krtuuri,osjokosk,jlvahlo}@jyu.fi
[2] Department of Languages, University of Helsinki,
P.O. Box 4, 00014 Helsinki, Finland
heli.tissari@helsinki.fi

Abstract. This paper presents an overview of and a brief critical reflection on game music's impact on players both within and beyond the context of gameplay. The analysis is based both on the current literature as well as on preliminary (work-in-progress) observations of our research project Game Music Everyday Memories. We consider how the functions and uses of game music potentially extend to people's everyday life, thus constituting a personally and culturally meaningful relationship with music that is not immediately connected to gameplay. On the other hand, we consider the ways game music and a person's attachment to the music are involved in gameplay motivation and potential game retention. As a conceptual thematization, four approaches for identifying the broader musical impact of games are suggested and discussed. To substantiate the discussion, we combine some preliminary observations from two different datasets gathered within the ongoing project: (D1) personal narratives of fond game music memories (N = 183), and (D2) survey-data on favourite game music (N = 785).

Keywords: Game music · Impact · Memories · Human-music interaction

1 Introduction

A game designer's task is to try to put together core gameplay loops and other game features that enable a desired type of game experience. It is well acknowledged that music has a significant role in this equation. Consequently, a person listening to game music is usually engaged in the specific interactional contexts of play. Therefore it makes sense that research on game music has mostly examined music and its meanings within and as a part of the game. Research in the field of ludomusicology has adopted traditional tools of musicology, treating music as a text and considering its function and meaning with respect to the narrative

This work is funded by Kone Foundation (grant number 201908388).

ⓒ IFIP International Federation for Information Processing 2021
Published by Springer Nature Switzerland AG 2021
J. Baalsrud Hauge et al. (Eds.): ICEC 2021, LNCS 13056, pp. 411–418, 2021.
https://doi.org/10.1007/978-3-030-89394-1_33

and mechanics of the game (see e.g., [10,23]). Besides the hermeneutic investigations, another line of research has taken an empirical approach and studied game music within a psychological framework, focusing on the effects and role of music in the gameplay experience (e.g., [12,19,25]). The existing body of research has acknowledged the crossmodal and interactive nature of game music [4]: In the course of the gameplay experience, music more or less becomes fused with different gameplay activities and the related physical or imagined environments. It thus potentially gets associated with certain indexes (e.g., events of the game) and functions (e.g., narration or mood management) within the game. The motivation of this paper, however, is to stretch our understanding of such game music's indexes and functions in a manner that extends well beyond the actual gameplay. Games in themselves inevitably become associated with mundane situations and events of life, yielding personal everyday meanings. Yet, so far, only very little research effort has been put into the impact of game music outside the gameplay functions.

Gasca's [6] PhD thesis was maybe the first study with the aim of showing that game music has "transcended the medium and is enjoyed by audiences beyond the game". According to the study, people value experiences of game music because of the memories they evoke. Many of such evoked memories were related to the gameworld, its events, feelings and aesthetics. But similarly to musically evoked memories in general [1], many of them included broader remembrances and associations of past times: nostalgic memories of family, friends, places and other autobiographically and socially significant experiences.

Although game music is composed for games, that is, specific activities performed with the game-medium, it is still largely an open question how game music differs from other types of music in terms of developing a personal attachment and meaningful relationships with it. So far practically no published studies exist that would have scrutinized whether game music's habitual connections to gameplay (i.e., the functional design within a game) would in some form extend into the more varying situational contexts outside the game (i.e., functions in everyday life). In other words, the question remains: what kind of role do games themselves and gameplay experiences have on the relationship a person develops with their music? This is one of the main motivations of our research project *Game Music Everyday Memories*, within which we are doing empirical research on how engagement with game music extends to people's everyday lives.

In order to promote future studies in the field, and to provide some work-in-progress observations on our ongoing research project, we will here conceptually formulate different ways to approach the phenomenon of constituting a personally and culturally meaningful relationship with game music both within and outside the gameplay. In the next section we will outline and describe four theory-based approaches. The first approach is built on the gameplay motivation perspective. The next two are inherent to music psychology and concern personal relationship with music and the use of music in everyday life. Finally, the fourth approach focuses on game music's impact on cultural conventions and habits. All approaches conform to Tia DeNora's [5] concept of human–music interaction as an all-embracing perspective that emphasises the action-oriented [13] and constructive [15] nature in the organization of both game and music related meanings. The perspective strongly correlates with Small's [21] term *musicking*, which frames music fundamentally as an activity and underlines the heterogeneity of activities through which music is meaningfully engaged with by people.

To back up the discussion in the following sections, we will reveal some preliminary observations from two currently unpublished datasets gathered within our ongoing project. Our intention here is not yet to present any comprehensive report, but rather, offer some glimpses of relevant information and general views on the basis of the ongoing analysis. The first dataset (D1) was collected in order to qualitatively investigate personal meanings of game music in everyday life. It consists of 183 spontaneous personal narratives of (self-selected) fond game music memories gathered through a public call for stories (elicited writing method, see [9]). The second dataset (D2) was collected in order to quantitatively study game music preferences. It contains survey responses from 785 participants about their favourite game music, the related gameplay situations and experiences, as well as ways of engaging with the music outside the game. Both data collections were conducted in Finland. It should be noted that the detailed analyses of both of the datasets are just currently underway and thus a subject of future publications. In the present paper, discussions either refer to simple descriptive statistical indicators, or preliminary typologies being built upon the analysis of written narratives of game music memories.

2 Approaches to Game Music's Impact

2.1 Music as a Motivator for Play

Although music and sounds are not typically implemented into the game mechanics directly (i.e., most games can be played muted), they are an important ingredient of the imaginative immersion of games. For instance, music adds to the feeling of "being there" and game sounds make the game environment feel more responsive and authentic [17]. They are both important for story-driven games and help the player to make sense of what is happening and is about to happen in the game. While game music and game sounds may be argued to have a mostly supporting function that "enhances", "enables", or "deepens" the game experience (i.e., they would be part of the "shell" of a game instead of its "core" in terms of gameplay dynamics, see [16]), in themselves, they may also provide an impactful motive for playing games in the first place. Hence, besides the assumed supporting role, we wanted to investigate whether music is also able to carry "core" meanings that players desire to live through and reminisce about. We asked in the D2 to what degree game music had influenced players' decision to play a game they had chosen to play. An average response was that this influence had been moderate. However, almost 40% of the respondents stated that game music had influenced their game choice quite much or very much. Later in the survey, more than 50% of the respondents stated that game music had been a reason for them to play the game again.

The attempt to understand play motivations has been a major vein of research in the overlap of game studies, media psychology, and human-computer interaction [24]. While the literature on player motives is growing rapidly, most models have not considered game music as a motive to engage with games or discussed how game music may be associated with overarching general play motives such as challenge, social interaction, or immersion. Our preliminary findings suggest, however, that game music and sounds might not just belong to the shell of the game experience, but that they might be something inseparable from its core. The data thus indicates that game music may have a significant impact both on the initial decision that players make when choosing a new game to be played, and on retention, that is, their continuous choice to keep on playing and coming back to the game.

2.2   Personal Attachment to Game Music

Both the gathering of elicited writings of fond game music memories (D1) and the survey about favourite game musics (D2) gained a respectable number of responses. The participants did not have any problems in naming their personal favourites. On the contrary, the willingness to share their fondly remembered experiences with game music implies that personal attachment to pieces of game music is not a marginal, but a more or less prevalent phenomenon. As Gasca's [6] study pointed out, and psychologists have previously documented [2], music is strongly interconnected with memories. It is certainly not far-fetched to argue that attachment to game music can be largely seen as a memory-related phenomenon, especially concerning memories that include biographical self-remembrance. Thus, a personal value of game music likely relates to music's ability to take a person back in time to meaningful moments and phases in life experienced with the music, and to the related feelings and sensations that accompany those memories [1]. Game music memories from D1 contained references, for example, to other people, certain places, activities and technologies, to autobiographical descriptions, as well as to some specific enjoyable moments with the music or the game itself. Moreover, the attachment to game music can also be examined through the language used in the written memories. The linguistic investigation revealed a prevalent use of metaphoric language, such as the use of a CONTAINER metaphor [14] in describing the memory. These linguistic depictions of a container referred, for example, to "my mind" or "heart" *in which* music-related experiences reside (or into which they come) – characterizing the intimate relationship with the music memory.

In many cases, informants indicated that their memories and the related imagery were appreciated, desirable, gratifying, or even inseparably belonging to their life. In terms of Huovinen and Tuuri's study on cherished music [7], such embraced memories of game music imply that the music-based memory is willingly and appreciatively being maintained, for example, through recurrent reminiscing. In D2 survey responses, reminiscing (i.e., "inner listening") interestingly appears to be the second most common activity the respondents do with the game music outside the game (the most common being regular listening).

2.3   Uses of Game Music in Everyday Life

In the D2 study, respondents were asked about their activities with their favourite game music outside the gameplay. Results quite clearly show that the majority of players (65%) have those kinds of musicking activities (e.g., listening, reminiscing, playing, singing), pointing out the relevance of the approach. When music's role is considered in people's everyday life, it is not only seen as an object of aesthetic appreciation, but as something that people do things with [5]. People use music in different everyday circumstances, for managing moods, for social bonding, and for self awareness [20]. Overall, music could be even taken as a resource for constituting our identity as the persons who we are [5]. From the personal narratives of D1 it is relatively easy to find examples of such usage of game music. In the following quotation from the data, a male participant summarises a collection of functions game music has in his life. This also exemplifies the potential intermix of music's functions between gameplay (e.g., energizing for a fight) and everyday life (e.g., energizing for sports).

> ...Game music has acted as background music for many social get-togethers (we have listened to a lot with friends, some also sang and danced with full participation, the best!), motivated me in sports (epic fight musics work well for this!), helped to cope when life felt difficult, speeded up everyday life (e.g., cleaning is nicer when a game soundtrack is playing in the background, such as Undertale), helped to fight the studies (with Bloodborne's Cleric Beast screaming in the ear, you just need to escape into the depths of an essay), made me find my favorite composer (Nobuo Uematsu) and generally get to know a wide variety of music around the world... (a quotation from D1)

2.4   Game Music Cultures

One of the prevalent themes in the personal narratives of D1 concerned how game music has had an effect on one's musical taste and music listening habits outside the gaming context. Some informants even pointed out a more established taste for game music with consumption practices resembling those of traditional music genres (e.g., buying original soundtracks and attending game music concerts). However, D1 writings also contained several mentions that point towards practices better considered as examples of participatory culture [8,22] such as listening to fan-made remixes, parodies or covers of game music on YouTube. In all, the most mentioned way of listening to game music outside the gaming context was through streaming services, often involving self-made playlists. Besides representing a musical category of its own, another aspect of game music's cultural impact is its symbiotic relationship with the music industry. This is evident, for example, in using licensed popular music in games [3] and in different cross-promotion strategies of marketing music and games [11]. In D1 there are mentions of how games with licenced music have introduced new bands and shaped the musical tastes of the informants but also how original (non-licenced) soundtracks have sparked an interest in previously unfamiliar styles of music. The potential synergy between game music and wider music culture is not only limited to music listening, as there are also games, such as *Guitar Hero* or *Electroplankton*, that incorporate music-making and other acts of musicking into the core dynamics of the gameplay (see [18]). While there were only few mentions about music games in D1, several respondents brought up how game music had inspired them to take up composing or playing an instrument, or even had a part in seeking for a career related to music.

3   Concluding Statements

In this paper, we have outlined four distinct approaches for identifying a broader impact of game music. Through discussing these approaches, our aim was to provide some new prospects for game music research that would inspire both the fields of music and game research alike. At this point, however, we are not yet suggesting any comprehensive theoretical model that would cover all potential dimensions of approaching game music's impact. Of course, more comprehensive results will be reported in future publications, as our research project proceeds in analyzing the gathered datasets. Nevertheless, we hope that this early discussion of the approaches here could serve as a rough thematization of potentially valuable dimensions of game music's impact.

The theoretical and methodological stance presented in this paper directly reflects the perspective of our ongoing research, in which we aim to triangulate different kinds of data for highlighting an interaction with game music in the processes of personal and cultural meaning-making. Our datasets provide a great deal of concrete examples of such processes. To mention but a few, one can consider the following questions as anecdotal examples:

- how is game music able to "teach" a person to use fighting music as a tool for personal emotional scaffolding (e.g., for overcoming life obstacles)?
- how do experiences of virtual skateboarding through empty industrial halls while listening to skate-punk give an opportunity to negotiate one's identity and the role of music in it?
- how does hearing symphonic pieces of music along with emotionally loaded game events provide ways for approaching and exploring classical music?

The talk about game music's impact might lead one to think of game music as an abstract force having an effect on the players and player communities. We would rather argue that the impact should be seen as a result of an interaction-based entanglement between game music and everyday life. Thus, we think we need to raise questions about how a particular music is actively made meaningful by using it in particular activities and in particular contexts. Through considering people's practical engagement with game music (as in the example questions above) we even argue that the distinction between in-game and out-game meanings becomes blurred – similarly to the way De Nora's acknowledgement of an active and self-reflective use of music has obscured the categories of intra- and extra-musical meanings [5]. While our focus has here been on music's meaningfulness, the adopted "in-action" perspective should also provide fruitful insights into video game research more generally. Similarly to music, the impact of video games is entangled in many kinds of personal and cultural activities that make our lives meaningful. From this perspective, it is particularly this experiential intermix between the inside and the outside of a game that is brought into focus.

References

1. Barrett, F.S., Grimm, K.J., Robins, R.W., Wildschut, T., Sedikides, C., Janata, P.: Music-evoked nostalgia: affect, memory, and personality. Emotion **10**(3), 390–403 (2010)
2. Belfi, A.M., Karlan, B., Tranel, D.: Music evokes vivid autobiographical memories. Memory **24**(7), 979–989 (2016)
3. Collins, K.: Grand theft audio? Popular music and intellectual property in video games. Music Moving Image **1**(1), 35–48 (2008)
4. Collins, K.: Playing with Sound: a Theory of Interacting With Sound and Music in Video Games. MIT Press, Cambridge (2013)
5. De Nora, T.: Music in Everyday Life. Cambridge University Press, Cambridge (2000)
6. Gasca, J.S.D.: Music beyond gameplay: Motivators in the consumption of videogame soundtracks. Ph. D. dissertation, Griffith University (2013)
7. Huovinen, E., Tuuri, K.: Pleasant musical imagery: eliciting cherished music in the second person. Music Perception Interdisc. J. **36**(3), 314–330 (2019)
8. Jenkins, H.: Fans, bloggers, and gamers: exploring participatory culture. New York University Press, New York (2006)
9. Johnstone, B.: Qualitative Methods in Sociolinguistics. Oxford University Press, Oxford (2000)
10. Kamp, M., Summers, T., Sweeney, M.: Ludomusicology: Approaches to Video Game Music. Equinox Publishing, Sheffield (2016)
11. Kärjä, A.-V.: Marketing music through computer games: the case of Poets of the Fall and Max Payne 2. In: Collins, K. (ed.) From Pac-Man to Pop Music: Interactive Audio in Games and New Media, pp. 27–44. Ashgate, Burlington (2008)
12. Klimmt, C., Possler, D., May, N., Auge, H., Wanjek, L., Wolf, A.L.: Effects of soundtrack music on the video game experience. Media Psychol. **22**(5), 689–713 (2019)
13. Krueger, J.: Enacting musical experience. J. Conscious. Stud. **16**(2–3), 98–123 (2009)
14. Lakoff, G., Johnson, M.: Metaphors We Live By. University of Chicago Press, Chicago (2008)
15. Matyja, J.R., Schiavio, A.: Enactive music cognition: background and research themes. Constructivist Found. **8**(3), 351–357 (2013)
16. Mäyrä, F.: An Introduction to Game Studies. Sage, Thousand Oaks (2008)
17. Nordahl, R., Nilsson, N.C.: The sound of being there. In: The Oxford Handbook of Interactive Audio, pp. 213–233 (2014)
18. Oliva, C.: Musicking with digital games. Ph.D. dissertation, University of Malta (2019)

19. Ribeiro, G., Rogers, K., Altmeyer, M., Terkildsen, T., Nacke, L.E.: Game atmosphere: effects of audiovisual thematic cohesion on player experience and psychophysiology. In: Proceedings of the Annual Symposium on Computer-Human Interaction in Play, pp. 107–119 (2020)
20. Schäfer, T., Sedlmeier, P., Städtler, C., Huron, D.: The psychological functions of music listening. Front. Psychol. **4**, 511 (2013)
21. Small, C.: Musicking: The Meanings of Performing and Listening. Wesleyan University Press, Middletown (1998)
22. Smith, J.W.: 'Wear people's faces' semiotic awareness in fan adaptations of the music from the legend of zelda: majora's mask. J. Sound Music Games **1**(4), 45–75 (2020)
23. Summers, T.: Understanding Video Game Music. Cambridge University Press, Cambridge (2016)
24. Vahlo, J., Hamari, J.: Five-factor inventory of Intrinsic Motivations to Gameplay (IMG). In: Proceedings of the 52nd Hawaii International Conference on System Sciences, pp. 2476–2485 (2019)
25. Zhang, J., Fu, X.: The influence of background music of video games on immersion. Journal of Psychology & Psychotherapy, vol. 5, no. 4 (2015)

Investigating Impact of Augmented Reality on Game Design to Facilitate Learning Experiences in Logistics Operations Using Immersive AR Interfaces

Sundus Fatima[1,3]([✉]), Jannicke Baalsrud Hauge[1,2] [iD], Prabahan Basu[1,3],
Jakob Baalsrud Hauge[1] [iD], Anindya Chowdhury[1,3], and Artem Schurig[1,3] [iD]

[1] BIBA – Bremer Institut Für Produktion und Logistik GmbH, Bremen, Germany
fat@biba.uni-bremen.de
[2] KTH-Royal Institute of Technology, Södertälje, Sweden
[3] Universität Bremen, Bremen, Germany

Abstract. Augmented Reality (AR) provides an immersive experience platform where players may interact with the real world. Virtual digital information details enhance this interaction with the physical environment. This paper focuses on investigating using Augmented Reality (AR) technology for player's interaction influences the game design (technical features and interactivity aspects mainly) that could facilitate its players to achieve its proposed Intended Learning Objectives when playing different scenarios for logistic operations. To achieve this, an initial mock-up is set up with simple AR interactions to analyse the overall immersive player's experience.

Keywords: AR · Game design · Immersive interactive interfaces · Logistics operations

1 Introduction

There is an increasing trend in using Augmented Reality (AR) in serious educational games as AR provides interactive interfaces for engaging learners and promotes active learning. Due to active involvement, AR can be an effective technology to visualise pedagogical paradigms and gain its learners' attention [1]. An advantage of AR is that it keeps the real world and, therefore, can maximise the experience by adding virtual objects providing the player with an interactive and prosperous environment with the possibility to place virtual objects anywhere without restriction to computer points to create unique immersive player experiences [2]. Within warehouse operations, some applications are using Virtual Reality (VR) and/or AR in an assistive way [3–6], but so far, the uptake both in training as well as in operative processes are limited [7–9]. Comparing the advantages and disadvantages of VR and AR and our experience with using such technologies [7, 10] in games, we will in this case study investigate AR in

© IFIP International Federation for Information Processing 2021
Published by Springer Nature Switzerland AG 2021
J. Baalsrud Hauge et al. (Eds.): ICEC 2021, LNCS 13056, pp. 419–426, 2021.
https://doi.org/10.1007/978-3-030-89394-1_34

more detail, since AR allows the combination of both virtual and real, letting players sense the real world. In contrast, VR provides a computer-generated immersive virtual environment to be experienced over either a computer screen or stereoscopic displays. VR enhances only a fictional reality, but AR enhances both the virtual and real world.

Player experiences in interactive, immersive and learning environments have become relevant in past years [11]. To create an immersive environment to improve the realisation of learning content, it is essential to make an appropriate selection of tools and technological devices that could support the creation of such an immersive educational environment where learners have first-person experiences [11]. To experience AR technology, proper devices and hardware are to be used.

The research problem encountered is how to select appropriate immersive interactive and cost-effective technical devices to realise the desired immersive environment. The selection of appropriate devices is necessarily crucial as to create such an interactive environment using AR technology. As mentioned earlier, this paper's focus is to see the impact of using AR technology on game design, mainly addressing technical features and interactivity. In this regard, it is to investigate if using tablet devices could provide users with the required immersive interactive environment for realising AR that could impact game design influencing overall player immersive experiences? To answer this question, an initial mock-up is set up with a tablet to realise basic AR interactions to observe player immersive experiences in terms of technology and interactivity aspects.

2   Game Design

The motivation behind the game is to give the players an experience as close as possible to the real-life one in a forklift driven scenario.

At the beginning of the game, a short introduction will be given to describe the game briefly. Once the game starts, the player will now be directed to the tutorial part, where they will learn about the basic controls and movement of the forklift. Considering this might be the first time the player plays an AR-based game, the tutorial is critical. In the tutorial, the player will learn how to control and move the forklift around in the given arena and get accustomed to the AR equipment. Once they are well accustomed to the available tools, they will be asked to perform basic tasks such as moving from one point to the other, picking up stuff, moving stuff from one point to the other within the stipulated area. This will ensure that the player is now comfortable with the movement and other actions available to them. The player requires to complete this part to be able to play the game.

The goal is to introduce sensor assistance and let the player explore how this assistance can enhance the performance or the quality of work in a warehouse scenario. With the improvement of technology, sensors have become an everyday tool in our lives. The target is to be able to integrate them into a forklift, benefit the logistics of a warehouse, and introduce the players to the implementations of these benefits. To maximise player possibilities and experiences that might help players while playing games using specific sensors to perform particular tasks in the warehouse environment. The sensors used for this purpose are 1. Ultrasonic sensors, 2. Vibration sensors, 3. Touch sensors.

The player will perform trivial actions of driving forward, backwards and steering the forklift. Different sensors have different purposes and are installed in the forklift to assist the performance. The player will be driving the forklift and performing tasks with sensor assistance and will experience the benefits of using sensors. Each assignment will comprise a sensor-specific action. For each of the sensors available in the game, the player will get to perform tasks specific to each of them to maximise their understanding of the working of the sensors, as mentioned above. The player will be able to use each sensor in real-time and understand the advantages of having a sensor assisted environment. The AR technology should be able to provide the players with a close to real-life experience.

3   Initial AR Prototype

The prototype needs proper testing. This will be held in early autumn 2021 as the prototype is still in the development phase. Here we will discuss the considerations, observations, initial testings, and its results during its development, which could provide a basic idea to understand how we intend to measure immersion in particular application when prototype would be implemented fully and tested then.

Since the goal is to measure the impact in player immersion, a sense of immersion in computer games is described for virtual environments, where the focus is to make the virtual world as authentic as possible. AR already gives a natural environment. The design focus is to make real interaction between virtual objects and the natural environment. By creating real interaction, we could measure the immersiveness based on the interaction between virtual and real environment which player would experience. Since development is in the initial phase with trivial UI and interactions not fully implemented, proper testing would be later in this mock-up. It was observed only to get an initial impression if the player could visualise and have the first impression of UI on the tablet screen, could control forklift using basic forward controls implemented, for the time being, initial interactivity impression and limitations in terms of usability been observed. However, it was pretty hard to measure or monitor immersiveness at this stage as proposed basic interactions are not entirely implemented.

The aim is to see immersive player experience using AR with a tablet which could increase engagement by using immersive learning techniques which could give players exciting new ways to interact with their environment. Since many years AR applications are developed, and the possibilities of AR applications are incredible, what we aim to achieve here with AR is more appropriate in terms of logistics operations as the knowledge could be offered in the space where learning or training needs occur using the cost-effective device (Tablet) to experience AR where the actual environment is augmented with information which can help the user learn or train for the specific skills within a safe environment avoiding the risks that real-world experiment may entail. The use of a cost-effective device to experience AR technology and the low probability of associated risks still make this approach appropriate and a good idea to be used for logistic operations.

A detailed introduction is provided in the pretest section to the players as the player will learn about the detail of the AR components of the game even if the player is experiencing the AR technology for the very first time. In the introduction, players will have some basic tasks that will teach them the basic controls of the forklift. During tutorial, the player will learn more about warehouse safety standards. This section should introduce the players to use the AR controllers to manage the forklift in the gaming scenario, which includes moving the forklift. The controllers will be on a tablet, which has the AR, and the player will be able to control the forklift through it. To develop that in the physical world, we use a model forklift and add sensors and motors. The forklift is operated, and the data collected by the sensors is transferred back.

Players will be using different sensors which have various purposes and are installed in the forklift to assist the performance. While selecting a sensor, the player will receive basic information about the sensor, like how the sensor works in natural environments and how the sensor can be of assistance.

4 Prototype

This chapter describes the current considerations related to the architecture of the MR-environment and which AR technology will be most suitable to achieve the intended interaction between player and gameplay.

4.1 Architecture

The technologies were implemented according to the current state of the art, focusing on simplicity, modularity, and expandability. Based on these requirements, a Raspberry Pi 4 Model B is used as a server and input device simultaneously. The UI developed with Unity Engine is running on an Android tablet. Its camera is used for environment recognition. The software accesses the real-time sensor data wirelessly via the REST interface. This data is presented to the player visually on display as an overlay using augmented technology (Fig. 1).

Technical Architecture

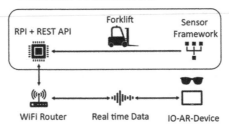

Fig. 1. Overview of technical architecture

4.2 Unity 3D Game Engine

Unity 3D game engine is used to develop interactive interaction as Unity is a multi-platform development tool used to generate 2D and 3D gaming and highly immersive experiences. It is used to make User Interface (UI) following the game art of simplicity for initial interactive mock-up. It would be a simple screen on tablet with basic controls where players could navigate the forklift.

4.3   Vuforia SDK

Vuforia is an Augmented Reality (AR) software development tool-kit is used to create dynamic user experiences. Vuforia utilises computer vision technology to see 3D objects in a real environment and is used to place virtual objects using camera viewfinders and positions objects in real surroundings. Using AR Camera GameObject from Vuforia is mainly used to realise augmented reality.

Fig. 2.   Initial Mock-up UI (Joysticks controllers and exit button)

5   AR Interactions and Players' Experience

This section discusses how AR interactions can improve the immersive user experience. The prototype still needs solid testing, which will take place during the summer 2021, so we just discuss the considerations. While Augmented Reality (AR) allows users to interact with things that are not physically present or may not be touched, it always has a component of "fiction". Due to this issue, Augmented Reality always requires the user to be open to such abstractions. While this usually presents no particular problem in a realistic environment, such as a computer simulation of living dinosaurs, this may present a high entry burden in more fictionalised settings, such as Pokémon Go.

As the presented game requires a realistic setting, the requirements in terms of imaging capabilities are low. Consequently, the entry barrier regarding user interaction is lacking. It is much more critical that the player can recognise the interaction through the AR device as a natural interaction similar to the one they already have in their daily work. Since many do not use sensors for this, it is essential that they can connect the interaction with the operations and system feedback they usually receive. The technical requirements, therefore, depend on the specific setting for the application. However, all AR applications require a mobile device. In this gameplay, one must walk around and interact with different physical environments precisely as they are used to from the real world.

Furthermore, any AR application results from programming that solidifies the requirement for a device capable of computing the inputs and presenting the resulting augmentation of reality. Our project also requires the digital device to possess an integrated camera to scan QR-codes. This eliminates the usage of some tablet computers, but most of the current portable devices have them. There is no need for a high-resolution camera. Unfortunately, there is a requirement regarding the processing power and random-access memory (RAM). The application has to process the user inputs and present the results instantly to allow optimal user interaction.

The mock-up provides immediate insight into the investigation of using Augmented Reality (AR) with the tablet. Using this AR technology would contribute effectively to immersive players' experience to achieve intended learning objectives while playing learning scenarios and could visualise its impact on game design.

6   Impact of AR Technology on Game Design

6.1   Technical Features

Technical features refer to both software and hardware used to make a game [4]. AR technology can give experience and immersive interaction as required if using appropriate, cost-effective devices [5].

We use a tablet to realise our desire environment, which supports ARCore. ARCore is used as an augmented reality-building interface, which has three features mainly: tracking and movement of entity, environment recognition and light and shadow identification, which is utilised effectively for interactive player participation. ARCore makes use of tablet cameras, processors and motion sensors to offer immersive experiences. Tablet offers a portable and wide display size experience where the player can freely visualise objects and environments efficiently and be immersive.

6.2   Interactivity

Interactivity refers to all possible interactions that could be possible in a game, which could give a live and interactive environment to the player [6]. For our initial interactive mock-up, basic AR interactions are implemented to navigate and move forklifts using tablets. Players hold a tablet, and on screen, the player has basic controls with trivial interactions to control forklift. Tablet is portable, and controlling forklift by basic commands with interactive interactions provide players with an immersive interactive experience.

AR technology is close to the real world as it runs in a real environment [7].

6.3   Proposed Interactions

Since the initial prototype is in the development phase, the proposed UI contains basic interaction components with tablets: 1) Joystick Controller1 to move forklift backwards and forward. 2) Joystick Controller2 to move forklift right and left. 3) Exit Button to stop the scene shown in Fig. 2. It is to observe player immersive experience when interacting with these trivial interactions.

One of the main aims of implementing these basic AR interactions using tablets is to give players an immersive experience. Specifications in tablet allow it to supports all AR interactions possible. The spatial relationship between player and gameplays a significant role in providing an immersive environment.

7 Conclusion

This paper focused on using AR technology in game design, specifically concerning the technical and interactivity features. The analysis was conducted by setting up an interactive prototype with a tablet selected as a cost-effective device to experience an immersive player experience. Using a tablet to experience AR technology its wide screen space and portability with the ability to support required building required immersive interface made it possible to achieve or provide players with the desired AR immersive experience with basic AR interactions. However, the research and mock-up are at initial phases to observe the overall progress of its implementation at this stage.

Acknowledgement. This work is funded by the German Federal Ministry of Education and Research (BMBF) through the project DigiLab4U (16DHB2113).

References

1. Wolf, M., Söbke, H., Baalsrud Hauge, J.: Designing augmented reality applications as learning activity. In: Geroimenko, V., (ed.) Augmented Reality in Education. SSCC, pp. 23–43. Springer, Cham (2020). https://doi.org/10.1007/978-3-030-42156-4_2
2. Söbke, H., Baalsrud Hauge, J.: User-Centered Evaluation of the Learning Effects in the Use of a 3D Gesture Control for a Mobile Location-Based Augmented Reality Solution for Maintenance (2020). http://ceur-ws.org/Vol-2685/paper5.pdf
3. Ginters, E., et al.: Mapping of conceptual framework for augmented reality application in logistics. In: 2020 61st International Scientific Conference on Information Technology and Management Science of Riga Technical University (ITMS), 2020, pp. 1–5 (2020). https://doi.org/10.1109/ITMS51158.2020.9259302.
4. Plakas, G., et al.: Augmented reality in manufacturing and logistics: lessons learnt from a real-life industrial application. Procedia Manufact. **51** 1629-1635 (2020). ISSN 2351–9789, https://doi.org/10.1016/j.promfg.2020.10.227
5. Matsumoto, T., et al.: Picking work using AR instructions in warehouses. In: 2019 IEEE 8th Global Conference on Consumer Electronics (GCCE), pp. 31–34 (2019). https://doi.org/10.1109/GCCE46687.2019.9015334.
6. Baalsrud Hauge, J., et al.: Employing digital twins within production logistics. ICE/ITMC **2020**, 1–8 (2020)
7. Hauge, J.B., Zafarzadeh, M., Jeong, Y., Li, Y., Khilji, W.A., Wiktorsson, M.: Digital and physical testbed for production logistics operations. In: Lalic, B., Majstorovic, V., Marjanovic, U., von Cieminski, G., Romero, D. (eds.) APMS 2020. IAICT, vol. 591, pp. 625–633. Springer, Cham (2020). https://doi.org/10.1007/978-3-030-57993-7_71
8. Sorko, S.R., et al.: Potentials of augmented reality in training. Procedia Manufact. **31**, 85–90 (2019). ISSN 2351–789, 10.1016/j.promfg.2019.03.014.(https://www.sciencedirect.com/science/article/pii/S2351978919303774)

9. Keepers, M., Romero, D., Hauge, J.B., Wuest, T.: Gamification of operational tasks in manufacturing. In: Lalic, B., Majstorovic, V., Marjanovic, U., von Cieminski, G., Romero, D. (eds.) APMS 2020. IAICT, vol. 591, pp. 107–114. Springer, Cham (2020). https://doi.org/10.1007/978-3-030-57993-7_13

10. Söbke, H.: Using a location-based AR game in environmental engineering. ICEC-JCSG **2019**, 466–469 (2019)

11. Brice, D., Rafferty, K., McLoone, S.: Usability of an input modality for AR. In: De Paolis, L.T., Bourdot, P. (eds.) AVR 2020. LNCS, vol. 12242, pp. 243–254. Springer, Cham (2020). https://doi.org/10.1007/978-3-030-58465-8_19

12. Wetzel, R., Mccall, R., Braun, A., Broll, W. : Guidelines for designing augmented reality games. In: Proceedings of the 2008 Conference on Future Play Re-search, Play, Share - Future Play 08 (2008). https://doi.org/10.1145/1496984.1497013

13. Liarokapis, F.: An exploration from virtual to augmented reality gaming. Simul. Gaming **37**(4), 507–533 (2006). https://doi.org/10.1177/1046878106293684

14. Guerrero Huerta, A.G., Hernández Rubio, E., Meneses Viveros, A.: Interaction modalities for augmented reality in tablets for older adults. In: Stephanidis, C. (ed.) HCI 2017. CCIS, vol. 714, pp. 427–434. Springer, Cham (2017). https://doi.org/10.1007/978-3-319-58753-0_61

15. Kirner, C., Zorzal, E. R., Kirner, T. G.: Case studies on the development of games using augmented reality. In: 2006 IEEE International Conference on Systems, Man and Cybernetics, vol. 2, pp. 1636–1641 (2006)

Amnesia in the Atlantic: An AI Driven Serious Game on Marine Biodiversity

Mara Dionísio[1,2(✉)] [iD], Valentina Nisi[1,3] [iD], Jin Xin[3], Paulo Bala[1,4] [iD],
Stuart James[5] [iD], and Nuno Jardim Nunes[1,3] [iD]

[1] ITI-LARSyS, Funchal, Portugal
{mara.dionisio,paulo.bala}@iti.larsys.pt
[2] Universidade da Madeira, Funchal, Portugal
[3] IST, Universidade de Lisboa, Lisbon, Portugal
{valentina.nisi,nunojnunes}@tecnico.ulisboa.pt
[4] FCT, Universidade Nova de Lisboa, Lisbon, Portugal
[5] Visual Geometry and Modelling (VGM) Lab and Pattern Analysis and Computer
Vision (PAVIS), Istituto Italiano di Tecnologia, Genoa, Italy
stuart.james@iit.it

Abstract. The use of Conversational Interfaces has evolved rapidly in numerous fields; in particular, they are an interesting tool for Serious Games to leverage on. Conversational Interfaces can assist Serious Games' goals, namely in presenting knowledge through dialogue. With the global acknowledgment of the joint crisis in nature and climate change, it is essential to raise awareness to the fact that many ecosystems are being destroyed and that the biodiversity of our planet is at risk. Therefore in this paper, we present Amnesia in the Atlantic, a Serious Game enhanced with a Conversational Interface embracing the challenge of critically engaging players with marine biodiversity issues.

Keywords: Interactive storytelling · Artificial intelligence · Conversational interfaces · Biodiversity · Nature conservation

1 Introduction

Over the years, we have witnessed that new Artificial Intelligence (AI) methods have become indispensable to orchestrate game dynamics. These range from the generation of storylines, game levels, enhanced graphics or to add intelligent behaviours to non-playable characters [5]. Conversational interfaces (CIs), also known as chatbots, are a form of AI created to have conversations with humans either by voice or by text [13]. This technology is becoming more and more intelligent and useful, and is implemented for multiple uses and contexts [1]. However, CIs have been an unexplored resource in games [7,16] even though they could be particularly relevant in Serious Games, where knowledge is passed through linguistic information in the form of spoken/written language [14]. Several studies highlight the positive impact of Serious Games in enhancing cognitive, skill-based, and affective abilities [17]. We are particularly interested in

© IFIP International Federation for Information Processing 2021
Published by Springer Nature Switzerland AG 2021
J. Baalsrud Hauge et al. (Eds.): ICEC 2021, LNCS 13056, pp. 427–432, 2021.
https://doi.org/10.1007/978-3-030-89394-1_35

how Serious Games target the player's environmental consciousness [4]; making intangible environmental issues more recognizable and aligned to players' experience and daily lives [9]. For marine environmental issues, this is a barrier since it often explores issues they have no knowledge of and underwater spaces that are not accessible. To overcome this, there is a need to engage players with novel and creative interfaces and gameplay strategies [9]. This is why in this paper, we explore the design space of incorporating CIs in Serious Games that engage users in nature conservation [2]. Interactivity through dialogue enhances text-based learning [17] and incorporating natural language interfaces is an active topic of interest [7]. With the use of CIs, we intend for players to be able to critically engage with the issues and recognize their role in the ecosystem. This paper contributes with the design of *Amnesia in the Atlantic (AmA)*, a Serious Game for marine environmental awareness, incorporating CIs as a conduit for knowledge of megafauna biodiversity of the Macaronesia region. Through the description of the design of the artefact, and the design decisions behind it, we delineate future directions of research for our artefact.

2   Related Work

2.1   Marine Environmental Conservation in Serious Games

The entertainment industry is engaging in increasing people's awareness regarding complex social issues, such as climate change and biodiversity conservation [15]. Benefits stemming from technological mediation of nature conservation include the engagement of larger audiences with the digital artifacts and their exposure to pro-environmental messages [6].

In particular, for marine biodiversity conservation, there are several examples of games [8] that aim at making users feel involved in restoring marine ecosystems by solving puzzles. In the narrative game *Beyond Blue* [19], the player takes on the role of a diver, that spends most of the time diving underwater and researching about marine creatures. The game narrative is used as an educational source to teach the players about marine biology. The *Ocean Rift* game [18], unlike the previous games, does not rely on puzzles or specific tasks to complete the game, but is rather an exploratory game of 12 underwater habitats, filled with a variety of animals and information about them [18]. These projects leverage immersion in the underwater world for player engagement. However, there is an opportunity to place the player in the role of the marine fauna, leveraging character persuasion and identification [11,12] to develop an emotional bond between the players and the marine species; this would allow for a better understanding of how ecosystem issues affect these animals. To accomplish this, we look at how CIs can add a new level of interactivity in the antromorphization of characters.

2.2   Conversational Interfaces in Serious Games

Conversational interfaces (CIs), have become popular as a means to create engaging human-computer interactions as they promise new ways to offer highly interactive and personalized experiences [1]. For example, social chatbots such as

Replika [13] can have deep conversations with the user while visual chatbots are created to have a conversation through the interpretation of images given by the user [3]. Since we are interested in CIs applied in the context of Serious Games, the work of Kowald et al. [10] is particularly relevant as it showcases three applications of CIs especially designed for learning through serious interactive fiction games. By analysing, three scenarios, the authors highlight the importance of having a clear idea of the specific application, the goals, and the target audience. Therefore, is vital to follow a good design process to ensure the quality of the CIs, and safeguard users' expectations against CIs' limitations. More recently, Göbl et al. [7] performed a literature review on CIs in Serious Games, where they analyse 30 works (from a broad range of applications domains) to understand the potential and future research directions of CIs in game-based learning. Their findings highlight an increased motivation and learning through social agents in the form of faces or embodied agents that also add non-verbal cues [7]. However, their research also exposes several limitations of CIs in Serious Games, such as users who initially showed engagement with the CIs, quickly would complain and give up when expectations are not met. Furthermore, the use of CIs in Serious Games is limited to what can be made with the available technical resources, budget, and of course, whether data-driven implementations can be built on sufficiently large data sets [7]. The literature in CIs applied to Serious Games is still quite limited, and there is still much do to in terms of design and evaluation, in order to derive general guidelines for future practitioners. Therefore, our goal is to contribute with the design of AmA to expand the body of work of Serious Games incorporating CIs, in particular, applied to the Marine Environmental Conservation cause.

3   Amnesia in the Atlantic

AmA, was inspired by Who Am I?, a guessing game where players use yes/no questions to guess the identity of a famous person or animal. In AmA, the players learn about the marine biodiversity of the Macaronesia ecosystem by trying to discover the characteristics of the animal that they are embodying. The game follows the simple narrative of a cetacean (aquatic mammal), that after being struck by a boat, is left wandering the Atlantic, affected by amnesia and in order to survive, needs to discover who they are. In each game, the player is randomly assigned to one of six species of cetaceans, and by exploring an underwater environment, representative of its marine ecosystem, the player has to uncover clues by talking to CIs, that lead to the discovery of who they are. The more they interact with the CI, the more they will know about themselves but also what kind of relationship they have in the marine ecosystem (e.g., feeding habits, symbiotic relationships, etc.). Looking into further details regarding the game play, Fig. 1 represents the interface flow of the game experience. After an initial 2D animation explaining the game goal, the player meets a non-playable character that will serve as a companion and advisor. This character, a turtle, is one of the most common species in the Macaronesia region. This first interaction serves as a tutorial, as this friendly turtle goes over the actions available

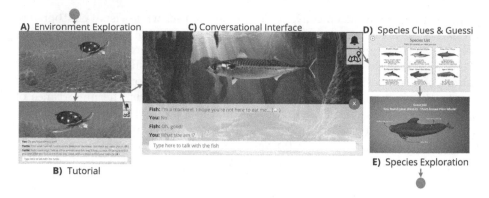

Fig. 1. Interface flow: while exploring environments (A), the player is introduced to the tutorial (B). Interacting with a species in the environment can establish a conversation (C). The game supports continued guessing (D) and a reward for the correct guess (E).

for the player, namely, navigation (in the 3D environment, and through a map interface), dialogue (by approaching an animal and asking questions) and how the player can guess their identity. After this initial tutorial, the player can explore different locations. These locations are showcased in the map and this exploration is non-linear. Currently, we envisage three locations with 3D environments expressive of the Macaronesia region, purposely representing different ocean zones to depict different ecosystems with different visual characteristics (e.g. orography, flora, and lighting). For example, a littoral environment near the coast will present different species than an environment in the deep sea. In this way, the player can learn about the Macaronesia underwater environment simply by space exploration. The characters in these environments are conversational agents, possessing character traits consistent with the species they are representing. By interacting with these species and through question formulation, the players will uncover clues about their identity. For example, this information can include clues about how they look like, how fast they swim, feeding habits or environmental threats that they might be facing. Once the player has retrieved enough information, they can try to guess their identity by clicking on the bell icon at the top right side of the screen. In case the player succeeds, more information about the species will be presented in a 3D exploratory view of the animal they were embodying. If they are not able to guess, then they can go back to the underwater environment to talk with more species (CIs).

AmA was designed by focusing on three pillars, (1) immersive environment, (2) characters, and (3) AI driven generative game play. Firstly, the immersive environments are intended to provide a realistic simulation of environments that are not accessible to players as humans. They also provide coded knowledge in the way they are visually presented and populated. Secondly, by embodying a marine species and playing in a first person view, we intend to dissociate the player from the experience of having a human body, while still being able to have character identification through role-playing. Moreover, the partial antromorphization of the characters as capable of dialogue is intended to allow character persuasion and identification. Thirdly, the random allocation of a character and the AI mechanic of conversational dialogue allows for generative game play promoting replayability. To fully understand the dynamics between cetaceans in the Macaronesia region, there are several species to discover and after finishing a game, players can go back to play as another species. The game also offers a personalised experience to each player, since the conversation with the marine species will be different from player to player.

4   Conclusion and Future Work

In this work in progress paper, we presented *AmA*, a Serious Game enhanced with a CI embracing the challenge of critically engage players with the marine biodiversity issues. *AmA* will be developed in Unity[1] for desktop computers, which allows for the creation of realistic simulation and easy input from mouse and keyboard devices. Dialogue with non-playable characters will be accomplished through a web-service (REST API) providing access to a question and answer agent. The separation allows the agent to run on independent computational resources for scalability and stability. The agent[2] will inspect a provided image of marine animal and attempt to answer questions about it.

While we develop a functioning prototype for *AmA*, a mid fidelity prototype will be tested with participants to uncover early design limitations and to understand dialogue within CIs in a game setting. By building on user's expectations, experience and tolerance to failure when interacting with CIs, we intend to understand how to prevail over the limitations of CIs and limit their impact on the overall game experience. In the long term, we plan to test the prototype to understand its impact in marine conservation awareness through the use of pro-environmental behaviour scales. With *AmA*, we contribute to the body of work in CIs used in Serious Games.

Acknowledgements. This work was supported by the project INTERTAGUA - MAC2/1.1a/385. We also wish to acknowledge the work of our fellow researcher Rui Trindade.

References

1. Adamopoulou, E., Moussiades, L.: An overview of chatbot technology. In: Maglogiannis, I., Iliadis, L., Pimenidis, E. (eds.) AIAI 2020. IAICT, vol. 584, pp. 373–383. Springer, Cham (2020). https://doi.org/10.1007/978-3-030-49186-4_31
2. Büscher, B.: Nature 2.0: exploring and theorizing the links between new media and nature conservation. New Media Soc. **18**(5), 726–743 (2016)
3. Das, A., et al.: Visual dialog (2016)

---

[1] Unity game engine - https://unity.com/.
[2] Visual Question and Answering - http://vqa.cloudcv.org/.

4. Fjællingsdal, K.S., Klöckner, C.A.: Gaming green: the educational potential of eco - a digital simulated ecosystem. Front. Psychol. **10**, 2846 (2019). https://doi.org/10.3389/fpsyg.2019.02846

5. García-Sánchez, P., Yannakakis, G.N., Togelius, J.: Artificial intelligence and games. Genetic Program. Evol. Mach. **20**(1), 143–145 (2018). https://doi.org/10.1007/s10710-018-9337-0

6. Gaver, W., et al.: My naturewatch camera: disseminating practice research with a cheap and easy DIY design. In: Proceedings of the CHI 2019, pp. 1–13 (2019)

7. Göbl, B., Kriglstein, S., Hlavacs, H.: Conversational interfaces in serious games: identifying potentials and future research directions based on a systematic literature review. In: Proceedings of CSEDU 2021, pp. 108–115 (2021). https://doi.org/10.5220/0010447301080115

8. Jepson, P., Ladle, R.J.: Nature apps: waiting for the revolution. Ambio **44**(8), 827–832 (2015)

9. Klöckner, C.A.: The Psychology of Pro-environmental Communication. Palgrave Macmillan UK, London (2015). https://doi.org/10.1057/9781137348326

10. Kowald, C., Bruns, B.: New learning scenarios with chatbots - conversational learning with Jix: from digital tutors to serious interactive fiction games. Int. J Adv. Corp. Learn. (iJAC) **12**(2), 59–62 (2019)

11. Minich, M.: The effects of narrative transportation and character identification on persuasion in the medium of comics. Ph.D. thesis, January 2017. https://doi.org/10.13140/RG.2.2.20322.79047

12. Moyer-Gusé, E.: Toward a theory of entertainment persuasion: explaining the persuasive effects of entertainment-education messages. Commun. Theory **18**(3), 407–425 (2008). https://doi.org/10.1111/j.1468-2885.2008.00328.x

13. Nima, N., Lee, T., Molloy, D.: Being friends with yourself: how friendship is programmed within the AI-based socialbot replika. Masters of Media (2017)

14. Picca, D., Jaccard, D., Eberlé, G.: Natural language processing in serious games: a state of the art. Int. J. Serious Games **2**(3), 77–97 (2015). https://doi.org/10.17083/ijsg.v2i3.87

15. Rands, M.R., et al.: Biodiversity conservation: challenges beyond 2010. Science **329**(5997), 1298–1303 (2010)

16. van Rosmalen, P., Eikelboom, J., Bloemers, E., van Winzum, K., Spronck, P.H.M.: Towards a game-chatbot: Extending the interaction in serious games. In: Felicia, P. (ed.) Proceedings of the 6th European Conference on Game-based Learning, Cork, Ireland, pp. 525–532. Academic Publishing International Ltd. (2012)

17. Stephanidis, C., et al.: Seven HCI grand challenges. Int. J. Hum. Comput. Interact. **35**(14), 1229–1269 (2019). https://doi.org/10.1080/10447318.2019.1619259

18. Takahashi, D.: The Ocean Rift in virtual reality is like relaxing in an IMAX theater - venturebeat. http://venturebeat.com/2016/04/09/the-ocean-rift-in-virtual-reality-is-like-relaxing-in-an-imax-theater/

19. Watts, R.: Beyond blue review a contemplative and educational diving sim. PC Gamer, June 2020

A VR-Based Serious Game Associated to EMG Signal Processing and Sensory Feedback for Upper Limb Prosthesis Training

Reidner Cavalcante[1] (ORCID), Aya Gaballa[2] (ORCID), John-John Cabibihan[2] (ORCID),
Alcimar Soares[1] (ORCID), and Edgard Lamounier[1(✉)] (ORCID)

[1] Federal University of Uberlândia, Uberlândia, Brazil
lamounier@ufu.br
[2] Qatar University, Doha, Qatar

Abstract. Using Serious Games (SG) in virtual rehabilitation is favorable since it allows users to evolve in their training process, while enjoying the tasks and challenges proposed. In this paper, the authors present a pilot test that uses an immersive Virtual Reality (iVR)-based Serious Game to simulate a myoelectric prosthesis, which is controlled by EMG signal processing (muscle activity reading). EMG signals, as in real life, control the opening and closing of the virtual prosthesis, and vibrational elements placed on the user's forearm provide sensory feedback to enhance the feeling of touching. Evidence presented in this work shows that users utilizing tactile feedback demonstrated improved performance and the Serious Game helped to accomplish the training tasks.

Keywords: Serious games · Prosthetic training · Immersive virtual reality · Sensory feedback · EMG signal processing

1 Introduction

Limb amputation is a traumatic event capable of triggering major changes in all areas of a subject's life. Usually, after amputation, a surgical procedure is performed to create new functional perspectives for the remaining segment of the amputated limb, usually referred to as stump [1]. With no previous training, the time to adapt and learn how to control the prosthetic device can take anywhere between three to twelve months. Studies have shown that such a lengthy and tiring process may contribute to prosthesis abandonment [2, 3].

The earlier the rehabilitation process starts, the greater its potential for success [4]. In several cases, adaptation to the prosthesis will be mentally and physically tiring, demanding considerable time over several weekly sessions in a clinic, and leading to loss of motivation [5, 12]. This drawback can be overcome with the association of Serious Games (SGs) and Virtual Reality (VR) techniques [5, 26].

Serious Games are becoming popular in various learning, health, education and training methods [6–9, 26, 27]. This technology seeks to go beyond simple fun, with

© IFIP International Federation for Information Processing 2021
Published by Springer Nature Switzerland AG 2021
J. Baalsrud Hauge et al. (Eds.): ICEC 2021, LNCS 13056, pp. 433–440, 2021.
https://doi.org/10.1007/978-3-030-89394-1_36

the purpose of influencing the thoughts and actions of players in real-life contexts. On the other hand, VR features allow high-level interactions and realistic responses to user actions, promoting user involvement by focusing on immersion [10, 15, 16]. However, most VR systems reported in upper-limb prosthetic training literature are based on non-immersive environments and lack sensory feedback [2–4, 11]. Furthermore, in many reported systems, users visualize the virtual prostheses at a distance on a flat screen [3, 17–20]. These include a first attempt by the authors for body empowerment prostheses [26]. Unfortunately, such an approach cannot deliver the natural and intuitive interactions for real training. In fact, immersive virtual environments have systematically shown to maintain the illusion of presence, which, in turn, positively impacts attention and engagement [21].

In addition, sole visual feedback drastically limits the immersive experience for the purpose of prosthesis training, which requires users to reach and manipulate various objects. The inclusion of sensory feedback, definitively would help in this matter. Such feedback is especially crucial for myoelectric prostheses (controlled by EMG signals [11, 13, 14]). In this paper, the development of a virtual training environment for rehabilitation of upper limb amputees based on serious games is presented. The idea is to evaluate this amputee training approach by using Serious Game with immersive VR, associated to EMG control and tactile feedback.

2   Game Development

A virtual training environment has been developed, based on a Box and Blocks test [21]. The user has to pick blocks, with the virtual prosthesis, in one side of a box and move them to the other side. Training sessions have been designed as game tasks, according to physiotherapists' recommendations.

2.1   System Architecture

The system's main components are: HTC Vive Pro, Vive Tracker, EMG controller (data acquisition and pattern recognition), vibrational armband, and a computer (Fig. 1). The user interacts with the virtual environment by moving and contracting the stump muscles. In case of nonamputee volunteers, forearm muscles are used.

The Vive Tracker, located in the arm, provides information so that the virtual prosthesis moves within the virtual environment as the user moves his arm. The EMG module processes the contractions of the stump (or forearm) muscles and sends setpoint values to the virtual environment to indicate how much the virtual prosthesis must open/close the hand. The vibrational armband, and the EMG sensors are also positioned on the user's forearm. Whenever the user grabs an object in the virtual environment, vibration feedback is sent to the user to convey touch.

2.2   Game Design Considerations

Six elements must be aligned with the use of a serious game: Purpose, Content and Information, Game Mechanics, Fiction and Narrative, Aesthetics and Graphics and Framing [9].

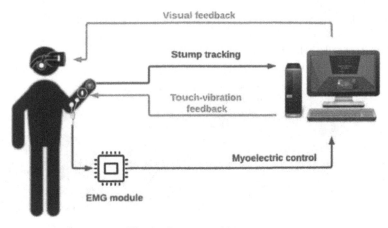

Fig. 1. System architecture.

The Purpose of this game is to help amputees to adapt to a myoelectric prosthesis, through game tasks related to physiotherapy protocols. As to Content and Information, there is a panel on the wall in front of the player and a clock, during the session, that indicates the score and time, respectively. Thus, the player can check this information without the need to lose the sense of immersion while playing. Also, the guidelines to prepare and start the game are shown in the panel. Most of the players, during a pilot test, stated that this information was very useful for the game.

The Game Mechanics involves tasks of grabbing and moving objects, as the user is supposed to do in real life. Yet, the player can move freely in the environment, accordingly to the real-world space available due to the Vive tracking area. A Narrative is constructed where the player went to a place to learn how to control a virtual prosthesis with objects, which faithfully mimic real ones – boxes and prosthesis (Graphics). As a result, participants mentioned that it was easy to understand how the game works.

The player gets points when he achieves certain game tasks. Studies have shown that with this scoring reward system, players can be motivated to improve their previous scores. This competitiveness factor stimulates the progress during the rehabilitation process [22]. Another Graphics aspect is related to the fact that the closest grabbable object to the Virtual Prosthesis (VP) will blink according to its distance. The closer the object is to the VP, the faster it will blink. This allows the player to have another visual reference to situate the VP in the environment.

A vibrational feedback is sent to the player when a grabbable object is correctly grabbed and will persist as long as the player continues to hold it. Once the object falls or the player release it, the vibrational feedback will stop. The vibrational feedback can be enabled or disabled before each session, according to the therapist's conduction.

Finally, Framing consists of aligning the elements already described in relation to the target audience and the experience of the target audience in relation to games. All these characteristics seek to ensure that the player has a good experience and the game is balanced in levels of difficulty and skills [9], also known as Flow [25]. Figure 2 shows a frame of the game with the virtual prosthesis in red. To train for prosthesis adaptation the

Box and Blocks (B&B) Test is one of the most commonly used measures for evaluating functionality and users' performance [21], along with the Hole Peg and the Clothespin Relocation Test [23, 24], which are also provided.

Fig. 2. Box & blocks environment (Left) and User Setup (Right).

3   Experimental Procedure

3.1   Participants

For this study, eight non-amputee male volunteers, ages between 20 and 40, were recruited. The volunteers were divided into two groups: G1 - performed the B&B tasks while receiving visual and vibrational tactile feedback; G2 - performed the B&B tasks while receiving only visual feedback, no tactile feedback.

3.2   Pilot Test

In this experiment, we performed four trials using the Box and Blocks environment with the experimental group receiving tactile feedback. No tactile feedback was given to the control group. Before the experiment, the volunteers received instructions related to the task including how they should use muscle contractions to control the virtual prosthesis, and the type of feedback to be expected in the case of G1. The volunteers sat comfortably while the devices were connected (Fig. 2).

The Vive Tracker and the vibrational armband were positioned side-by-side close to the wrist. Finally, the volunteer was equipped with the Vive headset.

Before use, the system must be calibrated to define the limits of the EMG envelop amplitude. This calibration is required only once to set the values for the fully closed hand (100%) or the fully opened hand (0%). For calibration, the user must rest the forearm muscles for 5 s and contract for another 5 s at a comfortable level ask consisted of four B&B trials. In each trial the volunteers were asked to move all blocks from one side of the box to the other as fast as possible. The time to complete each trial was registered.

Table 1. Time (in Seconds) for completion of trials by G1 – vibrational tactile feedback.

Volunteer	Trial 1	Trial 2	Trial 3	Trial 4
G1-V1	17.67	39.98	38.10	30.37
G1-V2	126.17	82.32	29.57	17.59
G1-V3	209.97	42.72	17.10	6.61
G1-V4	50.14	25.39	62.22	34.25
Average	100,99	47,60	36,75	22,21

Table 2. Time (in Seconds) for completion of trials by G2 – visual feedback only.

Volunteer	Trial 1	Trial 2	Trial 3	Trial 4
G2-V1	38.08	107.94	42.67	49.62
G2-V2	135.12	207.38	38.48	96.36
G2-V3	63.72	17.35	37.01	43.55
G2-V4	28.06	10.4	11.81	13.94
Average	66,25	85,77	32,49	50,87

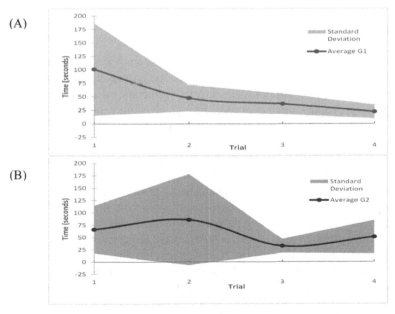

Fig. 3. Plotting completion time per trial of group G1(A) and G2 (B).

4 Results and Discussion

Tables 1 and 2 show the completion time of all trials performed by the volunteers in groups G1 and G2, respectively. In the first sessions, the volunteers learn how to control the virtual prosthesis, using myoelectric signals while adapting to the virtual environment.

Accordingly, the first two trials required a longer time to complete. As the trials progressed, especially for the volunteers in G1, completion time decreased steadily, from a of mean 100.99 s in the first trial to a mean of 22.21 s in the last one. In contrast, the mean completion times for the volunteers in G2 ranges from 66.25 s to 50.87 s.

Although the initial mean value for G1 was considerably higher than the initial mean value for G2 (mainly due to the very high time taken by G1-V3 to complete the first trial), the group using vibrational tactile feedback showed better performance overall. On average G2 took 2.3 times longer to complete the task at the fourth trial. A similar trend can also be seen in Fig. 3(A), where the G1 average completion times and standard variations per trial are plotted. Similarly, Fig. 3(B) reports those values for G2.

As for the utility of the game during training sessions, 7 participants mentioned that the game is useful and 1 participant mentioned that it is very useful. It is important to say that the presence of a therapist is still required, during first experiments and also due to devices' costs. However, the authors believe that in the near future, patients will be able to conduct the training session by themselves, at home, as the price of technology decreases. Also, we emphasize that the feeling of immersion with the challenge/Flow of the game can provide a different and more pleasant approach for training. Especially for children who lose their upper limbs in war zones.

5 Conclusions and Future Work

In this study, a virtual training environment for upper limb amputees based on serious gaming as a rehabilitation tool has been presented. The system allows the user to train how to use a myoelectric prosthesis. The game involves motivational aspects by presenting the user with the opportunity to achieve goals, through physiotherapy tasks. This encourages the user to minimize the time required to complete tasks and promotes patient-game interaction.

A pilot test using the Box and Blocks environment was performed. Although both the experimental and control groups showed improvement in the control of the myoelectric virtual prosthesis over the trials, participants using tactile vibrational feedback showed better performance as the trials progressed, compared with the group that did not use tactile feedback. Users reported that the game, with its content and mechanics, was very useful in learning how to control a myoelectric prosthesis.

These results indicate that sensory feedback can provide a better overall experience and performance in training sessions for amputees, during an immersive Virtual Reality experience, which is aided by a serious game. Also, the use of EMG signal processing to control opening/closing of the virtual prosthesis derives new directions for the virtual training of myoelectric devices, which requires more complex processing. As future work, more tests will be performed on the Box and Blocks environment as well as on the other two environments, also with real patients. Although recruitment of amputees during the COVID-19 pandemic requires time following ethic protocols, tests involving such volunteers will also be performed.

Acknowledgments. This study was financed in part by the Coordenação de Aperfeiçoamento de Pessoal de Nível Superior - Brasil (CAPES) - Finance Code 001, Autodesk Foundation and Qatar University under the grant IRCC-2019–001.

References

1. Global Lower Extremity Amputation Study Group Unwin N.: Epidemiology of lower extremity amputation in centers in Europe, North America and East Asia. J. Br. Surg. **87**(3), 328–37 (2000)
2. Mattioli, F.E.R., Lamounier, E.A., Cardoso, A., Soares, A.B., Andrade, A.O.: Classification of EMG signals using artificial neural networks for virtual hand prosthesis control. In: Proceedings of the Annual International Conference of the IEEE Engineering in Medicine and Biology Society, EMBS, pp. 7254–7257 (2011)
3. Putrino, D., Wong, Y.T., Weiss, A., Pesaran, B.: A training platform for many-dimensional prosthetic devices using a virtual reality environment. J. Neurosci. Meth. **244**, 68–77 (2015)
4. Li, K., Boyd, P., Zhou, Y., Ju, Z., Liu, H.: Electrotactile feedback in a virtual hand rehabilitation platform: evaluation and implementation. IEEE Trans. Autom. Sci. Eng. **16**(4), 1556–1565 (2019)
5. Sharma, A., et al.: A mixed-reality training environment for upper limb prosthesis control. In: 2018 IEEE Biomedical Circuits and Systems Conference Proceedings, pp. 1–4, IEEE. Cleveland, Ohio, USA (2018)
6. De Gloria, A., Bellotti, F., Berta, R.: Serious games for education and training. Int. J. Ser. Games **1**(1), (2014)
7. Sekhavat, Y.A., Nomani, P.: A comparison of active and passive virtual reality exposure scenarios to elicit social anxiety. Int. J. Serious Games, **4**(2), 3–15 (2017)
8. Garcia-Agundez, A., et al.: PDPuzzleTable: a leap motion exergame for dual-tasking rehabilitation in parkinson's disease. design and study protocol. In: van der Spek, E., Göbel, S., Do, E.-L., Clua, E., Baalsrud Hauge, J. (eds.) ICEC-JCSG 2019. LNCS, vol. 11863, pp. 402–406. Springer, Cham (2019). https://doi.org/10.1007/978-3-030-34644-7_35
9. Mitgutsch, N., Alvarado, K.: Purposeful by design: a serious game design assessment framework. In: International Conference on the Foundations of Digital Games Proceedings, pp. 121–128. ACM (2012)
10. Kuttuva, M., Burdea, G., Flint, J., Craelius, W.: Manipulation practice for upper-limb amputees using virtual reality. Presence: Teleoper. Virt. Environ. **14**(2), 175–182 (2005)
11. Melero, M., et al.: Upbeat: augmented reality-guided dancing for prosthetic rehabilitation of upper limb amputees. J. Healthcare Eng. (2019)
12. Churko, J.M., Mehr, A., Linassi, A.G., Dinh, A.: Sensor evaluation for tracking upper extremity prosthesis movements in a virtual environment. In: Annual International Conference of the IEEE Engineering in Medicine and Biology Society Proceedings. IEEE (2009)
13. Atzori, M., et al.: Electromyography data for non-invasive naturally-controlled robotic hand prostheses. Sci. data **1**(1), 1–13 (2014)
14. Blana, D., Kyriacou, T., Lambrecht, J.M., Chadwick, E.K.: Feasibility of using combined EMG and kinematic signals for prosthesis control: a simulation study using a virtual reality environment. J. Electromyogr. Kinesiol. **29**, 21–27 (2016)

15. Odette, K., Fu, Q.: A physics-based virtual reality environment to quantify functional performance of upper-limb prostheses. In: 41st Annual International Conference of the IEEE Engineering in Medicine and Biology Society Proceedings, pp. 3807–3810 (2019)
16. Phelan, I., Arden, M., Garcia, C., Roast, C.: Exploring virtual reality and prosthetic training. In: IEEE Virtual Reality, pp. 353–354. IEEE (2015)
17. Shibanoki, T., Nakamura, G., Tsuji, T., Hashimoto, K., Chin, T.: A new approach for training on EMG-based prosthetic hand control. In: 2nd Global Conference on Life Sciences and Technologies Proceedings, pp. 307–308. IEEE (2020)
18. Earley, E.J., Kaveny, K.J., Johnson, R.E., Hargrove, L.J., Sensinger, J.W.: Joint-based velocity feedback to virtual limb dynamic perturbations. In: 2017 International Conference on Rehabilitation Robotics, pp. 1313–1318. IEEE (2017)
19. Johansen, D., et al.: A comparative study of virtual hand prosthesis control using an inductive tongue control system. Assist. Technol. 28(1), 22–29 (2016)
20. Lamounier, E., Lopes, K., Cardoso, A., Andrade, A., Soares, A.: On the use of Virtual and augmented reality for upper limb prostheses training and simulation. In: 2010 Annual International Conference of the IEEE Engineering in Medicine and Biology Society, EMBC'10, pp. 2451–2454 (2010)
21. Johnson-Glenberg, M.C.: Immersive VR and education: embodied design principles that include gesture and hand controls. Front. Robot. AI 5, 81 (2018)
22. Burke, J.W., McNeill, M.D.J., Charles, D.K., Morrow, P.J., Crosbie, J.H., McDonough, S.M.: Optimising engagement for stroke rehabilitation using serious games. Vis. Comput. 25(12), 1085–1099 (2009)
23. Figueiredo, S.: Nine Hole Peg Test (NHPT). Stroke Engine
24. Kyberd, P., Hussaini, A., Maillet, G.: Characterisation of the clothespin relocation test as a functional assessment tool. J. Rehab. Assistive Technol. Eng. 5, 2055668317750810 (2018)
25. Alves, T., Gama, S., Melo, F.S.: Flow adaptation in serious games for health. In: 6th International Conference on Serious Games and Applications for Health Proceedings. IEEE (2018)
26. Cavalcante, R., Lamounier, E., Cardoso, A., Soares, A., de Lima, G.M.: Development of a serious game for rehabilitation of upper limb amputees. In 2018 20th Symposium on Virtual and Augmented Reality (SVR), pp. 99–105. IEEE, October 2018
27. Luo, T., Cai, N., Li, Z., Pan, Z., Yuan, Q.: VR-DLR: a serious game of somatosensory driving applied to limb rehabilitation training. In: Nunes, N.J., Ma, L., Wang, M., Correia, N., Pan, Z. (eds.) ICEC 2020. LNCS, vol. 12523, pp. 51–64. Springer, Cham (2020). https://doi.org/10.1007/978-3-030-65736-9_4

A Review on the Contribution of ClassDojo as Point System Gamification in Education

Rabab Marouf[✉] and Joseph Alexander Brown[ID]

Innopolis University, Innopolis 420500, Russia
`r.marouf@innopolis.ru`

Abstract. Maintaining students' engagement and classroom management have been among the major challenges teachers encounter in schools. Gamification of education has proposed solutions via online platforms to assist teachers in controlling students' behaviours by point system gamification. ClassDojo, as a point system platform, seems to limit its contribution to classroom behaviour without demonstrating evidence of its positive influence in attaining the learning outcomes. This paper reviews the effectiveness of ClassDojo and underpins the potential negative impact on students motivation and learning.

Keywords: Gamifcation · ClassDojo · Point system · Classroom discipline

1 Introduction

Classroom management is one of the biggest challenges in school environments. Teachers struggle between managing students' behaviour or covering the curriculum and meeting with the Intended Learning Outcomes (ILO). ClassDojo is a point system example of gamification in education that is argued to help teachers in classroom management and prevent the dilemma of time spent on behavioural disruptions. Teachers in the modern world are claimed to "be able to create a modern classroom" [8]. Despite the valuable role of educational games, they are short-term solutions in their best scenario [22]. [25] perceives these games as temporary solutions. This paper aims to address the following questions: (1) how efficient the point system gamification in education can be; (2) and what amendments can be implemented to bridge the existing gap in ClassDojo as a point system platform. This paper provides an overview of reward-based systems in education and examines the efficiency of ClassDojo in education. Finally, suggestions are provided for educators and system designers to address the potential negative influence on students' motivation and learning.

2 ClassDojo and Point Systems

ClassDojo is a popular online classroom which is actively used in 95% of all K-8 schools in the US and 180 other countries [11]. ClassDojo claimed that technology

© IFIP International Federation for Information Processing 2021
Published by Springer Nature Switzerland AG 2021
J. Baalsrud Hauge et al. (Eds.): ICEC 2021, LNCS 13056, pp. 441–448, 2021.
https://doi.org/10.1007/978-3-030-89394-1_37

is integrated into classrooms to facilitate everyday communication among teachers, students and families [11]. ClassDojo is argued to be the teacher's auxiliary in improving classroom behaviour. ClassDojo manual for teachers introduces a Toolkit that connects teachers with families, create positive classrooms, and share student learning [10, 23]. Upon demonstrating good behaviour, the teacher taps the students' name and selects the type of behaviour. Consequently, Dojo points are awarded.

2.1 Point System in Education

The rationale of introducing point system gamification in education is to motivate students, enhance their engagement, and reduce classroom disruptive behaviour. Moving to higher levels, in these systems, results from winning new points. 'levelling up' is 'satisfying' feedback for the player of a game [22]. Levelling up is as an accessible objective in comparison with the traditional letter-based grading system [25]. Prensky argues that this system can replace the 'negative stress' with 'positive stress. Whereas [19] does not justify gamifying schools "because it is the next fad, or because we believe students are motivated by points, or because we think badges will cause students to change the behaviours permanently".

In ClassDojo, point systems enable teachers to announce grades from (0–5). The points can be granted for behavioural or academic achievement. These digits from (0–5) can be respectively equivalent to what institutional manuals identify for teachers in regular classrooms: 'A excellent, B good, C adequate, D inadequate/unsatisfactory, F failing/unacceptable' [5]. Those points or grades are not significantly different, due to the absence of evidence of the efficiency of traditional letter grading or gamified points in meeting the ILO.

[22] and [25] have not provided evidence that demonstrates the effectiveness of these learning tools on students' constant engagement and deep learning. Seeking positive points in a competitive environment can be a reason for stress. Hence, Robinson [26] suggests involving students in the action of determining the behaviors ClassDojo evaluates. Wang and Holcombe [29] argued that in a competitive environment, student participation and their sense of belonging tend to decrease. Thus, students learning can be at risk.

3   ClassDojo in the Literature

This review covers the literature on ClassDojo and its contribution in education from 2016 until present. This review highlights significant evaluation of the point system's contribution in the educational environment. In [30], pre/post-quasi-experimental design recorded student behaviour and off-task disruptions. The analysis showed that ClassDojo did not have significagnt impact on student behaviour and off-task disruptions.

In terms of ClassDojo's associated noise, teachers regarded this noise as a drawback [6]. Another participant observed the correlation between positive/negative points and the likelihood of receiving good/lower grades. The effectiveness of ClassDojo to help students recognize and self-monitor behaviours during guided reading was examined in [9]. ClassDojo has shown positive impact on enabling students to be "more aware of their own behavioural choices".

Whereas, Dillon [13] investigated the impact of tootling [28] intervention with ClassDojo on the reduction of disruptive classroom behaviour and the increase of academically engaged behaviour. Tootling with ClassDojo was effective in decreasing disruptive behaviour and increasing academically engaged one. In another study, Williamson [31] investigated ClassDojo as a facilitator of psychological surveillance through gamification techniques. The study examined the correlation between ClassDojo's psychological concepts and the Physiological methods of Silicon Valley designers. ClassDojo was argued to be utilized in schools for giving priorities to governmental interests to achieve political goals.

The focus in Saeger's study [27] was whether ClassDojo can enforce student's positive behaviours and decrease the frequency of negative ones. Students demonstrated an enhancement of positive behaviour and a reduction of negative behaviour. However, the study has not addressed the influence of negative points on the emotional state of participants. Upon examining the efficiency of positive variation of the Good Behavior Game (GBG) [2], Ford [14] appraised, through ClassDojo, the increase of academically engaged behaviours and the decrease of disruptive ones. Whereas, for tracking the increase of prosocial behaviours and the decrease of disruptive ones, [15] examined the effect of ClassDojo on two neurotypical children. The findings demonstrated that near-baseline levels, disruptive behaviours remained the same.

According to Manolev et al. [20], the success of ClassDojo lies in connecting teachers, students, parents and schools. ClassDojo was used in [17] as a digital "badge-and-point" approach to enhance behavioural engagement and English acquisition. This program was compared to a non-digital token economy approach. Upon examining the effectiveness of ClassDojo against a paper-pencil method for students with behavioural and emotional disorders, Cravalho [12] observed academic engagement. Data was collected via Behavior Observation of Students in Schools (BOSS) software. Children in ClassDojo are "digital subjects, where their identities are evaluated through the kinds of metrics (e.g. like and points) of contemporary social media services". Students can be passive as they are not using the application, rather they are used by it [26].

In a recent study [18], the data was collected on how ClassDojo can influence student behavior, resulting from the teacher's observation. The result of Questionnaires of closed-ended items unfolded that students have a significantly negative attitude towards English as a subject. ClassDojo is utilized for improving the behavior scores without any correlation with those of the course.

This review uncovers the claim on the efficiency of integrating point system platforms in classrooms, as a means of managing behavior and consequently creating more engaging learning environments. Therefore, questioning the rationale for the existence of point system gamification in education emerges.

4   Reflection on Point Systems

If student's main focus is rewards, this connection between the reward and learning can create deep concerns on whether the absence of rewards can hinder learning or not [32]. Caillois in [7] argued that rewards and incentives decrease a person's intrinsic motivation in performing a task. Therefore, classroom engagement can be short-termed and the time spent for offering rewards can be pointless. The risk in reward system can be in the linkage between students performance and gaining tangible rewards. Students are extrinsically motivated and therefore the influence on their academic performance might not lead to life-long learning [1].

4.1   The Impact of Negative Points on Students Motivation

The influence of the competitive atmosphere, that point systems create, might enforce negative behaviour. Hence, students who earn negative points can be demotivated and consequently less engaged. Moreover, Displaying students points publicly in the classroom and sharing them with parents can be demotivating because students lose face for being losers among peers and teachers. Students can respond differently to these rewards [3]. A teacher participant in [6] reported that students were distracted when displaying their points. Whereas, student participants expressed that negative points can make them feel embarrassed, off task, far from that goal of earning rewards, being the winner in the classroom competition, angry, disappointed, and ashamed. The consequences of these negative feelings can influence students performance and consequently learning.

In point systems gamification, students tend to focus on being winners. Therefore, their motivation is influenced because they expect earning points or tangible rewards. McGeown et al. differentiated between the two types of motivation: intrinsic and extrinsic. Nevertheless, intrinsic motivation is argued to be an essential factor to academic success [21].

In schools, however, opportunities to try are few, and if students try, it is risky. Gamification might teach students that they should learn only when provided with external rewards [19]. ClassDojo's reliance on reward can make students less engaged at one point of their learning as engagement can diminish by time.

4.2   Time in ClassDojo

Teachers in ClassDojo can set timers, shuffle students randomly, make groups, check the noise meter and take attendance. The actual duration for using these features is not precise in comparison with that the same activities can require in the absence of such platforms. Thus, saving teacher's time in point system gamification can be questionable. The reviewed literature did not demonstrate actual evidence on how classDojo saved the classroom time, as the main constituent of the rationale for introducing ClassDojo into the classroom environment.

4.3   Point Systems and Teacher's Role

The teacher's role in the presence of point systems seems to be neutral because students are controlled by the behaviours labelled in the system as negative or positive. In addition, students are granted these points without receiving feedback on the significance of gaining or losing these points, how to enforce good behaviour and avoid the negative one, and most importantly how all these factors can contribute to better learning. The approach for classroom management is addressed via adding or reducing points. Furthermore, there is no sufficient information in the system on the alignment between points and teacher's feedback; whether verbal or written.

Choice and reflection are among the essential features Nicholson [24] prescribed for meaningful gamification. These features are missing in ClassDojo. Students need to reflect on the reason for earning negative points, how to evade disruptive behaviours to avoid losing points, and how to maintain positive points. Students should be provided the help needed to be decision makers and help themselves to be more engaged [4]. Teachers should take the lead to assist students not to take point systems for granted and to critically accept or discard certain features of such systems.

4.4   Point System Gamification and Teacher Centeredness

In the environment of a point system gamification, a teacher's centered pedagogy prevails. In such a model, the teacher is "the dominant leader who establishes and enforces rules in the classroom" [16]. The student is passive as they receive instructions, in which good and bad behaviours are labeled arbitrarily or because they seem to be responsible for creating inconvenience in the learning environment from the teacher's or educational institutions' perspective. The absence of participation in this disciplinary procedure during which positive and negative points/adjectives are given can negatively influence the learning process. In this environment, the students are passive and receiving knowledge is within the frame established by the teacher (who is dominated by the point system), upon labelling these behaviours. Moreover, all disruptive behaviours are equally associated with negative points and consequently students lose points. Educational institutions are responsible for involving students in the structure of such point system platforms to ensure more awareness of their objectives and thereby utilise them for achieving the ILO. Teachers seem to be unaware of the passive role they practice when giving the lead to the point system gamification in classrooms, thereby, leading to decrease teacher efficacy and consequently having a negative influence on students learning.

Proposal for Amendments in Point Systems. The following suggestions address the limitations in point Systems in education for both teachers and point system designers.

Suggestion for Educators

1. Using point systems as a contract of agreement between teachers and students and discussing the rationale for using this system beforehand.
2. Becoming familiar with the main features of point systems and its drawbacks; thereby saving classroom time and avoiding any potential negative influence on students' motivation.
3. Involving students in identifying and agreeing on a set of behaviour that can hinder or enhance learning.
4. Reflecting on the game-based learning classroom experience and documenting their observation meanwhile to maintain the strong features and avoid potential consequences of negative ones.
5. keeping the buzz sound off whether for positive or negative points to avoid distraction or de-motivation.
6. Avoiding the display of points on the screen to avoid students' distraction by the earned or deducted points.
7. Reflecting on the reasons for students disruptive behavior and allocating time to individually discuss the disruptive behaviour with students.
8. Attempting to address any behavioural issues that can be beyond control after referring to specialists.
9. Familiarising parents with the limitations of the point system and the negative potential influence on students.

Suggestions for Point System Designers. Point system designers must be aware of the potential for negative implications of rewards on learners, especially in the long run, when students reach the top levels of gaining or losing points. Point system designers can reward academic institutions with more educationally rewarding versions of game-based systems. Game designers can take the responsibility for conducting needs analysis that investigates the disruptive behaviours that can hinder learning. Such behavioural examples can be identified in the system and prevent teachers and academic institutions from subjectively classifying behaviours to be indicators of winning or losing in this unfortunately game-like environment.

Therefore, designers can attempt to integrate features that can deal with such implications on learning. The following are suggested features for point systems platforms:

1. Integrating platforms where students define positive and negative behaviour and mark the behaviours that can hinder their learning and distract their attention; in addition to the positive behaviors that can motivate students to learning;
2. Integrating platforms for teachers to reflect on individual behaviours and do follow-up on a regular basis;
3. Providing orientation pages to students, teachers and parents to reveal the point system as a friendly tool, the goal of which is enhancing learning, rather than recording points to punish or reward;

4. Enabling the feature of hiding the system from the screen to allow the teacher to access it for taking notes; without functioning as a 'spy' that can threaten students.

5   Conclusion

ClassDojo, as a popular example of point system gamification in education, does not meet its claims of providing the solutions in classroom management as it only addresses the student behaviour and neglects the motivation towards learning, students' emotions upon point deduction and consequently attaining the learning outcomes. Most evidence is either teacher centric or anecdotal responses. Moreover, these studies have not done any form of experimental design which conclusively shows any positive outcome from the software on the part of the learner. Further studies should examine the potential negative influence of point deduction on students motivation to learning.

References

1. Baranek, L.K.: The effect of rewards and motivation on student achievement. Master's thesis, Grand Valley State University (1996)
2. Barrish, H.H., Saunders, M., Wolf, M.: Good behavior game: effects of individual contingencies for group consequences on disruptive behavior in a classroom 1. J. Appl. Behav. Anal. **2**(2), 119–124 (1969)
3. Berridge, K.C.: From prediction error to incentive salience: mesolimbic computation of reward motivation. Eur. J. Neurosci. **35**(7), 1124–1143 (2012)
4. Bolitho, R., Carter, R., Hughes, R., Ivanič, R., Masuhara, H., Tomlinson, B.: Ten questions about language awareness. ELT J. **57**(3), 251–259 (2003)
5. Priyanvada, B.H.: Douglas abd Abeywickrama. Language Assessment Principles and Classroom Practices, Penguin (2011)
6. Michael, B.: The perception of the effectiveness of ClassDojo in middle school classrooms: A transcendental phenomenological study. PhD thesis, Liberty University (2015)
7. Roger, C., Barash, M.: Man, Play And Games, Transition. University of Illinois Press, Urbana (2001)
8. Sam, C.: Sam chaudhary cofounder of classdojo, June 7 2020. http://Inc.com/profile/classdojo http://Inc.com/profile/classdojo
9. Chiarelli, M.A., Szabo, S., Williams, S.: Using classdojo to help with classroom management during guided reading. Texas J. Literacy Educ. **3**(2), 81–88 (2015)
10. ClassDojo, Inc., Classdojo, June 7, 2020. https://www.classdojo.com/en-gb/resources/ https://www.classdojo.com/en-gb/resources/
11. ClassDojo, Inc., Classdojo, June 7, 2020. http://Inc.com/profile/classdojo http://Inc.com/profile/classdojo
12. Cravalho, D.A.: ClassDojo as a Token Economy Method. PhD thesis, UC Riverside (2019)
13. Melissa, M.D.: The tootling intervention with ClassDojo: Effects on classwide disruptive behavior and academically engaged behavior in an upper elementary school setting. PhD thesis, University of Southern Mississippi (2016)

14. William, B.F.: Evaluation of a positive version of the Good Behavior Game utilizing ClassDojo technology in secondary classrooms. PhD thesis, University of Southern Mississippi (2017). Dissertations. 1046. https://aquila.usm.edu/dissertations/1046 https://aquila.usm.edu/dissertations/1046

15. Valerie, F.: Using ClassDojo textregistered to Enhance School Age Students' Prosocial Behavior in a Classroom Setting. PhD thesis, Florida Tech (2017)

16. Hancock, D.R., Bray, M., Nason, S.A.: Influencing university students' achievement and motivation in a technology course. J. Educ. Res. **95**(6), 365–372 (2002)

17. Ryan, H., Khe, F.H., Cheng, Y.T.: Comparing digital badges-and-points with classroom token systems: Effects on elementary school esl students' classroom behavior and english learning. J. Educ. Technol. Soc. **21**(1), 137–151 (2018)

18. Güldeniz, K., Yusuf, İ.B., Göksu, İ., Özdaş, F.: Improving the positive behavior of primary school students with the gamification tool classdojo. Ilkogretim Online **20**(1), 1193–1204 (2021)

19. Lee, J.H.: Gamification in education: What, how, why bother. Acad. Exchange Q. **15**(2), 146 (2011). page 3

20. Manolev, J., Sullivan, A., Slee, R.: The datafication of discipline: classdojo, surveillance and a performative classroom culture. Learn. Media Technol. **44**(1), 36–51 (2019)

21. McGeown, S.P., Putwain, D., Simpson, E.G., Boffey, E., Markham, J., Adrienne, V.: Predictors of adolescents' academic motivation: personality, self-efficacy and adolescents' characteristics. Learn. Ind. Diff. **32**, 278–286 (2014)

22. Jane, M.: Reality is broken: Why games make us better and how they can change the world. Penguin (2011). page 121

23. Common Sense Media. common sense education, June 7, 2020. https://www.commonsense.org/education/website/classdojo https://www.commonsense.org/education/website/classdojo

24. Scott, N.: A recipe for meaningful gamification. In: Gamification in Education and Business, pp. 1–20. Springer (2015)

25. Prensky, M.R.: Teaching digital natives: partnering for real learning. Corwin Press, Thousand Oaks (2010). page 130

26. Bradley, R.: The classdojo app: training in the art of dividuation. International Journal of Qualitative Studies in Education, pp. 1–15 (2020)

27. Abigail, M.S.: Using classdojo to promote positive behaviors and decrease negative behaviors in the classroom. Master's thesis, Rowan University (2017)

28. Skinner, C.H., Skinner, A.L., Cashwell, T.H.: Tootling, not tattling. In: Twenty-sixth Annual Meeting of the Mid-south Educational Research Association, New Orleans, LA (1998)

29. Wang, M.-T., Holcombe, R.: Adolescents' perceptions of school environment, engagement, and academic achievement in middle school. Am. Educ. Res. J. **47**(3), 633–662 (2010)

30. Ward, J.J.: The effect of classdojo and go noodle on the behavioral and off-task disruptions of third grade students. Master's thesis, Goucher College (2015)

31. Williamson, B.: Decoding classdojo: psycho-policy, social-emotional learning and persuasive educational technologies. Learn. Media Technol. **42**(4), 440–453 (2017)

32. Gabe, Z., Christopher, C.: Gamification by design: implementing game mechanics in web and mobile apps. " O'Reilly Media, Inc." (2011)

Assessing the Support for Creativity of a Playground for Live Coding Machine Learning

Francisco Bernardo[✉], Chris Kiefer, and Thor Magnusson

Experimental Music Technology Lab, School of Media, Arts and Humanities,
University of Sussex, Brighton, UK
{f.bernardo,c.kiefer,t.magnusson}@sussex.ac.uk

Abstract. We present the ongoing research around the design of Sema, a live coding environment aimed at supporting live coding with machine learning in the modern web browser. Sema integrates custom dashboards with code editors, debugging and visualisation tools, reference documentation and interactive tutorials. We analyse survey findings applying the Creativity Support Index, which aimed at understanding how well Sema supports creativity across its subsystems, and discuss how the insights we obtained contributed to inform the following design iteration.

Keywords: Live coding · Sound · Music & performance · Machine learning · Creativity support tools

1 Introduction

Live coding practitioners typically engage in real-time composition and performance by programming with a domain-specific language (DSL) and community-developed open-source tools for audio and visual synthesis, algorithmic creation and instrument design [7]. Such tools can be considered as Creativity Support Tools (CST), a class of tools designed to assist users in creative work that includes, for instance, environments for software development, mathematics, music production, animation and visualisation [9]. Designing complex applications to support creativity with highly-technical domain-specific workflows presents difficult challenges, nevertheless, particularly when assessing prototypes for informing future design iterations. We present an assessment of the creativity support of Sema, a playground for live coding music and machine learning (ML) in the Web, using the Creative Support Index [4] with a sample of workshop participants that comprised novices and expert live coders.

2 System Overview

Sema [1,2] is an open source live coding system—such as SuperCollider [5], TidalCycles [6] or Gibber [8]—where code is used as the language and medium for

ⓒ IFIP International Federation for Information Processing 2021
Published by Springer Nature Switzerland AG 2021
J. Baalsrud Hauge et al. (Eds.): ICEC 2021, LNCS 13056, pp. 449–456, 2021.
https://doi.org/10.1007/978-3-030-89394-1_38

real-time composition and performance. Sema aims to support different musical practices and cultures, and empower users to shape the language to their own musical needs. It also aims to support users wanting to apply machine learning models that may generate interesting musical behaviour in their performance. Such models can be trained on small data sets interactively and in real time, or previously trained on big data sets and used through transfer learning.

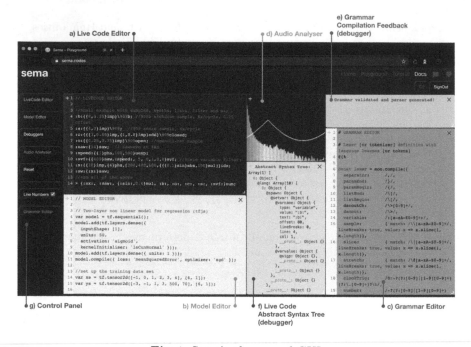

Fig. 1. Sema's playground GUI

Previous user-centred design iterations led us to integrate machine learning and language design workflows with a high-performance signal engine for real-time interactive audio in a low-entry-barrier environment available in the Web browser [1,2]. Sema integrates third-party ML libraries—e.g. Tensorflow.js [11] and Magenta.js [10]—that enable users to design and evaluate end-to-end ML pipelines. This includes creating training datasets, bespoke model architectures and hyper-parameters, and input and output channels that enable communication between the live coding languages and the signal engine. The user interface to ML is a code editor similar to Jupiter Notebooks where users can write and evaluate JavaScript code blocks in a non-linear fashion. The system provides machine learning exemplars for sound and music applications, including interactive machine learning for FM synthesis, reinforcement learning for sequencing beats, or pre-trained Magenta models for note sequencing. Sema also enables users to customise or create their live coding languages by inspecting, editing or specifying the different components of a language grammar (i.e. lexer, grammar rules and semantic actions) using the Bachus-Naur Form metasyntax notation.

Sema's user interface—version 0.5.0, used in the workshop (Fig. 1)—allowed users to navigate between two main areas: the Playground and the Tutorial. In the Playground, users could access a dashboard of customisable layouts and a library of dynamic components—code editors, visualisers, and debugging tools—and engage in a free, open-ended exploration of live coding, language design and ML workflows. In contrast, the Tutorial area makes a strong proposition with a constrained-layout environment and content structured with chapters and sections with gradually increasing challenge and granularity. The live coding editor (Fig. 1-a) provided users with the main tool to interact with the live coding languages, key bindings for code evaluation and real-time audio playback, suspension and resume, code commenting and text search.

3   User Study

The overall goal of the mixed-methods user study was to evaluate the creativity support, usability and utility of Sema. This study succeeded a previous study which assessed the first design iteration of Sema through a week-long co-located workshop [2]. For the scope of this paper, we focus on creativity support and delimit the description of methods, results and discussion accordingly, while providing as much context about the workshop as it is deemed reasonable.

3.1   Workshop

The "Sema: Live Coding With Machine Learning Workshop" was as a two-week long online workshop in late June–July 2020, which was conducted as part of a mixed-methods user-centred design study. The workshop was advertised using a blog post[1] that was disseminated on social media and personal contact networks two weeks before the event. The blog post described the target audience of beginners, with beginner-level JavaScript programming skills, and without required experience in Sema, machine learning, language design or music. The blog post described some of the affordances of Sema in live coding, language design and machine learning, and provided demonstration videos of live coding with three languages in Sema. Additionally, it described the workshop programme, with schedule and topics to cover, and included details about the registration and a link to the registration form.

In the first week of the workshop, we employed a flipped-learning approach [3] where, every day, we released introductory tutorial videos and provided two-hour long synchronous Zoom sessions (one hour of workshop tutorial followed by an hour of Q&A) and asynchronous Slack channel support. Participants would explore Sema and the instructional content on their own individual time. The

---

[1] Sema: Live Coding With Machine Learning Workshop http://www.emutelab.org/blog/semaworkshop.

second week of the workshop switched to hands-on project development, with three synchronous Zoom sessions and continued asynchronous Slack channel support over the week for people developing their projects.

The workshop was designed to give us data for further development of the project. For data collection, we employed several techniques that yielded a very substantial and rich primary data set comprising:

1. a record with all the interactions between workshop participants and facilitators in the Slack channel, with live code samples produced and shared by participants,
2. video recordings of the Q&A sessions and of semi-structured interviews conducted with a selection of 10 participants at the end of the workshop,
3. an online survey that included sections with the Creative Support Index completed by 23 participants by the end of the workshop.

The full analysis of all the elements of this data set is beyond the scope of this paper and will be published separately. Here we focus our analysis on the last element of the data set, the results of the Creativity Support Index.

3.2   Creativity Support Index

The Creativity Support Index (CSI) is a survey designed for the psychometric evaluation of the support for creativity of digital tools [4]. The CSI enables researchers to understand how well a tool supports creative work and what aspects of creativity support need improvement, through a quantitative assessment of six dimensions of creativity support—Exploration, Expressiveness, Immersion, Enjoyment, Results, Worth Effort, and Collaboration.

The CSI was administered to the participants at the end of the workshop, as part of an online survey in the Qualtrics platform. A preface survey section comprised a summary of the study goals, the participant information sheet, and a consent form that conditionally unblocked access to the remainder of the survey. Part A of the survey assessed participant demographics, background and experience on live coding, machine learning and language design. Part B.1 was compulsory and presented CSI agreement statements in two pages (with six items per page) followed by 15 pages of paired-factor comparisons. All paired-factor comparisons had 15 pages, with one pair per page. The remainder of the survey presented an optional section with open-ended qualitative questions.

3.3   Sample

The sample of participants consisted mostly of novices to Sema, but with extensive coding experience, particularly in live coding and creative coding tools, and a varying degree of machine learning experience. Twenty-one workshop participants engaged with the Qualtrics survey (17 males and 3 females, 1 non-binary, with an average age of 36 years old). The average reported coding experience was 9.14 years (SD = 8.71). One participant had participated on an early Sema workshop and had advanced skills in live coding, machine learning and language design. One participant reported having no live coding experience. The remainder of the respondents reported having experience with at least one live coding system or a combination of several (e.g. 'Chuck', 'Csound', 'Gibber', 'Supercollider', 'TidalCycles', etc.). Seven respondents reported never having used machine learning tools, while 14 respondents reported having experienced different creative ML tools, illustrating with examples (e.g. 'Wekinator', 'ml5js', 'Magenta', 'RunwayML', 'ML4A', etc.). Two respondents reported having had previous experience designing a programming language. Respondents reported having spent 19.62 h working with Sema on average (SD = 12.79).

3.4   Results

All the participants completed Part B.1 of the survey, which referred to the CSI of Sema's subsystem for live coding with the default language. Part B.1 generated an average score of 56.86 (SD = 20.84), which is a moderate score with a high standard deviation. This score indicates that the prototype assessed at the workshop provided support for creativity to novices to the system, in the task of live coding with the default language. The high standard deviation value indicates high variability across participants. On further inspection, Table 1 shows the average factor counts, average factor score, and average weighted factor score for each of the six factors of the CSI for Part B.1.

Table 1. CSI results from the live coding with the default language (N = 21)

Scale	Avg. factor counts (SD)	Avg. factor score (SD)	Avg. weighted factor score (SD)
Exploration	3.71 (1.10)	12.34 (5.00)	47.72 (26.42)
Expressiveness	3.55 (1.23)	11.72 (5.18)	39.83 (25.29)
Results worth effort	3.17 (1.47)	12.33 (5.58)	32.07 (29.60)
Enjoyment	2.48 (1.12)	14.19 (5.57)	34.9 (22.38)
Immersion	2.11 (1.08)	6.63 (4.43)	10.50 (10.26)
Collaboration	2.11 (1.54)	6.04 (6.02)	5.56 (13.29)

The average factor counts for live coding with the default language in Sema (Table 1, first column) show the importance that participants have given to the different CSI factors (in a scale between 0 and 5) independently of how well Sema supported them. Exploration and Expressiveness were considered the most important factors, followed by Results Worth Effort and Enjoyment, with more moderate importance. Collaboration and Immersion were considered the less important factors for the task by novice users. The factor score metrics indicate how well Sema supported the six factors for the task of live coding with the default language, in a scale between 0 and 20. The weighted factor scores show sensitivity to the importance that participants assigned to specific factors (factor counts) for the live coding task and how they affect factor scores, in a scale between 0 and 100.

The Enjoyment dimension received the highest score albeit a moderate good one. This indicates that, to some extent, participants became adept of live coding with the default language, despite having faced difficulties. These could relate to the design, level of polish of the system, or its complexity and steep learning curve. In a system with complex workflows and a steep learning curve, enjoyments ratings usually start low and increase over time, as the user learning experience progresses [4].

The Exploration, Expressiveness, and Results Worth Effort dimensions received moderate scores. The Exploration score (12.34) suggests that users found challenging to try out new ideas, different possibilities or versions, and that system support for versioning, branching, and duplication of user content should be developed. The Expressiveness score (11.72) suggests that users found limitations in the space of possibilities offered by the system, or in the ability to express their ideas when live coding with the system. It also suggests the need for developing system features that align with the goals and needs of novice users of a live coding system. The Results Worth Effort score (12.33) suggests that, for the results obtained, the effort required to live code with the default language may be too high, or involve too many steps. This could point to the verbosity or low abstraction level of the language. Both Collaboration and Immersion paired-factor comparisons scored very low against the remaining factors. Collaboration received a low value with 8 respondents marking the collaboration statements as non-applicable (which coded Collaboration statements as 0). Given that the prototype was not designed with collaboration features (except for the ordinary Copy & Paste to share code) this score was expected. Nevertheless, we decided to keep this factor in the survey to apply a standard CSI version. The low Immersion score points out to potential disruptions to the workflow, which could be due to bugs, lack of feedback or visibility, or the necessity to look for help resources outside the system.

In general, we found the results obtained through the CSI were reasonable given the level of system complexity and skill levels of the sample of participants. However, we also recognise that these point out mostly to the need for deeper research around the causes of the moderate factor scores and to general improvements to the system.

4   Discussion

The results of the CSI score and factor breakdown analysis indicated that Sema required substantial improvements to achieve a good creativity support level. This was anticipated as, at the time of the workshop, despite successfully integrating rather complex subsystems and workflows (to a good extent), Sema was a functional high-fidelity prototype that presented 'rough edges' and bugs of varying severity (e.g. UI layout rendering, code editor interactions, debugger compilation error reporting, a malfunctioning delay line). More critically, there were important functional and non-functional features lacking, such as a well-designed and encompassing documentation system, comprehensive error handling and feedback in all workflows, and data persistence mechanisms.

Despite these shortcomings, participants showed interesting accomplishments, including creating a new language (e.g. STX), porting an existing language to Sema (e.g. QuaverSeries), extending ML examples to new applications (e.g. neural arpeggiator), integration of an euclidean rhythm generator, etc. Five participants used Sema in a live coding performance at the Networked Music Festival, one week after the workshop. All these examples of issues and successful usage were captured through complementary methods (interviews, open-ended sections of the survey, Slack content) as part of the broader mixed-methods user study. The CSI was useful as a structured framework and complementary design assessment tool for uncovering how novices valued the different factors for creativity support, and for using the resulting insights to influence the directions of improvement and re-design.

Worthwhile of reflection and note are the challenges found with the application of the CSI. The CSI has been previously applied to CSTs with relatively simple tasks, where even the most complex examples are typically well-defined and self-contained tasks with high-level interfaces. In contrast, in CSTs with highly complex workflows and subsystems that interact, that are difficult to learn and master, and that aim to support end-user goals with non-linear, variable or unknown underlying tasks like Sema, the CSI provides an analysis that seems to park at a rather superficial level. CSI authors [4] point out that tool complexity and user skill level can impact CSI scores, and they acknowledge that new system complexity metrics are required to support deeper investigations into these relationships.

Furthermore, it was difficult to account for the effect that the communication used in the workshop advertisement might have had in building up overly inflated user expectations about the tool, and how this in turn may have affected the creativity scores. On experimental designs with more scoped tasks and constrained environments, this might be easier to account for. However when applying discount usability methods or testing CSTs in the wild with workshops [2] this seems to be an additional aspect to consider in the final evaluation outcome.

5   Conclusion

We have applied the CSI and computed scores for the task of live coding with the default language in Sema. We also carried out a breakdown analysis of the CSI factors. The scores were moderate which could be explained by the shortcomings of the high-fidelity prototype. They also suggested room for substantial improvements to the creativity support of Sema. On one hand, the CSI is relatively straightforward to apply, to analyse, and provides a limited but useful set of insights. On the other hand, we question the efficacy and applicability of CSI in assessing highly complex, hard to learn workflows and systems, which aim to support unknown, non-linear or variable tasks, such as live coding, language design or machine learning.

For future work, we will release the more extensive results of the mixed methods user study, further identify and improve on the issues that undermine creativity support in Sema, and apply the CSI as a tool to complement assessment of the different workflows in future design iterations.

Acknowledgements. We would like to thank the workshop participants and our MIMIC project colleagues. This work was supported by two UKRI/AHRC grants: MIMIC-Musically Intelligent Machines Interacting Creatively (ref: AH/R002657/1)- and Innovating Sema-Community-building of Live Coding Language Design and Perfor mance with Machine Learning (ref: AH/V005154/1).

References

1. Bernardo, F., Kiefer, C., Magnusson, T.: A signal engine for a live coding language ecosystem. J. Audio Eng. Soc. **68**(10), 756–766 (2020)
2. Bernardo, F., Kiefer, C., Magnusson, T.: Designing for a pluralist and user-friendly live code language ecosystem with sema. In: Proceedings of International Conference on Live Coding, pp. 41–57 (2020)
3. Bergmann, J., Sams, A.: Flip your classroom: reach every student in every class every day, pp. 120–190, Washington DC. International Society for Technology in Education (2012)
4. Carroll, E., Latulipe, C.: Quantifying the creativity support of digital tools through the creativity support index. ACM Trans. Comput. Hum. Interact. **21**(4), Article 21, 25 (2014). https://doi.org/10.1145/2617588
5. McCartney, J.: Rethinking the computer music language: SuperCollider. Comput. Music J. **26**, 61–68 (2002). https://doi.org/10.1162/014892602320991383
6. McLean, A.: Making programming languages to dance to: live coding with tidal. In: Proceedings of the First ACM SIGPLAN Workshop on Functional Art, Music, Modeling - FARM 2014, pp. 63–70 (2014). https://doi.org/10.1145/2633638.2633647
7. Magnusson, T.: Herding cats: observing live coding in the wild. Comput. Music J. **38**, 91–101 (2014). https://doi.org/10.1162/COMJ
8. Roberts, C., Kuchera-Morin, J.A: Gibber: Live coding audio in the browser. Proc. Int. Comput. Music Conf. **2012**, 64–69 (2012)
9. Shneiderman, B.: Creativity support tools: accelerating discovery and innovation. Commun. ACM **50**(12), 20–32 (2007)
10. Roberts, A., Hawthorne, C., Simon, I.: Magenta.js: a JavaScript API for augmenting creativity with deep learning. In: Proceedings of the 35th Joint Workshop on Machine Learning for Music (ICML) (2018)
11. Smilkov, D., et al.: TensorFlow.js: machine learning for the web and beyond. In: Proceedings of the 2nd SysML Conference (2019)

Safety Risks in Location-Based Augmented Reality Games

Munir Makhmutov$^{(\boxtimes)}$(iD), Timur Asapov, and Joseph Alexander Brown(iD)

Innopolis University, Innopolis 420500, Russia
{m.makhmutov,t.asapov,j.brown}@innopolis.ru

Abstract. Location-based augmented reality games occur with a player moving through public spaces, which carries risks. The inattention of the player is one such hazard. Additionally, as seen in many news reports, players of these games have also engaged in trespassing, playing while driving, playing in places of worship, etc. These actions have led to public outrage, and in some well-known cases, arrest and legal consequences. These instances bring forward issues for developers to consider to ensure players' ethical development and safety while using modern location-based AR games. To evaluate the current safety problems of these games, we provide a comparison of popular AR games.

Keywords: Augmented Reality · Location-based games · Safe games

1 Introduction

The world is an inherently dangerous place. We learn this from a young age, and we protect ourselves via risk mitigation, such as wearing a seat belt in a car. This is problematic for new technologies, as technological development moves faster than a risk assessment and mitigation is put in place. Further, there are the *unknown unknowns*, which only become apparent over the life cycle. Over the past few years, augmented reality (AR) technology made a giant leap in development. Such developments have not been well examined in terms of risks, leading to incidences of arrests, detainment, potential physical harm, and emotional damage for both users and non-participants, which we will examine later in this article. AR is the environment with the addition of digital data to the physical world employing digital devices. The scope of AR is rather extensive, and it includes mobile technology, medicine, military, computer games, etc. AR applications and limitations are described in detail in [32].

In 2018, the global law firm *Perkins Coie LLP* issued the report comparing Augmented Reality and Virtual Reality (VR) in 2016 and 2018 [4]. About 39% of respondents indicated that AR and VR technologies are more prevalent in game development. In 2016, only 18% of respondents were concerned about safety issues. However, in 2018, the number of respondents concerned about safety issues has increased to 42%, which shows that the AR and VR markets require a

J. Baalsrud Hauge et al. (Eds.): ICEC 2021, LNCS 13056, pp. 457–464, 2021.
https://doi.org/10.1007/978-3-030-89394-1_39

solution for this problem. This growth portrays the relevance of the study about safety issues in AR games. Later in 2020, *Perkins Coie LLP* issued the newer report, where the safety issues in AR and VR games are of concern to 41% of respondents, which participated in this survey [5]. This survey was conducted with startups, established tech firms, advisers, and outside consultants.

In his book Wassom raises questions about the ethical side of AR technologies [33]. The author states that the AR may change our relation to privacy and ethics [29]. This is already happening, and cases of arrests and fines because of AR games demonstrate that this process is not smooth (see Sect. 2). AR provides the extension of different parts of reality. This paper focuses on game content generation based on location and aims to discuss safety and ethical problems.

2   Background

One of the pioneers of mobile multiplayer location-based AR games (LBGs) is *Ingress* released in 2012 by *Niantic Labs*. This game's main idea is to join one of two existing teams and, on the real-world map, conquer game objects linked to specific locations, which are called portals. To conquer portals, players must physically reach them. The players were allowed to create new portals. However, some players created portals in unethical and unsafe places, including cemeteries, temples, dangerous places, etc. To prevent it, developers have forbidden the creation of new portals in 2015. Later in 2017, this functionality was returned to players with some limitations: high-level players had to approve new portals. It does not imply that all high-level players are highly educated people who understand ethical problems, which some players can cause. The game's positive side is that it allowed people to get a new playing experience, pushing them to go outside. More extensive research about *Ingress* can be read in [3,12].

In 2016 *Niantic Labs* released a new LBG called *Pokémon GO*, which became the most popular AR game in the world. The idea of this game is to catch imaginary creatures called *pokémon* located on the map, upgrade them and fight with other *pokémon*. Similarly to *Ingress Pokémon GO* pushes players to move. The *Pokémon GO* has *pokéstops* and gyms located on map. Their locations are taken from *Ingress* portal locations. *Pokémon GO* revealed the ethical and safety problems of this game concept. Some of the locations resulted in people questioning the ethics of a specific location being integrated into the game space.

It is impolite to see someone playing games in temples during prayers. This can distract and make worshipers feel uncomfortable. The world contains many places where playing games may be considered inappropriate and even illegal. For example, the director of public affairs at the Holocaust museum states that it is unacceptable to play *Pokémon GO* in a memorial to the victims of Nazism [27]. After such incidents, *Niantic Labs* had to exclude some of the museums from possible places of *pokémon* generation. Nevertheless, the problem did not disappear. More discussion about catching *pokémon* is provided in [15].

Mobile application stores allow publishing games separately for different countries. This will enable developers to focus on chosen markets. Also, some games and applications are not authorized by governments to be published. In some cases, games and apps can even be blocked [18] in those countries' mobile application stores. One of the possible reasons for it is a conflict with the laws of those countries. For example, *Pokémon GO* remains blocked in Iran, Kuwait, etc.

Sometimes illegal behaviour caused by AR games may lead to jail. Players can be officially arrested for playing in some territories; this happened to Ruslan Sokolovsky while playing in Russia in Yekaterinburg's Orthodox church [29]. Therefore, it is imperative to know the country's laws while playing LBGs.

Generation of game content in water, near volcanoes, and other places can endanger life. In [16] authors consider five LBGs and claim that in *The Walking Dead: Our World* content can be generated in the water and in *Draconius GO* even on high traffic motorways. Unfortunately, dangerous areas can be everywhere if players are too distracted by the game. There are plenty of situations when *Pokémon GO* players died or were traumatized while playing [11,19].

In their paper, Colley et al. [6] reported the results of a mixed-methods study of the geography of *Pokémon GO*. It includes a five-country field survey of 375 *Pokémon GO* players and a large-scale geostatistical analysis of game elements. Authors claim that *Pokémon GO* has geographically-linked safety risks. The authors found out that *Pokémon GO* causes people to visit new locations on an unprecedented scale with some degree of distraction-related risk. The results have shown that more in-game content is generated in urban places than in rural areas. Over one-third of respondents reported some form of near-miss or actual collision with an object while playing the game. Mainly those players reported bumping into signs, poles and other people. The most severe awareness problem is raised when they come into conflict with road traffic. In this respect, 11% of participants recalled situations in which they had put their safety at risk by, for example, crossing the street without looking. About 13% of respondents did report feeling unsafe in an unknown place while playing *Pokémon GO*. Authors reported that three approaches could be used to increase the safety of AR game players: notification about dangerous areas, avoidance of game content appearing across a road from the player's location and stricter game prohibitions while driving. Also, the authors state that movements are more dangerous than places in LBGs. Some gamers' carelessness and indifference will always be a problem in LBGs. Still, there is a chance to reduce the deaths and traumas using some universal rules for forbidding game content generation in dangerous areas. Thus, this paper should examine hazardous locations for game content generation.

The popularity of *Ingress* and *Pokémon GO* led to the greater interest of gamers in LBGs; it has been claimed that these games created a new game genre [30]. And this stimulates the market to develop a more considerable amount of new LBGs in the nearest future. It can be assumed that future games should somehow change game content generation to prevent problems with laws in different countries and issues with dangerous places. Therefore, game developers should pay attention to laws. Some countries considered *Pokémon GO* inappropriate from a religious point of view. Some countries were afraid of revealing military object locations, etc. We believe that the lack of algorithms preventing the generation of game content in dangerous and inappropriate places increases the risk of traumatizing people and breaking the laws in LBGs.

According to [16] generation of content in LBGs happens in points of interest (PoIs), which can be created manually or automatically. Authors claim that in *Draconius GO* automatically generated PoIs may appear in restricted areas making the game unsafe because of trespassing to forbidden territories. Millard et al. discuss the responsibilities of mixed reality designers for using places in their applications [20]. These responsibilities include avoiding physical trespass, respecting cultural norms of behaviour, etc. The application of the automatically generated PoIs can lead to ignoring those two responsibilities because virtual objects may occur in private territories or unethical places.

Some safety issues can be solved by using audio cues [26]. *Songs of North* is a LBG released in 2004, where users can get a sound notification while playing in a dangerous situation. The audio cues are more deeply discussed in Ekman et al. [7]. The sounds in *Songs of North* emphasize the surroundings, which allows a player to percept the game and other players without staring at the phone.

Other problems may arise while playing LBG with a specific device on the head, as described in the paper of Broll et al. [2]. The authors describe the head-mounted AR system with monocular or binocular for the augmented view of the world. Even though the system can superimpose the real world with virtual objects, using such a system outdoors risks a malfunction and wearing a sizeable head-mounted unit in many places in a church might not be appropriate.

In 2019, a new COVID-19 virus emerged [31]. Due to this, countries were obliged to maintain social distancing and self-isolation, which almost excluded playing outside. It has been widely publicized that some players of *Pokémon GO* were fined for playing outdoors [8]. In 2020, *Niantic Labs* announced the changes in their games to encourage home AR gaming [23,25]: walking inside home began counting as the achievements progress; the paid pass to participate in *Pokémon GO* raids was introduced; the amount of content for *Harry Potter: Wizards Unite* was increased; the need of interaction with *Ingress* portals was reduced.

3   Comparison of LBGs

To understand the advantages and disadvantages of LBGs in terms of safe and ethical content, we provide a comparison of several popular games: *Ingress, Pokémon GO, Jurassic World Alive* and *Harry Potter: Wizards Unite*. All of those games were released in different years, which allows for a focus on LBGs evolution. Other LBGs are omitted in comparison because it is work-in-progress. *Ingress* is chosen for comparison as a pioneer in the field of LBGs. The *Pokémon GO* is chosen for being the most popular LBG. *Jurassic World Alive* was released in 2018 by *Ludia Inc.* This game's idea is close to *Pokémon GO*. Another setting and game content differs from *Pokémon GO*. Visually *Jurassic World* looks different from *Pokémon GO*, mechanics of catching of dinosaurs do not copy the mechanics of *pokémon* catching. In 2019 *Niantic Labs* and *WB Games San Francisco* released *Harry Potter: Wizards Unite*. It has the same backbone as *Pokémon GO*. As a result, the game suffers from the same problems: generation of the game content depends on the time of the day and weather, the neighbourhood's density, which results in a lack of content in rural areas.

People tend to overcome their opponents by reaching generated content faster than others. However, it could lead to traumas while using vehicles [14]. Therefore, all the abovementioned games have a speed limit for players. We believe that the speed limit may differ for the compared games, affecting the safety level.

The number of extreme weather conditions rises exponentially year over year [9]. However, with the current quality of life, the amount of people suffering from the consequences of extreme weather conditions is decreasing. From 2006 until 2010, in the United States, 10649 deaths were related to adverse weather conditions such as heat and cold [1]. The LBGs may be played outdoors, so they impose restrictions on movement in extreme weather conditions.

Due to the lack of visibility, a human makes more mistakes at nighttime than daytime [28]. The street robbery rate is higher at night, as stated by the US Department of Justice [21]. Moreover, the night also worsens the visual perception of obstacles, which can lead to traumas. Gold mentions that some people were awakened at 3 AM by crowds of *pokémon* catchers bumping into things [10]. Therefore, playing LBGs during the night may be unsafe and unethical.

By trespassing private, unethical, and unsafe areas, players put themselves and people around at risk [22]. The LBGs should prevent the generation of in-game content in such areas. The experience of *Ingress* shows that two or more players competing nearby can negatively affect their health [13]. Thus, Player vs. Player (PvP) distance is vital for the safety of the players.

Since the developers of considered games have not provided the exact information about the speed limit for playing, all of the measurements were done empirically. Information about other criteria was gathered from considered games' safety rules, community guidelines, terms of service and observed game features. The results of our observations are collected in Table 1. Previously described games are compared according to the criteria: speed limits, extreme weather conditions, nighttime, trespassing alerts, and PvP distance.

Table 1. Comparison of chosen LBGs

	Ingress	Pokémon GO	Jurassic World Alive	Harry Potter: Wizards Unite
Speed limit alert	50 km/h	50 km/h	15 km/h	15 km/h
Extreme weather alert	Weather	Weather	General	Weather
Nighttime alert	No	No	No	No
Trespassing alert	General	General	General	General
PvP distance	Proximity	No matter	No matter	N/A

It can be seen that *Jurassic World Alive*, and *Harry Potter: Wizards Unite* have the lowest speed limit for playing the game, which makes driving during the game almost useless. Therefore, these two games are better for the safety of drivers. However, all games allow skipping the warning by answering that they are passengers. We believe that more strict rules have to be applied for players exceeding the speed limit, whether they are drivers or passengers. The game should be locked in such cases to prevent cheating by playing drivers.

Each compared game gives a general warning to avoid private and unsafe areas. Nevertheless, notification during trespassing is not provided. We assume that the detection of such a variety of spaces can work better than a general warning. In the ideal case, games should not generate content in such areas or close to them. This should become an essential direction for LBGs to make them safer and protect players from breaking the laws. Currently, all considered games allow sending reports about unsafe and inappropriate places.

Extreme weather conditions are differently processed in considered games. All games of *Niantic Labs* give extreme weather condition warnings while *Jurassic World Alive* gives only a general notice, which is less safe. We believe that warnings can help some players to stop playing. For others, they may be ineffective. The ultimate solution is locking the game during extreme weather conditions.

None of the considered games notifies players about increased danger during the night. The presence of this feature could allow preventing playing outdoors at night. Moreover, *Pokémon GO* has unique creatures appearing during nights, pushing some players to go outdoors. We assume that night game content generation in LBGs has to be minimized or even excluded to make games safer.

PvP was added to *Pokémon GO* in 2020, and developers claim that the opponents for PvP are chosen from the entire world [24]. We may assume that this decreases the chance of matches between players located nearby. According to claims of developers, the choice of opponents for PvP in *Jurassic World Alive* does not depend on distance [17], which prevents physical contact between players because of game conflicts. Currently, PvP in *Harry Potter: Wizards Unite* does not exist. Therefore, *Ingress* has the highest safety risk among others because of possible conflicts between players located near to each other.

Thus, it can be said that games of *Niantic Labs* have partially evolved in terms of safety because of having lower speed limit alert in their last published game *Harry Potter: Wizards Unite* and because of not having proximity condition for PvP in *Pokémon GO*. Supposedly, developers of *Jurassic World Alive* have considered the experience of *Niantic Labs* with playing drivers and also used a lower speed limit. However, they did not pay that much attention to extreme weather condition warnings and used only general warnings.

4   Conclusions

This study has considered the ethical and safety problems of content generation in LBGs. The comparison of modern LBGs was done. This paper demonstrates that the current state of LBGs contains many safety risks related to playing while driving, in extreme weather conditions, during nights, on private territories, etc. Therefore, it requires changes to motivate players to enjoy the game safely. Specific actions could decrease this.

Future work would be to develop and test the LBG following the provided recommendations and contain safe content generation algorithms that can exclude hazardous places. Furthermore, surveys should be conducted to understand how effective risk warnings are for the user and if they will be heeded.

References

1. Berko, J.: Deaths attributed to heat, cold, and other weather events in the United States, 2006–2010. Nat. Health Stat. Report **30**(76), 1–15 (2014). US Department of Health and Human Services, CDC
2. Broll, W., Ohlenburg, J., Lindt, I., Herbst, I., Braun, A.K.: Meeting technology challenges of pervasive augmented reality games. In: Proceedings of 5th ACM SIG-COMM Workshop on Network and System Support for Games, p. 28-es (2006)
3. Chess, S.: Augmented regionalism: ingress as geomediated gaming narrative. Inf. Commun. Soc. **17**(9), 1105–1117 (2014)
4. Coie, P.: Augmented and virtual reality survey report. Perkins Coie, pp. 1–20 (2018)
5. Coie, P.: Augmented and virtual reality survey report. Perkins Coie, pp. 1–32 (2020)
6. Colley, A., et al.: The geography of pokémon go: beneficial and problematic effects on places and movement. In: Proceedings of the 2017 CHI Conference on Human Factors in Computing Systems, pp. 1179–1192 (2017)
7. Ekman, I., Ermi, L., Lahti, J., Nummela, J., Lankoski, P., Mäyrä, F.: Designing sound for a pervasive mobile game. In: Proceedings of the 2005 ACM SIGCHI International Conference on Advances in Computer Entertainment Technology, pp. 110–116 (2005)
8. Gilbert, B.: 'I have to hunt the pokémon': a man in Italy gets charged for ignoring the coronavirus lockdown to play 'pokémon go' (2020). https://www.businessinsider.com/pokemon-go-have-hunt-pokemon-coronavirus-outbreak-italy-2020-3. Accessed 15 July 2021
9. Goklany, I.M., Morris, J.: Wealth and Safety: The Amazing Decline in Deaths from Extreme Weather in an Era of Global Warming, 1900–2010. Reason Foundation (2011)
10. Gold, S.: When Pokemon GO(es) too far: augmented reality and Tort law. Whittier L. Rev. **38**, 161 (2017)
11. Hernandez, D.: 'Pokémon go' players fall off 90-foot ocean bluff (2016). https://www.sandiegouniontribune.com/sdut-pokemon-go-encinitas-cliff-fall-2016jul13-story.html. Accessed 15 July 2021
12. Hulsey, N., Reeves, J.: The gift that keeps on giving: Google, ingress, and the gift of surveillance. Surveill. Soc. **12**(3), 389–400 (2014)
13. Hunzaker, M.A.: Intent or Misinterpretation? Disruptive Behaviors within Ingress. Master's thesis, NC State (2016)
14. Jacob, J.T.P.N., Coelho, A.F.: Issues in the development of location-based games. Int. J. Comput. Games Technol. **2011**, 495437 (2011)
15. Judge, E.F., Brown, T.E.: Pokémorials: placing norms in augmented reality. UBCL Rev. **50**, 971 (2017)

16. Laato, S., Pietarinen, T., Rauti, S., Laine, T.H.: Analysis of the quality of points of interest in the most popular location-based games. In: Proceedings of the 20th International Conference on Computer Systems and Technologies, pp. 153–160 (2019)

17. Ludia Inc.: How are my battle arena opponents selected? (2020). https://ludia. helpshift.com/a/jurassic-world-alive/?s=about-battles&f=how-are-my-battle-arena-opponents-selected&l=en. Accessed 15 July 2021

18. Mans, S.: Who owns the playground?: Urban gamification and spatial politics in Pokémon GO. ESTI Developers (2017)

19. McCormick, R.: Driver distracted by Pokémon go kills woman in Japan (2016). https://www.theverge.com/2016/8/25/12637878/pokemon-go-driver-kills-woman-japan. Accessed 15 July 2021

20. Millard, D.E., Hewitt, S., O'Hara, K., Packer, H., Rogers, N.: The unethical future of mixed reality storytelling. In: Proceedings of the 8th International Workshop on Narrative and Hypertext, pp. 5–8 (2019)

21. Monk, K.M., Heinonen, J.A., Eck, J.E.: Street robbery. U.S. Department of Justice, Office of Community Oriented Policing Services, Washington, DC, USA (2010)

22. Neustaedter, C., Tang, A., Judge, T.K.: Creating scalable location-based games: lessons from geocaching. Pers. Ubiquit. Comput. **17**(2), 335–349 (2013)

23. Niantic Inc.: Embracing real-world gaming from home (2020). https://nianticlabs. com/blog/stay-safe/. Accessed 15 July 2021

24. Niantic Inc.: Go battle league (2020). https://niantic.helpshift.com/a/pokemon-go/?s=gyms-battle&f=go-battle-league&l=en&p=web. Accessed 15 July 2021

25. Oe, H.: Discussion of digital gaming's impact on players' well-being during the COVID-19 lockdown. arXiv preprint arXiv:2005.00594 (2020)

26. Paavilainen, J., Korhonen, H., Alha, K., Stenros, J., Koskinen, E., Mayra, F.: The Pokémon GO experience: a location-based augmented reality mobile game goes mainstream. In: Proceedings of the 2017 CHI Conference on Human Factors in Computing Systems, pp. 2493–2498 (2017)

27. Peterson, A.: Holocaust museum to visitors: please stop catching Pokémon here. Washington Post, 12 July 2016

28. Plainis, S., Murray, I., Pallikaris, I.: Road traffic casualties: understanding the night-time death toll. Inj. Prev. **12**(2), 125–138 (2006)

29. RT: Russian blogger arrested for 2 months for playing 'Pokémon go' in church (2016). https://www.rt.com/viral/358174-blogger-arrested-pokemon-church/. Accessed 15 July 2021

30. Söbke, H., Baalsrud Hauge, J., Stefan, I.A., Stefan, A.: Using a location-based AR game in environmental engineering. In: van der Spek, E., et al. (eds.) ICEC-JCSG 2019. LNCS, vol. 11863, pp. 466–469. Springer, Cham (2019). https://doi.org/10. 1007/978-3-030-34644-7_47

31. Van Bavel, J.J., et al.: Using social and behavioural science to support COVID-19 pandemic response. Nat. Hum. Behav. **4**, 460–472 (2020)

32. Van Krevelen, R., Poelman, R.: A survey of augmented reality technologies, applications and limitations. Int. J. Virtual Reality **9**, 1 (2010). (ISSN 1081-1451). https://doi.org/10.20870/IJVR.2010.9.2.2767

33. Wassom, B.: Augmented Reality Law, Privacy, and Ethics: Law, Society, and Emerging AR Technologies. Syngress, Waltham (2014)

Workshops

Virtualization of Digital Location-Based Experiences

Jannicke Baalsrud Hauge[1,2](✉) ⓘ, Heinrich Söbke[3] ⓘ, and Ioana A. Stefan[4] ⓘ

[1] BIBA – Bremer Institut für Produktion und Logistik GmbH, Hochschulring 20, 28359 Bremen, Germany
baa@biba.uni-bremen.de
[2] Royal Institute of Technology, Kvarnbergagatan 12, Södertälje, Sweden
jmbh@kth.se
[3] Bauhaus-Institute for Infrastructure Solutions (B.Is), Bauhaus-Universität Weimar, Goetheplatz 7/8, 99423 Weimar, Germany
heinrich.soebke@uni-weimar.de
[4] Advanced Technology Systems, Str. Tineretului Nr 1, 130029 Targoviste, Romania
ioana.stefan@ats.com.ro

Abstract. Digital location-based experiences, such as app-guided digital scavengers, depend on users being on-site. The requirement to be on-site is a virtue, but it can also be a shortcoming of location-based experiences, such as in the COVID 19 pandemic. This workshop addresses the possibilities of eliminating the on-site requirement, thus extending the potential application of location-based experiences. First, virtualization approaches will be presented, which allow eliminating the need to be on-site, such as the usage of 360° technologies or the employment of videoconferencing software. Further, various challenges, such as the application of existing design principles for location-based experiences and instructional design for virtualized location-based experiences, are discussed and options to overcome the limitations imposed by the virtualization. This paper provides insights into theoretical foundations relevant to solving the aspects of virtualizing location-based experiences. The workshop results are intended to provide lasting advancements to eliminating the on-site requirements for location-based experiences.

Keywords: Location-based · Serious games · 360° technology · Virtual field trips · Smart city

1 Introduction

Digital location-based experiences (LBEs), in the scope of this paper, are the place-based extension of reality with the help of digital technologies. The extension can refer to the digital generation of optical sensory stimuli, for example, and the provision of interaction options depending on the respective position of the user contributes to digital LBEs. A prominent group of digital LBEs are location-based augmented reality (AR) games, which have received increasing attention in the recent decade. Examples of these

© IFIP International Federation for Information Processing 2021
Published by Springer Nature Switzerland AG 2021
J. Baalsrud Hauge et al. (Eds.): ICEC 2021, LNCS 13056, pp. 467–474, 2021.
https://doi.org/10.1007/978-3-030-89394-1_40

AR games include INGRESS [1], Pokémon GO [2], Minecraft Earth [3], and Harry Potter: Wizards Unite [4]. Yet apps that support geo-caching [5] and scavenger hunt activities [6] also enable digital LBEs. In this paper, LBEs are considered in a broader sense, and not limited to gaming LBEs.

There is a multitude of positive implications of digital LBEs. Across location-based games, Laato et al. [7] analyze corresponding game mechanics and potential effects. In another work [8], Laato et al. observe an association between playing a location-based game and players' psychological well-being. Also, location-based games are used as a tool in Citizen Science initiatives [9, 10]. Furthermore, LBEs are part of a smart city, increasing quality of life and more efficient use of resources [11]. Important potential use of LBEs is also evident in learning contexts [12–15], not only because a wide variety of learning approaches are supported, such as inquiry-based learning, project-based learning, or situational learning [16].

Despite all benefits, however, the characteristic of being tied to a specific location also has a limiting effect. For example, Minecraft Earth has been discontinued at the end of June 2021 [17], among other reasons due to the COVID 19 pandemia caused the number of users to fall short of expectations [18]. Especially in learning contexts, it may be too costly and time-consuming to be on-site physically, so the LBE might not be conducted at all [19]. On these grounds, it may be beneficial to de-couple LBEs from the need to be on-site. This is the point this workshop addresses. The workshop aims to present approaches to virtualizing LBEs, e.g., using 360° technologies or video conferencing systems. Virtual field trips (VFTs) [20] might be considered as a subgenre of virtualized LBEs. Overall, the workshop intends to contribute to making the tool LBE more versatile by lowering the on-site requirement. The workshop can be seen as a continuation of previous workshops at IFIP ICEC in Vienna, Austria in 2016 about pervasive gamified learning [21], in Arequipa, Peru in 2019 about designing serious location-based games [22], and in Xi'an, China in 2020 about facilitating serious location-based games [23]. The research questions that will guide the workshop include the following:

RQ 1: What are the technical options for freeing LBEs from the need to be on-site, i.e., for digitizing LBEs?
RQ 2: In how far may existing frameworks for designing LBEs also be applied to virtualized location-based experiences?
RQ 3: How may the limitations caused by the virtualization of LBEs be compensated?

In the following Section, two, foundations for addressing these research questions are presented. After that, in Section three, limitations are discussed and conclusions drawn in Section four.

2   Location-Based Experiences in the Light of Virtualization

2.1   Technical and Organizational Options for Virtualization of LBE

Virtualization of LBEs can be achieved through various methods, such that a reality-virtuality continuum [24] might also apply to LBEs. Methods that lead to differentially latitudinal positioning of an LBE on the reality-virtuality continuum towards the virtuality pole include:

- **Modification of interaction mechanics.** Interaction mechanics in LBEs that require on-site presence might be redesigned to eliminate the need for on-site presence, e.g., remote trading in Pokémon GO [25]. While this does not eliminate the need for on-site presence for users, it may significantly reduce the intensity of on-site presence.
- **Location spoofing.** GPS spoofing allows location-based apps to simulate being at a specific location [26]. While this technique is perceived as cheating in various games [27], it may help in virtualizing LBEs: Users remain in a fixed location yet interact with apps as if they were on-site. This method might need to complement other methods if the LBE requires sensations that can only be obtained on-site, such as the current temperature on-site.
- **Replicating real worlds.** The creation of virtual worlds used for LBEs is one of the methods that may lead to completely virtualized LBEs. There are various technical measures for creating virtual worlds. 360° video technology allows the creation of worlds close to reality but may not be completely navigable, with comparatively little effort. Geometric modelling of virtual worlds is more complex but will enable users more positioning freedom. As alternative options adding spatial information to 360° models, the use of laser scanners and the creation of geometric models by photogrammetry may be considered. Additional information, which would otherwise be given via location-based apps, must be integrated into the worlds created. It is also conceivable to implement further interactions, such as talking to people simulated by chatbots.

Interaction mechanics in LBEs may be differentiated according to the different interaction target groups: the users of LBEs may interact with (a) the location-based app, (b) additional co-users and (c) the real world. For each of these interaction target groups, there is a demand for virtualization: the location-based app (a) may be directly integrated into the virtual world; for example, by replicating the app controls, co-users (b) may be supported either in virtual worlds providing multi-user features or manually via screen sharing in a video conferencing software. Interactions must replace interactions with the real world (c) with the corresponding virtual world.

2.2 Design Principles for LBE Virtualization

There are several design frameworks for LBEs whose applicability for virtualized LBEs still needs to be reviewed [28–30]. As an example, the aspects of the Pervasive Game Design Framework (PGDF) [21] will be discussed in the following regarding possible interference with virtualization:

- **Pervasive Context.** A pervasive game should reflect a pervasive context. In terms of LBEs, this seems to be a challenging requirement: the location-based context has to be represented virtually, at least in the LBE-relevant aspects.
- **Pedagogical Objective.** The learning goals of an educational LBE may be impacted by virtualization. It has to be investigated which learning goals are no longer achieved or by what adaptations of the LBE the learning goals become achievable.
- **Assessment Metrics.** Virtualising LBEs might also eliminate assessment metrics (e.g., distance walked) and might need to be replaced by other metrics (e.g., virtual

distance walked). It may also be necessary to adjust the assessment metrics, e.g., the time users spend in an LBE could be reduced by the walking distance saved that could be completed faster virtually.

- **Difficulty Level.** The difficulty level could be affected by virtualization since not all information might be collectable in a virtualized LBE in the same way as in reality. On the other hand, information can also be made more accessible through virtualization.
- **User Skills.** The skills of the users of the LBE are not dependent on whether LBEs are on-site or virtual. However, the virtualization of LBEs could provide better accessibility for impaired users.
- **Social Interaction.** Ensuring social interactions in virtual LBES appears to be a significant challenge as many virtual environments are not designed for multi-user operation. There is also a lack of uninvolved externals, which are crucial for some LBEs, e.g., as described in [31].
- **Motivation.** Although there is evidence that LBEs cause high motivation in their users [19], it remains likely that there are different preferences for virtualized or real LBEs depending on the user profile. If appropriate, virtualized LBEs must be explicitly designed for optimizing motivation.

This non-exhaustive discussion suggests that the virtualization of LBEs is not an automated process but that further design decisions deserve careful consideration. Suppose LBEs are designed for learning, for example. In that case, the cognitive theories of multimedia learning [32], the Cognitive Load Theory [33], and the Cognitive Affective Model of Immersive Learning [34], which builds on them, are essential theoretical frameworks that are to be accounted for in the design of virtualized LBEs. For example, Petersen et al. [35] present a VFT and its instructional design-oriented integration into an educational virtual LBE. Yepes-Serna et al. [36] discuss principles relevant for virtualizing learning scenarios in general.

2.3   Overcoming Limitations of Virtualized LBEs

Shifting elements of the LBE from reality to virtuality may change or limit the LBE. In such cases, it becomes necessary to investigate to what extent organizational or technical changes may compensate for the limitations. In the following, some examples are presented:

- Due to the COVID pandemic, the game mechanics of Pokémon GO were changed, among others, to limit player contacts [37]. This led to considerations of how to change the game mechanics in a manner that would affect the original game experience as little as possible [25].
- In virtualized LBEs, recognizing the characteristics of reality that are important to the LBE may become more complicated, among other things. For example, in a learning scenario for planning sewage infrastructure, it is essential to recognize the slope of the terrain. However, this is more challenging in 360° models, to begin with [19]. Coloured markings in the 360° models may provide a remedy for these difficulties.
- Slingerland et al. [31] present an LBE in which interactions are an essential part of the game, both with other users and with strangers on the street. Special arrangements

need to be made for the potential virtualization of this LBE, such as how strangers on the street can continue to be part of the game. Chatbots would undoubtedly be an approach to be validated.

3 Limitations

The LBEs and their virtualizations considered include neighbouring manifestations that will not be considered as much in this workshop. These manifestations include pervasive games [38], where absolute positioning in the real world might be not an integral part of the game but rather a relative positioning to other players. Similarly, there are intersections with mixed reality sports platforms [39], though here, too, absolute positioning in the real world is less important. Likewise, not covered are the usages of LBEs to serve human health, especially in times of the COVID pandemic [40]. Not included in this workshop are the affordances of using LBEs to manage the player population in pandemics [41].

4 Conclusions

Location-based experiences (LBEs) have characteristics that turn them into successful learning tools, such as supporting exploratory learning. Virtualizing LBEs, i.e., eliminating the need to be on-site, increases the variability of the possible uses of LBEs. The COVID pandemic or travel constraints due to cost and time eliminate the need to be on-site. This article, which is the basis of a workshop on virtualizing LBEs, technical options for virtualization, the applicability of design frameworks, and mitigating limitations of virtualized LBEs compared to LBEs, were presented as relevant fundamentals of virtualizing LBEs. It is to be assumed that the virtualization of LBEs requires a non-negligible effort. The workshop intends to contribute to a topic that has so far been insufficiently covered in the literature.

Acknowledgement. This work has been partly funded by the German Federal Ministry of Education and Research (BMBF) through the projects DigiLab4U (No. 16DHB2113) and AuCity2 (No. 16DHB2131).

References

1. Niantic Labs: Ingress. http://www.ingress.com/
2. Niantic Inc.: Pokémon GO. http://www.pokemongo.com/
3. Mojang Studios: Minecraft Earth. https://www.minecraft.net/en-us/about-earth/
4. Warner Bros. Entertainment Inc.: Harry Potter: Wizards Unite. https://www.harrypotterwizardsunite.com
5. Fornasini, S., Dianti, M., Bacchiega, A., Forti, S., Conforti, D.: Using geocaching to promote active aging: qualitative study. J. Med. Internet Res. **22**(6), e15339, (2020). https://doi.org/10.2196/15339

6. Hutzler, A., Wagner, R., Pirker, J., Gütl, C.: MythHunter: gamification in an educational location-based scavenger hunt. In: Beck, D., et al. (eds.) iLRN 2017. CCIS, vol. 725, pp. 155–169. Springer, Cham (2017). https://doi.org/10.1007/978-3-319-60633-0_13

7. Laato, S., Pietarinen, T., Rauti, S., Sutinen, E.: Potential benefits of playing location-based games: an analysis of game mechanics. In: Lane, H.C., Zvacek, S., Uhomoibhi, J. (eds.) CSEDU 2019. CCIS, vol. 1220, pp. 557–581. Springer, Cham (2020). https://doi.org/10.1007/978-3-030-58459-7_27

8. Laato, S., Islam, A.K.M.N., Laine, T.H.: Playing location-based games is associated with psychological well-being: an empirical study of Pokémon GO players. Behav. Inf. Technol. 1–17 (2021). https://doi.org/10.1080/0144929X.2021.1905878

9. Celino, I.: Location-based games for citizen computation. In: Michelucci, P. (ed.) Handbook of Human Computation, pp. 297–316. Springer, New York (2013). https://doi.org/10.1007/978-1-4614-8806-4_25

10. Loureiro, P., Prandi, C., Nunes, N., Nisi, V.: Citizen science and game with a purpose to foster biodiversity awareness and bioacoustic data validation. In: Brooks, A.L., Brooks, E., Sylla, C. (eds.) ArtsIT/DLI -2018. LNICSSITE, vol. 265, pp. 245–255. Springer, Cham (2019). https://doi.org/10.1007/978-3-030-06134-0_29

11. Nijholt, A.: Towards playful and playable cities. In: Nijholt, A. (ed.) Playable Cities. GMSE, pp. 1–20. Springer, Singapore (2017). https://doi.org/10.1007/978-981-10-1962-3_1

12. Schneider, J., Schaal, S., Schlieder, C.: Integrating simulation tasks into an outdoor location-based game flow. Multimedia Tools Appl. 79(5–6), 3359–3385 (2019). https://doi.org/10.1007/s11042-019-07931-4

13. Schaal, S.: Location-based games for geography and environmental education. In: Walshe, N., Healy, G., (eds.) Geography Education in the Digital World: Linking Theory and Practice, p. 54. Routledge (2020)

14. Wolf, M., Wehking, F., Söbke, H., Londong, J.: Location-based Apps in environmental engineering higher education: a case study in technical infrastructure planning. In: Söbke, H., Baalsrud Hauge, J., Wolf, M., Wehking, F., (eds.) Proceedings of DELbA 2020 - Workshop on Designing and Facilitating Educational Location-based Applications co-located with the Fifteenth European Conference on Technology Enhanced Learning (EC-TEL 2020) Heidelberg, Germany , Online, 15 September 2020. CEUR Workshop Proceedings (2020)

15. Avouris, N.M., Yiannoutsou, N.: A review of mobile location-based games for learning across physical and virtual spaces. J. UCS. 18, 2120–2142 (2012)

16. Zydney, J.M., Warner, Z.: Mobile apps for science learning: review of research. Comput. Educ. 94, 1–17 (2016). https://doi.org/10.1016/j.compedu.2015.11.001

17. Mojang Studios: Minecraft Earth coming to an end. https://www.minecraft.net/en-us/article/minecraft-earth-coming-end

18. Kumbarak, G.: Minecraft Earth will shut down in June. https://techcrunch.com/2021/01/05/minecraft-earth-will-shut-down-in-jun

19. Springer, C., Wehking, F., Wolf, M., Söbke, H.: Virtualization of virtual field trips: a case study from higher education in environmental engineering. In: Söbke, H., Baalsrud Hauge, J., Wolf, M., and Wehking, F. (eds.) Proceedings of DELbA 2020 - Workshop on Designing and Facilitating Educational Location-based Applications co-located with the Fifteenth European Conference on Technology Enhanced Learning (EC-TEL 2020) Heidelberg, Germany, Online, 15 September 2020. CEUR Workshop Proceedings (2020)

20. Tuthill, G., Klemm, E.B.: Virtual field trips: alternatives to actual field trips. Int. J. Instr. Media. 29, 453 (2002)

21. Baalsrud Hauge, J., Stanescu, I.A., Stefan, A.: Constructing and experimenting pervasive, gamified learning. In: Entertainment Computing – ICEC 2016 15th IFIP TC 14 International Conference Vienna, Austria, 28–30 September 2016 (2016)

22. Baalsrud Hauge, J., Söbke, H., Stefan, I.A., Stefan, A.: Designing serious mobile location-based games. In: van der Spek, E., Göbel, S., Do, E.-L., Clua, E., Baalsrud Hauge, J. (eds.) ICEC-JCSG 2019. LNCS, vol. 11863, pp. 479–484. Springer, Cham (2019). https://doi.org/10.1007/978-3-030-34644-7-49

23. Baalsrud Hauge, J., Söbke, H., Stefan, I.A., Stefan, A.: Applying and facilitating serious location-based games. In: Nunes, N.J., Ma, L., Wang, M., Correia, N., Pan, Z. (eds.) ICEC 2020. LNCS, vol. 12523, pp. 104–109. Springer, Cham (2020). https://doi.org/10.1007/978-3-030-65736-9_8

24. Milgram, P., Takemura, H., Utsumi, A., Kishino, F., Fumio, K.: Augmented reality: a class of displays on the reality-virtuality continuum. In: SPIE Proceedings Volume 2351: Telemanipulator and Telepresence Technologies, pp. 282–292 (1994).

25. GamePress: It's Time for Niantic to Allow Remote Trading in Pokemon GO

26. Larcom, J.A., Liu, H.: Modeling and characterization of GPS spoofing. In: 2013 IEEE International Conference on Technologies for Homeland Security (HST), pp. 729–734 (2013). https://doi.org/10.1109/THS.2013.6699094

27. Paay, J., Kjeldskov, J., Internicola, D., Thomasen, M.: Motivations and practices for cheating in Pokémon Go. In: MobileHCI 2018 - Beyond Mob. Next 20 Years - 20th International Conference Human-Computer Interaction with Mobile Devices Services Conference Proceedings, pp. 1–13 (2018). https://doi.org/10.1145/3229434.3229466

28. Rauschnabel, P.A., Rossmann, A., Tom Dieck, M.C.: An adoption framework for mobile augmented reality games: the case of Pokémon Go. Comput. Human Behav. **76**, 276–286 (2017). https://doi.org/10.1016/j.chb.2017.07.030

29. Hamari, J., Malik, A., Koski, J., Johri, A.: Uses and gratifications of pokémon go: why do people play mobile location-based augmented reality games? Int. J. Hum. Comput. Interact. 1–16 (2018). https://doi.org/10.1080/10447318.2018.1497115

30. Söbke, H., Baalsrud Hauge, J., Stefan, I.A.: Prime example ingress: reframing the pervasive game design framework (PGDF). Int. J. Serious Games, **4**(2), 39–58 (2017). https://doi.org/10.17083/ijsg.v4i2.182

31. Slingerland, G., Fonseca, X., Lukosch, S., Brazier, F.: Location-based challenges for playful neighbourhood exploration. Behav. Inf. Technol. 1–19 (2020). https://doi.org/10.1080/0144929X.2020.1829707

32. Mayer, R.E.: Cognitive theory of multimedia learning. Camb. Handb. Multimedia Learn. **41**, 31–48 (2005)

33. Sweller, J., Ayres, P., Kalyuga, S.: Cognitive Load Theory. Springer, New York, NY, USA (2011). https://doi.org/10.1007/978-1-4419-8126-4

34. Makransky, G., Petersen, G.B.: The Cognitive affective model of immersive learning (CAMIL): a theoretical research-based model of learning in immersive virtual reality. Educ. Psychol. Rev. 1-21 (2021). https://doi.org/10.1007/s10648-020-09586-2

35. Petersen, G.B., Klingenberg, S., Mayer, R.E., Makransky, G.: The virtual field trip: investigating how to optimize immersive virtual learning in climate change education. Br. J. Educ. Technol. **51**, 2098–2114 (2020). https://doi.org/10.1111/bjet.12991

36. Yepes-Serna, V., Wolf, M., Söbke, H., Zander, S.: Design principles for educational mixed reality?: adaptions of the design recommendations of multimedia learning. In: Akcayir, G., Demmans Epp, C., (eds.) Designing, Deploying, and Evaluating Virtual and Augmented Reality in Education, pp. 76–99. IGI Global (2020)

37. Laato, S., Laine, T.H., Najmul Islam, A.K.M.: Location-based games and the COVID-19 pandemic: an analysis of responses from game developers and players. Multimodal Technol. Interact. **4**(2), 1–25 (2020). https://doi.org/10.3390/mti4020029.

38. Oppermann, L., Slussareff, M.: Pervasive games. In: Dörner, R., Göbel, S., Kickmeier-Rust, M., Masuch, M., Zweig, K. (eds.) Entertainment Computing and Serious Games. LNCS, vol. 9970, pp. 475–520. Springer, Cham (2016). https://doi.org/10.1007/978-3-319-46152-6_18

39. Westmattelmann, D., Grotenhermen, J.-G., Sprenger, M., Rand, W., Schewe, G.: Apart we ride together: the motivations behind users of mixed-reality sports. J. Bus. Res. **134**, 316–328 (2021). https://doi.org/10.1016/j.jbusres.2021.05.044
40. Ellis, L.A., Lee, M.D., Ijaz, K., Smith, J., Braithwaite, J., Yin, K.: COVID-19 as 'game changer' for the physical activity and mental well-being of augmented reality game players during the pandemic: mixed methods survey study. J. Med. Internet Res. **22**(12), e25117 (2020). https://doi.org/10.2196/25117
41. Laato, S., Islam, A.K.M.N., Laine, T.H.: Did location-based games motivate players to socialize during COVID-19? Telemat. Inform. **54**, 101458 (2020). https://doi.org/10.1016/j.tele.2020.101458

Artificial Intelligence and Entertainment Science Workshop: Towards Empathic Entertainment Technology

Mohd Nor Akmal Khalid[1]([✉]), Hiroyuki Iida[1], Umi Kalsom Yusof[2], and Ruzinoor Che Mat[3]

[1] School of Information Science, JAIST, Nomi, Ishikawa, Japan
{akmal,iida}@jaist.ac.jp
[2] School of Computer Sciences, University of Science Malaysia, George Town, Penang, Malaysia
umiyusof@usm.my
[3] School of Creative Industry Management and Performing Arts (SCIMPA), Universiti Utara Malaysia (UUM), Bukit Kayu Hitam, Kedah, Malaysia
ruzinoor@uum.edu.my

Abstract. The intersection of artificial intelligence and entertainment science via games had led to fruitful development in both fields. Empathic technology in the entertainment medium is a promising trend that bridges both worlds. This workshop provides the discussion space for those interested in its application, societal issues, risks, and best practices.

Keywords: Artificial intelligence · Entertainment · Technology · Empathy

1 Background

Billions of people have been enlightening with the joy of the entertainment industry via movies, games, books, and music. Today's production and marketing budgets for entertainment products often exceed \$100 million and can reach up to \$500 million for a single new movie or video game [5]. *Entertainment Science* built on the assumption of the modern world with almost unlimited data and great computational resources, the combination of intelligent analytics and powerful theories would provide valuable insights in supporting decision making.

The notion of *robust* AI had been advocated, which involves applying its knowledge to a wide range of problems systematically and reliably, synthesizing knowledge from a variety of sources such that it can reason flexibly and dynamically about the world, able to transfer what it learns from one context to another

Electronic supplementary material The online version of this chapter (https://doi.org/10.1007/978-3-030-89394-1_41) contains supplementary material, which is available to authorized users.

© IFIP International Federation for Information Processing 2021
Published by Springer Nature Switzerland AG 2021
J. Baalsrud Hauge et al. (Eds.): ICEC 2021, LNCS 13056, pp. 475–481, 2021.
https://doi.org/10.1007/978-3-030-89394-1_41

and build the sense of trust [13]. An overview of the game design and study of human-based phenomena that induce emotional reactions and people's motivation in digital games had been explored by [12]. Similarly, emotionally sentient systems would also enable AI agents to perform complex tasks more effectively, making better decisions, and offered more practical and effective services [14].

With the recent rise of artificial emotional intelligence, empathy becomes the new buzzword term. With the establishment of *Empathic Computing* framework [3], a machine can recognize human feelings and states, understand user intents, and respond to user needs dynamically [22]. Such a framework becomes the enabler for prominent applications such as the empathic conversations in healthcare [7], social [22], and both [4]. Another study utilized such frameworks in mediating judgment, explored the effect of metaphors on evaluating AI agents while managing expectation and perception [9]. In addition, combinations of sympathetic actions and explanation types would assist AI agents to adapt in multiple human-computer interaction scenarios [8].

Based on the advancements outlined by the previous works, empathic technology is currently a nascent field. The general trend focuses on the development of emotional AI agents and technologies surrounding it [14], describing the AI performance and its implications to interaction design [15], realizing computational creativity and humor [20], and bridging physical and virtual sensations and interactions [2,11]. However, empathic computing was adopted alongside AI technology while its influence and interactions, physically, emotionally, or virtually, remained unexplored from the entertainment science perspective. As such, empathic technology from an entertainment point-of-view could potentially produce robust, humorous, explainable, and perceptive AI systems. Such niche is the primary motivation of this workshop, which could observe and bring a heightened experience of interactions, collaborations, and co-creations, in human-machine relations and beyond.

2   Workshop Objective

Artificial intelligence (AI) had enabled the establishment of a platform for the development of intelligent search techniques [19] and general language description [16] in competitive settings. However, such research studies emphasize functional utility and performance optimization. In contrast, the motion in mind concept [6] synthesized the foundation of entertainment science by considering the analogy of physics and motions with the game-playing process by aggregating value functions and reward systems [10,21]. Nevertheless, such a concept lacks experimental validation and empirical verification because of its subjective properties.

A recent study showed that AI search applied in a game environment provided the utility to identify entertaining elements as a new form of scientific venture [17]. Bringing together AI and entertainment science, establishing common interests is vital to understand better how those fields interact. In particular, in what ways does AI becomes entertaining? How can entertainment benefit from

AI applications? Nevertheless, such questions address one side of the equation. More importantly, how can both fields come together as beneficial to humanity? In such a situation, having a common interest that resonates in both fields requires understanding the needs and challenges faced by the experts of the fields and the users.

Dale Carnegie argued that a person's success is impacted more by the ability to "deal with people" than by professional knowledge, as outlined in his classic book *How to Win Friends and Influence People* [1]. However, such "people skills" are not easy to come by. For many, it takes years of practice and learning to get along with others, especially when the people's interests are not aligned with ourselves [15]. This situation describes the notion of "empathy," and its importance in human interactions, which is an essential component in the coming age of *artificial emotional intelligence* [18]. In essence, this workshop would be interested in technology-related development and encourages multi-disciplinary efforts while being neither purely technical driven nor purely qualitative research.

This workshop aims to bring together researchers, designers, and practitioners under the umbrella of the workshop organized alongside the 20th International Federation for Information Processing–International Conference on Entertainment Computing (IFIP-ICEC 2021). The workshop aimed to establish a panel of discussion at the intersections of AI and entertainment science areas by utilizing entertainment computing activities such as video games, digital arts, or film media. The niche area of empathic entertainment, which focuses on intertwining empathic computing and entertainment science, provides a unique approach to humanizing AI applications. A novel entertainment-based empathic technology can be developed and established, which is centralized on the notion of empathy and how it influences technological advancements that benefit people and their surrounding community. Best-practice experience and successful initiatives can be identified, while empirical outcomes and novel designs can be determined to build up and strengthen the community of interest in empathic entertainment technology. In addition to building an international community, the workshop aims to identify challenges and opportunities related to empathic entertainment technology in games or non-game contexts.

3   Deliverable and Organization

Participants will be asked to submit a two (2) pages extended abstract to present their work, and the organizers will invite them to present such works as a short or poster presentation. An extended version of their research works will be considered for publication in a special issue journal. The materials and results of the workshop will be made available to all participants. Other intended results are the formation of networks for project proposals or further common activities. As a follow-up, the workshop organizers will summarize the workshop's outcomes in a paper, preferably published in the *IFIP-ICEC 2021* or the *Entertainment Computing* journal. We also want to collect relevant literature and successful initiatives to be shared on the workshop's website. Follow-up activities also include joint research activities and subsequent publications.

The profiles of the expected participants were from the background of computer science, engineering, and technology-related fields. A minimum number of 10 participants and a maximum of 20 participants will be expected. The scope of the topics include, but are not limited to:

1. **Theoretical contributions** that lead to or deliver empathic entertainment.
2. **Presentation and experience** of empathic AI agent and empathic simulation.
3. **Perception and acceptance** related to empathic experience and its entertainment context.
4. **Specific aspects** of human-AI interactions and empathic play in games or non-game context.
5. **Examples** of entertainment medium, designed and developed for better empathetic experience.
6. **Examples** of empathic game design or processes that integrate empathetic design.
7. **Examples** of empathic AI-based support tools for creating an entertaining experience.

4   Program Structure and Important Dates

The workshop will be organized as **a full day session (about 8 h)**. The program includes the keynote speech from two invited speakers and an expected 10 participants with short presentations (each given about 10 min presentation and 5 min question and answering session). The program starts with an opening speech by the organizers (about 15–30 min), followed by the first keynote speech (about 1 h and 15 min). Then, the participant's presentation will be conducted in two sessions (totaled into two and a half hours) before summarizing the program and ending the workshop. In the event of more participants, parallel sessions will be conducted for the participants. Meanwhile, in the event of fewer participants, plenary speakers will potentially be conducted by one or more program committee members. More information is outlined in https://aies.info/.

Submission deadline: 30th September 2021
Notifications of acceptance: 7th October 2021
Workshop program: 2nd November 2021

5   Organizers

Mohd Nor Akmal Khalid is an assistant professor in the School of Information Science at the Japan Advanced Institute of Science and Technology (JAIST) and a part-time Research Fellow in the School of Computer Sciences, University of Science Malaysia (USM), Malaysia. His work focuses specifically on methods and developments in the fields of entertainment technology and operational research. His topics of interest include but are not limited to manufacturing systems, advanced scheduling and planning, artificial intelligence techniques, game analytic and informatics, search algorithms, bio-inspired optimization techniques, and machine learning methods. He was also involved in organizing scientific, social activities such as research writing workshops, student colloquiums, and academic talks.

Hiroyuki Iida is a Japanese computer scientist and computer game researcher focusing on game refinement theory, opponent-model search, and computer shogi. Hiroyuki Iida is the Trustee and Vice President for educational and student affairs at the Japan Advanced Institute of Science and Technology (JAIST), Director of the Global Communication Center, and head of the Iida laboratory. He is a member of the ICGA as Secretary-Treasurer and a Section Editor of the ICGA Journal. Previously, he was affiliated with Shizuoka University, Hamamatsu, and was a guest researcher at Maastricht University. He is a professional 7-dan shogi player, coauthor of the shogi program Tacos, and a four-time gold medal winner at the ICGA Computer Olympiad. He also had the pleasure of becoming the organizer of several International Computer Games Association (ICGA) in 2002, 2010, and 2013, and the program committee of 2021 International Joint Conferences on Artificial Intelligence (IJCAI), as well as the founder of the International Conference of Entertainment Computing (ICEC). His research interests include artificial intelligence, game informatics, game theory, mathematical models, search algorithms, game refinement theory, game tree search, and entertainment science.

Umi Kalsom Yusof currently an Associate Professor and a Senior Lecturer with the School of Computer Sciences, USM. She has previously worked in Petronas, Toyota, ASE Electronics, and Motorola before joining the academia in 2008. She also co-organized several local conferences from 2007 to 2011, and international conferences from 2013 to 2015, while actively involved as a reviewer in local and international journals. Her research interests are related to artificial intelligence, machine learning, computational intelligence, multi-objective optimization, evolutionary computing, Web engineering, manufacturing optimization, crowd behavior in an emergency evacuation, and health-related and global warming effect studies. She has published research articles in national and international journals, conference proceedings, and book chapters.

Ruzinoor Che Mat is an Associate Professor at the School of Creative Industry Management and Performing Arts (SCIMPA), Universiti Utara Malaysia (UUM). He has developed numerous products on an online 3D system for agriculture, teaching and learning, mobile Augmented (AR), and Virtual Reality (VR). He was also actively involved in many research competitions at local and international which were awarded 23 medals. He has 18 years of experience in teaching and has taught about 30 subjects in various disciplines from four different faculties and invited to teach at Open University Malaysia (OUM) and Universiti Malaysia Sabah (UMS) as a part-time lecturer. He had also successfully procured funds, leading six research projects and 15 others as a team member. He is also an expert in 3D visualization and game engine, where he had published scientific papers in refereed journals, proceedings, academic books, and actively involved as a reviewer of several high impact journals such as Remote Sensing and GIS. His research interests are on 3D GIS, terrain visualization, game engines, remote sensing, GIS application, Virtual Reality, Augmented Reality, Gamification, computer graphics, and visualization.

References

1. Carnegie, D.: How to win friends & influence people. e-artnow (2017)
2. Dey, A., Piumsomboon, T., Lee, Y., Billinghurst, M.: Effects of sharing physiological states of players in a collaborative virtual reality gameplay. In: Proceedings of the 2017 CHI Conference on Human Factors in Computing Systems, pp. 4045–4056 (2017)
3. Fung, P., et al.: Towards empathetic human-robot interactions. In: Gelbukh, A. (ed.) CICLing 2016. LNCS, vol. 9624, pp. 173–193. Springer, Cham (2018). https://doi.org/10.1007/978-3-319-75487-1_14
4. Goel, R., Vashisht, S., Dhanda, A., Susan, S.: An empathetic conversational agent with attentional mechanism. In: 2021 International Conference on Computer Communication and Informatics (ICCCI), pp. 1–4. IEEE (2021)
5. Hennig-Thurau, T., Houston, M.B.: Entertainment science. In: Data Analytics and Practical Theory for Movies, Games, Books, and Music, pp. 1–865. Springer, Cham (2019). https://doi.org/10.1007/978-3-319-89292-4
6. Iida, H., Khalid, M.N.A.: Using games to study law of motions in mind. IEEE Access **8**, 138701–138709 (2020)
7. James, J., Balamurali, B., Watson, C.I., MacDonald, B.: Empathetic speech synthesis and testing for healthcare robots. Int. J. Soc. Robot., 1–19 (2020). https://doi.org/10.1007/s12369-020-00691-4
8. Kampik, T., Nieves, J.C., Lindgren, H.: Explaining sympathetic actions of rational agents. In: Calvaresi, D., Najjar, A., Schumacher, M., Främling, K. (eds.) EXTRAAMAS 2019. LNCS (LNAI), vol. 11763, pp. 59–76. Springer, Cham (2019). https://doi.org/10.1007/978-3-030-30391-4_4
9. Khadpe, P., Krishna, R., Fei-Fei, L., Hancock, J.T., Bernstein, M.S.: Conceptual metaphors impact perceptions of human-AI collaboration. Proc. ACM Hum. Comput. Interact. **4**(CSCW2), 1–26 (2020)
10. Khalid, M.N.A., Iida, H.: Objectivity and subjectivity in games: understanding engagement and addiction mechanism. IEEE Access **9**, 65187–65205 (2021). https://doi.org/10.1109/ACCESS.2021.3075954
11. Lee, Y., Masai, K., Kunze, K., Sugimoto, M., Billinghurst, M.: A remote collaboration system with empathy glasses. In: 2016 IEEE International Symposium on Mixed and Augmented Reality (ISMAR-Adjunct), pp. 342–343. IEEE (2016)
12. Lopes, P., Boulic, R.: Towards designing games for experimental protocols investigating human-based phenomena. In: International Conference on the Foundations of Digital Games, pp. 1–11 (2020)
13. Marcus, G.: The next decade in AI: four steps towards robust artificial intelligence. arXiv preprint arXiv:2002.06177 (2020)
14. McDuff, D., Czerwinski, M.: Designing emotionally sentient agents. Commun. ACM **61**(12), 74–83 (2018)
15. Oudah, M., Rahwan, T., Crandall, T., Crandall, J.: How AI wins friends and influences people in repeated games with cheap talk. In: Proceedings of the AAAI Conference on Artificial Intelligence, vol. 32 (2018)

16. Piette, É., Soemers, D.J.N.J., Stephenson, M., Sironi, C.F., Winands, M.H.M., Browne, C.: Ludii - the ludemic general game system. CoRR arXiv:1905.05013 (2019)
17. Primanita, A., Khalid, M.N.A., Iida, H.: Computing games: bridging the gap between search and entertainment. IEEE Access **9**, 72087–72102 (2021). https://doi.org/10.1109/ACCESS.2021.3079356
18. Schuller, D., Schuller, B.W.: The age of artificial emotional intelligence. Computer **51**(9), 38–46 (2018)
19. Song, Z., Iida, H., van den Herik, H.J.: Probability based proof number search. In: ICAART, no. 2, pp. 661–668 (2019)
20. Veale, T.: Sympathetic magic in AI and the humanities. J. Artif. Intell. Hum. **2**, 9–38 (2018)
21. Xiaohan, K., Khalid, M.N.A., Iida, H.: Player satisfaction model and its implication to cultural change. IEEE Access **8**, 184375–184382 (2020)
22. Zhou, L., Gao, J., Li, D., Shum, H.Y.: The design and implementation of Xiaoice, an empathetic social chatbot. Comput. Linguist. **46**(1), 53–93 (2020)

Aesthetic Perspectives on Computational Media Design

Rui Craveirinha$^{(\boxtimes)}$ ⓘ, Luís Lucas Pereira ⓘ, Mariana Seiça ⓘ,
and Licínio Roque ⓘ

Department of Informatics Engineering, Centre for Informatics and Systems of the
University of Coimbra, University of Coimbra, Coimbra, Portugal
{lpereira,marianac,lir}@dei.uc.pt

Abstract. The main goal of this workshop is to open a collaborative
space for reflection and debate on how Aesthetics can inform the design of
computational media, in an attempt to grasp the multiplicity of aesthetic
dimensions that can influence the reception, experience, and interpretation of such sociotechnical objects and experiences. We will approach the
goal from the entertainment computing field where such concerns are of
vital influence.

Keywords: Aesthetics · Computational media design · Digital media ·
User experience

1 Introduction

Computer technologies have entered our everyday lives as structural tools for our
professional, personal and social dimensions. Society has become an information
society, as the need to grasp, apprehend and manage information has inevitably
entered our daily routines. It is this process for creating, changing and inter-
nalising this constant info-stimulus that Manovich [5] called info-aesthetics, in
a "global information society (...)" where the use of computers for design and
production gives rise to new cultural forms".

Aesthetics emerged as a relevant field to help us understand how we can
creatively and innovatively expand universes of experience in a new digital world.
But the plethora of dimensions in Aesthetics has centuries of expanding concepts
and diverse perspectives. From the Greek *aisthētikós*, which means "something
of or for the perception of the senses", we will take it here broadly, to include any
contribution relevant to understand how we perceive objects and their context,
but also how they influence our *being-in-the-world* [14].

Notions of beauty and aesthetics have been intrinsically linked with long-
held views of what constitutes an artistic object and an aesthetic experience.
For example, an artistic object can be somewhat simplistically defined by its
capacity to move subjects emotionally and prompt them to reflect critically on a
given subject [3]. Yet, such aesthetic experiences are not only sought out in the

© IFIP International Federation for Information Processing 2021
Published by Springer Nature Switzerland AG 2021
J. Baalsrud Hauge et al. (Eds.): ICEC 2021, LNCS 13056, pp. 482–488, 2021.
https://doi.org/10.1007/978-3-030-89394-1_42

context of artistic object fruition. Just as a film, or a painting, can be praised for its ability to convey emotion and sprout critical reflection – for being beautiful, for being artistic, for its aestheticness – so can a TED talk on the impending climate crisis, a play from the world's top football player, a video game about the loss of a loved one, a medium article on the rise of new authoritarianism, a university's lecture on identity discrimination, a civil rights discussion on Twitter, a Facebook story showing a wedding proposal, a viral cat meme, a face swapping photo app, an algorithm that generates poetry and music, etc., etc., etc.... all these things can move us, touch us emotionally, make us think, change our lives. They can be aesthetic; they can be beautiful.

Understanding the nature of this elusive aesthetic value, how it can be conceptualised, studied, and nurtured within digital media creation practices is therefore of the utmost relevance. What are the new Aesthetics? How does digital media's interactive nature shape them? What exquisite new shapes do Aesthetics take in the digital space? What objects do they encompass? And how can Aesthetics elevate our relationships with computational artefacts? With this workshop, we intend to reflect upon this challenges, resulting in a collective research manifest submission to a journal such as Entertainment Computing.

2   Plurality of Perspectives

With this workshop, we will explore several perspectives on how aesthetics can inform the design of computational media artefacts/experiences:

A. How can its experience shape subjective perceptions of digital artifacts;
B. How can it inform the process, tools and models used in designing digital artifacts;
C. How can it offer a lens to both conceptualise and evaluate the subjective experience with digital artifacts.

These are just the perspectives we have studied in the past, and wish to expand upon in the future. We will start with three examples of perspectives we pursued in our recent work. With these, we aim to illustrate and invite others to bring in their research contributions and unique perspectives on how aesthetics can inform the design of computational media.

2.1   Perspective A

Seiça et al. [12] propose an alternative view over Aesthetics applied to Sonification, rooted in the foundational applications in HCI of the human as a bodily, multisensorial agent. Driven by the notion of aesthetic experience that may offer an expansion of the perception field for the experiencer, it is based on a model proposed by Pelowski and Akiba [6] describing a 5-stage cognitive flow that leads to self-transformation. The differing piece of this model is the need for discrepancy to occur: in a circular process of understanding-evaluating the artefact, it rises when the comparison between what is expected and what is perceived fails. This failure raises doubts and uncertainties that demands a reevaluation of her own expectations and former knowledge, inviting her to look outside the problem and out of herself. This is the transformational stage that leads to the essence of an aesthetic experience, from which a new, expanded self emerges.

The notion of expanded self is built over Merleau-Ponty' statement that "perception requires action" [14]. To fully grasp the behaviour and inherent meaning(s) of an artefact, one must look, listen, touch, embody and interact with it through a sequence of interpretive exchanges. As a conceptual space for this to occur, systemism [1] and the living systems theory emerged with Capra's six perceptual shifts [2] for designing sustainable societies based on nature's ecosystems. We propose an alternative to classical sonification, grounded on the concept of a sonification as a living system, designated as a **systemic sonification**.

A systemic sonification is regarded as a dynamic, ever-evolving system, composed by an ensemble of intertwined sound beings who actively respond to changes in its environment and interactions with surrounding elements. These constant exchanges determine the course of evolution of the system, with which each human can engage with and weave his/her own experience. The intertwined bonds born in these interactions allow for unique experiences to arise for each human, surpassing initial expectations, enabling perceptions and insights over the dataset and, ultimately, an internal transcendental process which offers an aesthetic experience of sonification. The experience itself becomes the purpose of a systemic sonification, and the exploration of emergent elements and sonic universes that adapt and transform to each participant, while being transformed as well with each interchange. Aesthetics embodies the role of an entity that drives the multiple acoustic journeys for each individual, offering the expansion of perceptual horizons and consciousness of each participant.

2.2 Perspective B

The Participation-centered Gameplay Experience Model [7] consists of both a player experience model and a set of canvases intent on supporting the game design activity. While competing theories focus on psychological motivation or how games can be designed to drive engagement or stimulate hedonic experiences, this model sought to assist designers in conceptualising gameplay as a form of player participation.

Inspired by postmodern artistic and poetic practices, the player is conceived as an active, meaning-making participant in the experience. Games are framed as artifacts, networks of mediators that enable said participation. Designers were then asked to think, formulate and plan out their design in the form of intentions for player participation. Once expressed, these intentions could guide the creation of the artifact and its qualities.

To assist in that process, six participatory dimensions were outlined, 3 of which being inherently aesthetic in their nature:

1. **Sensoriality**: the videogame as a context of multisensory involvement; participation as feeling, perceiving, contemplation, sensorial expression, wondering, etc.
2. **Embodiment**: the videogame as a context of physical participation, both virtual and real; participation as physical performance, physical involvement, physical coordination, movement, dancing, etc.
3. **Sensemaking**: the videogame as a context of significant participation, of creation of meaning; participation as interpretation, understanding, role-playing, self-expression, critical-thinking, etc.

In trying to support the education of a new generation of designers so as to leave the comfort zone of familiar objects, the model's inspiration in artistic practices helped reframe pre-existing assumptions of what constitutes a game and its constituting elements (as that might constrain the designer's creativity) and thus push for the creation of imminently aesthetic artifacts. Aesthetics was, in that sense, both premise and goal for the model. Several design exercises were carried out [8–10] with the model and its support tools, resulting in innovative artifacts and aesthetic experience.

2.3 Perspective C

In [4], the authors set out to study how the presence of traditional game rules could impact the perceived artistic valuation of a videogame experience. Aesthetic theories provided both grounds for the research question, and the basis for a player self-report method for evaluating player experience, beyond hedonic facets of player experience. This research project ended up testing (among other things) if Aesthetic Theories of Art – which define art in terms of the attitude objects elicit in their audience – had any empirical basis, when applied to a specific videogame.

'Aesthetic' theories postulate that object perception is shaped by the function we attribute to them. They conceive of two different attitudes: the aesthetic and the practical. When engaging in a practical attitude, our attention swerves from the object towards our goal of use – *"I see a pen as something I can write with"* [13]. Conversely, if we are engaged in an aesthetic attitude, we pay attention to the object only, in disinterested and complacent manner, to *"enjoy its visual features, the way it sounds, or feels to the touch"* [13]; and only in those cases can an aesthetic experience emerge.

To verify these theories merits in the context of video game appreciation, the authors created two versions of renowned interactive art-game experience Passage [11], one which gave players explicit tasks to achieve (to stimulate a practical attitude), and one with no such goals (to stimulate an aesthetic attitude). A self-report based on cluster art theories was used to assess players' aesthetic experience.

Results showed that the perception of the video game's meaning decreased in the practical version of the game, suggesting that aesthetic theories of art had at least some empirical confirmation: that the perception of meaning was dependent on the nature of the task the user was involved in. Thus, for an experience to be deemed aesthetic, users may need to approach it with an aesthetic attitude, a "contemplation of the object for its own sake".

3   Process (at the Workshop and Beyond)

The overall goal of this process is to prepare a collective research manifest submission to a major journal such as the Entertainment Computing, to be drafted from contributions at the workshop and subsequent interactions. As a collaboratively created research manifest, it will feature an integrative reflection with new questions for a renewed research program in computational media design. Participants are invited to submit a positional statement or case study of their own research practice into how aesthetics impacted digital artifact creation in their research practice. They will be invited to give a short introduction of their position as preparation for the debate during the workshop. For the expected duration, unless we receive a great volume of contributions, we expect that 4h should be enough to run through the meeting process (step 2 below).

1. *Call for and Gather Contributions*:
   (a) Individual presentations of each participant, covering their definition of aesthetics and research influence;
2. *Group Debate of Contributions*:
   (a) Discussion among groups of participants lead by questions designed to spark group interaction and mapping of bridges between research strands;
   (b) Summary of group work and joint debate of positions presented;
   (c) Draft from contributions and emergent questions for the production of a submission draft;
3. *Aggregate and Update Perspective*:
   (a) Collective update of an aesthetics framework within the field and how it can influence digital artifact creation, experience and research;
4. *Propose Integration of Perspectives*:
   (a) Outline research avenues for the future based on the framework;

4   Profile of Participants

Intended participants will be any researcher or practitioner interested in the role of aesthetics in computational media design and experience. Participants interested in contributing with an aesthetic perspective should make the organizers aware of that intention by submitting a position paper in the workshop call.

5   Proponents Info

Common Affiliation: University of Coimbra, Centre for Informatics and Systems of the University of Coimbra, Department of Informatics Engineering.
Common Address: Pólo II - Pinhal de Marrocos, 3030-290 Coimbra.

5.1   Rui Craveirinha

Email: rui.craveirinha@gmail.com
Biography: Rui Craveirinha is a Games User Researcher at Player Research. He has lectured HCI, Game Design and Game Criticism courses at the University level. His research interests cover both the study of artistic experiences in video games and conceptualising authorial approaches to procedural content generation in games. He also loves cats and memes, which is to say, he loves cats twice.

5.2   Luís Pereira

Email: lpereira@dei.uc.pt
Biography: Luís Pereira is pursuing his PhD studies in the field of HCI, focusing on the notion of participation as a key perspective in game design. Having developed an hexadimensional model of participation from which he created and tested a design canvas, his work tries to address game design from an aesthetic perspective, rather than the more usual object mechanics. Luís is also a lecturer in interactive multimedia project courses with experience in multimedia development processes.

5.3   Mariana Seiça

Email: marianac@dei.uc.pt
Biography: Mariana Seiça is an audiovisual designer, with a Master's Degree in Design and Multimedia from the University of Coimbra. She is currently pursuing a PhD in Information Science and Technology, studying the influence of aesthetics on interactive systemic sonifications. Her research and artistic practices focus on sound as a communication tool, embodying her enthusiasm for musical forms that travel between the fields of Sonification, Sound Design, Human Computer Interaction and Computational Music.

5.4   Licínio Roque

Email: lir@dei.uc.pt
Biography: Licínio Roque is an Associate Professor, coordinator of the CISUC Information Systems group and Computational Media Design PhD Program. Current research focuses on Participatory Media, mainly the design and evaluation of shared computational media objects to empower creative collaborations. He was principal researcher on various research/industry projects, and has an extensive methodological and training experience in the areas of HCI, SE, ISD, Interaction Design, Game Design and related technologies. He was also an Associate Professor at Carnegie Mellon University, visiting professor at Aarhus University's CMA group, co-Founder of SPCVIDEOJOGOS and Tapestry Software.

References

1. Bunge, M.: Emergence and Convergence: Qualitative Novelty and the Unity of Knowledge. University of Toronto Press, Toronto (2003)
2. Capra, F.: Speaking nature's language: principles for sustainability. In: Ecological Literacy: Educating Our Children for a Sustainable World, pp. 18–29 (2005)
3. Carroll, N.: Philosophy of Art: A Contemporary Introduction. Routledge, Milton Park (1999)
4. Craveirinha, R., Roque, L.: Impact of game elements in players artistic experience. In: Extended Abstracts of the 2019 CHI Conference on Human Factors in Computing Systems, CHI EA 2019, pp. 1–6. Association for Computing Machinery, New York (2019). https://doi.org/10.1145/3290607.3313049
5. Manovich, L.: Introduction to info-aesthetics, pp. 333–344 (2008). https://doi.org/10.1215/9780822389330-022
6. Pelowski, M., Akiba, F.: A model of art perception, evaluation and emotion in transformative aesthetic experience. New Ideas Psychol. **29**(2), 80–97 (2011)
7. Pereira, L.L., Craveirinha, R., Roque, L.: A canvas for participation-centered game design. In: Proceedings of the Annual Symposium on Computer-Human Interaction in Play, CHI PLAY 2019, pp. 521–532. Association for Computing Machinery, New York (2019). https://doi.org/10.1145/3311350.3347154
8. Pereira, L.L., Portela, M., Roque, L.: Machines of disquiet: textual experience in the LDoD archive. MATLIT: Materialidades Da Literatura **6**(3), 59–71 (2018)
9. Pereira, L.L., Roque, L.: Fátima postmortem. Online-Heidelberg J. Relig. Internet **5** (2014)
10. Pires, D., et al.: The blindfold soundscape game: a case for participation-centered gameplay experience design and evaluation. In: Proceedings of the 8th Audio Mostly Conference, AM 2013. Association for Computing Machinery, New York (2013). https://doi.org/10.1145/2544114.2544122
11. Rohrer, J.: Passage. Game [PC] (2007)
12. Seiça, M., Roque, L., Martins, P., Cardoso, F.A.: A systemic perspective for sonification aesthetics. In: Proceedings of the 26th International Conference on Auditory Display (ICAD 2021). Georgia Institute of Technology (2021)
13. Stolnitz, J.: A atitude est?tica. In: D'Orey, C. (ed.) O que ? a Arte, A Perspectiva Anal?tica. Carmo d'Orey e Dinalivro (2007)
14. Svanaes, D.: Interaction design for and with the lived body: some implications of Merleau-Ponty's phenomenology. ACM Trans. Comput. Hum. Inter. (TOCHI) **20**(1), 8 (2013)

Workshop: Challenges for XR in Digital Entertainment

Esteban Clua[1]($\boxtimes$), Thiago Porcino[1,2], Daniela Trevisan[1], Jorge C. S. Cardoso[4], Thallys Lisboa[1], Victor Peres[1], Victor Ferrari[1], Bruno Marques[3], Lucas Barbosa[1], and Eder Oliveira[1]

[1] Universidade Federal Fluminense, Niteroi, Brazil
esteban@ic.uff.br
[2] Dalhousie University, Nova Scotia, Canada
[3] Universidade Federal do ABC, Sao Paulo, Brazil
[4] University of Coimbra, CISUC, DEI, Coimbra, Portugal

Abstract. Extended Reality as a consolidated game platform was always a dream for both final consumers and game producers. If for one side this technology had enchanted and called the attention due its possibilities, for other side many challenges and difficulties had delayed its proliferation and massification. This workshop intends to rise and discuss aspects and considerations related to these challenges and solutions. We try to bring the most relevant research topics and try to guess how XR games should look in the near future. We divide the challenges into 7 topics: Cybersickness, User Experience, Displays, Rendering, Movements, Body Tracking and External World Information.

Keywords: Extended Reality · Virtual Reality · Digital entertainment · Head-mounted displays · UX

1 Introduction

Extended Reality (XR) platform can be considered as an increment of Virtual Reality in relation to immersion and interaction aspects. While VR platforms are mostly dedicated to visual issues, XR includes more external elements and senses, such as movements, tactile, haptics and the usage of the real environment as the application stage [29]. According to the Milgram Continuum, the virtual immersion is a result that comes not only from accurate visual aspects, but mostly from a precise combination of all human senses, orchestrated in such a way that all of them enhances each other. While many progresses had been achieved in graphics, audio, tracking and interfaces issues, there are still many remaining challenges, mostly related to a correct combination on adaption to recent XR hardware devices.

In this workshop we propose a division of areas for these challenges. We believe that for a real consolidation for entertainment within this platform it is necessary to have robust solutions in each field. We divide the challenges into

© IFIP International Federation for Information Processing 2021
Published by Springer Nature Switzerland AG 2021
J. Baalsrud Hauge et al. (Eds.): ICEC 2021, LNCS 13056, pp. 489–498, 2021.
https://doi.org/10.1007/978-3-030-89394-1_43

7 topics: Cybersickness (CS), user experience and design guidelines, Display and Fovea, Image quality and rendering, movements and redirect walking, body tracking and finally External world information and acquisition.

2   Cybersickness

Motion sickness (MS) is defined as the discomfort felt during a forced visual movement (without body movement), which typically happens in airplane trips, boats, or land vehicles. Such discomfort is also experienced in virtual environments and is called VIMS (Visually Induced Motion Sickness). MS can be split into two subcategories [16]: transportation sickness, which is tied to the real world and simulator sickness, which is associated to the virtual world and includes CS, as shown in Fig. 1.

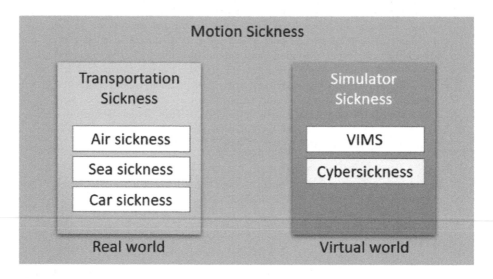

Fig. 1. Motion sickness and its subcategories according to environments and trigger mechanisms.

XR environments that use head-mounted displays (HMDs) are strongly related to common indications of discomfort [18]. Among the potential causes, CS deserves special attention as it is the most common and is usually associated to long exposures to HMDs. Additionally, more than 60% of HMDs usability problems are considerably related to discomfort [18]. The most persistent symptoms caused by CS are general discomfort, headache, stomach awareness, nausea, vomiting, sweating, fatigue, drowsiness, disorientation, and apathy [7]. These symptoms influence the user experience and impact the profit and coverage of XR game manufacturing. In addition, discomfort symptoms can vary over people, where some individuals are more susceptible than others. Several studies have been conducted using deep learning models to predict and mitigate CS, such as convolutional neural network (CNNs) and recurrent neural networks (RNNs) [12,17]. Although deep learning classifiers are the most suitable approach for CS prediction, deep neural networks are black boxes that are very difficult to grasp. In contrast, a recent approach apply techniques to make deep learning models explainable [31]. However, the literature is still not strongly affirmed. Furthermore, symbolic machine learning algorithms enable a straight understanding of decision paths [23]. Another critical problem in CS researching is associated with data labeling. In general, researchers collect verbal, haptic, or brain signal feedback to construct the ground truth of sickness. While verbal feedback is highly subjective and different from each participant, collecting haptic feedback when participants are under discomfort can often be corrupted by the delay associated with participant feedback. A straightforward challenge is related to gender differences tied to XR tasks. Some works [6,9] pointed out that specific tasks can produce different results of CS for different user-profiles and groups. Overcoming these issues will help designers to produce better XR content and improves the user experience and retain users for longer XR exposures.

3 User Experience

Since XR is a new technology and there are many people experiencing it for the first time, it is important that XR designers make their experiences as intuitive and memorable as possible. The game UX accounts for the whole experience players have with a game, from first hearing about it to navigating menus and progressing in the game. The question is: How to make a better game user experience (UX)? Celia Hodent [11] says UX is about understanding the gamer's brain: understanding human capabilities and limitations to anticipate how a game will be perceived, the emotions it will elicit, how players will interact with it, and how engaging the experience will be. As Celia said we believe that UX and cognitive and behavioral psychology can provide very concrete and easy-to-use guidelines to anticipate and even solve design problems. Additionally, techniques from HCI domain such as users interviews, surveys, usability heuristics, analysis of physiological signals, wizardOz [21], among others, need to be properly studied and applied to understand and evaluate the whole UX in the XR context of usage.

4 Displays, Foveated Rendering

Computational needs for game rendering in XR systems have grown faster. The advent of wider Field of View and higher resolutions HMDs have amplified shading complexities [2]. These features bring a computing power bottleneck, requiring some sort of optimization for keeping target frame rates. Knowing that the human eye has a non regular distribution of cones and rods, some studies have suggested to create non regular pixel distribution (Foveated Rendering). While it is already being explored by rendering engines, there still many challenges for optimizing and customizing it. Foveated Rendering technique exploits human visual system to render the best resolution possible only where the user looks, as in Fig. 2. According to Swafford et al. [27], since the human eye perceives more detail at the center of vision, this uniformity in resolution, regardless of user focus, is a waste of valuable resources such as computing power.

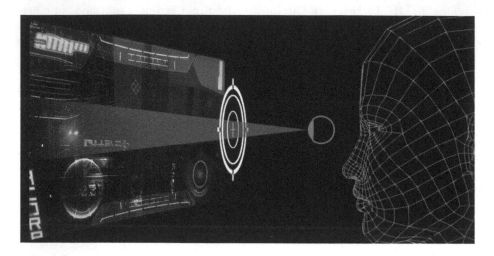

Fig. 2. Foveated rendering simulation. Source: [1]

Besides finding a correct balance for the foveated areas, there are still many challenges, such as understanding how this impacts human perception, color distortions and dynamic factors according with the game scene (games with constant colors in large areas naturally requires less pixels to be rendered and enhances the foveated optimizations). It is also important to create robust factors for measuring and better calibrating rendering parameters. Finally, we believe that this concept can also be transposed for different refresh rates for each foveated area, taking into consideration that rods are more dense at the peripheral human vision area.

5   Image Quality and Rendering

Traditional rasterized rendering algorithms are limited for achieving photo-realism, which is many situation is desirable for a high immersive environment. Path tracing achieves a higher degree of realism due to the global illumination effects, with a Monte Carlo integration method. Still, it is computationally costly to render a 3D scene at an HMD's resolution. In 2018, with the RTX architecture, access to GPUs capable of optimizing the intersection calculation of a ray with a polygon and thus accelerating realistic rendering became available. With this, some areas of research have been reignited. One of them is the use and optimization of path tracing or hybrid rendering (with rasterization and

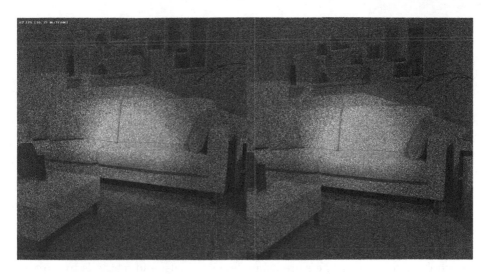

Fig. 3. Path traced scene rendered in dual screens using foveation, before denoiser.

path tracing) algorithms for virtual reality devices such as HMDs, although they remain changeable. By using the properties of vision such as the concentration of cone distribution in the fovea and devices that allow tracking of the user's gaze, we can avoid rendering parts of the screen with such sharp details or rendering at a reduced spatial sampling frequency. Previous studies have experimented with users to define what an optimal distribution would be, with probabilistic selection of which pixels will be selected by rays, thus decreasing the amount of traced rays and optimizing the algorithm [30]. Similarly, other studies use a fixed texture for ray selection.

Not least, reconstruction algorithms called denoisers, which are already commonly used in path tracing rendering, are even more relevant with the fovea distributions, as in Fig. 3. The few works that have made approaches in this regard try to adapt reconstruction to be compatible with log-polar space rendering as well.

6   Movements and Redirect Walking

Providing the user the capacity to explore a virtual environment is one way to enhance and create a sense of belonging. Therefore, to create a satisfactory experience, there is a necessity to let users interact with their surroundings. Moving is another form people unconsciously and continuously interact with their surroundings, and developers invented several techniques to move in XR. The problem with this kind of interaction is that while developers can create infinite worlds, users play in confined spaces. Hence, the locomotion, made in real life, can't be mimicked in the virtual world. The literature indicates a growing search to solve this issue [3].

Artificial Movement is one example of a solution. It consists of moving the character with a button or joystick and allows the user the freely roam the virtual area. However, it creates severe cybersickness because of the divergence between the seen and felt movement. Another known solution is teleportation. With a self-explanatory name, this technique transfers the player's position to a desired new one. When developers use this solution, they avoid problems with the cybersickness, but it breaks the immersion since people can't do this in real life. With these two examples, we can set the scene and understand what researchers struggle with within this field. One solution that has the purpose of creating, in the user, the feeling of mimicking his movement by misleading his senses is Redirect Walking [14], which is based on tricking the user's perception and make him feel that is walking forward, but in reality, he is walking in a curved path. The main problem with this solution is how to shift the virtual environment without triggering the user's perception, which can cause cybersickness and break the immersion [5]. Instead of only divert the player's movement or turn the whole scenery, researchers are using devices, tools, and methods to improve Redirect Walking. Methods such as pointed by [26] recognizes when is happening the saccade movement of the eye and shifts the scene at the same time. Redirect Walking is the least used method of movement in VR applications mainly because of the necessity of bigger spaces to fully reach its potential of making the user unperceptive by the reorientation of his movement [5]. Matsumoto et al. [20] measured that it needs a circular arc of 22 m to avoid perception, but [24] managed to do constrain the movements to an area of 6 m × 6 m. Even though there is an evolution in this topic, it is needed to develop methods that can use smaller spaces, and it is computed fully in the HMD so this method can become more universally available.

7 Body Tracking

XR games must provide users with an immersive experience with a sense of presence and satisfying natural interaction. Body tracking allows reconstruction of the body movement needed to achieve a satisfying natural interaction [15], especially in multiplayer games [13], enabling users to observe other players' movements. A virtual body is crucial for a good level of immersion, and when the user identifies himself with this virtual body, we can see the feeling of presence [25]. Although there are many important works related to the subject [4], most are related for showing only floating hands or VR controllers, due to the lack of movement data. In the application domain, XR in Games, vision-based body tracking remains a challenge because of the sudden change in object motion, cluttered background, partial occlusion, and camera motion [8]. The hands are the most used body parts in XR in Games, as they provide a robust form of interaction. Vision-based hand-tracking is an object of interest of several researchers. Most work on hands-tracking focuses on the use of depth cameras [28] or RGB [21]. Depth-based approaches present results that are superior to RGB-based approaches. A depth camera provides hand geometry in terms of a

2.5D point cloud, and the model-based approaches can reliably fit a hand mesh to the reconstructed point cloud [28]. Using hand tracking input with mobile technology is a problem mainly due to the high energy consumption. Han et al. [10] present a real-time tracking system that uses four egocentric monochrome fisheye cameras to produce 3D hand pose estimates and run not only on PC but also on mobile processors (Fig. 4). The system presents failures in hand-hand and hand-object interactions showing that grasping objects and training data generation are still open issues in mobile hand tracking interactions.

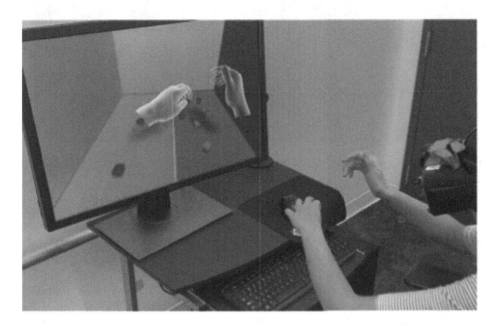

Fig. 4. A real-time hand-tracking system using four monochrome cameras mounted on a VR headset. Source: [10]

8   External World Information

Acquiring and processing the external world information is an essential and challenging aspect of XR applications. The real-world data acquisition for XR applications comes from different sources such as motion sensors, cameras, depth sensors, and other hardware. Aggregating and incorporating this data into meaningful information for XR games is not a trivial task.

Considering the visual features of XR applications, one crucial aspect is the consistent appearance between virtual and real-world objects. One of the main characteristics that drive the consistent appearance is the lighting between virtual and real-world objects. One possible approach to solve this problem is the

Fig. 5. Left: rendering of XR scene with inconsistent lighting. Right: relighting of XR scene with consistent environment lighting.

relighting of real-world objects into a specific lighting setting [22]. However, relighting the entire scene is still an open challenge. Another possible approach is the relighting of virtual objects (Fig. 5) into a lighting setting that matches the environment lighting [19]. Both of those approaches require the estimation of environmental lighting from the external world. Usually, all the lighting information is estimated from images of the environment, captured in real-time, thus posing as a computer vision problem. With the advances in deep learning, those methods are able to estimate the lighting information and provide a way to improve the XR experience regarding visual fidelity. Extracting and estimating external world information is still considered a difficult task. Developments regarding the representation of the information, including the recent advancements in computer vision methods, can dramatically improve XR environments by allowing new forms of interaction between the virtual and the real world.

9   Conclusion

Extended Reality as a game platform has an incredible potential, due its high immersive conditions. However, it is a totally new computational and ubiquitous environment and brings many challenges and problems, some of them not trivial. In this workshop we categorize these issues in 7 different topics, although there can be many others. This classification is not exhaustive and there are many other aspects that could also be included, such as audio, new interfaces devices and collaborative environments.

References

1. Fove's $250,000 kickstarter campaign wants to bring eye-tracking control to virtual reality, April 2021. https://thenextweb.com/news/foves-250000-kickstarter-campaign-wants-to-bring-eye-tracking-control-to-virtual-reality. Accessed 28 July 2021

2. Albert, R., Patney, A., Luebke, D., Kim, J.: Latency requirements for foveated rendering in virtual reality. ACM Trans. Appl. Percept. (TAP) 14(4), 1–13 (2017)

3. Cannavò, A., Calandra, D., Pratticò, F.G., Gatteschi, V., Lamberti, F.: An evaluation testbed for locomotion in virtual reality. IEEE Trans. Vis. Comput. Graph. 27(3), 1871–1889 (2021). https://doi.org/10.1109/TVCG.2020.3032440

4. Caserman, P., Garcia-Agundez, A., Göbel, S.: A survey of full-body motion reconstruction in immersive virtual reality applications. IEEE Trans. Vis. Comput. Graph. 26(10), 3089–3108 (2019)

5. Cherni, H., Métayer, N., Souliman, N.: Literature review of locomotion techniques in virtual reality. Int. J. Virtual Reality 20(1), 1–20 (2020). https://doi.org/10.20870/IJVR.2020.20.1.3183, https://ijvr.eu/article/view/3183

6. Curry, C., Li, R., Peterson, N., Stoffregen, T.A.: Cybersickness in virtual reality head-mounted displays: examining the influence of sex differences and vehicle control. Int. J. Hum.-Comput. Inter. 36(12), 1161–1167 (2020)

7. Dennison, M.S., D'Zmura, M.: Cybersickness without the wobble: experimental results speak against postural instability theory. Appl. Ergon. 58, 215–223 (2017)

8. Dutta, A., Mondal, A., Dey, N., Sen, S., Moraru, L., Hassanien, A.E.: Vision tracking: a survey of the state-of-the-art. SN Comput. Sci. 1(1), 1–19 (2020)

9. Grassini, S., Laumann, K.: Are modern head-mounted displays sexist? A systematic review on gender differences in HMD-mediated virtual reality. Front. Psychol. 11, 1604 (2020)

10. Han, S., et al.: MEgATrack: monochrome egocentric articulated hand-tracking for virtual reality. ACM Trans. Graph. 39(4), 87 (2020)

11. Hodent, C.: The Gamer's Brain: How Neuroscience and UX Can Impact Video Game Design. CRC Press (2017). https://books.google.com.br/books?id=JzyhDwAAQBAJ

12. Jeong, D., Yoo, S., Yun, J.: Cybersickness analysis with EEG using deep learning algorithms. In: 2019 IEEE Conference on Virtual Reality and 3D User Interfaces (VR), pp. 827–835. IEEE (2019)

13. Jiang, F., Yang, X., Feng, L.: Real-time full-body motion reconstruction and recognition for off-the-shelf VR devices. In: Proceedings of the 15th ACM SIGGRAPH Conference on Virtual-Reality Continuum and Its Applications in Industry, vol. 1, pp. 309–318 (2016)

14. Jonathan, E., Roberts, C., Presentation, S., Razzaque, S., Kohn, Z., Whitton, M.: Redirected walking. In: Proceedings of Eurographics (2001)

15. Kasahara, S., et al.: Malleable embodiment: changing sense of embodiment by spatial-temporal deformation of virtual human body. In: Proceedings of the 2017 CHI Conference on Human Factors in Computing Systems, pp. 6438–6448 (2017)

16. Kemeny, A., Chardonnet, J.R., Colombet, F.: Getting Rid of Cybersickness: In Virtual Reality, Augmented Reality, and Simulators. Springer, Cham (2020). https://doi.org/10.1007/978-3-030-59342-1

17. Kim, J., Kim, W., Oh, H., Lee, S., Lee, S.: A deep cybersickness predictor based on brain signal analysis for virtual reality contents. In: Proceedings of the IEEE International Conference on Computer Vision, pp. 10580–10589 (2019)

18. Kolasinski, E.M.: Simulator sickness in virtual environments. Technical Report. DTIC Document (1995)
19. Marques, B.A.D., Clua, E.W.G., Vasconcelos, C.N.: Deep spherical harmonics light probe estimator for mixed reality games. Comput. Graph. **76**, 96–106 (2018). https://doi.org/10.1016/j.cag.2018.09.003
20. Matsumoto, K., Ban, Y., Narumi, T., Yanase, Y., Tanikawa, T., Hirose, M.: Unlimited corridor: redirected walking techniques using visuo haptic interaction. In: ACM SIGGRAPH 2016 Emerging Technologies, SIGGRAPH 2016. Association for Computing Machinery, New York (2016). https://doi.org/10.1145/2929464.2929482
21. de Oliveira, E., Clua, E.W.G., Vasconcelos, C.N., Marques, B.A.D., Trevisan, D.G., de Castro Salgado, L.C.: FPVRGame: deep learning for hand pose recognition in real-time using low-end HMD. In: van der Spek, E., Göbel, S., Do, E.Y.-L., Clua, E., Baalsrud Hauge, J. (eds.) ICEC-JCSG 2019. LNCS, vol. 11863, pp. 70–84. Springer, Cham (2019). https://doi.org/10.1007/978-3-030-34644-7_6
22. Pandey, R., et al.: Total relighting: learning to relight portraits for background replacement. ACM Trans. Graph. (TOG) **40**, 1–21 (2021). https://doi.org/10.1145/3450626.3459872
23. Porcino, T., Rodrigues, E.O., Silva, A., Clua, E., Trevisan, D.: Using the gameplay and user data to predict and identify causes of cybersickness manifestation in virtual reality games. In: 2020 IEEE 8th International Conference on Serious Games and Applications for Health (SeGAH), pp. 1–8. IEEE (2020)
24. Rietzler, M., Gugenheimer, J., Hirzle, T., Deubzer, M., Langbehn, E., Rukzio, E.: Rethinking redirected walking: on the use of curvature gains beyond perceptual limitations and revisiting bending gains, pp. 115–122 (2018). https://doi.org/10.1109/ISMAR.2018.00041
25. Slater, M., Wilbur, S.: A framework for immersive virtual environments (five): speculations on the role of presence in virtual environments. Presence: Teleoper. Virtual Environ. **6**(6), 603–616 (1997)
26. Sun, Q., et al.: Towards virtual reality infinite walking: dynamic saccadic redirection. ACM Trans. Graph. (TOG) **37**(4), 67 (2018)
27. Swafford, N.T., Iglesias-Guitian, J.A., Koniaris, C., Moon, B., Cosker, D., Mitchell, K.: User, metric, and computational evaluation of foveated rendering methods. In: Proceedings of the ACM Symposium on Applied Perception, pp. 7–14 (2016)
28. Taylor, J., et al.: Articulated distance fields for ultra-fast tracking of hands interacting. ACM Trans. Graph. (TOG) **36**(6), 1–12 (2017)
29. Valente, L., Feijó, B., do Prado Leite, J.C.S., Clua, E.: A method to assess pervasive qualities in mobile games. Pers. Ubiquitous Comput. **22**(4), 647–670 (2018)
30. Weier, M., et al.: Foveated real-time ray tracing for head-mounted displays. In: Computer Graphics Forum, vol. 35, pp. 289–298. Wiley (2016)
31. Xie, N., Ras, G., van Gerven, M., Doran, D.: Explainable deep learning: a field guide for the uninitiated. arXiv:2004.14545 (2020)

Interactive Entertainment/Experiential Works

"The Woods" AR Game

Scott Swearingen$^{(\boxtimes)}$, Kyoung Swearingen$^{(\boxtimes)}$, Fede Camara Halac$^{(\boxtimes)}$, Sruthi Ammannagari, and Matt Hall$^{(\boxtimes)}$

The Ohio State University, Columbus, OH 43210, USA
{swearingen.16,swearingen.75,camarahalac.1}@osu.edu,
{Ammannagari.1,hall.2586}@buckeyemail.osu.edu

Abstract. While loneliness in our real lives is increasingly recognized as having dire physical, mental and emotional consequences, cooperative games have been shown to build empathy and provide positive social impact. In this paper, we present "The Woods", a local cooperative, mixed-reality game using augmented reality and 4-channel audio spatialization panning that provides players with face-to-face interactions in pursuit of a shared goal. This paper discusses the narrative, mechanical, and sonic components of the game, as well as the players' experiences. The goal of our team is to develop a narrative-driven AR game that promotes collaborative problem-solving and engages players in an emergent physical and digital experience.

Keywords: Networked AR · Cooperative game · Multiplayer · Mixed reality · Sonic experience · Collaboration · Social good

1 Introduction

"The Woods" is a mixed-reality, two-player cooperative game that addresses the perils of social isolation by promoting connections between people and actively engaging them through play. Using Augmented Reality (AR) and 4-channel audio spatialization panning, players choreograph their movement in real-world space while interacting with birds, clouds and other objects in virtual space. In pursuit of a shared goal, players experience an immersive sonic narrative of rumbling storm clouds and disconnected voices that culminate in stories of hope and reconciliation. The design intent behind "The Woods" is to illuminate human connections to others and to celebrate this through collaborative play while communicating the importance of fostering positive social interaction through face-to-face engagement and the power of the human voice. [1–4].

2 Narrative

The narrative of "The Woods" is built around the broken relationship of two adult brothers who have been separated and out of contact with each other for a considerable

© IFIP International Federation for Information Processing 2021
Published by Springer Nature Switzerland AG 2021
J. Baalsrud Hauge et al. (Eds.): ICEC 2021, LNCS 13056, pp. 501–504, 2021.
https://doi.org/10.1007/978-3-030-89394-1_44

amount of time. One of the brothers in a desperate attempt to reach out and reconcile with the other brother is heard leaving a voicemail. In the beginning of the game, players hear only fragments and distorted chunks of the message and are unable to decipher meaning or intent. However, as the game progresses through player collaboration, the message becomes clearer. This narrative of reconciliation between these estranged brothers informs the mechanics of the game itself, with the players coordinating their efforts to one another in pursuit of a common goal. The game is designed such that it is not enough for one player to do all of the work. Rather, success requires the combined work of both players. As players engage one another and contribute to the goal together, the game rewards them with the unfolding narrative of the brothers reconnecting to one another (see Fig. 1).

Fig. 1. Two players playing "The Woods" together

3   Mechanics

As a two-player game, "The Woods" is unique in how it enables players to physically collaborate with their whole bodies. A client-server model exists between the players' phones and the Photon Unity Network where each client renders the game based on its shared positional data. We accomplish this by tracking the positions of each phone relative to an AR marker located on the floor as players move about the 12-foot diameter game space with their positions synched over the network. Based on the calculated positions of each client, we connect the players together by placing a virtual branch at their midpoint (see Figs. 2 and 3). As players move their phones through physical space, the branch simultaneously moves accordingly in virtual space. Thus, players must choreograph their movement and, by extension, the branch to provide a perch for the virtual birds to land on. The game checks for collisions between the branch and two other virtual objects. If a collision occurs between the branch and a bird, then the bird will land on the branch and a new fragment of the aforementioned voicemail will play. Alternatively, if a collision occurs between the branch and a storm cloud, then a crash of thunder erupts, and any birds that had been caught scatter and fly away. Moreover, the flight path of the birds and clouds are randomly generated to maintain interest and avoid players exploiting the game. As a metaphor, these game mechanics are designed to parallel the narrative of the isolated brothers who are navigating their own obstacles in order to reconnect with one another.

Fig. 2. In-game screenshots of "The Woods"

4 Comparison to Other AR Games

"The Woods" promotes face-to-face interactions over screen-based interactions. It can only be played in person because the game is built upon the players' adjacency to one another. Furthermore, the phone as an AR device is not the focus of interaction with the other player. After the start of the game, there is no direct interaction of the player with the phone other than holding it and using it as a viewport. In "The Woods", the player's interaction with the other player extends beyond the phone and into the space in which they are playing together. There are no touch-based or gesture-based interactions. Rather, the primary purpose of the phone in "The Woods" is to provide the players with feedback and encourage verbal and physical collaboration as they negotiate the game environment together, locating birds in flight, moving the branch towards birds to provide a perch for them to land on, and evading storm clouds.

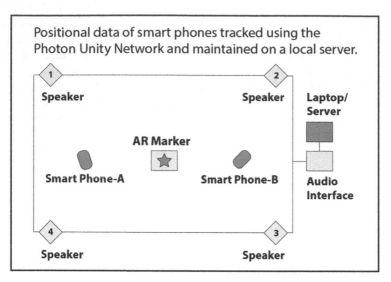

Fig. 3. Systems diagram of "The Woods"

5   Conclusion

The strength of cooperative games is that they promote social interaction, build empathy and improve personal relationships by encouraging players to work together to achieve a common objective. "The Woods" further expands this by promoting real-world, physical space interactions over screen-based interactions, made possible through our unique design of AR and audio spatialization. By highlighting the importance of physical interaction and collaboration, our intent is to provide a positive social impact by illuminating our human connections to one another through prompting our players to coordinate their efforts, discover what connects them, and work together in pursuit of shared goals.

References

1. Velez, J.: Extending the theory of bounded generalized reciprocity: an explanation of the social benefits of cooperative video game play. Comput. Hum. Behav. **48**, 481–491 (2015).https://doi.org/10.1016/j.chb.2015.02.015
2. Jin, B., Park, N.: Mobile voice communication and loneliness: cell phone use and the social skills deficit hypothesis. New Media Soc. **15**(7), 1094–1111 (2013). https://doi.org/10.1177/1461444812466715
3. https://www.floridatechonline.com/blog/psychology/how-smartphones-are-contributing-to-the-loneliness-epidemic/
4. Bekker, T., Sturm, J., Barakova, E.: 2004 2nd workshop on design for social interaction through physical play. In: Gross, T., et al (eds.) Human-Computer Interaction – INTERACT 2009. Lecture Notes in Computer Science, vol. 5727, pp. 952–953. Springer, Berlin, Heidelberg (2009). https://doi.org/10.1007/978-3-03548-3_127

Sentenced to Transportation: An iDoc for Australia's Convict Past

Nicole Basaraba[(✉)][iD]

Maastricht University, Studio Europa, Maastricht, The Netherlands
n.basaraba@maastrichtuniversity.nl

Abstract. An interactive web documentary (iDoc) was produced to highlight multinational perspectives and give users the option to choose their own experience by exploring different narrative paths about convict transportation to the 11 UNESCO World Heritage Australian Convict Sites. The iDoc prototype provides a map-based main menu, an alternative "stories" footer menu, and a traditional linear progression. It brings 11 physical locations into the digital landscape and provides a series of "stories" from the perspectives of female convicts, Irish convicts (and their famous escape stories, convicts' life in prison), and the impact of colonialism on the Indigenous populations. The iDoc also addresses the issue of growing public rejection of experts' presentation of history through a bottom-up approach of remixing user-generated (i.e., non-expert) content with curated archives and tourism marketing content. The public can interact with the work through a web browser (preferably Chrome) with an internet connection by clicking on the hyperlinks in the interface.

Keywords: iDoc · Virtual tour · Transmedia · Edutainment · Colonial narratives

1 Introduction

This paper presents an 'edutainment' experiential work in the form of an interactive web documentary developed for UNESCO World Heritage Sites (WHS), which were chosen as the narrative focus because they are recognised as culturally significant to the world rather than a single culture. These sites also allowed for the inclusion of multiple perspectives and the communication of worldwide shared heritage. Furthermore, WHS designation involves a rigorous selection process based on a set of criteria and UNESCO, being a world-recognised organisation, provides a common frame of reference to situate cultural heritage as a

This research was conducted during PhD candidature with the financial support of the ADAPT Centre for Digital Media Technology at Trinity College Dublin, Ireland, which is funded by Science Foundation Ireland through the SFI Research Centres Programme and is co-funded under the European Regional Development Fund (ERDF) through Grant 13/RC/2106.

J. Baalsrud Hauge et al. (Eds.): ICEC 2021, LNCS 13056, pp. 505–508, 2021.
https://doi.org/10.1007/978-3-030-89394-1_45

concept. At the time the case study was selected, there were 1072 designated UNESCO WHS, of which 832 were categorised as cultural, 206 as natural, and 35 as mixed [1]. The list of cultural sites was reduced to those with some tourism infrastructure to ensure that user-generated content exists and to sites where the majority of content is available in the English-language. After applying these selection criteria and doing preliminary research on the amount of existing content produced by the tourism industry, experts in related fields, and Internet users, the 11 UNESCO World Heritage Australian Convict Sites were selected.

This case study actually consists of 11 smaller location-based case study narratives connected by the central theme of convict transportation. This more recent history (1788–1868) presents opportunities for a vested personal interest on behalf of the public today whose ancestors may have been transported or moved as free immigrants to Australia and this history has a long-term impact on national identity. For example, it was referred to by some in certain contexts as "the convict stain" [2,3]. The 11 UNESCO WHS featured in the iDoc include four sites in New South Wales—Hyde Park Barracks, Cockatoo Island, Old Government House, and Old Great North Road; five in Tasmania—Port Arthur Historic Site, Cascades Female Factory, Coal Mines Historic Site, Brickendon and Woolmers Estates and Darlington Probation Station; one located in Perth—Fremantle Prison; and one on Norfolk Island—Kingston and Arthur's Vale Historic Area [5].

2   Bottom-Up Remix Method for iDoc Development

The iDoc prototype was developed through remixing existing content from multiple different sources into a narrativized cultural heritage system [4]. The goal was to allow users to select the story options provided that most piqued their personal interests. This bottom-up approach followed Lawless et al.'s [6] best practices for tailoring access to content which included: modelling users, modelling content, and then creating an adaptive system through the four steps of guiding, exploring, suggesting and reflecting [6].

Three corpora were selected for a multimodal data analysis to capture specific perspectives (based on the producers) and the rhetorical purposes of the content. The first corpus was produced by the tourism industry, which focuses on marketing experiences to generate capital. The second corpus included user-generated content produced by the general public who post on social media posts for a variety of intrinsic (e.g., help others) and extrinsic (e.g., monetisation) reasons. The third corpus was expert-produced content (e.g., scholars, governments, and professional writers) who publish primarily for educational reasons. This bottom-up'big data' analysis of the three corpora let the data speak to what themes are of interest to the primary target audience of cultural heritage tourists and the results led to the formation of a narrative content model for the iDoc prototype titled, "Sentenced to Transportation: A Virtual Tour of Australia's Convict Past."

3   Results from Content Modelling

Documentary genre conventions were referred to for creative inspiration if the narrative production process based on the content model. Penz [7] outlined that the common narrative layers for documentaries about cities are: the story and history of the buildings, the narratives and points of view of the city planning process, the tales and personal stories embodied by passers-by, and the narrative intentions of the film itself. The results of the multimodal data analysis highlighted that visitors to the 11 UNESCO Australian Convict WHS are interested in tangible heritage, natural heritage, and intangible heritage in terms of literature, arts, and dark tourism. It also led to a content model with six thematic narrative layers, namely: (1) natural heritage and the site's 'sense of place,'; (2) infrastructure and the settlement's chronological timeline; (3) the rationale for UNESCO designation and cultural significance of the heritage site; (4) convict narratives, related artworks, novels, and other media such as mobile apps; (5) nearby tourist attractions and modern-day usage of the WHSs that are no longer functioning prisons; (6) the convicts' daily life as prisoners; and finally the colonial impact on Australian history and national identity. There were also six main points of view included in the iDoc, which are: British convicts, Irish convicts, Female convicts, New Zealand convicts, juvenile convicts, Aboriginal Australians, and the historical Australian authorities (e.g., British magistrates, governors, ship captains). This allows users to select a particular convict site to explore or a narrative path from the perspective of a specific sub-group.

Two user surveys for this iDoc prototype were conducted and the results showed that (1) users preferred video content and historical photography; (2) the narrative structure provided freedom for exploration and encouraged non-linear navigation but its unfamiliarity caused some confusion; (3) the ability to measure agency was inconclusive due to contradictory survey responses and the difficulty of measuring this academic concept through simple survey questions; and (4) users were inspired to physically visit one or more WHSs and related nearby attractions, to view additional materials, and to share their travel experiences and the iDoc with their networks [4].

4   Conclusion

The user experience surveys highlighted the revisions/updates required prior to a public launch of the iDoc for edutainment purposes. These revisions include: adding more narration to further connect the 290 different nodes of content, performing additional user testing on the non-linear narrative structure to visually map the level of user accomplishment within the iDoc, further improving the user experience (UX) design for the iDoc genre, and providing user training on new interactive digital narrative interfaces. This iDoc prototype demonstrates how a bottom-up remix can create a new narrative about cultural heritage sites; how a map-based main menu can be used as the primary navigation mode and be supplemented by both alternative branches and a linear progression option, and finally a non-linear narrative structure can lead to unique emergent narrative experiences for each user, thus increasing the iDoc's replay value.

5   Link to iDoc

The iDoc prototype is available at: http://nicolebasaraba.com/Australian-convicts-prototype/.

6   Technical Requirements

The technical requirements are minimal. The optimal viewing experience would be using a Chrome web browser on a laptop with headphones. Since there are embedded videos a strong internet connection would help for faster buffering. Since this is a prototype, it is noted that the Google Maps menu is also in a prototype view due to the expired API funding, but it still functions when an item is selected.

References

1. UNESCO Criteria. http://whc.unesco.org/en/criteria/. Accessed 27 May 2021
2. Lambert, R.D.: Reclaiming the ancestral past: narrative, rhetoric and the 'convict stain'. J. Sociol. **38**(2), 111–127 (2002)
3. Tranter, B., Donoghue, J.: Convict ancestry: a neglected aspect of Australian identity. Nations Nationalism **9**(4), 555–577 (2003)
4. Basaraba, N.: Remixing transmedia for cultural heritage: the rhetoric, creative practice and evaluation of digital narratives (2020)
5. UNESCO Australian Convict Sites. https://whc.unesco.org/en/list/1306/. Accessed 11 Mar 2020
6. Lawless, S., Conlan, O., Hampson, C.: Tailoring access to content. In: A New Companion to Digital Humanities, pp. 171–184 (2016)
7. Penz, F.: Towards an urban narrative layers approach to decipher the language of city films. CLCWeb: Comp. Lit. Cult. **14**(3), 7 (2012)
8. Basaraba, N.: Sentenced to transportation: a virtual tour of australia's convict past iDoc (2020). http://nicolebasaraba.com/Australian-convicts-prototype

Casa das Máquinas: An Artificial Dialogue of Portuguese Poetry

Mariana Seiça[1]($\boxtimes$)(iD), João Couceiro e Castro[1](iD), Sérgio Rebelo[1](iD),
Pedro Martins[1](iD), Ana Boavida[2](iD), and Penousal Machado[1](iD)

[1] University of Coimbra, Coimbra, Portugal
{marianac,srebelo,pjmm,machado}@dei.uc.pt, jccastro@student.dei.uc.pt
[2] Department of Informatics Engineering, Centre for Informatics and Systems
of the University of Coimbra, Coimbra, Portugal
aboavida@fba.pt

Abstract. *Casa das Máquinas* is an audiovisual confrontation between
two artificial engines—*Máquina de Ouver* and *Máquina Canora*—in a
multimodal dialogue that explores the poetic language of Mário de Sá-
Carneiro. The poems *Epígrafe*, *Anto* and *Fim*, serve as feedstock to the
machines, with their words oiling the internal engines of both entities,
pulsating their mechanical universe and stimuli.

Keywords: Media art · Installation · Typography · Sonification ·
Poetry · Mário de Sá-Carneiro

1 Introduction

Over time, poets and writers explored the visual arrangement of typography to
insert expressiveness into their works. Although this practice was already visible
in the work of some Ancient Greek poets, some Modern artists, such as Futurists
and Concrete poets, typeset their work in nonstandard, dynamic and non-linear
layouts to fully transmit the emotional charge of their works [2, 3].

Casa das Máquinas is an audiovisual installation that generates and presents
audiovisual artefacts, aiming to bring its audience into a sensory, emotional
experience of the textual inputs, based on the perceptions of these contemporary digital "machines". Two artificial beings, *Máquina de Ouver* and *Máquina
Canora*, appropriate and explore the work of Portuguese Poet Mário Sá-Carneiro
(1890–1916), each revealing its own interpretative dimensions of his work.

2 The Engines

Máquina Canora is a confrontation between two mechanical entities, in a pulsating and vocal conversation, that breathes the poetic language of Mário de Sá-
Carneiro. In the installation, three of his poems are presented, namely *Epígrafe*
[4, p. 4], *Anto* [4, p. 30], and *Fim* [4, p. 78]. These poems serve as feedstock for

© IFIP International Federation for Information Processing 2021
Published by Springer Nature Switzerland AG 2021
J. Baalsrud Hauge et al. (Eds.): ICEC 2021, LNCS 13056, pp. 509–512, 2021.
https://doi.org/10.1007/978-3-030-89394-1_46

(a) Frame example of the poem *Epígrafe*   (b) Frame example of the poem *Fim* by
by *Máquina de Ouver*   *Máquina Canora*

Fig. 1. Examples of the two engines

these two machines that, with each word, nurture their internal gears with these futuristic stimuli that naturally refer to this mechanic universe.

Entitled *Máquina de Ouver* (tr. Listening/Seeing Machine) and *Máquina Canora* (tr. Singing Machine), the two react in contrasting ways to the same textual content, chanting audiovisual odes that seek to highlight distinct dimensions of these poems: the first, with an extensive acoustic analysis of declamations for creating typographic compositions that convey the plasticity of the human voice; and the second, focused on the extraction of emotions inherent in each verse for creating musical compositions that reflect these emotional universes.

The interpretation of each machine is, thus, exposed as a dialogue or antithesis, with the two alternatively revealing their language reacting to poetry and redefining Sá-Carneiro's poetic imaginary under a mechanical-generative view.

2.1 *Máquina de Ouver*

Máquina de Ouver is based on a computational system [1] that analyses sound recordings of human speech and creates a visual representation for its expressiveness through typographic features (see Fig. 1a).

This experimentation process uses poetry performances as the system input, as they are one of the most dynamic and richest forms of speech in terms of expressiveness. It receives the speech recording and its transcription, analyses the acoustic qualities, the speed variations in the speech, the pauses, and then maps these values to typographic features (*e.g.* size, weight, or leading). In this version, we can hear the poet's words through the voice of Paula Couceiro.

2.2 *Máquina Canora*

Máquina Canora is an audiovisual machine that unveils the underlying emotions within the poetic language. The acoustic environment is generated by a computational system named ESSYS [5], that composes musical pieces representing eight emotions: joy, anticipation, trust, fear, anger, disgust, surprise and sadness.

Fig. 2. First public exhibition of *Casa das Máquinas*

These emotions travel melodically and harmonically through timbres of immersiveness, mystery, and mechanic ambience, in a constant dialogue with the typography that reveals the most influential words. The typographic animation reflects the meaning of each verse in a "linotypic dance" of almost visual poetry (see Fig. 1b), with each word establishing an unexpected connection between the machine and the emotional universe.

3   The Installation

The debate between these two engines demands an immersive, darkened and enclosed environment for them to co-exist, while inviting each participant to enter and experience this audiovisual space of poetry. Each machine, physically existing in its own display, stand side by side, addressing each other while also addressing the audience, facing each seated spectator to embrace them in their audiovisual universe. The first exhibition of this piece took place in the first edition of the Portuguese Poetry Festival MAP (see Fig. 2), in June 2021.

4   Conclusion

Casa das Máquinas offers a singular experience, presenting distinctive and artificial reactions from mechanical-generative engines to poetry, which may, in turn, entice novel perspectives from each spectator. We believe these new perceptions may elevate the rich, emotional value intrinsic to the work of Sá-Carneiro, which in turn increases the conceptual and historic value of the installation, as one of the most influential Portuguese poets from the earlier twentieth century and one of the pioneers of the modernism movement in Portuguese poetry.

As insatiable entities, *Máquina de Ouver* and *Máquina Canora* can feed themselves with any kind of written language, fostering future iterations with expanded poetic universes, literature dimensions or even, as an ultimate challenge, the individual, single expression of each visitor who enters this space.

5   Video

The full artefact of *Casa das Máquinas* can be seen in https://cdv.dei.uc.pt/2021/casa-das-maquinas.mp4.

6   Technical Requirements

The proposed installation consists of two audiovisuals artefacts, functioning alternately in two distinct displays. The technical requirements for the implementation of *Casa das Máquinas* are the following: (I) a computer (*e.g.* Windows 10 Pro Machine with, at least, an Intel® Core™ i7-9700, or similar, 8 GB RAM and 125 GB of disk storage); (II) two landscape-oriented digital screens (preferably full-HD 43" screen); and (III) two active speakers. The computer should be connected to the network. Alternatively, video projectors may be used instead of digital screens. Also, the computer should be connected to the two video outputs (either monitors or video projectors) via display port or HDMI, and to the two audio outputs (loudspeakers) via TRS audio cable. If necessary, the author can provide some of the needed technical material.

7   Physical/Space Requirements

The installation should be presented in a relatively isolated space, either in terms of audiovisual stimuli, or sources of light, to provide an immersive environment. This space should be, at least, five meters wide and five meters in length. The displays can either place one facing the other, or side by side.

If any kind of spatial and/or logistic limitations arise, the exhibition organisation and curators can suggest a new arrangement of the artwork.

References

1. Castro, J.A.C., Martins, P., Boavida, A., Machado, P.: «máquina de ouver» - from sound to type: finding the visual representation of speech by mapping sound features to typographic variables. In: Proceedings of the 9th International Conference on Digital and Interactive Arts. ARTECH 2019, Association for Computing Machinery, New York (2019). https://doi.org/10.1145/3359852.3359892
2. Meggs, P.B., Purvis, A.W.: Meggs' History of Graphic Design, 6th edn. John Wiley & Sons, New York (2016)
3. Polkinhorn, H.: Visual poetry: an introduction. Vis. Lang. **26**(4), 390–393 (1993)
4. de Sá-Carneiro, M.: Indícios de Oiro. Edições Presença, Oporto (1937)
5. Seiça, M., Lopes, R.B., Martins, P., Cardoso, F.A.: Sonifying twitter's emotions through music. In: Aramaki, M., Davies, M.E.P., Kronland-Martinet, R., Ystad, S. (eds.) CMMR 2017. LNCS, vol. 11265, pp. 586–608. Springer, Cham (2018). https://doi.org/10.1007/978-3-030-01692-0_39

Student Game and Interactive Entertainment Competition

Designing an Arts-Based, Collaborative Mystery Game to Improve Players' Motivation and Confidence as Storytellers

Simone Downie$^{(\boxtimes)}$ (ID)

The Ohio State University, Columbus, OH 43210, USA
`downie.42@osu.edu`

Abstract. Literacy is a complex term that involves an array of inter-twined processes, including motivation. Students who lack this internal willingness often fail to engage with books and other literacy-related content, which in turn negatively effects their learning outcomes. *Murder on Mansion Hill* is a digital tabletop game that weaves together arts-based strategies shown to improve students' involvement in reading - including storytelling, collage, and co-design - in a cohesive manner. By blending these strategies with the motivational benefits of gameplay, *Mansion Hill* encourages players to take a highly active role in developing and sharing imaginative narratives, helping them to view stories as an enjoyable and rewarding outlet they can share with friends. In playtests, players overcame fear of judgment, enjoyed engaging with narrative in multimodal ways, and bonded with peers.

Keywords: Educational games · Storytelling · Literacy · Collage · Co-design

1 Introduction

While there are well-documented benefits to students spending time with book-related content, there is also a notable lack in some of their desire to do so. This phenomenon, known as aliteracy, is unfortunately on the rise as students spend less and less time reading for pleasure [1]. This reluctance can be caused by a variety of factors, from students fearing they will be considered "dumb" for making a mistake [2], to viewing reading as a submissive, boring act that fails to consider their creativity and desires [3], to feeling constrained by traditional text and tools that don't support ways students make meaning and express themselves to peers [4].

Electronic supplementary material The online version of this chapter (https://doi.org/10.1007/978-3-030-89394-1_47) contains supplementary material, which is available to authorized users.

© IFIP International Federation for Information Processing 2021
Published by Springer Nature Switzerland AG 2021
J. Baalsrud Hauge et al. (Eds.): ICEC 2021, LNCS 13056, pp. 515–520, 2021.
https://doi.org/10.1007/978-3-030-89394-1_47

Murder on Mansion Hill was developed to help combat these aliteracy-related factors by encouraging players to view stories as interactive social acts, and themselves as capable storytellers. To achieve this, the game leverages the motivational benefits of gameplay [5], storytelling [6], collage [7], and co-design to support players as they craft imaginative stories in a group-based setting. It gives participants greater control over game construction and story through the use of arts-based collaborative tools, with the goal to motivate players to approach narrative in new visual ways and recognize that stories can be rewarding and fun. By engaging with stories crafted within the game, players gain hands-on experience using multimodal techniques that can help them form a positive relationship to literacy-related content.

2   Technology

Murder on Mansion Hill is setup and delivered digitally on a web-based whiteboarding platform called Miro (alongside a video-chat application such as Zoom or Discord). Because Miro is intended for team-based collaboration and visualization, it lacks many automation and coding features found in game development software. However, its lack of technical complexity also makes it a promising platform for tabletop games as it enables quick iteration, is accessible and free to any internet-connected device, and is easy to use. These features support the creation of a remote game that connects family and friend who may not live in the same location or are socially distanced.

Because Miro lacks automation, some set up is required by the lead Game Master (GM). The game materials can be made from scratch or the GM can use pre-packaged templates that include: one design Miro board; one gameplay Miro board; 150 story cards pre-populated with places, items, characters, and actions; 52 poltergeist cards; collage building assets; avatar tokens; and pre-determined links between collage items and story cards (described in Fig. 3). The remaining story cards are left blank to be filled in later by players. Links to the Google Drive documents that populate these blank cards are provided in each player's workspace within the design template. The GM may modify the story cards, the collage assets, and the cards to which the collage items are assigned.

3   Aesthetics

Despite the inclusion of the word murder in the title, the tone of the game is lighthearted and appropriate for nearly all ages, focusing more on mystic fantasy than gore. To support this tone, visuals are simplistic, with brightly colored cards with icon-based designs and illustrated avatars of fantasy races. Most of setting is conveyed visually by the board that holds the interior rooms of the Mansion, which is crafted by players using collage. Though players are in some ways limited by the collage images included in the game template, which reflect an opulent yet neglected estate, it is still entirely up to players whether they want to create rooms that are more fanciful, serious, or even comedic. The GM may also introduce pictures of her own to influence the potential tone of the rooms.

4   Narrative

Players take on the role of psychic medium students who are given their final assignment to uncover what happened to the Master of the Mansion at the top of the hill, who recently disappeared in a mysterious fashion. The first group to successfully get in touch with their spooky side and correctly solve the murder gets infinite bragging rights and an automatic A. What exactly happens during the game is entirely up to the players as they use their imagination to describe their journey through the mansion, the interesting characters they interact with, and any other observations or actions of note. Players should think of the game as a story, and themselves and their fellow teammates as the storytellers, building on-the-fly narratives to search around and decipher clues.

5   Mechanics

Pre-Game Design Session. A major goal of the game is to give players heightened creative control, including over physical game components. In a pre-game design session, which takes 30–45 min, players use collage to construct the board and determine contents of the story card deck. Figure 1 provides a view into the collage workspace, Fig. 2 highlights collages made by playtesters, and Fig. 3 diagrams the process of how these visuals influence game structure. This phase most closely resembles a co-design session with the GM guiding others through the activity, ensuring the group is moving at the same pace and staggering tasks to reduce complexity and answer questions. Tackling tasks together encourages casual conversation, helping build social bonds.

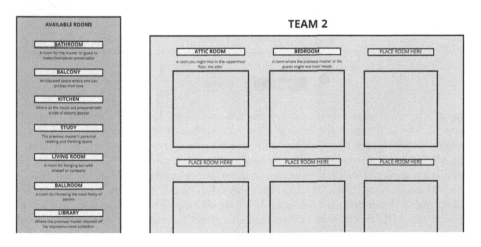

Fig. 1. Closeup view of collage workspace. Collages are built within each square using a provided collection of visual assets

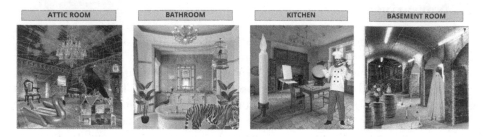

Fig. 2. Examples of rooms created by players using collage techniques.

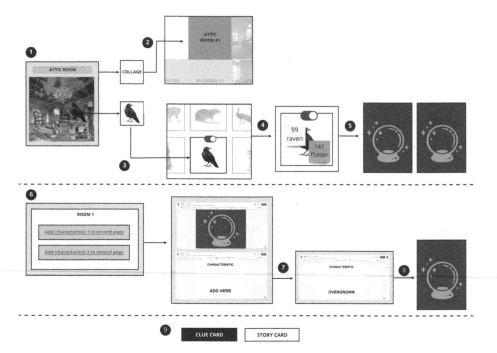

Fig. 3. Player collages influence game content as follows. 1: Player 1 collages the attic room. 2: The GM places the collage on the game board beneath its tile. 3: The GM assesses which elements are 'in use' (marked by a toggle the player set to active). 4: The GM looks at the notes hidden beneath the active element. These notes list the story cards assigned to that element (as determined by the template or the GM) 5. The GM copies these cards into the gameplay Miro board. 6. Player 1 follows the first link included in her collage workspace to open a Google Drive document. 7. Player 1 replaces the ADD HERE text with a word that describes the room. 8. Player 1 repeats this two times per room. Each Google Drive document is linked to a characteristic story card; when changes are made to the document, they also appear on the card. The GM refreshes the characteristic cards and deletes any not in play. 9. The GM chooses two place, action, and item cards at random and deals them to a member of each team to become their clue card. The rest are shuffled into the deck to become story cards.

Playing the Game. Once the design stage is finished, it's time to play (Fig. 4). Players act as psychics working in two competing teams to determine how the eccentric owner of the mansion was killed, in what room, and with what item. To accomplish this, players navigate their avatars around the mansion while using the story cards in their hand and the visual contents of the board to tell a story. For example, if you have the story cards witch, cauldron, and basement, and a room with green smoke, you may describe a scene in which you move to the basement and uncover an old witch stirring a smoking cauldron full of suspiciously green liquid.

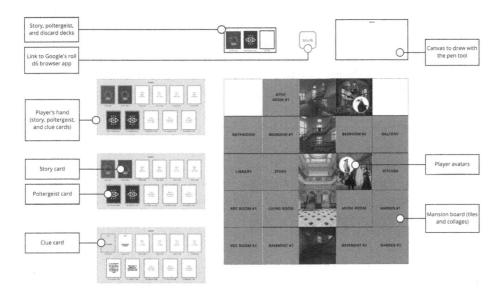

Fig. 4. Diagram of murder on mansion hill board.

Each player also has a secret clue card that contains the answer to one piece of the mystery. When the current narrator says a word related to a story card in a teammate's hand, that teammate is overtaken by his psychic powers; he rolls a die to determine in what creative way he must hint at the contents of his clue card, such as by writing a riddle or drawing a picture. But look out, other players may use their poltergeist cards to make the clue-giving process just a bit trickier. Once a team correctly guesses all three clues, they win by crafting one final sentence describing what caused the Master's ultimate end.

6   Player Insights

According to feedback and survey results, players across three playtest groups greatly enjoyed the collage making process and felt the collages postively impacted their experience, with several players especially liking the social conversation that blossomed as the group moved through the design activity. The visual board provided a way to keep track of the game's narrative, while the character avatars added to a sense of immersion. On several occasions, and unprompted, players introduced their characters and provided a backstory and personality, and then used those personas throughout the game. Players also felt more invested in the game due to their creative contribution and found that playing with their own assets was rewarding and exciting. Nearly all players also found that they became more comfortable with their role as a storyteller, in large part due to growing more comfortable with the group and recognizing that no one was there to judge, as well as having the cards and board to provide creative guidance. However, players were hesitant to say whether the game helped them feel more comfortable sharing stories outside of the game context. Players suggested that more engagement with the game could have this benefit. If not, future improvements should focus on making this learning transfer more explicit to build a positive bridge between the game and an outside context.

7   Conclusion

Murder on Mansion Hill blends together elements of co-design, collage, and group storytelling to create a game-based experience in which players feel motivated to explore their narrative creativity together with peers. It gives players control and agency to create and play a game based on their imagination, balancing player-made assets with pre-made designs in a way that allows for player input while providing a guiding foundation of rules and goals. The whimsical setting, visual collages, and story cards work together to help players view themselves as capable storytellers and the process of weaving unique stories as an enjoyable, lighthearted social experience. Future improvements can help bridge the gap between positive experiences within the game environment and outside literacy-related contexts.

References

1. De Naeghel, J., Van Keer, H., Vansteenkiste, M., Haerens, L., Aelterman, N.: Promoting elementary school students' autonomous reading motivation. J. Educ. Res. **109**(3), 232–252 (2016)
2. Johnston, P.H.: Opening Minds. Stenhouse Publishers, Portsmouth (2012)
3. Wilhelm, J.: Reading is seeing: using visual response to improve the literary reading of reluctant readers. J. Read. Behav. **27**(4), 467–503 (1995)
4. McGlynn-Stewart, M., Brathwaite, L., Hobman, L., Maguire, N., Mogyorodi, E., Park, Y.U.: Inclusive teaching with digital technology: supporting literacy learning in play-based kindergartens. Lear. Landscapes **11**(1), 199–216 (2017)
5. Rapp, A.: Designing interactive systems through a game lens: an ethnographic approach. Comput. Hum. Behav. **71**, 455–468 (2017)
6. Diamant-Cohen, B.: First day of class: the public library's role in school readiness. Child. Libr. **5**(1), 40–48 (2007)
7. Siegel, M.: Rereading the signs: multimodal transformations in the field of literacy education. Lang. Arts **84**(1), 65–77 (2006)

An Introduction to ChemiKami AR

Tengjia Zuo$^{(\boxtimes)}$ ⓘ, Erik D. van der Spek ⓘ, Max V. Birk ⓘ, and Jun Hu ⓘ

Systemic Change, Industrial Design, Eindhoven University of Technology,
Eindhoven, The Netherlands
{t.zuo,m.v.birk,e.d.v.d.spek,j.hu}@tue.nl

Abstract. ChemiKami is an Augmented Reality card game aiming to introduce chemical elements to students before they are formally being taught chemistry. We designed an avatar representation for each chemical element as well as an application card related to each element. Players can complete the game task by putting the correctly matched avatar card and application card together and having them scanned by an AR device. This game presents several applications of chemical elements in a fantasy setting. Using the idea of employing endogenous fantasy in AR game-based learning, we aim to explore the effect of fantasy on the player's motivation and working memory. As virtual and game-based learning becomes a leading trend of education, research using ChemiKamiAR helps designers identify the role of fantasy in AR game-based learning.

Keywords: Fantasy play · Game-based learning · Working memory · Augmented Reality · Serious Games

1 The Design of ChemiKamiAR

ChemiKami is a portmanteau of two words. Chemi represents this game's learning goal—chemistry, while Kami is a Japanese word meaning spirits or avatars with supernatural powers [1]. We designed the AR-game-based learning application ChemiKami AR to help and encourage beginners to learn chemistry and scrutinize the effects of fantasy elements such as anthropomorphic representations on motivation and learning. Each chemical element is designed into an avatar, with different characterizations, voices, and magical powers, embellishing the element's daily application with fantastical representations. Traditionally, learning chemistry, especially memorizing the names of the chemical elements and their associated traits from the Periodic Table of the Elements [2] is difficult and requires a lot of effort [3]. With the idea of enhancing one's working memory on chemical elements, we implement anthropomorphisms into our design in a fantastical way. Previous research indicates that anthropomorphisms create more emotional and cognitive interests among players [4, 5]. We will research the effect of fantasy on the player experience and learning effects through design research in future work.

Electronic supplementary material The online version of this chapter (https://doi.org/10.1007/978-3-030-89394-1_48) contains supplementary material, which is available to authorized users.

© IFIP International Federation for Information Processing 2021
Published by Springer Nature Switzerland AG 2021
J. Baalsrud Hauge et al. (Eds.): ICEC 2021, LNCS 13056, pp. 521–526, 2021.
https://doi.org/10.1007/978-3-030-89394-1_48

1.1 Mechanics and Systems

The game is developed using Unity 3D 2020.2.7F1, Vuforia Engine 9.7. The application needs to be installed on an Android phone with camera access and sound on, and a set of cards needs to be printed out to be able to play.

Players will be introduced to two kinds of cards: an Element card and an Application card. Both cards can be scanned by a phone individually or side by side, and show a 3D overlay with an animation. The application card is about a real-life application domain that requires one of the chemical elements. For example, it could show a sign without any color, which then needs an element that often exists in pigment (Fig. 1, left). Scanning the Application card alone, players would see a scene of daily life without the existence of a certain chemical element (in this case a sign that is not very visible). The Element card is designed with a picture of the avatar representing the element, the name, and a short description of that chemical element. Scanning the Element card alone, players will see an avatar representing the element, introducing themselves with the description printed on the card. By reading or listening to that description, players can find hints for pairing the Element card and the Application card, e.g., Bismuth is an element in the Bismuth yellow pigment (Fig. 1, Right). Reading this description, players may find this chemical element can play a role in the card of "the sign with no color."

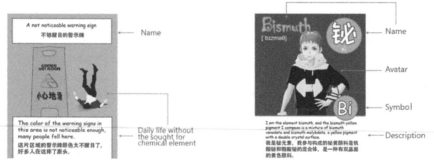

Fig. 1. The application card (left) and the role card (right), which are available in both English and Chinese

Fig. 2. Animation under AR device when two cards are paired correctly

After pairing the right combination, players can have both cards scanned by the AR camera. If correctly paired cards are scanned simultaneously, the avatar will cast the "magic of chemistry" and complete the task on the Application card. For example, when cards in Fig. 1 are correctly paired, the Bismuth avatar will cast a magic spell to make the sign noticeable with a bright yellow color. Then the man who is about to fall notices the sign and watches out for the slippery ground (Fig. 2).

1.2 Game Design Theories

There are few game design theories we apply in ChemiKami AR. Using the idea of fantasy play [6], we turn knowledge of facts into thematic fantasy and the traditional memorizing processing into playing and making believe [7]. Fantasy play can positively affect social competence like peer skill achievement and affective role play [8, 9]. With the affordance of Augmented Reality, this game tries to create a context of what Stapleton defines as Mixed-fantasy [10]. In his Mixed-fantasy continuum, AR games enable a lasting impression of the gameplay experience. Such experiences should persist if players interact with only the physical object without AR because their imagination plays a leading role. We are curious if such Mixed-fantasy will influence players' motivation and learning outcomes.

The emotional design principles were introduced for designing ChemiKami AR. Mayer et al. coined emotional design as "redesigning the graphic in a multi-media based learning to enhance the level of personification and visual appeal of the learning content." In ChemiKami AR, we design each chemical element into an avatar, with different voices, magical powers and characterizations. Aiming to increase learners' motivation, this game has the potential to improve their learning outcomes through appropriate cognitive processing in learning [4].

2   Interaction and Social Learning

2.1   Single-Player and Multiple Players

ChemiKamiAR can be played single-player or multi-player. For a single-player, there is no tension of competition. It takes three steps to complete each task, as shown in Fig. 3. The key to completing the game task is to find the right connection between chemical elements and their application.

Fig. 3. Three steps of play

The multiplayer mechanics are generally the same as in single-player, with the addition of competition and cooperation. A stack of Element cards with their backside facing up will be placed on the center of the table. In addition, each player holds a set of Application cards. For each turn, one player starts the game by flipping one Element card. Once the game starts, players need to find the correct Application card pairing from their decks as soon as possible and place them next to the Element card in the middle of the table. The one who has both cards scanned under (an) AR camera (s) first, triggering the successful narrative, will win this turn and take the Element card. Additionally, there could always be cooperation with more players on both sides. For example, while one player is holding a phone and scanning cards, others can look for cards, solving the puzzle together (Fig. 4).

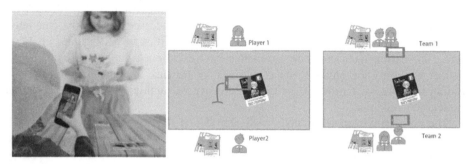

Fig. 4. Social learning and play

2.2 Interaction Design

We emphasize tangible interaction in game design since prior research indicates that tangible interactions may offer a more enjoyable experience than screen touch for the user via a sequence of intuitive and natural interactions [11]. Focusing the players' attention on tangible interaction with cards makes it easier for them to play in the absence of AR. Enabling play alternately with and without AR may foster children's imagination through mixed-fantasy [10], therefore possibly enhancing their memorization of chemical elements.

2.3 Social Learning

We introduce competition and cooperation through multiplayer game modes. Previous research indicates competition will increase players' immersion [12], while cooperation will encourage communication and social connection in gameplay [13]. Both aspects have the potential to improve players' play and learning motivation [14]. Additionally, the tangible part of ChemiKami AR helps build the social connection around this game. Players can collect and exchange cards they gain from the social gameplay mode. Research indicates collecting objects makes players enjoy the gameplay [15]. Furthermore, research shows that collecting and exchanging chards increases children's learning motivation and can improve learning outcomes [16].

3 Future Work and Possible Contribution

There is frequently a discussion about serious game design and how to design a motivating and practical learning experience [17–19]. With ChemiKami AR, we would like to explore the potential effect of Mixed-fantasy, and how the fantastical anthropomorphisms and emotional design influence motivation and learning in an AR game context. In addition, we are curious to see if this game would have a lasting effect after gameplay so that players can be motivated to memorize more through imagination without the help of AR. We are furthermore curious to see if other game principles like social play, competition and collection would play a positive role in this game.

Virtual learning has become a leading solution for geography and time issues in education [20]. Learning outcomes and motivation have become a major concern when the physical and social connection is often absent in most virtual learning [21]. We hope the design of ChemiKami AR would benefit students and educators who try to seek motivational ways of introducing chemistry knowledge. Additionally, we hope game design researchers would benefit from strategies of employing mixed fantasy in serious game design, which we would figure out using ChemiKami AR in our future research.

References

1. Oh, D.-I.: The surface and the inside of japanese feature-length animation: focused on the characteristics of signification. J. Digit. Contents Soc. **15**, 701–710 (2014)
2. Siegfried, R.: From elements to atoms: A history of chemical composition (2002)
3. Torrens, F., Castellano, G.: Reflections on the nature of the periodic table of the elements: Implications in chemical education (2014)
4. Mayer, R.E., Estrella, G.: Benefits of emotional design in multimedia instruction. Learn. Instr. **33**, 12–18 (2014)
5. Park, B., Kn, L., Orzer, €, Plass, J.L., Brünken, R.: Emotional design and positive emotions in multimedia learning: an eyetracking study on the use of anthropomorphisms. Comput. Educ. **86**, 30-42 (2015)
6. Pellegrini, A.D., Galda, L.: The effects of thematic-fantasy play training on the development of children's story comprehension. Am. Educ. Res. J. **19**, 443–452 (1982)
7. Fein, G.G.: Pretend play in childhood: an integrative review. Child Dev. 1095–1118 (1981)
8. Connolly, J.A., Doyle, A.B.: Relation of social fantasy play to social competence in preschoolers. Dev. Psychol. **20**, 797–806 (1984)
9. Zuo, T., Feijs, L., Van Der Spek, E.D., Hu, J.: A classification of fantasy in serious games. In: CHI Play 2019 - Extended Abstracts Annual Symposium Computer Interaction Play, pp. 821–828 (2019)
10. Stapleton, C.B., Hughes, C.E., Moshell, J.M.: MIXED FANTASY: Exhibition of entertainment research for mixed reality. In: Proc. - 2nd IEEE ACM International Symposium 6 Mixed Augment Reality, ISMAR 2003, pp. 354–355 (2003)
11. Li, J., Van Der Spek, E.D., Hu, J., Feijs, L.: Turning your book into a game: improving motivation through tangible interaction and diegetic feedback in an AR mathematics game for children. In: CHI Play 2019 – Proceedings of Annual Symposium Computer Interaction Play, pp. 73–85 (2019)
12. Li, J., Van Der Spek, E.D., Yu, X., Hu, J., Feijs, L.: Exploring an augmented reality social learning game for elementary school students. Proc. Interact. Des. Child. Conf. IDC **2020**, 508–518 (2020)

13. Al Mahmud, A., et al.: AMAZEd: designing an affective social game for children. Proceedings of the 6th International Conference on Interaction Design and Children IDC 2007, pp. 53–56 (2007)
14. Despain, W., et al.: 100 Principles og Game Desing (2013)
15. McCall, R., Wetzel, R., Löschner, J., Braun, A.K.: Using presence to evaluate an augmented reality location aware game. Pers. Ubiquitous Comput. **15**, 25–35 (2011)
16. Toups, Z.O., Crenshaw, N.K., Wehbe, R.R., Tondello, G.F., Nacke, L.E.: The collecting itself feels good: towards collection interfaces for digital game objects. In: CHI PLAY 2016 - Proceedings of the 2016 Annual Symposium on Computer-Human Interaction in Play, pp. 276–290. Association for Computing Machinery, Inc (2016)
17. Wouters, P., Van Nimwegen, C., Van Oostendorp, H., Van Der Spek, E.D.: A meta-analysis of the cognitive and motivational effects of serious games. J. Educ. Psychol. **105**, 249 (2013)
18. Zuo, T., Birk, M. V., Van Der Spek, E.D., Hu, J.: Exploring fantasy play in MathMythos AR. In: CHI Play 2020 - Extended Abstracts 2020 Annual Symposium Computer Interaction Play, pp. 413–417 (2020)
19. Birk, M. V., Mandryk, R.L., Miller, M.K., Gerling, K.M.: How self-esteem shapes our interactions with play technologies. In: CHI Play 2015 - Proc. 2015 Annual Symposium Computer Interaction Play, pp. 35–46 (2015)
20. Molnar, A., et al..: Virtual Schools in the U.S. 2019: Exec. Summ. Natl. Educ. Policy Center **0249** (2019)
21. Garbe, A., Ogurlu, U., Logan, N., Cook, P.: Parents' experiences with remote education during COVID-19 school closures. Am. J. Qual. Res. **4**(3), 45–65 (2020)

¡Juéguelo!: An Interactive Compilation of Traditional Colombian Games*

Andrés Felipe Daza Díaz, Luis José García Mojica,
Luisa Mariana Rodríguez Cifuentes, and Pablo Figueroa(✉)

Universidad de los Andes, Cra 1E #18A 40, Bogotá, Cundinamarca, Colombia
{af.daza,lj.garciam1,lm.rodriguezc2,pfiguero}@uniandes.edu.co
https://sistemas.uniandes.edu.co

Abstract. Traditional Colombian games are slowly being lost to time
due to a waning oral tradition and the popularization of modern media.
We seek to maintain and propagate these ludic manifestations by means
of a video game, made possible through an engineering team effort. Each
traditional game is represented in a microgame that contains abstracted
and transformed characteristics from the source material, upholding its
crux nevertheless. An MVP (minimum viable product) is disclosed amid
early development stages to gather valuable feedback. The game's implementation is then continued based on the collected comments, suggestions, and data.

Keywords: Traditional games · Microgames · Oral tradition ·
Abstraction · Serious games

1 Motivation

Through the development of a video game and in the context of an engineering project, we seek to persist and communicate Colombian ludic traditions not
only to those who don't know about them, but also to those who want to experience them again. We believe that a video game is the best approach to achieve
this goal, since their interactive nature allows the player to experience to a certain degree what it is like to have the real involvement. This is unachievable
with written or recorded media. Likewise, we share a fascination for video game
development and we would like to generate a product that, besides being fun,
accomplishes our communicative goals.

Supported by Universidad de los Andes.

Electronic supplementary material The online version of this chapter (https://
doi.org/10.1007/978-3-030-89394-1_49) contains supplementary material, which is
available to authorized users.

J. Baalsrud Hauge et al. (Eds.): ICEC 2021, LNCS 13056, pp. 527–533, 2021.
https://doi.org/10.1007/978-3-030-89394-1_49

1.1 Problem Statement

Oral tradition has been a determining factor for the preservation of traditional games, since they cannot be found in many documents or books and cannot be bought in conventional game or toy stores [1]. However, in recent years, this tradition is rapidly being lost. Bañol [2], warns that due to globalizing tendencies and the surge of new mass media, attention has been deviated to other forms of entertainment and in consequence, cultural transmission between generations has been diminishing. Having this in mind, it is of great importance to adapt traditional ludic models to ways compatible with new media, in such a way that their cultural preservation is encouraged and facilitated.

1.2 Goals

The project's primary goal is to communicate and preserve some of the various traditional games of Colombian culture and the way they are played through the narrative and playability constructed in a video game. More specific goals include: design an organic narrative surrounding Colombian tradition that captivates the player in such a way they obtain the complete game experience, encourage the players to challenge themselves through a global leader board, create a playability that generates fluidity between each component of the game through the abstraction of the most relevant aspects of traditional Colombian games, create an immersive game environment true to Colombian culture with the use of art and music and build a game experience accessible to a diverse audience, regardless of age, experience and context.

2 Game Experience

For the purpose of this section, it is necessary to know the following definitions: a mini game is a small, self-contained game that focuses on a defined theme and, in most cases, takes a small amount of time to complete [3]. With this in mind, a microgame is defined as a mini game characterized by having very simple mechanics and lasting a considerably small amount of time (usually a few seconds). Note that microgames, despite being self-contained experiences, are rarely found individually thanks to their simplicity and briefness. *WarioWare* is a well known example of such collections, and a significant influence on how we design microgames. Since the term "mini game" includes a great variety of experiences with variable complexity, it is important to categorize microgames as their own subset.

2.1 Abstraction

Traditional games, like every game, are complex models that are governed under numerous rules (each with innumerable distinctions and regional variants) and that can be affected by several stochastic variables. Likewise, computational engines present their own restrictions. In addition, traditional games can range from a simple handheld toy to a national sport. With that being said, it is necessary to abstract each traditional game to include it in the project. Wolf [4] defines abstraction as the action of simplifying and reducing something in such a way that its essential components and basic forms are maintained. The most important characteristics and mechanics of each game are decomposed in atomic components and implemented in objects that exist in a two-dimensional environment.

For each microgame included in *¡Juéguelo!*, an abstraction process was made. In these, key aspects of the corresponding traditional game were taken into account: game rules, ways to play the game, used material, etc. The final goal of this process is to generate a two-dimensional microgame that maintains the essence of the original game.

2.2 Game Structure

¡Juéguelo! is composed of two main game modes: a story campaign and a game gallery.

Story Campaign In order to encourage the player to experience the game thoroughly, a game mode based on a simple, yet riveting narrative was implemented. The narrative is divided in three acts, in which the player will start out as a novice to traditional games and build their skills up to become the grand master. Concerning this, the microgames in each act are notably more difficult than the last. Due to the segmented nature of this mode, each act serves as an appetizer for the next one, in such a way that the player remains entertained.

Each act involves a series of pseudorandomly selected microgames, which are sequentially presented to the player, and a finite amount of life points. A life point is taken each time the player loses at a microgame (Fig. 1). If the player manages to complete a certain number of microgames without depleting all life points, they will complete the act and gain access to the next one, with exception of the third act. In this final act, the player will instead be given the option to keep playing at an incremental difficulty, in order to achieve the highest score possible. These scores will be ranked and displayed in a global leaderboard.

Game Gallery In this section, the player can freely select each of the traditional Colombian games implemented in *¡Juéguelo!* in order to obtain detailed information about the selected game. The information shown will be: alternative names, game overview, demonstrative video and how to play it both in reality and in its abstraction as a microgame.Additionally, the player will be able to play the selected game in any of its three difficulties (easy, medium and difficult) (Fig. 2).

It should be noted that, both in story campaign and in the game gallery the player can pause the microgame to access additional information about the microgame that is currently paused or to return to the main menu.

Fig. 1. Act two of the story campaign

Fig. 2. Game Gallery

2.3   Aesthetics

The art of *¡Juéguelo!* was made alongside the development of each microgame by separate members of the team. This way, every microgame has a distinctive and independent identity. A single member of the team illustrated the scenes that narrate the events in story campaign in order to keep narrative and aesthetic consistency, as well as to showcase certain aspects of Colombian culture. It is worth noting that the game's development was an engineering based project, ergo art was not a main focus. Since this project revolves around Colombian tradition, it is relevant to complement it with local music from all around the country. This music[1] must also uphold the dynamism of the video game events (Fig. 3).

2.4   Microgames

Coca. The *Coca* is a wooden or plastic toy that consists of a handle attached to a perforated sphere or barrel through a string. To win this microgame, the player must insert the barrel in the handle by moving the mouse before the time expires.

---

[1] The music was composed and produced by fellow student AlejandroCuevas.

Fig. 3. Microgames

Fuchi. This game consists of performing tricks with a hacky sack without dropping it to the ground. In the microgame, the player must prevent the ball from touching the ground by clicking on the ball. In order to win, it must be kicked at least 6 times before time runs out.

Jackses. This game is played using pieces called *Jackses*, a ball and a flat surface. In this microgame, the player shall drop the ball by clicking on it and collect the pieces before the ball bounces for the second time. Once all the pieces are collected, the player must grab the ball by clicking on it. All this needs to be done before the time expires.

La Olla. *La Olla* is a game for a large group of players that is played with a light ball. In the microgame, the player will control one on-screen character, and must spike the ball when prompted in such a way that it strikes the character in the middle.

Piquis. *Piquis* is one of the names given to marbles in Colombia. In order to win at the microgame, the player must aim and thrust a marble so that all marbles in screen are struck at least once before time runs out.

Rana. This game is played with a *Rana* (frog) table and metallic rings. In this microgame, the player must throw the rings to insert them in one of the table's openings. To throw the ring, the player sets the direction and force using the displayed meters. Victory is given to the player if they score enough points in time and within the given number of throws.

Tejo. *Tejo* is a sport that consists of throwing a metal disc onto clay-filled boxes to make a gunpowder envelope explode. In the microgame, the disc must be thrown by clicking on the arrow to set the direction and then the strength must be selected by clicking on the screen.

Trompo. A *trompo* is a traditional top, often made of wood. In the microgame, the player must prevent the toy from toppling over by clicking on either side to apply torque. The player will win if the top remains upright for the whole duration of the microgame.

Yermis. This team-based game is played using bottle caps, a ball and in some cases bats. The player must throw the ball towards the bottle cap tower. If the tower is knocked down, the player must hit the characters shown within a limited number of throws. Otherwise, the player must evade the balls thrown at them using the mouse (Fig. 4).

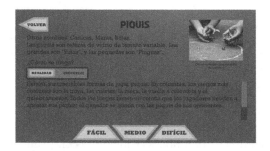

Fig. 4. Microgame information

3   Our Solution

There are multiple video games that are related to assorted Colombian aspects such as history and geography. However, there is a scarce amount of video games that communicate traditional ludic models. The only video game that explores traditional Colombian games is *Virtual Tejo*[5], which is focused on a singular traditional game (*tejo*).

To the extent of our knowledge, our project is the first video game to represent and cluster multiple traditional Colombian games in the same digital experience, some of which have never been represented in this way before. In addition, a significant effort was made to channel and streamline the way such greatly different games are played in reality in order for them to be playable solely with a mouse.

3.1   Results

A demo of the game was publicly released as well as a survey to collect player feedback. In the course of two weeks, approximately 80 game sessions were recorded. Information of each game session was persisted in a database to analyze the players' performance with the intention to balance difficulty and improve the game experience. The feedback received through the survey was mostly positive and suggestions were taken into account for the development of the full release. We have recorded over 300 game sessions[2] since. We have also received comments from players stating their unawareness about certain games or relevant aspects and how they have learned more about them by playing *¡Juéguelo!*.

References

1. Millan, M.: Juegos tradicionales del Valle del Cauca: Las tradiciones lúdicas y los valores acercan a las generaciones. (2003)
2. Bañol, G.: Juego tradicional colombiano: una expresión lúdica y cultural para el desarrollo humano. (2008)
3. Zaman, B., et al.: Concepts and Mechanics for Educational Mini-Games. (2012)
4. Wolf, M.: Abstraction in the video game. (n.d.)
5. Virtual Tejo-Apps in Google Play. (n.d.). Accessed 12 May 2021. https://play.google.com/store/apps/details?id=me.alexsosa.virtualtejo&hl=es_419&gl=US

---

[2] as of 20 of June, 2021.

ICEC Tutorial

Cross-Sector and Cross-Discipline Project Planning for Serious Interactive Digital Narratives

Nicole Basaraba ⓘ

Maastricht University, The Netherlands
n.basaraba@maastrichtuniversity.nl
http://www.nicolebasaraba.com

Abstract. This tutorial will provide participants with an overview of a theory-based project planning process, namely a "seven-phase framework" for creating nonfiction edutainment experiences from the ground up. The types of "serious digital stories" can take various formats (e.g., serious games, mobile apps, interactive web exhibitions/documentaries, AR/VR) depending on the interests and needs of the project developers. The target audience that would most benefit from this tutorial would be collaboration teams from institutions (e.g., museum, NGO, news reporters), research groups, creative industries, and (preferably) one member from each group. By the end of this tutorial a team of collaborators could develop a drafted project proposal for future academic funding application or a series of "next steps" for carrying out an research and development project.

Keywords: Non-fiction · Edutainment · Project planning

Background on the Theoretical Approach

As more participatory narratives are being developed by scholars, creative industries, and members of the public and they are increasingly using digital media, it raises the challenge of authorial control of the resulting emergent narrative(s). This challenge to authorial control has been termed the "narrative paradox" by Aylett in 1999 [1] who introduced the difficulty of "retaining the original narrative" because the audience is actively involved, such as in the case of virtual environments where the audience becomes a "user," "interactor" or even a "co-producer" of the narrative. The level of control is two-fold in that the first question for the narrative creator is how much of the narrative can be relaxed, or opened-up to change, and secondly how much the "user" can participate in the narrative [1]. The level of control on either side, namely the authorial or public (i.e., "user" in digital media) is a key aspect of how successful the resulting product is in terms of whether the desired narrative is actually communicated. When interactive narratives are co-produced by experts across sectors and the public, there needs to be a larger underlying theme, communication goal, and rationale for constructing the project. Strong authorial control on behalf of experts has been the most common approach to date because they can solicit input from the public rather than

© IFIP International Federation for Information Processing 2021
Published by Springer Nature Switzerland AG 2021
J. Baalsrud Hauge et al. (Eds.): ICEC 2021, LNCS 13056, pp. 537–539, 2021.
https://doi.org/10.1007/978-3-030-89394-1

completely putting the narrative in their hands, but new opportunities lie in project planning and cross-sector collaboration.

As an example, public history and cultural heritage projects in recent years have begun sharing authority with members of the public who are contributing to narrative production in a variety of ways. The most-frequently seen methods of public participation in these types of projects to date are crowdsourcing oral histories, archives, and community heritage information [2]; civic labour in the contribution of helping "read" historical documents or categorise archives; user-testing and/or civic engagement and interaction through online forums and social media responses to interactive narratives; and bottom-up and collaborative co-authorship in transmedia narratives [3]. These participatory co-constructive approaches will be discussed and some popular themes for digital interactive narratives development such as, the protection/preservation of cultural heritage sites; environmental storytelling (e.g., conscious consumerism, sustainable tourism); and transmedia journalism to educate the public about detecting "fake news" and/or sensational articles by developing their digital literacies.

Description of Tutorial Content

The first 30-minutes will be an introduction to the seven-phase development framework [4]. This framework includes a "ludonarrative toolkit" and evaluation model, which will be useful for participants while they think about their own projects. This will be followed by a presentation of a few examples of "serious interactive digital narratives" on non-fiction topics to inspire creativity amongst participants. For example, participatory methods will be contextualised within examples of digital humanities projects, virtual museum exhibitions, mobile applications, and interactive web documentaries.

Participants will then be broken up into small groups or pairs to work with their colleagues (if present) or they will be paired up to achieve (where possible) a cross-sector and cross-disciplinary mixture of backgrounds. Participants will work for 1.5 h to outline (or visually map out) the seven phases of their project idea. Note: participants can develop a brand new idea or work on mapping an existing idea/project into the respective phases.

After the 'hands-on' working session, 30 min will be allocated for groups to report back on:

- their reflections on the process of collaborative project development
- what type of project and topic they developed, and
- one key challenge they identified in their potential project such as, access to software/digital media, access to funding, narrative structure, difference of opinion across sectors/disciplines, etc.

Then a 30 minute discussion will follow on these identified challenges and participants will, as a large group, brainstorm ideas to include in their individual "action plans" to problem-solve some solutions prior to departing the tutorial.

References

1. Aylett, R.: Narrative in virtual environments-towards emergent narrative. In: Proceedings of the AAAI Fall Symposium on Narrative Intelligence, pp. 83–86 (1999)
2. Museums and the Web 2014. Modelling Crowdsourcing for Cultural Heritage. https://mw2014.museumsandtheweb.com/paper/modeling-crowdsourcing-forcultural-heritage/. Accessed 13 Aug 2021
3. Spurgeon, C., Burgess, J., Klaebe, H., McWilliam, K., Tacchi, J. A., Tsai, Y. H.: Co-creative media: theorising digital storytelling as a platform for researching and developing participatory culture. In: Communication, Creativity and Global Citizenship: Refereed Proceedings of the Australian and New Zealand Communication Association Conference 2009, pp. 274–286 (2009)
4. Basaraba, N.: A framework for creative teams of non-fiction interactive digital narratives. In: Rouse, R., Koenitz, H., Haahr, M. (eds.) Interactive Storytelling. ICIDS 2018. LNCS, vol. 11318, pp. 143–148. Springer, Cham (2018). https://doi.org/10.1007/978-3-030-04028-4_11

Author Index

Printed in the United States
by Baker & Taylor Publisher Services